D0834096

THE ECONOMICS AND POLITICS OF CLIMATE CHANGE

The Economics and Politics of Climate Change

Edited by

DIETER HELM AND CAMERON HEPBURN

OXFORD
UNIVERSITY PRESS

Great Clarendon Street, Oxford OX2 6DP

Oxford University Press is a department of the University of Oxford.
It furthers the University's objective of excellence in research, scholarship,
and education by publishing worldwide in

Oxford New York

Auckland Cape Town Dar es Salaam Hong Kong Karachi
Kuala Lumpur Madrid Melbourne Mexico City Nairobi
New Delhi Shanghai Taipei Toronto

With offices in

Argentina Austria Brazil Chile Czech Republic France Greece
Guatemala Hungary Italy Japan Poland Portugal Singapore
South Korea Switzerland Thailand Turkey Ukraine Vietnam

Oxford is a registered trade mark of Oxford University Press
in the UK and in certain other countries

Published in the United States
by Oxford University Press Inc., New York

First published 2009

British Library Cataloguing in Publication Data
Data available

Library of Congress Cataloging in Publication Data
Data available

Typeset by SPI Publisher Services, Pondicherry, India
Printed in Great Britain
on acid-free paper by
CPI Antony Rowe Chippenham, Wiltshire

ISBN 978–0–19–957328–8

3 5 7 9 10 8 6 4 2

Acknowledgement

Chapters 3, 4, 5, 6, 7, 8, 10, and 16 originally appeared in *Oxford Review of Economic Policy:* volume 24, number 2, Summer 2008, 'Climate Change.' Oxford Journals, Oxford University Press (www.oxrep.oxfordjournals.org).

Contents

PART V. INSTITUTIONAL ARCHITECTURE

List of Figures

List of Tables

List of Boxes

List of Contributors

Krister P. Andersson As an assistant professor in environmental policy on the Environmental Studies Program at the University of Colorado at Boulder, Krister Andersson studies the politics of environmental governance within two main policy domains: forestry activities in developing countries and climate-change mitigation strategies. He received his PhD in Public Policy from Indiana University in 2002 with a dissertation comparing the conditions for effective local governance of natural resources among 50 municipal governments in Bolivia. His research has appeared in a number of journals and his books include *The Samaritans' Dilemma* (Oxford University Press, 2005), which examines the institutional incentive structures of development aid, and *Rural Development and Local Government* (University of Arizona Press, 2009), which analyses the conditions for effective local provision of public services in Latin America. In 2007, he was awarded the Giorgio Ruffollo Research Fellowship by Harvard University's Sustainability Science Program.

Scott Barrett Scott Barrett is Lenfest-Earth Institute Professor of Natural Resource Economics in the School of International and Public Affairs at Columbia University in New York City. He is also a research fellow with CESifo (Munich), the Beijer Institute (Stockholm), and the Kiel Institute of World Economics. When he wrote the chapter for this book, he was at the Johns Hopkins University School of Advanced International Studies in Washington, DC. He was previously on the faculty of the London Business School, and a member of the academic panel for the Department of Environment in the UK. He has been an advisor to many international organizations, and was a lead author with the Intergovernmental Panel on Climate Change. His first book, *Environment and Statecraft: The Strategy of Environmental Treaty-Making*, was published by Oxford University Press in paperback in 2005. His most recent book, *Why Cooperate? The Incentive to Supply Global Public Goods*, was published by Oxford University Press in 2007.

Kjell Arne Brekke Kjell Arne Brekke is an economist, specializing in behavioural and environmental economics and, in particular, the impact of moral and social norms on environmentally relevant behaviour. He is Professor at the University of Oslo. He is also an affiliate research fellow at the Ragnar Firsch Centre for Economic Research, and part of the ESOP—Centre of Equality, Social Organization, and Performance, which is funded by the Research Council of Norway as a Norwegian Centre of Excellence.

Ying Chen Dr Ying Chen is an associate research fellow at the Research Center for Sustainable Development, Chinese Academy of Social Sciences (CASS). She is also an associate professor at CASS Graduate School. She received her PhD from the Department of Chemical Engineering of Tsinghua University in 1997.

Since then, she has been involved in the field of climate change and worked on energy policy, climate-change mitigation, and sustainable development. Her research interests also include environmental economics, international environmental governance, etc. She has co-authored two books, about 30 papers in books and academic journals, as well as a number of reports, analyses, and articles.

Paul Collier Paul Collier is Professor of Economics and Director of the Centre for the Study of African Economies at Oxford University. During 1998–2003 he directed the research department of the World Bank, and is currently Co-director of the International Growth Centre. He is the author of *The Bottom Billion*, which in 2008 won the Lionel Gelber, Arthur Ross, and Corine Prizes. He has worked on African economies for over 30 years and was a founding editor of the *Journal of African Economies*.

Gordon Conway Sir Gordon Conway is Professor of International Development at Imperial College, where he is working on a Bill and Melinda Gates Foundation grant to improve European support of agricultural development in Africa. He is an agricultural ecologist by training and was a pioneer of Sustainable Agriculture in North Borneo in the 1960s. He has worked and lived in many countries in Asia and Africa. Highlights of his career include Chair of the Centre for Environmental Technology at Imperial College, Representative of the Ford Foundation in New Delhi, Vice-Chancellor of the University of Sussex, President of the Rockefeller Foundation, Chief Scientific Adviser to the UK Department for International Development, and President of the Royal Geographical Society. His books include *The Doubly Green Revolution; Food for all in the 21st Century* (Cornell University Press). He is a KCMG, HonFREng, and FRS.

Joanna Depledge Joanna Depledge is Sutasoma Research Fellow at Lucy Cavendish College, and Associate at the Centre of International Studies, at Cambridge University. She has published several papers on climate-change politics, and is a regular contributor to the journal *Environmental Policy and Law* on a range of environmental issues. She is the co-author of *The International Climate Change Regime: A Guide to Rules, Institutions and Procedures* (2004) and author of *The Organization of Global Negotiations: Constructing the Climate Change Regime* (2005). She has worked for the UN Climate Change Secretariat, and also as writer/editor for the *Earth Negotiations Bulletin*.

Ross Garnaut Professor Ross Garnaut is a vice chancellor's fellow and a professorial fellow (Faculty of Economics and Commerce) at the University of Melbourne, as well as a distinguished professor of the Australian National University. In addition to his distinguished academic career, Professor Garnaut has also had longstanding and successful roles as policy advisor, diplomat, and businessman. He was the Senior Economic Adviser to Australian Prime Minister R. J. L. Hawke (1983–5) and subsequently the Australian Ambassador to China (1985–8). He is currently Chairman of a number of international companies and research organizations, including the International Food Policy Research Institute

(Washington, DC) and the Papua New Guinea Sustainable Development Program (Singapore). In addition, he is a director of Ok Tedi Mining (Papua New Guinea) and a member of the board of several international research institutions, including the Lowy Institute for International Policy (Sydney) and the China Centre for Economic Research at Peking University (Beijing). In September 2008, Professor Garnaut presented the Garnaut Climate Change Review to the Australian Prime Minister. This review, commissioned by the Australian government, examines the impact of climate change on the Australian economy and provides potential medium- to long-term policies to ameliorate these.

Arunabha Ghosh Arunabha Ghosh is currently Oxford–Princeton Global Leaders Fellow at the Niehaus Center for Globalization and Governance, Woodrow Wilson School, Princeton University. His work focuses on monitoring, surveillance, and compliance systems in international regimes, particularly climate change and global trade. He is also working on technology transfer and trade and climate linkages. He has worked previously at the United Nations Development Programme as Co-author of three Human Development Reports, and at the World Trade Organization. He has led research on transboundary water basins, intellectual property and the rights of indigenous people, violent conflict, and extremist movements, and has undertaken/advised research projects on aid, financial crises, and trade negotiations for DfID (UK), IDRC (Canada), and the Commonwealth Secretariat. His advocacy efforts for human development span a documentary on water broadcast out of Africa, presentations to the Indian Parliament and other legislatures, training of ministers in Central Asia, and public lectures in Australia, Germany, Spain, and the United States. He is on the editorial board of the *Journal of Human Development and Capabilities.*

Richard Green Richard Green is an economist, specializing in the economics and regulation of the electricity industry. He is Professor of Energy Economics and Director of the Institute for Energy Research and Policy at the University of Birmingham. He has previously worked at the Universities of Cambridge and of Hull, and at the Office of Electricity Regulation. He has acted as a specialist advisor to the House of Commons Trade and Industry Committee, and the House of Lords Economic Affairs Committee. He has been a member of the Conseil Economique of the French Commission de Regulation de l'Electricité, and is a member of the Academic Advisory Panel of the Competition Commission.

Dieter Helm Dieter Helm is Professor of Energy Policy at the University of Oxford and a fellow of New College. He holds a number of advisory board appointments, including Chairman of the Academic Panel of the Department of Environment, Food and Rural Affairs and Member of the Advisory Panel on Energy and Climate Security, Department for Energy and Climate Change. He was a member of the DTI Sustainable Energy Policy Advisory Board (2002–7) and of the Prime Minister's Council of Science and Technology (2004–7). He is an associate editor of the *Oxford Review of Economic Policy.* Dieter Helm's career to date has spanned academia, public policy, and business. He founded Oxera in 1982 and has published extensively on environmental, energy, infrastructure, and regulation topics.

Cameron Hepburn Dr Cameron Hepburn is a senior research fellow at Oxford University's new Smith School of Enterprise and the Environment. He has advised several governments and international institutions on climate and environmental policy, and he currently serves on the Academic Panel of the Department of Environment, Food and Rural Affairs. He is an associate editor of the *Oxford Review of Economic Policy*, a research fellow at New College, Oxford, and he has over a decade's experience working on environmental issues and climate change, with a particular focus on emissions trading and carbon markets. He holds a DPhil in economics from Oxford, and undergraduate degrees in law and engineering from the University of Melbourne.

Howard Herzog Howard J. Herzog is a principal research engineer in the MIT Energy Initiative. He received his undergraduate and graduate education in chemical engineering at the Massachusetts Institute of Technology (MIT). He has industrial experience with Eastman Kodak (1972–4), Stone & Webster (1975–8), Aspen Technology (1981–6), and Spectra Physics (1986–8). Since 1989, he has been on the MIT research staff, where he works on sponsored research involving energy and the environment, with an emphasis on greenhouse-gas mitigation technologies. He was a coordinating lead author for the IPCC Special Report on 'Carbon Dioxide Capture and Storage' (released September 2005), a co-author on the MIT *Future of Coal* study (released March 2007), and a US delegate to the Carbon Sequestration Leadership Forum's Technical Group (June 2003–September 2007).

Stephen Howes Professor Stephen Howes is at the Crawford School of Economics and Government at the Australian National University. In 2008, he worked on the Garnaut Climate Change Review. Prior to that, he was Chief Economist with the Australian Agency for International Development (AusAID). From 1994 to 2005, he was with the World Bank, most recently as Lead Economist for India. Professor Howes has a PhD in Economics from the London School of Economics, and has conducted extensive research over the last 20 years into the economies of the Asia-Pacific region.

Olof Johansson-Stenman Olof Johansson-Stenman is a professor of economics at the School of Business, Economics and Law, University of Gothenburg. His current research interest is behavioural economics in a broad sense, both theoretically and empirically exploring deviations from the purely selfish, rational, and atomistic 'homo economicus'. Several of his journal publications deal with relative income and consumption concerns, i.e. that we tend to derive utility not only from the absolute amount of consumption, but also from the relative amount compared to others. He is also interested in environmental economics, transport economics, public economics, risk, welfare economics, happiness research, and normative economics more generally.

Vijay Joshi Vijay Joshi is a fellow of St John's College, Oxford and an emeritus fellow of Merton College, Oxford. His research interests cover international economics, development economics, and Indian economics, and he has published widely in scholarly journals and elsewhere on these topics. His publications on India include three major books: *India's Economic Reforms 1991–2001* (co-authored with Ian Little), Oxford University Press, 1996; *India: Macroeconomics and Political Economy 1964–1991* (co-authored with Ian Little), Oxford University Press, 1994; and *India: The Future of Economic Reform* (co-edited with Robert Cassen), Oxford University Press, 1995. His career has included stints as Economic Adviser to the Ministry of Finance, Government of India and as Special Adviser to the Governor, Reserve Bank of India. Since 1996, he has been a director of the J. P. Morgan India Investment Trust.

Frank Jotzo Frank Jotzo is an environmental economist specializing in climate-change economics and policy, including design of post-2012 international climate policy and options for engaging developing countries, Kyoto Protocol mechanisms, and emissions trading design. He also works on broader issues of development and international economics, particularly in the Asia-Pacific region. Frank works at the Australian National University (ANU), where he is a research fellow at the College of Asia and the Pacific, and Deputy Director of the ANU Climate Change Institute. In 2008 he worked as Economic Advisor for the Garnaut Climate Change Review. He holds a PhD and Masters from ANU, and an honours degree from Humboldt University Berlin. He previously worked with the Australian Bureau of Agricultural and Resource Economics, and has collaborated with and consulted for organizations including Stanford University, the World Bank, and Australian government agencies.

Nathaniel Keohane Dr Nathaniel Keohane is the Director of Economic Policy and Analysis in the Environmental Defense Fund (EDF)'s Climate and Air Program. He oversees EDF's analytical work on the economics of climate policy, and helps to develop and advocate the organization's policy positions on global warming. Prior to joining EDF, Dr Keohane was an associate professor of economics at the Yale School of Management; he is currently an adjunct professor at NYU Law, teaching a class on climate-change policy. His academic research has focused on the design and performance of market-based environmental policies. He has published articles on environmental economics in academic journals including the *Journal of Public Economics*, the *RAND Journal of Economics*, the *Journal of Environmental Economics and Management*, and the *Harvard Environmental Law Review*. He is also the co-author of *Markets and the Environment* (Island Press, 2007) and co-editor of *Economics of Environmental Law* (Edward Elgar, forthcoming).

Jiahua Pan Jiahua Pan is currently Director of the Institute for Urban and Environmental Studies at the Chinese Academy of Social Sciences (CASS), and Professor of Economics at CASS Graduate School. He received his PhD from Cambridge University in 1992. He has worked for the UNDP Beijing Office as an advisor on environment and development. He was lead author of the IPCC Working

Group III 3rd and 4th Assessment Reports on Mitigation; a member of the China National Expert Panel on Climate Change; and Advisor to the Ministry of Environment Protection. He is Vice President of the Chinese Society of Ecological Economists. He was co-editor of *Climate Change 2007: Mitigation of Climate Change*, published by Cambridge University Press, and is the author of over 200 papers, articles, and books in both English and Chinese.

Urjit R. Patel Urjit R. Patel is an economist with interests in Indian macroeconomics, energy, infrastructure and climate change. He spent a decade working in the Indian financial sector, specializing in funding private infrastructure projects. In 2006–7, he was Non-resident India Economics Fellow at the Brookings Institution. He is currently a member of the Advisory Committee of the Competition Commission of India, and previously served on the Expert Committee on Integrated Energy Policy and the Task Force on Direct Taxes, both constituted by the Government of India. He has also worked at the International Monetary Fund and as an adviser to both the Reserve Bank of India and the Ministry of Finance, New Delhi. He serves as an independent member on the board of Gujarat State Petroleum Corporation, and he is currently on an assignment with Reliance Industries Limited.

Annie Petsonk Annie Petsonk is International Counsel at the Environmental Defense Fund (EDF). She coordinates EDF's advocacy efforts on international environmental law, international agreements, and institutions, working to develop international laws that provide economic incentives for environmental protection. Ms Petsonk previously worked in the environmental law unit of the United Nations Environment Programme and served as a trial attorney for the US Justice Department. She holds a JD from Harvard Law School and is an adjunct professor at George Washington University Law School in Washington, DC.

Jonathan Phillips Jonathan Phillips is a political economist, working in the fields of development and environmental economics. He is currently a fellow of the Overseas Development Institute, working in the Office of the Senior Special Assistant to the President on Millennium Development Goals in the Federal Government of Nigeria. He is focusing on the oversight of Nigeria's Virtual Poverty Fund and the design of conditional grants from the federal government to state governments to encourage the implementation of pro-poor projects and improved public-service delivery. Previously, he worked for Oxera and Vivid Economics in Europe, providing advice on regulatory, transport, competition, and climate-change policy, and in Cameroon for a non-governmental organization promoting agroforestry and rural development. His published articles have critically evaluated the UK's climate-change record, analysed the international responsibility for carbon emissions from Chinese production for export, and scrutinized regulatory incentives in the UK rail and air transport industries.

Andrew J. Plantinga Dr Andrew Plantinga is Professor of Agricultural and Resource Economics at Oregon State University. He received a PhD in Agricultural and Resource Economics from the University of California–Berkeley in 1995, an MS in Forestry from the University of Wisconsin–Madison in 1988, and a BA from Grinnell College. His research focuses on econometric modelling of land-use decisions, land price analysis, and the economics of carbon sequestration and biodiversity conservation. Dr Plantinga has authored or co-authored articles appearing in the *American Journal of Agricultural Economics* (*AJAE*), the *Journal of Environmental Economics and Management* (*JEEM*), *Land Economics*, the *Journal of Urban Economics*, and the *Proceedings of the National Academy of Sciences*. He currently serves on the editorial councils of the *AJAE* and *JEEM*. His research has been supported by the National Science Foundation, the US Department of Agriculture, the US Forest Service, and the US Department of Energy.

Kenneth R. Richards Kenneth Richards is an associate professor of environmental and energy policy and law at the School of Public and Environmental Affairs and Adjunct Professor of Law at the Maurer School of Law, Indiana University. His research interests include climate-change policy, environmental policy implementation, and terrestrial and geological carbon sequestration. Professor Richards is Director of the IU at Oxford Program, and Associate Director of both the Richard G. Lugar Center for Renewable Energy in Indianapolis and the Center for Research in Energy and the Environment in Bloomington, Indiana. He holds a PhD in Public Policy from the Wharton School and a JD from the Law School, University of Pennsylvania; an MSCE in Urban and Regional Planning and a BSCE in Environmental Engineering from Northwestern University; and a BA in Botany and Chemistry from Duke University.

Peter Sheehan Professor Peter Sheehan is Director of the Centre for Strategic Economic Studies in the faculty of Business and Law at Victoria University, Australia. He has spent 25 years in economics research and eight years working in government. His research interests include strategies for economic development, health and pharmaceuticals, energy, and climate change. He has made a substantial contribution to the studies of the global knowledge economy, and of its Australian and international ramifications. From 1987 to the late 1990s he was actively involved, as Chairman or Director, in a number of technology-based companies.

Steve Sorrell Steve Sorrell trained as an electrical engineer and spent four years working in industrial R&D laboratories before gaining an MSc in Science and Technology Policy in 1990. Since joining SPRU (Science and Technology Policy Research) at the University of Sussex, he has undertaken a range of research on energy and environmental policy, with particular focus on energy modelling, energy efficiency, and emissions trading. This work is primarily informed by economics and has included case studies, econometric analysis, and modelling. Steve has published three books, 18 papers in refereed journals, 12 book chapters, and more than one hundred research reports. He has acted as Consultant to the European Commission, the Department of Environment, Food and Rural Affairs, the Department of Trade and Industry/ Department for Business, Enterprise &

Regulatory Reform (BERR), the Environment Agency, the Sustainable Development Commission, private-sector organizations, and non-governmental organizations. Steve is currently Deputy Director of the ESRC-funded Sussex Energy Group and co-managing the Technology and Policy Assessment function of the UK Energy Research Centre.

Robert N. Stavins Robert N. Stavins is the Albert Pratt Professor of Business and Government at the Harvard Kennedy School, Director of the Harvard Environmental Economics Program, Director of Graduate Studies for the Doctoral Programs, Co-Chair of the Harvard Business School-Kennedy School Joint Degree Programs, and Director of the Harvard Project on International Climate Agreements. He is a university fellow of resources for the Future, a research associate of the National Bureau of Economic Research, Editor of the *Review of Environmental Economics and Policy*, Co-editor of the *Journal of Wine Economics*, and a member of the Board of Directors of Resources for the Future and of numerous editorial boards. He was Chairman of the US EPA Environmental Economics Advisory Committee and Lead Author of the Intergovernmental Panel on Climate Change. He holds a BA in philosophy from Northwestern University, an MS in agricultural economics from Cornell, and a PhD in economics from Harvard.

Nicholas Stern Lord Stern of Brentford, Kt, FBA is IG Patel Professor of Economics and Government at the London School of Economics, where he is also Head of the India Observatory and Chairman of the Grantham Research Institute on Climate Change and the Environment. He has held academic posts at the Universities of Oxford, Warwick, and the LSE, was Chief Economist for the European Bank for Reconstruction and Development and subsequently Chief Economist and Senior Vice President at the World Bank. He has held visiting posts at the People's University of China, the Indian Statistical Institute, MIT, and the Ecole Polytechnique in Paris. From 2003 to 2007 he was Head of the UK Government Economic Service and in 2004–5 he led the writing of the Report of the Commission for Africa. In 2005, he was appointed by the UK government to conduct the influential Stern Review, which analysed the economic costs of climate change. His most recent book is *A Blueprint for a Safer Planet* (in the USA, *A Global Deal*).

Anthony J. Venables Tony Venables is Professor of Economics at Oxford University where he also directs the Oxford Centre for the Analysis of Resource Rich Economies. He is a fellow of the Econometric Society and of the British Academy. Former positions include Chief Economist at the UK Department for International Development, Professor at the London School of Economics, Research Manager of the trade research group in the World Bank, and Advisor to the UK Treasury. He has published extensively in the areas of international trade and spatial economics, including work on trade and imperfect competition, economic integration, multinational firms, and economic geography. Publications include *The Spatial Economy; Cities, Regions and International Trade*, with M. Fujita and

P. Krugman (MIT Press, 1999) and *Multinationals in the World Economy* with G. Barba Navaretti (Princeton, 2004).

David G. Victor David Victor is Professor of Law at Stanford Law School and Director of the Program on Energy and Sustainable Development. His current research focuses on the role of state-controlled oil companies in the oil market, the design of effective strategies for protecting the global climate, and the emerging global market for coal. He is also Adjunct Senior Fellow at the Council on Foreign Relations, where he was Senior Adviser to the Council's task force on climate change (chaired by Governors George Pataki and Tom Vilsack) and leads study groups on energy security and on regulation of climate geoengineering. He is author or editor of seven books and more than one hundred articles on issues and energy and environmental policy. His PhD is from the Massachusetts Institute of Technology (Political Science and International Relations), and his BA is from Harvard University (History and Science).

Gernot Wagner Gernot Wagner is an economist in the Environmental Defense Fund (EDF)'s Climate and Air Program. He focuses on global greenhouse-gas emission-reduction pathways, and works on developing and applying economically sound climate policy in the USA and internationally. Prior to the EDF, he worked for the Boston Consulting Group, focusing on the energy and sustainable development practice areas, and wrote for the editorial board of the *Financial Times* in London as a Peter Martin Fellow, where he covered economics, energy, and the environment. He received his PhD in Political Economy and Government and his AB from Harvard University, and holds an MA from Stanford.

James S. Wang James Wang is an atmospheric scientist with the Environmental Defense Fund in New York. He conducts research and educates policy-makers and the public on scientific and policy aspects of global warming, air quality, and anthropogenic perturbation of the nitrogen cycle. He specializes in climate-change physics and impacts on society and ecosystems, and the emissions, transport, and chemistry of air pollutants, with a focus on greenhouse gases. He has published a dozen peer-reviewed scientific papers and spoken at various conferences. He received his PhD in Earth and Planetary Sciences from Harvard University, and joined the staff of the Environmental Defense Fund in 2003.

Ngaire Woods Ngaire Woods is Professor of International Political Economy at the University of Oxford and Director of the Global Economic Governance Programme. She was educated at Auckland University and Balliol College, Oxford. She taught at Harvard University before taking up her Fellowship at University College, Oxford. In 2005–6 she was appointed by the IMF Board to a three-person panel to report on the effectiveness of the IMF's Independent Evaluation Office. Since 2002 she has been an adviser to the UNDP's Human Development Report. She was a member of the Helsinki Process on global governance and of the resource group of the UN Secretary-General's High-Level Commission into Threats, Challenges and Change, and a member of the Commonwealth

Secretariat Expert Group on Democracy and Development, established in 2002, which reported in 2004. Her most recent publications are *The Politics of Global Regulation* (with Walter Mattli, Princeton University Press, 2009) and *Networks of Influence* (with Leonardo Martinez, Oxford University Press, 2009).

Farhana Yamin Farhana Yamin is Fellow of the Institute of Development Studies at the University of Sussex. She is an international environmental lawyer with nearly two decades of experience of international negotiations, multi-disciplinary research, legal advice, and consultancy work for governments, international organizations, and non-governmental organizations. She has been a lead author for the IPCC since 1994 and has written numerous books and articles covering climate change, development, and carbon markets. Her research interests are international negotiations, including post-2012 frameworks, intellectual property, and governance and international justice.

1

Introduction

Dieter Helm and Cameron Hepburn

As climate change has moved from the possible to the probable, and as scientists have both refined our knowledge of the processes and the predictions of the consequences, climate-change policy has not kept pace. To date, international agreement on a credible climate-change framework remains elusive, and while the process is intensifying in the run-up to the end of the first Kyoto period, emissions continue to rise and the concentrations of carbon dioxide (CO_2) in the atmosphere are rapidly approaching 400 parts per million (ppm) (from a pre-industrial 275ppm). Behind this growth lies an expansion (and corresponding lock-in) of high-carbon electricity generation from the world's coal burn, both absolutely and relative to other energy sources.

There is then an urgency to the negotiations towards a post-2012 regime. And while it is true that progress has been painfully slow, it is not for want of solutions. The economics and politics of climate change have both been revolutionized in recent years as research has accelerated. The aim of this volume is to bring together some of the main insights from this research and the lessons learnt from the policy instruments deployed so far.

Our starting point is to consider why so little has yet been achieved (Helm, Ch. 2). What is it about the economics and the politics which makes it all so difficult?

The economics of climate change was the focus (and title) of the now famous Stern Review (Stern, 2007). There are three key components to the Review's economic assessment: the estimated damage that climate change may cause; the discount rate and the weight that current generations should place on the well-being of the future generations which will suffer the damage; and the costs of partially mitigating climate change. This economic framework is set in the context of a broad policy consensus that the target ought to be stabilization at around 450–550 ppm, which is thought to give roughly 50 per cent odds of around 2°C warming.

The Review provides an excellent framing of the economic issues, and its various dimensions are explored in this volume. In estimating the damages from climate change, very profound and challenging problems are posed not just for policy-makers but for economists, too. The very process by which the climate system relates to economic growth is poorly understood. Is the climate just another factor input or does it create binding constraints not only on growth, but on other factors of production? If it is the latter, can we continue to substitute for it with man-made capital? This basic conceptual issue divides environmentalists from many conventional neoclassical economists, and leads to questioning of the basic assumption that economic growth will continue ever upwards over this century and beyond, making us ever richer in aggregate even if the environment deteriorates.

Furthermore, in valuing the damages, deep ethical debates on our obligations to future generations remain relevant. The arguments have often focused narrowly on whether a particular utility discount rate appropriately reflects considerations of intergenerational equity and efficiency. Frank Ramsey's famous and much quoted remark to the effect that discounting future utility represents a failure of the imagination is a statement of his own ethical position, but not a convincing critique of others. The Stern Review did not duck this issue—and, indeed, the conclusions from its quantitative modelling hang on it—and critics have not failed to challenge the Review head on. Notable among these critics have been Nordhaus (2007*a*) and Weitzman (2007), who have stressed the significance of market data in formulating views on intergenerational allocation. Hepburn and Stern (Ch. 3) have replied to a number of these challenges, putting forward a range of reasons why they find market data to provide inadequate guidance to questions of justice between generations. Brekke and Johannson-Stenman (Ch. 6) consider the same set of issues from the perspective of behavioural economics: as market data simply reflect the aggregate of human behaviour of participants, understanding this behaviour and its normative significance is relevant to thinking about discounting, just as it is relevant to the design of climate-change policy.

The mitigation costs appear to have been rising as the complexity of the design of climate-change policy has been gradually revealed. While economists have the tools to analyse efficient outcomes, the policy process is much messier, involving the interaction of politics and rent-seeking lobby groups, and the difficulty of forming policy consensus. The 1 per cent cost so widely quoted from the Stern Review may turn out to be very optimistic, given the underlying assumptions about technologies and costs, and the associated learning effects. Garnaut, Howes, Jotzo, and Sheehan (Ch. 5) argue that, notwithstanding the financial crisis, rapid economic growth has driven faster emissions growth, making the effort required even greater. Furthermore, these costs are subject to policy bias and will increase with a more realistic view of policy that accounts for the absence of a smooth coordination between policy deployment, manufacturing capability, market power, and the underlying costs of capital. Furthermore, concerns about enforcement persist (Barrett, Ch. 4), and weak compliance with the new deal may further increase costs. The policy costs cannot be divorced from the political process, and it is evident that the economics of climate-change policy cannot be considered independently of the politics.

The politics does, however, have to start with the interests of the main players, which are also addressed in this volume. The aim is not to be comprehensive—there are, after all, over 190 countries involved. Rather, it is to see how the impacts of climate change vary and how the interests of the players link up with their economic and political circumstances. Individual chapters consider key issues relevant to the USA (Stavins, Ch. 10), the EU (Helm, Ch. 11), China (Pan, Phillips, and Chen, Ch. 8), India (Joshi and Patel, Ch. 9) and Africa (Collier, Conway, and Venables, Ch. 7). The interests of the forestry nations, such as Brazil and Indonesia, are highlighted by the proposal for a national inventory of forest carbon, advanced by Andersson, Plantinga, and Richards (Ch. 15). What emerges from these chapters is the sheer complexity and variety of interests. For the USA, a cap-and-trade approach has considerable political and economic attractions for what is an economy modelled along Anglo-Saxon lines, with a deep institutional market structure, and the experience of sulphur trading behind it. But for China and India, such approaches are much less likely, and although Joshi and Patel (Ch. 10) put forward a well-argued case for an Indian cap, agreement about a binding cap is unlikely in the short term. China and India matter enormously, both because of their current and future industrialization and, in both cases, the doubling of their populations by 2050. The third area where population is also doubling is Africa (China, India, and Africa are all projected to have populations of two billion by 2050, out of a total for the world of nine billion). The African position is extremely diverse, with widely differing climate-change impacts and, in most cases, very weak governmental and institutional structures.

Given that the energy needs of the developing world will increase dramatically in the coming decades, development and deployment of low-carbon technologies and, indeed, carbon sinks, will be critical. Those in the nuclear industry are preparing for a renaissance, provided the appropriate policy framework can be put in place (Helm, Ch. 12), and carbon capture and storage is the best hope for a reconciliation of the coal industry with the notion of low-carbon growth (Herzog, Ch. 13). Renewables—particularly solar—promise rapid cost reductions, but in most instances still remain uncompetitive (Green, Ch. 14). And although investment in energy efficiency does, indeed, appear to make economic sense, there are reasons to be cautious about the claimed emission reductions. Most studies barely, if at all, account for the potentially serious rebound effects, addressed by Sorrell (Ch. 17). If nuclear, carbon capture and storage, renewable, and energy efficiency fail to deliver the necessary emission reductions, and even if they do not, it may be that the costs and benefits of deliberately engaging in planetary-level control of Earth's atmosphere and/or ocean systems should be considered. Victor (Ch. 16) argues that norms to govern deployment of geoengineering systems are needed, which might arise through intensive research organized by the academies of sciences in key countries.

Just as critical as the available technologies are the policy instruments that are put in place to incentivize their deployment. They are inevitably shaped both by the economics and by the politics, which influences the choice of policy instruments to a much greater degree than economists tend to allow for. A set of chapters considers the various policy options and how far they require international cooperation. 'Quantity instruments', such as cap and trade, have been adopted ahead of 'price instruments', such as carbon taxes. This has been driven by significant political reasons, rather than economic reasons, and it appears desirable to design cap-and-trade schemes to be as 'price like' as possible (Hepburn, Ch. 18). Encouraging developing countries to join in establishing cap-and-trade schemes will be difficult, and Wagner, Keohane, Petsonk, and Wang (Ch. 19) advance the 'docking stations' proposal as a way of transitioning to a global carbon market. In the interim, at the crux of a global deal on climate change is a mechanism efficiently to transfer finance from developed to developing countries to pay for the latter's emission reductions. Various mechanisms might serve this function, including multilateral funds or a reformed Clean Development Mechanism (Hepburn, Ch. 20). Asymmetric information causes difficulties for both approaches, and the resulting mechanism is guaranteed to be messy and 'second-best' until coverage of cap and trade is more comprehensive.

Policy for research, development, and deployment of low-carbon technologies is similarly challenging, and there is relatively little high-quality economic and political analysis of how to allocate resources to and between research, development, and deployment. And yet, in the long term, the massive reductions in emissions implied by the target of at least 80 per cent reductions for developed countries by 2050 will require significant advances in low-carbon technologies. Indeed, the most critical technology may not yet have been invented. Further work on the economics of support for low-carbon research and development, following the lead of Victor (Ch. 16) on geoengineering, would be welcome.

What chance then is there of agreement? There is much experience of international treaty negotiations to draw upon, and the institutions supporting them. From these we can learn much about the sculpting of an international climate-change agreement. There is a considerable literature on the ozone layer initiatives and notably the Montreal Protocol, but perhaps less on the non-environmental international treaties. Depledge and Yamin (Ch. 21) and Ghosh and Woods (Ch. 22) consider the broader lessons to be learned from long experience with existing institutions designed to address climate change and other multilateral challenges.

As politicians and policy-makers struggle with perhaps the greatest challenge yet to face the planet, this volume is not intended to provide simple answers. Rather the intention is to illustrate why it has so far proved so intractable—why, so far, the emissions just keep going up. Yet recognition of just how difficult it all is—of the complexity, the costs, and the problems of cooperation—is a necessary step towards crafting a credible policy regime. The promise of a relatively cheap transition to a low-carbon economy has seduced politicians into avoiding the very hard issues that confront them of explaining to their electorates just how substantial the challenge we face will be. There has never been a problem like climate change before, and unsurprisingly it takes time—and probably climate crises—to face up to these requirements. If, in the meantime, a more immediate economic crisis comes along, the temptation is to prevaricate and 'muddle through'. At the same time, a major economic recession reduces growth and emissions, creating a pause in the rise in emissions, risking yet further delays in taking action. We broadly know what has to be done. Doing it remains the difficult part.

Part I

Revisiting the Economics of Climate Change

2

Climate-change Policy: Why has so Little been Achieved?

*Dieter Helm**

I. INTRODUCTION: THE SCALE OF THE PROBLEM

Few now doubt that climate change is occurring, and that it is human activity that is a prime cause. The science of the greenhouse effect has been well known for a century, but the complexity of the climate makes any precise prediction of the relationship between specific concentrations of particular greenhouse gases and changes in global temperatures extremely difficult. We are condemned to live with the uncertainty.

But that uncertainty is not unbounded, and we have already had significant temperature changes and, in the Arctic, fairly rapid climate change. The prospect of an ice-free North Pole in summer is not far away, and the Arctic Ocean is opening up for shipping through the Northeast and Northwest Passages.

While the science of the climate and the empirical evidence mount up, the policy responses have so far had little or no impact on the build-up of emissions. A concentration of 400 parts per million (ppm) of carbon dioxide[1] equivalent (CO_2e) will soon be reached (the pre-Industrial Revolution level was around 273ppm). A doubling of concentrations is all but inevitable, and 750 ppm by the end of the century is predicted on a business-as-usual scenario.

Business-as-usual is, indeed, what is most likely for some time to come. Emissions are not being stabilized, but rather are on a path of rapid increase. Fossil-fuel consumption is going up, there is plenty left to exploit, and the dirtiest fossil fuel—coal—is expanding its share. Energy-related carbon emissions are predicted to rise by around 45 per cent by 2030 (IEA, 2008*b*), on the back of a similar rise in energy demand. There is no global decoupling of the energy ratio. Indeed, global warming is making new sources of oil and gas easier to exploit—notably, in the northern regions (Canada and Russia, in particular) and in the Arctic seas as the ice retreats. There are also abundant (highly polluting) tar sands to exploit

* New College, Oxford.

Comments from, and discussions with, Chris Allsopp, Robin Smale, Cameron Hepburn, Christopher Bliss, and Paul Klemperer are gratefully acknowledged. Any errors remain mine, unfortunately.

[1] Throughout carbon dioxide (CO_2) is used as a proxy for greenhouse gases.

(in Canada, again), and most oil reservoirs are abandoned after half or less of the oil has been extracted. More worrying from a climate-change perspective, there is enough coal to last well beyond this century—and, given recent oil price increases and the wide dispersal of coal reserves, it is not surprising that coal is increasingly the fuel of choice for electricity generation. China and India's power sectors account for 85 per cent of the increase in global coal consumption in the IEA's reference scenario. This translates into perhaps 1,000GW of new coal electricity generation in China by 2030. There are, in short, far more fossil-fuel reserves than the capacity of the atmosphere to absorb them, and little evidence that they will be left in the ground in at least the short to medium term.

The global response so far has been meagre. The United Nations Framework on Climate Change Convention (UN FCCC), agreed in 1992, built upon the Intergovernmental Panel on Climate Change (IPPC) which had been established in 1988—an unprecedented international scientific collaboration.[2] It also kicked off the process which culminated in the Kyoto Protocol (UN FCCC, 1998), built around the fixing of national greenhouse-gas emissions-reduction targets for some developed countries. But Kyoto has so far delivered little: it has not made *any* appreciable difference to climate change—nor would it have done, had it been fully implemented and the targets delivered. The framework does not include binding caps on the USA, and provides no targets for India and China. Indeed, it only became operational because the Europeans bargained World Trade Organization (WTO) membership and other concessions with Russia.

In its defence, it is claimed that the Kyoto agreement provides a tentative step towards a post-2012 framework and, within Europe, it enabled the European Union Emissions Trading Scheme (EU ETS) to get under way as a prototype for a global emissions-trading regime. This defence rests, however, on the assumption that Kyoto is, in fact, a well-designed approach and that EU ETS could not have been started without Kyoto. Neither, arguably, turns out to be correct.[3]

So why is there such a disconnect between the science and the evidence on the one hand, and the policy response on the other? The disconnect is all the more surprising because it has been widely claimed—notably in the immensely influential Stern Report (Stern, 2007)[4]—that the costs of action now are comparatively small; smaller even than the typical annual differences between forecast and actual GDP. A 1 per cent GDP cost to stabilize emissions is perhaps less, even, than the current impacts of the credit crunch. Indeed, some claim that mitigating climate change is actually GDP-positive, and such a possibility is included in the Stern Report ranges.

One possible answer is that the disconnect is a function of education, information dissemination, and lags in the political process. According to this view, it is not at all surprising that it has taken a couple of decades for the evidence to be

[2] The IPCC has produced a series of reports (IPPC, 1995, 2001*a*, 2007*a*), and reactions, notably House of Lords (2005), but as an exercise in *international* collaboration, it is unprecedented.

[3] Indeed, the UK set up its own emissions-trading scheme to address its domestic 2010 carbon target. See Marshall Task Force (1998).

[4] The references throughout are to the 2007 version of the Stern Report.

gathered and analysed, and for politicians to absorb and lead the public towards new policy initiatives, but now action will follow quickly, as indeed witnessed by the recent Bali Conference, the new EU climate-change package announced in January 2008 and agreed in December 2008, and moves in the USA after the 2008 presidential election. A second possibility is that the Stern Report analysis is flawed, that the costs are much higher than estimated, and that the political economy of climate-change policy is much more constraining. On this view, the easy compatibility between economic growth and climate change, which lies at the heart of the Stern Report, is an illusion. And, given higher costs and serious threats to economic growth, the fact that politicians have founded their arguments to the public on the basis of low costs has been counterproductive. This chapter explores this second view, for, if it is correct, the necessary task of education and information needs to be recast.

The climate-change policy optimists work not only on the assumption that the costs of mitigation are low, but also that there will be a global agreement based upon the Kyoto principles after 2012, with *binding*, *tight*, and *credible* carbon caps. Again there is another more pessimistic view: that the prisoner's dilemma will make a credible top–down global carbon cartel very difficult to achieve, and that any agreement will require very significant fiscal transfers from Europe and the USA to China, India, and other developing countries. Some countries—notably in the Arctic regions—may actually experience some gains from climate change, and hence also require considerable financial inducements to join in.

This chapter considers why the disconnect between science and policy exists. In section II, the serious adverse trends are noted, especially in the energy and transport sectors. Section III explains why Kyoto has achieved so little. Section IV turns to the key concepts. Kyoto is based upon carbon production, not consumption, which conveniently places the burden of emissions reduction on those countries which *produce* energy-intensive goods, rather than those which *consume* them. The relationship between carbon consumption, sustainability, and economic growth is reconsidered. Section V considers the Stern Report, its economic framework, and, in particular, its estimates of the damage and mitigation costs. It is argued that both may be significantly underestimated. Section VI looks at the negotiations for a post-2012 framework. Section VII concludes.

II. THE CONTEXT: ADVERSE TRENDS

Current climate-change policy has been designed on the basis of the current economic structures and how marginal emissions reductions can be made from this starting point. It begins with where we are and then aims to reduce emissions towards future targets—notably, in 2020 and 2050. These, in turn, are based upon an overarching global ambition to halt the rise of emissions to around 450–550ppm CO_2e, a concentration that is roughly linked to limiting global warming to around 2° centigrade. There is no convincing analysis to suggest that this is an 'optimal' target, but rather an assumption that it could, in principle, be achieved and that two degrees may be a containable warming, which will not trigger rapid subsequent change.

These global targets are being translated into a plethora of sub-targets set at the European level, at the state level in the USA, and adopted by a number of localities and municipalities. It is the approach embedded in the Kyoto framework, and in the European ambitions for the post-Kyoto framework, and was the one at the centre of debates at the Bali Summit in 2007. But are these various targets enough? And is there any evidence that they are likely to be realized?

Unfortunately, global trends in the causes and levels of emissions—population growth, energy demand, and transport—suggest otherwise. The starting point is population and human consumption. Climate change has accompanied industrialization and a rapid increase in population, both of which have been facilitated by the harnessing of fossil fuels. The world population tripled in the twentieth century from two to six billion. Between now and 2050, it is projected to increase from six to nine billion—to add more extra people than the entire world population in 1950. These additional people will be overwhelmingly concentrated in China, India, and Africa—each with a total population of roughly two billion by 2050. The first two are expected to continue their rapid economic growth, with China perhaps matching current US consumption levels by 2050. China and India will in the process probably add around 1 billion cars, and will require the associated energy to sustain their much higher levels of consumption. Africa may be a different story.[5]

Energy-demand patterns do not simply map on to population-growth projections, though the correlation is closest for China and India. The IEA (2008*b*) reference scenarios are helpful in this regard, less for their predictive precision than for their value in setting out the parameters of the trends and policy contexts. Furthermore, the IEA focuses on 2030, which is midway to the 2050 target—and this is the period within which technological progress will have limited impacts on the capital stocks. It is the timeframe within which scientists say urgent action must be taken to avoid irreparable damage.

The IEA predicts a 45 per cent increase in global energy demand by 2030—i.e. in just over two decades' time—with China and India accounting for just over half of that increase. These enormous increases map almost exactly on to projected CO_2 increases. Both energy demand and carbon emissions are rising faster than population growth. The IEA (2007*a*) constructed an 'alternative energy scenario' in which all the current policies that governments around the world have devised to combat climate change are implemented and even then CO_2 emissions still rise by 25 per cent by 2030. In other words, we are heading substantially—and rapidly—in the wrong direction.

There is, in fact, very little reason to place much reliance on the alternative scenario. Much of the capital stock which will be in use in 2030 in the energy sector is already in place. Asset lives in the electricity industry are typically around

[5] See Chapter 7 by Paul Collier, Gordon Conway, and Tony Venables in this volume.

30 years or above—indeed, some coal generation in Europe and the USA is up to 60 years old. And in the replacement cycle for the energy capital stock, the relevant decisions to change the marginal carbon intensity for 2030 (and even to a considerable extent for 2050) are likely to be made in the next decade, and these reflect a substantial bias towards coal- and gas-fired generation. Germany and the UK are both, for example, considering new coal-fired power stations. New nuclear investments will have a marginal impact when set against nuclear plant closures up to 2030, and there is little prospect over this time horizon of carbon sequestration and storage making much impact.[6] The impact of global recession will offset some of the growth in emissions, but the lower the growth rates, the lower the oil price. IEA (2008*b*) assumes US$100 a barrel for 2008–15, rising to US$120 for 2030.

Indeed, in the energy sector, the key global shift in the fuel mix is adverse—towards coal. With the increase in oil (and therefore gas) prices since 2000, and with growing concerns about security of supply as oil and gas production is increasingly concentrated in the hands of autocratic governments, the share of coal projected in the IEA reference scenario in total energy demand rises from 26 to 29 per cent. Most of this is in China and India—with China (currently with nearly 80 per cent coal-fired generation) adding about two large coal power stations per week at present, and projected to add perhaps 1,000GW of new coal plant by 2030. (To put this into perspective, the total capacity of electricity generation in the UK (all fuels) is around 80GW.) China's generation by 2030 will be equivalent to current levels of the USA and Europe combined.

The position on transport is not encouraging either. While it is true that some of the capital stock turns over a bit faster, and there are significant fuel economies that can be made (and some scope for hybrid and electric cars), these trends are swamped by the increased demand for cars. Chamon *et al.* (2008) suggest that car ownership remains low up to a *per capita* annual income of about US$5,000, and then takes off rapidly above that level. They estimate that 'the number of cars worldwide will increase by 2.3 billion between 2005 and 2050, and that the number of cars in emerging and developing countries will increase by 1.9 billion'.[7] The trends in developed countries are adverse, too. In the UK, new car registration increased 13 per cent between 1996 and 2006, while air passenger numbers increased by 54 million between 2001 and 2006 (Office of National Statistics, 2008). Recession may provide some respite, but in the timescale of climate change, this is likely to be temporary.

The importance of the embedding of carbon-intensive production capacity in the capital stock in China and elsewhere is not just in respect of power stations and cars. It applies to energy transmission and distribution systems, which may be designed for large- or small-scale technologies, and it applies, too, to the transport sector. New airport capacity causes demand to increase for aviation. China has

[6] Nuclear power stations have a typical lead time of around ten years. Given that existing nuclear plants are reaching the end of their lives in a number of European countries (notably Germany and the UK), plant closures and output reductions are likely to exceed new plants coming into the systems in Europe until at least the mid- to late 2020s.

[7] IMF (2008, p. 10, box 4.1). The current number is around 0.5 billion.

recently been reported to be increasing its regional airports capacity in the order of some 97 new regional airports by 2020,[8] and it is notable across Europe that governments are encouraging new runway and terminal capacity.[9] The expansion of road networks encourages car use, too. Once these infrastructures are built, the marginal costs are significantly below the average costs, and marginal cost pricing leads to greater utilization. A carbon economy embeds fossil fuels into the fabric of its infrastructure.

The implication of these broad (and often crude) IEA scenarios is that the rapid economic growth (and associated population increases) of China and India is at the core of any serious attempt to decarbonize the world economy. Whether China builds 1,000GW of coal-fired electricity generation and whether it adds half a billion cars with conventional engines is of an order of magnitude more important to climate change than virtually any other trend. The corollary is obvious, too: climate-change policies matter largely insofar as they address these global trends, and local policies such as wind generation in remote locations are relevant largely insofar as they have an impact on behaviour in these developing economies. It does not, of course, follow that developed countries should not reduce their own emissions—indeed, on the contrary, as we will see, much of this growth in emissions in countries such as China is driven by developed countries' demand. The point here is that, so far, climate-change policies have had virtually no effect on these trends.

We return below to the China question and who is responsible for this growth of emissions and who should pay to decarbonize the Chinese economy. But before we do this, we need to consider whether this projected increase in China's emissions is really likely to materialize (and, to a lesser extent, the impacts of other rapidly developing countries). Three countervailing factors are relevant here. The first, and probably the most important, is whether China's economic growth—and therefore the derived demand for carbon—can be sustained. Are there any reasons why the projections of GDP growth of some 10 per cent per annum for the foreseeable future may turn out not to be delivered?

The answer is complex and beyond the scope of this chapter to scrutinize in any detail. However, it is worth noting the possible causes of a much lower growth path. The first is world demand. China is an export-oriented economy (exports comprise some 45 per cent of its GDP). Like Japan in the 1970s and 1980s, it exports significantly to the USA, and then, in effect, lends the money to the USA to pay for these goods (with roughly a 50 per cent domestic savings ratio). The serious recession in the USA represents a setback for the Chinese economy (as it did for the Japanese at the end of the 1980s).

[8] General Administration of Civil Aviation, China, January 2008. Chinese passenger air traffic grew 16 per cent in 2007, and is projected to increase by 11.4 per cent p.a. until 2020. Freight is projected to grow at 14 per cent p.a. over the same period.

[9] In the UK, major airport expansions are planned for Heathrow and Stansted. The 2003 White Paper, 'The Future of Aviation' reports that UK air travel has increased fivefold in the last 30 years (Department for Transport, 2003). Half the population now flies at least once a year. Unconstrained (by capacity) forecasts are for demand to *double* or *triple* by 2030.

A significant adjustment in exchange rates might also reduce the demand for Chinese exports—and, indeed, this is already under way. But there would be offsetting factors. Domestic consumption might absorb some of the demand shock, and then there are alternative markets in Europe and elsewhere. China's competitive advantages—notably cheap land and cheap labour—may erode somewhat. Yet they are likely to remain powerful engines for growth—especially when the doubling of its population to 2050 is taken into account.

A second possibility is that an oil-price shock may disproportionately affect China since it is energy-intensive. So far, however, the increase in oil prices from around US$10 a barrel in 1999 to over US$140 (and then the return to US$40) in 2008 appears to have had little impact. Furthermore, the oil-price effect is inversely related to the effect of the US recession—since the latter weakens oil demand and hence leads to lower prices (and, indeed, the fact that oil is priced in dollars exaggerates the scale of the price increase). To an extent, too, China has some strategic options in responding to higher oil prices, some of which are already being deployed. These include the scramble for resources (notably in Africa and the Caspian, but also in enhanced relations with the Middle East exporters), and, of course, further exploitation of coal reserves.

Some argue that, however intense the dash-for-resources, China (and others) will fail because they will run out. In other words, what will decarbonize the world economy is that there will not be enough carbon resources left to deplete. A particular version of this argument is called 'peak oil'.[10] It is argued that the peak of conventional oil production has been already reached, and that production will decline over the coming decades, just as demand rises. Prices will, therefore, increase very sharply, setting off a significant substitution effect. From a climate-change perspective, it is argued that this would be good news, but there are major weaknesses with the peak-oil hypothesis. There may well be lots more resources to discover, notably in an increasingly ice-free Arctic Ocean, and then in Antarctica (as well as elsewhere). Existing 'depleted' oil wells typically retain over half the initial reserves, and new technologies (not least using CO_2 to increase pressure through oil-enhanced recovery) may be effective.[11] Then there are many near substitutes which may be available, notably tar sands. Once these are included, Canada, for example, becomes one of the top three oil-reserve countries. These sources may be even more polluting than conventional ones. There is also lots of coal.

A third possibility is a political implosion as part of a revolt against communism and authoritarian state power. But even in this scenario (and twentieth-century Chinese history has examples of major political turmoil and consequent stagnation), it is worth bearing in mind the attraction of higher consumption

[10] The concept is associated with the *Hubbert Curve*, named after M. King Hubbert, who predicted in 1956 that US oil production would peak between 1965 and 1970. He subsequently predicted that global oil production would peak in 1995–2000.

[11] Oil-enhanced recovery (OER) is already a deployed technology in Norway (see http://www.Norway.org.vn/business/oil/carbonemissions.htm).

to the wider population and, therefore, that such events may not do more than temporarily reduce economic growth.

It would, therefore, be prudent to assume, for the purpose of designing credible climate-change policy, that none of these is likely *sufficiently* to derail China's economy in such a way as to offset the projected emissions growth—at least in the medium term to 2030. We are, therefore, left with the question of whether climate-change policies can facilitate a benign decarbonization of the Chinese, Indian, and other rapidly developing economies over the next two decades or so—against the adverse trends identified above. This is the central challenge for the negotiations for a post-2012 international climate-change agreement: to achieve a significant and rapid *reduction* in emissions in the context of a sharply *rising* trend.

III. POLICY HAS ACHIEVED VERY LITTLE SO FAR—KYOTO AND ALL THAT

Faced with these powerful adverse trends, how much progress has been made so far to slow down the rate of growth of carbon emissions, and how far has the groundwork been laid for a coherent and credible global response? The answer on both counts is worryingly little.

The starting point was the so-called Rio Earth Summit in 1992, which gave rise to the UN Framework Convention on Climate Change (UN FCCC, 1992). At this summit, there was a very widespread agreement to act—and this consensus was achieved largely because the Convention did not, in fact, mandate much by way of immediate and binding actions or economic impacts on the nation states. It was an agreement without many immediate political or economic consequences. It promised much and cost little. What was, however, achieved was to set up a process and a negotiating forum, and the role of the IPCC was reinforced, being tasked to examine the science and policy options, with a view to creating a consensus on the facts, the forecasts, and the policy recommendations that would form the basis for the development of international agreements to limit greenhouse-gas emissions.

The IPCC processes and reports have, not surprisingly, been controversial, but the IPCC has largely achieved its main aims. It has provided the international scientific forum for analysis and debate, and although its conclusions have had to be negotiated, they have proved remarkably robust. Dissenting academics and others have from time to time cried foul, and in important respects they have been proved right. However, it is notable that this dissent has been more heavily focused on the economics and policy aspects and less on the pure science.[12]

But the success of the IPCC has not been matched by the development and implementation of policies to reduce emissions. It provided for a periodic

[12] See, for example, House of Lords (2005) and Lawson (2008).

'conferences of the parties' (COP) process, with the most important outcome being at the third COP, which produced agreement on the Kyoto Protocol, signed in 1997 (UN FCCC, 1998). This had two main dimensions: the setting of targets for the reduction of emissions from industrialized countries; and the establishment of a framework for the evolution of wider and deeper reductions subsequently.

Let's start with the targets. There are several considerations here. First, do the targets set make any noticeable difference to global warming? The targets cover the main industrialized countries (excluding the USA after its withdrawal in 2003). In practice, this means the EU—Canada is not making much progress on meeting its targets (emissions up by over 20 per cent since 1990), and Australia is outside.[13] The Japanese position is not good, despite low economic growth (emissions rose 8.1 per cent by 2005 from the 1990 level). The targets for new members from the former Soviet block left lots of headroom, as their economies contracted in the 1990s after the collapse of the Berlin Wall, and this provided the 'hot air' which the other EU members could trade into.

For the EU, it is important to specify the counterfactual—what would have happened to greenhouse-gas emissions up to 2012 in the absence of the Kyoto targets? There are three parts to this counterfactual: the dash-for-gas, and the reduction in coal-burning activities in a number of core countries (notably the UK and Germany); the migration of energy-intensive industries offshore to the developing countries; and the impact of higher oil prices since 2000. Counterfactuals cannot, of course, be observed, but it is reasonable to assume that the outcome would not have been markedly different. The first two had little to do with climate change, and the oil price increases were unrelated, too. The targets themselves are more typically being overshot than met, as Table 2.1 indicates. Only a lengthy (unanticipated) recession might close the gap.

The Kyoto Protocol and the COP process as currently constructed are not delivering significant aggregate greenhouse-gas emissions reductions in the EU, *sufficient* to have a noticeable effect on global warming. And these numbers flatter the true underlying position. The Kyoto targets do not included aviation and shipping, which are merely noted items.[14] In both cases, these have risen strongly since 1990, and given the greater damage caused by emissions in the atmosphere from aviation, its growth is alone enough to undermine the limited reductions claimed as directly caused by the Kyoto Protocol targets.

What about the second part of Kyoto—the evolutionary framework towards an eventual deeper and wider agreement? The defenders of Kyoto suggest that the COP process has been successful in bringing together a coalition of parties incrementally adding more body to the climate-change negotiations, and that, at Bali, the USA signalled a willingness to participate, and that at Copenhagen in 2009, the main players will all come on board for a new agreement for the

[13] Within the EU, Spain and Portugal had by 2002 both *increased* their emissions by over 40 per cent above the 1990 levels.

[14] See NAO (2008) for a discussion of the various measurement issues, and Helm *et al.* (2007).

Table 2.1. Kyoto targets and outcomes for EU member countries (%)

	Kyoto target	2005[a] outcome
Austria	−13.0	18.1
Belgium	−7.5	−2.1
Cyprus	No target	63.7
Denmark	−21.0	−7.8
Finland	0.0	−2.6
France	0.0	−1.9
Germany	−21.0	−18.7
Greece	25.0	25.4
Ireland	13.0	25.4
Italy	−6.5	12.1
Luxembourg	−28.0	0.4
Malta	No target	54.8
Netherlands	−6.0	−1.1
Portugal	27.0	40.4
Spain	15.0	52.3
Sweden	4.0	−7.4
United Kingdom	−12.5	−15.7
Former Communist states		
Bulgaria	−8.0	−47.2
Czech Republic	−8.0	−25.8
Estonia	−8.0	−52.0
Hungary	−6.0	−34.5
Latvia	−8.0	−58.0
Lithuania	−8.0	−53.1
Poland	−6.0	−32.0
Romania	−8.0	−45.6
Slovak Republic	−8.0	−33.6
Slovenia	−8.0	0.4

Note: [a] 2005 is the latest full year for which data are available.
Source: EEA (2007).

post-2012 period. They point, too, to the initiative by the EU to pre-announce that it will unilaterally reduce its emissions by 20 per cent by 2020 and offer 30 per cent by 2020 if others take similar measures (EU, 2008).

There are, however, two counter-claims: that Kyoto demonstrated how difficult it is to bring on board the major players; and that a better and more comprehensive agreement could be achieved without the Kyoto architecture getting in the way.

As Victor (2001) and Barrett (2003), among others, have demonstrated, the problem of climate change does not easily lend itself to a global agreement to reduce emissions. The analysis of the conditions for such a top–down agreement to work tolerably well have been researched by international-relations specialists for decades, and, in the environmental field, the Montreal Protocol on ozone depletion has provided a pertinent (and much misunderstood) case study (Barrett, 2003, ch. 8). Climate change is so intractable because the basic conditions for agreement—and for compliance and enforcement—are largely absent. To name but a few of the problems: the allocation of responsibility for the existing stock of carbon in the atmosphere (which developing countries point out was put there by the industrialized countries) is complex; carbon emissions per head are low in those countries most rapidly increasing their emissions; some countries (and, particularly, some countries' political élites) may actually benefit from climate change, and generally the effects vary greatly between countries; there are powerful—multidimensional—free-rider incentives; the measurement of emissions (including, to list just a few, rain-forest depletion, soil erosion, methane from permafrost melting, aviation and shipping, agriculture, and ocean and other sink depletion) is at best weak; and there are, at present, no serious enforcement mechanisms. It is hard to think of an international problem which lends itself less to a coherent, credible, and sufficiently robust and comprehensive general agreement.[15] To put it in perspective, limiting nuclear proliferation is trivial by comparison.

It is further complicated by the fact that these problems all arise in the context of negotiating a climate-change agreement as a stand-alone exercise. But international negotiations are not only multilateral but over a multiple number of issues. Thus climate change sits alongside trade negotiations, nuclear weapons negotiations, and migration and human rights negotiations. Russia, for example, ratified Kyoto in the context of WTO and other EU-related discussions.

Some of these problems can be addressed through the Kyoto discussions. But those which are core—notably basing an agreement on national emissions-production-based reduction targets—are not so straightforward in Kyoto and, indeed, may prove a hindrance. Targets may have to be flexible, they may require the development of global financial-transfer mechanisms, and they may require linkages to the WTO trade framework and even to military mechanisms. New institutions may be needed, too. And the linking factor here—a serious weakness of Kyoto—is that what matters for an international agreement is the consumption of carbon, not its geographic production (as we shall see in the next section). Of course, Kyoto provides a forum, but it is far from obvious that it is the only, or best, one.

These considerations lead to two conclusions: that little has, in fact, been achieved in terms of emissions reductions under Kyoto; and that Kyoto at best provides a forum for debate going forward. But a gradual widening of the number of countries adopting national emissions targets, and a gradual tightening of these targets is unlikely to do much to address the urgency of the climate-change problem. What may be required is to go back to the fundamental problems of the climate-change negotiations, and to address in particular the problems of major international fiscal transfers—in other words, how to craft an agreement in which industrialized countries pay developing countries not to increase emissions, and provide them with the technology to achieve this. But to consider how to do this, we need to step back and look at the underlying economics of

[15] A series of proposals for a post-Kyoto agreement are set out in Aldy and Stavins (eds) (2007).

climate change—in particular, the consumption (as opposed to production) of greenhouse gases, and the relationship between carbon consumption, economic growth, and sustainability.

IV. CARBON CONSUMPTION, ECONOMIC GROWTH, AND SUSTAINABILITY

(i) Consumption, Not Production

The Kyoto Protocol employs the measurement of emissions based on the UN FCCC methodology. It takes a geographical approach to emissions responsibility—all (and only) emissions generated from *production* activities within a country's territory are attributable to that country's emissions total. And, as noted above, the UN FCCC approach is not comprehensive: among other things, it excludes aviation and shipping.

From this accounting methodology, the Kyoto targets follow. If the methodology fails to provide an appropriate basis for the assignment of responsibility between national states then any agreement based upon this foundation is unlikely to prove credible. And since, as we shall see, it does not, Kyoto is (perhaps fatally) flawed.

A country (for example, the UK) could have a relatively low production of greenhouse gases, but at the same time have a high consumption level. It could produce low carbon-intensive goods (such as services, rather than manufacturing), but import and consume high carbon-intensive goods (steel, aluminium, glass, and chemicals). In the UK's case, the shift of high carbon-intensive production to China, India, and other developing countries has had this effect. Furthermore, it could achieve a given Kyoto target by moving energy-intensive industries offshore—without making any noticeable difference to climate change.

Some numbers indicate the scale of these effects. On the UN FCCC basis, the UK's record is impressive, having already surpassed the Kyoto target of a 12.5 per cent reduction by 2008–12. Just adding back in aviation and overseas activities of UK residents puts a dent in this performance—emissions have fallen only 11.9 per cent. Even this adjustment puts the UK's meeting of the Kyoto target in jeopardy. But taking all greenhouse gases embedded in imports and subtracting greenhouse gases embedded in exports, Helm *et al.* (2007) provide a crude estimate that emissions between 1990 and 2003 have *increased* by 19 per cent.[16] Consider the impact on Kyoto, and its two claimed advantages: that it commits the developed countries to reducing emissions; and that it provides a framework going forward. It is immediately apparent that it fails on both counts.

[16] NAO (2008) argues in response that because the calculation of carbon consumption is more complex—and hence uncertain—we should *therefore* continue to use production-based measurements. In other words, it is better to be more precisely wrong than approximately right (Wiedmann *et al.*, 2008).

Industrialized countries can increase (and have been increasing) their carbon consumption (probably significantly), and developing countries are unlikely to agree that the industrialized countries' responsibilities are exhausted by addressing their current and future carbon production. As China has pointed out, although it might *produce* high emissions, these are *on behalf of* consumers in developed countries, and therefore the consumers should pay for the relevant reductions. The polluter is the consumer, not the producer.[17]

Just to complete the criticisms of the production-based Kyoto framework, note that, in addition to failing on both counts above, it creates major distortions in efficiency terms, too, making it a high-cost method of reducing emissions (we return to these policy costs below). In the Kyoto world, countries have differential greenhouse-gas caps. Given that emissions are closely tied to energy intensity, energy-intensive industries face a distortion on the basis of geographical location, which is a function of policy not underlying costs. Hence the problem of 'carbon leakage': production simply shifts from high cap to low (or no) cap locations, thereby, in the process, exacerbating the gap between carbon production and consumption.

(ii) Carbon Consumption and Economic Growth

If current carbon consumption provides a better measure of the responsibility for global warming (leaving out, for the moment, the past consumption), it follows that the scale of the compensating financial transfers from industrialized countries to developed ones will have to be on a scale significantly greater than currently under discussion following Bali. To put it into perspective, the USA comprises around 25 per cent of the world economy, with the EU at around 20 per cent. Adding in Canada, Japan, and Australia takes the number over 50 per cent. If the carbon intensity of consumption in industrialized countries were similar to that in developing countries (it may, indeed, in aggregate be greater since the latter tend to be labour-intensive), the share of the total costs of meeting the global targets would be at least half.[18]

The policy implications of this point are considered later. But first the implications for economic growth that this focus on carbon consumption illustrates need to be explored. In the conventional approach—as, for example, used in the Stern Report—economic growth is measured by GDP. Estimates of the costs of climate change and the costs of mitigation are expressed in terms of GDP forgone. Behind these estimates lies a series of assumptions about the counterfactual—what would happen in the absence of climate-change and abatement measures.

Though this framework is one in which climate-change policy is typically addressed, it is important to recognize that GDP is not a particularly useful indicator. Indeed, it is hard to think of the relevant climate-change policy question to

[17] See Chapter 8 by Jiahua Pan, Jonathan Phillips, and Ying Chen in this volume.

[18] The exception here is China, where since 2000 there has been a shift *towards* energy and carbon intensity. See Rosen and Houser (2007).

which GDP is the answer. GDP is particularly inappropriate for the consideration of environmental issues, and for longer-term contexts (Dasgupta 2001, 2008*a*). It has no asset counterpart, and hence no account is taken of asset depreciation. For example, for the UK, the GDP performance in the last two decades has no offset for the depletion of North Sea oil and gas. In environmental economics, changes in the stock of non-renewable assets (often referred to as natural capital) are a core component of economic performance: indeed, it is often argued that much of apparent economic growth is, in large measure, the depletion of natural capital. As Dasgupta (2008*a*, p. 6) puts it: 'GDP . . . is not a measure of long run human well-being, meaning that movements in GDP . . . are a poor basis for judging economic progress.'

There are a number of measures which improve upon GDP. Net national product (NNP) takes account of assets and depreciation. Then there are attempts to incorporate shadow prices for environmental services.[19] If assets are incorporated, then it matters greatly what substitution between different types of assets—particularly between natural and man-made capital—is assumed. In the conventional approach, this is one-for-one: non-renewable assets can be depleted provided there is a commensurate investment in man-made capital to compensate. Such an assumption lies at the heart of the sorts of calculations made in the Stern Report analysis: thus we can carry on getting better off by, say, 3 per cent p.a. GDP growth *ad infinitum* as we gain more and more man-made capital to compensate for the loss of environmental assets. So a reduction of the species on the planet by, say, 50 per cent by the end of this century (a distinct possibility) can be compensated for by an offsetting improvement in whatever replaces iPods and other new and existing technologies.

Once it is assumed that the substitution effect is less than unity, the GDP 3 per cent growth rate becomes unreliable. In due course, the feedback mechanisms from the reduction in natural capital reduce the ability of the economy to function, as (environmental) costs rise. The feedback in conventional accounting is indirect through costs rather than assets since, as noted, GDP does not value assets. Climate change is likely to be one such cost escalator, together with the related loss of habitat and biodiversity (some of which is caused by climate change, and some independently by population growth and other effects). Over the short run, these effects make little perceived difference; over the longer run, their effects can be profound. Hence, the assumed GDP growth may not materialize. It is at best a short-run indicator—and climate change is a long-run process.

These considerations are important for two separate reasons: GDP may not be a proxy for the level of consumption that is consistent with a sustainability criterion—the prevention of the consumption possibilities of future generations falling below our own (non-decreasing utility over time); and the GDP measure of the costs of climate change which the Stern Report gives may be a significant underestimate, because climate change (and biodiversity loss and all the other environmental damage from economic activities) may lower the growth rate.

[19] See Dasgupta and Mäler (2000) and Dasgupta (2001) for a more detailed discussion.

We deal with the second issue in the next section, and concentrate here on the sustainability criterion.

Sustainability is an interpretation of a principle of equity over time. It measures the consumption possibilities over time against a constraint: they must not deteriorate. People in the future will have better technology (we can assume that technical progress will continue and saturation effects are unlikely). In this sense, they will be better off. The supply function will continue to shift outwards. But with ever more people, and with biodiversity loss and climate change, their consumption possibilities (per head, and even in aggregate) may be reduced. The oceans are already highly polluted, agricultural land is being affected by salinization and desertification, and global warming will have serious effects on the areas where population is most heavily concentrated. There will be some compensating benefits from increased temperatures to some agricultural areas (and from high-carbon concentrations in the atmosphere benefiting some plant growth). And there will be the gains from new technology. But the net effects of these factors are captured by some measure of economic well-being which incorporates the depreciation of natural capital (including the climate and biodiversity) and the associated costs.

The kinds of information necessary to construct this sort of measure do not exist in conventional GDP accounts. Nevertheless, some conjectures can be made about the impact of a more comprehensive measure which can be linked back to the argument made above about carbon consumption. The IPCC target of stabilization at 450–550ppm is not based on any explicit optimization exercise, but it can be taken as a proxy. Beyond that level, climate change may have 'dangerous' consequences, and it may not be easy to control. In other words, once this level is reached, we are into the 'fat tail' of the probability distribution of global temperature outcomes—of really big economic effects from more dramatic climate change. One way of thinking about this is that, as the concentration of greenhouse gases rises, so the substitution between natural and man-made capital declines.

The IPCC (and the UN FCCC) argue that we should avoid this prospect, and should do this through a stabilization of emissions now. Since we are, by definition, on a business-as-usual path, the implication is that the current consumption path does not meet the sustainability criterion. By how much are we over-consuming? On the IPCC's analysis, the answer is: by the costs of reverting to the 450–550ppm path, adjusted first for the outward movement out of the supply function owing to man-made capital appreciation, human capital, and technical change over the same period, and adjusted second for other related and unrelated environmental damage. What would it take to revert to the 450–550ppm path? The answer is: the reduction of carbon consumption to the preferred path. How far are we above it? This is the amount measured by the path of carbon consumption over time, incorporating the aviation and shipping, and the net carbon composition of imports and exports. From the calculations referred to above, in the UK case, it may perhaps be more than 30 per cent when the difference between consumption increases are compared with the required consumption falls. The EU and the USA may not be greatly different. This is the gap which scientists tell us must be urgently addressed in the next decade or two.

Consideration of these conceptual measurement problems suggests some radical conclusions. Emissions should be measured on a consumption not production basis. On a consumption basis, current emission-reduction targets for industrialized countries are comparatively trivial in comparison to the gravity of the problem, a shortfall which Kyoto underwrites. It is, therefore, unsurprising that Kyoto has made no significant difference to climate change. GDP provides little guidance to the climate-change problem, and the claim that climate change can be addressed without significant impacts (the widely quoted 1 per cent GDP number to which we return below) relies on an assumption that the accumulation of man-made capital, human capital, and technical progress is fast enough to offset the depletion of natural capital, of which the climate is a part. There is no good reason to accept this assumption, certainly over the time period scientists advise in which the increase in carbon emissions needs to be halted and then reversed. And the starting point is a level of GDP which does not account for the responsibility in respect of current carbon consumption. If past contributions were to be added to the responsibility calculation, a significant reduction in consumption levels in developed countries is implied.

V. REVISITING THE STERN REPORT

The assumptions about growth and consumption are, unfortunately, not the only problems with the conventional approach to the economics of climate change. The focus here is on the Stern Report—notably because it provides a conventional approach, but also because its conclusions have been widely taken up by politicians and commentators, to the extent that it has become the new conventional wisdom on the economics of climate change. In addition to the possibility that the growth rate may be lower (possibly much lower) later in the century (and hence the predicted GDP measured loss of perhaps 5–25 per cent GDP by the end of the century may be higher), there are two other dimensions of Stern's arithmetic which are questionable: the costs and the discount rate.

(i) The Costs of Mitigating Climate Change

The Stern Report devotes just two chapters to addressing the costs of mitigation, to substantiate the claim that these will be between −1.0 and +3.5, with an average estimate of just 1 per cent to stabilize at 500ppm. This matters, because the 1 per cent is the most widely quoted number from the Report, particularly by politicians, and provides the basis for the claim that economic growth need not be much harmed by reducing emissions to stabilize at 450–550ppm.[20]

The two chapters purport to provide microeconomic and macroeconomic justification of the 1 per cent, and each is seriously flawed in important, but different ways. The microeconomic chapter is, in turn, based upon a single supporting paper (Anderson, 2006), itself largely derivative of a series of papers on technology costs, and it is hard to reproduce its results.[21] In essence, the microeconomics is not based upon economic cost factors, but more narrowly on technology. An 'optimal' supply function of technologies is presented on the basis of conventional models (which go under the general name of MARKAL), which provide a least-cost solution to the mitigation target.

The essence of MARKAL-type models is the assumptions: the assumed costs of each of the technologies considered and the learning and technology assumptions going forward. The optimal supply function is merely the transformation of the assumptions that are made about the costs of each selected technology. Such estimates are obviously vulnerable to appraisal optimism, and there are numerous lobbyists with vested interests in the numbers, since these influence policy and the associated allocation of the economic rents that result. A serious analysis would focus largely on the evidence for the assumed costs. Unfortunately, the Stern Report chapter and the supporting paper provide very little by way of guidance as to the reliability of these assumptions, and in particular do not report how past sets of assumptions have performed against out-turns. As a result, little (or indeed no) reliance should be placed upon them. Strictly, on this basis, the Stern Report's 1 per cent on which politicians are relying is an *assumed* number.

But even if the underlying assumptions were soundly grounded, and supported by empirical evidence, the derived supply function is essentially restricted to the 'optimal' costs of the technologies, and takes no account of the fluctuations in the costs of the technologies as market conditions vary, and assumes that the policy framework will lead to their costless deployment. It is the (least) costs of the equipment, not the cost of producing the outputs. Neither turns out to be well-founded. A rapid least-cost roll-out of low-carbon technologies assumes that the manufacturing capability anticipates demand, and hence prices do not reflect imbalances between demand and supply. They are always in equilibrium. The evidence is to the contrary: for example, the prices of wind turbines have risen sharply as the dash-for-wind has been embedded in renewables policy; and now there is evidence in the sharply rising prices of new nuclear development technologies as manufacturing production lags demand. These price effects are of a significant order of magnitude—rendering the cost numbers in the Stern Report all but useless for the purposes of public policy design and implementation.

[20] A few examples include Baroso, Blair, Brown, and Sarkozy in Europe. US politicians have been less willing to endorse this number.

[21] Nordhaus's criticism that the Stern Report has not been subject to the normal process of peer review is particularly important in respect of this chapter and the supporting paper (Nordhaus, 2007).

The technology costs assume that the energy systems are optimally designed to facilitate their deployment. No account is taken in the Stern Report of the costs of system-wide changes to the transmission and distribution, for example, and, in the case of wind, the assumptions about availability and back-up supplies are optimistic. While these may not matter at the margin, with large-scale deployment of these technologies, they are likely to be significant. Given the scale of the switch from high- to low-carbon technologies implied by the overarching targets, non-marginal deployment should be taken into account.[22]

Then comes perhaps the greatest gap in the Stern Report cost calculations—the policy costs.[23] There is a voluminous literature of government failure, regulatory capture, and the impact of rent-seeking behaviour within the policy process. Climate-change policy may or may not be the biggest externality, as the Stern Report suggests (actually it is a public bad), but it is likely to be one of the largest sources of economic rents from policy interventions. There is a large and growing climate-change 'pork barrel'.[24] It is highly unlikely that the policy costs will be zero. Indeed, there are good reasons to suppose otherwise—at every level of climate-change policy.

The starting point in analysing climate-change policy costs is Kyoto and its associated distorting incentive structure. Its design encourages two sorts of rent-seeking behaviour: by countries seeking advantage from their individual quotas; and by companies seeking to arbitrage between different geographic production caps. Every country has an incentive to overstate its costs of compliance and underestimate its opportunities for abatement. The very measurement base has economic rents attached to it. Countries also have an incentive to misreport performance. Companies have incentives to switch locations to minimize their carbon costs. These distorting incentives have been a common feature of negotiations since the UN FCCC, and there is no reason to suppose that they will go away.

To these policy costs in the overall design of international climate-change agreements need to be added the costs of specific policy interventions. In this respect, the UK is an interesting and instructive example. The incoming Labour government in 1997 committed itself to a unilateral domestic CO_2 target of a 20 per cent reduction by 2010 from 1990 levels (Labour Party, 1997). This was presented as an exercise in 'leadership': the UK would demonstrate that this target could be achieved, and at low cost, thereby providing an example which would be used to persuade the USA to accept Kyoto carbon caps.[25]

[22] It is interesting to note that Cameron Hepburn and Nicholas Stern (Ch. 3 in this volume) correctly place significance on the non-marginal nature of climate-change impacts on the one hand, but do not recognize the non-marginal nature of mitigation policies to achieve the sharp reductions in emissions on the other.

[23] Stern himself acknowledges this gap in his analysis. In the *Financial Times* (16 April 2008), he is quoted as saying: 'I probably would have emphasized the importance of good policy [if writing the report again today] and how bad policy puts up the costs [of cutting emissions]'.

[24] This rent-seeking behaviour is also prevalent in the allocation of R&D funding. See Cohen and Noll (1991).

[25] The case was summarized by Tony Blair in *The Economist*: 'A year of huge challenges', 29 December 2004.

It has been a failure in all three respects: it is very unlikely to be achieved, even with the recession; it has been (very) high-cost; and it has not persuaded the Bush administration of the virtues of Kyoto.[26] Here the main concern is the costs. The UK set out a climate-change strategy to achieve this target through renewables (the Renewables Obligation and the Renewables Obligation Certificates) and energy efficiency, with some support from emissions trading (the UK ETS and then the EU ETS). These approaches were deemed preferable to nuclear power, which was effectively ruled out, notably in the 2003 Energy White Paper (DTI, 2003*a*). Much of the energy-efficiency programme was claimed to be net present value (NPV)-positive, while the estimates for renewables from the MARKAL model (discussed above) pointed to limited additional cost burdens.[27]

In practice, energy efficiency has not had a significant take-up and, in particular, individuals and companies have not been noticeable in their adoption of the claimed positive-NPV investments.[28] Indeed, an improvement in energy efficiency take-up appears to be more likely to result from the sharp increase in energy prices (which were not anticipated when the policy was set out—the 2003 White Paper assumed US$25/barrel oil for the foreseeable future). Subsequent falls may reverse some of these gains, although the recession may have an income effect on energy demand. But it is on renewables where the costs of the policy have turned out to be orders of magnitude greater than indicated by the MARKAL modelling. A study by the National Audit Office (NAO, 2005, p. 4) found that the Renewables Obligation 'is several times more expensive than other measures currently being implemented by the government'. Compared with EU ETS carbon prices in the range £20–£30 per tonne of carbon, the UK renewables programme is staggeringly expensive. At the early 2009 level, below £10 per tonne, it is even worse. Perhaps only the Italian renewables programme looks more expensive. Recently it has begun to be appreciated that current biofuels policy may be even worse—not only in terms of costs, but also in terms of the very limited carbon savings and the impact on agriculture.

Taking account of these policy costs at both the international level and in national policy design, and adding them on to the technology optimism in the MARKAL numbers, adjusted upwards further for the lag in manufacturing of the technologies which is an inevitable part of a rapid decarbonization process, is likely to produce a number well above the Stern Report's 1 per cent. To produce an alternative estimate in terms of percentages of GDP is not only well beyond the scope of this chapter, but conceptually very difficult. It requires an estimate of the scale of future policy costs, which in turn requires an analysis of the incentives in public-policy design and in implementation processes, and how lobbying interests seek out the economic rents from policy. It is illustrated by specific examples of policy failure—such as the renewables example in the UK. These examples might

[26] Nor, indeed, any other senior US politicians on *the basis of the British policy approach*.

[27] An accompanying technical paper to the 2003 White Paper set this out (DTI, 2003*b*).

[28] On behavioural approaches and explanations, please see Chapter 6 by Kjell Arne Brekke and Olof Johansson-Stenman.

indicate several percentage points higher—but once recognized as non-trivial, there would be a feedback in terms of either better policy design, or greater reluctance to act at all. These very broad political economy effects are probably beyond precise statistical estimation—and, indeed, such estimates are probably unhelpful, not least because politicians are led to believe that there is more certainty than merited and, in consequence, are ill prepared for unanticipated cost shocks.

There is a final twist to these costs. Above we noted that, on a consumption basis, the implied cuts in the industrialized countries would be much greater. There would, therefore, be a more rapid deployment of low-carbon technologies, and many existing carbon-intensive assets would be stranded. The (non-marginal) disruption costs of the transition might be very considerable—for example, electricity security of supply might be seriously impaired if existing coal plants were rapidly shut down. There would be significant price effects, without a drawn-out period for individuals and firms to adjust.

Taken together, it can be concluded that the costs of mitigation from a microeconomic perspective are likely to be significantly higher than those predicted by the MARKAL modelling exercises. Indeed, the MARKAL model is best regarded as an idealized solution. This makes it all the more remarkable that the Stern Report should place reliance on such an approach—and the corollary is that policy-makers should place no reliance on the 1 per cent number.

The Stern Report, however, provides an alternative way of calculating the costs—one grounded in macroeconomics. Aggregate income is made up of consumption plus investment. The decarbonization process represents an enormous investment opportunity, and, as investment goes up, so too will aggregate income. Thus, it is argued that mitigation is a growth-inducing activity. This is a beguiling argument and, as with the MARKAL approach, it has an element of credibility. It is true that as investment goes up, *ceteris paribus* so too does aggregate income. But this is true of *any* investment. The important point is whether the investment—compared with other investments that might have been made—increases wealth in a way which increases the level of sustainable consumption (see Dasgupta, 2001). Energy-generating technologies are derived demands, and the microeconomic point raised above is that low-carbon technologies are probably higher-cost than the current carbon technologies. Furthermore, it is not even clear that the aggregate level of investment goes up: for a given demand for energy there is a vector of alternative ways of meeting it through different capital stocks. The low-carbon investment opportunity is mirrored by a declining high-carbon investment opportunity. The net effect on growth is unclear.

Then there is the consumption element of aggregate demand. If costs rise for (low-carbon) energy, and if energy demand is relatively inelastic, household budgets will contract, reducing aggregate consumption. Add to this the impact of the consumption-based measurement of emissions and the sharper emissions-reduction targets implied for industrial countries, and the impact on growth may be much more significant.

The implication of these considerations on the macro and micro approaches is that the costs of mitigating climate change are likely to be significantly higher than indicated by the Stern Report, with a resulting reduction in the sustainable level of consumption in industrialized countries. They are also inherently uncertain. The happy political message that we can deal with climate change without affecting our standard of living—which is a key implicit message from the Stern Report on which politicians have publicly focused—and do so in a sustainable way, turns out, unfortunately, to be wrong.

(ii) Discounting

The Stern Report has one more variable in deriving its result: that the discount rate to be used in marrying up the damage in the future to the costs now of mitigation should be low. This turns out to be needed because, if the discount rate were to reflect the evidence from current behaviour, the Stern Report calculations would indicate, even on its 1 per cent costs, that we should do little about climate change—since future people are going to be so much better off than us as a result of the compounding of 2–3 per cent economic growth for a century, and we currently discount their future utility at a positive (and significant) rate. By 2100, when the Stern Report expects that the damage may be equal to between 5 and 25 per cent GDP, the nine billion or more people will have been on this 2–3 per cent p.a. growth scenario for the century and hence will all be living at or above the current consumption patterns of the industrialized countries. And in industrialized nations, people will be consuming at levels more than four times their current levels.[29] We should not now, on this basis, sacrifice some of our relative low levels of consumption to people in the future who will be much better off than we are now, just to avoid them being a little less than staggeringly better off than us.

This compound GDP growth rate is one part of the calculation. But it is on the discounting of future utility where the Stern Report deviates from observed behaviour. By using a sufficiently low time-preference rate over future utility, the balance can be tipped in favour of action now. That is what the Stern Report does, and it has been challenged on at least two broad levels. First, following Nordhaus (2007), there is little evidence that the sort of discounting practice the Stern Report advocates matches what we actually do. Thus, the Stern Report's discount rate relies upon a *moral* argument. However, moral judgements are, of course, open to dispute, and moral philosophers disagree about the principle of strict equity, which gives the Stern Report its zero (or rather 0.1, reflecting extinction risk) time preference—either as a principle of equity itself, or because other non-equity considerations count, too. Second, the 'fat tailers' argue that the real source of the claim that we should act now comes not from the discount rate, but rather from the possibility that the probability distribution of outcomes has a nasty sting

[29] Note, however, that these growth rates are unlikely to be uniformly distributed. Indeed, lower growth rates may well occur where damage is highest.

in it—the 'fat tail', the low probability of a rapid and damaging climate change. Weitzman (2007*a*) leads this critique.

These discounting issues have been the subject of a long and distinguished literature. From the perspective of climate-change *policy*, and in particular in crafting a post-Kyoto framework, it is important to separate out those issues which turn on welfare judgements and moral philosophy, and those which are matters of scientific dispute and evidence of behaviour. For while the Stern Report—and, indeed, Ramsey (1928) on whom the Stern Report leans, quoting his famous remark that to discount at other than zero reflects a lack of imagination—might argue that public policy *ought* to be based upon a deep principle of equity, the post-Kyoto discussions will be grounded more heavily in the self-interest of the participants, more or less enlightened. So, while moral education may be important in improving the behaviour of voters and governments, and even if there was moral agreement on the principle of zero discounting (which there is not), it would be a considerable mistake to expect that it will, in fact, determine the outcome. This is to assume a rapid success for education and public persuasion overcoming the gap between the science and the (lack of) policy response. There is, as yet, sadly no evidence that such persuasive arguments are leading to individuals or countries changing their behaviour towards lower discounting of future utility.

Indeed, it is important to realize just how controversial the ethical foundations of the zero time-preference arguments are. The claim is that we should be indifferent as to the time period in which consumption takes place—that the interests of future generations count equally with our own. The sustainability criterion goes even further: it requires that they should be at least as well off as ourselves, and since there is uncertainty, this implies a slightly negative time-preference rate.

Why should this be? Is the claim even coherent? Does it apply thousands of years into the future, or are we more concerned with those in closer time proximity to those more remote? Is it limited by population? Would a faster rate of population growth mean that more resources should be sacrificed to the future? And is the underlying claim to equality robust? The claims to equality between existing people have had a mixed philosophical reception: why then should we apply them into the future when we clearly do not do so for current people?[30]

So the moral case for a zero time discounting should not be taken as given, but rather as highly contentious, and, not surprisingly, it is unlikely to be a prime motivation to the negotiations on future climate-change policy. In practice, we do not take equality between people in different locations now very seriously: few politicians would be elected on a platform of a major transfer of wealth from the industrialized nations to the developing countries necessary to equalize current living standards. One per cent GDP contributions to aid budgets remains the meagre global ambition. This matters, because any plausible set of policies to stabilize emissions at the IPCC-recommended levels will require significant transfers from industrialized to developing countries, and such transfers based

[30] See Hepburn and Stern (Ch. 3) for further discussion.

upon self-interest are likely to be very different from those based on the idea of inter-generational equity.

Behaviourally, then, there is little basis for assuming that voters and governments will in fact use a zero time-preference rate. The case for urgent action now rests rather on the non-discounting reasons: that the damage is likely to be great, and, indeed, that the fat-tail argument should be taken seriously. Where the discounting issue matters is not so much in time-preference assumptions but rather in the impact of global warming on economic growth—the 2–3 per cent per annum growth assumption. Because of the direct damage, because environmental capital and man-made capital are not such easy substitutes, future generations may not be so much better off—and so they will not be so well placed to offset the environmental damage with their greater man-made capital and associated technologies. As argued in section IV, economic growth may not be so easily compatible with the effects of, and mitigation costs of, climate change. So, although the time preference rate may be higher, the growth component may be lower.

In summary, the Stern Report framework provides a useful coat hanger on which to examine the economics of climate change. But it is open to challenge in respect of its main components: the damage is likely to be greater and so are the costs of mitigation. The impacts on economic growth rates are likely to be more severe. We will not, therefore, be as well off in the future as we would have been on the basis of the 2–3 per cent GDP compound growth rates. What the Stern Report does is give a very conventional analysis, which points away from doing much about climate change now, only to rescue its conclusion with a dose of highly debatable moral philosophy. What remains, however, is the conclusion—that we should take urgent action now—which is correct, but for reasons almost entirely diametrically opposite to those of the Stern Report. What makes action necessary now is that, contrary to the Stern Report, there are good reasons for believing that the substitution of man-made capital to compensate for the damage to the environment (including climate change and its environmental consequences for biodiversity) is not unity, but rather less, and probably declining. The fat tail of more rapid and damaging climate change lurks, like the hidden underside of an iceberg.

VI. AFTER 2012

Present international negotiations are based around the follow-up to the COP at Bali in December 2007 and the EU policy package discussed above. At Bali, the main action focused on getting the USA to declare that it would participate actively in the next phase of the process leading up to the Copenhagen Conference in December 2009. In this limited, but important, aim, it was successful.

The core issues for these negotiations remain those which have been on the table since the UN FCCC was agreed in 1992: how to get a global carbon cartel in place which commits the main emitters to an aggregate programme of credible carbon emissions reductions consistent with stabilizing emissions at the 450–550 ppm concentrations. The challenges to this undertaking are well known, and little has changed the basic incentives and trade-offs. At the core is the prisoner's dilemma—it is in the interests of each party that the others reduce emissions, rather than themselves. That way, it is possible to gain the benefits of others' actions without bearing the costs oneself. No single party can on its own achieve the outcome of stabilization,[31] and all share in the benefits.

Matters are made worse than the simple characterization in the prisoner's dilemma by virtue of the distributions of costs and benefits. Some countries arguably actually gain from a warmer climate, while others are badly affected. Key participants are not democracies, and the interests of their political élites may be particularly badly affected by mitigation policies and their costs—including: China, whose élite is heavily reliant of fast GDP growth based on energy-intensive industries to retain power; and Russia, whose élite is heavily dependent on, and personally financially involved in, the main fossil-fuel industries.

Given the concentrated location of emissions growth, an inevitable part of any new agreement is that there will have to be significant financial flows from industrialized to developing countries. Yet this looks very hard to achieve: in particular, despite the change in leadership, it is hard to imagine the USA making significant payments to communist China to pay for a lower-carbon industrialization which may have a further impact on competition between the two countries. This, indeed, has been a stumbling block since 1992, and the major reason why the USA pulled out of Kyoto. A minimum condition for the USA has been that China (and others) adopt binding caps on emissions. A condition for the Chinese is that the burden should not fall heavily on them, as their *per capita* carbon emissions are still low, it has been the USA and other industrialized countries that are largely responsible for the stock of greenhouse gases currently in the atmosphere, and (as noted above) its carbon-intensive exports are a response to US and European consumption demand.

As we have seen above, the Chinese argument has considerable merit when emissions are based upon a consumption rather than production basis. However, this does not in itself *solve* the problem: even if the parties could agree on the principles for responsibility, it would remain to establish a credible regime which could be monitored and, indeed, enforced. What incentives would the parties have to comply *ex post*? The free-riding incentives owing to the prisoner's dilemma would remain.

These difficulties appear immense, and are unlikely to be resolved any time soon. Indeed, it could be argued that the way the negotiations are being framed *ex ante* is unlikely to produce a solution to the climate-change problem. Getting an agreement only constitutes a solution if it actually results in a reduction and then arrest of the growth of emissions—and fairly quickly. But, as we have seen, Kyoto

[31] As Victor (Ch. 16) argues, geo-engineering may be an exception. See also Chapter 4 by Scott Barrett.

is designed in such a way as to exclude the most important components. Being based upon geographical production, excluding aviation and shipping, shapes the negotiations in an inherently conservative and inefficient way. So even if tighter geographic production caps are agreed, the net result for developed countries will not meet the scale of the task—and, as a result, developing countries (which produce and export carbon) will find themselves asked to do proportionately more than their own carbon consumption dictates.

Kyoto is skewed, too, to the shorter term, within which there is little that can be done on a large scale. The key issues are *post*- not pre-2020—with the deployment of large-scale technologies between 2020 and 2030, and new technologies thereafter. As a result, large-scale programmes for R&D may have more impact on the climate-change problem than shorter-term targets for renewables and biofuels—as pursued by the EU at the heart of its proposed approach to climate change.[32] Indeed, the EU programme is skewed heavily to areas of more marginal significance to the overall problem. The exception is, perhaps, the EU ETS, but even here it is the use of the revenues—the income effect—which is probably more important than the substitution effect in the period to 2020, and these revenues are unlikely to make much impact on large-scale R&D. Politically demanding renewables targets may appear more attractive than longer-term R&D programmes—or even CCS and nuclear.

These difficulties have arisen in the context of a conventional wisdom which has built up around the Stern Report—that the problem as a whole can be tackled with just 1 per cent GDP cost. If even this number is proving a difficult political obstacle to progress in the developed countries then a recognition that the scale of the burden on the developed countries should be much higher—on a consumption basis—*and* that the costs of the problem as a whole may be much higher than 1 per cent indicates an almost insuperable obstacle. A coldly rational and objective analysis of the problem facing international negotiators is that the sort of agreement that could be signed up to by the main players is one that almost certainly will not solve the problem—in other words, like the Kyoto Protocol, agreement is more likely to be achieved if its impacts are marginal.

What would it take to overcome these incentive problems? One approach is to persuade people of the ethics of climate change—an approach which is embedded in the Stern Report, and which is manifest in egalitarian proposals such as equal personal carbon budgets and GDP-per-head emission targets.[33] The chances of agreement on this basis in time to have an effect on the problem are remote. A second approach is to change the incentives themselves—the damage pay-offs in particular. If the science reveals that the fat tail is actually quite probable (that it is not, in fact, in the tail of the distribution), bringing forward the damage from climate change into the nearer term, with all its associated problems of migration, conflict, sea-level rises, and the direct effect of higher temperatures, then the perceived trade-off between damage and costs would shift. This is not

[32] See Chapter 11 by Helm.

[33] House of Commons Environmental Audit Committee (2008).

an impossibility, and underlines the importance of the scientific research to the policy process.

A third option is to take away from the national dimensions some elements of sovereignty, as the UN has in wider conflict resolution. This might involve a delegation of the negotiations to a new international body. Already the move from the national level has helped in Europe: arguably the EU has managed to force member countries into tougher action than would have occurred had they engaged in the within-EU prisoner's dilemma debates. Such an international body might function analogically to the WTO, and, indeed, membership and compliance could then be linked to wider international issues—such as trade. By broadening the pay-offs through multiple international engagements and agreements, greater leverage might be gained, thereby weakening the free-riding incentives. Even net gainers from climate change—such as the Russian élites—might face costs from failure to reduce emissions, for example through international carbon taxes or trade discrimination for its carbon-intensive exports. Access to the benefits of technology transfer may also be easier in the context of an international body, as, too, might enforcement of agreements.

But to agree about the design of such an institution, and to set it up, would take time—perhaps a decade—a serious obstacle it shares with the other two options. Moral education is a long-term endeavour, on a par with gender equality and the abolition of slavery. Science, too, takes time: as noted at the outset, we are condemned to uncertainty over the relevant time period within which action needs to be taken.

VII. CONCLUSIONS

It is very grim. The trends are in the wrong direction, the timescale is short, and a Kyoto-style new agreement from 2012 is unlikely to make much difference to the underlying (upwards) trends in emissions. Without a fundamental rethink, we are likely to be doomed to significant increases in emissions, and the corresponding uncertain warming of the climate. The science suggests that it is probably more likely than not that rapid climate change will result later in the century with potentially quite catastrophic results.

Recognition of this likely outcome from the current approach to climate-change negotiations and policies is the first step to finding a more palatable outcome. The starting point is the economics of climate change—the title of the Stern Report. The core elements of that report have become the new conventional wisdom of climate change—and all three of the main ones are open to serious challenge. The damage is likely to be much greater than the numbers generated by assuming that there is a straight substitution between environmental and man-made capital, and that therefore economic growth can continue indefinitely adding to our wealth and consumption possibilities as long as man-made capital is created faster than the environment is depleted. The costs of mitigation are likely to be higher too—if only because the Stern Report assumes away policy costs. Zero time preference may be an admirable moral principle (though contentious even as a moral principle), but it is not reflected in behaviour, nor likely to be so.

Thus the case for urgent action—the Stern Report's recommendation—needs to be grounded on an economics which presents the problem of climate change to the politicians and the public in more robust terms—by analysing the consequences of a harder constraint on the substitutability of the environment for man-made capital, and with cost assumptions based upon empirically observed data rather than idealized technical supply functions. These jointly reduce the growth rate which is likely as global warming continues and mitigation measures are put in place, and it is this consequence rather than an idealized time-preference rate which dictates the case for urgent action.

Having recast the economics of the problem of climate change, the next step is to analyse the problem of international negotiations in terms of consumption rather than production—to get the accounting sorted out. The consequence is that, for developed countries, it is not only that the costs of mitigation will be (significantly) higher, but the amount required will be higher, too.

This representation of the nature of the problem and assignment of responsibility will initially make the process of gaining an international agreement harder to achieve. But a Kyoto-based approach will, in any event, probably achieve agreement at the price of not making much meaningful progress towards addressing the underlying problem. This, in turn, opens the door to alternative approaches—including the couching of the negotiations themselves in an international context, with a new international institution, and thereby helping to internalize the endemic free-rider problems. It also opens up the possibility of bringing other aspects of international relations into play, notably trade, and focusing on international R&D and more longer-term technological options. These steps will take time—hence the grim prospects—but they represent one way of eventually closing the gap between the science and climate-change policy. Unfortunately, time is, according to the scientists, of the essence.

3

The Global Deal on Climate Change

Cameron Hepburn and Nicholas Stern***

I. INTRODUCTION

Climate change may not turn out to be the greatest challenge humanity faces in the twenty-first century, but there is no doubt it requires extremely serious and sustained global attention. The basic structure of the problem is now well known: humans emit greenhouse gases (GHGs), particularly carbon dioxide (CO_2), but also methane, nitrous oxide, and hydrofluorocarbons (HFCs), through consumption and production. These flows of emissions accumulate into stocks of GHGs in the atmosphere. The rate of accumulation depends upon Earth's 'carbon cycle', whereby CO_2 is reabsorbed into the oceans and land. Over time, the accumulated GHGs trap heat and the result is global warming. As the planet warms, the climate changes, which affects human and animal life through rising sea-levels and events such as storms, floods, and droughts. While the fundamental science has long been clear, the specific processes and impacts (both positive and negative) involve considerable uncertainty. Many of the impacts will be felt in the distant future, but it is also likely that serious impacts will be felt by many people currently alive.

While the basic science of global warming is simple, the causes and likely impacts of climate change are highly complex. This creates a major communication challenge—significant proportions of citizens in both Britain and America still do not believe that the world is warming owing to human activity (see the beginning of section III(v)). Formulating appropriate policy in the face of scientific complexity, an ambivalent general public, and a major international prisoner's dilemma, is exceptionally challenging. Solutions require an understanding of many disciplines beyond economics, including philosophy,

* Smith School of Enterprise and the Environment and New College, Oxford.

** Grantham Institute, India Observatory, and STICERD at the London School of Economics and Political Science.

The authors are grateful to Claire Abeillé, Dennis Anderson, Alex Bowen, Sebastian Catovsky, Peter Diamond, Simon Dietz, Ottmar Edenhofer, Sam Fankhauser, Graham Floater, Su-Lin Garbett, Ross Garnaut, Roger Guesnerie, Geoffrey Heal, Daniel Hawellek, Claude Henry, Paul Joskow, Jean-Pierre Landau, James Mirrlees, Ernesto Moniz, Steven Pacala, Nicola Patmore, Vicky Pope, Laura Ralston, Mattia Romani, John Schellnhuber, Matthew Skellern, Robert Socolow, Martin Weitzman, Dimitri Zenghelis, and all of those who worked on and guided the Stern Review team. Particular thanks to Simon Dietz, Dieter Helm, Tim Jenkinson, Robert Ritz, and participants in the *Oxford Review of Economic Policy* seminar in February 2008.

politics and international relations, business, law and international development, to name but a few. The inherent interdisciplinary nature of the problem creates great challenges in bringing all the relevant analytical tools to bear in an appropriate manner.

The economics of climate change is still relatively young, and needs to mature swiftly if we are rapidly to develop appropriate policy responses. GHG emissions are classified as a global public bad, possibly the most significant yet in human history. The economics required goes well beyond that of Pigou (1932) and Coase (1960). For instance, our conventional shortcuts break down over long time horizons, under Knightian uncertainty, and for non-marginal challenges. Transitioning from business-as-usual to stable atmospheric concentrations of GHGs is not a small perturbation around an existing path; it requires shifting from one growth path to another and, in so doing, changing relative prices across the global economy.

The intellectual challenges are substantial; the practical challenges are enormous. Global emissions are currently increasing, driven by growing use of power generated by coal, which is abundant and cheap. In the next 20–25 years, under business-as-usual, China alone will emit cumulatively more than the USA and Europe combined over the last one hundred years, driven in large part by its coal consumption. As energy security continues to move up the political agenda, coal will become increasingly appealing, despite the carbon downside. This provides an indication of the necessity of agreeing an international response quickly, and the fifteenth Conference of the Parties (COP) in Copenhagen in December 2009 provides a critical opportunity to do so.

Section II discusses the ethics and economics behind a global emissions-reduction target for climate change—no global deal is possible without one—including consideration of developments since the Stern Review. Section III sets out the shape of a global deal that would put the world on a path towards achieving a 450–550 ppm target, starting from the world target declared at Heiligendamm, Germany, and confirmed at Toyako, Japan, of 50 per cent reductions by 2050, with rich countries contributing at least 75 per cent of the reductions. Section IV examines the key instruments needed to implement the global deal. These include global emissions trading (IV(i)); reform of the clean development mechanism (CDM) to scale up emission reductions on a sectoral or benchmark level (IV(ii)); scaling up of R&D funding for low-carbon energy, particularly carbon capture and sequestration (IV(iii)); an agreement on deforestation (IV(iv)); and adaptation finance (IV(v)). Section V concludes.

II. GLOBAL TARGETS

(i) The Inescapability of Ethics

Any global deal will be based upon one or more global climate-change targets, inevitably requiring consideration of normative, and specifically ethical, issues

(Broome, 1992; Beckerman and Hepburn, 2007; Dietz *et al.*, 2008). By emitting GHGs, humans in the past and the present cause harm to other humans in the present and the future. While reducing emissions is costly for the current generation, continuing to emit will be costly for future generations. Balancing the different interests at stake raises questions that are fundamentally and inescapably ethical. This is true of many, if not all, policy areas where individual interests come into conflict, but it is particularly salient in climate policy, where the conflicts of interest are also international and intergenerational. Ethics is also important from a pragmatic perspective: nation states will not sign up to an agreement they perceive to be unfair, and focusing exclusively on efficiency will do little to guarantee fairness or equity.

In the economic analysis of domestic policy, equity implications are often ignored or downplayed on the basis that they can be addressed separately through the taxation and transfer system. This intellectual shortcut can be appropriate as a theoretical device, sharpening the focus on important questions of efficiency. However, it provides only limited guidance to domestic policy formulation, because national taxation and transfer systems are subject to important constraints.

There are two reasons why the limitations of taxation and transfer systems are particularly relevant to climate change. First, there are no simple mechanisms to redistribute wealth to future citizens, nor can they be represented in current deliberations, yet the conflict of interest is precisely between future and present generations. Second, it is impossible to apply taxation and transfer systems across international borders, yet climate policy involves conflicts of interests between citizens of different countries.

For these reasons, equity cannot be ignored. Yet some commentators suggest that a 'descriptive' approach, which focuses on determining the efficient outcome, and which generally advocates the use of current interest rates to do so, is plausible for climate change policy formulation (e.g. Baker *et al.*, 2008). Even if efficiency were the sole objective, current interest rates are inadequate, for several reasons. First, in imperfect economies, Drèze and Stern (1987, 1990) show that it will not generally be true that the private rate of return on investment (PRI) will be equal to the social rate of return (SRI), and, similarly, private discount rates (PDRs) can diverge from the social discount rates (SDRs). In the general case, PDR $\neq$ SDR $\neq$ SRI $\neq$ PRI, and current market interest rates provide imperfect guidance to efficient social discount rates. Second, given uncertainty over long time horizons, the efficient certainty-equivalent discount rate will eventually decline through time (Weitzman, 2001, 2007*a*). Third, current marginal interest rates will not yield efficient results for a non-marginal problem such as climate change (see section II(ii)).

Hence a 'descriptive' approach that employs current interest rates will not even yield the efficient future discount-rate path, let alone resolve the difficult ethical issues created by climate change. Instead, it is necessary to adopt an approach that directly accounts for the five challenges noted above: international ethical issues; intergenerational ethical issues; economic imperfections; compounding uncertainty over time; and non-marginality.

The fact that an economic assessment of climate-change policy must incorporate an explicit ethical analysis does not mean that we should insist on one particular ethical route. A number of ethical perspectives can, and should, be brought to bear. Approaches that focus directly on the consequences of climate change, such as cost–benefit analysis, command attention; so do procedural approaches highlighting rights, freedoms, and the prevention of harm, as well as approaches based on needs and virtues. Because of their importance, these value judgements must be made explicitly and directly, in a process that is open for public discussion and critical scrutiny (Sen, 1999, p. 80). Universal agreement on the appropriate value judgements is impossible. There is no easy technocratic solution, such as the recommendation that ethical parameters should simply be consistent with today's marketplace (e.g. Nordhaus, 2007*a*).

How should we decide which of the competing ethical frameworks should be employed to develop a global climate-change target? Moral and political philosophers have proposed various methods for determining and aggregating moral values.[1] Given the impossibility of universal agreement on values, and even on the method of aggregating values, and given the centrality of ethics to climate change, sensitivity analysis over ethical frameworks and parameters is very important. Such analyses can actually aid the development of our ethical intuition by clarifying the consequences of particular ethical standpoints.

Stern (2007) discussed a range of plausible ethical perspectives, although arguably still did not do justice to a rich and evolving field of thought (Beckerman and Hepburn, 2007). In making a concrete proposal for a specific, quantitative global climate-stabilization target, on which a global deal might be based, Stern (2007) adopted a largely utilitarian perspective, and determined that the recommendation of strong action to mitigate climate change was robust to a range of different ethical parameters within a utilitarian framework. Utilitarianism is one of many approaches, and it is not necessarily favoured by moral philosophers, but the broad recommendation of strong action to mitigate climate change by reducing GHG emissions would be supported by many tenable ethical viewpoints.

(ii) The Consequences of Non-marginality

Even ignoring equity (which, as we have just argued, is impossible), the shortcuts of cost–benefit analysis encounter further problems in that mitigating climate change does not constitute a small perturbation around business-as-usual, but,

[1] Some of the more influential approaches include the 'reflective equilibrium' notion of Rawls (1971), the 'argument from received opinion' discussed by Hare (1971), the use of opinion polls (Miller, 1999), the theory of 'discourse ethics' (Habermas, 1990), and works by Barry (1995), Griffin (1996), and others. See Dietz *et al.* (2008) for further discussion in the climate-change context, and Saelen *et al.* (2008) for a specific application which aggregates stated public preferences through an Internet survey of 3,000 people.

instead, involves a shift from one economic growth path to another. In this context, the most basic mistake made by many commentators is to use a marginal concept (e.g. an exogenous interest rate) to make non-marginal comparisons between different macroeconomic paths. Climate policy will shift the pattern of growth for a whole collection of capital goods, particularly natural capital, and thus change the interest rate on manufactured, natural, and other types of capital (Sterner and Persson, 2007). Each path has an implied set of discount factors and rates associated with it (Hepburn, 2006; Stern, 2007, pp. 27–31). Thus it is incorrect to apply past interest rates, which refer to a given historical path, to vastly different future paths. Even if a 'descriptive' approach were adopted (but see above), it would need to compare the appropriate general equilibrium rates in a forward-looking manner, along different future paths, rather than simply use current or historical interest rates.

As a result, analogies with the theory of marginal investment under certainty are problematic. Concluding that climate mitigation is an 'inferior investment', compared with the short-term pay-off from investing resources elsewhere, is unsafe; the next 200 years are highly uncertain, and the underlying structure of the economy will be transformed as changes to our climate alter the human and physical geography of the planet. The relative prices that apply along a business-as-usual pathway are significantly different to the relative prices applicable to a growth path with strong mitigation, or to a hypothetical path with no climate change whatsoever. For climate policies with impacts over 200 years, specifying the relevant path, and its associated relative prices, matters enormously to the analysis.

(iii) Recent Developments and the Global Target

While Stern (2007) did not identify a specific numerical stabilization target, the analysis strongly suggested that the upper limit to the optimal stabilization range should not be above 550 ppm CO_2e, and that stabilization below 450 ppm CO_2e would be excessively difficult and costly. Hence, a stabilization range of 450–550 ppm CO_2e was identified. Since the Stern Review, there have been several advances and developments in the science and economics of climate change. The following sections examine how these developments impact the global target proposed by the Review.

The Risks of Climate Change

Various commentators asserted that the Review drew heavily on studies that were pessimistic in their assessment of climate change and its impacts, giving relatively little attention to more optimistic views (Tol and Yohe, 2006; Baker *et al.*, 2008) If anything, however, recent developments suggest the opposite. In retrospect, the Review could be viewed as being overly optimistic in each of the four steps linking human emissions to climate change: (i) future emissions growth; (ii) the carbon cycle linking emissions (flows) to concentrations (stocks); (iii) the climate sensitivity, linking concentrations to temperature increases; and (iv) damages from a given temperature increase.

First, the Review was probably optimistic, not pessimistic, in its assumptions about future emissions. Chapter 6 of the Review (Stern, 2007, pp. 173–88) employs the second highest of the four scenarios—the A2 scenario—in the Intergovernmental Panel on Climate Change (IPCC) Special Report on Emissions Scenarios, or SRES (IPCC, 2000*a*). However, the highest of the four scenarios—the A1F1 scenario—is probably the best description of business-as-usual emissions not withstanding the recent global financial crisis, as indicated by Garnaut *et al.* (Ch. 5), as well as Pielke *et al.* (2008). This is primarily due to rapid growth in the developing world, particularly China and India, driven by increases to coal-fired power generation (ECIEP, 2006).

Second, the Review was optimistic in the assessment of the links between human emissions and atmospheric carbon stocks. It did not take into account the fact that the carbon cycle is likely to weaken as a result of, for example, the possible collapse of the Amazon forest at temperature increases of above 3–4°C, or the decreasing absorptive capacity of the oceans. Further, the Review did not account for the fact that a thawing of the permafrost is likely to result in additional methane release. Omitting these positive feedbacks in the carbon cycle may have led to a significant underestimate of the risks.

Third, the Review was optimistic in its assumption of how increased carbon stocks affect temperatures. The Review employed the PAGE2002 model, with triangular distributions for the climate sensitivity parameter, implying that the highest (and hence worst) possible values were cropped. The full spread from *all* (100 per cent) of the Review's Monte Carlo runs is roughly coincident within the IPCC Fourth Assessment (AR4) Report 'likely' (66 per cent confidence interval) range. The Review was therefore more optimistic than the IPCC on climate sensitivity. Other research indicates that much higher values still of the climate sensitivity cannot be ruled out (e.g. Stainforth *et al.*, 2005; Meinshausen, 2006).

Fourth, the Review might be seen to have been optimistic in its mean estimates of damages from climate change. It was calculated that a 5°C warming would reduce *welfare* by the *equivalent* of a reduction of 5 per cent of GDP (Stern, 2007, p. 180). However, as Stern (2008) notes, a temperature increase of 5°C would most likely transform the physical and human geography of the planet, leading to massive human migration and large-scale conflict. As such, welfare reductions of this magnitude appear likely significantly to underestimate the damages from climate change from 5°C warming (Stern, 2008).

In summary, while the analysis in the Review provided a fair picture of the damages from climate change given the scientific and economic knowledge available at the time, it is arguable in retrospect that the Review was, if anything, too optimistic in its assessment of the risks of climate change.

The Costs of Mitigation

The world economy will probably have grown three-fold by 2050, so absolute emission reductions of around 50 per cent would require cuts of 80–85 per cent in emissions per unit of output. Further, since emissions from some sectors (in particular agriculture) will be difficult to cut back to anything like this extent, and since richer countries should make much bigger proportional reductions than poor countries (see section V), richer countries will need to have close to zero emissions in power (electricity) and transport by 2050.

Clearly, this is no small challenge. However, technology that is already available makes close-to-zero emissions in power by 2050 possible, if costly. Furthermore, a large-scale increase in R&D, coupled with reasonable long-term carbon prices, is likely to deliver further advances in zero-carbon power. Close-to-zero emissions in power would deliver close-to-zero emissions for most of the transportation sector. This would, however, require radical changes to the source and use of energy, including much greater energy efficiency.

In this context, costs will be a strong function of three endogenous variables. First, policy is very important—bad policy will lead to the uptake of more expensive options. Second, increasing the rate of low-carbon technical progress is very important to reducing costs, and this should be promoted by a dramatic scaling up of funding for R&D (see section IV(iii)), so that the range of options is widened and costs are reduced. Third, costs are also strongly dependent upon the speed at which emission reductions are necessary. Starting now allows more time for planned choices, gradual replacement of capital stock, and discovery of new options. This is the measured, lower cost approach. Delaying further, and then eventually moving in haste if and when damaging climate impacts change public opinion, is likely to be the expensive option.

The Stern Review reported results from two different approaches to estimating the costs of moving on to a pathway consistent with stabilization at 450–550 ppm. The first approach, based on bottom–up costs of specific technologies, suggested average costs of around 1 per cent, with a range of −1 to 3.5 per cent (Anderson, 2006; see also IEA, 2006). The reported results were based on good policy, specifically the assumption that costs would be kept down through pricing mechanisms that provided for flexibility in the type, timing, and location of emissions reduction.

The second approach looked at top–down macro modelling of costs of emissions reductions (see also Barker *et al.*, 2006). Both the bottom–up (Ch. 9) and the top–down (ch. 10) studies produced numbers in similar ranges, with mean estimates of around 1 per cent of world GDP. There is considerable uncertainty in these estimates. Bad policy or delayed decisions could give higher numbers. Stronger technical progress could give lower numbers, particularly in the context of an efficient emissions-trading scheme that provides firms with flexibility to take advantages of shifting cost curves, as experience with sulphur dioxide in the United States demonstrates (Carlson *et al.*, 2000). This uncertainty reflects the fact that policy-makers cannot predict *ex ante* the cheapest ways to achieve emission reductions.

Since the Review was published there have been a number of new studies, both bottom–up and top–down. Examples of the former are those from McKinsey (Enkvist *et al.*, 2007) and the International Energy Agency (IEA, 2007*a*), both of which indicated costs either in the region suggested by the Review, or somewhat lower. Similar conclusions are drawn in the AR4 (IPCC, 2007*a*). These types of analyses, while limited, are nevertheless useful in that they provide an indication of where carbon prices should be. In particular, for stabilization at 550 ppm CO_2e, it follows that by 2030 cuts at the world level would have to be of the order of 20 Gt CO_2e, suggesting a CO_2 price of around €30 per tonne (Enkvist *et al.*, 2007), assuming the cost curves are accurate.

In summary, the evidence and analysis that emerged in the year following the Review has been consistent with the range of cost estimates for stabilization expressed in the Stern Review, or has even indicated that they may be on the high side. Fundamental to all these studies is that good policy and timely decision-making are crucial to keeping costs down. Whether or not we have good policy is, of course, not exogenous to the analysis. Pessimists look at certain policies and point to high costs. Optimists point to the experience with previous environmental trading schemes and argue that they serve as an incentive for innovation and often provide low-cost solutions that policy-makers had not expected.

Implications for the Global Target

We have seen that while Stern (2007) may have underestimated the risks of climate change, the mitigation cost estimates appear consistent with subsequent analyses, although the range of possible estimates remains wide. While the appropriate global target remains in the 450–550 ppm CO_2e range suggested by Stern (2007), it is perhaps more narrowly within the 450–500 ppm CO_2e range (Stern, 2008). The interim review by Garnaut (2008*b*) indicated that Australia is now likely to seek agreement on an international target of 450 ppm, at the bottom end of that range. Given the conclusion that business-as-usual emissions are likely to follow the A1F1 scenario, a 450 ppm CO_2e scenario is very ambitious, and this target is almost impossible to meet without some overshooting.

More recently, some climate scientists have expressed the view that global targets are not ideally expressed in equilibrium quantities (e.g. Frame *et al.*, 2006). They argue this is because: (i) equilibrium is many centuries, if not millennia, into the future; (ii) equilibrium parameters, such as climate sensitivity, remain poorly understood and difficult to estimate (Allen and Frame, 2007); and (iii) the transition to equilibrium will produce most of the damage. It may be that a cumulative CO_2 emissions target (Broecker, 2007; Wigley, 2007), may provide better guidance than targets expressed in terms of equilibrium parts per million of CO_2e in the atmosphere.

III. THE GLOBAL DEAL

A response to climate change will be more effective if it is organized globally and when it involves international understanding and collaboration. This need not necessarily involve a formal process such as the World Trade Organization (WTO), founded in legal structures and where no one is bound until the full deal is done, but can rather be based on a looser set of cooperative arrangements between states, built on a shared appreciation of the scale of the challenge. These arrangements should seek to minimize the costs of emission reductions, and ensure that the burdens are shared equitably in ways which take account of wealth, ability, and historical responsibility.

(i) Global Emission-reduction Targets

Starting from the view that an appropriate stabilization target is around 500 ppm, the first broad necessary area of agreement is on the rough pathway of global emission-reduction targets. The international discussion has already made significant progress, and a global target of 50 per cent reductions by 2050 was agreed at the combined summit of the Group of Eight (G8) and Group of Five (G5) nations, chaired by Germany in Heiligendamm in June 2007, and confirmed in June 2008 at the summit chaired by Japan in Toyako. While the base date was not specified, and other details were not spelled out, this serves as clear guidance. The 50 per cent target is for the world as whole and it is generally agreed that richer countries should take responsibility for greater reductions, in the spirit of the Kyoto language of 'common but differentiated treatment'. Taking responsibility implies paying for the emission reductions—it is less relevant whether the emission reductions occur within a particular national boundary.

(ii) Target Sharing

Currently global emission flows are around 40–45 billion tonnes of CO_2e each year. The world population is around six billion, so average global *per capita* emissions are around seven tonnes. Reducing emissions by 50 per cent by 2050, to an aggregate flow of around 20 Gt CO_2e, will require *per capita* emissions to be around two tonnes, given that the world population will be around nine billion by 2050. Even if emissions in rich countries fall to zero, people in poor countries will still need to emit only 2–2.5 tonnes, because eight billion of the global population will live in currently poor countries. This basic arithmetic shows that the currently poor countries must be at the centre of any effective global deal.

This arithmetic is presented in terms of equalizing future *per capita* emissions, for simplicity, but this fails to account for emissions that have occurred over the last 200 years. The currently rich countries are responsible for around 70 per cent of the current stock of GHGs, and are continuing to contribute substantially more to increasing the stock than developing countries. The United States, Canada, and Australia emit around 20 tonnes of CO_2e *per capita*, Europe and Japan around ten tonnes, China around five tonnes, and India around two tonnes, while most of sub-Saharan Africa emits much less than one tonne. Figure 3.1 illustrates *per capita* CO_2 emissions (but excluding other GHGs) from 1990 to 2004 for several countries.

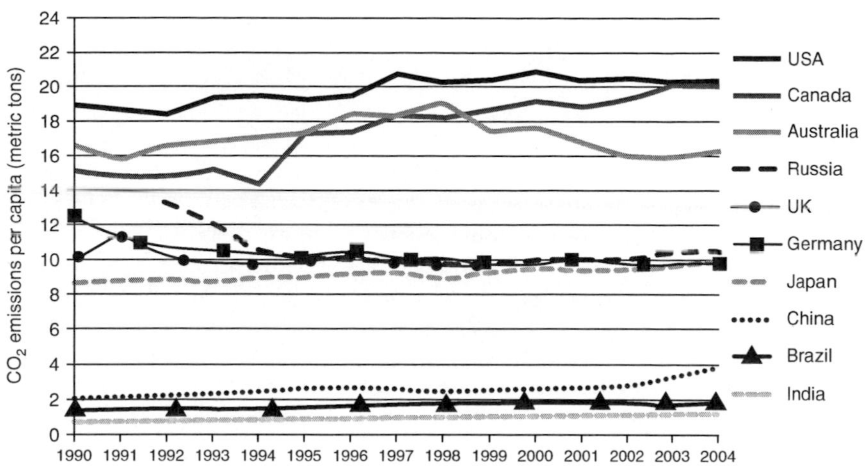

Figure 3.1. *Per capita* CO_2 emissions (in tonnes)

Source: US Department of Energy's Carbon Dioxide Information Analysis Center (CDIAC) for the United Nations Statistics Division.

In the lower part of Figure 3.1 are three big developing countries. China is experiencing extraordinarily rapid growth, fuelled in large part by coal-fired power, and is already above five tonnes *per capita* once all GHGs from all sources are accounted for (Figure 3.1 shows only CO_2 emissions up to 2004). It is likely that China will reach current European emission levels within 20 years or so, even with fairly conservative estimates of China's growth under business-as-usual.

With 80 per cent reductions by 2050, Europe and Japan would be around the required two tonnes global average level in 2050, if the 50 per cent overall reduction is achieved. At current emissions of around 20 tonnes *per capita*, the USA, Australia, and Canada would need a reduction of 90 per cent by 2050 to achieve emissions at the global average of two tonnes. Thus a 50 per cent overall reduction and an 80 per cent rich-country reduction would still leave average rich countries flows above the world average in 2050.

This does not reflect a strong commitment to equity on the part of the rich countries. A target of equal allocations of emissions by 2050 (allowing for trade) may be seen as being a fairly pragmatic one, on which it might be possible to obtain agreement. If the entire globe is subject to caps, then whether the caps are on the basis of production or consumption matters only to the initial allocation. Either way, rich countries will most likely continue to emit more than the poor, but they will pay poor countries to purchase these rights.

(iii) National Targets

Many nations and sub-national states have already adopted targets consistent with emission reductions along this pathway. California has a target of 80 per cent reductions by 2050. France has its 'Facteur Quatre': dividing by four, or 75 per cent reductions by 2050. The UK has a 60 per cent target, but in November 2007 the Prime Minister indicated that this may be increased to 80 per cent. Australia, under the new government elected at the end of November 2007, has now signed the Kyoto Protocol, and has a target of 60 per cent, and at the time of writing 80 per cent was under consideration after the publication of the Garnaut Review.

But setting long-term targets is the easy part; achieving them will be altogether more difficult. Action is required immediately, so shorter-term targets are being set. At the 2007 European Spring Council, 20–30 per cent targets were set for 2020, and Germany has set 40 per cent targets by 2020. At Bali, many were pressing for rich countries to accept 25–40 per cent cuts by 2020. While extremely ambitious, this is nevertheless the appropriate range for 80 per cent cuts by 2050 for rich countries. However, experience with shorter-term targets gives pause for thought—the UK government's impending failure to meet its domestic 20 per cent CO_2 target provides but one example.

Given the scale of the challenge, some have argued that developing countries should also take binding national emission caps in the short term. Yet the only acceptable targets for poor countries at this stage would be very loose, generating 'hot air' and reducing the carbon price on international markets. Moreover, these loose targets might end up determining the baseline for subsequent negotiations. However, by 2020 developing countries will need to take on binding national targets, and current policies should be framed with this objective in mind. Some fast-growing middle-income developing countries may need to take on early sectoral targets, and possibly binding national targets, before 2020.

(iv) Agreement is Challenging but Feasible

Obtaining an agreement at Copenhagen, or subsequently, will be no easy task. That said, it is notable that the understanding of the challenge is increasingly shared by policy-makers around the world, and the national targets above are consistent with a broader shared goal. Based on this understanding, a framework should emerge that allows all countries to move quickly along what they see to be a responsible path. Building a deal upon a formal WTO structure, where nothing is implemented until everything is agreed, would appear to be a dangerous route. The fundamental challenge, however, is that the negotiations reflect a complex and asymmetric prisoner's dilemma, where, crudely speaking, it is in the interests of each nation to do little other than observe, while other nations bear the costs of reducing their emissions. Nevertheless, there are at least four considerations that suggest that reaching agreement, while difficult, may not be impossible.

First, there is an enormous collective pay-off if agreement is reached and collusion can be maintained. Given the scale of the costs of climate change, the collective prize for overcoming narrow self-interest and reaching a Pareto-efficient coalition is great indeed. Second, the possibility of side agreements on issues other than climate change expands the scope for agreement. Russia joined the Kyoto

Protocol in part owing to concessions granted by the EU on WTO membership. Third, while the assumption of self-interested action by nation states is surely the best starting point, it is also clear that nation states are also motivated by other considerations, some reflecting the concerns of their particular leaders, others reflecting important notions of responsibility, capability, national pride, and self respect. Fourth, climate change will redistribute wealth around the world, both within and between nations. If and when the transition to a low-carbon economy occurs, countries which have been slow to move will find that their high-carbon assets are stranded owing to shifts in the full cost of dirty production processes. Indeed, it is not impossible, given the magnitude of the gains from 'winning' in critical low-carbon technologies, that a competitive dynamic will develop where countries race to develop the leading low-carbon technology. Given the significance of coal to the business-as-usual growth path of the global economy, at present carbon capture and sequestration would appear to be one of these critical technologies.

These reasons suggest that hope is far from lost, and agreement may well be reached. But even if it is reached, enforcement of the agreement is another matter. Developing and implementing systems of punishment for nations who fail to meet their targets is difficult. Indeed it seems likely that more than one nation will fail to adhere to its Kyoto target. Unless punishing defection is credible, selfish nation states might be expected to continue emitting at the trigger level of defection.

Public discussion and opinion may serve as one form of enforcement mechanism, even in non-democratic countries such as China, where the Communist Party is increasingly sensitive to popular opinion. The former Prime Minister of Australia was voted out of office in November 2007 in part because of his perceived weakness on climate policy. Politicians recognize the strength, and often breadth, of public interest and demand on this issue from an increasingly vocal civil society. Climate change has become a unifying and defining issue in the structures of Europe. Significant changes in perception in the key countries, the USA, China, and India, have also been observed over the last 12 months.

(v) Anticipating Roadblocks

Public Opinion

Just as public opinion may have already begun to serve as an enforcement mechanism at the ballot box, so too may it serve as a roadblock to sustained commitment to reduce emissions. When cuts become deeper, and as costs are incurred, country-by-country political support will be necessary in order to sustain climate-mitigation policies over time. This will require a robust and shared public understanding of the science, and agreement that action is warranted, irrespective of short-term economic conditions.

Recent polls provide conflicting indications as to whether this agreement is present or not. For instance, a majority (56 per cent) of those interviewed by a

2007 IPSOS/Mori poll in the UK agreed that 'many leading experts still question if human activity is contributing to climate change', and more than 40 per cent of Britons and Americans think that warming is not due to human activity (*The Economist*, 29 March 2008, p. 35). Boykoff (2007) argues that confusion persists because the media, at least in the United States, effectively have an incentive to portray conflict rather than coherence in scientific explanations of climate change. However, a BBC World Service poll of 22,000 people in 12 countries in September 2007 found that 'large majorities around the world believe that human activity causes global warming and that strong action must be taken, sooner rather than later, in developing as well as developed countries'.[2] The same poll claims to find majority support (73 per cent on average) in ten of the 12 countries polled for an agreement in which developing countries would limit their emissions in return for financial assistance and technology from developed countries.

While it is clear that awareness of the problem has been gradually increasing over the last two decades,[3] even the otherwise encouraging BBC World Service poll shows challenges ahead; for instance, only 47 per cent of Indians believe that human activity is a significant cause of climate change. While supportive public opinion is clearly no guarantee of good climate-change policy, it is probably a necessary condition to sustain the move to a low-carbon economy, and in some important instances this condition does not yet seem to be satisfied.

Political Economy of Financial Transfers

It was noted in section III(iii) that the currently poor countries must be at the centre of a global deal if it is to be effective. However, the developing countries are neither responsible for creating the problem, nor are they capable of immediately addressing it; they have other urgent priorities for their limited resources. That being so, unless the rich countries provide the finance for the extra costs of reducing carbon, developing countries are extremely unlikely to join the effort on the scale and at the pace required. The developing world rightly argues that they should not be asked to slow their economic growth just at the point when they are beginning to make progress in overcoming poverty. Financing from the rich countries, together with technology demonstration and transfer, will be necessary to convince them to move to a low-carbon growth path.

However, it is very unlikely that the public sector of rich countries will be able to provide the financial flows on the scale required to incentivize appropriate action. The political appetite for flows on the magnitude required—at least several tens of billions—is low. The challenges in extracting resources for Overseas Development

[2] The survey was conducted for the BBC World Service by the international polling firm GlobeScan together with the Program on International Policy Attitudes (PIPA) at the University of Maryland. GlobeScan coordinated fieldwork between 29 May and 26 July 2007.

[3] Nisbet and Myers (2007) sifted through 20 years of polls in the USA, and found that awareness of global warming as a problem has increased steadily from 39 per cent in 1986, to 58 per cent by 1988, 74 per cent by 1990, and reaching 91 per cent in 2006.

Assistance (ODA) at the level agreed to in the Millennium Development Goals serve as a clear warning against relying upon public financial flows. Furthermore, public aid will be strained still further by the challenge of adaptation, discussed below.

The carbon-trading system is the most feasible model for supporting private financial flows on the scale necessary for the developing world to reduce its emissions on the scale required. Already, as noted below, the CDM is transferring several billions of euros to the developing world, contributing to reducing the costs of compliance in Europe and other developed countries, and reflecting the fact that, given the irrelevance of where reductions occur, firms in rich countries have a strong incentive to finance them in the cheapest location, which is often in the developing world (Hepburn, Ch.20). Carbon trading provides a legitimate and coherent rationale for financial transfers on the scale necessary to shift China, India, and other developing economies on to cleaner growth pathways.

IV. CLIMATE INSTRUMENTS

Implementing the global deal will require the use of a range of different policy instruments at the international, national, and sub-national levels. There are five key components: carbon pricing; support for low-carbon R&D; financial support to reduce deforestation; other domestic instruments; and finance for adaptation.

(i) Carbon Pricing

Any satisfactory global deal will place a price on GHG emissions, both to provide an incentive to reduce them and also to minimize the costs of abatement. Indeed, a carbon price would be sufficient to internalize the greenhouse externality in a world without any other imperfections. But, in our imperfect world, a carbon price alone is inadequate, given the urgency of reducing emissions, the inertia in decision-making, and the other market imperfections, including those relating to low-carbon R&D. So a carbon price is a necessary, but not a sufficient, component of the global deal.

Putting a price on GHG emissions can be done in three main ways: carbon taxes; carbon trading; and implicit pricing via regulations and standards. Each of the three approaches has different advantages and disadvantages, and all three are likely to be used in some form at some level of government. For instance, a great deal of research indicates that the uptake of energy efficiency by individual consumers is relatively insensitive to energy prices (Oxera, 2006). Carbon pricing would, therefore, be expected to do relatively little to increase the uptake of domestic energy efficiency measures. In contrast, behavioural change is likely to be better stimulated by policies that provide information, reduce cognitive costs, hassle costs, and transactions costs. Pricing will do little to overcome these hidden costs and information imperfections. This is not to say that explicit carbon pricing via taxes or trading is not necessary—it is clearly a core part of appropriate climate policy—but rather that it is not sufficient to capture all economic reduction opportunities.[4]

Taxes and trading are 'dual' instruments: they provide identical results under idealized conditions with no uncertainty. Where there is uncertainty, taxes fix the carbon price but leave the quantity of emissions uncertain, such that, for instance, setting taxes too low would lead emissions to overshoot their target. The science makes clear that overshooting on emissions is dangerous. In contrast, carbon trading can guarantee that a particular emissions target is achieved. The European Union Emissions Trading Scheme (EU ETS) covers around one-half of European emissions with relatively low administrative burdens by focusing on major emitting industries. However, an implication of carbon trading is price uncertainty and volatility, and firms would ideally prefer clear and simple signals for decision-making and investment, which a tax provides. With learning and readjustment of policy the difference in effects between carbon taxes and carbon trading can be reduced. However, continual policy readjustment creates further uncertainty for firms that increases the cost of capital for low-carbon investments.

Carbon trading has been selected as the instrument of choice because of its appealing political characteristics. By starting with allocations which are not paid for, and moving to auctions, trading schemes have been accepted by industry because they allow for a less dramatic adjustment than a carbon tax. Free allocations based on historical emissions have significant drawbacks. First, they create a perverse incentive for firms to increase emissions in order to get more permits. Second, they lead to a sluggish management response since there are no immediate balance-sheet pressures. Third, they can give competitive advantages to incumbent firms, who may succeed in getting large quota allocations, and thus reduce competition and promote rent-seeking (indeed, intensive lobbying occurred in Europe, and windfall profits as a result of allocation hand-outs were observed). Finally, they lose public revenue. Thus moving to auctioning over time has strong advantages and should be a clear and transparent policy (Hepburn *et al.*, 2006*b*).

A further feature of carbon trading is its role in international efficiency and collaboration. International trading reduces costs, from the usual gains from trade, and provides an incentive for poor countries to participate in the global deal. The importance of these arguments, on cost and collaboration, is a central reason why there should be a very substantial element of carbon trading in policy in rich countries, with openness to international trade, backed by strong rich-country targets for reductions, in order to maintain prices at levels which will give incentives both for reduction at home and purchase abroad.

Price volatility is also a potential problem with carbon trading, when the market rules are unclear and when trading is narrow and thin, rather than broad and deep. The first phase of the EU ETS (2005–7) is sometimes cited as an example,

[4] See Hepburn (2006) for an overview of the advantages and disadvantages of taxes and trading.

but in fact the primary problem in that scheme was that too many allowances were allocated, resulting inevitably in a price collapse. Prices in the second phase (2008–12) of the EU ETS have so far been more stable, and are currently over €20 per tonne. Greater trading across sectors, periods, and countries should also reduce volatility.

Difficulties may arise in trading emissions with countries with low price ceilings or with overly generous allocations and correspondingly lower carbon prices. Linking of different trading schemes will need to address these issues, and ensure consistency of definitions and units of account. Further difficulties may arise when trading goods with countries which have not adopted strong measures against climate change. There is, in principle, a case for levying appropriate border taxes, or requiring the purchase and retirement of carbon allowances, on goods from such countries which do not otherwise embody a carbon price. A system analogous to the operation of the border procedures for VAT could be envisaged. However, this is a second-best alternative and care would be necessary to ensure that border adjustments did not generate a round of protectionist policy.

One further advantage of carbon trading, when conducted over relatively long time periods, is that the market establishes a forward price for allowances. Investors buy or sell forward emissions allowances until a forward price curve emerges that causes the expected return from holding an allowance to equal that on alternative investments, as reflected by the opportunity cost of capital. The whole price curve—the spot price and all of the forward prices, together—embodies the market's expectations on what will be necessary to comply with the future pathway of agreed emission reductions. The forward price curve provides stability to the market, with opportunities for hedging price risks and adjusting quickly to new information.

Trading over longer periods also provides firms with 'when' flexibility as well as 'where' flexibility—firms can use their carbon allowances at the point when they have greatest value. Many of the low-carbon investments that are needed now, to avoid high-carbon lock in, are long lived. A market that provides long-term certainty of a reward for low-carbon investment will reduce the cost of capital for these investments.

(ii) Reforming the CDM

The current system for trading between rich and poor countries, the Clean Development Mechanism (CDM), was established by Kyoto and operates at the level of a project in a poor country (so-called 'non-Annex I' country in the Kyoto Protocol). If a firm in a rich country (an 'Annex I' country) is part of a trading scheme (such as the EU ETS) which recognizes the CDM, then that firm can buy an emissions reduction achieved by the project, provided the project employs approaches and technologies from an admissible list, amounting to the requirement that the project would not have occurred in the absence of the funds from the CDM. The amount of the notional reduction is determined by comparing the project with a counterfactual, or baseline, which sets out what might otherwise have happened. Approval of a project goes through the rich and poor country authorities and the CDM Executive Board in Bonn.

In some respects, the CDM has been the success story of carbon trading to date. It has delivered emissions reductions from thousands of projects and generated billions of euros of investment in a short space of time, producing emission reductions at relatively low cost. It has also provided an important platform for engaging the developing world in efforts to mitigate climate change. As a market, the CDM is functioning as one would expect it to. Despite relatively high transaction costs and bureaucratic barriers, the private sector has developed a wide range of methodologies to reduce emissions, which have been submitted for approval to the CDM Executive Board, and efforts have focused on picking the 'low hanging fruit', or the cheapest emission reductions. In short, the CDM market has directed private-sector efforts to the short-term efficient outcome.

The short-term efficient outcome, however, involves emission-reduction projects being concentrated in relatively few countries, particularly China and India, and further being focused on gases other than CO_2 in relatively few industry sectors—in particular, on HFC-23 from refrigerant manufacturing. As such, the CDM has done relatively little to address the crucial long-term need to reduce CO_2 emissions from the energy sector at a time when high-carbon capital assets are being locked in. For instance, the CDM has done little to stop China from rapidly increasing coal-fired power-generating capacity, most of which is likely still to be operating in several decades, and most of which may be costly to retrofit with carbon capture and sequestration (CCS) technology. Second, it is contributing very little to sustainable development in the poorest countries, which was one of the original objectives of the mechanism. In particular, projects in Africa constitute a tiny percentage of the total.

Another significant problem arises because of the reliance upon defining a baseline, or counterfactual, to determine whether the project would have happened anyway. Here, the mechanism faces difficult challenges of asymmetric and uncertain information. Firms applying for carbon credits under the CDM, called 'certified emission reductions' (CERs), have more information about this hypothetical baseline than the regulator, because they are more likely to know what they would have done if the CDM had not existed. Unsurprisingly, these problems of asymmetric information have generated opportunities for gaming, coupled with classic symptoms of moral hazard and adverse selection. The net result is that a small proportion of CERs have been issued to projects which probably would have happened without the CDM.

The CDM also created some perverse incentives. Governments would have an incentive not to impose regulations on emissions if this meant that lucrative CDM projects were incorporated into the baseline. In other words, the CDM reduced the incentives of developing-country governments to enact policies reducing emissions (see Hepburn, Ch. 20). Project participants have an incentive to design projects so that they just, at the margin, fail to be economically sensible without the support of carbon finance through the CDM.

The two key objectives of CDM reform are to scale up the mechanism, so that it can deliver significantly greater finance and emission reductions, and to ensure the integrity of the mechanism, by reducing information problems and perverse incentives. Scaling up will require a much simpler, 'wholesale' CDM. Wholesale measures might include sectoral benchmarks, so that firms would receive credits for achieving a stipulated emissions intensity per unit output, or technological benchmarks, such as employing CCS (which is currently excluded from CDM). Standardized emissions-intensity factors for specific sectors would improve upon the relatively slow and costly case-by-case nature of the current CDM. Because the mechanism would remain one-sided, providing a 'no-lose' mechanism for participating countries, so that there are benefits for reducing emissions but no penalties for business-as-usual, these benchmarks could be set very ambitiously.

Defining benchmarks is complicated, however, by the need to recognize specific local circumstances. For instance, local factor prices of labour and natural capital, including energy endowments (e.g. wind, water, geothermal, etc.), will strongly determine the feasibility of achieving particular benchmarks. In some industries, the entire supply chain may have to be covered to ensure that carbon-intensive activities are not simply outsourced. Data availability may also prove to be problematic if companies and countries prove unwilling to share data for commercial reasons.

Sectors where benchmarks might work include most emissions- and energy-intensive industries, including electric power, refining, pulp and paper, metals, and cement. In sectors that are particularly subject to international competition, such as aluminium and steel, the benchmarks would probably mirror the efficiency levels expected from firms in industrialized countries (for example, those used in the allocation of allowances in an emissions-trading scheme). In some sectors this might take the form of global sector agreements. Standardized benchmarks would help to reduce the risk of carbon leakage, alleviate competitiveness concerns, and thereby help to preserve free trade in these sectors.

(iii) Research and Development

Public support for R&D in energy has fallen dramatically since the early 1980s, as Figure 3.2 illustrates. This trend needs to be rapidly reversed in order to stimulate a portfolio of new technology options that are ready for deployment to reduce emissions from 2030 and in the longer term. Large-scale contributions from the public finances will be necessary to ensure the optimal levels of investment, because research has public-good characteristics. The fruits of research into low-carbon technologies will not necessarily be fully protected by the patent regime, and each country's public efforts to support low carbon R&D will benefit other countries, leading to inadequate financing in the absence of an international agreement. Furthermore, private- and public-sector R&D spending on energy have been closely correlated in the recent past, so partnerships where the public

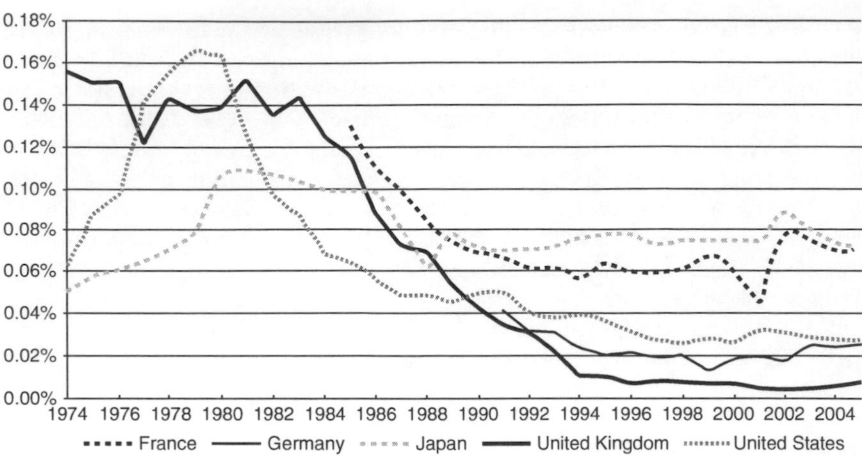

Figure 3.2. Public energy R&D investments as a share of GDP

Source: Stern (2007, p. 401).

and private sectors each bear different risks may enhance both private and social returns.

In addition to support for fundamental research, the commercial demonstration and sharing of existing technologies is urgent. Demonstration of CCS for coal is particularly urgent given the abundance and low cost of coal reserves (Helm, Ch. 2). While there are a couple of dozen demonstration plants at different levels of maturity, there are no current commercial plants using CCS for coal. Stern (2008) argues that, from 2015 or 2020, most new coal-fired generation globally will need to be fitted with CCS for there to be any chance of realizing the 2050 targets. He argues that feed-in subsidies, world-wide, of around US$5 billion p.a. could support over 30 plants over the next seven or eight years across a portfolio of specific technologies and countries. Note that this does not require every individual country to run its own CCS portfolio, and individual countries might aim to develop expertise in specific CCS technologies. Certainly, we need to know soon whether CCS will be relatively cheap or expensive on the necessary scale, so that alternative cost-effective strategies can be developed if necessary.

Other technologies should also be supported, with a variety of policies as set out by Stern (2008). One of the most significant challenges will be to avoid a low-carbon technology pork-barrel. The last few years have seen several potentially promising developments, including new materials and technologies for solar photovoltaics (other than silicon), various biotechnologies to sequester carbon, along with industrial carbon-capture processes. But governments have a poor record at picking the winning technologies and, indeed, the crucial low-carbon technology may yet to be invented. To the extent possible, technology-neutral mechanisms need to be employed, including prizes, tournaments, auctions, and distribution of grants through university channels.

Financial resources must be rapidly committed, and institutional arrangements designed to ensure those resources are delivered. Garnaut (2007) proposes that countries above a given threshold of GDP *per capita* should spend a fraction of their GDP above that threshold on public support for 'research, development and commercialization of new technologies relevant to the transition to a low-emissions economy'. Much of this funding might be raised through hypothecation of revenues from auctioning national emission allowances.[5] Each government would determine which specific technologies it would support, subject to meeting agreed criteria for the public-good or global-benefit nature of the spending on technological development.

(iv) Deforestation

Emissions from global land-use change probably amount to 5–8 Gt CO_2e per annum, implying that up to 20 per cent of current emissions are from this category, primarily deforestation in Brazil and Indonesia. Deforestation occurs because the value of the logged timber, coupled with the value of converting the forest to agriculture (including for production of commodities such as soy and palm oil), is greater than the value of the standing forests. Reducing these emissions requires a framework that accounts for the full opportunity costs of land and provides the institutional, administrative, and enforcement measures necessary.

Stern (2008) estimated that emissions from deforestation could be roughly halved for around US$5 per tonne of CO_2, at a total of US$15 billion per annum. The estimates are somewhat uncertain: estimated opportunity costs alone range from US$3 billion (Grieg-Gran, 2006) to US$33 billion (Obersteiner, 2006) annually. These estimates will now be much higher, given recent increases in agricultural commodity prices. Implementation of a scheme to reduce emission from deforestation and degradation (REDD) will be challenging. Property rights need to be strengthened, as do democratic institutions which are needed to protect the poor and to resolve and arbitrate between competing usage claims. This is extremely important, because an estimated 1.6 billion people depend on forests for their livelihoods (World Bank, 2004). Administrative costs of delivering funds through a national payment scheme, one of the possible alternatives, may be up to US$1 billion annually (Grieg-Gran, 2006). Institutions, such as the World Bank's Forest Carbon Partnership Facility, will be needed to support capacity in rainforest nations, to develop national deforestation strategies, and to put in place monitoring systems to ensure objectives are met. The private sector, which currently provides 90 per cent of the total forest finance (Tomaselli, 2006), also has a major role to play in reducing deforestation rates, potentially

[5] Hypothecation may not be considered credible when 'new' revenues are, in fact, merely allocated to pre-existing programmes, with the funds for the pre-existing programmes returning to the general budget. Here, however, the new financial flows from allowance auctions would significantly exceed existing flows to low-carbon R&D, thereby guaranteeing a net R&D increase.

through the voluntary and, in the longer term, the compliance-based carbon markets.

Cost will be as low as possible when programmes are coordinated internationally and are as large-scale as possible; this reduces the risk that reduced deforestation in one country is simply displaced into deforestation activities in another country. Developing alternative sources of supply for existing demand that drives deforestation is critical. Given capital requirements, public-sector funds will need to be combined with private-sector flows, with a view to ultimately working towards the trading of credits earned through preserving forests.

As with the political economy considerations of international financial transfers more generally (see section III(v)), large payments for avoided deforestation could become unpopular in the countries buying permits if the funds are not directed towards achieving clear development goals. As such, a development framework to support payments for avoided deforestation would need to be agreed as an important component of a global deal on reduced emissions from deforestation and degradation.

(v) Adaptation Finance

Even if the ambitious global emission reduction targets to 2050 are achieved, Earth will warm by another 1–2°C, and it will be necessary for humans to adapt to a changing climate. This will be particularly difficult for poor countries, which lack the resources to prepare for and respond to these changes. The UNDP Human Development Report has estimated additional costs for developing countries of around US$86 billion annually by 2015 (UNDP, 2007), while the UN FCCC (2007*a*) estimates adaptation costs to be US$28–67 billion annually by 2030.

Delivering this level of adaptation finance will be difficult. Indeed, it is already proving difficult to achieve the official development assistance (ODA) promises of the UN Financing for Development conference in Monterrey in 2002, in connection with the Millennium Development Goals. If, as many have promised, the OECD countries move to providing 0.7 per cent GDP in ODA by 2015, this would generate US$150–200 billion in additional development finance annually. However, the Millennium Development Goals did not adequately address climate change. If support for climate adaptation is added, then delivering ODA of 0.7 per cent GDP would only barely meet the responsibilities of the rich nations to the poor. Beyond 2015, assessments of the appropriate level of development assistance should account for the likely additional costs from climate change. Much more detailed risk and impacts information will be necessary to ensure development proceeds in a fashion that is resilient to climate changes.

It is important that financial assistance for climate adaptation be integrated into development spending more generally. Countries with good governance and successful diversified economies are less vulnerable to shocks of all kinds, including those related to climate impacts. Spending should be directed to developing broader social resilience to environmental changes, rather than being earmarked for climate-specific adaptation projects, which may not yield social returns as high as other development priorities.

V. CONCLUSION

Reaching a new climate agreement is both urgent and important, and will be exceptionally challenging. Many of the trends are adverse (Helm, 2008), but a new global deal on climate is nevertheless possible. The international community now has a broadly shared understanding of the objective, with the basic outlines coming into focus. A new global deal should seek to stabilize atmospheric concentrations of GHGs at around 500 ppm CO_2e, or place an equivalent limit on cumulative emissions of CO_2e. Achieving that broadly requires setting a pathway to reduce global emissions by 50 per cent in 2050, with rich countries reducing their emissions by at least 75 per cent.

The instruments required to achieve this are feasible. Global emissions trading, built by linking existing and new emissions-trading schemes, will establish a shared global carbon price to reduce costs. The reform of the CDM is crucial to both scale up emission reductions on a sectoral or benchmark level, and to deliver the necessary finance to the developing world. Similarly, a dramatic scaling up of R&D funding for low-carbon energy is necessary to ensure that new technologies have been invented and are in place by the time they are needed from 2030 and beyond. In the shorter term, an agreement on deforestation is important to capture large-scale emission reductions at relatively low cost. Finally, in the longer term, the demands for finance to adapt to inevitable climatic changes will continue to grow, irrespective of the success or otherwise in agreeing a new global deal.

4

Climate Treaties and the Imperative of Enforcement

*Scott Barrett**

I. INTRODUCTION

Though the Kyoto Protocol entered its implementation phase only in 2008, attention has already turned to negotiating the next climate agreement. One reason for this is that Kyoto terminates in 2012 and it will take time to negotiate a follow-on agreement, to bring this agreement into force, and for its parties to pass the domestic or EU legislation needed to implement it. The more important reason, however, is that the Kyoto Protocol will have no discernable impact on the climate. More needs to be done.

How much more? There is broad agreement among economists that emissions should be reduced below the 'business as usual' level, today and in the future. There is also broad agreement that greenhouse-gas concentrations should not be allowed to increase without limit.[1] Even 'gradual' climate change will eventually melt Greenland ice, causing sea level to rise several metres over many centuries. 'Abrupt and catastrophic' climate change is more uncertain, but would cause greater damage, and is more likely to occur as concentrations climb. So, eventually, concentrations must be capped, and this can only be done if emissions are reduced very substantially.[2]

To stabilize atmospheric concentrations, the amount of carbon dioxide (CO_2) emitted into the atmosphere has to equal the amount that is taken up by the oceans. The balance of CO_2 between the atmosphere and the oceans depends on the rate at which surface waters mix with the deep ocean. Currently, the system is in disequilibrium; the oceans are absorbing CO_2. For the oceans and

* Columbia University.

I am grateful to Christopher Allsopp, Dieter Helm, Cameron Hepburn, Paul Klemperer, and David Victor for comments on a previous draft.

[1] Nicholas Stern (2007) and William Nordhaus (2007*a*) disagree about the level of emission reductions that should be undertaken immediately and the desirable future emissions path.

[2] Even if we stabilize concentrations at 1,000 parts per million CO_2-equivalent—and no economist I know is recommending this—emissions would need to peak before the end of this century and then decline after this (IPCC, 2007, p. 15).

the atmosphere to approach equilibrium (over a period of a few centuries), (net) emissions to the atmosphere must fall to zero, to equal the rate of uptake by the oceans, which must be zero in equilibrium. I want to stress that this qualitative picture is true for any stabilization target. Eventually, stabilizing concentrations will require a technological revolution.

The important treaty design question is whether this long-run goal can be achieved by merely tightening Kyoto's emission caps, leaving the treaty's basic architecture unchanged, or whether more fundamental change is needed. In this article I explain why fundamental change is needed.

Climate change may or may not be the most important problem the world has ever faced, but it is certainly the greatest challenge for collective action. As I shall explain in this paper, this is true both in theory and in practice. It has certainly been true in practice thus far. In 1988, at a quasi-political conference held in Toronto, participants concluded that global carbon-dioxide (CO_2) emissions should be reduced 20 per cent from the 1988 level by 2005. Through 2004, however, and despite two climate treaties having entered into force, global emissions increased 32 per cent.[3] A gap this big (50 per cent), opening up over a period of just two decades, hints at the magnitude of the collective-action challenge.

The Toronto target is important not only because it was the first target ever proposed but because it was a global target, and only global emissions matter. The problem with global targets, however, is that everyone is responsible for meeting them—meaning, of course, that no one is responsible for meeting them.

What about individual targets? After the Toronto meeting, Austria, Denmark, Italy, and Luxembourg all pledged to meet the Toronto target individually (by reducing their individual emissions 20 per cent from the 1988 level by 2005). In the end, however, none did so.[4] (The Labour Party's 1997 manifesto pledged to reduce Britain's emissions 20 per cent from the 1990 level by 2010, but this target is also expected to be missed.) These (and many other) individual targets were not met because reducing emissions unilaterally is costly and doing so promises little benefit to the country that shoulders this cost. Of course, if every country fails to reduce its emissions, atmospheric concentrations will keep on rising (they have been rising steadily since the first measurements were taken in the late-1950s), and all countries will be worse off (at least in the longer term). Put concisely, this is the collective action problem.

In February 2007, the European Union unilaterally set the goal of reducing emissions 20 per cent from the 1990 level by 2020.[5] The EU pledged to reduce its emissions by 30 per cent (again, from the 1990 level), provided the United States and other industrialized countries agreed to the same target. By making its own (higher) target contingent on other countries, the EU may have been aiming

[3] See http://cdiac.ornl.gov/ftp/ndp030/global.1751_2004.ems.

[4] The targets are summarized in International Energy Agency (1992).

[5] In 2005, EU-27 emissions were almost 8 per cent below the 1990 level; see European Environment Agency, *Annual European Community Greenhouse Gas Inventory 1990–2005 and Inventory Report 2007*, Technical Report No. 7, 2007.

to create an *incentive* for other countries to reduce their emissions, it may have been trying to address the collective action challenge. But will its offer change the behaviour of these other states?

History is not encouraging.[6] According to the *Guardian*, EU officials called the proposal an 'opening bid' for the post-Kyoto negotiations.[7] Over ten years ago, European officials travelled to Kyoto with another opening bid—a proposal to cut their emissions 15 per cent if the other OECD countries did so, too. That offer was rejected, and Europe eventually agreed to reduce emissions by just 8 per cent. In 1992, the European Community proposed a mix of measures, including a carbon/energy tax, to stabilize EC emissions at the 1990 level. Like the EU's recent proposal, the EC's tax was made contingent on other OECD countries adopting the same tax. The other OECD countries rejected the offer; the EC dropped the tax.

The idea of making obligations contingent is also a feature of the Kyoto Protocol. Its emission limits only become 'binding' (in the legal sense of the word) on each of its parties if the agreement enters into force, and entry into force depends on the ratification decisions of a substantial number of countries. Unfortunately, and as explained later, this mechanism also has done little to change behaviour.

II. KYOTO PROTOCOL

The logic of the Kyoto Protocol goes something like this: The Kyoto Protocol was intended to be a first step. It requires small (about 5 per cent, on average) reductions in the emissions of industrialized (Annex I) countries for a short period of time (2008–12). Kyoto was to be followed by a sequence of other agreements—a second step, a third step, and so on—with each new agreement progressively lowering the limit on the emissions of Annex I countries. It was expected that, in time, the non-Annex I countries would also agree to limit their emissions. Eventually, it was hoped, every country would be subject to an emission cap.

Associated with these country-specific caps would be a price on greenhouse-gas emissions. This price would be a 'shadow price' if emissions were regulated domestically. It would be a market price if the caps were implemented by a tradable emission entitlement scheme. It would be a tax rate if countries chose to implement their obligations by means of a carbon tax. However countries sought to reduce their emissions domestically, the treaty's 'flexible mechanisms' would ensure that the price on emissions would be equal internationally, making

[6] As well, to call for identical percentage cuts in emissions from the same base year is to ignore differences among countries. The EU-27 includes countries in economic transition. The emissions of these countries are already substantially below the 1990 level for reasons of restructuring. For other OECD countries to meet the same target would not reflect 'equal sacrifice'. This is the 'comparability' problem, discussed later in this chapter.

[7] Traynor and D. Gow, 'EU Promises 20% Reduction in Carbon Emissions by 2020', the *Guardian*, 21 February 2007.

global abatement cost-effective. As the caps were progressively tightened in future agreements, this world price on greenhouse-gas emissions would increase, stimulating a range of activities from energy conservation to fuel switching. Expectations about its future growth would encourage energy R&D. Eventually the rising price path would lead to substitution of renewable or nuclear energy for fossil-fuel energy. Alternatively, fossil fuels would continue to be burned but with the emissions captured and stored. Kyoto did not specify the technological means by which emissions would be cut; its purpose was to support a collective end: a limit on atmospheric concentrations. In particular, Kyoto's purpose was to lay a foundation for meeting the goal of the Framework Convention on Climate Change (FCCC)—to ensure that concentrations would be stabilized 'at a level that would prevent dangerous interference with the climate system'.

This is an elegant and audacious construct. Can it work? An effective international agreement for climate-change mitigation must do three things; Kyoto, unfortunately, does none of them.

First, a treaty must attract broad *participation*. This is not only because all countries emit greenhouse gases. It is also because, should only some countries reduce emissions, comparative advantage in the carbon-intensive industries will shift to the other countries, causing *their* emissions to increase—a phenomenon known as 'trade leakage'. Kyoto failed to deter the United States from not participating, partly because of US concerns about leakage. It may seem that the USA is an outlier, but China, India, and the other developing countries only participated in the Kyoto Protocol because the agreement does not require that they reduce their emissions. Similarly, Russia and the economies in transition participated because they were given a surplus of emission entitlements—'hot air' (see Table 4.1, where the economies in transition are set off in bold). Under Kyoto, very few countries are required to reduce their emissions.

Second, a treaty must create incentives for *compliance*. Canada is a party to the Kyoto Protocol, required to reduce its emissions 6 per cent below the 1990 level through 2008–12. In 2005, however, Canada's emissions were 30 per cent *above* this target, and Canada's current government has given up on the idea of meeting the Kyoto target. It aims instead to reduce the rate of growth in emissions, hoping that Canada's emissions will peak around 2010, the mid-point of Kyoto's implementation period. A government-funded roundtable, however, has concluded that the government's policies will not meet even this modest goal.[8] Canada's previous government—the one that ratified Kyoto but that did not adopt the policies needed to comply with it—predicted that Canada's emissions would exceed the Kyoto target by 45 per cent by 2010 (Government of Canada, 2005). This still remains distinctly possible.[9] Canada's situation is extreme, but it is not the only Kyoto party in jeopardy of non-compliance. As shown in Table 4.1, the

[8] For the relevant section of the roundtable's report (see http://www.nrtee-trnee.ca/eng/publications/c288-response-2007/section4-c288-response-2007-eng.html).

[9] The current government's projections are that Canada will exceed Kyoto's limits by around 34 per cent; again (see http://www.nrtee-trnee.ca/eng/publications/c288-response-2007/section4-c288-response-2007-eng.html).

Table 4.1. The Kyoto compliance gap

Annex I country	Kyoto cap from base year	Excluding LULUCF		Including LULUCF	
		Change from base year to 2005	Gap	Change from base year to 2005	Gap
Australia	+8	25.6	17.6	4.5	−3.5
Austria	*−13*	*18.0*	*31.0*	*13.6*	*0.6*
Belgium	*−7.5*	*−1.3*	*6.2*	*−0.6*	*6.9*
Bulgaria	**−8**	**−47.2**	**−39.2**	**−59.3**	**−51.3**
Canada	−6	25.3	31.3	54.2	60.2
Croatia	−5	−3.4	1.6	−10.2	−5.2
Czech Rep.	**−8**	**−25.8**	**−17.8**	**−27.5**	**−19.5**
Denmark	*−21*	*−7.0*	*14.0*	*−9.8*	*11.2*
Estonia	**−8**	**−50.9**	**−42.9**	**−61.4**	**−53.4**
EC	−8	−1.5	6.5	−4.0	4.0
Finland	*0*	*−2.5*	*−2.5*	*−22.8*	*−22.8*
France	*0*	*−1.6*	*−1.6*	*−7.1*	*−7.1*
Germany	*−21*	*−18.4*	*2.6*	*−19.5*	*1.5*
Greece	*+25*	*26.6*	*−1.6*	*25.3*	*0.3*
Hungary	**−6**	**−30.7**	**−24.7**	**−32.7**	**−26.7**
Iceland	+10	10.5	0.5	0.3	−9.7
Ireland	*+13*	*26.3*	*13.3*	*24.9*	*11.9*
Italy	*−6.5*	*12.1*	*18.6*	*7.4*	*13.9*
Japan	−6	6.9	12.9	7.1	13.1
Latvia	**−8**	**−58.9**	**−50.9**	**−161.5**	**−153.5**
Liechtenstein	−8	17.4	25.4	18.4	26.4
Lithuania	**−8**	**−54.1**	**−46.1**	**−64.8**	**−56.8**
Luxembourg	*−28*	*0.4*	*28.4*	*0.4*	*28.4*
Monaco	−8	−3.1	4.9	−3.2	4.8
Netherlands	*−6*	*−0.4*	*5.6*	*−0.4*	*5.6*
New Zealand	0	24.7	24.7	22.7	22.7
Norway	+1	8.8	7.8	−23.1	−24.1
Poland	**−6**	**−32.0**	**−26.0**	**−33.8**	**−27.8**
Portugal	*+27*	*42.8*	*15.8*	*40.3*	*13.3*
Romania	**−8**	**−45.6**	**−37.6**	**−53.5**	**−45.5**
Russia	**0**	**−28.7**	**−28.7**	**−27.7**	**−27.7**
Slovakia	**−8**	**−33.6**	**−25.6**	**−32.5**	**−24.5**
Slovenia	**−8**	**0.4**	**8.4**	**−20.1**	**−12.1**
Spain	*+15*	*53.3*	*38.3*	*59.8*	*44.8*
Sweden	*+4*	*−7.3*	*−11.3*	*−8.2*	*−12.2*
Switzerland	−8	1.7	9.7	4.6	12.6
Ukraine	**0**	**−54.7**	**−54.7**	**−58.7**	**−58.7**
United Kingdom	*−12.5*	*−14.8*	*−2.3*	*−15.4*	*−2.9*
United States	−7	16.3	23.3	16.3	23.3

Note: The countries in italics were the 15 states covered under the European bubble. The countries in bold are in transition. These countries were allowed to choose an alternative base year to 1990.

Source: http://unfccc.int/resource/docs/2007/sbi/eng/30.pdf

compliance gap is significant for many countries, including New Zealand and Japan. The caps for some members of the European Union also appear challenging. Spain has the largest gap of any country. Denmark is well off its individual target. However, thanks to the European 'bubble,' these countries are not bound by their individual limits so long as the original 15 members of the European Union meet their collective limit. Australia recently ratified the Kyoto Protocol, but as Table 4.1 shows, after taking land use, land-use change, and forestry (LULUCF) activities into account, Australia is within its Kyoto limit; Australia will have to do very little to comply.[10]

Third, a treaty must somehow get countries to participate in and to comply with an agreement in which global emissions are to be reduced substantially. Participation in the FCCC is nearly full (the only non-participants are Andorra, the Holy See, Iraq, and Somalia). Moreover, compliance with this agreement is perfect. However, the Framework Convention does not require that parties reduce their emissions. Kyoto requires that some parties reduce their emissions—but, overall, these requirements are exceedingly modest and short term. Even if participation in Kyoto were full and compliance perfect, global emissions of greenhouse gases would keep on rising.

These problems with Kyoto are more easily understood by contrasting this agreement with one that works well.

In 2002, the United States imposed tariffs on steel imports. The European Union, supported by other countries, complained to the World Trade Organization (WTO) that the US tariffs were in non-compliance with WTO rules. A WTO panel convened to hear this case agreed. So did an appeals panel. Under WTO rules, the USA was at this time obligated to remove its tariffs. It did not. Also under WTO rules, however, the EU was permitted to 'rebalance' the effect of the US tariffs, given that the USA failed to comply. The EU put together a rebalancing package that targeted politically sensitive products such as citrus fruit from Florida—an astute calculation, since the tariffs were scheduled to be imposed in December 2003, less than a year before the next US presidential election (recall that Florida was a 'battleground' state in the contested 2000 election). As it happened, shortly before the EU tariffs were to be imposed, President George W. Bush lifted the US tariffs on steel imports. In the event, the EU tariffs were never imposed. They did not need to be imposed; the credible threat that they would be imposed was enough to make the USA comply (after a delay) with the WTO ruling.

This is an example of a treaty arrangement that works. The agreement creates an incentive for the EU to punish the USA for not complying, and it creates an incentive for the USA, when facing this punishment, to comply. The agreement also creates incentives for the EU and the USA to participate in the agreement. At no point during this dispute did the USA (or the EU) contemplate withdrawing from the WTO. This incentive to participate is attributable to the very substantial

[10] LULUCF is normally treated differently because of various accounting and incentive problems. For example, carbon accumulated in forestry may later be released.

reduction in trade barriers agreed by the WTO—a favourable treatment that could be denied to non-parties.[11]

It is widely acknowledged that Kyoto's emission limits are inadequate, but tightening these limits (as the EU has proposed) will have no effect unless the other two problems with Kyoto (participation and compliance) are also addressed. We have already seen evidence of how the three different requirements play off one another. After the USA announced that it would not ratify Kyoto, Canada and Japan, worried about leakage, insisted upon a generous accounting of their 'sinks' as a condition for their ratification. This renegotiation increased participation at the cost of reducing the overall effect of the agreement. Similarly, compliance can be achieved fairly easily today if countries take advantage of the Protocol's 'flexible mechanisms', thanks again to post-Kyoto negotiations lifting restrictions on emissions trading. But if compliance is achieved by the purchase of 'hot air', global emissions may not fall at all relative to 'business as usual'.

To sum up, a climate treaty must achieve three things. It must get countries to participate; it must get participants to comply; and it must do both of these things even as it requires that parties reduce their emissions substantially. The Kyoto Protocol satisfies none of these conditions. It would be easy to design a treaty that satisfied one or two of the conditions, but success depends on meeting all three of them—no exceptions.

III. ENFORCEMENT

Deterring non-participation and non-compliance requires enforcement. As explained previously, trade measures have been used successfully to enforce the WTO; so, why not use trade restrictions to enforce Kyoto? The idea is alluring (Stiglitz, 2006). Would it work?

Trade restrictions in a climate agreement have two justifiable purposes.

First, trade restrictions could be adopted to neutralize leakage. Suppose emissions at home are reduced by means of an economy-wide tradable permit scheme and that emissions abroad are not subject to any controls. Then leakage will be neutralized if exporters are given a rebate at the border, and importers are made to pay a tax at the border, equal to the market price of domestically traded permits times the amount of greenhouse gases emitted in the manufacture of the traded good. Under this arrangement, domestic producers would not be harmed in international markets, and foreign producers would not have an advantage in the home market. By neutralizing leakage, 'border tax adjustments' would also

[11] This is not to say that the WTO is flawless. For example, it is a problem that the USA found it in its interests to violate the trading rules in the first place. The incentive for the USA to do so is probably due to the long lag between tariffs between imposed and rebalancing being threatened. As well, while the WTO has reduced trade barriers in manufactured goods, it has not done so for agriculture—the focus of the most recent round of negotiations.

help to promote participation in a treaty aiming to reduce emissions. However, the free-riding problem would remain.

Second, trade restrictions could be designed to deter non-participation directly. If participation were full, and if emissions everywhere were reduced by means of Kyoto's flexible mechanisms, then the price of emissions would be uniform worldwide; there would be no leakage and no need for border tax adjustments; there also would be no free riding.

Which approach is best? Border tax adjustments would need to be comprehensive and based on how products were made.[12] But how to calculate the emissions released in the manufacture of individual products? That would be difficult. Two identical products, manufactured in the same country, might have very different 'carbon footprints' (depending, for example, on how the electricity input had been generated). Cruder calculations might be contemplated, but sector-specific taxes would also be hard to calculate.[13] Crudely designed trade restrictions may also be less effective at reducing leakage (see Oliveira-Martins *et al.*, 1992).

Trade restrictions intended to deter free riding can be blunt by design. Their aim, after all, would be to coerce. Ideally, they would not need to be imposed at all; the credible threat to impose them would be sufficient to make every country want to participate. To be effective, however, the restrictions would have to be severe in addition to being credible, and punishments typically become less credible as they become more severe (see Barrett, 2005*a*). Another problem is the legitimacy of such an action. Who should decide what a particular country ought to do? Who should decide the type and severity of punishment that ought to be imposed upon a country that fails to fulfil this obligation? The use of blunt trade restrictions to enforce an unfair climate agreement would lack legitimacy; it may only spur retaliation—a trade war. When Britain decided to debate climate change at the United Nations Security Council, three of the other permanent members (China, Russia, and the United States) responded with indifference, but many countries not represented on the Security Council were angry; they felt that the issue should remain with the General Assembly, where every country has one vote, not the Security Council, where a small number of countries call the shots. At the end of the day's debate, no resolution was presented, no statement issued.

Another problem with trade restrictions of either type is that they would need to apply to countries that failed to comply as well as those that failed to participate. Otherwise, participation would become a route for avoiding having to reduce emissions. Climate negotiators actually agreed to adopt a compliance mechanism in 2001. But according to Article 18 of the Kyoto Protocol, any compliance mechanism 'entailing binding consequences' must be approved by amendment. An amendment is akin to a new agreement. It would only be binding on the parties that ratified it, provided at least three-quarters of the parties to the Kyoto Protocol

[12] Even if the domestic policy were not economy-wide, there would be general equilibrium effects, and these would need to be taken into account at the border.

[13] For example, Hoel (1996) shows that there is no simple relationship between fossil-fuel intensity and the optimal sector-specific carbon tax.

also ratified it. So far, no such amendment has been adopted. The mechanism agreed in 2001 is thus non-binding.

Even if the mechanism were binding, it would have no effect. The main component of the mechanism is a 30 per cent penalty. A country that emits, say, 100 tonnes more than the treaty allows in the first 'commitment period' (2008–12) must make up for this by reducing its emissions by an additional 130 tonnes in the next period. This reduction is 'additional' relative to this country's next-period cap. This cap, however, is subject to the approval of the country having to pay the penalty. That country can, therefore, insist on a generous cap as a condition for joining, and so get away with paying a 'phantom' penalty. Alternatively, it could ratify the new treaty and then fail to comply again—the current arrangement essentially carries forward the penalty indefinitely. The reason this penalty system cannot deter non-compliance is that its punishments must be self-inflicted. This is to be contrasted with the WTO enforcement mechanism described previously. The WTO compliance mechanism works by enabling an injured party to impose rebalancing tariffs against a party found to have violated the rules. It was the threat by the EU to impose tariffs against the USA that impelled the USA to drop its illegal steel tariffs.

The Kyoto compliance mechanism just mentioned does allow one non-self-inflicted punishment. It permits other parties to the Kyoto Protocol to suspend the trading privileges of a country found to be in non-compliance. Would other countries impose this punishment? There is good reason to believe they would not, at least in some important cases (Kallbekken and Hovi, 2007). If a large seller of permits were in non-compliance, withdrawal of its trading privileges would push up international permit prices, harming net importers; the latter countries may therefore be unwilling to impose the punishment. If a large buyer of permits were punished in this same way, international permit prices would fall, harming net exporters; *these* countries may therefore also be unwilling to impose the punishment. In short, the threat to punish may not be credible. Of course, in each of the cases I just mentioned, some countries would gain by imposing the punishments (net exporters in the first instance, net importers in the second). But with some countries gaining and some losing, activation of the sanction could spark conflict among the countries that had complied. This is in contrast to the WTO punishment mentioned previously, in which the retaliatory trade restriction harms only the target country.[14]

Another point: it cannot be assumed that every other aspect of a treaty will remain unchanged should an effective enforcement mechanism be adopted. Adding enforcement penalties, for example, may make parties want to water down the agreement, to ensure that the punishments are not imposed. As I said before, to be effective a treaty must not only deter non-participation and non-compliance;

[14] The essential difference between enforcing a trade agreement and a climate agreement is that trade is a bilateral activity whereas climate-change mitigation is a global public good. Bilateral agreements are easy to enforce; multilateral agreements seeking to supply a global public good are much harder to enforce.

it must do both of these things even as it gets countries to change their behaviour significantly. Usually an attempt to address one of these dimensions only displaces the free-rider problem, putting pressure on one or both of the other dimensions.

To sum up, should the focus of negotiations be on setting even tougher targets and timetables without addressing the underlying enforcement challenge, the outcome is likely to be more of the same—meaning, little if any success in reducing global emissions. Should the focus be on strengthening the enforcement mechanism—by allowing trade restrictions, for example—different challenges will emerge. We cannot be sure that the outcome will be any more satisfactory.

IV. THE MONTREAL PROTOCOL AS A CLIMATE-CHANGE TREATY

While efforts to address climate change directly have failed, we have succeeded in addressing climate change indirectly—almost without anyone noticing.

The relationship between stratospheric ozone depletion and climate change is complex. Ozone in the stratosphere is a greenhouse gas (protecting the ozone layer will thus add to climate change), but so are the chemicals that deplete stratospheric ozone (reducing these emissions will thus help mitigate climate change). Making matters more complicated, some of the substitutes for these ozone-destroying gases are also greenhouse gases. The Montreal Protocol on Substances that Deplete the Ozone Layer, which aims to protect stratospheric ozone by banning ozone-depleting gases, could thus dampen or aggravate global climate change.

What is the net effect? A recent study has done the accounting and shown that the overall effect of the Montreal Protocol is helpful to the climate (Velders *et al.*, 2007). Indeed, the study calculates that the Montreal Protocol has been, and will continue to be, much more helpful in addressing climate change than the Kyoto Protocol, even assuming that Kyoto is implemented perfectly and with full participation. Already, this study estimates, the Montreal Protocol has reduced greenhouse-gas emissions four times as much as the Kyoto Protocol aspired to do.

In September 2007, on the Montreal Protocol's 20th anniversary, the parties to this extraordinary treaty met again in Montreal to accelerate and expand the phase-out of hydrochlorofluorocarbons (HCFCs), an ozone-depleting substance that happens also to be a greenhouse gas. HCFCs are especially important because the manufacture of these compounds produces hydrofluorocarbons (HFCs) as a byproduct. HFCs do not deplete the ozone layer, and are not regulated directly by the Montreal Protocol; but they are a very potent greenhouse gas, covered under the Kyoto Protocol. By one estimate, the adjustment negotiated in Montreal in September 2007 will have about the same impact on the climate as the Kyoto Protocol was designed to achieve (Kaniaru *et al.*, 2007, p. 4).[15] I stress that this is

[15] The example of reducing HFCs exposes another flaw in the Kyoto Protocol. It turns out that most emission reductions under the treaty's Clean Development Mechanism (CDM) have involved HFCs.

on top of the larger effect Montreal has already had in reducing the concentration of greenhouse gases.

V. WHY MONTREAL WORKS

Why has the Montreal Protocol succeeded where the Kyoto Protocol has failed? Part of the reason is that the environmental problems are very different.[16] However, the treaty itself also made a huge difference. It is really only in hindsight that protecting the ozone layer appears easy.

First, the Montreal Protocol limits not only the production of chlorofluorocarbons (CFCs) and related chemicals; it also limits the consumption of these substances (defined by Montreal as production plus imports minus exports). We speak of 'Britain's carbon emissions' and 'China's carbon emissions' but when Britain imports energy-intensive products from China, which country is responsible for the emissions released in the manufacture of these products, China or Britain? If participation were universal, the distinction would not matter. When participation is incomplete, limiting consumption as well as production helps to reduce leakage. For that reason, it also promotes participation.

Second, the Montreal Protocol requires *all* countries, rich and poor alike, to cut back on their production and consumption of CFCs. Developing countries were given easier, initial limits, but they were expected to get to the same final end-points as the rich countries (an early example of rich and poor countries having 'common but differentiated responsibilities'). Under the Kyoto Protocol, the emissions of developing countries are unconstrained—a bizarre situation when you consider that China has added more coal-fired electricity capacity in a single year than Britain's entire installed capacity.

Third, Montreal's cuts are permanent whereas Kyoto's last only five years. Five-year targets are entirely unsuited to bringing about lasting change. The coal

This would not matter except that too much is being paid for the reductions. One consequence of this is that less is being achieved than could be achieved for the same money. According to Michael Wara (2007, p. 596), HFCs could be phased out for less than €100 million, saving €4.6 billion 'in CDM credits that could be spent on other climate-protecting uses'. Wara (2007, p. 596) also notes an allied problem—'HFC-23 emitters can earn almost twice as much from CDM credits as they can from selling refrigerant gases—by any measure a major distortion of the market'. The distortion creates incentives for production of HCFCs to expand so that the manufacturers can earn CDM credits for cutting back on their emission of HFCs.

[16] For example, ozone depletion harms all countries. Catastrophic climate change (such as a break-up of the West Antarctic Ice Sheet) would similarly harm all, or nearly all, states, but 'gradual' climate change would create winners as well as losers. As well, the damages from ozone depletion are substantial (primarily owing to increased deaths from skin cancer) and the costs of substituting for ozone-depleting substances modest, whereas for climate change the benefit–cost comparison is less attractive (Barrett, 2007*b*). Finally, it also happened that the companies manufacturing ozone-destroying chemicals were best placed for developing and manufacturing their replacements, and the treaty deftly opened new markets for the substitutes as it shut the old markets down. Altogether, the 'initial conditions' for addressing ozone depletion were unusually favourable.

plants being built today will last 40 or 50 years. The energy and transportation infrastructure being built now will last even longer. Because of path-dependence, the effects of these investments may endure longer still. An effective climate agreement must impose obligations that can be ratcheted up, and that are immune to backsliding.

Fourth, the Montreal Protocol, as amended in 1990, creates positive incentives for developing countries to participate. Essentially, Montreal compensates developing countries for their compliance costs. These costs are paid out of the Multilateral Fund, which is financed by rich countries according to the United Nations scale of assessments.[17] Kyoto's Clean Development Mechanism offers limited incentives for developing countries to reduce their emissions. However, CDM 'offsets', being project-based, are burdened by high transactions costs. Their quantity is also too small to be transformational.[18] The Montreal Protocol used financing to get developing countries on to an ozone-friendly development path. An effective climate agreement needs to get poor countries, especially the fast-growing poor countries, on to a climate-friendly (carbon-free) development path.

Finally, Montreal created strong incentives for countries to participate and to comply. The main incentive is a trade restriction: Montreal bans trade between parties and non-parties in ozone-depleting substances and products containing these substances. Originally, the treaty also intended to ban trade in products made using these same substances, but experts determined that this was impracticable, and this last ban was never adopted. Fortunately, it was not needed. (As explained previously, trade restrictions based on how products are made would be needed to enforce a climate treaty, if their purpose was to limit leakage.) Importantly, Montreal's trade restrictions have not been imposed. The threat to impose them, made credible by the leakage that would be avoided by the restrictions, has sufficed to change behaviour.[19] As explained previously, it is not obvious that climate-related trade restrictions, at least if applied across-the-board, would work as conveniently.

VI. MONTREAL'S LESSONS

Like the Kyoto Protocol, Montreal establishes targets and timetables. In Montreal's case, however, these instruments served as a means, not an end. Their purpose was not to reduce emissions by an exact amount on a particular date. Their purpose was to effect a technological transformation. An effective climate treaty system must do the same thing.

The Kyoto Protocol limits more than the emissions of CO_2; it also caps the emissions of methane (CH_4), nitrous oxide (N_2O), and three industrial

[17] As of July 2007, US$2.27 billion has been contributed (see http://www.multilateralfund.org). See Barrett (2007*b*) for a discussion of the United Nations scale.

[18] See also the comments in footnote 15.

[19] This makes Montreal's punishment mechanism better than the WTO's, which has needed to be imposed, as explained previously. See also footnote 11.

gases—HFCs, perfluorocarbons (PFCs), and sulphur hexafluoride (SF_6). Economists have celebrated Kyoto's 'comprehensive' design. By throwing all these gases in the same basket, as it were, Kyoto has facilitated cost-effective abatement (that is, it has allowed the marginal cost of reducing concentrations, after adjusting for each gas's contribution to climate change, to be equal for every gas). The problem is that cost-effectiveness has been achieved at the cost of lowering the emission reductions that Kyoto is able to sustain. Montreal has shown that emissions could have been cut more if the different gases included in Kyoto had been treated separately. It seems very possible that the three industrial gases mentioned above could have been controlled more effectively by a separate agreement styled after Montreal rather than being lumped together with all the other gases in the Kyoto Protocol.

In 1998, 11 years after Montreal was first negotiated, the agreement was not only well into its implementation phase; it had already been adjusted and amended seven times. In 2008, 11 years after Kyoto was negotiated, that agreement has only just entered its implementation phase. In 1998, it was clear that the ozone layer would be protected, and nearly to the maximum extent achievable. The agreement would be amended one more time (in 1999) and adjusted twice more (in 1999 and, as mentioned before, in 2007), but by 1998 the main work of the Montreal Protocol had already been accomplished; certainly an effective architecture was firmly in place. In 2008, by contrast, the future of the climate regime remains very uncertain. Kyoto expires in 2012 and we don't know what kind of regime will succeed it. The current plan is to negotiate a successor by late 2009, but this is an ambitious timetable, particularly as the US negotiating team will be replaced midway through this process, and a new regime, if it is to be effective, must include the USA as a key and enthusiastic party. At the same time, delays in negotiating a successor to Kyoto will put more pressure on the existing agreement; compliance with Kyoto may suffer further.

Where to go from here? The parties to the Framework Convention mapped out a plan—a 'roadmap'—in Bali in December 2007. I turn to this next.

VII. BALI

In Bali, the European Union urged rich countries to accept 'binding commitments' for reductions in greenhouse gases—a plan that would retain Kyoto's essential structure. Specifically, the EU pushed for rich countries to cut their emissions 25–40 per cent by 2020 (a higher level than the EU had recommended before; see the introduction to this chapter). This proposal is consistent with the view that Kyoto's only problem is that its caps are too generous. Kyoto's caps are too generous, but as I have explained, simply tightening Kyoto's existing caps while leaving the rest of the agreement unchanged will not increase the treaty's effectiveness—indeed, it is likely to make no difference at all. Incentives must also be created for developing countries to reduce their emissions. Most importantly, the obligations of the new agreement need to be enforced.

The Bali Action Plan admits a wider range of possibilities. In particular, it identifies five key areas: (*a*) 'a shared vision for long-term cooperative action, including a long-term global goal for emission reductions'; (*b*) 'enhanced... action on mitigation'; (*c*) 'enhanced action on adaptation'; (*d*) 'enhanced action on technology development and transfer to support action on mitigation and adaptation'; and (*e*) 'enhanced action on the provision of financial resources and investment to support action on mitigation and adaptation and technology cooperation'. This agenda is broader than Kyoto's. It also provides an opportunity to address many of Kyoto's failings. I discuss each of these five issues in turn below.

(i) Long-term Goal

What should be the long-term global goal? In 1996, the Council of the European Union decided that the goal should be to ensure that mean global temperature increase does not exceed 2°C. Why this level? The Council reasoned that, 'once global warming exceeds 2°C, climate impacts on food production, water supply and ecosystems are projected to increase significantly and irreversible catastrophic events may occur'.[20] The Council's rationale is significant. The FCCC says that the world should avoid 'dangerous anthropogenic interference with the climate system', and do so 'within a time frame sufficient to allow ecosystems to adapt naturally to climate change, to ensure that food production is not threatened and to enable economic development to proceed in a sustainable manner'. The EU goal of limiting climate change to 2°C was meant to quantify the agreed qualitative goal.

Will other countries accept it? There are a number of problems with this goal; three are especially important. First, because of 'climate uncertainty', there is a probability distribution of concentration levels associated with meeting any particular temperature target. This means that, given our present knowledge, we have to ask with what degree of certainty we should aim to limit temperature rise to 2°C. With probability equal to one? That would require reducing concentrations below the current level. With probability one-half? Two-thirds? (Allied to this question is a related one: Should this concentration level be an upper bound or a long-run target? Should 'overshooting' be allowed?) Second, the goal seems to have been determined without considering the consequences of having to meet it.[21] Would it matter if the goal were met by a massive expansion in nuclear power? Nuclear power would have consequences for very long-term waste storage and

[20] 'Questions and Answers on the Commission Communication, *Limiting Global Climate Change to 2°C*', Memo/07/17.

[21] This need to account for the consequences of acting or not acting to address the threat of global climate change underlies the analyses of both Nordhaus (2007*a*) and Stern (2007). I noted in footnote 1 that these economists agree that emissions need to be reduced now and that they need to be reduced very substantially later. They disagree as to whether 2°C is the 'right' target.

proliferation; not every country agrees that nuclear power should be expanded. What about carbon capture and deep ocean storage on a massive scale? This may introduce new risks to the marine environment. Would countries agree that these risks are worth taking to avoid the risk of greater climate change? Meeting the goal will also be costly. Will countries agree that the cost is worthwhile? Will some developing countries argue that development deserves a higher priority? Will they say that the target for temperature increase needs to be determined jointly with arrangements for adaptation assistance?

Finally, this goal can only be met by the collective actions of all countries. Will agreeing on a collective goal help? It would if the following were feasible. Having agreed on a maximum allowable temperature change, having agreed on the concentration level needed to avoid exceeding this temperature target (with some probability), and having determined the best emission trajectory for reaching this concentration level (where 'best' might be the cost-effective emissions path), all the countries of the world are also able to agree how to allocate annual emission limits among them such that the sum of all their limits equals the required global total precisely (this division, you will notice, is a zero-sum game; it assumes that countries can 'solve' the participation problem). Then, provided each country stayed within its emission limit (that is, that the treaty also 'solves' the compliance problem), the temperature-change goal would be met (again, with some probability). But will countries stay within these limits? Will they consent to this arrangement? Will they be able to reach agreement? There have been numerous proposals for a programme like the one just outlined.[22] But the logic underpinning these proposals presumes a degree of global solidarity and a capability to enforce individual behaviour that simply does not exist.[23]

Choosing a long-run goal only helps if there is a reasonable prospect of the goal being met. As I noted earlier, the world has set collective goals before (recall the Toronto target from 1988) and missed them by a mile. Agreeing on a goal only helps if it is also possible to enforce the actions needed to ensure that the goal is actually met. This, in my view, should be the focus of negotiations.

Interestingly, the Vienna Convention for the Protection of the Ozone Layer (ozone's equivalent to the FCCC) does not specify a collective goal, even in qualitative terms. Instead, it enjoins countries 'to take appropriate measures ... to protect human health and the environment against adverse effects resulting or likely to result from human activities which modify or are likely to modify the ozone layer'. This is what a climate regime needs to do. It needs to focus the world's attention on the need to take appropriate measures: to take action rather than to set goals.

[22] The most recent is by Barnes *et al.* (2008).

[23] There is one exception to the situation described here. Imagine that damages (benefits) were discontinuous at the global target: should the world cross this threshold, the consequence would be truly catastrophic for every country. Then avoiding the threshold would be sustainable; it would be a Nash equilibrium. This situation resembles the challenge of averting a certain catastrophic asteroid strike; see Barrett (2007*b*). Unfortunately (or fortunately!), global climate-change damages do not, so far as we know, have this feature. They are not catastrophic in the same sense.

This is why the other four elements of the Bali roadmap are important. They all focus on the taking of actions. I turn to these next.

(ii) Enhanced Mitigation: The Merit in Sectoral Approaches

According to the Bali roadmap, 'enhanced mitigation' is to include 'measurable, reportable and verifiable nationally appropriate mitigation commitments or actions, including quantified emission limitation and reduction objectives, by all developed country Parties, while ensuring the comparability of efforts among them, taking into account differences in their national circumstances.' Developing countries are now also expected to contribute. They are to undertake 'nationally appropriate mitigation actions ... in the context of sustainable development, supported and enabled by technology financing and capacity-building, in a measurable, reportable and verifiable manner'. Importantly, the mitigation actions of all countries may include 'cooperative sectoral approaches and sector-specific actions'.

Bali thus permits a range of treaty designs.[24] It could lead to negotiation of a Kyoto look-alike treaty. It could allow some countries to adopt targets and timetables even as others chose a different approach—tradable permits with a price escape valve, perhaps, or a carbon tax, or technology standards. Though the type of action can vary, the actions adopted by different developed countries must be comparable. The Kyoto emission caps only had the illusion of comparability. They were calculated relative to an atypical base year (making matters worse, the economies in transition were able to choose their preferred base year). The gaps identified in Table 4.1 do not reflect different efforts to reduce emissions so much as different initial conditions. They are meaningless as an indicator of 'comparability'. So, Bali was right to draw attention to comparability, though it will be difficult for countries to define what the term means.

While the emphasis of Kyoto was on economy-wide emission reductions, it is not a fully comprehensive agreement. It excludes emissions from aviation, marine transport, and deforestation. Of course, it also fails to impose emission obligations on developing countries. Various proposals have been made for integrating these omitted areas in a new agreement. Doing so would aid cost-effectiveness. However, it may also compromise enforcement. With all gases and sectors bundled together, enforcement of the system as a whole may depend on its weakest links.

An alternative approach would address the parts and not—or not only—the whole. My suggestion earlier that the three industrial gases be treated separately is an example of this approach. For the main greenhouse gas, CO_2, this approach would commend a focus on sector-level actions.[25]

Implementation of Kyoto has so far been sectoral by choice. No country has a single, economy-wide policy for meeting its Kyoto obligations. The European

[24] A number of alternative approaches have been proposed. For a particularly good collection and analysis, see Aldy and Stavins (2007).

[25] After the Bali meeting, Japan proposed a sectoral approach.

Emissions Trading Scheme (EU ETS) covers less than half of EU emissions. Sweden arguably has the most well-developed climate-change policy of any country, and its approach involves both 'sector integration' (every sector plays a part towards meeting the overall goal) and 'sector responsibility' (different sectors play different parts). Even Sweden's economy-wide policies differentiate by sector. Its carbon tax, for example, offers relief for energy-intensive industrial operations (Ministry of Sustainable Development, 2005). The reason, of course, is fear of trade leakage.

In not requiring that developing countries reduce emissions, Kyoto has created incentives for its emissions-constrained parties either to offer preferential treatment to the trade-sensitive sectors or to adopt trade restrictions. Preferential treatment undermines the objective of cost-effectiveness—the main reason for adopting an economy-wide approach in the first place. Economy-wide trade restrictions, as noted previously, are likely to introduce new tensions (the legitimacy problem). They may also fail (the credibility problem).

Sectoral agreements would need to be inclusive; developing countries would be expected to participate in these agreements, to meet the same industry standards, but they would also be offered financial assistance, to aid their compliance. This arrangement would recognize that rich and poor countries alike have common but differentiated responsibilities. Sectoral agreements would also need to be enforced—by trade restrictions. Trade restrictions in this context would be legitimate, since developing countries would be compensated for participating and the aim of the restrictions would be to enforce an agreement establishing a 'level playing field' for a global industry. Trade restrictions applied to sector-specific agreements are also more likely to be credible. Parties to a sectoral agreement would not want non-parties to have an 'unfair' advantage in international trade. Moreover, by definition, these sectors would be especially vulnerable to leakage. Applying trade restrictions to non-parties would reduce leakage, and thus help to make credible the threat to apply the restrictions. Enforcement would be further helped if the treaty's obligations were expressed in terms of consumption and not only production.

The aluminium sector is a prime candidate for a separate agreement.[26] It is a concentrated industry: 12 countries account for 82 per cent of global production; ten companies produce more than half of world output. The industry employs just two smelting technologies, and emissions can be reduced substantially by re-melting aluminium scrap (the former is 95 per cent less greenhouse-gas-intensive than primary aluminium production). Finally, 26 companies, making up 80 per cent of world output, belong to the International Aluminium Institute, which has already adopted voluntary intensity targets. There exists a basis here for negotiating new global standards for the industry, backed by international enforcement. Other candidates for sectoral agreements include steel and cement.[27]

[26] I am drawing here from the excellent study by Bradley *et al.* (2007), especially pp. 37–8.

[27] Again, see Bradley *et al.* (2007).

Emissions from the power sector must be cut substantially. Electricity is rarely traded internationally; it is not trade-sensitive in the same way as are the aluminium, steel, and cement sectors. Indeed, that is why many countries have already adopted, or are now in the process of adopting, policies to reduce emissions from the power sector. Control of the emissions of the trade-sensitive sectors in separate global agreements should help these efforts (aluminium production, for example, is very electricity-intensive), while at the same time lessening incentives to adopt across-the-board trade restrictions (since the sectoral agreements would be enforced using trade restrictions). The industrialized countries should continue to focus on reducing emissions from electricity production domestically. They should do this by relying on domestic enforcement and international comparability, not international enforcement. Beyond this, international cooperation is needed for R&D into, and the demonstration of, new electricity-generation technologies. I discuss this challenge in section VII(iv).

Transportation is another sector that may benefit from separate treatment, but for a different reason than aluminium and electricity. I discuss it also in section VII(iv).

The Kyoto Protocol enables parties to generate credits for afforestation and reforestation, but subject to substantial restrictions. No credits are allowed for avoided deforestation. The latter category, however, is responsible for around 18 per cent of global emissions of greenhouse gases (Bradley *et al.*, 2007, p. 44), and there is wide agreement that the deforestation 'loophole' needs to be closed. However, there are good reasons why avoided deforestation was left out of the Kyoto Protocol. Forest loss is sometimes beyond the control of individual parties (forest fires), the potential for leakage is huge, the benefits of avoided deforestation are reversible, and establishing a baseline for agreement is a tricky business. Policies to reduce deforestation will be imperfect. One reason for addressing deforestation in a separate agreement is to ensure that such policies do not drag down efforts to reduce emissions from other sectors.

(iii) Adaptation

The climate will change, no matter how successful we are at reducing emissions Countries will therefore need to adapt.

Countries have exceptionally strong incentives to adapt. In contrast to mitigation, the benefits of adaptation are excludable. Much adaptation will be done 'automatically' by the market. Much of the rest will require the supply of local public goods (augmenting the Thames Barrier is an example), the benefits of which will be largely internal to the countries that supply them.

Unfortunately, many poor countries lack the capability to adapt. Adaptation requires the same institutions as development. Poor countries have weaker market institutions, and their governments routinely undersupply basic local public goods. Poor countries are also less accustomed to cooperating with each other to address cross-border challenges such as malaria, which may spread (largely to higher altitudes) with climate change. The failure to supply regional public goods is especially important for adaptation in Africa (see Ch. 7 by Collier *et al.*), a highly fragmented continent.

Mitigation will depend mostly on the efforts of the richest countries (not only as regards their own abatement but also their financing of abatement by other countries). However, these countries are also more able to adapt. The rich countries may, therefore, substitute the local public good of adaptation for the global public good of mitigation, leaving poor countries more vulnerable still. Climate change thus has the potential to widen existing inequalities. I discuss this challenge further in section VII(v).

(iv) Technology R&D and Diffusion

Emissions can be reduced significantly using existing technologies. Reducing emissions very, very substantially, however, will require fundamentally new technologies (Hoffert *et al.*, 2002).

Kyoto provides a modest 'pull' incentive for innovation. By constraining emissions, Kyoto makes emissions costly, stimulating demand for technologies that can allow users to avoid this cost. This demand in turn creates an incentive for innovation. As already mentioned, however, Kyoto is unable to raise the price on emissions significantly. The incentives it creates for innovation are exceedingly weak.

Kyoto also fails to create a 'push' incentive for innovation. The discovery, development, and demonstration of 'breakthrough' technologies (such as carbon capture and storage, space solar power, and nuclear fusion) require basic research—the fruits of which cannot be patented. Like mitigation, the knowledge arising from basic research is a global public good.

The incentives to undertake basic research are mixed. We know the incentives to conduct research into nuclear fusion are strong, because countries have already invested in this research.[28] Fusion power, however, would yield national benefits quite apart from the benefits for climate-change mitigation. The incentives to undertake R&D into carbon capture and storage are much weaker. They depend on the prospects of the knowledge emerging from this research being embodied in new technologies that are actually diffused, and these depend on the incentives for countries to cut their emissions (Barrett, 2006). As noted previously, these incentives are weak unless a way can be found to address the enforcement challenge.[29]

[28] The International Thermonuclear Experimental Reactor, being built now in France, is a cooperative endeavour, supported by the European Union, China, India, Japan, South Korea, Russia, and the United States—the same countries that will need to cooperate in addressing climate change.

[29] The United States had planned to build a 'clean coal' pilot project called FutureGen. The plant was to produce hydrogen and electricity from coal while using carbon capture and storage to sequester the CO_2 underground. The initiative was launched in 2003. In December 2007, a site was selected. A month later, the project was cancelled, ostensibly because the cost had risen from US$1 billion to US$1.8 billion. See M. L. Wald, 'Higher Costs Cited as US Shuts Down Coal Project',

Intriguingly, some technologies have features that can aid enforcement. The incentives for new technologies to spread depend on more than their cost of production (relative to the alternatives). They depend also on whether use of these technologies entails network effects. Suppose that there are two technologies, A and B. The current technology, A, is cheaper; the alternative technology, B, is more expensive but results in zero emissions. Full cooperation requires that the world switch from A to B (the benefits of reducing emissions exceed the costs of switching). But there are two obstacles. The first is the usual one: the incentive for countries to free ride (perhaps exacerbated by trade leakage.) The second is that, due to network effects, the cost to any country of switching to B is exorbitantly high when few if any other countries switch to B. This double penalty will prevent any country from switching to B unilaterally. However, should 'enough' countries switch to B, and should network effects be very strong, it may pay all the remaining countries to switch to B, despite free-rider incentives (Barrett, 2006).

Though emissions from international marine transport are excluded from Kyoto, this sector may be an attractive candidate for switching to hydrogen fuel (Farrell *et al.*, 2003). One reason for this is that ports are often close to refinery operations, where hydrogen is already produced and where cargo vessels already refuel. Helped by network effects, ocean shipping has already been transformed. For example, the standard for oil tankers has evolved—first, by requiring separate oil and ballast water tanks; and, second, by requiring double hulls (Barrett, 2007*b*). Parties to the International Maritime Organisation could establish a new standard for hydrogen-powered container ships. This would require that ports make the fuel available and that individual governments ban ships (above a certain size) that were not powered by hydrogen. As more countries imposed this standard, the incentives for others to impose it would increase. Moreover, should hydrogen become viable for this one sector, further network effects may help to spread the technology to other forms of transportation (Farrell *et al.*, 2003).

The economics of hydrogen for automobile transportation are less attractive, but this sector also exhibits strong network effects, particularly as regards refuelling. Moreover, substituting an alternative fuel for petrol may yield local environmental benefits—a further inducement for spread. The current high price of petrol makes the economics of substitution more attractive still. Currently, the electric vehicle seems to be a particularly attractive option, with the plug-in hybrid possibly acting as a kind of bridge to a full-electric future. Network effects would include the availability of electrical outlets for recharging and of replacement batteries for long-haul travel. Of course, a switch to electric vehicles makes it even more imperative that emissions from electricity generation be cut very substantially.

New York Times, 31 January 2008 (available at http://www.nytimes.com/2008/01/31/business/31coal.html?ref=environment&pagewanted=all). The Obama administration has reversed this decision. It appears that FutureGen will now go ahead.

(v) Financing

Financing for mitigation actions undertaken in developing (non-Annex-I) countries is already available under the Clean Development Mechanism (recall that the CDM allows rich countries to fulfil their emission-reduction obligations by obtaining credit for the emission reductions they finance in poor countries). As noted previously, however, there are a number of problems with this means of financing. Most importantly, the effectiveness of this mechanism depends on Kyoto's emission limits being enforced and, as I have explained, Kyoto's enforcement arrangements are very weak. Canada, for example, has no plans to comply with Kyoto by purchasing CDM credits. To stabilize concentrations, it is imperative that fast-growing developing countries such as China be put on to a different kind of development path. Doing so, however, will require financing. Since this financing is just another means of supplying the global public good of mitigation, its provision will depend on an agreement to finance mitigation in such countries being enforced.

It is typically assumed that industrialized countries must transfer their technologies to developing countries. However, developing countries may require different kinds of technology than rich countries. The ecological, economic, and social context in developing countries is different. So is the installed base of infrastructure. At the very least, developing countries must be able to determine the technologies they need, whether the technologies available from rich countries have to be adapted to suit local circumstances, and how these technologies should be deployed and used. All of this requires a degree of technical and scientific capability that many developing countries currently lack. Assistance is needed to help developing countries obtain this capability.[30]

Rich countries have already accepted that they are obligated to assist poor countries to adapt. Article 3 of the FCCC says that rich-country parties to the convention shall 'assist the developing country Parties that are particularly vulnerable to the adverse effects of climate change in meeting costs of adaptation to those adverse effects'. The Kyoto Protocol makes a first attempt to implement this obligation. It established an adaptation fund, financed by a levy on CDM transactions. However, this arrangement is inadequate. The amounts of money that will be needed for adaptation bear no relation at all to the amounts raised by CDM transactions. Moreover, taxing CDM transactions penalizes efforts to reduce emissions. Finally, since the United States is not a party to this treaty, its obligation to assist developing countries, accepted under the Framework Convention, cannot be fulfilled by this mechanism. Here again, a different approach is needed.

[30] The International Task Force on Global Public Goods and, more recently, the Club of Madrid have proposed creating a Consultative Group on Clean Energy Research for this purpose. The proposal was inspired by the successful Consultative Group on International Agricultural Research, which gave rise to the 'green revolution' (see http://www.gpgtaskforce.org/uploads/files/227.pdf and http://www.unfoundation.org/files/pdf/2007/GLCA_Framework2007.pdf).

The Bali roadmap underlines 'the urgent and immediate needs of developing countries that are particularly vulnerable to the adverse effects of climate change, especially the least developed countries and small island developing States'. It allows a new approach to be prepared but it does not mention how much money ought to be provided or the basis for determining this amount or for assessing contributions. Unfortunately, while a strong moral argument can be made for international assistance (the rich countries, after all, are largely responsible for the accumulation of greenhouse gases in the atmosphere), the direct incentives rich countries have to provide assistance are weak. Adaptation assistance is likely to become an increasing source of friction in international relations particularly if mitigation efforts continue to stumble.

VIII. CONCLUSIONS

Climate change is arguably the greatest collective-action problem the world has ever faced. We should not be surprised that we have failed to address it thus far. Climate change emerged as a major global challenge soon after the Montreal Protocol was negotiated. Understandably, many people believed at that time that climate change could be addressed as easily as stratospheric ozone depletion. They were wrong. Climate change is a much harder problem.

A more instructive exemplar may be the efforts taken to address pollution of the world's oceans by oil dumping.[31] The first international conference on this issue was held in 1926. An agreement was reached but never signed. In 1935a new agreement was negotiated, but it also never entered into force. In 1954, the world tried again. This time a treaty to protect the oceans entered into force. However, it had no effect; it failed to address the enforcement challenge. The agreement was amended in 1962 and again in 1969, but these changes also made little difference because the amendments, like the underlying treaty, could not be enforced. Finally, in the 1970s, a different approach was tried. Instead of trying to reduce oil dumping by means of performance standards, countries negotiated technical standards, which were much easier to enforce. These agreements entered into force in 1983 and have been a great success. Climate change is a much harder problem than oil dumping, but it need not take us 50 years to discover how to address it. The lesson of the history of oil dumping is not that effective agreements take decades to negotiate. It is that, should one approach to addressing a problem fail, we should be open to trying another.

The European Union has proposed styling a post-Kyoto agreement after the original agreement, the key difference being that the EU wants the emission limits in the new agreement to be more ambitious. Greater cuts in emissions are needed, but, as I have explained in this chapter, tighter caps will not help unless the treaty also creates incentives for participation and compliance. President Sarkozy, among

[31] See Barrett (2005*a*), especially ch. 9.

others, has suggested that trade restrictions be imposed against non-participants. Such measures may not work as intended. They are also likely to introduce new tensions.

As explained here, a superior strategy may be to break the problem up, relying on separate agreements to address different gases and sectors. Kyoto lumps everything together—an approach that helps ensure cost-effectiveness but that also ensures that enforcement is only as effective as the agreement's weakest individual component. By breaking the problem up, different pressure points can be exploited—trade restrictions coupled with financial assistance for developing countries for the trade-sensitive sectors, technical standards, again with financial assistance for developing countries, for sectors characterized by network effects, and so on. This alternative strategy will not sustain a first best. Given the nature of this challenge, however, a first best is unattainable. The motivation for recommending separate agreements is that it would be superior to the approach tried thus far.

5

The Implications of Rapid Development for Emissions and Climate-change Mitigation

*Ross Garnaut, Stephen Howes, Frank Jotzo, and Peter Sheehan**

I. INTRODUCTION

The world has entered a period of exceptionally fast economic growth, with rapid economic development especially in China, followed by India and many other low-income countries. This is the 'Platinum Age', to use the terminology of Garnaut (2008*a*), who notes that recent rates of economic growth have been even higher than the average in the 'Golden Age' of the 1950s and 1960s. The global financial crisis of 2008 has derailed global growth temporarily, but is not expected to alter fundamentally the strong developing and global growth outlook of the early twenty-first century.

The developments of the early 2000s have not yet been fully incorporated into the projections and scenarios of future greenhouse-gas emissions. The most influential projections used in climate-change analysis are still the *Special Report on Emissions Scenarios* (SRES; Nakiçenovic and Swart, 2000) of the Intergovernmental Panel on Climate Change (IPCC), which provide a wide range of future emissions paths out to 2100 under four different 'storylines' about growth and technology.

The SRES authors did not assign likelihoods to particular scenarios, but rather argued that they were all equally plausible. In practice, most attention has been given to low- and mid-range emission-growth scenarios. For example, the video presentation by the Chairman of the IPCC, Rajendra Pachauri, at the Conference

* The first three authors are at Australian National University; Peter Sheehan is at Victoria University, Melbourne.

The first three authors worked on the Australian Garnaut Climate Change Review. We would like to thank colleagues, in particular Elizabeth Edye, at the Garnaut Climate Change Review (www.garnautreview.org.au) for useful discussions, and for their contributions to the Garnaut Report (Garnaut, 2008*c*) which we draw on in parts of this chapter. Anonymous peer-reviewer comments, feedback from Peter Downes, Dieter Helm, Cameron Hepburn, Warwick McKibbin, and from seminar participants at the Australian National University and at ICRIER, Delhi also helped improve the chapter.

of the Parties in Bali, referred to a range of possible temperature increases, but placed more emphasis on the lowest end of the range represented by scenario B1 (Pachauri, 2007). Other analyses give all SRES scenarios equal weight, rather than asking which ones are more soundly based. Reliance on only the more pessimistic IPCC scenarios, that is the ones with more rapid emissions growth, is seen as 'unbalanced'. One of the criticisms of the Stern Review has been that the SRES scenario the Review relied on showed 'high range greenhouse gas emissions' (Baker *et al.*, 2008, p. xi). Stern himself, however, in his recent Ely lecture (2008*a*) has noted that his Review underestimated the likely growth of emissions.

The SRES scenarios have been criticized for not applying an economic framework that adequately reflects sources of economic growth and endogenous structural change (McKibbin *et al.*, 2004). A specific criticism of the SRES scenarios in the literature has been that they overstate emissions growth, either because they fail to adopt purchasing power parity (PPP) measures for GDP (Castles and Henderson, 2003) or because the more rapid emission growth SRES scenarios are inconsistent with long-term (Hansen *et al.*, 2000) or recent (van Vuuren and O'Neill, 2006) trends in emissions. Post-SRES scenarios reflect these criticisms of the SRES scenarios. Thus GDP growth, total energy use, and carbon-dioxide (CO_2) emissions are all lower in the median post-SRES non-intervention scenario than in the median pre-SRES/SRES scenario (Fisher *et al.*, 2007).

This chapter builds on earlier work by Garnaut (2008*c*) and Sheehan *et al.* (2008) to make the case that, in the absence of a serious policy response to climate change, even the most pessimistic SRES and post-SRES scenarios may underestimate future emissions growth and levels.

The chapter examines the evolution of greenhouse-gas emissions in recent decades and then projects their 'business as usual' path out to 2030, i.e the path they would take in the absence of any further response to climate change. The focus on the period to 2030 is for three reasons. First, it is the period that matters for the policy issue at hand. As we show in the concluding section, if concentrations of greenhouse gases are to be kept to acceptable levels, action will need to be taken well before 2030. Second, it is the period for which we can have greater confidence in our projections. Third, it is the period covered by the International Energy Agency *2007 World Energy Outlook*, and (roughly) the period used by a number of projection exercises.

Most of the analysis of the chapter is in terms of CO_2 emissions from fossil fuels. We discuss trends in those emissions and their drivers (section II), before presenting our alternative projections (section III). Section IV analyses non-CO_2 emissions (contributing a quarter of global anthropogenic greenhouse-gas emissions) and CO_2 emissions from land-use change and forestry (another sixth). Section V summarizes our results, and compares them to existing projections. Section VI examines the implications of ongoing rapid growth in emissions for the global approach to climate-change mitigation, and section VII concludes.

Table 5.1. A comparison of GDP, energy, and CO_2 emissions growth rates and elasticities for the world, OECD, and non-OECD countries

Average annual growth rates and elasticities	**1971–90**	**1990–2000**	**2000–5**
World			
Emissions growth (%)	2.1	1.1	2.9
GDP growth (%)	3.4	3.2	3.8
Energy growth (%)	2.4	1.4	2.7
Emissions/GDP elasticity	0.62	0.35	0.76
Energy/GDP elasticity	0.71	0.43	0.69
Emissions/energy elasticity	0.87	0.82	1.10
OECD			
Emissions growth (%)	0.9	1.2	0.7
GDP growth (%)	3.2	2.7	2.1
Energy growth (%)	1.5	1.6	0.8
Emissions/GDP elasticity	0.28	0.45	0.31
Energy/GDP elasticity	0.48	0.61	0.38
Emissions/energy elasticity	0.59	0.73	0.80
Non-OECD			
Emissions growth (%)	4.2	0.9	5.5
GDP growth (%)	3.8	4.0	6.2
Energy growth (%)	3.8	1.0	4.6
Emissions/GDP elasticity	1.10	0.23	0.88
Energy/GDP elasticity	0.98	0.25	0.74
Emissions/energy elasticity	1.12	0.90	1.18

Notes: Emissions growth is CO_2 from fossil fuels (excluding industrial processes). Energy growth is total primary energy supply measured in million tonnes of oil equivalent (mtoe). GDP growth is measured using 2000 US$ PPP.

Source: IEA (2007*b*).

II. TRENDS IN THE GROWTH OF CO_2 EMISSIONS FROM FOSSIL FUELS

CO_2 emissions from fossil-fuel burning increased by only 1 per cent a year on average in the 1990s, but grew by 3 per cent a year from 2000 to 2005 (Table 5.1). Through the Kaya identity,[1]

$$CO_2 = GDP^*(Energy/GDP)^*(CO_2/Energy), \qquad (1)$$

emissions growth is a function of economic growth, growth in energy intensity (of GDP) and growth in carbon intensity (of energy). Summary data for these variables are presented in Table 5.1. It can be seen that there has been a worldwide

[1] Kaya and Yokobori (1997). The Kaya identity further decomposes economic growth into population growth and growth in income *per capita*.

acceleration this decade in the growth of all three of these variables (see also Raupach *et al.*, 2007).[2]

Disaggregating between OECD (developed) and non-OECD (developing including transition) countries shows that it is the latter group that is driving global trends. In the early 1970s, non-OECD countries were responsible for roughly one-third of global emissions, energy, and output. In 2005 they were responsible for just over half of global energy use and emissions, and 45 per cent of global output. Since 2000, non-OECD emissions have been growing almost six times as fast as OECD emissions, accounting for 85 per cent of the growth in emissions.

The OECD countries show a slowdown in growth in emissions, GDP, and energy in this decade (2000–5) compared to the last. In the non-OECD countries, the rate of growth in all three has increased significantly this decade.

There has also been a significant reduction among the OECD countries in the rate of decline of the energy intensity of economic activity and the carbon intensity of energy use. The 1990s saw a rapid decline in energy intensity in the non-OECD group. Energy grew at only a quarter of the rate of GDP, and emissions grew slightly more slowly than energy. This decade has seen the resumption of energy-intensive and carbon-intensive growth in the developing and transition world: energy use has grown at three-quarters the rate of GDP, and carbon emissions at a rate a fifth faster than energy use.

Figure 5.1 shows just how differently energy intensity (the energy/GDP ratio) has behaved in OECD and non-OECD countries. Though it has fallen in both, in the developed world one sees a smoothly and continuously declining energy/GDP curve. In the developing world, energy intensity fell only slowly over the 1970s and 1980s, plunged in the 1990s, and has now flattened out, at around 70 per cent of its 1971 level. The elasticity of energy use to GDP in non-OECD countries was nearly one in the 1970s and 1980s, only 0.25 in the 1990s, and is at 0.74 for 2000–5.

The carbon intensity (emissions/energy) curve shows greater consistency across the two sets of countries. In the developed world, the emissions/energy curve declined to the mid-1990s but has now flattened out at around 85 per cent of its 1971 level. In the developing world, the emissions/energy curve has been flat throughout most of the period and is now actually rising.

These results appear paradoxical in two regards. First, the reduction in energy intensity appears to contradict the finding that the energy elasticity for most developing countries is one or more (Sheehan, 2008). Second, the flattening and increase in the carbon intensity of energy seems odd in light of the large price increases in oil and other fossil fuels seen in the first half of this decade. The resolution to these paradoxes lies, respectively, in China and coal.

Figure 5.2 shows energy intensity separately for China, other developing countries, and the transition countries. It shows that energy intensities are remarkably constant for developing countries once China is excluded. China started out with

[2] Since energy intensity and carbon intensity are declining, an acceleration for them means that they are declining less rapidly.

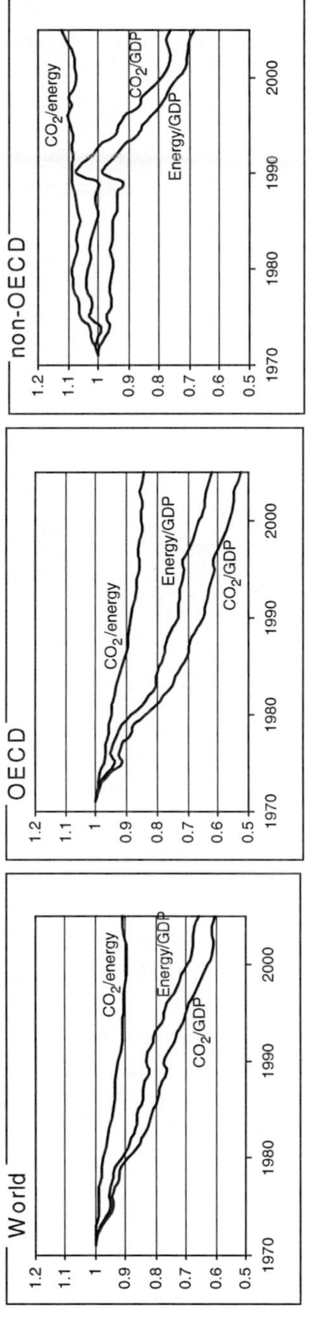

Figure 5.1. Emissions/GDP, energy/GDP, and emissions/energy for the world, OECD, and non-OECD countries, 1971–2005 (1971 = 1)

Notes and Source: As per Table 5.1.

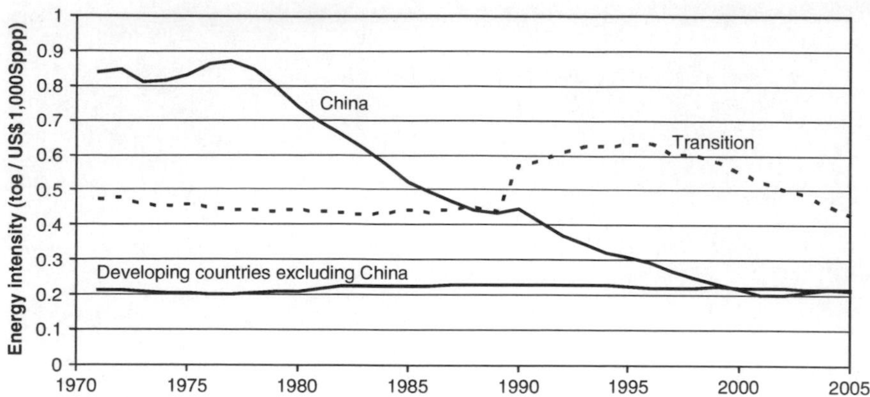

Figure 5.2. Energy intensities of GDP for China, other developing countries, and transition countries, 1971–2005

Notes and Sources: As for Table 5.1. Prior to 1990, transition economies are defined residually as non-OECD non-developing countries. GDP measured in US$ PPP in 2000 prices.

an enormously high energy intensity which declined through the 1980s and 1990s, due to a shift away from subsidized prices and central planning, flattening only at the turn of the century (Sheehan and Sun, 2007).

The transition countries show constant energy intensity up to the 1990s, then a rising energy intensity (as GDP collapsed faster than energy use), and in recent years a fall in energy intensity, which is continuing.

On the second paradox, the increasing reliance on coal, which is more carbon-intensive than oil and gas, has kept the carbon intensity of energy roughly constant in recent years.[3] While increasing demand and limitations on expansion of production lifted oil prices to exceptional levels prior to the onset of the financial crisis, there is no similar scarcity constraint on coal. Coal prices rose, but only reflecting short-term capacity constraints, rather than long-term resource limits. In the 1980s and 1990s, a reduction in the share of oil in total energy demand was made up for by a corresponding increase in gas. But since 2000, the share of gas has remained constant, and the share of coal has increased.

As Table 5.2 shows, the same trends in relation to coal are evident in both developed and developing regions, though in much more dramatic terms in the latter. Between 2000 and 2005, coal use increased in developing countries on average by 9.5 per cent per year, and by 11.7 per cent in China.[4] In 2005, 61 per cent of the world's coal was consumed in developing countries, up from 51 per cent just 5 years earlier. In 2005, coal provided 63 per cent of China's energy,

[3] The EIA (1998*a*) reports that, on average, oil emits 40 per cent more CO_2 than gas, and coal 27 per cent more than oil, per unit of energy input.

[4] In 2006, China's coal consumption grew by 11.9 per cent and in 2007, according to preliminary estimates, by 7.8 per cent (see NBS, 2007*a*, *b*).

Table 5.2. Coal, oil, and gas growth in the world, OECD, and non-OECD countries, 1980–2005 (%)

	World		OECD		Non-OECD	
	1980–2000	2000–5	1980–2000	2000–5	1980–2000	2000–5
Coal	1.3	4.8	0.6	0.7	1.5	9.5
Oil	0.8	1.9	0.5	0.6	1.5	3.8
Gas	2.7	2.4	1.9	0.8	3.6	4.2
Total fossil fuel	1.4	2.9				
Total energy demand	1.3	2.7				

Source: IEA (2007*a*).

39 per cent of India's energy, and only 17 per cent of the rest of the world's energy (IEA, 2007*a*).

In summary, the acceleration of emissions this decade has been caused by three factors: the rapid acceleration of growth in the developing world; the ending of the period of rapid decline in energy intensity in China, which lasted from the 1970s to the 1990s; and the end to the decarbonization of energy supply in both the developed and (especially) the developing world.

Long-term emission forecasts produced by the International Energy Agency have been relatively stable in recent years. The IEA projected an average annual growth of 1.8 per cent in CO_2 emissions from fossil fuels out to 2030 in 2002, and did so again in 2007. Over the same period, average annual GDP growth was revised from 3 to 3.6 per cent.[5] The implied downward revision of the emissions intensity of GDP is not consistent with recent experience. A re-examination of emissions projections is warranted.

III. CARBON-DIOXIDE EMISSIONS FROM FOSSIL FUELS OUT TO 2030

This section projects fossil-fuel-related CO_2, CO_2(FF) for short, emissions out to 2030, under a 'business-as-usual', constant-policy approach. Policies already in place to reduce emissions are assumed to continue, but no new ones are assumed to be put in place, even if a government has committed to do so. We start from the most recent International Energy Agency (IEA) *2007 World Energy Outlook* (WEO) projections, which make use of extensive information on energy systems in a partial equilibrium framework. Using an emissions growth decomposition framework, we then make adjustments, based on the analysis presented in the

[5] The projection period in the 2002 WEO was 2000–30, and in the 2007 WEO 2005–30. The 2007 WEO does include a rapid growth scenario with higher emissions growth (2.1 per cent per annum over 2005–30), but this is not the reference case.

paper, to selected macroeconomic assumptions, namely GDP growth in non-OECD countries and the intensity of energy use with regard to GDP in China. The strength of this approach is that it builds on the specialist knowledge of the IEA, and makes clear what assumptions might need rethinking. Its limitation is that it does not capture the general equilibrium effects that would derive from the changes in assumptions.

(i) Economic Growth

We review WEO growth rates for the three most populous developing countries, China, India, and Indonesia, and then for other developing and transition regions.

China deserves special attention. In 2005, China was responsible for 19 per cent of global CO_2(FF) emissions. China has averaged about 10 per cent GDP growth per annum since 1990. The latest figures, for 2006 and 2007, are 11.6 and 11.9 per cent growth respectively.[6] Our growth forecasts for China draw on the growth accounting framework of Perkins and Rawski (2008). We accept the Perkins–Rawski projections for education-enhanced labour, and assume a figure of 3.1 per cent total factor productivity (TFP) growth for the entire period, which is the rate of TFP growth in the last decade. Perkins and Rawski assume a slowdown in the rate of capital formation. But investment rates are rising, and Garnaut and Huang (2005) argue that investment rates are, in fact, likely to rise even higher than current levels. We assume investment stays at 45 per cent of GDP to 2015 and then falls to 40 per cent by 2025. Embedding these assumptions into the Perkins–Rawski framework results in growth of 9 per cent from 2005 to 2015 and 6.8 per cent for 2015–25 (Table 5.3).[7] Considered against China's recent performance, and its good prospects for continued double-digit growth (Garnaut and Huang, 2005, 2007), we consider this projection to be relatively conservative.

Growth first lifted in India in the 1980s. It averaged about 6 per cent from 1980 to 2000. It accelerated again starting around 2004, and has averaged 8.9 per cent between 2004 and 2007. This new higher-growth trajectory is soundly based, supported by strong trade performance and a growing savings rate. Our growth projection for India is based on Oura (2007), which surveys a range of growth-accounting exercises and possible assumptions and finds potential growth for India for the medium term in the range of 7.3–9.5 per cent. Oura defines the medium term only out to 2012, but there is plenty of evidence that these rates of growth can be sustained for much longer (see Rodrik and Subramanian, 2004, for example). We use 7.5 per cent for 2005–30 as a conservative projection.

Indonesia, an example of a large developing country outside the fastest growing parts of the developing world, also has reasonable prospects for growth, albeit not at the same speed as China or India (see Hofman *et al.*, 2007). Indonesia

[6] See China's National Bureau of Statistics, 'Announcement on Verified GDP Data in 2006 and 2007', (available at http://www.stats.gov.cn/english/newsandcomingevents/t20080410_402473201.htm) 10 April 2008.

[7] We extend the latter projection out to 2030.

Table 5.3. Growth accounting projections for China, 2005–25

Annual average growth (%)	2005–15		2015–25	
	Perkins-Rawski	Platinum Age	Perkins-Rawski	Platinum Age
Labour growth	2.0	2.0	1.0	1.0
Capital growth	9.8	11.0	5.6	7.3
Capital share	0.43	0.43	0.43	0.43
TFP growth	3.6	3.1	3.0	3.1
GDP growth	9.0	9.0	6.0	6.8

Notes: All 'Platinum Age' (current paper) assumptions from Perkins and Rawski (2008) unless otherwise stated. Note that Perkins and Rawski's 3.6 per cent TFP growth figure for 2005–15 is not presented as a realistic estimate, but derived by the authors to show what, given their projected capital and labour growth, it would take to achieve 9 per cent GDP growth.

has a strong resource base and potential for expansion in both manufacturing and service sectors, but has been hampered in recent years by low investment. After prolonged adjustment to the 1997 Asian financial crisis and political and institutional change, including far-reaching decentralization, Indonesia's recent growth rate has increased to 6 per cent, after averaging 4.7 per cent from 2000 to 2005. This is well below growth rates in previous decades, and future growth may be somewhat higher. Van der Eng (2006) shows a mid-point estimate of the potential growth rate until 2030 of 6.5 per cent. This is the GDP growth rate we assume in our projections.

Rapid GDP growth over several decades of 7 per cent or more, consistent with sustained high TFP growth, has not been achieved by many countries, but was achieved in Asia in the past by Indonesia, Japan, Korea, and Taiwan. As Perkins and Rawski (2008) note, growth slowed in the last three of these countries when their income *per capita* reached about US$13,000 in PPP (2005 prices). According to our projections, China will reach that level in about 2020 (Table 5.4). If Perkins and Rawski are correct, a slow-down in growth could occur at US$13,000. However, with the frontier income level also increasing, it is possible that today faster growth can be sustained at higher levels of income. Under our projections, by 2030 the ratio of China's, India's, and Indonesia's income *per capita* to that of the United States will be below the ratios for Japan, Taiwan, and Korea at the points of deceleration of growth in those countries.

The recent acceleration of growth in the developing world has extended well beyond China, India, and Indonesia. The growth acceleration is most evident from the period 2004–7, during which time all developing and transition regions grew at 5 per cent per annum or more (Table 5.5). We see this acceleration of growth in developing countries as owing much both to better policy settings, and to the spillover effect of rapid Chinese growth, and therefore as sustainable. WEO projections again seem on the low side. For example, the 'rest of developing Asia' region (excluding China and India) is projected to grow at 4.6 per cent for 2005–15, which is lower than the average for 1990–2005, and much lower than

Table 5.4. Historical and projected GDP *per capita* for the United States, China, India, and Indonesia

Per capita GDP	**In 2005 PPP USD**			**USA = 100**		
	2005	**2015**	**2030**	**2005**	**2015**	**2030**
United States	42,096	54,414	75,418	100.0	100.0	100.0
China	4,067	9,068	23,194	9.7	16.7	30.8
India	2,139	3,836	9,776	5.1	7.0	13.0
Indonesia	3,132	5,282	12,219	7.4	9.7	16.2

Notes: US$ in PPP, 2005 prices. GDP assumptions as per Table 5.5. Population from the IEA 2007 WEO. These figures use baseline PPP GDP data from ICP (2008), that is, they use the new PPP data; the rest of the chapter uses older PPP numbers to be consistent with the IEA 2007 WEO.

Table 5.5. GDP growth by region: historical data and alternative projections

GDP (USD PPP 2000), annual average growth (%)	Actual				2007 WE0		Platinum Age	
	1971 to 1990	1990 to 2000	2000 to 2005	2004 to 2007	2005 to 2015	2015 to 2030	2005 to 2015	2015 to 2030
OECD	3.2	2.7	2.1	2.8	2.5	1.9		
OECD North America	3.3	3.3	2.4	2.9	2.6	2.2	as per WEO	
OECD Europe	2.7	2.3	1.9	2.7	2.4	1.8		
OECD Pacific	4.3	2.2	2.2	2.8	2.2	1.6		
Transition	2.6	−2.5	5.4	7.0	4.7	2.9	5.5	4.3
Developing Countries	4.3	5.5	6.3	7.8	6.2	4.4	7.1	6.1
Developing Asia	5.7	7.3	7.8	9.4	7.0	4.8	8.0	6.7
China	7.8	10.2	9.4	10.8	7.7	4.9	9.0	6.8
India	4.5	5.5	7.0	8.9	7.2	5.8	7.5	7.5
Indonesia	7.1	4.2	4.7	5.6	4.6	3.1	6.5	6.5
Other	4.3	4.7	5.5	6.7	4.6	3.1	5.3	4.3
Latin America	3.2	3.1	2.6	5.4	3.8	2.8	4.3	3.7
Middle East	2.9	3.7	4.3	5.8	4.9	3.4	5.2	4.2
Africa	2.8	2.5	4.3	5.9	4.5	3.6	5.0	4.4
Dev'ing countries excl China	3.6	3.9	4.7	6.1	5.2	4.0	5.7	5.4
World	3.4	3.2	3.8	5.2	4.2	3.3	4.6	4.4

Note: IEA projections are not provided separately for Indonesia, but are included in other developing Asia.

Source: IEA (2007*b*) for actuals; 2004–7 data from IMF (2007, 2008).

the 7.1 per cent achieved in 2004–7. Our alternative projections for developing countries other than China, India, and Indonesia, are a weighted average of WEO projections (two-thirds) and performance of the last four years (one-third). This is admittedly *ad hoc* but captures conservatively the idea that official projections are not adequately reflecting recent experience.

Growth data, WEO projections, and our 'Platinum Age' or rapid growth projections are shown in Table 5.5. Growth rates are in terms of purchasing power parities. OECD growth rates are taken from the reference scenario of the WEO 2007. We do not make downward adjustments in light of the recent economic slowdown (see postscript). Equally we do not represent possibly growth-enhancing flow-on effects from future higher growth in China and elsewhere to OECD countries.[8] Growth rates outside the OECD are adjusted upwards from WEO projections as per the above discussion.

The growth rates of all countries and regions in Table 5.5 appear reasonable in the light of recent experience. All developing and transition countries are projected to be growing faster than they were in the latter decades of the last century, but slower than at rates observed over 2004–7, with the exception of Indonesia. The growth rates for China, India, and Indonesia are supported by our growth-accounting analysis, and the assessment of the authors, whose expertise in development covers these three countries.

(ii) Energy Intensity

The 2007 IEA WEO projects significant falls in the energy intensities—the ratio of total primary energy supply to GDP, measured using PPP—of developing countries from current levels (Table 5.6). Until 1990, energy intensities increased for the developing world excluding China, and since then they have stayed roughly constant (Figure 5.2). Yet, as Table 5.6 shows, the IEA projects an annual average decline of just under 2 per cent for energy intensity in the developing world (excluding China) over the next 25 years. Some of the contrasts between the historical record and projections for particular regions are stark. For example, energy intensity in the Middle East is expected to shift from a 1–4 per cent annual growth to a 1 per cent annual reduction, or in Africa from unchanged levels to a 2 per cent annual reduction. Energy intensities in China and India also fall sharply in the IEA projections: these countries are projected to lead the world in both economic growth and energy de-intensification.

What lies behind the assumptions of declining energy intensity in the 2007 WEO? It is mentioned that energy intensity 'resumes its steady downward path in China' (p. 120). But we saw in section II that the sharp reduction in China in energy intensity in the 1980s and 1990s was more in the nature of a one-off adjustment than a 'steady downward path' (see also Garnaut and Song, 2006). The 2007 WEO also argues that energy intensity will fall as the structure of the Chinese economy shifts from heavy to light industry. However, normally the opposite would be expected as an economy develops with a high level of investment (extraordinarily high in China's case) underpinning a shift in comparative advantage towards more capital-intensive manufacturing.

[8] We do not take the assumptions of the WEO 2007 'high growth' scenario as the default because they are not provided in detail.

Table 5.6. Energy intensity levels and growth by region: historical data and WEO projections

Primary energy supply (Mtoe)/ GDP (billion USD PPP 2000)	Levels			Annual average growth rates (%)			
	Actuals	IEA 2007 WEO		Actuals		IEA 2007 WEO	
	2005	2015	2030	1971 to 2000	2000 to 2005	2005 to 2015	2015 to 2030
OECD	0.18	0.16	0.13	−1.4	−1.3	−1.3	−1.3
OECD North America	0.21	0.19	0.15	−1.8	−1.7	−1.3	−1.4
OECD Europe	0.15	0.13	0.11	−1.4	−0.7	−1.7	−1.4
OECD Pacific	0.17	0.16	0.14	−0.4	−1.4	−0.8	−1.1
Transition	0.36	0.26	0.19	−0.3	−4.2	−2.9	−2.0
Developing Countries	0.22	0.17	0.13	−0.8	−0.7	−2.3	−2.2
Developing Asia	0.21	0.16	0.11	−2.2	−0.9	−2.5	−2.4
China	0.22	0.17	0.11	−4.5	−0.1	−2.5	−2.8
India	0.16	0.11	0.08	−1.0	−3.5	−3.3	−2.1
Indonesia	0.24	0.20	0.18	−1.0	−0.3	−1.6	−1.4
Other	0.23	0.20	0.16	−0.1	−0.3	−1.6	−1.4
Latin America	0.16	0.14	0.12	−0.3	−0.7	−1.2	−0.8
Middle East	0.37	0.33	0.28	3.8	1.0	−1.0	−1.1
Africa	0.29	0.23	0.17	0.6	−0.7	−2.6	−1.8
Dev'ing countries excl China	0.22	0.18	0.14	0.2	−0.9	−2.1	−1.6
World	0.21	0.17	0.13	−1.2	−1.1	−1.8	−1.8

Source and Notes: IEA (2007*b*) for actuals. Prior to 1990, transition economies are defined as non-OECD non-developing countries.

It is true that China is already explicitly targeting a reduction in energy intensity, and has put in place a number of policies to achieve this (e.g. taxes on energy-intensive exports). But it has been missing its targets, and will continue to do so without an intensification of policy effort (Sheehan, 2008). Energy intensity remained unchanged between 2000 and 2005. Energy intensity fell in 2006 by 2 per cent.[9] First half figures for 2007 indicated a fall in energy intensity of 2.8 per cent.[10]

In India, energy intensity has fallen slowly since 1970, and rapidly this decade as growth accelerated in the service sector. However, with the more recent pick-up of industrial growth, it is far from clear that energy intensities will fall from their current extremely low levels. Rectifying the currently low level of rural electrification will lead to a surge in energy demand. India's current energy intensity is lower than that of other major countries and regions, and comparable to that in Japan and the more low-energy European countries. The expert committee headed by Kirit

[9] In 2006, energy consumption grew by 9.6 per cent, and GDP by 11.6 per cent. Energy figures from NBS (2007*a*) (consumption of energy). For GDP figures, see footnote 7.

[10] See NBS (2007*b*). Provisional figures for 2007 indicate energy consumption growth of 7.8 per cent (NBS, 2008). This would imply a faster reduction in energy intensity (−3.7 per cent), but GDP has been revised upwards since the energy figures were released.

Parikh (2006) projects growth in commercial energy demand in India between 5.6 and 7.2 per cent per annum over 2006/7 to 2031/2. Even with our higher estimates of economic growth, applying the IEA energy-intensity assumptions gives energy growth of only 4.7 per cent over this period.

Analysis of the historical experience of Japan, Taiwan, and Korea shows only small decreases in energy intensity as *per capita* income increases, with energy intensity roughly flattening out at or above 0.15 toe/US$1,000. Even at GDP *per capita* levels in excess of US$15,000 (USD 2000 PPP), energy intensity remained flat rather than declining to around or under 0.10 toe/US$1000 as projected by the WEO for China and India. Figure 5.3 illustrates. The different OECD regions show continued downward trends in energy intensity, but levels are still above 0.15, even at the prevailing very high *per capita* incomes in these countries.

One reason why energy intensities might fall in the future in developing countries (unlike in the past) is that, although the world has abundant coal supplies to support rapid, energy-intensive expansion, high energy prices and constraints around the supply of oil might force greater energy efficiency. For example, the IEA projects that, for its reference case, oil exports from the Middle East will have to increase from 20m barrels a day in 2006 to almost 40m by 2030 (see Figure 1.7 in IEA, 2007*a*). There must be a question whether such expansion will materialize. Substitution from oil to shale oil and coal will be possible (and, with an abundant

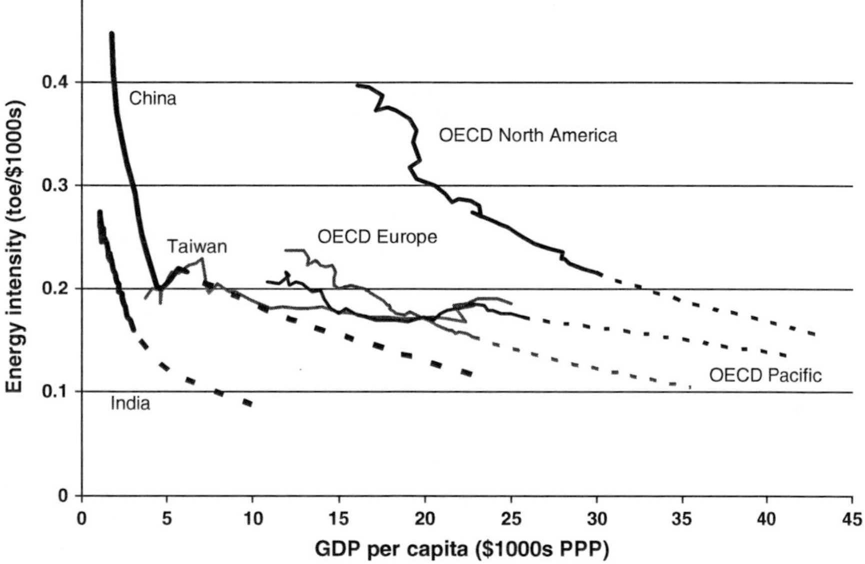

Figure 5.3. Energy intensity and GDP *per capita* for various countries and regions: historical (solid lines) and projected by the 2007 WEO (dashed lines)

Sources and Notes: IEA (2007*b*). GDP measured in US$ PPP in 2000 prices; years for actuals (solid lines) are from 1971 to 2005 except for China (from 1990); IEA 2007 WEO projections (dashed lines) run from 2005 to 2030 (see Table 5.6); 'toe' are tons of oil-equivalent.

supply, coal prices are not expected to rise in the long term) but permanently higher prices for oil and its close substitutes may drive improvements in energy efficiency and so dampen growth in energy use. However, a decline in energy intensity for this reason is not inevitable. It is possible that current high prices will induce such high levels of investment in coal production that coal prices fall relative to oil, encouraging greater use of coal rather than less use of energy in total.

Given the uncertainties, we do not make across-the-board adjustments to the WEO's projected energy intensities. However, the WEO's energy intensities for China appear particularly implausible, especially given recent experience. The WEO projects energy intensity in China to fall faster than in any other developing country/region, at −2.7 per cent a year over the projection period. Even with our more rapid growth, this implies annual average growth of 4.8 per cent in energy supply between 2005 and 2030, significantly below the 6.4 per cent annual growth estimated by Sheehan and Sun (2007).[11] The WEO emission-intensity projections for China are also low relative to what is projected for developed countries. Energy intensity in China, which today is almost 40 per cent above that of OECD Europe, is projected to have almost converged with OECD Europe by 2030 (Figure 5.3). Given China's specialization in manufacturing, and continued high investment levels, it is hard to see how the energy intensity of the Chinese economy could fall relative to Europe's.

For China, we instead assume that energy intensities decline at two-thirds the rate assumed by the IEA (Table 5.7). This gives China a rate of energy intensity reduction still equal or below the developing country average. It gives energy elasticities for China of 0.8 for 2005–15 and 0.7 for 2015–30, consistent with or below the work of Sheehan and Sun (2007). Auffhammer and Carson (2008), in dynamic statistical models for China's emissions based on regional data, forecast a CO_2 emissions elasticity with regard to income of around unity until 2010, which implies no reduction at all in energy intensity.

(iii) Carbon Intensities of Energy and Other Assumptions

For the carbon intensity of energy use (CO_2/total primary energy supply), we adopt WEO projections, which assume that carbon intensities stay broadly constant (Table 5.8). This is a conservative approach on two accounts. First, in recent years, emission intensities have in fact been increasing in the developing world, owing to the shift to coal (Figure 5.1). The tighter supply constraints on oil, and the associated tendency for the relative price of coal to decline, suggest that this may continue. Second, if energy use does turn out to be higher than projected by the IEA (as we argue it will), then a disproportionate amount of the extra demand will be met by (emissions-intensive) coal. For example, our projections

[11] Without changing the growth assumption, the WEO forecast for China is only 3.2 per cent for annual average energy growth between 2005 and 2030.

Table 5.7. China energy intensity, historical data, and alternative projections

	Base			WEO		Platinum Age	
	1990	**2000**	**2005**	**2015**	**2030**	**2015**	**2030**
Energy intensity	44.7	21.8	21.6	16.9	11.0	18.3	13.8
		1990 to 2000	**2000 to 2005**	**2005 to 2015**	**2015 to 2030**	**2005 to 2015**	**2015 to 2030**
Annual average growth in energy intensity		−6.9%	−0.1%	−2.5%	−2.8%	−1.6%	−1.9%
Energy/GDP elasticity		0.25	0.98	0.66	0.40	0.80	0.71

Note: Energy intensity levels are in Mtoe/billion USD (2000 prices, PPP).

Table 5.8. Carbon intensity of energy levels by region: historical data and IEA projections

Emissions ($MtCO_2$)/Primary energy supply (Mtoe)	Actual			2007 WEO	
	1971	2000	2005	2015	2030
OECD	2.8	2.3	2.3	2.3	2.2
OECD North America	2.7	2.4	2.4	2.4	2.3
OECD Europe	2.9	2.2	2.2	2.1	2.1
OECD Pacific	2.7	2.3	2.4	2.3	2.1
Transition	2.6	2.5	2.4	2.4	2.2
Developing Countries	1.7	2.2	2.3	2.4	2.4
Developing Asia	1.7	2.3	2.5	2.6	2.6
China	2.0	2.7	2.9	3.0	3.0
India	1.3	2.1	2.1	2.3	2.5
Indonesia	0.7	1.8	1.9	1.9	2.1
Other	1.6	1.7	1.8	2.0	2.0
Latin America	1.8	1.9	1.9	1.9	1.8
Middle East	2.4	2.5	2.5	2.5	2.4
Africa	1.3	1.4	1.4	1.4	1.5
Dev'ing countries excluding China	1.5	1.9	1.9	1.9	2.0
World	2.5	2.3	2.3	2.4	2.4

Notes and Source: As for Table 5.6.

have emissions growing at the same rate as energy in the non-OECD world (about 5 per cent), whereas we know coal has been growing at 9 per cent p.a. from 2000 to 2005, compared to energy growth for the same region and period of 4.6 per cent.

Indonesia's experience of fuel switching towards coal is instructive. In 1990, oil constituted 59 per cent of total energy use (excluding energy from biomass and waste), falling to 51 per cent in 2005, while the share of gas fell from 32 to 24 per cent. The share of coal over the same period increased from 7 to 20 per cent, a more than sixfold increase in level terms (IEA, 2007*c*). The shift to carbon-intensive coal is expected to continue apace, with industrial plants substituting coal for gas (which fetches high prices in export markets) and planned expansions in electricity generation predominantly using low-grade coal (Narjoko and Jotzo, 2007).

There are two final inputs needed to complete these projections. Energy from fuel used to power ships (marine bunkers) is included in the IEA projections (though not aviation fuel). We use the 2007 WEO projections unchanged. Second, unlike the IEA projections, SRES projections for CO_2 emissions from fossil fuels also include CO_2 emissions from industrial processes. These in theory cover non-fossil-fuel CO_2 emissions from iron and steel, lime, and cement production, but in practice only emissions from cement tend to be covered. To make our projections comparable with SRES projections, we also provide projections for cement. Cement emissions are equivalent to about 4 per cent of fossil-fuel emissions. Emissions in cement have tracked world growth fairly closely over the last three decades, and were ahead in the first half of this decade. We assume that cement growth is proportional to global economic growth (for actual figures see Table 5.9).

(iv) Platinum Age Projections for CO_2 Emissions from Fossil Fuels

Incorporating our revised growth assumptions for the developing world, and energy intensities for China, as well as our projections for cement emissions gives a projection of annual average emissions growth of 3.1 per cent from 2005 to 2030. Table 5.9 shows the contribution of different countries and regions to this result.

Note the emerging dominance of China in the global emissions profile. Under these projections, by 2030, China will be responsible for 37 per cent of global emissions, up from 19 per cent currently. This is a product of China's exceptionally high growth, population, and carbon intensity (Table 5.8). In terms of *per capita* emissions, China will catch up with Europe by 2015, and almost reach North American emissions levels by 2030. The developing world excluding China increases its weight in global emissions more slowly, from 21 per cent in 2005 to 26 per cent in 2030.

Total business-as-usual CO_2 emissions from fossil fuels (excluding cement) are 8 per cent higher under Platinum Age assumptions than under 2007 WEO ones by 2015, and 34 per cent higher by 2030. China is responsible for almost two-thirds of this difference. By 2030, emissions are 85 per cent higher in China under Platinum Age than under 2007 WEO assumptions.

Figure 5.4 puts this result into perspective, by showing average growth rates for CO_2 emissions from fossil fuels for a number of SRES and post-SRES scenarios for the period c. 2005–30, as well as average emission growth in the 1970s and 1980s, the previous decade, and so far in this decade (2000–5).

Table 5.9. Emissions of CO_2 (FF) in 2005 and projected: growth, shares in global total, and *per capita* emissions

	Annual average growth (%)			Share of total excluding cement (%)		*Per capita* emissions (t)	
	2005–15	2015–30	2005–30	2005	2030	2005	2030
OECD	0.8	0.5	0.6	48.3	26.8	11.0	11.6
OECD North America	1.1	0.7	0.8	25.3	14.7	15.6	15.6
OECD Europe	0.3	0.5	0.4	15.3	8.0	7.6	7.9
OECD Pacific	1.0	0.0	0.4	7.8	4.1	10.3	11.7
Transition	2.1	1.8	1.9	9.8	7.4	7.7	13.2
Developing countries	5.8	4.4	5.0	39.8	63.3	2.2	5.4
Developing Asia	6.7	4.8	5.5	28.6	51.9	2.3	6.9
China	7.5	4.7	5.8	19.1	37.4	3.9	14.5
India	4.9	5.8	5.4	4.3	7.6	1.0	3.0
Indonesia	4.6	6.4	5.7	1.3	2.4	1.5	4.9
Other	4.7	2.9	3.6	3.9	4.5	1.4	2.4
Latin America	3.0	2.8	2.9	3.5	3.4	2.1	3.3
Middle East	4.1	3.0	3.4	4.6	5.1	6.6	10.1
Africa	2.3	3.0	2.7	3.1	2.9	0.9	1.1
Developing countries excluding China	4.0	3.9	4.0	20.8	25.9	1.5	2.8
Marine bunkers	7.8	1.3	3.9	2.0	2.5		
				Gt CO_2			
World total excluding cement	3.3	2.8	3.0	26.7	56.4	4.2	6.9
Cement	4.8	4.4	4.5	1.0	3.1	0.2	0.4
World total including cement	3.4	2.9	3.1	27.8	59.6	4.3	7.2

Source: Population data from IEA (2007*a*, *b*). Cement from CDIAC (2007): 2005 is an estimate for cement based on 2004 actuals.

Most emissions projections for growth out to 2030 forecast annual average growth of about 2 per cent. Our Platinum Age projections predict that, without a shift in policies, global emissions growth in the coming decades will be basically a continuation of what has been seen since 2000—growth of around 3 per cent. Although economic growth and energy intensity are both projected to fall from the rates of 2000–7, the rising weight of the rapidly growing developing economies in the global economy combined with their higher emissions intensity of output will cause the rate of growth of emissions to stay high.

If China's energy intensity is not adjusted from WEO projections, and only non-OECD economic growth rates are adjusted as per Table 5.5, the projected growth rate of global emissions is 2.7 per cent. This is still in excess of the A1FI SRES scenario (2.5 per cent growth for 2000–30), which depicts a high-growth, fossil-fuel-intensive scenario for the world and has to date been generally considered 'extreme.'[12]

[12] See for example Agerup (2004): 'The A1FI scenario depicts an extremely unlikely future.'

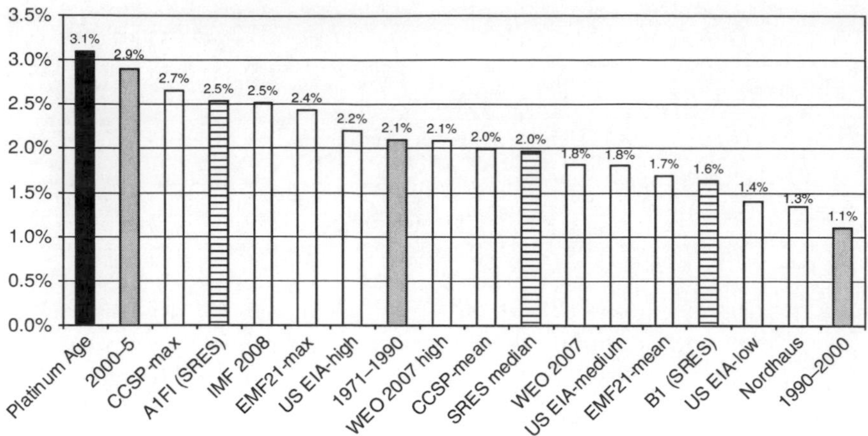

Figure 5.4. A comparison of annual projected growth rates in SRES and post-SRES scenarios (c. 2005–30) with historical data for global CO_2 emissions from fossil fuels and the Platinum Age projections (2005–30).

Note: The grey bars show average annual emissions growth for various historical periods. The striped bars show various SRES scenarios, and the transparent bars post-SRES scenarios. The black bar gives the projections of the authors. Historical data are from Table 5.1. The SRES scenarios (Nakiçenovic and Swart, 2000) used are: A1FI (AIG MINICAM), which shows the most rapid emissions growth, both to 2030 and to 2100; B1 (BI IMAGE), which is at the lower end of the range; and the median SRES scenario (which is defined as the median for each variable and each decade of the four SRES marker (or main) scenarios). The SRES scenarios give projections for every ten years from 1990 to 2100; we report here projections for 2000–30. Post-SRES scenarios included are: the mean and maximum emission baselines from the EMF-21 (Energy Modelling Forum) project (Weyant *et al.*, 2006), which included 18 different emission projection models for 2000–25; the mean and maximum projections from the US Climate Change Science Program (CCSP) (Clarke *et al.*, 2007), which used three models; the base case from the well-known Nordhaus (2007*b*) model for 2005–35; projections for 2005–30 from the IEA 2007 *World Energy Outlook* (both the base case and a rapid-growth scenario with higher growth projected for China and India); the high, medium, and low projections from the US EIA (2007) for 2004–30; and the IMF *World Economic Outlook* baseline for 2002–30 (IMF, 2008).

This is a broad-brush, illustrative projection. We do not regard it as an unreasonable one, and point out that our adjustments to IEA projections are both conservative and restricted to selected countries and regions. Growth rates and energy and emission intensities could all be higher than we have projected. While we have not attempted explicitly to quantify the substitution away from energy in an era of high and increasing energy prices, the energy intensities projected embody a powerful effect of rising energy prices on energy use.

IV. OTHER EMISSIONS

According to the IPCC Fourth Assessment Report (Rogner *et al.*, 2007), in 2004, CO_2 from fossil-fuel use and industrial processes contributed 59 per cent of greenhouse-gas emissions. CO_2 from land-use change and forestry contributed

Table 5.10. Projections of methane (CH_4) and nitrous-oxide (N_2O) emissions growth

Measured in CO_2-e, % growth	CH_4	N_2O	$CH_4 + N_2O$
SRES projections (2000–30)			
AIFI	1.4%	1.5%	1.4%
SRES median	1.1%	0.3%	0.9%
B1	0.6%	0.5%	0.6%
EMF projections (2000–25)			
EMF-21 mean	1.3%	1.0%	1.2%
EMF-21 max	2.0%	2.2%	2.0%
EMF-21 min	0.7%	−0.1%	0.5%
EPA projections (2000–20)	1.5%	1.3%	1.5%
Platinum Age (2005–30)	1.8%	1.9%	1.8%
2005 level (Gt CO_2-e)	6.6	3.3	9.9
2030 level (Gt CO_2-e)	10.3	5.3	15.6

Notes and Sources: For SRES and EMF projections, see Figure 5.5. EPA projections are from EPA (2006). Platinum Age projections adjust EPA forecasts using the methodology set out in the text. They extrapolate EPA projections to 2020 out to 2030, and use a 2005 starting point.

17 per cent, and non-CO_2 emissions contributed the remaining 23 per cent. This section considers these latter two sources of greenhouse gas emissions.

(i) Non-CO_2 Greenhouse Gases

Methane (CH_4) and nitrous oxide (N_2O) are the two most important non-CO_2 greenhouse gases. They constitute, respectively, 14 and 8 per cent of total emissions in CO_2-e terms (Rogner *et al.*, 2007). [13]

Firm historical data for non-CO_2 gases are only available till 2000.[14] Projections for non-CO_2 gases from 2000 onwards are shown in Table 5.10. The very detailed, recent US Environmental Protection Agency (EPA) projections show annual growth in non-CO_2 gases of 1.5 per cent, slightly higher than the rate of growth seen in the SRES A1FI scenario.

EPA projections for developed and transition countries are largely based on official national projections. For developing countries, a 'Tier 1' method is used, generally by applying IPCC emissions coefficients to projections of economic drivers based on EIA (2002) or from other official sources. The EIA (2002) projections for GDP growth and for energy use are definitely by now outdated.

[13] Fluorinated compounds (F gases) are not included in these projections owing to their small size (about 1 per cent of greenhouse-gas emissions) and the difficulties of making comparisons with the SRES scenarios using these gases.

[14] IEA (2007*b*) does publish data for non-CO_2 gases for 2005. However, some of these data appear identical to 2000 data (including for major countries such as China and India). There are varying estimates of non-CO_2 emission levels. For example, EPA (2006) has combined CH_4 and N_2O emissions in 2000 of 9.1 Gt CO_2-e; IEA (2007*b*) of 10.5 Gt CO_2-e.

We adjust the EPA projections for CH_4 emission from energy (about a third of the total) by the ratio of our growth rates for a given country or region (in section II(i)) to the corresponding EIA (2002) estimates. For other non-CO_2 emissions, we assume that growth rates will be partly but not entirely responsive to higher GDP growth. Hence we adjust the EPA projections by half of the differential between our growth projections and the corresponding EIA (2002) figures. These broad adjustments lead to a projected annual average growth rate of CH_4 and N_2O combined of 1.8 per cent a year.

(ii) CO_2 Emissions from Land-use Change and Forestry

Emissions of CO_2 from land-use change and forestry (LUCF) are large, poorly measured, difficult to project, and highly variable (Nabuurs *et al.*, 2007). CO_2 (LUCF) emissions, as defined here, are made up of three types: emissions from biomass burning (reported by IEA, 2007*b*); emissions from peat fires and decay of drained peat soils (from Hooijer *et al.*, 2006); and emissions from decay of above ground biomass that remains after logging and deforestation (which is derived residually from Rogner *et al.*, 2007, figure 1.1).

CO_2 (LUCF) emissions are more extensive than thought earlier. In particular, only recently have peat-related emissions, mainly originating from Indonesia (Page *et al.*, 2002; Hooijer *et al.*, 2006) been taken into account. Table 5.11 demonstrates this by comparing CO_2 (LUCF) emissions assumed in the SRES and

Table 5.11. CO_2 emissions from land-use change and forestry: latest estimates, earlier estimates, and projections

Gt CO_2	Estimates			Projections
	1990	2000	2005	2030
A. Latest estimates				
Biomass burning	2.4	3.3	3.5	3.5
Biomass decay	1.5	1.8	2.0	2.0
Peat decay and burning	1.7	1.9	2.0	2.1
Total	5.6	7.0	7.5	7.6
Period ave. growth rate (%)		2.3	1.3	0.05
B. Earlier estimates				
Total	4.1	3.4		

Notes and Sources: Biomass burning from IEA (2007*b*). Peat decay and burning from Hooijer *et al.* (2006). Biomass decay is estimated from Rogner *et al.* (2007, figure 1.1), and is actually for 2004. 2030 projections for biomass burning from Hooijer *et al.* (2006). Zero growth assumed for other sources. Earlier estimates are, respectively, the SRES baseline (1990) and the mean EMF baseline (2000) for CO_2 (LUCF). For sources for these projections, see Figure 5.4.

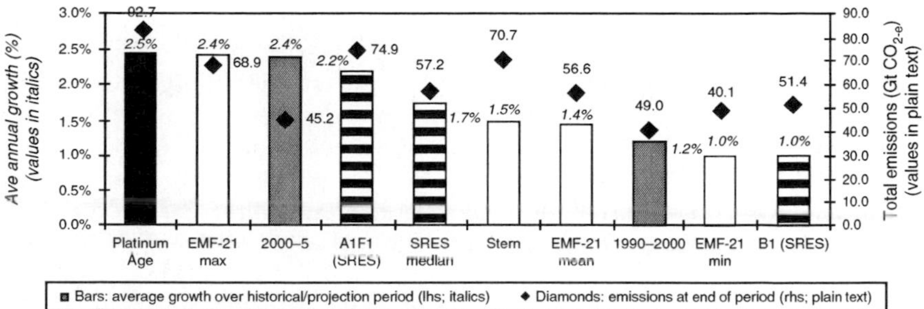

Figure 5.5. Comparison of Platinum Age greenhouse-gas projections with other projections and historical data in terms of average growth rates (bars; italics; left axis) and total emissions (diamonds; plain text; right axis)

Notes: The striped bars are the SRES scenarios; grey are actuals; transparent are post-SRES projections; black is the Platinum Age projection. Growth rates are for the projection or historical period; values are end-of-period. The mean, maximum, and minimum EMF-21 projections are composites of different projections: they use the projections with the mean/maximum/minimum projected growth rates for CO_2(FF), CO_2 (LUCF), NO_2, and CH_4, respectively, and combine them. The Stern projection is the business-as-usual projection from ch. 7 of the Stern Review: this is a composite projection based on various published projections for different sources of global warming (it is different from the A2 SRES scenario which Stern uses elsewhere in his report). To obtain a 2030 total emissions figure for EMF-21, we extrapolate to 2030 using the average growth rate for 2000–25. For more details on the SRES scenarios, and for all sources, see notes to Figure 5.4. There are not as many projections in this figure as in Figure 5.4 because only a subset of projections go beyond CO_2(FF) to project other sources of global warming.

EMF-21 base years (1990 and 2000, respectively) with latest estimates for those years (see Figure 5.5 for more details on these two well-known sets of projections). The latter are 40–100 per cent higher. Earlier, LUCF emissions were thought to contribute about 10 per cent of greenhouse-gas emissions. They are now thought to contribute 15–20 per cent.

It is very difficult to project CO_2 emissions from land-use change and forestry. Historical growth is significant: 2.3 per cent in the 1990s and 1.3 per cent in the first half of this decade, though there are large margins of error around these numbers. SRES and EMF-21 projections forecast both positive and negative growth. Houghton (2003), who is widely cited, has slightly higher emissions in 2000 (7.6 Gt CO_2) but declining to about 6.2 Gt in 2030.[15] Sathaye *et al.* (2006) have a reference case where annual deforestation emissions slowly increase until 2030, then slowly decline. Projections for peat decay and fire are available from Hooijer *et al.* (2006), who projects growth of about 1 per cent per year out to 2020, and then a period of slow negative growth. For want of better information, no growth is assumed in the other two categories from the 2005 base, consistent with the approach taken in Jotzo and Pezzey (2007). The results are shown in Table 5.11.

[15] Canadell *et al.* (2007) who update Houghton's work have a lower CO_2 (LUCF) value for 2000 (5.05 Gt CO_2).

V. SUMMARY OF RESULTS

Platinum Age projections give annual average growth in greenhouse-gas emissions of 2.5 per cent over the period 2005–30—lower than the 3 per cent for CO_2 emissions from fossil fuels largely because of the assumed low growth in CO_2 emissions from land-use change and forestry. This overall growth rate is slightly above the upper-end of existing scenario growth rates (Figure 5.5).

End-period emissions are significantly higher than in existing rapid-growth scenarios because of the higher forestry emissions built into the base. We project annual emissions of 83 Gt CO_2-equivalent by 2030, almost double their current level, 11 per cent higher than the 'extreme' A1FI scenario, and a level of emissions reached only in 2050 in the business-as-usual scenario used by the Stern Review (Stern, 2007, p. 202).

VI. IMPLICATIONS FOR POST-KYOTO NEGOTIATIONS

The importance of an urgent response to the threat of climate change is noted in the Bali Action Plan agreed in December 2007 to guide climate negotiations on the UN Framework Convention on Climate Change. What these new projections make clear is that an effective urgent response has to be an ambitious one. To illustrate this point, consider Box 13.7 from the IPCC Fourth Assessment Report (Gupta *et al.*, 2007) made famous by the prominence given it in the Bali negotiations. At one point, a summary of this box was to appear in the agreed text arising from these international negotiations; it ended up being referred to in a footnote (UN FCCC, 2007*b*). This box (which we will call the 'Bali Box') gives the extent of cuts in emissions required by both Annex I and non-Annex I countries by both 2020 and 2050 if various stabilization targets are to be achieved. It quantifies cuts required for Annex I countries (developed and transition countries), and gives qualitative assessments of what is required for the other countries. Cuts for Annex I countries are given relative to 1990. Cuts for other countries are given relative to the baseline.

Sheehan (2008) examines the 16 studies which are surveyed to produce the famous box. He notes that 15 of these undertake empirical analysis, and that all of these 15 are 'within the SRES marker scenario range'—that is, predicting significantly lower emissions growth and levels up to 2030 than now appears reasonable (i.e. significantly lower than the Platinum Age projections).

With higher business-as-usual or baseline emissions, to achieve a given emissions target, one of two adjustments must be made. Either higher deviations from the baseline will be required (for non-Annex-I countries) or higher cuts from 1990 levels (for Annex I countries.) Given our new projections, by how much will Annex I and non-Annex I countries have to cut emissions by 2020 to achieve the stabilization targets set out in the Bali box?

Table 5.12. Extent of deviations required from business-as-usual baseline by non-Annex-I countries assuming given reductions from 1990 levels by Annex I countries

	Scenarios	Stabilization pathways			
		450 ppm CO_2-e		550 ppm CO_2-e	
		Annex I deviation by 2020 from 1990		Annex I deviation by 2020 from 1990	
		−25%	−40%	−10%	−30%
		Implications for non-Annex-I countries			
IPCC synthesis ('Bali Box')	**Deviation from baseline (for range of Annex I cuts above)**	**Substantial deviation from baseline (in most regions)**		**Deviation from baseline (in some regions)**	
SRES median marker	Deviation from baseline (2020)	−15%	−4.7%	−8%	5.6%
	Annual average growth (2005–20)	2.1%	2.9%	2.6%	3.6%
Platinum Age	Deviation from baseline (2020)	−40%	−33%	−35%	−26%
	Annual average growth (2005–20)	0.0%	0.7%	0.5%	1.4%

Sources and Notes: Annex I countries under the UN Framework Convention on Climate Change include most developed and transition economies. Gt CO_2-e targets from Stern (2007, figure 8.4): 40 Gt CO_2-e for the 450 CO_2-e ppm target; and 45 Gt CO_2-e for the 550 CO_2-e ppm. IPCC Synthesis from the 'Bali Box' (box 13.7 in Gupta *et al.*, 2007). For SRES median marker, see Figure 5.5; Annex I median calculated separately from the four marker scenarios. For Platinum Age projections, CO_2(FF) emissions from Table 5.9 (bunker and cement emissions allocated as per national fossil-fuel emissions); CO_2 (LUCF) emissions from Table 5.11 (all emissions in this category allocated to non-Annex-I countries); non-CO_2 emissions from Table 5.10 (emissions allocated to Annex I (actually, OECD and transition countries) and non-Annex I (all other) countries as per baseline data from EPA and growth rules described in text).

To answer this question, we need a pathway of global emissions towards atmospheric stabilization. Of course, there can be many, and so this answer is only illustrative. We use the stabilization paths given by the Stern Review (2007, Figure 8.4) associated with the 450 and 550 ppm CO_2-e concentration targets.[16] Baseline emissions are allocated between the two groups of countries (Annex I and non-Annex I) based on the data and projection methods described in the previous two sections. Note that the analysis only goes out to 2020, and so conclusions can be reached with greater confidence than they can for 2030.

We compare for given Annex-I reduction targets (at the bottom and the top of the Bali Box range), the implied cuts for non-Annex-I countries for two projections: one, the SRES median marker scenario; and, two, the Platinum Age projections.

[16] As per the Bali Box, and the Stern Review, since it is impossible to stabilize at 450 ppm CO_2-e without overshooting, we consider a 450 target with temporary overshooting of that target to 500 ppm CO_2-e.

If the SRES median scenario is used, the Bali Box write-up for the implications for non-Annex-I countries seems reasonable (Table 5.12). Even for Annex-I country cuts at the bottom of the respective ranges, modest reductions from the baseline are required for other countries. For example, a 10 per cent cut by Annex I countries relative to 1990 requires a cut of 8 per cent from the non-Annex-I baseline if the 2020 target arising from the 550 ppm CO_2-e stabilization path is to be adhered to. This would still allow annual average emissions growth of 2.6 per cent in developing countries.

However, if the Platinum Age projections are used, the picture changes completely. Consider the results based on the top-of-the-range level of cuts for Annex I countries: 30 per cent for the 550 stabilization path, and 40 per cent for the 450 one. Even then the 450 path will require a 33 per cent cut from the non-Annex-I baseline by 2020, which allows for annual growth of only 0.7 per cent between 2005 and 2020. The 550 path, and its 2020 target, will require a 26 per cent cut from baseline for non-Annex-I countries, which limits annual average emissions growth in these countries to 1.4 per cent. This would imply no growth in *per capita* emissions in the developing world.

VII. CONCLUSION

Projecting business-as-usual greenhouse-gas emissions decades out from now requires difficult judgements. No doubt the projections we have presented could be improved in various ways. Nevertheless, there is clearly a compelling case that existing emissions projections are unduly conservative, and that, in the absence of effective mitigation over the coming decades, emissions will be significantly higher in terms of both growth and level than previously thought.

If this conclusion is accepted, then two implications for climate-change mitigation follow. First, it will be extremely difficult to adhere to pathways consistent with stringent stabilization targets (such as stabilization at 450 ppm CO_2-e), even with some overshooting. Second, even given moderate stabilization targets, and greater back-end loading of the stabilization task than used in the example of the previous section, large cuts for developed countries will be required, and developing countries will need to bring down emissions substantially below business as usual.

Cuts below baseline growth of such dimensions will not be made in a framework of voluntary commitments and selective policies. They will only be made if major developing countries also become subject to quantified national targets. The terms of the climate-change discussion need to be shifted. There is no room any longer for defending the view that the 'differentiation' of effort called for in the United Nations Framework on Climate Change Convention between developing and developed countries should be based on the application of emissions targets and comprehensive policies to the latter, and not the former. Differentiation is critical, but should enter the frame through developed countries taking on more stringent targets, and through their provision of finance to back mitigation efforts in developing countries. Differentiation within the group of non-Annex I countries is also critical, with middle-income countries shouldering greater effort and high-income countries currently part of the non-Annex I group graduating to taking on full binding commitments. Without all major emitters accepting economy-wide targets and implementing comprehensive policies, given rapid emissions growth, the prospects for the global climate-change mitigation effort are bleak.

POSTSCRIPT: THE GLOBAL FINANCIAL CRISIS

This chapter was written before the onset of the main recessionary impact of the global financial crisis (GFC) in late 2008. In early 2009, the GFC is beginning to have a large impact on economic growth, energy use, and emissions. Emissions are falling in absolute terms in developed countries, and emissions growth is falling in developing countries, and for a while might turn negative as well. Oil prices have also fallen from their historic highs in the first half of 2008.

We have not revised our projections to take into account the impact of the GFC. If we did, we would certainly revise our global growth forecasts downwards in the short term. At the same time, we would expect that, after a period of low growth, the global economy will recover, and rapid growth in the developing world will resume. At that point of time, oil prices would be expected to rise again. There is no reason to expect that longer-term economic growth rates, or the relationship between economic growth, energy use, and carbon output, would be significantly changed. In other words, we see Platinum Age growth as being put on hold, rather than permanently derailed.

How much of a difference to total emissions could the GFC make? There is, of course, massive uncertainty about both the severity and length of the impact of the GFC on global growth. To illustrate possible impacts, assume that there is no growth in global emissions of CO_2 emissions from fossil fuels between 2007 and 2010—which would amount to a very strong and prolonged break from past trends—but that before[17] and after this emissions grow at the annual average rates forecast by us first to 2015, and then to 2030. Then the annual average growth in CO_2(FF) emissions for 2005–30 would be 2.6 per cent instead of the 3.1 per cent calculated in the paper.[18] This is a significant difference, but note that 2.6 per cent

[17] The Netherlands Environmental Assessment Agency (2008) reports that global emissions of CO_2 from fossil-fuel use and cement production increased by 3.5 per cent in 2006 and 3.1 per cent in 2007, which is broadly in line with our 2005–15 projection of 3.4 per cent annual average for 2005–15. The above calculations in the text exclude cement.

[18] In this context, it is worth noting that our biggest disagreement with the WEO concerns the post-2015 rather than pre-2015 period. Our annual average emissions growth rate for 2005–15 is 40 per cent higher than the 2007 WEO's: 3.3 per cent compared to 2.5 per cent. But our annual average emissions growth rate for 2015–30 is double that of the 2007 WEO: 2.8 per cent compared to 1.4 per cent.

is still above the 2.5 per cent annual average growth rate for CO_2 in the A1FI SRES scenario, the most 'extreme' of the SRES scenarios.

Another way of gauging the effect of economic slowdown is to ask at what time a particular level of emissions would be reached. Assuming that the GFC resulted in a three-year halt in emissions growth, and 'business-as-usual' growth resumed thereafter, then the emissions levels projected for 2030 (2015) would be reached in 2033 (2018).

Our main conclusions, that the SRES scenarios as a whole underestimate future business-as-usual emissions growth, and that scenarios of future emissions growth once considered extreme now appear reasonable, remain intact.

We do not exclude altogether the possibility that the disruption to global growth that began in 2008 will turn out to be deeper and more prolonged than assumed in this postscript, and will have a larger effect on total emissions for many years ahead. This is possible, but unlikely.

6

The Behavioural Economics of Climate Change

Kjell Arne Brekke and Olof Johansson-Stenman***

I. INTRODUCTION

The effects of climate change and their remedies are frequently discussed both in the media and among politicians and the general public. Interest in the problems at hand has increased steadily in the last few years, and today the issue is very high on the political agenda worldwide; large initiatives have been and will be taken to handle the problem effectively.

Within economic science we have, parallel to this development, witnessed a dramatically increased interest in behavioural economics (BE) in the last decade or so. First, compared to conventional economic theory, BE emphasizes the notion that people have cognitive limitations, and that, at least partly for this reason, they sometimes make seemingly irrational decisions. There is, in particular, much empirical evidence with respect to choices under risk and over time. Second, much work in BE follows Adam Smith (Ashraf *et al.*, 2005; Evensky, 2005), in particular *The Theory of Moral Sentiments*, but also *The Wealth of Nations*, in emphasizing the idea that people's behaviour is not solely motivated by their own material pay-offs, and that issues such as perceived fairness and social norms often influence human decisions to a large extent. Third, again contrary to conventional economic theory but following Adam Smith, BE often highlights the notion that we act in a social context, and that issues such as social approval and status are central motivators of human behaviour.

Crucial issues in the economics of climate change concern how to deal with long-run choices over time, as well as problems under risk, i.e. issues where BE has identified that conventional theory may provide poor predictions of human behaviour. Although the uncertainty regarding the consequences of climate

* University of Oslo.

** School of Business, Economics and Law, University of Gothenburg.

We are grateful for useful comments from Cameron Hepburn, David Hendry, Steffen Kallbekken, Åsa Löfgren, Snorre Kverndokk, Thomas Sterner, Asbjorn Aaheim, Olle Häggström, Tobias Schmidt, an anonymous referee, and participants at a seminar arranged by the *Oxford Review of Economic Policy* in Oxford. We also gratefully acknowledge financial support from the Swedish International Development Cooperation Agency (Sida).

change appears to have decreased somewhat lately, since most researchers now at least agree that the changes in the climate that are starting to appear are, indeed, largely due to human activity, the overall extent of the changes and their distributional impact are still highly uncertain. Moreover, how people deal with choices under risk has important implications for the discussion of the appropriate discount rate, an issue that is of crucial importance in the economics of climate change.

Given this, it is surprising that BE has had so little influence on the economics of climate change so far. This chapter is a modest attempt to do just this: bring central insights from BE into the economics of climate change. Section II deals with the crucial issue of discounting in a world where people are not time-consistent expected-utility maximizers, whereas section III looks into the issue of human cooperation in general, and implications for climate negotiations in particular. Section IV provides some concluding remarks.

II. DISCOUNTING, RISK, AND TIME

One of the major discussions in the literature on climate policy is the choice of discount rates. The discount rate may be determined from both the consumption and production sides of the economy. From the consumption perspective, the interest rate reflects the marginal rate of substitution between consumption now and next year, and follows from the parameters in the utility function as given by the Ramsey rule,

$$r = \rho + g\sigma$$

This equation states that the rate of return should equal the pure time discount rate, ρ, plus the changes in marginal utility over time, determined by the consumption growth rate, g, and the intertemporal elasticity of substitution $(1/\sigma)$. One of the most controversial features of the Stern (2007) report concerns the choices of these parameters ($\rho = 0.1\%,\ g = 1.3\%,\ \sigma = 1$), which yield an annual interest rate of 1.4 per cent.

The parameters of the Ramsey rule may be estimated from market data or evaluated based on ethical considerations. For example, Dasgupta (2008*b*) argues that the implied weight on redistribution between rich future generations and the poorer current generation is unreasonably low. Alternatively, one may compare the result, r, with estimates from the production side, e.g. market data on return on investment. Nordhaus (2007*a*) criticizes the choice in the Stern report on the grounds that the market real return on investment is about 6 per cent per year.

A problem with the latter approach is that there are so many rates of return, and they vary much more than we are able to explain. For example, Mehra and Prescott (2003) report the return on relatively riskless securities (treasury bills) and stock-market indices for different periods, datasets, and countries. For the USA in the period 1926–2000, where the best data are available, the mean risk-free return is

0.4 per cent, while the mean return on stocks is 8.8 per cent, i.e. an 8.4 percentage point difference—the equity premium. It should be noted that many estimates of the premium are less dramatic, but still considerable.[1] So why compare the 1.4 per cent with the return on investment and not with the risk-free rate of return?

To answer this question we need to know why the equity premium is so large. For a long time, the standard answer used to be risk aversion, with the theoretical justification from the capital asset pricing model (CAPM) (Sharpe, 1964; Lintner, 1965; Mossin, 1966). One of the main insights of the CAPM is that the risk associated with an asset is not the variance of the asset return. A well-diversified investor will own many assets, and in contemplating whether to buy a particular asset, the crucial risk question is not the variance of the asset in question but rather how the overall portfolio risk is affected. It then turns out that the relevant measure of risk is the covariance with the market portfolio, since that is the portfolio that well-diversified investors will hold. An asset that does not add to the overall risk is, from a well-diversified investor's perspective, equivalent to a risk-free asset, and the required rate of return should then equal the risk-free rate (0.4 per cent with the numbers above). An asset that reduces the risk of the portfolio is even better; now the required rate of return is less than the risk-free interest rate, and may even be negative. However, the average asset is perfectly correlated with the market portfolio and should therefore have a return equal to the market portfolio, i.e. 8–9 per cent.

The same logic applies for climate change; if we invest in reduced carbon-dioxide (CO_2) emissions, how will this affect the overall risk in the society? The answer depends on how climate damages are expected to co-vary with future consumption, which is far from self-evident. Consider first the case where future damage is simply proportional to economic activity (and where climate damage decreases with abatement investments). Then the return to climate investment will correlate perfectly with the market portfolio, and there will be no reason to have different discount rates for abatement and other investments. This is consistent with Nordhaus (2007*a*), who assumes that climatic investments share the risk properties of other capital investments.

Weitzman (2007*a*, pp. 713–14), on the other hand, uses a model with several sectors and argues that climate damage affects only a minor sector, the 'outdoors', and hence argues for a lower but still positive correlation. The resulting discount rate would then be larger than the risk-free rate but lower than the mean return on stocks. However, we think it is important to consider different kinds of risks and, more specifically, that climate investments presumably reduce the risk and severity of natural catastrophes in terms of, for example, hurricanes or drought. Since the reduction of a catastrophe would be larger for larger catastrophes, we may obtain a negative correlation between the outcomes of abatement investment and the rest of the economy. Consider the extreme alternatives of complete abatement with

[1] In Merha and Prescott's (2003) survey, the highest risk-free rate is 3.2 per cent for Germany, 1978–97, and the lowest equity premium is 3.3 per cent for Japan, 1970–99. Dimson *et al.* (2007) argue that the premium tends to be overestimated, but that the puzzle nevertheless remains.

no man-made climate change and business as usual with no abatement. Then the question of correlations corresponds to whether the future consumption is less or more uncertain with man-made climate change. Less uncertainty with no potential climate change corresponds to returns to abatement being negatively correlated with future consumption. Whether the overall discount rate for climate change should be larger or smaller than the risk-free rate will then depend on the relative size of these components; see also Howarth (2003) who conducts a simple simulation yielding zero correlation. In this perspective, the interest rates in the Stern (2007) report are not obviously low.

However, a problem here is that the CAPM account of the equity premium is hardly plausible in the first place. Transferring wealth from bonds to equity increases both the return on a portfolio and the associated risk, but, as demonstrated by Mehra and Prescott (1985), the difference in return is simply too high to be explained only by risk aversion—the equity premium puzzle. They argue that, based on reasonable parameter assumptions, CAPM can explain less than one percentage point of the equity premium. Since their seminal paper, many attempts have been made to explain the puzzle, but reviews such as Kocherlakota (1996) and Mehra and Prescott (2003) conclude that we still lack a good explanation. It is worth noting that each of the possible explanations would have implications for the choice of discount rate for climate policy. In most cases these implications are not explicitly analysed. One exception is a recent cut at the problem by Weitzman (2007*b*) who argues that, since we do not know the distribution of asset return but have to estimate it, the tail tends to fatten and the perceived risk increases—to the extent that it becomes unclear why anyone saves in risky assets at all. Weitzman (2007*a*) then argues that if this account of the puzzle is correct, the implications for climate policy are far more dramatic than the Stern review suggests. The reason is similar to why CAPM may suggest a discount rate below the risk-free rate: continued large greenhouse-gas emissions constitute a gamble as the future consequences are not known, and if Weitzman's argument is correct, then the reason for avoiding the gamble is much stronger than in conventional models.

Here we will only discuss one of the possible explanations of the equity premium puzzle in some detail; it is one derived from BE and is the one that we consider to be the most plausible.[2] Benartzi and Thaler (1995) explain the equity premium using Kahneman and Tversky's (1979) prospect theory (PT). According to the review in Starmer (2000), cumulative PT is the theory that best predicts the data we have on choices under uncertainty, so it is a natural candidate to explain also the effect of uncertainty on the return on financial instruments. One of the main elements of PT is the concept of loss aversion, where it is argued that losses are valued much more highly than gains (typically more than twice as high). A highly stylized representation[3] of this theory is to assume that individuals

[2] We do not suggest that all other explanations are wrong. Indeed, we consider it likely that several contribute to our understanding, albeit to different extents.

[3] This formulation disregards two important elements of prospect theory. First, people are assumed to be risk-averse for gains and risk-seeking for losses. With the calibrated version used in Benartzi

maximize the expected value of the value-function $v(x)$ where,

$$v(x) = \begin{cases} x & \text{for } x > 0 \\ 2.25x & \text{for } x < 0 \end{cases}.$$

This introduces a kink in the value function around the *status quo*. At the kink the slope makes a discrete jump, so that local 'risk aversion' is infinite. In expected utility theory, the utility function has no similar kink, hence it is almost linear for sufficiently small variation, implying risk neutrality for small gambles (Rabin, 2000; Rabin and Thaler, 2001). Consider, for example, a gamble with equal probability of $-Z$ and $+2Z$. With the PT preferences above, this gamble will be turned down irrespective of Z, while a risk-averse expected-utility maximizer will accept if Z is small but may reject if Z is sufficiently large. One way to think about the failure of expected utility theory (EU) to explain the equity premium is that holding assets involves too small gambles.

Another major difference between EU and PT is how they view repeated gambles. Samuelson (1963) points out that if a gamble is turned down once (at any level of wealth), then expected utility implies that n repetitions of the same gamble should be turned down, too. If the subject does not watch as each gamble is played out, PT on the other hand allows the subject to turn down the single gamble but accept the repeated one. The intuition is that the main risk aversion in PT is due to the kink in the value function, and that the accumulated pay-off in the repeated gamble will move away from the kink. Thus, risk aversion is much lower for repeated gambles.

Now, what has all this got to do with the equity premium? The point is that the stock market can also be seen as a series of gambles. Each day, even each minute, may be seen as a lottery when you own stocks. PT predicts very high risk aversion toward small lotteries, so if each day is seen as a separate lottery, the PT individual will turn down the lottery. But as the lotteries are repeated they become increasingly attractive to the PT individual. It turns out that if each year in the asset market is seen as one lottery, then that generates exactly the amount of risk aversion needed to explain the equity premium. The reference point must thus move once a year; not once a month or once per quarter, and not once every second year. While this may, of course, be questioned, Benartzi and Thaler (1995) argue that resetting the reference point every twelfth month is plausible, as investors have to file their tax reports yearly. There is some experimental support for the Benartzi and Thaler explanation: Gneezy and Potters (1997) and Gneezy *et al.* (2003) find that investors are indeed more risk averse when evaluation periods are experimentally manipulated to be more frequent, and Eriksen and Kvaløy (2008) find similar results for investors managing other people's money, e.g. fund investors.

and Thaler (1995), these effects are weak. Second, people are assumed effectively to overestimate low probabilities and underestimate large ones. This is disregarded in Benartzi and Thaler's analysis.

Now, if this is the true explanation for the equity premium puzzle,[4] then what is the appropriate discount rate for climate abatement projects? To assess climate risk according to PT we need to specify a reference point. What changes will be perceived as gains and losses? The canonical choice is to use the *status quo*. If the Maldives are flooded, it would be seen as a loss and not as an absence of a gain (the gain being the continued habitation of the Maldives). But if all changes are seen as losses, then the kink in the value function does not matter. With the value function above, we would be on the linear part of the value-function implying risk neutrality and, hence, a risk-free discount rate, even if climate investments do lower the society's overall risk.[5] This accounts for the equity premium puzzle and thus also indicates a discount rate close to the risk-free rate (see also Howarth, 2009).

Thus far we have only considered the use of market data to infer the correct interest rate. An alternative approach is to consider the parameters in the Ramsey equation directly. The central parameter is then the elasticity of intertemporal substitution (EIS), corresponding to $1/\sigma$ above. Vissing-Jørgensen (2002) finds that EIS differs between stock holders (0.3–0.4) and bond holders (0.8–1.0). With the parameters in Stern this amounts to interest rates in the 3.3–4.4 per cent range for stock holders and 1.4–1.7 per cent for bond holders. Similarly, Mehra and Prescott (1985) argue (without explicit statements about σ) that a direct assessment of r based on estimates of EIS should yield an interest rate of about 4–4.5 per cent.

The difference between the observed risk-free rate and the assessed risk-free rate based on EIS is itself a puzzle—the 'risk free rate puzzle' (Weil, 1989)—which is closely related to the equity premium puzzle. The literature has been somewhat more successful at explaining this puzzle, where habit formation and liquidity services of treasury bills are possible explanations. Again, the explanations of the puzzle have implications for the choice of discount rate. For example, if treasury bills provide liquidity services, then the direct EIS approach may provide a more reliable estimate of the risk-free return than the observed return on treasury bills.

As argued above, the question of discount rates in the assessment of climate abatement cannot be disentangled from the discussion of the equity premium puzzle. Here, BE offers one potential piece of the explanation, with important implications for the choice of discount rates.

[4] Recent alternative (partial or complete) explanations of the equity premium puzzle include: disasters with non-negligible probabilities (Barro, 2006), which is somewhat similar to the explanation by Weitzman (2007*b*) mentioned above; transaction costs (Jang *et al.*, 2007); habit formation (Pijoan-Mas, 2007); and incomplete risk sharing among stockholders resulting from the combination of aggregate uncertainty, borrowing constraints, and idiosyncratic shocks (Gomes and Michaelides, 2008).

[5] Actually, the PT predicts that individuals are risk-seeking when it comes to losses. Hence the predicted required rate of return should be slightly higher than the risk-free rate, since we should like to increase risk when risk-seeking. The claimed convexity is, however, very weak and the effect should be very small.

(i) Self Control and Social Discount Rates

A separate question concerns the problems of self-control and the relationship between observed behaviour and the social optimum. Many people prefer US$10 today to US$11 tomorrow, but at the same time prefer US$11 paid on day 15 to US$10 paid on day 14. In other words, the discount rate is high in the very short run, but low in the long run. One possible account of this result is presented in Fudenberg and Levine (2006), extending an idea of Thaler and Sherfin (1981). The self is represented by a sequence of myopic 'doers' and one 'long-term planner'. The doers will rule the game unless the planner exerts an effort of self-control. The cost of making the doer deviate from the myopic optimum depends on the short-run cost of deviating. The current doer has no opinion about money paid out in the future; hence, it takes no self-control to make him choose US$11 over US$10. However, the current doer strongly prefers US$10 now to nothing now (and US$11 tomorrow). To make the doer choose US$11 tomorrow is thus costly in terms of self-control, and the cost may exceed the US$1 gain.

This model of choice is consistent with more recent literature showing that long-term considerations are given less weight under a high cognitive load. For example, Shiv and Fedorikhin (1999) found in an innovative experiment that the subjects were more likely to choose a cake over a fruit salad when they had to remember seven digits in order to get anything, while they chose the fruit salad when they only had to remember two digits. Presumably, the cognitive part of the brain (primarily the prefrontal cortex) realizes that fruit salad is better in the long run, but when this part of the brain—or the planner—is occupied, another part takes over.

Now, assume that we observe that subjects turn down a 10 per cent daily return. Should we then, respecting consumer sovereignty, use a 10 per cent daily discount rate? Or would the person be better off with US$11 tomorrow rather than US$10 today? Now suppose that the planner's true preferences amount to a zero pure time preference. In a situation where the cost of self-control is low, the subject will save at a 1 per cent yearly rate, while turning down a 10 per cent daily rate. For example, the person would happily choose a saving programme forcing him to save at a 1 per cent yearly return starting next year (avoiding the cost of controlling current doers). Similarly, the person would vote for a public project that is profitable at a 1 per cent discount rate.

Above, we have questioned the common claim that saving is lower than what a 0.1 per cent pure time preference would imply. Let us still, for the moment, accept that claim. There are then two possible interpretations of such a finding: saving is lower than the planner would have liked it to be, owing to the cost of self-control; or, the planner may have a pure rate of time preference above 0.1 per cent. Without further analysis we cannot rule out one in favour of the other.

Note finally that with multiple selves (the planner and many doers) the question arises: who represents the person's *true* preferences? Above, we have taken for granted that the planner is the one to listen to, but that is not obvious. Still, according to Harsanyi (1982, p. 55), whereas choices may be 'based on erroneous factual beliefs, or on careless logical analysis, or on strong emotions that at the moment greatly hinder rational choice', what he denotes 'true preferences' are the preferences that an individual would have had if 'he had all the relevant factual information, always reasoned with the greatest possible care, and were in a state of mind most conducive to rational choice'. He argues that it is the true preferences that carry moral significance, which would presumably correspond to the planner's preferences in our case. See also Karp (2005) for a recent analysis of global warming and hyperbolic discounting.

(ii) The Ethics of Discounting

One possible view of the Ramsey rule is to take an explicitly ethical point of view. At the most fundamental level, it is clear that the weight we should attach to the consequences for future generations is ultimately an ethical question. However, this does not necessarily imply that ethics should guide the parameter choices. Indeed, if one could compensate future generations in some other way, it may still be optimal to choose an 'efficient' market interest rate irrespective of the ethics argument. Nevertheless, if one considers such compensations unlikely, it still makes perfect sense to discuss the Ramsey rule from an ethical perspective, even if this results in a discount rate that differs from the market interest rate, whether viewed from the consumption or the production side.

BE in itself has not very much to contribute to ethics. However, insights from BE are sometimes also used in normative analysis. For example, as mentioned, much evidence suggests that people have self-control problems, and this is suggested as one of the reasons behind the fact that many smokers continue to smoke even though the majority would like to quit, and have even tried to quit. Gruber and Köszegi (2001) argue that this justifies a substantial tax on the 'internalities' of smoking. This is based on the idea that in a situation where people are not necessarily doing what is best for themselves, it is their experienced utility, or well-being, rather than their decision utility, as reflected by their choice, that matters from a normative perspective (see Kahneman *et al.*, 1997; Kahneman and Thaler, 2006). Similarly, there is an emerging literature on 'soft paternalism', suggesting that it is often possible to help people make better decisions for themselves without compromising their liberty to choose (Camerer *et al.*, 2003; Thaler and Sunstein, 2003). The most obvious example is to change the default alternatives, which has been shown sometimes to have dramatic effects on people's choices (Thaler and Bernartzi, 2004). We believe that this has implications also for the climate-change problem (see Thaler and Sunstein, 2008). What ultimately matter are the welfare implications, and these cannot always be inferred from revealed behaviour.

The Stern (2007) review clearly uses ethics to justify the low δ, i.e. the pure time preference. However, as pointed out by Beckerman and Hepburn (2007), Dasgupta (2008*b*), and Dietz *et al.* (2009), ethics is involved in choosing the σ-parameter, too. To illustrate, suppose we let $\delta = 0$, and assume, first, that there is no consumption growth in the next 100 years. Those living 100 years from now will then be just as wealthy as we are, no richer and no poorer. A cost of US$1 billion will presumably hurt them just as much as it hurts us, and the costs are therefore given equal weight irrespective of when they occur.

However, if we assume, like Stern (2007), that consumption grows at a rate of 1.3 per cent per year, then those living 100 years from now will be 3.6 times as rich as we are. Hence, a billion-dollar loss will hurt them less in welfare terms (provided that the representative utility function is concave). It is debated whether it is, in principle, possible to observe how much less they will be hurt in welfare terms; this relates to the classical debate about the extent by which it is possible to make interpersonal comparisons of well-being. The literature discussing these parameters assumes interpersonal comparisons, and in this perspective it follows that the larger the σ, the lower the weight to the future, provided that they are richer than we are. Stern (2007) assumes that $\sigma = 1$, so that the marginal utility of income is inversely proportional to income itself. This implies that the well-being of an additional billion dollars today corresponds to the well-being of US$3.6 billion 100 years from now.[6] This also implies that a 1 per cent consumption increase of the rich will *per se* be perceived to be equally as valuable as a 1 per cent consumption increase of the poor. Dasgupta (2008*b*) argues that this puts too little emphasis on the needs of the poor.[7]

We do, however, think that an ethical assessment also needs to take into account the distribution of income *within* each generation (cf. Azar and Sterner, 1996; Anthoff *et al.*, 2009). In particular, climate change will most likely cause the most serious damage to the relatively poor in the future, too. The average income for the poorest third of the world's population is currently around US$500 per year. Assuming a very optimistic consumption growth rate for the poor of 3 per cent annually, the descendants of these people will earn about US$9,600 per year 100 years from now. However, this is still less than the current OECD consumption average of at least US$15,000 per year.[8] This means that if one applies the ethical reasoning behind the Ramsey formula, while ignoring the pure rate of time preference for a moment, then the weight of the future costs (the future poor part of the world) relative to the present costs (in OECD countries) equals $(15,000/9,600)^{\sigma}$ (see Johansson-Stenman, 2005). With $\delta = 0.1$ and $\sigma = 1$, as suggested by Stern, this corresponds to a negative annual discount rate of -0.3 per cent per year. Moreover, with $\delta = 1.5$ and $\sigma = 2$, as suggested by Nordhaus (2007*a*) as the baseline discount rate in his DICE-2007 model, the implied discount rate increases, but only slightly, to 0.6 per cent per year. The reason is that the higher δ is offset by the higher σ, which here implies a higher weight for the future. These simple

[6] Including the pure time preference of Stern, $\delta = 0.1$, one billion today corresponds to four billion 100 years from now.

[7] However, as pointed out by Dietz and Stern (2008), most cost–benefit analyses do not use welfare weights at all, corresponding to $\sigma = 0$.

[8] Based on the GDP *per capita* of US$27,700 from OECD (2005), together with the conservative assumption that consumption constitutes 60 per cent of GDP.

calculations are intended to illustrate the danger of ignoring the distribution within generations when discussing the distribution among generations.[9]

(iii) Summary of the Discount Rate

To summarize our discussion thus far, we would argue that if interest rates are to be determined from the production side, the CAPM would indicate an interest rate that is hardly higher than the risk-free rate, as global warming presumably adds to future uncertainty. While it is not entirely clear how different explanations of the equity premium would change this conclusion, none of those discussed here pulls in the direction of an interest rate above the risk-free rate. Determining the risk-free rate is another matter, where at least treasury bills yield a remarkable low return. From the demand side, the parameters of the Ramsey equation are essential, and some estimates suggest that $\sigma > 1$, and is even closer to 2. On the other hand, self-control issues may lead to overstatements of σ, as people would have liked commitment devices to allow them to save more. Finally, it is not obvious that individual time preferences should be used in matters of distribution among individuals. A high σ then implies a higher discount rate, but also much more emphasis on damages that affect the poor. The latter effect may very well dominate the former, if it is taken into account that the damage of climate change will most likely affect the relatively poor in the future, too.

III. SOCIAL PREFERENCES AND THE BEHAVIOUR OF INDIVIDUALS AND NATIONS

The climate can be seen as a global public good, since we can all benefit from it and we cannot hinder others from benefiting, too. This is also the core of the problem, since what is rational for a single country in isolation is globally suboptimal. If each country has to pay for its own abatement costs of reducing the greenhouse-gas emissions, while all countries now and in the future will share the benefits, then there is clearly room for free-riding so that each country may continue to emit much more than is globally optimal. In order to prevent this, we need multilateral negotiations to obtain a cooperative solution.

By now there is a relatively large game-theoretic literature on negotiations related to transnational pollution (see, for example, Carraro and Siniscalco, 1998; Asheim *et al.*, 2006). Some of this literature concerns repeated games, i.e. that negotiations do not occur only once but several times, and some take into account that the negotiating parties are asymmetric, since some countries are much bigger

[9] We do not suggest that it is necessarily advisable to lump both aspects of distribution into one single parameter. Sensitivity analysis in Stern (2007) also finds that the present value can be non-monotonic in σ.

and more powerful than others. Moreover, parts of the literature concern the possibility for collusions, i.e. that some countries may cooperate against others, and other parts, so-called differential games, deal with both the strategic interaction and the complicated dynamic optimization simultaneously. However, a common denominator in almost all of this literature is the assumption that each negotiating country (or unit) will solely take into account its own material pay-off in the negotiations (Barrett, 2005*b*), which mimics the conventional microeconomics assumption for individual behaviour.

(i) Conditional Cooperation, Reciprocity, and Social Norms

By contrast, in BE there is a large experimental literature at the individual level in which attempts are made to understand under what conditions people cooperate, even when it is not in their own material interest. Many experimental results can be interpreted in terms of *conditional cooperation*, suggesting that many people are willing to choose the cooperative alternative, but only if others do, too (Gächter, 2007). For example, Fischbacher *et al.* (2001) found that a large fraction of subjects increased their contributions in a one-shot public-good game if others did so too. Similarly, and perhaps more importantly given that laboratory environments are rather artificial (Levitt and List, forthcoming), there is much evidence from the field suggesting that people's willingness to contribute to good social causes increases with their perception of the contribution of others. For example, Frey and Meier (2004) analysed the behaviour of students in Zurich who had the opportunity to contribute to two social funds every semester, and found that they gave higher contributions after being informed that many other students were contributing. Shang and Croson (2006) and Alpizar *et al.* (2008) investigated how contributions to good causes (a public radio station and a natural park, respectively) are affected by information about a typical contribution by others; both studies found a positive relationship.

There is also much evidence from laboratory experiments consistent with reciprocity, in the sense that people reward kind and punish unkind actions *towards them* (cf. Rabin, 1993; Falk and Fischbacher, 2006). Note that this meaning of reciprocity does not presuppose that people necessarily reciprocate in order to gain in the long run. On the contrary, Fehr and Gächter (2000*a*) provide much evidence, both from experiments and real life, suggesting that people often reciprocate also in one-shot interactions. Falk (2007) and Alpizar *et al.* (2008) present the only field experiments of which we are aware that study reciprocity directly. Both studies found that people contribute more to charity after a small gift has been given to them. Cialdini (2001) provides a number of real-world examples, from fund raising to politics, where the principle of reciprocity plays an important role. There is also evidence that the perceived kindness of an action is generally not only evaluated in terms of the consequences of the action; perceived intentions matter, too (Dufwenberg and Kirchsteiger, 2004; Falk *et al.*, 2008). Thus, kind actions are less likely to be reciprocated if the intentions behind them are perceived as bad.

Reciprocity can be seen as an example of a rather fundamental *social norm.* Such norms can also be more specific, e.g. the norm to recycle. Environmental labelling, or eco-labelling, is a policy instrument that makes use of people's willingness voluntarily, or perhaps partly influenced by peer pressure, to behave in an environmentally friendly fashion; see Stephan (2002) for an overview. In a situation where people are motivated by social norms, it is important to consider how conventional policy instruments, such as command-and-control and environmental taxes, influence the mechanism of the social norms. Sometimes external policy instruments strengthen the norms, typically denoted a *crowding-in effect*, and sometimes they weaken the norm, i.e. a *crowding-out effect*; see Frey and Oberholzer-Gee (1997), Gneezy and Rustichini (2000), and Brekke *et al.* (2002).

(ii) Individual Cooperation *vs* Group Cooperation

While it is certainly not straightforward to generalize the experimental findings from individuals to a multi-country negotiation setting, we do believe that some of the insights are transferable, if not quantitatively at least qualitatively. First, there is an emerging literature on group decision-making. From this literature, however, it is ambiguous as to whether people become more 'cooperative' in a group decision situation compared to when acting as individual decision-makers. An often-cited reference is Cason and Mui (1997), who found teams to be more altruistic and other-regarding than individuals. However, Luhan *et al.* (2009) argue that the Cason and Mui study constitutes an exception, and that most studies, including their own, find that groups of people are typically less altruistic or cooperative than individuals. On the other hand, Dannenberg *et al.* (2007) found in an experimental study that climate-policy negotiators have stronger preferences for equity compared to students who are typically used as subjects.

Second, there is an economic literature on voting behaviour. The conventional rational-actor voting model has been unsuccessful both in explaining *why* people vote, since the expected benefit from voting is so small compared to the time cost and effort of voting, and in explaining *how* people vote, since there is much empirical evidence that we *do not* solely vote in our own material self-interest (e.g. Mueller, 2003). So, why do we vote? According to Brennan and Hamlin (1998, 2000), one reason is that there is a utility gain from expressing an opinion through voting; see Sobel and Wagner (2004) and Tyran (2004) for empirical and experimental evidence. If the expressive motive is important it also seems more likely that people are more concerned with society as a whole when voting, rather than with what is good solely for themselves. Indeed, as found by, for example, Brekke *et al.* (2002), most people seem to prefer a self-image that reflects social responsibility rather than pure self-concern, and Tyran and Sausgruber (2006) found that self-centred inequality aversion, as suggested by Fehr and Schmidt (1999), can explain much of the voting behaviour in a voting experiment. Taken together, the evidence suggests that the case for actions beyond the narrow self-interest is most likely often present also at the country level, although it is unclear whether or not countries are likely to act more cooperatively than individuals.

(iii) The Darker Side of Human Behaviour

However, it should be emphasized that BE does not only bring good news about human behaviour. For example, there is much systematic evidence in favour of *self-serving bias*. Babcock and Loewenstein (1997) observed that in wage negotiations, both parties (employers and employees) seem to accept that the wage level for comparable groups is a relevant factor in determining local wages. They then asked employers and employees to list comparable work places. Not surprisingly, the average wages at the work places on the employers' list were lower than those on the employees' list. This is one example of the phenomenon that when facts or principles are ambiguous, we tend to pick the ones that favour our own self-interest. Babcock and Loewenstein also found that the larger the differences in wages between the lists, the higher the probability of a conflict in the wage negotiations. Thus, although people typically care quite a bit about fairness, our perception of what is fair tends to be influenced by what is in our own interest, and this often affects our actions, including how we tend to vote. According to Elster (1999, p. 333): '*Most people do not like to think of themselves as motivated only by self-interest.* They will, therefore, gravitate spontaneously towards a world-view that suggests a coincidence between their special interest and the public interest' (italics in original). Although a preference for equity may improve the possibilities for cooperation in climate negotiations (see Lange and Vogt, 2003), this is much less clear when the equity principles used are influenced by self-serving bias (Lange *et al.*, 2007).

Similarly, much evidence suggests that people tend to deceive themselves into believing that they are in various ways 'better' than they really are (Baumeister, 1998), including in ethical issues, in order to improve or preserve their self-image. Related to this, there is evidence that we often try to avoid situations where we know that we will feel the pressure to act in accordance with the norms, e.g. due to shame, if these norms are in conflict with our own material self-interest. For example, Dana *et al.* (2006) offered their subjects the choice between playing a US$10 dictator game and an exit option in which the subject receives US$9 instead of playing the game; if the dictator chose the exit option the receiver was not told about the existence of a game (and a potential sender). Many subjects chose the exit option. Broberg *et al.* (2007) provide similar results. This can obviously not be explained by standard selfish preferences, in which case all subjects should have preferred the US$10 dictator game and kept everything for themselves. Nor can it be explained by a combination of preferences for own pay-offs and pay-offs for the other player (or distribution of pay-offs). Rather, it seems that people dislike it when others think badly of them, even in cases like this when the game was anonymous. Somewhat similarly, Dana *et al.* (2007) provide evidence that when there is a certain amount of uncertainty induced between people's actions and the resulting outcomes, subjects tend to use this 'moral wiggle room' to behave more self-interestedly. This can also imply that people, including policy-makers and politicians, in the richer parts of the world simply try to avoid some of the ethical discussions related to climate change. For example, it is hard to come up with a defendable ethical theory suggesting that just because the poorer countries have emitted less greenhouse gases in the past they are obliged to do so also in the future, unless they are adequately compensated for this.[10] Yet, this is what many global emission reduction plans suggest.

There is also much evidence in favour of what psychologists term 'cognitive dissonance' (Festinger, 1957), which suggests that inconsistency between beliefs and behaviours causes an uncomfortable psychological tension, sometimes implying that people change their beliefs to fit their behaviour, instead of changing their behaviour to fit their beliefs (as is conventionally assumed). With respect to climate, this may imply that people who cause large greenhouse-gas emissions, e.g. many people in the USA, tend to believe that the climate-change problems are overstated; see, for example, Stoll-Kleeman *et al.* (2001). Thus, it may not only be that those who believe that climate change is a serious threat for this reason adapt their behaviour accordingly and emit less; the causality is also likely to go in the other direction.

In addition, there is experimental evidence that people's behaviour in repeated games tends to become less cooperative over time and converges towards the conventional Nash equilibrium, unless there is a possibility of punishing free-riders (Fehr and Gächter, 2000*a*, *b*) so that cooperation can be maintained. Kroll *et al.* (2007) showed experimentally that voting alone does not increase cooperation, but that if voters can punish violators, then contributions increase significantly. On the other hand, Dreber *et al.* (2008) found that costly active (destructive) punishment (as in Fehr and Gächter, 2000*a*, *b*) is far less effective than punishment in terms of lack of continued cooperation (such as tit-for-tat). Ostrom (1990) provides extensive real-world evidence that sanction possibilities are essential for successful common-property resource management, and Gürerk *et al.* (2006) present experimental evidence that people tend to prefer an institution where they have the ability to punish free-riders, compared to an institution without this possibility.

(iv) Implications for Climate Negotiation

Taken together, what can we learn from the BE literature on cooperation for climate negotiations? First, people, and also countries, are able to make decisions

[10] One straightforward way of incorporating an adequate compensation mechanism would be to introduce a global system of tradable permits, where the initial allocation is proportional to the population size in each country. Or, with a very similar distributional implication, impose a global tax on the emission, where the revenues are distributed back in proportion to population size. Furthermore, one may argue that poorer countries should have the right to emit more than the richer countries in the future, in order to compensate for their lower emissions in the past. However, that this appears ethically reasonable (e.g. Kverndokk, 1995) does not, of course, imply that it is politically feasible.

that are not in their own material interest if they have other sufficiently strong reasons for doing so, such as obtaining a situation that is overall socially desirable and if this can be obtained in a way that is perceived as reasonably fair. Second, when individual parties analyse what a fair outcome should look like, they are typically influenced by self-serving bias, and this makes it more difficult to reach agreements. Third, negotiating parties are likely to avoid looking at information that would force them to reflect over ethical issues. A potential policy implication is, therefore, to emphasize such information to the point where it is impossible for the negotiators to ignore it (Nyborg, 2007). Fourth, the possibility of using sanctions and punishments seems essential for the longer term effectiveness of a climate agreement. The Kyoto protocol and the forecasts for the next agreement currently lack this possibility. This serious drawback was emphasized by Barrett (2003, 2007*b*); see also Stiglitz (2006) for a suggestion of linking the climate and trade negotiations, leading to countries that fail to act responsibly in the climate area being punished by tolls. The potential success of the latter strategy is also consistent with the experimental evidence of Dreber *et al.* (2008), but there are, of course, large political obstacles that need to be solved before an effective system of sanctions can be agreed upon.

IV. CONCLUSION

In this chapter we have incorporated some important aspects of BE into the economics of climate change, in particular with respect to the discount rate and climate negotiations. We have argued that the choice of discount rate cannot be disentangled from the explanations of the equity premium puzzle, and that a discount rate closer to the risk-free rate than to the average return on investments is advisable, both when we use the classical CAPM and when a BE explanation of the equity premium is used. We also discussed the ethics of discounting, noting, for example, that climate changes will likely harm the future poor. If the future poor are poorer than the rich are today, then their marginal utility of income would be correspondingly larger, implying a higher weight according to the basic logic behind the Ramsey discounting rule. Overall, there are several reasons why it appears advisable to choose a substantially lower social discount rate than the average return on investments.

We have also discussed climate negotiations where BE has a positive message, as studies have found that humans are less self-serving than the economic man. The evidence suggests, however, that cooperation is conditional, underlining the importance of sanctioning mechanisms in negotiated agreements. Thus, although taking social preferences into account seems to increase the possibilities of obtaining international agreements, compared to the standard model, there are also effects going in the opposite direction, such as self-serving biases.

Naturally, there are many important aspects that lack of space has prevented us from discussing. For example, global climate change implies risks of potentially very substantial damages. Indeed, according to the palaeontologist Peter Ward (2006), in the last 500 million years most life forms on earth simply died out at five different points in time, four of which were probably due to global warming from endogenous (although, of course, not anthropogenic) changes on earth.[11] There is clearly much beyond the standard theory, and beyond what we have touched upon here, to be said about how people react to catastrophic and other risks.

The issue of political feasibility, i.e. what makes people support some measures but not others, is another important area where insights from BE and psychology are important. Moreover, as noted by many great economists in the past (including Adam Smith, John Stuart Mill, Arthur Pigou, and John Maynard Keynes), people do not only derive utility from their absolute income, but also from their income relative to others; see, for example, Brekke and Howarth (2002) and Aronsson and Johanson-Stenman (2008). This suggests that the welfare effects associated with abatement costs may be substantially lower compared to the base case when not taking relative income effects into account.

Finally, researchers are also, of course, affected by the same psychological mechanisms. For example, there is much evidence suggesting a *confirmatory bias*, i.e. a tendency to search for or interpret information in a way that confirms one's preconceptions and to avoid information and interpretations that contradict prior beliefs; see, for example, Rabin and Schrag (1999). While we as scientists tend to think of research as a process where our conclusions follow from our assumptions and perceptions of the world, the existence of confirmatory bias suggests that the link sometimes may go in the opposite direction. This perspective suggests that economists who, for whatever reason, consider it important to take drastic action against climate change today (coincidentally, the authors of this chapter belong to this group), would tend to believe that low parameter values in the Ramsey discounting formula are more appropriate. Similarly, those who believe the climate issue to be overstated, and that there are many other issues that we should prioritize instead, would tend to believe that high parameter values are more appropriate. Of course, we try our best to present balanced arguments, and knowing the difficulty in this we are particularly focused on finding important arguments against our own main conclusion (as other participants in scientific discussions do). Still, we leave it to the readers to judge whether or not we have been affected by confirmatory bias in our arguments for relatively low discount rates. We strongly encourage more research that incorporates BE into the economics of climate change.

[11] The fifth, and the one that killed off the dinosaurs, was according to the same source largely due to a meteor impact. We are grateful to David Hendry for directing us to this research.

Part II

The Global Players and Agreements

7

Climate Change and Africa

Paul Collier, Gordon Conway,** and Tony Venables****

I. INTRODUCTION

Climate change has implications for Africa which are highly distinctive. Its climate is likely to be affected more severely than that of other regions. This is compounded by the far greater exposure of its economy to climatic variation. In contrast to this atypically severe exposure to effects on production, Africa's role in emissions of carbon is atypically minor. Its past economic activity has not contributed to the accumulated global stock of carbon, its current activity accounts for only a trivial proportion of global emissions, and future projections suggest that it will continue to be marginal. Hence, whereas in other regions the key issues concern how to reduce carbon emissions, in Africa they concern the adaptation of production to changing, and mostly deteriorating, opportunities. Further, whereas for other regions the main adverse consequences of global warming occur only far in the future and are uncertain, in Africa many of the adverse consequences are already apparent.

At the root of climate change is global warming caused by anthropogenic emissions of carbon dioxide (CO_2), methane, and other greenhouse gases. The warming occurs worldwide and temperatures are rising on the African land mass and in the surrounding oceans. But Africa is distinctive in the combination of climate-change effects. First, there is evidence that Africa is warming faster than the global average and this is likely to continue. The recent data for Africa are given in Figure 7.1.

Second, because Africa is such an enormous landmass, stretching from about 35°N to 35°S, the climatic effects are very different according to location within the continent: there is no Africa-wide climate effect. Some areas of Africa will become drier, others wetter, and some regions may derive economic benefit, while most are adversely affected. And because mainland Africa is divided into

* Centre for the Study of African Economies, Oxford University.

** Imperial College London and UK Department for International Development.

*** Department of Economics, University of Oxford.

Views expressed are those of the authors and do not represent institutional positions. Thanks to the editorial board of the *Oxford Review of Economic Policy* and to Aditi Maheshwari and Malcolm Smart for helpful comments.

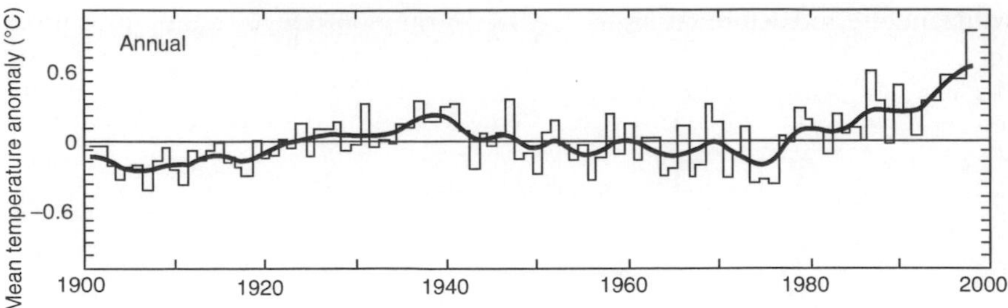

Figure 7.1. African annual mean temperature anomalies °C for the past 100 years

Source: Hulme *et al.* (2001).

50 countries, these geographic variations imply not just some people gain while others lose, but that these redistributions are essentially between countries.

Third, agriculture is the largest single economic activity in Africa, accounting for around 60 per cent of employment and, in some countries, more than 50 per cent of GDP. Some of this activity is already close to the limits of plant tolerance, so changing climate will have an immediate and direct effect, beyond that in many other regions of the world. Charting these likely impact effects is the subject of section II.

The economic consequences of these climate-induced technological changes depend upon human responses. A complex set of changes, most adverse but some advantageous, create scope for reducing the adverse effects and even making some net gains as long as the opportunities for adaptation are fully realized. However, over the past half-century, Africa's economies have not displayed a high degree of adaptability. Although households have considerable experience of coping with temporary shocks, such defensive flexibility has not been combined with sustained ability to adapt to new circumstances or adopt new technologies. At the macroeconomic level, factor reallocation between sectors has been far more limited than in other regions despite the prominence of 'structural adjustment'. One manifestation of this is Africa's continued dependence upon the same narrow range of commodity exports. At the microeconomic level, technical progress has been slower than in other regions, both among farms and manufacturing firms. An implication is that a key reason to fear that the consequences of rising carbon levels will in aggregate be highly adverse for Africa is that adaptation will be inadequate, with contingently adverse effects being realized and opportunities for gain missed. Thus, while attention is usually focused on the overall adverse exogenous effects of climate change on Africa—the region as a victim of circumstances beyond its influence—it might be more important to consider how capacity to adapt can be enhanced. This is the subject of section III.

Globally, attention on climate change is predominantly focused not on adaptation but on carbon and methane emissions and mitigation. While there are some actions that Africans can take to reduce their emissions—particularly to do with land use and deforestation—by far the most important aspects of mitigation for Africa are the implications of the mitigation strategies chosen by the rest of the world. At one extreme, some strategies for global mitigation have serious adverse consequences for Africa and so would be damaging for the region even if they succeeded in arresting global warming. At the other extreme, some strategies create new income-earning opportunities for Africa, although whether these opportunities are harnessed is again contingent upon human response. This is the subject of section IV.

II. IMPACT

Attempting to understand the effects of climate change on Africa is fraught with difficulties. While some things are known and relatively well understood there is still great uncertainty about the key climatic processes. There is also much that is simply unknown.

The African climate is determined at the macro-level by three major global drivers (the Inter Tropical Convergence Zone, the El Niño–Southern Oscillation (ENSO), and the West African Monsoon), but how they interact and how they are affected by climate change is poorly understood. What we can be sure of is that global warming affects their outcomes, increasing the incidence and severity of the droughts, floods and other extreme weather events that they produce. In general, the drier subtropical regions will warm more than the moister tropics. Northern and southern Africa will become much hotter (4°C or more) and drier (precipitation falling by 10–20 per cent or more). In eastern Africa, including the Horn of Africa, and parts of central Africa average rainfall is likely to increase (by 15 per cent or more). In general the best assumption is that many regions of Africa will suffer from droughts *and* floods with greater frequency and intensity. The risk of drought in southern Africa is related to the occurrence of the El Niño phenomenon in the Pacific, and there has been a tendency for these to become more prolonged and frequent (Figure 7.2).

Despite these strong likelihoods, there is much that we do not know. For example, the countries of the Sahel may get wetter or remain dry. The Sahel has experienced many multidecadal periods of drought since the last glaciation (Brooks, 1998). We are in one such period now (Figure 7.3). Whether this current period is another natural episode or is the result of environmental degradation or of global warming we do not know. Probably it is a combination of these factors. Global warming is likely to exacerbate droughts such as these, increasing their frequency and intensity, but whether the current drought will continue is uncertain.

We are also unsure about the future flows of several of Africa's major river systems. Conflicting models of the flow of the Nile suggest it may be greater or less. In the Sahel and in southern Africa even a uniform decrease in rainfall will hit the river flows disproportionately hard. In wetter areas a 10 per cent reduction in

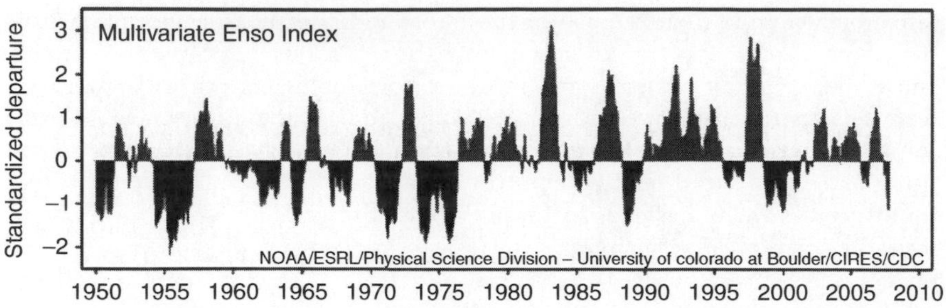

Figure 7.2. The alternation of La Niña (below the line) and El Niño (above the line) events

Note: The Multivariate ENSO Index is based on six variables measured across the Pacific.

Source: Available at http://www.cdc.noaa.gov/people/klaus.wolter/MEI/

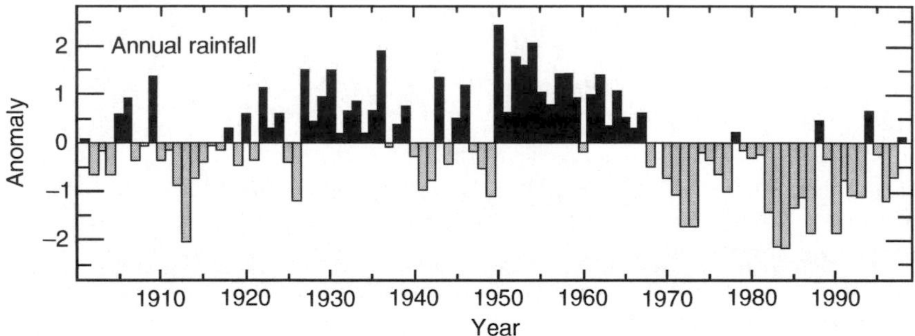

Figure 7.3. Annual rainfall anomalies representing the region 10–20°N; 25°W–30°E, roughly corresponding to the Sahelian zone

Source: Brooks (2004).

rainfall would have virtually no effect on the perennial drainage density, whereas in drier areas, for example in the basins of the Zambezi and the Limpopo, its effect would be far greater than 10 per cent.

How will these climatic changes affect African economies? By far the most important effects will be on agriculture, although these effects are also the least certain. The IPCC concludes that current conditions of chronic hunger are likely to be made worse. This is, in large part, because the proportion of arid and semi-arid lands is expected to increase (by 5–8 per cent by the 2080s) and partly because of depleted water resources. Impacts on agricultural output vary from country to country, with the IPCC projecting reductions in yield in some countries of as much as 50 per cent by 2020, with small-scale farmers most vulnerable (Boko *et al.*, 2007).

Higher temperatures will directly change crop yields. The area suitable for agriculture, the length of growing seasons, and yield potential, particularly along the margins of semi-arid and arid areas, are expected to decrease. Many crops in Africa are grown close to their limits of thermal tolerance. We already know that just a few days of high temperature near flowering can seriously affect yields of crops such as wheat, fruit trees, groundnut, and soybean (Challinor *et al.*, 2006). Such extreme weather is likely to become more frequent with global warming, creating high annual variability in crop production. But more prolonged high temperatures and periods of drought will force large regions of marginal agriculture out of production. The maize crop over most of southern Africa already experiences drought stress on an annual basis. This is likely to get worse with climate change and extend further southwards, perhaps making maize production in many parts of Zimbabwe and South Africa very difficult if not impossible. Wheat yields in North Africa are also likely to be threatened.

These adverse effects need to be combined with the potentially benign 'carbon fertilization effect' on plant growth caused by elevated levels of carbon dioxide. Greenhouse and field chamber experiments show that the carbon fertilization effect is capable of producing substantial increases in yields. But the latest analyses of more realistic field trials suggest the benefits of carbon dioxide may be significantly less than initially thought—an 8–15 per cent increase in yield for a doubling of carbon dioxide for responsive species such as wheat, rice, and soybean; but not all crops are responsive—in particular, maize and sorghum. Hence this offsetting factor may be less than has previously been assumed (Warren *et al.*, 2006). The most significant effect may be in eastern and north-east Africa, where rainfall is likely to rise by 10–20 per cent, and the carbon fertilization could produce higher agricultural productivity. Estimates of yield losses elsewhere (including CO_2 fertilization) are 18 per cent for wheat in northern Africa and 22 per cent for maize in southern Africa (Warren *et al.*, 2006). Proximity to the equator and low elevation amplify negative effects, and in worst affected countries (such as Senegal and Sudan) yield losses reach 50 per cent (Cline, 2008).

In general, the ideal conditions for a crop is evidently crop-specific, and since the existing choice of crops can be presumed to be appropriate for current conditions, changing conditions will tend to reduce yields in the absence of adaptation, but may open as many possibilities as they close once adaptation is considered. While a farmer who continues to grow maize will not benefit from the rising levels of carbon, farmers who switch from maize into a responsive crop and are able to reproduce experimental conditions would reap significant gains.

While the effects on agriculture are likely to predominate, there are three other effects of significance. Higher temperatures, and higher peak temperatures, will also affect health. High peak temperatures (above 30°C) will increase mortality, particularly in large conurbations, although the effect is modest in the overall context of African mortality. The effects via disease will probably be more substantial owing to the increase in disease-carrying insects. For example, the geographical distribution and the rates of development of mosquitoes are highly influenced by temperature, rainfall, and humidity. We may expect an extension of the range of malaria-carrying mosquitoes and malaria into higher elevations, particularly above 1,000 m. There have been resurgences of malaria in the highlands of East Africa in recent years. Many factors are probably involved—poor drug-treatment implementation, drug resistance, land-use change, and various socio-demographic factors, including poverty. But there is also a strong correlation with climate change (Pascual *et al.*, 2006). The temperature in the highlands of East Africa has risen by 0.5°C since 1980—much faster than the global average—and this is correlated with a sharp increase in mosquito populations.

Both malaria and dengue are expected to spread substantially unless countered. Malaria already inflicts enormous costs on Africa, over and above its direct effects on health. Gallup and Sachs (2001) argue that, controlling for other factors, the impact of intensive malaria is to reduce income by two-thirds; a 10 per cent reduction in malaria is associated with 0.3 per cent p.a. higher growth. Hence the spread of malaria, and the concomitant increase in the difficulty of its control, may imply high though currently unquantifiable long-term costs.

The rise in global temperatures will in turn lead to a rise in sea levels, by a metre or more by the end of the century. Such a rise would affect some 6m people in the Nile Delta. Sub-Saharan Africa is likely to be less affected because it does not yet have large urban population concentrations in deltas. Again, however, the extreme sub-division of Africa into many small countries implies that even these modest effects are highly concentrated in a few countries: in Ghana the coastal zone occupies less than 7 per cent of the land area, but contains 25 per cent of the population and so even relatively small rises could have damaging effects on the economy; and the tiny state of Gambia is at risk of having its capital city entirely submerged.

Finally, greater exposure to flooding will have severe effects on infrastructure, most notably on the road system, which is currently predominantly unpaved and therefore particularly vulnerable to erosion from flooding. Although it is not possible to quantify the cost of the increased proneness to climatic shocks, the typical such shock in a developing country reduces GDP in the year of the shock by around 0.4 per cent (Collier and Goderis, 2008*a*).

We now turn to how Africa can best adapt to these changing conditions.

III. ADAPTATION

While most of the effects described above are adverse, some are potentially favourable. The carbon fertilization effect is positive and East Africa appears likely to benefit from wetter climates. However, the most general implication is that the consequences will depend upon the capacity to adapt to change. Even the potentially favourable carbon fertilization effect will not benefit those farmers currently growing non-responsive crops unless they switch to responsive crops. The adverse effects, such as the increased incidence of drought, could have disastrous consequences unless appropriate defensive action is taken. In this section we consider in turn the responses of three distinct classes of actor: the African private sector; the African public sector; and international actors, some regional and others global.

At an overarching level the key effects are changes in the relative productivities of different locations within the region, and an increase in production risk. Adaptation to these effects will predominantly be by private actors and can take three broad forms: people can move location, workers can change sector, or, if they remain in the same sector, they can change technique—the way in which they engage in their economic activity. We first discuss these possibilities, and then discuss how they can be induced.

Evidently, an appropriate response to changes in the relative productivities of location is the relocation of labour and capital towards the relatively favoured places. However, African conditions present several impediments. The movement of people is constrained both by the informal restrictions of strong ethnic identities and the formal restrictions of national boundaries. Africa is even more subdivided into ethnic groups than it is into countries, so that ethnic identities create barriers to movement even within a country. There is currently controversy over the extent to which population movements owing to the drought in the Sahel have contributed to the conflict in Darfur, as pastoralists seeking water resources clash with sedentary arable farmers. Cross-border migration on a mass scale can be stymied by political restrictions, and even where it is permitted has the potential for violent conflict. For example, the movement of population from arid and landlocked Burkina Faso to coastal Côte d'Ivoire at its peak was so large that around 40 per cent of Ivoirian residents were Burkinabe. This facilitated a populist politics that was instrumental in triggering a political collapse into civil war.

Even where people are able to migrate across ethnic or national boundaries, they may not be able to gain access to land. In most of Africa land rights still reflect some ancestral claim and are not readily marketable.

The reduced productivity of many locations is largely specific to agriculture, the sector which accounts for more than 60 per cent of the African labour force: in major parts of Africa farmers are going to be faced by technological regress. Further, the adverse effect of climate change on agriculture is much more pronounced in Africa than in other regions. The climatic variation will be more severe in Africa, and African agriculture is still overwhelmingly rain-fed and so more vulnerable. This has two important implications, one macroeconomic, the other concerning comparative advantage and the inter-sectoral allocation of resources.

The macroeconomic issue is that African economies will become more prone to shocks. Collier and Goderis (2008*b*) analyse which structural policies in factor markets are most appropriate to reduce the macroeconomic consequences of natural disasters. They find that disasters have less severe macroeconomic consequences if employment legislation permits greater flexibility, enabling easier hiring and firing of workers. A related significant structural policy is the case with which firms can be established and closed: greater flexibility reduces the cost of natural calamities. The pay-off to flexibility is substantial. Hence, labour-market liberalization and a lighter regulatory burden on firms look to be appropriate responses to the threat of climate change, although such considerations have been entirely omitted from the now voluminous economic literature on climate change.

The inter-sectoral issue is that climate change will shift Africa's comparative advantage away from agriculture. The efficient response would therefore be to shift resources out of agriculture into other activities that are less vulnerable to climate. Potentially, this socially optimal reallocation of resources will occur simply through normal market processes. However, to date the pace of inter-sectoral resource reallocation has been modest. African economies remain predominantly agricultural because other sectors have not generated many opportunities. Much of the growth in the services sector has been due either to public-sector employment, which is fiscally constrained, or is in informal activities, such as petty vending, which are perhaps more a symptom of limited alternative opportunities than a sign of dynamism. The industrial sector has generally been in relative decline, reflecting the retreat from the costly cul-de-sac of protectionism. In an earlier phase governments attempted to force industrialization through trade restrictions, but domestic markets were far too small for this to be viable. Hence, on the basis of past evidence, technical regress in agriculture is likely to be reflected predominantly in a decline in agricultural incomes rather than in a reallocation of factors to other sectors. This suggests that a policy priority in responding to climate change should be to raise the factor absorption capacity of the non-agricultural sectors.

There is considerable scope for such increased absorption. Export-oriented manufacturing offers a way to achieve this sectoral shift, but Africa has to face the obstacle of the dominance of Asian countries in these markets. To date, many African governments have severely handicapped both industrial and service sectors. One indicator of this poor policy environment is the annual *Doing Business* survey of the World Bank, which provides a wide range of precisely comparable performance measures. Most African countries are far down the international rankings on these measures, implying that all tradable activities, other than those which depend upon locationally specific advantages, are liable to be uncompetitive. Examples of impediments to business are unreliable electricity, long delays at ports, and expensive telecommunications. Other developing regions used to have similar problems, but governments have been more vigorous in addressing them. Even in Bangladesh, where overall governance is very poor, the government has done enough to enable the garments sector to flourish in export markets, resulting in more than two million jobs. Similarly, in India, well-functioning international telecommunications and attention to quality in education have enabled the e-services sector to create millions of export-orientated jobs. Matching these sector-specific policy achievements of Bangladesh and India are surely feasible goals for most African governments. They may well be the most important response to climate change.

Were such a strategy of sectoral reallocation from agriculture to succeed, an implication is that the rate of urbanization would increase. Africa is currently the least urbanized region and would be urbanizing even without climate change, so accelerated urbanization would take it along a well-trodden development path, although possibly at rates of expansion that are exceptionally high. In China such a relocation of population has occurred rapidly and on a massive scale, driven not by climate change but by other reasons for changing relative economic opportunities. Much of this migration has been towards coastal areas, an option impeded in Africa by the extreme sub-division of the continent and the large number of landlocked countries.

While faster inter-sectoral resource allocation is desirable, it is clear that a substantial proportion of the African labour force will remain in agriculture for decades to come. These households will need to adapt their agricultural techniques. Substitutions between crops and crop varieties can reduce income losses and even lead to overall gains. Evidently, substitution should be towards those crops and crop varieties that are most responsive to increased carbon dioxide and those best suited to changed local climatic conditions.

In addition to the trend change in relative yields, there will also be increased year-on-year variability. Adaptation to the increase in production risk could potentially be either through holding relatively liquid assets or through insurance. The liquidity option is problematic. Often financial assets carry negative real interest rates, and real liquid assets either have high costs of storage, such as grain, or are themselves vulnerable to climatic shocks: notably, during a drought the price of livestock will decline owing to synchronized pressures to sell (Dercon, 2002).

In the absence of transactions costs, insurance would always be the first-best response to risk, but it is well understood that agricultural insurance is problematic. Other than through neighbours it is costly to observe effort levels and so there is a severe risk of moral hazard. At the moment, overwhelmingly the most important form of crop insurance in Africa occurs informally, within small communities which can readily observe behaviour. Unfortunately, such neighbourhood insurance is inappropriate for climatic shocks since they are covariant across the community. It may be possible to develop insurance instruments which work in the conditions of rural Africa, such as insurance policies under which specified variation in a local rainfall index will trigger payments. A number of pilots are under way, varying in whether payment is made to government for disaster relief, to individual farmers, or to banks to allow the write-off of farmers' debts. However, designing such insurance contracts requires both that there is a long historical record of climate data, and that this record is expected to be a good guide to future probabilities. The former condition is absent in much of Africa, and the latter is threatened by climate change itself.

Hence, the best available responses to risk may be costly changes in production, notably switching production towards crops that are drought resistant, such as cassava, and spreading production over a wider range of crops—diversification. However, as with all insurance strategies, the greater safety inevitably comes at the loss of average income. A further agricultural adaptation strategy is investment in irrigation. As rainfall becomes lower and more peaked, the return to storing it increases. Farm-level investments in irrigation are not well suited to functioning as collateral because the benefits are highly location-specific, and so credit-constrained households may underinvest.

These adaptations depend upon the decisions of individual firms and households. Will they happen naturally as people learn about rising carbon levels, or should public action attempt to induce them? One reason for believing that much of the adaptation will happen without government inducements is that the impact occurs only very gradually. Private decision-takers are not caught by surprise by some sudden event of which the government has foreknowledge. Private actors are naturally forward-looking and so gradual change need not imply any especial difficulty. However, private actors can be presumed to respond appropriately to changing conditions only if they have adequate information, appropriate incentives, and an economic environment conducive to investing in the required changes. Hence, the most promising strategy for government is to ensure that these three conditions are met.

One key role of the public sector is thus to provide the information and incentives that private actors need in order to induce adaptation. The most information-intensive aspects of adaptation are likely to be changes between crops and crop varieties. It is well understood that the generation of information is an important market failure in smallholder agriculture: the incentives to free-ride are too strong. This is why governments around the world provide agricultural extension services. The need for adaptation increases the pay-off to public agricultural extension services. It also shifts the focus of the related agricultural research from yield-enhancement of existing crops. However, just as individual African farmers face an acute free-rider problem in the financing of research, so do individual African governments: agricultural research in Africa is a regional public good.

In addition to providing information, government needs to ensure that the private sector has the incentive to adapt. In many cases this requires that government (and donors) commit *not* to act. While the public sector should be pro-active in responding to the need for information, it should be cautious in directly trying to mitigate increased risks. In particular, interventions by government or aid donors that soften the consequences of adverse shocks have the inadvertent consequence of weakening the incentive to reduce exposure to them.

In respect of one key public good, the road network, climate change constitutes technical regress. Increased climatic variation, and, in particular, intense bouts of rainfall, can dramatically erode unpaved surfaces. The appropriate response here is to an extent ambiguous. Overall, the return on investment in roads is lower and so the appropriate size of the road network is smaller than would otherwise be the case. However, because the cost of maintaining a road network of any given size increases, the appropriate level of expenditure on roads may well rise. This is just one example of how the provision of public infrastructure will have to be adapted to climate change. As it becomes clearer what form climate change will take in particular countries, so action will have to be taken to 'climate-proof' infrastructure investments.

Are there areas where more direct government intervention in support of adaptation is valuable? The balance here is between market failures that impede the private sector's ability to adjust and public-sector failure. For example, the difficulty faced by credit-constrained farmers in investing in irrigation opens a further role for public provision. In general, the record of African government investment in large-scale irrigation suggests that there are major difficulties with this approach, although there may be more scope for financing smaller scale, local-level cooperation. Potentially, the government could require change by means of effective regulation. However, the history of agricultural regulation in Africa suggests that usually the regulatory route would meet such strong resistance as to have only limited effect. Most African governments lack the administrative capacity to enforce complex agricultural changes that are against the private interests of farmers.

We now turn to international cooperation to assist adaptation, starting with cooperation between governments within the region. As we have argued, the shocks to the region as a whole are considerably smaller than those to individual countries. This suggests that there might potentially be benefits from regional integration, and these could be derived through several different channels. The first is that regional integration might facilitate migration. However, we have already pointed to some of the difficulties here. Even where free movement of labour is part of long term regional integration plans, as in the East African Community, very little progress has been made to date. The second channel is trade. Countries may become more dependent on food trade both because of changing patterns of comparative advantage and because of the need to integrate markets to pool risk. Given the radically higher costs of land transport over sea transport, coastal Africa may be more cheaply integrated into global food markets than into the markets of landlocked neighbours. Further, regional trade in food is proving to be so vulnerable to political intervention that it is unreliable. For example, in response to the rise in global food prices the government of Tanzania has imposed restrictions on food exports to Kenya, despite both belonging to the East African Community. The third potential benefit of regional integration derives from improved cooperation on non-market inter-country linkages, in particular water. While increased rainfall in East Africa may increase flow in the Nile, drier and hotter conditions in Southern Africa may reduce the flow of the Zambezi significantly. There is potential for inefficient and inequitable water use—and, ultimately, conflict—unless regional cooperation is established.

International actions to assist African adaptation have both an ethical and a practical rationale. The ethical rationale is evidently that the rising levels of carbon dioxide are not attributable to Africa but to economic activity elsewhere, and so there is a strong case that the costs of African adaptation to these adverse externalities should be borne by others. In practical terms, some of the public goods required for adaptation are regional in nature, such as climate information, agricultural research, and transport infrastructure. Africa's extreme political subdivision means that it faces intense problems in supplying regional public goods, and international assistance can usefully substitute for these missing public goods. Assistance for adaptation also needs to be seen more broadly in the context of development policy. Climate change is likely to make development more difficult and diversification out of agriculture more necessary. This suggests that

OECD trade preferences for African non-agricultural exports might become more important (Collier and Venables, 2007). Aid flows might need to be reallocated between sectors to support such diversification, and reallocated geographically to target those societies most severely affected. Finally, the most elementary step would be for the international community to do no harm. The prohibition by the European Union of genetically modified crops has slowed African use of genetic modification lest it precludes exports to Europe. Yet genetic modification is a useful means of speeding African agricultural adaptation.

IV. MITIGATION

Historically and to the present day Africa has made little contribution to the stock of greenhouse gases in the atmosphere. Data for *per capita* emissions of CO_2—excluding land-use change—indicate that in most African countries emissions are less than 0.5 tonnes *per capita*, one-twentieth that of the UK. Sub-Saharan Africa, with 11 per cent of the world's population, accounts for just 3.6 per cent of world emissions of CO_2e (CO_2 equivalent), reflecting low levels of income and of energy consumption.

Nevertheless, mitigation is an important topic for Africa, for two reasons. The first is that the mitigation response of the rest of the world will have an impact on Africa. Future international frameworks for mitigation, in particular for emissions trading, create opportunities for Africa. And even without this channel, energy-related innovation and changes in the prices of fuels and other goods will change the economic and technological opportunities open to Africa. The second reason is that there is one area where Africa is fast becoming a major greenhouse-gas emitter. This is from land-use change, in particular deforestation (Figure 7.4) for which Africa now accounts for 20 per cent of world emissions (with world emissions from land-use change amounting to around 20 per cent of total anthropogenic emissions). Much of this comes from land-use change in the Congo basin, in particular the Democratic Republic of the Congo. A framework is needed that balances lower carbon emissions with productive use of forest areas, and which can operate in politically difficult environments.

We look first at the design of international mitigation frameworks and their treatment of deforestation, turning then to the impact on Africa of mitigation in the rest of the world.

Under an idealized cap-and-trade emissions-trading scheme, each citizen would be endowed with a right to emit a specified quantity of CO_2e (or each country endowed with the corresponding national total) and would be able to sell rights in excess of own emissions. Were emissions monitorable at the level of the individual citizen or country, such a scheme would provide incentives for reductions in CO_2e. Depending upon the allocation of emissions rights, it might also create a distinct channel for resource flows to low-emission countries. In the hypothetical extreme in which each person was endowed with the

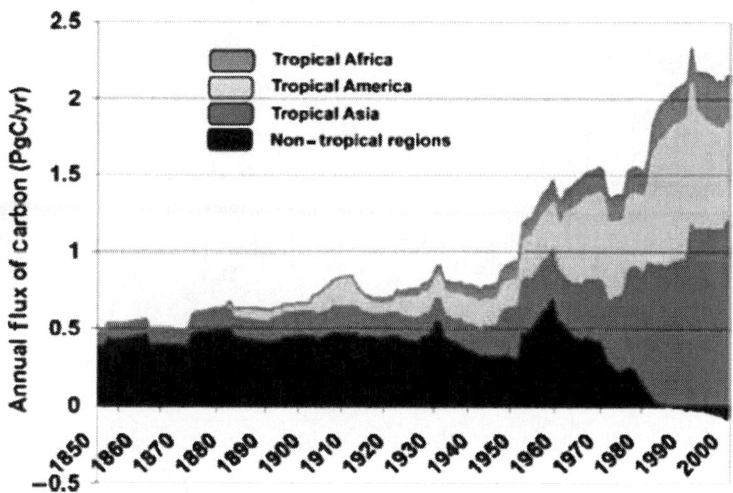

Figure 7.4. Annual emissions of carbon from changes in land use

Note: Vertical axis is gigatonnes carbon (1 Pg of C = 1 GT of C). One gigatonne of carbon is 3.67 GT of CO_2.
Source: Houghton (2005).

same emission rights, the financial flows to Africa resulting from sales of carbon rights might be of comparable size to its current aid receipts of around $40 billion p.a.[1] In effect, the allocation of carbon rights to Africa would *become* its aid programme. The abrupt creation of such valuable rights without reference to existing patterns of usage is, of course, entirely implausible. Somewhat more realistically, 'contraction and convergence' schemes propose national emissions quotas that would start from current levels and very slowly converge—over several decades—to being proportional to population. Since, over this time frame, international economic convergence would substantially reduce disparities in usage, the redistributive aspect of carbon trading would be correspondingly reduced.

While a new channel for massive transfers to Africa may appear attractive both to African governments and to aid advocates, it is likely to prove illusory. A realistic political economy of public international financial transfers would suggest that transfers through emissions trading might largely substitute for existing financial transfers rather than supplement them, since both provide budgetary resources. Such a switch might be welcomed by African governments: in particular, it would release them from conditionality. In effect, were Africa to export carbon rights the revenue consequences would be analogous to the export of oil. Unfortunately, to date, Africa's oil revenues have been less well used than its aid receipts, so this substitution need not be beneficial (Collier, 2006). Further, while the allocation of aid within the continent is purposive and so broadly related to need

[1] If two tonnes of CO_2e per head were sold at US$30 per tonne.

and governance, revenues from carbon rights would be unrelated: Angola would receive approximately as much *per capita* as Uganda.

In between entitlements based on existing usage and equal entitlements *per capita*, is an equal entitlement per unit of GDP. This would create an incentive to reduce the carbon-intensity of GDP without discouraging the growth of GDP itself. For example, it would penalize a carbon-profligate economy, such as America, and reward a carbon-efficient economy, such as France. Unfortunately, on this metric Africa looks like America. Its low carbon emissions are entirely due to its poverty: its structure of income generation is highly carbon-intensive.

While the above arrangements are hypothetical, the Clean Development Mechanism (CDM) already functions as an institution by which developing countries can earn income from reducing CO_2e emissions. Unfortunately, Africa barely participates in this scheme. Of the US$2–US$3 billion p.a. currently being traded through the CDM, just 2 per cent of payments go to Africa. Even this grossly overstates the participation of low-income Africa. As of January 2008 there were 21 CDM projects in Africa (out of around 1,000 worldwide), all except two of which were in either North African countries or South Africa (the exceptions being a gas-recovery project in Nigeria and the West Nile Electrification project in Uganda).

There are several reasons for the virtual absence of the CDM in low-income countries across Africa. One is limited African capacity to prepare or implement credible CDM proposals. Such proposals require detailed and complex project documents, construction of baselines, and arrangement of the financial packages necessary for CDM participation. CDM projects often have elements of foreign direct investment and attracting such investments requires that the investment climate as a whole is attractive, a factor lacking in many African countries. As a market mechanism the CDM has attracted large-volume/low-cost sources of emissions, and most African countries do not have the volume to justify the high transactions costs. Another reason is that, within the CDM, the approved methodologies for project selection are heavily biased towards energy and industrial and synthetic gas sectors, all areas in which Africa has relatively little presence. On the energy side, Africa has potential for hydro, for reducing energy losses in transmission and distribution, and for unconventional schemes for using natural sources of methane as a power source. Yet none of these is easily handled by existing CDM methodologies. Deforestation remains outside the CDM, and afforestation/reforestation projects are not accepted by the European Union Emissions Trading Scheme (EU ETS)—the world's largest carbon market.

To move forward, several lines of action are needed. The first is to develop African capacity to participate in the CDM as presently constituted. There is a role here both for knowledge dissemination and for skills development. Aid has a role in providing technical assistance for project preparation and also in levering finance for environmental projects.

The second is to broaden the CDM to include a wider range of potential African projects—in the power sector, waste disposal, and, above all, in avoided deforestation. At present afforestation and reforestation schemes are eligible for the CDM, but forest management and conservation projects are excluded. The difficulty of handling avoided deforestation illustrates clearly the fundamental design problems of the CDM. A CDM project requires a 'baseline scenario' or counterfactual against which payments can be made. For a forest project this is the rate at which the particular area of forest would be cut down in the absence of the CDM intervention. There is no reasonable way to establish such a baseline; and, if there were, it would create perverse incentives as people sought to signal that—in the absence of CDM project status—they would have been likely to cut down the forest. The project-level basis of the CDM also creates acute problems of 'leakage'; preserving one area of forest is of no value if another area is cut down instead. These arguments point to the need to switch from a project-based to a programmatic approach. Such an approach would operate at a much wider level than separate projects, perhaps at the national or regional level. The baseline could be constructed on the basis of estimates of historical emissions, and payments made for emissions reduction below these baseline levels.

Steps in this direction are being taken by the Forest Carbon Partnership Facility, based at the World Bank, which has two elements. The first is to assist countries in building up estimates of the baseline levels of their current forest stocks and forest emissions. The second is to pilot national schemes for reducing forest emissions below baseline levels. Under such schemes countries would receive payment if actual forest emissions were below the baseline. Of course, many problems remain; even if a government is participating in such a scheme and has set targets for reduced forest emissions, there are still problems both in monitoring outcomes and in enforcing measures to reduce deforestation. Any scheme which depends upon government preventing people from taking up profitable opportunities may require a degree of effective and honest governance beyond the capacity of many African governments.

While carbon-trading arrangements will create incentives for mitigation within Africa, Africa will also be affected by the mitigation efforts of the rest of the world. There are two main channels. One is a diversion effect, arising as developed countries switch their patterns of expenditure in pursuit of lower carbon consumption. The other is a creation effect, as technological change raises the efficiency of new green technologies.

The diversion effect is already evident. One manifestation is consumer concern with 'food miles' and the potential damage that this could do to African suppliers of non-traditional agricultural exports. Another more important one is changes in relative prices, including the current high prices of cereals and many other food crops. While the main factors driving the higher prices are increased food consumption (particularly in Asia, with associated use of cereals as animal feed) and drought in some food-producing regions, the conversion of food-producing land to biofuel production is a further element. Ten per cent of world maize production now goes to biofuel production, and the startling fact is that, with current technology, the opportunity cost of filling the tank of an SUV with gasoline is enough food to feed a person for a year. Since Africa is a net food importer, these price changes are having a significant negative effect on the terms of trade of many African countries. The fundamental problem here is not with biofuel production *per se*, but with the fact that production subsidies in some OECD countries are causing inappropriate biofuel crops to be grown in the wrong places. In the USA biofuel production displaces maize otherwise destined for food supply. In contrast, the opportunity cost of Brazilian biofuel production from sugar cane is much lower, while in Mozambique just 9 per cent of arable land is at present cultivated, and much of the rest is suitable for biofuel production from sugar cane or jatropha with little or no impact on food production.

On the technology side, world mitigation efforts will lead to a shift in the pattern of R&D towards the development of low-carbon energy sources. This is a slow-moving process that will affect a very wide range of technologies. New biofuels will use more advanced technologies (cellulosic or algae based) with much less impact on food production. There are prospects for much improved plant varieties, possibly genetically engineered, able to cope with drought and other environmental changes. In some areas there may be a prospect of technological 'win–wins' for Africa. The analogy is sometimes made between new green technologies doing for electricity supply what mobile telephones did for communications in Africa. Instead of having to invest in landlines—or large-scale power-distribution networks—decentralized power supply based on small-scale hydro or solar power might be able to bring power to new areas in a manner that is both greener and cheaper. Whether such 'win–win' technologies will emerge remains unclear, although two general points can be made. One is that Africa may have a latecomer advantage, and be able to leapfrog technologies that are in use in the developed world, going straight to more efficient technologies in a number of areas. The other is that, while new technologies will be developed in high-income countries, adapting them to be suitable for Africa is likely to involve some costs, and will remain bedevilled by the small size of African markets.

V. CONCLUSIONS

Climate change is not a problem of Africa's making, yet parts of Africa stand to be particularly hard hit because of their geography, their agricultural dependence, and because of difficulties that adaptation will face, as outlined in this chapter. These observations point to a range of actions that need to be pursued by African governments and by the international community.

In the long term, world mitigation that is effective in stabilizing atmospheric levels of CO_2 will be valuable to Africa, as it will for the rest of the world. For the next half-century the key development issues are African adaptation to future climatic deterioration and opportunities for African participation in schemes for mitigation. World mitigation efforts will also affect Africa indirectly via price effects and technical change. Here, as in other contexts, production subsidies to OECD farmers can damage developing country interests. Shaping new technologies so they are applicable in Africa, and developing regions more widely, may require public financial support.

The impact of climate change is already being felt in Africa and strategies for facilitating adaptation need to be developed. The private sector has been adapting to technical progress for centuries, but will now have to adapt to technical regress in some areas. The role of government is primarily to supply information, to maintain incentives, and to increase the flexibility of the economic system both to secular change and to short-run shocks. There is also a public role for support for agricultural research, and there will be growing demands on public expenditure as it becomes necessary to design infrastructure to cope with a harsher climate.

In addition to their mitigation responsibilities, developed countries and the donor community must recognize that climate change will make poverty reduction objectives more difficult and more expensive. There will be direct financial burdens (e.g. from infrastructure needs) and a particular role for donors in providing the regional public goods which Africa lacks.

8

China's Balance of Emissions Embodied in Trade: Approaches to Measurement and Allocating International Responsibility

Jiahua Pan, Jonathan Phillips,** and Ying Chen****

I. INTRODUCTION

Thirty years after its 'opening and reform', China has earned its reputation as the 'factory of the world'. China's rise to become, according to some reports,[1] the largest single emitter of greenhouse gases is closely linked to its economic growth, and particularly the export sector that has driven this growth. Export volumes accounted for 40 per cent of GDP in 2006, with the majority consisting of intermediate or consumption goods destined for developed countries' markets. Under current Kyoto Protocol accounting rules, the emissions associated with these exports are fully attributable to China, since they took place within its territory. As China and other developing exporters watch their emissions increase rapidly relative to the OECD countries, they are beginning to question why they are criticized for such rising emissions by the very consumers whose market demands they are supplying. On top of their historic responsibility for cumulative emissions, a central question for a post-Kyoto framework is whether developed countries should take responsibility for a portion of *current* emissions from developing exporters like China. This is an

* Research Centre for Urban and Environmental Studies, Chinese Academy of Social Sciences.
** Overseas Development Institute, London.
*** Research Centre for Sustainable Development, Chinese Academy of Social Sciences.

This chapter is based on a study on embodied energy with financial support from the World Wide Fund for Nature China Office and the Chinese Academy of Social Sciences. The authors would like to acknowledge with thanks the research assistance and discussion provided by Laihui Xie, Yan Zheng, and Olivia Macdonald. In the process of research, the authors benefited from comments from experts from the China Institute of International Trade, the Energy Bureau of the National Development and Reform Commission of China, and Research Centre on Environmental Policy of the Ministry of Environmental Protection, and from participants in workshops in Bali, Beijing, Washington, DC, and Berlin during the period from September 2007 to November 2008. However, remaining errors are the sole responsibility of the authors.

[1] Netherlands Environmental Assessment Agency (2007); see also IEA (2007*a*).

argument that was raised by senior Chinese officials at the Bali conference in December 2007.[2]

This chapter makes three contributions to our understanding of the role of Chinese trade in the response to climate change. First, it estimates the scale of emissions embodied in China's current trade pattern, demonstrating the magnitude of the difference between emissions accounts based on production rather than consumption. In doing so, it extends the range of country studies carried out (for example, Machado *et al.* (2001) on Brazil and Mukhopadhyay (2004) on India) and complements international comparative studies (Ahmad and Wyckoff, 2003; Ward, 2005). We show that China was a net exporter of 1,660 mt of carbon dioxide (CO_2) in 2006, a figure that is growing rapidly. These emissions are incurred to support consumption elsewhere, but establishing specific counterfactuals is difficult since production patterns and energy intensities are endogenous to historical development trajectories. However, for illustration, directly transferring responsibility for emissions from producer to consumer would have raised US CO_2 emissions by 2.6 per cent in 2002.

Second, the chapter improves on the methodologies used in previous studies of China, including Shui and Harriss (2006), and Li Hong *et al.* (2007), Wang and Watson (2007), by taking account of total energy intensity in upstream production and changes in energy intensity over time. This illustrates that a reliable consumption-based accounting methodology is feasible and could improve our understanding of emissions responsibility in a post-Kyoto framework. Third, it assesses the economic factors, national policies, and international frameworks that explain the current pattern of emissions in trade. While producers' locational decisions have been influenced by Chinese policies such as a depressed exchange rate and export tax rebates, we argue that complementary policies of deindustrialization in developed countries, trade liberalization, and the failure to harmonize international climate-change policy have also contributed to the emissions surplus.

These considerations lead us to conclude that, if Chinese production has merely substituted for production in developed countries, recent emissions reductions in developed countries may lack credibility. Reported Kyoto emissions performance may be a poor guide to the sacrifices that countries are making and the actual environmental impact of their consumption activities. Attributing full responsibility to China (and other developing countries) for historical emissions surpluses may then be unfair according to some normative criteria. Further, the current Kyoto production methodology does not create appropriate incentives for *global* decarbonization, but permits extensive leakages through trade. Consequently, as the distribution of abatement efforts comes to the fore in post-Kyoto negotiations, we stress that close attention should be paid to emissions embodied in trade

[2] The issue was first raised on 4 June 2007 by Ma Kai, Director of the National Development and Reform Commission, at a press conference on China's National Programme on Climate Change. It was reiterated at the Bali conference by his deputy, Xie Zhenhua, the head of the Chinese delegation to the 13th Conference of Parties to the United Nations Framework Convention on Climate Change (UN FCCC) Serving as the 3rd Meeting of the Parties to the Kyoto Protocol (COP13/MOP3).

if future methodologies are to be simultaneously equitable and able to provide effective abatement incentives.

Section I summarizes alternative emissions accounting methodologies and provides a framework for understanding the multiple effects of an expansion of trade on emissions. Section II estimates the emissions embodied in Chinese trade and national emissions on an alternative (consumption accounting) basis. Our methodology and results are also contrasted with previous studies. Section III discusses how we might efficiently and equitably re-assign responsibility for these emissions, evaluating the merits of a consumption basis for emissions accounting.

II. ACCOUNTING FOR GREENHOUSE-GAS EMISSIONS

(i) Trade and Emissions

There are many links between international trade and emissions, including direct effects from transportation and more subtle links from foreign investment and ownership. In this chapter we focus only on the emissions embodied in traded goods themselves. The expansion of international trade has led to a significant divergence between the incidence of production and consumption. Just as countries with a balance-of-trade surplus export more than they import, countries run a surplus on the balance of emissions embodied in trade (BEET) where the emissions involved in producing the goods they consume (including those produced abroad) are less than the emissions from domestic production.

However, there are a number of differences between trade in goods and in emissions. First, the two do not always coincide—a country running a trade deficit could nevertheless have an emissions surplus if its exports embodied more CO_2 per unit of value than its imports. Second, there are equilibrating forces at work in goods markets to ensure countries cannot remain net goods importers or exporters in the long run (even if recent experience suggests imbalances can be prolonged and large). By contrast, these adjustments are impotent in the emissions trade as there are no international mechanisms to enforce settlement of 'loaned' emissions. Additionally, intertemporal balancing of trade accounts need not imply balancing of emissions accounts, since technological advances imply future production will be less carbon-intensive. So a country may be a net emissions importer without ever having to be a net emissions exporter.[3] Third, while there are well-developed accounting systems for valuing the level of trade, measuring the emissions embodied in goods along a global value chain is still a nascent discipline.

[3] Since an emissions deficit in one country is a surplus for another country, this cannot imply a reduction in global emissions, but does affect the distribution between countries.

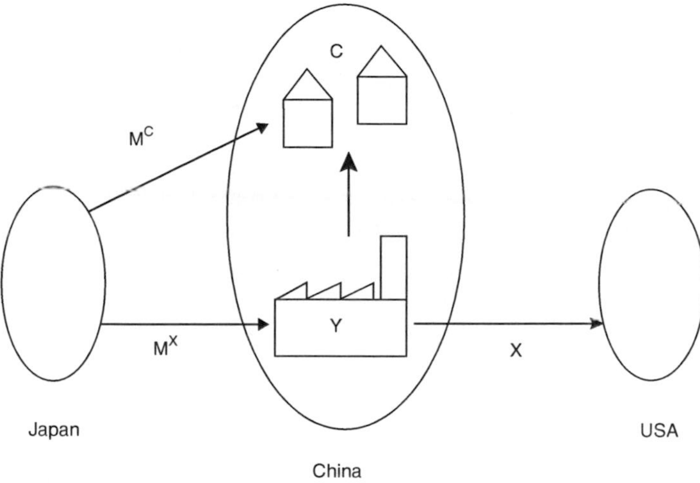

Figure 8.1. Components of emissions embodied in trading relationships

(ii) The Components of Different Emissions Accounting Bases

If trade in emissions does not coincide with trade in goods, it is important to understand how traded emissions can be estimated. Figure 8.1 illustrates the components of emissions embodied in trading relationships. On a production basis—the prevailing Kyoto methodology—emissions are attributed to countries on the basis of territory; all emissions from China's *domestic* production, labelled Y, are included. Domestic production includes goods exported for foreign consumption, X, and the emissions associated with their production are the emissions embodied in exports. Symmetrically, imported goods M^C, though consumed domestically, embody emissions from production processes that take place abroad.

In evaluating emissions on a *consumption* basis, we mean the emissions embodied in the complete production process of goods consumed by an entity, regardless of the geographical location of production. As Figure 8.1 illustrates, in moving from the production to the consumption account, it is therefore necessary to subtract emissions embodied in exports and attribute them to recipient countries (in this example, the USA, as the largest export partner), while adding emissions embodied in imports (in this example, Japan, as the largest import partner).

The principal complication illustrated in Figure 8.1 is that some imports, M^X, may be inputs to domestic production of goods that are subsequently exported. We describe this as the 'processing trade' and attribute the emissions embodied in these imports (and any additional emissions embodied in their processing for export) to the country consuming the final exports (the USA in this case). Hence, imports for consumption must be included in the consumption account, but imports for the processing trade must be excluded.

When dealing with many sectors of the economy, estimation of both accounting bases must combine data from input-output tables with emissions-intensity data. We explain the measures algebraically below.

In goods terms, the output vector Y_i of any sector i can either be used as an input to another sector j, forming the matrix Y_{ij}, or, for final use, forming the vector Z_i, which includes consumption, investment, and exports. Final use of all goods, excluding imports, is then represented by Z. This allows us to write sectoral domestic output as the vector $Y_i = \sum_{j=1}^{n} Y_{ij} + Z_i = \sum_{j=1}^{n} a_{ij} \cdot Y_i + Z_i$ where the matrix $a_{ij} = \frac{Y_{ij}}{Y_i}$ is the direct use coefficient. The Leontief Matrix, A, of a_{ij} represents the economy-wide production function. Total domestic output is then given by the scalar $Y = (I - A)^{-1}Z$, where $(I - A)^{-1}$ is the Leontief inverse matrix.[4]

We define the *direct* unit emissions intensity of production processes within a sector as the vector $S_i = \frac{E_i}{Y_i}$ (where E_i represents aggregate sectoral emissions). The Leontief inverse matrix can then be used to construct the *total* unit emissions intensity vector $\hat{S} = S \cdot (I - A)^{-1}$, taking into account embodied emissions in the upstream value chain.

On a production basis, emissions are measured as $E^P = \hat{S} \cdot Z$: total emissions intensity per unit of output multiplied by output for final use. Note that E^P includes emissions from production for export but excludes emissions embodied in imports.

There are two complications in extending this model to the consumption accounting basis. First, goods exports $X = \sum_1^n \sum_1^G X_{ig}$ and imports $M = \sum_1^n \sum_1^G M_{ig}$ for each sector i are assessed over G countries.[5] The gross emissions embodied in exports are given by the scalar $E_X = \hat{S} \cdot X$. However, to get an estimate of the exported emissions *from domestic production* it would be necessary to subtract imported goods that make up the processing trade. This would be achieved using the import coefficient matrix $N_i = M_i/(Z_i + M_i - X_i)$ to obtain the vector $\hat{S}' = S \cdot (I - (I - N)A)^{-1}$, which we term the *total domestic* unit emissions intensity. Thus, our estimate of exported emissions from domestic production would be the scalar $E_{X'} = X \cdot \hat{S}'$. However, in the absence of sectoral level data on the break-down between imports used for the processing trade and the proportion of export value that this accounts for, we use the gross measure E_X. While this is a limitation of the analysis, inducing over-estimation of exported emissions, the magnitude of the error is limited by the concentration of exports in sectors such as textiles that are only partially dependent on the processing trade. Additionally, the bias is counteracted by the re-importation of some goods into China, which may be wrongly incorporated at foreign rather than Chinese emissions intensity.

Second, since imports arrive from many countries with varying emissions intensities of production, an accurate estimate of imported emissions would

[4] I represents the identity matrix.

[5] Note that M here includes all imports, whether for domestic consumption or the processing trade.

be the scalar $\hat{M} = \sum_1^G \sum_1^n S_{ig} \cdot M_{ig}$. However, sectoral-level emissions-intensity data for every trade partner are not readily available. Some studies of ecological footprints, for example Li Hong *et al.* (2007), have made the simplifying 'import substitution' assumption that the emissions intensity of foreign production is equivalent to domestic production, such that $\hat{M}^* = \sum_1^n S_i \cdot M_i$. This approach fails to capture potentially important national differences in both the energy intensity of foreign production and the carbon intensity of energy consumption. The compromise we adopt here is to assume that the national average emissions intensity is representative of that country's exported goods, so $\hat{M}' = \sum_1^G S_g \cdot M_g$. Imported emissions are then represented by the scalar $E_{M'} = M' \cdot \hat{S}$. The limitation of this approach is that bilateral trade is often concentrated in particular sectors which may be more or less intensive than the national average. Specialization according to comparative advantage would reduce the risks of divergence, but in practice such specialization is incomplete.

Drawing these arguments together, emissions measured on a consumption basis can be expressed as the scalar $E^C = E^P - E_X + E_{M'}$. The difference between the production and consumption estimates, the scalar $E^B = E^P - E^C$, represents the BEET.[6] This is our estimate of emissions that take place in Chinese territory but are *not* attributable to Chinese consumption. Equivalently, it is a measure of emissions attributable to foreign consumption.

(iii) Decomposing Changes in the BEET

Whether a country has a BEET in deficit or surplus depends on whether the goods it consumes embody more or less emissions than the goods it produces. To understand the economic *causes* of any imbalance, we extend Copeland and Taylor's (1994) decomposition of changes in production emissions to more than one polluting sector. Produced emissions by sector are represented by the vector $E_i^P = \hat{S}_i \cdot Z_i$ and both vectors S_i and Z_i can be rewritten to reflect economy-wide values weighted by the share of the sector in emissions, $\hat{S}_i$, and output, z_i, such that $E_i^P = (\hat{S} \cdot \frac{\hat{S}_i}{\hat{S}}) \cdot (Z \cdot \frac{Z_i}{Z}) = (\hat{S} \cdot \hat{s}_i) \cdot (Z \cdot z_i)$. We rewrite $\hat{s}_i \cdot z_i = d_i$, which is the weighted average share of output of a sector, where the weights are the relative emissions of the sector. The vector d_i serves as an index of the concentration of the economy in relatively emissions-intensive or low-emissions activities. Then $E_i^P = \hat{S} \cdot d_i \cdot Z$ for a sector, and $E^P = \hat{S} \cdot d \cdot Z$ for the economy. This can be approximated in differential form as $\Delta E^P = \Delta\hat{S} + \Delta d + \Delta Z$.

This shows that a change in production emissions can be decomposed into (i) a technology effect from changes in the emissions intensity of production; (ii) a composition effect, reflecting the share of 'dirty' versus 'clean' sectors in total output; and (iii) a scale effect from the growth or contraction of the economy. Each effect assumes all other factors are held constant; for instance, if emissions

[6] See Muradian *et al.* (2002).

intensity and the size of the economy are stable, production emissions may still increase if 'dirty' sectors—those that have higher emissions intensities than average—are expanding, while 'clean' sectors are contracting.

The same decomposition can be applied to consumption emissions. The three components remain, but their interpretation now refers to changes in the technology, composition, and scale of *consumed* goods. We argue, therefore, that the BEET will evolve to reflect the *differences* between production and consumption in a country along these three effects.

(i) *Technology effects*: Progress made in reducing emissions intensity in domestic industry may differ from other countries. A rise in the BEET may therefore reflect faster technical progress in abatement by import partners relative to domestic production.

(ii) *Composition effects*: If domestic production is shifting towards emissions-intensive sectors, while consumption goods maintain a relatively stable emissions intensity, the BEET will grow. Trade facilitates this decoupling of production and consumption, and comparative advantage suggests that specialization is likely to push an economy towards concentration in particular sectors that may be above or below the emissions intensity of consumption.

(iii) *Scale effects*: The BEET will be growing where the scale of production is increasing faster than the scale of consumption. This situation represents a growing balance-of-trade surplus. So while trade imbalances in the goods and emissions contexts need not coincide, a trade surplus in goods makes it more likely that a country will have a surplus BEET.

A surplus BEET must be offset by a deficit elsewhere, and the above effects therefore describe the *distribution* of emissions between countries. However, the literature has also identified potential reasons for aggregate changes in emissions arising from trade. First, if trade shifts out the global production possibility frontier, the increased economic activity may have a 'global scale effect', boosting both production and emissions. Offsetting this expansion of emissions there may be an income effect that increases the demand for low-emissions production. This depends on an endogenous policy response and the turning point of the relationship, labelled the Environmental Kuznets Curve (EKC), varies significantly between countries and pollutants, and also depending on the 'deep' determinants of trade, such as factor endowments and distance between markets (Brock and Taylor, 2004).

Second, composition effects need not be zero-sum; while trade could lead to specialization by one country in emissions-intensive production, it could also allow each country to specialize in the goods it produces most efficiently. As Hayami and Nakamura (2002) found for trade between Japan and Canada, 'global composition effects' may reduce both countries' emissions, with Japan exporting manufactured goods it produces at very low energy intensity and Canada exporting energy-intensive products using energy from hydroelectric power with a very low carbon intensity. Such efficiency gains are more likely where emissions are appropriately and universally priced, so that specialization takes into account a country's carbon efficiency. Where there are asymmetries between countries' environmental policies, the 'pollution haven effect' may arise. In this case, the location of dirty industries is determined by lax environmental policy and not just comparative advantage. Not only could this concentrate dirty industry in particular countries and increase their BEET, it could also produce an aggregate increase in emissions by undermining the global composition effect. In practice, variation in labour costs, political risk, and the stage of industrialization (Pan, 2008) are likely to be overwhelming influences on locational decisions, but we merely wish to argue that trade plays an ambiguous role in shaping both the distribution and total level of emissions, particularly where environmental policies are not harmonized.

Third, trade facilitates a diffusion of technology that can produce a 'global technology effect' as best practices diffuse, and may even spur greater technological progress.

The net impact of these effects is ambiguous; free trade is neither inherently good nor bad for the environment, and changes in a country's BEET depend on patterns of trade that are shaped by comparative advantage and national economic policies.

III. CHINA'S EMISSIONS EMBODIED IN TRADE

(i) Data Sources

The key data for estimating China's emissions using an input-output methodology are the *Input-Output Tables of China in 2002* (NBS, 2006). We use energy consumption data from the *China Statistical Yearbooks* (NBS, various years) and carbon intensity data from the International Energy Agency (IEA) and the World Resources Institute (WRI). In the absence of comprehensive data on energy sources, we assume that the carbon intensity of energy use for exports is the same as for domestic production and the same across sectors. Data on trade in goods are sourced from the UN Commodity Trade Statistics. Matching data sources required the classification of 122 sectors in the input–output tables and the Standard International Trade Classification (SITC) into the 37 traded sectors in the energy consumption statistics.

(ii) Energy-intensity Calculations

Following the methodology in section I, Table 8.1 details the direct (S) and total ($\hat{S}$) energy intensities for a selection of sectors and across the economy in 2002, the same year for which we have comprehensive input–output tables. It illustrates

Table 8.1. Selected energy-intensity measures by sectors in China, 2002

	Direct energy intensity (tce/10,000 yuan)	Total energy Intensity (tce/10,000 yuan)
Farming, forestry, animal husbandry, fishery	0.23	0.80
Manufacture of textiles	0.33	1.54
Extraction of petroleum and natural gas	1.38	1.90
Smelting and pressing of ferrous metals	1.71	3.45
Raw chemical material and chemical products	1.38	3.07
Electronics and communications equipment	0.06	1.17
Average energy intensity in all 43 sectors	0.42	1.08
Average energy intensity in 37 traded sectors	0.57	1.13

the increase from direct to total energy intensity as upstream activities' embodied energy is included. The differences vary by sector, with primary-sector activities, such as the extraction of petroleum, showing little variation and downstream sectors with long production chains, such as electronics and communications equipment, showing much greater variation.

The national average energy intensity derived by this method across all 43 sectors is 1.08 tonnes of coal equivalent (tce)/10,000 yuan RMB, which is identical to official estimates.[7] Reflecting the higher energy intensity of traded sectors over non-traded services, the average energy intensity in the 37 traded sectors is 1.13 tce/10,000 yuan.

Our assumption that the carbon intensity of energy use is the same across all sectors means the same pattern characterizes carbon intensity. The value for Chinese carbon intensity per unit of energy we adopt is the 2002 figure of 2.13 tonnes of CO_2 per tonne of coal equivalent.[8] This figure, and all the estimates we present are based on CO_2 emissions alone and not a broader measure of greenhouse gases.

(iii) Emissions Embodied in Exports

Calculating the emissions embodied in exports is simply a case of combining the total emissions intensity with the value of exports in each sector. Here, for consistency with the input-output tables, we provide the estimates only for 2002; time-series estimates are discussed in section II (v). In 2002, China's exports totalled US$326 billion, embodied energy of 410 mtce, and embodied emissions of 880 mt CO_2 (million tonnes of CO_2). Domestic energy embodied in exports

[7] *China Statistical Yearbook 2006* (NBS, various years). Note that there are nevertheless sectoral differences between our estimates and reported figures because we estimate intensity per unit of final demand while official statistics are based on unit of value added.

[8] This conversion rate is based on CAIT (Climate Analysis Indicators Tool, an information and analysis tool on global climate change developed by the WRI, cait.wri.org). The conversion factor between toe and tce is approximately 1:1.43.

Table 8.2. Emissions embodied in exports, 2002

	Export volumes (%: sector value of exports / total exports)	Emissions embodied in exports (%: sector total emissions / total export emissions)
Manufacture of textiles	17.41	13.41
Smelting and pressing of ferrous metals	1.02	2.32
Electronics and communications equipment	11.80	12.52
Raw chemical material and chemical products	3.53	7.13

therefore amounts to approximately 28 per cent of total Chinese primary energy consumption and exported emissions around 24 per cent of production emissions.

Table 8.2 shows the sectoral share of exports in volume and total emissions. As expected, emissions-intensive sectors, such as raw chemical materials, are responsible for a larger proportion of emissions embodied in exports than their share in the value of exports. High-value but low-emissions sectors, such as electronics and communications equipment, are responsible for a smaller proportion of exported emissions. Interestingly, this sector has even less responsibility when imports are removed, reflecting the importance of the processing trade to cleaner sectors. 'Dirty' sectors, such as smelting and pressing of ferrous metals, rely predominantly on domestic inputs of raw materials.

The top ten recipients of these exported emissions, who account for over 70 per cent of total exports, are listed in Table 8.3. In most cases, embodied emissions correspond closely to export volumes. However, minor differences can arise owing to the structure of a country's imports; South Korea's imports of around 4.97 per cent of exported emissions are higher than its share of export volumes because it receives around 16.9 per cent of Chinese exports of emissions-intensive non-ferrous metals. The USA is the largest importer of both Chinese goods and emissions, closely followed by Hong Kong SAR (Special Administrative Region), although in the latter case one would expect the vast majority of goods to be re-exported.[9] This illustrates the importance of adopting a global approach to any assessment of trade in emissions, since if these re-exports from Hong Kong were destined for consumption in the USA, then the energy ultimately embodied in Sino-US trade would be even greater than the estimate made here.

(iv) Emissions Embodied in Imports

It is straightforward to calculate imported emissions according to the simplistic import-substitution approach, where the energy intensity of imports is assumed

[9] Hong Kong operates an independent trading system, but since April 2003 has been a party to the UN Framework Convention on Climate Change (FCCC) as a part of China.

Table 8.3. Recipients of exported emissions, 2002

Recipient	Chinese export volumes (%: country value of exports / total exports)	Emissions embodied in Chinese exports (%: country total emissions / total export emissions)
USA	21.49	20.64
HK (SAR)	17.96	17.81
Japan	14.88	14.12
South Korea	4.76	4.97
Germany	3.49	3.41
Netherlands	2.80	2.82
UK	2.48	2.50
Australia	1.41	1.44
Canada	1.32	1.33
Russia	1.08	0.95
Total for top 10	71.66	70.00

to be the energy intensity of domestic production. Our estimate on this basis of 440 mtce of imported embodied energy is slightly higher than the exported value of 410 mtce, suggesting China is a net *importer* of embodied energy. We illustrate below that simply by accounting for differences in the average energy intensity of trade partners, this story is dramatically reversed.

Estimates of total energy intensity in each import partner are taken from primary energy intensity per unit of GDP.[10] We examine the top 32 import partners (those exporting over US$1 billion to China in 2001), which account for 93.4 per cent of total imported value. Assuming that these 32 partners also accounted for 93.4 per cent of imported energy and emissions, we infer that the total energy embodied in imports is around 170 mtce. On the basis of emissions embodied in traded goods, China is then a net energy *exporter* of 240 mtce. Total imported emissions are estimated at 257 mt CO_2.

Table 8.4 illustrates the share of import volumes, energy, and emissions for the top ten import partners. The degree of variation is striking compared to the export partners. One cause is the greater diversity in emissions intensity for import partners, while all exported energy is produced at the same (Chinese) emissions intensity. Additionally, as theories of comparative advantage and specialization suggest, it is likely that while the structure of Chinese exports is relatively constant across export partners, the structure of its *imports* and hence their emissions content, is likely to vary much more sharply. Accordingly, while Japan is the largest import partner by volumes, the energy and emissions embodied in its goods

[10] We attribute this energy intensity to the full value of imported goods, assuming away any role for the processing trade in the country of origin. These linkages are hard to trace for single-country studies, but would emerge naturally from a comprehensive study that combined the input–output tables of all countries.

Table 8.4. Imported goods, energy, and emissions, 2002

	Imports volume (%)	Energy embodied in imports (%)	Emissions embodied in imports (%)
Japan	18.11	5.27	5.28
Taiwan, China	12.89	10.74	11.52
South Korea	9.67	9.08	8.62
USA	8.98	5.43	5.82
Germany	5.92	2.80	2.93
China (reimport)	5.07	11.49	14.21
HK (SAR)	3.62	0.92	0.90
Malaysia	3.15	4.61	4.51
Russia	2.85	16.26	15.78
Indonesia	1.52	3.62	2.97
Total for top 10	71.78	70.22	72.54

represent a much smaller share of imports owing to both the relatively 'clean' nature of the imported goods and the relatively low emissions intensity with which these were produced. By contrast, Russia accounts for less than 3 per cent of the value of imports, but the concentration of these in raw materials and the high emissions intensity of their production make it the largest source of imported energy and emissions.

(v) The Balance of Trade in Emissions

It was noted earlier that the import-substitution approach implies China is a net importer of energy. However, subtracting our methodology's estimate of imported energy of 170 mtce from the exported estimate of 410 mtce suggests that China is a net *exporter* of some 240 mtce of energy, around 16 per cent of its total energy consumption. The same is true of the balance of emissions: subtracting total imported emissions of 257 mt CO_2 from total exported emissions of 880 mt CO_2 suggests China was a net exporter of approximately 623 mt CO_2, about 19 per cent of its production emissions in 2002. Net exports to the USA alone account for 165.1 mt CO_2, about 5 per cent of China's reported production emissions in 2002. Attributing these emissions to the USA would have increased US emissions by 2.6 per cent in 2002.

Table 8.5 illustrates the geographical distribution of these flows of goods, energy, and emissions. In all but one case, China is running an energy and emissions surplus. With Russia, its deficit reflects the import of high emissions-intensity raw materials and the export of comparatively 'cleaner' goods at lower emissions intensity.

Table 8.5. China's balances of trade with key partners, 2002

	Balance of trade in:		
	Goods (US$ billion)	**Embodied energy (mtce)**	**Embodied emissions (mt CO_2)**
Australia	−1.26	3.31	7.86
Russia	−4.88	−25.69	−32.35
Canada	0.67	3.21	9.05
HK (SAR)	47.8	70.90	153.10
South Korea	−13.04	5.11	21.13
UK	4.72	9.46	20.63
Netherlands	7.54	10.95	23.90
Japan	−5.03	48.94	109.65
Germany	−6.09	9.16	22.19
USA	43.48	75.24	165.14
Total	31.01	241.74	623.02

(vi) The Balance of Trade in Emissions Over Time

Input–output tables are estimated only every five years, so to conduct a time-series analysis we assume that changes in national energy intensity apply equally to all sectors. It is also necessary to make adjustments for exchange-rate movements over time, although this is simplified by the pegging of the yuan against the dollar until 2005. The methodology for assessing imports is unchanged when looking at the time-series data.

Figure 8.2 illustrates the balance of trade in goods, embodied energy, and emissions (the BEET) between 2001 and 2006. All are in surplus and rising rapidly, with emissions trends closely tracking changes in embodied energy.

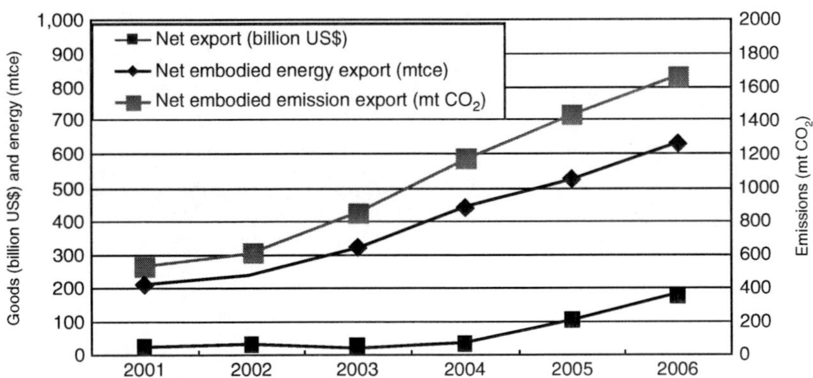

Figure 8.2. China's balances of trade

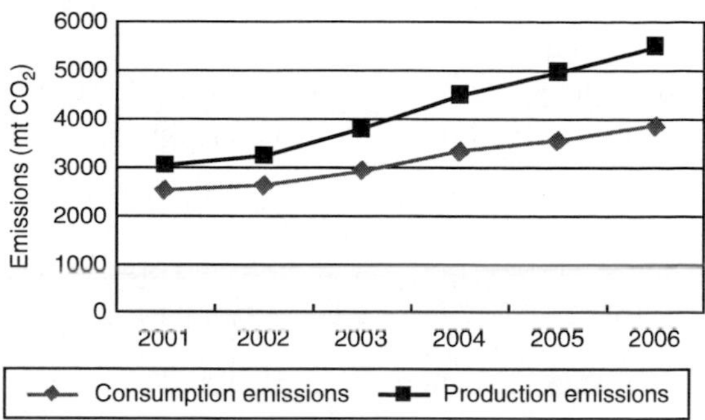

Figure 8.3. China's emissions on different accounting bases

To a large extent, growth in exports has driven both the trade surplus and associated energy and emissions surpluses. In 2006, exports reached US$969 billion, a 27 per cent increase on the previous year, while imports stood at US$792 billion, a 20 per cent increase on 2005. The share of exports in GDP has grown from 24.4 per cent in 2001 to about 40 per cent in 2007. However, the BEET rose substantially in 2001–4 when the trade balance was stable, which leads us to believe that composition and technique effects, rather than just scale effects, are important.

(vii) Emissions on a Consumption Basis

In this section we compare China's emissions on a *production* basis and a *consumption* basis. The current Kyoto figures reflect the production basis, and are obtained from the World Resources Institute and estimates for 2005/6 from the Netherlands Environmental Assessment Agency. Our methodology allows us to estimate emissions on a consumption basis by subtracting the BEET, $E^C = E^P - E^B$.[11] The results are displayed in Figure 8.3. For 2006, produced emissions were around 5,500 mt CO_2. Subtracting the 1,660 mt CO_2 BEET surplus implies consumption emissions of 3840 mt CO_2, some 30 per cent lower.[12] Just as importantly, the difference has grown over time, suggesting that if we are even partially interested in consumption measures of emissions responsibility, the production accounting method is becoming increasingly misleading. From 2001 to 2006, production emissions have increased from 3,050 mt CO_2 to 5,500 mt CO_2, indicating that 47 per cent of the growth in production emissions between

[11] As noted earlier, there are many components to a consumption account, of which the emissions embodied in trade estimated here are only one. Others include transportation and tourism.

[12] According to WRI CAIT, the emission factor in 2006 is 0.86tC/toe, larger than the figure of 0.83tC/toe in 2002. Using WRI emissions factor, total emission of CO_2 from fossil-fuel combustion is estimated at 5,500 mt CO_2, which is lower than the figure 6,200 mt given in the study by the Netherlands Environmental Assessment Agency (2007). Please note our figure does not include emission from industrial processes, such as cement production and methane.

2001 and 2006 is due to the increase in the BEET, with the remaining 53 per cent reflecting increased levels of Chinese consumption.

(viii) Comparison with Other Estimates

Wang and Watson (2007) conducted a similar analysis and estimate the net export of emissions from China in 2004 at around 1,109 mt CO_2, above our estimate of 748 mt CO_2. This is surprising, since Wang and Watson only undertook an analysis of direct energy intensity in traded goods, rather than the total energy intensity (including upstream inputs) considered here.

Ahmad and Wyckoff's (2003) comparative study estimated China's trade emissions surplus at around 12 per cent of production emissions in 1995. Given the growth in export volumes since that time, our estimate of 19 per cent in 2001 and 30 per cent in 2006 is not inconsistent with this estimate. The study incorporated detailed data, including Chinese input–output tables and country-specific emissions-intensity figures. However, its time-series estimates assumed unchanged energy technologies.

Shui and Harriss (2006) focused on USA–China trade. Their methodology adjusts for national differences in the fuel mix of energy production, but assumes the energy intensity of Chinese production is the same as in the USA, omitting the influence of different technology levels. Given that Chinese energy intensities are, in practice, higher, we would expect this method to provide underestimates. However, they estimate gross exports to the USA at 449 mt CO_2 in 2002, which is much larger than our own estimate of 167 mt CO_2. The principal reason is that the authors use a purchasing power parity (PPP) adjustment to capture the fact that 'the same dollar value of a US product and a Chinese export in the same/similar category can represent different quantities of merchandise produced in each country'. So the use of PPP exchange rates goes some way to capturing the higher energy use per traded dollar of output in China—simply because more goods must be produced in China for US$1 million worth of exports than for US$1 million worth of US production. The adjustment is necessary because US energy intensity is clearly a poor proxy for Chinese energy intensity under a very different industrial structure. Yet, it is a blunt adjustment, since PPP measures capture differences in the *prices* of non-tradable inputs, which need not be directly related to differences in energy used to produce a particular dollar value of exports. Our use of direct energy-intensity figures is therefore preferable and avoids the need for (notoriously unreliable) PPP adjustments.

Li Hong *et al.* (2007) provide results which contradict our own, suggesting that China has consistently been a net *importer* of embodied energy since 2000. While their data rely on earlier input–output figures, from 1997, and they assume constant energy intensity across time, the crucial difference is the adoption of the import-substitution approach to assess the energy intensity of imports. The approach is chosen because the authors' objective is to assess the ecological footprint of China and the impact of trade on energy use, rather than to quantify real energy flows.

(ix) Decomposing Changes in The BEET

In section I we showed that changes in the BEET can be decomposed into scale, composition, and technique effects.

Scale effects are unambiguous. Chinese nominal GDP has grown at an average annual rate of 13.7 per cent p.a.—10 per cent in real terms—between 2001 and 2006. So it is not surprising that both production and consumption emissions show an upward trend. Moreover, the BEET has risen because production growth has outpaced consumption growth. This is directly reflected in the growing balance-of-trade surplus, which has risen from US$22 billion in 2001 to US$177 billion in 2006. For 2007 there has been a further jump to US$262 billion, 48 per cent higher than the previous year.

Composition effects are harder to detect, but the data suggest that there has been a gradual change in the sectoral composition of exports, most strikingly away from textile and clothing, which made up 22.69 per cent of exports in 1998 and only 13 per cent in 2006, towards electronics and communications, which has risen from 6.05 per cent of exports in 1998 to 12.76 per cent in 2006. Given the greater energy intensity of textiles manufacture, this is significant. However, in the most intensive sectors, such as ferrous metals, there has been a gradual increase in exports, from 2 to 4 per cent, which has offset this trend. Rosen and Houser (2007) document an economy-wide shift from light to heavy industry. We are not aware of any estimates of composition effects arising from emerging consumerism, although Rosen and Houser note that any trend towards carbon-intensive activities, such as vehicle ownership, is extremely recent and limited to wealthier coastal provinces.

Technique effects are assessed at the national level, and it is apparent that energy efficiency has contributed significantly to a reduction in energy-intensity figures. IEA data show that world total primary energy supply per unit of GDP has only decreased slightly from 0.365 kgoe/US$ (kg of oil equivalent, 2000 prices) in 1990 to 0.315 kgoe/US$ in 2005, while for China the fall has been from 1.941 kgoe/US$ in 1990 to 0.908 kgoe/US$ in 2005.[13] Had it not outpaced world efficiency improvements, China's BEET would have been even higher. However, more recently the trends may have become adverse. China's energy intensity has, in fact, risen from 0.844 kgoe/US$ in 2002 while world trends have been stable. Garnaut *et al.* (Ch. 5) revise IEA projections upwards on the basis that this trend is likely to persist. Moreover, the carbon intensity of energy use has been rising, from 3.03 t CO_2 per tonne of oil equivalent (toe) in 2000 to 3.23 t CO_2/toe in 2004.[14]

[13] If purchasing power parity (PPP) is used, the figures for China would be close to world averages. For example, in 2005 the world average was 0.209 kgoe/US$ PPP and 0.219 kgoe/US$ PPP.

[14] WRI CAIT.

As Garnaut *et al.* explain, this reflects a growing reliance on coal-fired electricity generation and could have placed the BEET on an upward trajectory.

(x) Has Chinese Trade Caused an Aggregate Increase in Emissions?

Our estimate of the growth of consumption emissions illustrates that, even abstracting from its export role, China's rapid economic growth has not been decoupled from CO_2 emissions. There is no evidence that China is anywhere near the downward-sloping part of the EKC. Yet, a 'global scale effect' is unclear because the counterfactual of Chinese growth in the absence of trade cannot be assessed.

There is some evidence of a global composition effect having increased aggregate emissions. The pure relocation of production from developed countries to China has increased emissions because Chinese heavy industry has, in static terms, a 20–40 per cent higher energy intensity than its OECD counterparts (Wan, 2006). Accordingly, Shui and Harriss (2006) find that emissions avoided in the USA owing to imported Chinese goods were 314 mt CO_2 in 2002, while China incurred significantly higher emissions of 449 mt CO_2 in the process of exporting to the USA. So even if only a fraction of industry relocates, carbon leakage to higher-intensity production locations may rapidly cancel out any reductions achieved in developed countries.

Finally, the evidence does not permit us to separate a 'global technique effect' from domestic efficiency improvements. We have seen that global efficiency gains have been limited in recent years, but it is plausible that the gains have been concentrated in countries such as China.

A formal evaluation of aggregate effects is more difficult because (i) it is unclear how to specify the relevant counterfactual and (ii) we do not know whether China could have raised living standards so sharply without opening to trade. If China had never undertaken its 'opening and reform', production may have been substituted either in developed countries, affecting both the mix of goods produced and national emissions intensity, or in other developing countries with potentially higher emissions intensities. In short, the scale, composition, and techniques of the world economy have all been endogenous to China's trade openness, making an assessment of its aggregate emissions impact difficult and uninformative. What is of interest is how we determine responsibility for emissions *given* the pattern of trade that has emerged.

IV. ALLOCATING RESPONSIBILITY FOR EMISSIONS

(i) Responsibility for the Existing Pattern of Emissions

The current international framework attributes responsibility for emissions to China on a production basis. However, China is not yet required to make binding emissions reductions and an alternative accounting basis could still be adopted in any post-Kyoto agreement. Given our decomposition of the various effects that have created a BEET surplus, the causes can be traced to the unique role that China has claimed in global trade. China has grown rapidly on the basis of a comparative advantage in relatively emissions-intensive goods consistent with its self-image as the 'factory of the world'. Garnaut *et al.* (2008) anticipate, contrary to the assumptions the IEA has made in its forecasts, further restructuring towards heavy industry in line with China's exceptionally high levels of investment. In turn, this role has been shaped by national and international policies.

At the international level, the absence of any global carbon-pricing framework has permitted trade patterns to develop without regard to environmental comparative advantage. Since appropriate carbon pricing would have encouraged a shift of production to countries with lower emissions intensities, current trade patterns are partly a reflection of global coordination failures.

By contrast, the liberalization of international trade has been a comparatively successful endeavour. Copeland and Taylor (2003) distinguish the 'pollution haven effect', owing to changes in environmental regulation, from the 'pollution haven hypothesis' that trade liberalization encourages relocation to places where production is dirtier. They find little evidence to support the 'pollution haven hypothesis'. However, trade liberalization could also affect the emissions pattern through the more potent force of comparative advantage. Grether *et al.* (2006) find evidence of significant changes in the pollution content of imports owing to differences in factor endowments, though they do not assess CO_2 emissions. This supports our argument that changes in the location of production can have strong distributional impacts on emissions, and may even affect aggregate emissions. However, the promotion of free trade has been a partnership between developed and developing countries, with developed countries sharing directly in the benefits through higher levels of consumption. The problem has not been trade *per se*, but that emissions related to trade have evolved autonomously from the negotiated Kyoto process.

A slightly more compelling argument is that China's *national* policies have artificially boosted its heavy industry and that it should therefore be responsible for the resulting emissions. Rosen and Houser (2007) lay the blame on microeconomic policies, including the granting of tax rebates; 'the abnormalities in costs and capital flows that have promoted energy intensive industry in China have altered the global distribution of production' (Rosen and Houser, 2007, p. 35). The economic and environmental stresses of these policies have encouraged the government to repeal them. Since 2004, the government has taken extensive steps to reduce or eliminate these rebates. From July 2007, the tax rebate was specifically lifted from 553 energy- and pollution-intensive goods.[15] Perhaps most significantly, the artificial depression of the Chinese exchange rate has been explicitly motivated by the desire to encourage export-based growth. However, our analysis

[15] Based on the *Shanghai Securities Daily*, 22 June 2007.

suggests that, in all these cases, responsibility for the resulting emissions need not automatically transfer to China.

Our decomposition of effects from trade underlines the complexity. To focus on bilateral trade with the USA, if the depressed exchange rate has attracted exporting industries and increased the scale of China's economy, or shifted its composition towards dirtier goods, then there would be a corresponding decrease in the scale of US production and a shift in its composition towards cleaner goods. The relocation of production is still meeting the same US consumer demand, and the counterfactual would have been the same pattern of consumption but with emissions produced in the USA.[16]

However, if relocation to China creates *additional* emissions relative to what would have occurred under US production, China may still bear some responsibility. The lower energy efficiency of Chinese industry may have created a global composition effect by replicating US production at higher emissions intensities. Any boost to aggregate economic activity may also have produced a global scale effect that has increased emissions. Yet, the relocation may at the same time have improved the efficiency of Chinese industry through a global technique effect, with potential spillovers to other sectors, even if this trend has recently slowed.

Estimating these effects is difficult, but it may be possible to isolate a global composition effect using our data. Consider the net export of US$43 billion of goods, 53 mtce of energy, and 167 mt CO_2 of emissions from China to the USA in 2002. If the same energy had been used in the USA at its domestic *carbon* intensity, emissions would have been 133 mt CO_2. If the same goods had been produced in the USA at its domestic *energy* intensity, emissions would have been 25 mt CO_2. So while the bulk of net exported emissions are attributable to more carbon-intensive and more energy-intensive Chinese production, some emissions would have been unavoidable.[17] While such an analysis is not a good basis on which to attribute responsibility—since the counterfactual is open to dispute and many other effects are omitted—it highlights the significant role that carbon leakage could play in boosting the emissions embodied in trade.

It is not only China's policies which have affected the pattern of emissions. At the same time as China has 'pulled' production within its own borders, Helm *et al.* (2008) argue that developed countries have 'pushed' dirty production abroad by undertaking complementary policies of deindustrialization. The UK's success in meeting its Kyoto targets and sustaining high levels of consumption have been premised on the possibility of displacing production of dirty goods to developing countries such as China. Low savings and budget deficits in the USA have also contributed towards a sustained trade deficit; just as the USA is consuming beyond its current income, it is consuming beyond its Kyoto footprint in emissions terms. In general, as part of a complex but rapid process of globalization, developed

[16] Of course, we are abstracting from transportation emissions which necessarily rise when production is relocated abroad.

[17] The exercise is only a hypothetical one; in practice, had the USA produced these goods the structure of its economy would be altered and its energy intensity would be endogenous to the alternative pattern of trade and industrial structure.

countries have been willing partners in the relocation of production and the growth of China's BEET, and they may even have benefited from 'abatement through trade'.

These arguments question the credibility of emissions reductions achieved by developed countries. On the one hand, if reductions have been premised on emissions increases in developing countries as industry has relocated, using the production account to allocate the burden of future emissions reductions may be unfair because 'easy' reductions have already been achieved by developed countries. One of the dimensions of equity referred to by Ashton and Wang (2003) is 'comparability of effort' and seems to rule out precisely this scenario in an equitable climate-change response. Additionally, developing countries may be unable to follow the same strategy when binding reductions are required; locked into their emissions-intensive comparative advantage, abatement may be disproportionately costly. On the other hand, the ability of developed countries to live outside of their carbon budgets by consuming emissions beyond their produced emissions implies that consumption has yet to be decoupled from emissions. Since there is not necessarily an equilibrating force in the BEET, the distributional transfer embodied in the BEET may dwarf offsetting financial transfers, such as the Clean Development Mechanism (CDM).

A related argument is made by Copeland and Taylor (2003) who emphasize that the EKC evidenced in developed countries might be an artefact of their encouraging dirty industry to relocate, rather than of domestic abatement efforts. If this is the case, 'even if an EKC exists for rich countries, the newly industrializing countries may not replicate the experience' (Copeland and Taylor, 2003, p. 22); dirty industry must be located somewhere, and if it is located in developing countries then eventual abatement investments will place a much larger burden on their economies. In the context of a global public bad, such as climate change, it is difficult to see how an equitable response can be created in the presence of such a fallacy of composition.

(ii) Responsibility for Future Emissions

While there is a strong case for giving at least some weight to a consumption basis when assessing historic emissions, accounting bases will have a more important role in shaping our ability to make future reductions. Especially as the cost of abatement rises, the scope for reducing emissions will depend not on their geographical location, but on tackling their *economic* causes. Allocating responsibility to producers or consumers directly affects the incentives for emissions reductions, the distribution of this burden, and its political feasibility.

Incentives and Opportunities for Abatement

A major advantage of the consumption basis is that it avoids international spillovers arising from trade, including both carbon leakage and 'abatement through trade'. To the extent that these have diluted environmental policy by displacing rather than reducing emissions, consumption accounts can help replace the pollution haven effect with a positive global composition effect that encourages carbon- and energy-efficient production in *each* country, just as it has between Japan and Canada. Additionally, as Peters and Hertwich (2008) stress, a consumption basis would solve allocation problems for international transportation, for which no one is currently responsible, and carbon capture and storage.

However, the value of attributing emissions to producers is that they are physically in control of emissions production and have the most information about feasible abatement opportunities. Just as in the management of risk, responsibility is usually best placed with the agent most able to control the outcome. A consumer basis would leave countries responsible for emissions at all points in a potentially long global value chain, but with no direct control over abatement. Indirect forms of consumer choice can be effective; just as individuals can choose between similar goods on the basis of both price and quality, countries can source their imports from countries with both low prices and low emissions. Indeed, Peters and Hertwich argue that this generates an intrinsic incentive for countries to transfer technology to their import partners, enhancing the CDM. Nevertheless, a natural policy counterpart to consumption accounts is the delegation of emissions responsibility to *individual* consumers in the form of personal carbon budgets (Pan, 2008). The conditions for this to be effective are stringent, with consumers requiring information on the emissions embodied in imported goods if they are to discriminate between foreign producers.

Distribution of Burden

We have shown that China's emissions in 2006 would be 30 per cent less if measured by consumption. Even in 1995, Ahmad and Wyckoff (2003) concluded that OECD countries' emissions on a consumption basis were 550 mt CO_2 greater than on a production basis. We have argued that beyond the historic responsibility for emissions that developed countries bear, they may be responsible for a significant proportion of *current* emissions at present attributed to developing countries such as China.

A proliferation of equity concepts makes it difficult to assess what a fair distribution of the burden would require. Yet our analysis is not independent of these concepts; for example, proposals for a regime of 'contraction and convergence' could have very different implications depending on whether *per capita* emissions are assessed on a consumption or a production basis. Footloose global production will cause these indicators to continue to diverge. When the moment comes for China to make binding emissions reductions, the accounting basis used should be consistent with the economic role it plays in the global economy. If China continues to run both a balance-of-trade and a BEET surplus, its role in supporting consumption in developed countries while postponing its own consumption suggests that it would be unfairly penalized by using a production methodology.

As Ashton and Wang (2003) stress, 'there are equity grounds for the proposition that those who receive the benefits from the emissions (or "embedded carbon") associated with the production of such goods should carry the cost'. This would be particularly important if current failures in the international environmental architecture reinforced the specialization of certain countries in emissions-intensive sectors; if countries are locked into these trade patterns, a shift to more 'efficient' international policies could entail high and concentrated burdens.

These arguments question the sovereignty sometimes attributed to the 'polluter pays principle'. This principle has become popular more for its simplicity and advocacy properties than its economic rationale. In a discussion of equity issues related to climate change, Ashton and Wang (2003) use the specific example of trade in carbon-intensive goods to stress the ambiguity of the principle. Where benefits and damage are spread widely, and in complex chains of economic causation, an individual 'polluter' cannot be determined merely by the location of emissions release.

Of course, in theory it is possible to separate out the allocation of emissions responsibility from the financing of abatement efforts. Transfers of technology and finance are likely to play a role in any post-Kyoto agreement; what our analysis shows is that if a production-based methodology is retained, these transfers would have to play a much larger role to compensate for the increased burden that developing countries such as China will face.

Political Feasibility

A political barrier to consumption accounts is that countries would become liable for the dirty production techniques of their import partners, and switching options may be limited or costly. Set against this, however, Peters and Hertwich note that the consumption approach would address competitiveness concerns which have been a major barrier to previous international agreements. While the precise effects depend on the method of implementation, if UK consumers were required to make their consumption choices taking into account embodied emissions, UK firms would not be penalized any more than French or Chinese firms, whose goods the consumer can choose between. Indeed, this system creates a competitiveness boost for developed countries since emissions intensities are usually lower and domestic production inevitably minimizes transportation emissions. In this way, environmental performance would become an element of a country's comparative advantage. One issue in the competitiveness debate has been the value of border tariff adjustments to supplement domestic carbon pricing. By extending national responsibility for emissions up the value chain, a consumption methodology provides a more natural basis for countries to impose such adjustments on countries that fail to implement robust carbon pricing.[18]

[18] However, the legality of border tariff adjustments remains unclear. See Deal (2008) for a summary.

Tariff adjustments may even help overcome the practical difficulties in exercising control over foreign abatement noted earlier.

Consumption accounting is also likely to enhance the scope to bring developing countries into an effective post-Kyoto framework. According to the IEA, China's production emissions will constitute 30 per cent of global emissions increases until 2030.[19] However, even on a production basis, *per capita* emissions are likely to remain below OECD averages, so participation by developing countries will need every encouragement.[20] A consumption methodology would both extend developed countries' control over emissions growth beyond their own borders and allow developing countries to grow into their responsibilities as their consumption rises.

A persistent challenge is perceived to be the difficulty of measuring emissions on a consumption basis. We have demonstrated that, by using readily available input–output tables and emissions-intensity data, an informative estimate can be produced. Many other national studies are now accumulating, including of India, Brazil, Australia, Vietnam, Thailand, South Korea, Spain, Japan, Finland, Norway, and Italy.[21] Crucially, there are increasing returns to the approach, since sectoral emissions intensities estimated for one country can be used to classify more accurately the emissions embodied in imports received by all other countries. While there are challenges, these are no longer insurmountable and, operating in parallel with production accounts, the improved understanding of emission flows would contribute greatly to our understanding of the drivers of emissions increases and the political economy of emissions reductions. Even if full consumption accounts proved intractable, estimating the BEET might facilitate adjustments to emissions accounts to reflect emissions-trade imbalances, mimicking the equilibrating forces present in the goods trade.

V. CONCLUSION

Estimating China's emissions on a consumption rather than a production basis both lowers its responsibility for CO_2 emissions in 2006 from 5,500 mt CO_2 to 3,840 mt CO_2 and reduces the growth rate of emissions from an average of 12.5 per cent p.a. to 8.7 per cent p.a. between 2001 and 2006. Emissions growth from China's transition to a consumer society has therefore been significantly slower than real income growth rates of 10 per cent.

[19] IEA *World Energy Outlook 2006*, Summary, p. 3.

[20] Standard *per capita* emissions measures are undertaken on a production basis and so fail fully to reflect equality in emissions *consumption* that they usually aim to express. For example, with a population of 1.3 billion, our analysis suggests that Chinese consumption emissions *per capita* would be 3.5 t CO_2 in 2006, compared to 4.8 t CO_2 on a produced-emissions basis.

[21] Lenzen (1998); Machado *et al.* (2001); IGES (2002); Straumann (2003); Mukhopadhyay (2004); Sánchez-Chóliz and Duarte (2004); Chung (2005); Mongelli *et al.* (2006); Nguyen and Keiichi (2006); Limmeechokchai and Suksuntornsiri (2007); and Mãenpãã and Siikavirta (2007).

China's role as a net exporter of goods has made it responsible under the Kyoto protocol for a large volume of emissions—1,660 mt CO_2—which support consumption abroad, primarily in developed countries. Conversely, developed countries' emissions have been lower than if they had continued to produce these goods domestically; for the USA, 2002 emissions would have been 2.6 per cent higher.

The magnitude of these differences is large and rising because (i) China runs a large and growing balance of trade surplus; (ii) China has a comparative advantage in relatively energy-intensive production (although contradictory trends in low-emissions electronics and high-emissions raw materials may alter this); and (iii) China's emissions intensity of production remains high, with efficiency improvements stalling since 2001.

By taking account of total energy intensity in upstream production and changes in energy intensity over time, our analysis shows that consumption accounts are both feasible and informative. A limitation of our approach, and an appropriate starting point for further research, is that the role of the processing trade is not fully accounted for, and the bias may increase as global production becomes increasingly fragmented.

Our analysis is also informative for the energy market. In contrast to the findings of other studies and to popular perceptions, when the energy embodied in traded goods is taken into account, China is a net exporter of energy. This suggests that a more subtle interpretation of China's impact on commodity prices is required, since its energy hunger has been as much to meet global demand as for domestic consumption. None the less, a plateau in energy-intensity reductions will make controlling energy use a long-term challenge.

While appropriate counterfactuals are difficult to specify, it is possible that China's unique role in global trade has boosted global emissions. Yet this has been tightly bound up in the relocation of dirty industry away from developed countries. China's depressed exchange rate and export tax rebates may have played some role in attracting industry, although these policies have recently been diluted. At the same time, policies of deindustrialization in developed countries have pushed dirty industries abroad, while a lack of international coordination has failed to price emissions efficiency into industry's locational decisions. So while China may hold some responsibility for the additional emissions that its production has generated, the bulk of its emissions from trade have merely substituted for developed countries' production and supported their consumption. By allocating the full BEET to China's emissions account, the Kyoto Protocol fails to reflect the complexities of global trade and these distributional concerns. Indeed, reported Kyoto emissions performance may be a poor guide to the sacrifices that countries are making and the actual environmental impact of their consumption activities.

In chapter 5, Garnaut *et al.* (2008) stress the degree to which stabilization scenarios, even at 550 ppm-CO_2e, will require sharp reductions in the growth rate of emissions from developing countries. We have argued that the current production methodology creates leakages through trade that may do more to displace than to reduce emissions. This both reduces the efficiency of abatement and places a disproportionate burden of responsibility on developing countries. Just as importantly, it could also cast doubt on the credibility of the abatement efforts so far undertaken by developed countries and which have allowed them to sustain growing levels of consumption. At the very least, acknowledgement of countries' emissions embodied in trade could play an important role in bridging the gap between the concerns of developed and developing countries, and encourage the active participation of key players such as China in a post-Kyoto framework.

9

India and Climate-change Mitigation

Vijay Joshi and Urjit R. Patel***

I. INTRODUCTION

While global warming can be argued to be a matter of urgency, it is also a long-horizon, protracted transformational challenge distinguished by a 'cascade of uncertainty', encompassing climate science, technology breakthroughs, and economic thresholds. The volatile (or fickle) economics can be appreciated within contemporary developments, for example, when the fluctuation in oil prices in 2008 is juxtaposed with the affordability of alternatives; petrol at US$4/gallon means that a hybrid petrol-electric car would pay for itself in two to three years, but at below US$2/gallon, the payback is seven to eight years. Since natural gas prices are tied to oil prices, the recent sharp decline in these prices has thrown into doubt the economics of forms of (cleaner/low-carbon-emitting) generation that compete with natural gas, including nuclear and renewables such as solar and wind.[1] An even more important backdrop for the goal of climate stabilization, is the current bleak outlook for the global economy; it is unclear whether the OECD constituency for pricing carbon (either through a direct levy or a cap-and-trade) will have the stomach to accept, when economic activity and

* St John's College, Oxford.
** Reliance Industries Limited, Mumbai.

We dedicate this chapter to the memory of Sudhir Mulji. We are grateful to Wilfred Beckerman, David Bevan, Simon Dietz, Arunabha Ghosh, Cameron Hepburn, Benito Mueller, Stephanie Ockenden, and Mattia Romani for useful conversations, and to Anjani Kumar, Hemendra Mankad, Arbind Modi, Claire Casey, and Allison Carlson for their help. The chapter has benefited from the comments and suggestions of participants at the New Delhi conference on 'India's Options in Climate Change Negotiations' organized by the University of Pennsylvania and the Centre for Policy Research. The views expressed here are personal and should not be attributed to the institutions to which the authors are affiliated.

[1] Price evolution of other commodities over the business cycle, on the other hand, has helped alternatives recently. For 25 years the cost of solar panels declined, sliding to US$3.15/Watt-peak ($W_p$) by 2004. Then global demand soared, and the spot price of polysilicon, normally less than US$200/kg, jumped to more than US$450/kg, which pushed the price of solar panels to US$5/$W_p$. However, polysilicon manufacturers are bringing into production new capacities in 2009 (more than 50 companies have entered the market in the last two years); in addition, the global crisis and a severe slowdown in some key markets has taken its toll on demand; therefore spot prices of polysilicon have plunged and the price of solar panels has sunk to US$3/$W_p$, with more declines predicted.

incomes are declining, permanently higher prices for energy sourced from hydro carbons.[2]

The consensus among climate scientists is that there are significant risks of a negative feedback from higher temperatures and concomitant catastrophic changes if global average temperatures rise by more than 1–2°C. Atmospheric concentrations of carbon dioxide (CO_2) and other greenhouse gases (GHGs) are increasing rapidly, and are held largely responsible for increasing the earth's average surface temperature by 0.7°C over the past century (IPCC, 2007*b*).[3] Levels of CO_2 have continued to increase during the past decade since the Kyoto treaty was agreed and they are now rising faster than even the worst-case scenarios from the Intergovernmental Panel on Climate Change (IPCC). In the meantime, the natural absorption of CO_2 by the world's forests and oceans has decreased according to scientists. Some scientists argue that the failure to curb emissions of CO_2, which are increasing at a rate of 1 per cent a year, has created the need for an emergency 'plan B' involving research, development, and possible implementation of a worldwide geoengineering strategy.

Recently, the fresh and favourably disposed US administration that took office in January 2009 has given impetus to the likelihood of a global agreement effective post-2012 to succeed the Kyoto Protocol, which was negotiated in 1997 and went into force in 2005.[4] Towards the end of 2008, the EU agreed (after much public haggling from the former East European bloc) on commitments for a 20 per cent reduction in emissions and to source 20 per cent of energy from renewable sources by the end of the second decade of this century.

The Bali Action Plan, which set the terms for long-term cooperative action for the post-2012 period, reiterated the equity principle of 'common but differentiated responsibilities' and emphasized the need for 'positive incentives for developing country Parties for the enhanced implementation of national mitigation strategies and adaptation action'. The UN Conference of the Parties (COP 15) in Copenhagen towards the end of 2009 could be decisive in determining the post-2012 policy scaffolding as well as the operational next steps and the associated institutional architecture.

The current state of play regarding global action on climate mitigation can be summarized as follows.

- The Kyoto Protocol emissions target for 2008–12 agreed by advanced countries will almost certainly not be met.
- Advanced (Annex I) countries' emissions in recent years have increased in absolute terms and in *per capita* terms (Government of India—GoI, 2008*d*).

[2] The International Energy Agency (IEA) reckons that, even by 2030, coal, oil, and gas will satisfy up to 80 per cent of the world's energy demand.

[3] Another 0.6°C increase is widely accepted as inevitable owing to the GHGs which have already been emitted.

[4] The Kyoto Protocol set a target for developed countries at about 5 per cent below the 1990 level of the six GHGs. Even this modest target will not be reached by any signatory according to data in Table A10 of the US Energy Information Administration's *International Energy Outlook 2008* (EIA, 2008*a*).

- Except for the flow of funds through the Clean Development Mechanism (CDM), advanced countries have done practically nothing to alleviate developing-country anxiety that they will not be helped financially—adequately in a predictable and sustainable manner—for meeting the (seriously) expensive twin challenges of mitigation and adaptation.
- The recent EU 20-20-20 commitment[5] may come to rely substantially on offsets from developing countries rather than actual reduction in emissions. (EU plans for combating global warming is reminiscent of Soviet planning—missed targets have spurred even more ambitious ones next time round!)
- Not much by way of material and durable outcomes can be gauged, in terms of emissions reduction from current levels, until 2020 or thereabouts.

Despite this unpromising beginning, there is now a growing consensus among governments that aggressive climate-change mitigation would be desirable, though they remain bitterly divided about how the associated burden should be shared.[6] India's position in climate negotiations, like that of most developing countries (DCs), has been largely negative. The Government of India has made a commitment not to allow the country's *per capita* emissions to rise above *per capita* emissions in the advanced countries (ACs) (GoI, 2008*c*).[7] But this commitment, however honest and well-intentioned, is vacuous, given India's unwillingness or refusal to join a treaty and take on internationally agreed binding targets. We argue below that India should reconsider its stance and negotiate to join a mitigation treaty, say in 2020, *if* it can negotiate a fair deal.

We take it for granted in this chapter that aggressive mitigation would be desirable from a global perspective.[8] An important India-specific point should be noted, however. India is more vulnerable to climate change than the USA, China, Russia, and, indeed, most other parts of the world (apart from Africa).[9] The losses would be particularly severe, possibly calamitous, if contingencies such

[5] The EU is committed to reducing its overall emissions to at least 20 per cent below 1990 levels and increasing the share of renewables in energy use to 20 per cent by 2020.

[6] The influential Stern Report (Stern, 2007) estimated the cost of mitigation to be around 1 per cent of global GDP. It has been cogently argued by Dieter Helm (Ch. 2 in this volume) that this is an underestimate. Note also that the Stern Report does not allow for the important possibility that the shadow price of capital may be greater than unity.

[7] In other words, if ACs reduce their *per capita* emissions to level x, India is committed not to allow its *per capita* emissions to exceed x. India's National Action Plan on Climate Change has succinctly documented changes in climate parameters in India, and the implications of these.

[8] Adaptation is an inadequate response on its own, because there are severe limitations to human ability to adapt to climate change. Our chapter ignores the important topic of adaptation to climate change and the need for international assistance to DCs to help them adapt.

[9] See Nordhaus and Boyer (2000), Mendelsohn *et al.* (2006), and IMF (2008, ch. 4). More widely, research has indicated that tropical geography has a substantial negative impact on output density and output *per capita* compared to temperate regions (Sachs, 2001). Effects of higher temperature are also felt in growth (and not just level) of output; Dell *et al.* (2008) estimate a panel-data-based relationship based on historical temperature and precipitation readings and find that higher temperatures may reduce economic growth substantially in poor countries, but have little effect in rich countries.

as the drying up of North Indian rivers and disruption of monsoon rains came to pass. Consequently, India has a strong national interest in helping to secure a climate deal.

The plan for the rest of the chapter is as follows. Section II outlines the criteria that a global mitigation agreement would need to satisfy and explains the importance of cap-and-trade as the keystone of that agreement. Section III underscores the inescapability of ethics in determining the fair distribution of the costs of mitigation and argues that there is a strong moral case for all or most of the global costs being borne by the ACs. Section IV discusses the implications of some specific permit-allocation schemes under cap-and-trade, and reviews recent attempts to model them and the financial transfers that are implied. Section V reviews India's energy and emissions profile, with particular reference to the electricity sector, and highlights the country's energy (electricity) challenge. Furthermore, it draws attention to the fact that India is an efficient user of energy (in broad GDP terms), and is not shy of imposing taxes on energy. Section VI attempts, against the background of wide dispersal of 'global/macro' estimates of abatement costs,[10] a bottom–up calculation for a key Indian sector—specifically, coal- and natural-gas-fired power generation—of the cost of abating carbon when carbon capture and sequestration (CCS) technology becomes available for deployment.[11] It also examines ways to finance CCS-inclusive investment in India's power sector through a mitigation treaty or via an expanded CDM. Section VII sets out our concluding thoughts on India's negotiating position in future climate bargaining.

II. ARCHITECTURE AND INSTRUMENTS OF GLOBAL MITIGATION POLICY

A global policy framework for mitigation must satisfy certain basic, widely agreed criteria. These are outlined below in an order that reflects expositional convenience, not intrinsic importance.

First, the framework should be global and comprehensive; in other words, it must cover all countries, or at least all significant emitters. The Kyoto agreement glaringly failed to do so since the USA did not join. In future agreements, participation by the USA and Europe will not be enough. The DCs need to be brought in because they are expected to contribute two-thirds of global emissions in the rest of this century in a business-as-usual (BAU) scenario. A comprehensive agreement is important for two further reasons. The first is the problem of 'leakage'. An agreement with partial coverage would lead to the migration of carbon-intensive industries to non-members, thereby negating the emissions reductions in participant countries. The second is that if significant trading partners were

[10] Prominent estimates include Stern (2007, 2008*b*) and the *World Energy Outlook* (WEO) (IEA, 2008*b*). Associated with the range of costs are diffused estimates of social marginal damages and optimal carbon taxes—see, for instance, Nordhaus (2005), IPCC (2007*b*), and Metcalf (2008).

[11] Globally, electricity generation has to be virtually decarbonized for meaningful progress by 2050.

excluded, competitiveness concerns would erode the willingness of companies in the participating countries to comply with emissions targets.

The second criterion is that the framework should be efficient. To this end, it is important that it should operate predominantly through the market and strive to achieve a worldwide common price for emissions. This would lead both to cost-effective emissions reductions and to appropriate price signals for the development of carbon-clean technology. But there remains an important choice: whether the common emissions price should be achieved by a global uniform carbon tax (CT) or a global cap-and-trade (CAT) system. We discuss this further below and conclude that CAT scores heavily over CT overall, and especially so from India's standpoint.

Third, the framework should be equitable. The major equity issue concerns burden-sharing. Mitigating global warming is costly. Distributing the cost fairly is important on moral grounds and also for obtaining participation and compliance by nation-states. It is not easy to specify or agree on what is 'fair', but that issue cannot be evaded. In practice, there will doubtless have to be a compromise between fairness and realism.

The fourth criterion is that the framework should be enforceable. It must have some meaningful disincentives for non-compliance.[12]

We discuss the equity criterion in some detail in the next two sections since it is critical in considering India's participation. In the rest of this section we focus on a major issue highlighted above. Should the centrepiece of the mitigation framework be a globally harmonized CT or a comprehensive global CAT system of emissions permits? A global uniform carbon price set at the right level would induce economic agents to carry abatement to the point where its social marginal cost equals its social marginal benefit. Under certain 'ideal' conditions, it does not matter for efficiency whether this uniform price is achieved by CT or CAT. The incentive to save energy and to innovate would be the same under the two alternatives, if CT is set at a level that induces the volume of emissions equal to the cap on the quantity of carbon emissions rights or permits under CAT. However, under non-ideal conditions, the effects of CT and CAT differ. Two of these qualifications are particularly important. The first relates to uncertainty, for example about the costs of abatement. If costs change, CT keeps the price of carbon unchanged but leaves the quantity of abatement undetermined. CAT fixes the quantity but leaves the price undetermined.[13] It may be thought that CAT is preferable in the climate-change context, since a quantity mistake would be especially dangerous. Then again, this consideration is not of great significance since the tax rate could be changed periodically. Certainty about the flow of emissions in a specific period

[12] See Scott Barrett (Ch. 4 in this volume) and Keohane and Raustiala (2008). The disincentives may eventually take the form of trade-related penalties. This is a complex issue, which we do not pursue in this chapter.

[13] A credible CAT system will require some safety-valve mechanism which prevents extreme fluctuations in permit prices. There are many suggestions for achieving this. (See IMF (2008, ch. 4) and Cameron Hepburn—Ch. 18 in this volume.) We assume throughout this paper that CAT systems incorporate this essential feature.

is not critical, since what ultimately matters is the stock of emissions, and that changes slowly. The second 'non-ideal' consideration is that administrative costs, as well as corruption are likely to be higher with a CAT than with CT. On balance, CT would probably be preferable to CAT, if efficiency were the sole objective.

Efficiency is, however, only one desideratum of a good climate-change regime. The overwhelming superiority of CAT with respect to equity and compliance issues trumps any efficiency advantages that CT may possess. In a CAT system, trading of *any* initial allocation of permits would lead to economic efficiency. This extra degree of freedom means that the allocation can be chosen to deliver equity as well as to offer inducements for compliance. The implied transfers would take place automatically, as part and parcel of the working of the carbon trading market. With CT, a uniform international tax would have to be agreed—difficult enough, but only half the battle. Other aims, including equity, could only be achieved by explicit, visible, government-to-government transfers, which would be impossible politically to deliver.[14]

Since an equitable burden-sharing arrangement is the indispensable condition of Indian participation in a climate treaty, it is clear that India's interests would be much better served by CAT than CT. Luckily for India, it is probable, given the head start that CAT has had in Europe, that it will be 'the only game in town' in future climate negotiations.

III. ETHICS OF BURDEN-SHARING

A global climate-change agreement has to be equitable; it must spread the cost of supplying the public good of mitigation justly and fairly. Philosophers have argued since time immemorial about the concept of justice without agreeing on any overarching theory. Even so, a strong moral case can be made for the proposition that the ACs should pay *all* the costs of global mitigation—'strong' in the sense that it can plausibly be based on several different and competing theories of justice.

We start with libertarianism. This is a non-consequentialist doctrine in which justice has nothing to do with outcomes or consequences. Libertarians care about the natural rights of individuals. Justice consists of nothing more or less than the protection of these rights. The right to property is a natural right and must not be violated. A person should not be deprived of property that she justly holds. Any holding of property is just that is acquired by just acquisition or transfer. A transfer is just if it is voluntary, not coercive. The definition of just initial acquisition is more complex since, as the progenitor of libertarianism John Locke put it, the 'earth and its contents belong to mankind in commons'. Common property can be justly converted into private property by the addition of labour, provided, to quote Locke again, 'enough and as good is left for others'. Acquisition of property is

[14] Note that even in the domestic context, efficiency is not the sole criterion for choosing economic instruments. For example, corporations are taxed, despite the fact that personal income taxes would be more efficient, because the public finds the former more acceptable.

unjust if the Lockean proviso is not fulfilled. It then follows that corrective justice requires restitution or compensation.

The application of this theory to the climate-change problem is that the finite safe capacity of the atmosphere to absorb greenhouse gases is a common resource that belongs to all human beings but was 'expropriated' in large part by the ACs. The DCs deserve compensation for that, not as a matter of charity but as a matter of justice. It is what they are *owed*. The above argument for compensation does, however, have a major weakness. This is that the perpetrators of the expropriation acted under the impression that the atmosphere was an infinite resource. They could not even be accused of negligence because the relevant scientific knowledge did not exist. Moreover, if the perpetrators were culpable, they are long since dead and gone. It may be unjust to visit their sins on their descendants, even if they could be identified. These objections significantly weaken the claim that *past* expropriation constitutes a ground for just compensation.[15] Even so, 'equal *per capita* emissions rights' remains a morally appealing principle in considering the just *future* allocation of carbon space between individuals (and countries).

The strength of libertarianism is that it appeals to the moral intuition that cause, history, and process are important. But it ignores outcomes, consequences, and 'end-states' entirely. Even extreme poverty would not count as a ground for just redistribution if liberty rights have not been violated. Many people would find this morally objectionable. Some other moral theories take the view that large inequalities of wealth are unjust, even if they have arisen out of entirely legitimate processes. We consider below two major strands of ethical thinking which reach egalitarian conclusions. The first is utilitarianism, a consequentialist ethical doctrine in which the rightness of actions depends solely on their consequences for individual 'utilities' or satisfactions. A right action is simply that which maximizes the sum of individual utilities. Utilitarianism is in some ways an attractive doctrine for public policy: it is an appealing notion that policy should promote overall satisfaction, in which each individual's satisfaction counts equally. Utilitarianism is radically egalitarian if we assume that income has diminishing marginal utility and that people are alike in their tastes and preferences. It then follows that an extra dollar is worth more to a poor person than to a rich person. The logic of this argument implies that incomes should be redistributed from the rich to the poor, unless inequality can be justified as helpful for increasing the sum-total of utility—due to incentive effects, say.

The proviso about incentives is indicative of the point that utilitarianism is not foundationally egalitarian. It would sanction redistribution from the poor to the rich if that could be shown to increase total utility—say because the rich were better converters of income into personal utility.[16] However, when modest

[15] But they do not, in our judgement, refute the claim entirely.

[16] Utilitarianism also suffers from another crucial defect. It has no place at all for natural rights. This offends against some powerful moral intuitions. For example, it would be wrong to kill an innocent man who is widely thought to be guilty, even if we suppose that it would increase total utility because of its deterrent effect. Many people, therefore, find undiluted utilitarianism an unacceptable doctrine.

redistributions from the very rich to the very poor are the issue, such arguments are unpersuasive. Plainly, utilitarians would be in favour of the ACs shouldering the whole burden of climate-change mitigation.

We have noted that utilitarianism offers only indirect support for redistribution from rich to poor. Egalitarian moral theories, which underlie the use of 'ability to pay' criteria in public finance, do so directly. Some of these are based on non-libertarian rights. It has been argued, for example, that individuals' natural rights include not only negative rights to life, liberty, and property, but also some positive rights to a minimum standard of living. A theory of justice based on positive rights can, however, be criticized on the ground that it is unclear whose duty it is to honour these rights. But this charge is not persuasive. For example, in the case of climate-change mitigation, the duty-bearers are quite plausibly the (governments of) ACs. Given the huge incidence of abject poverty in the DCs, governments of ACs have a moral obligation to bear the cost of climate-change mitigation as well as the power to discharge that obligation.

An important strand of egalitarianism locates the grounds for distributive justice in social relations—for example, in a hypothetical social contract. John Rawls's influential theory envisages a contract set up under a hypothetical 'veil of ignorance' in which participants do not know anything about themselves. (The 'veil of ignorance' is a device to ensure impartiality.) Rawls argues that the veiled contractors would choose a social framework in which would be enshrined a principle of individual liberty, followed by a principle of distributive justice, viz. 'the difference principle', stipulating that benefits and costs be distributed so as to maximize the welfare of the worst-off individuals. The theory is egalitarian but not equalitarian; inequalities would be permitted if they were to the advantage of the worst-off. Despite this proviso, it is obvious that the theory would endorse ACs defraying the entire cost of global mitigation. The world's worst-off individuals are mostly to be found in DCs and it is highly implausible that their lot would be improved if some or all of the burden of mitigation was borne by the DCs rather than the ACs.

We must note, however, that Rawls himself did not think of his theory in cosmopolitan terms. In his view the concept of justice makes sense only in a 'scheme of cooperation', such as a nation-state, and the world as a whole does not satisfy this description. But others have extended the Rawlsian theory to the world level by postulating a hypothetical contract that covers all human beings, an extension that yields a 'global difference principle'.

The preceding paragraph alerts us to an important question which was begged in the above discussion: what is the *domain* of justice? Is it the whole world or the nation-state? Strictly speaking, utilitarian and natural-rights-based theories have cosmopolitan premises, which regard national boundaries as morally arbitrary. Just as justice between individuals must ignore distinctions of colour, race, or sex, it must ignore distinctions of nationality. Nevertheless, despite obvious inconsistency, the dominant moral perspectives have been nation- or state-centric. Utilitarians, libertarians, and egalitarians have all, in practice, limited the domain of justice largely to the nation-state. Globalization, however, powerfully challenges this parochial standpoint. The fact and the perception of global interconnectedness, of which climate change is an archetypical example, has shown that the world should be regarded for many important purposes as one community. Our erstwhile values were the product of circumstances in which the atmosphere could be thought of as an unlimited resource. These circumstances no longer obtain, and a purely nationalist ethical perspective no longer makes sense.[17] The minimum requisite change to our ethical perspectives is to move towards a weakly cosmopolitan position, viz. compatriots have priority but there are some (though weaker) duties of justice towards non-compatriots. Such a moral outlook is sufficient to reach the conclusion that the ACs should shoulder the whole burden of global climate-change mitigation.[18, 19]

IV. ALLOCATION OF EMISSIONS PERMITS

We have seen in section II that global CAT would achieve efficiency, whatever the initial distribution of emissions permits. That leaves the vital issue of how to allocate permits in a manner that satisfies equity criteria but is also realistic.[20]

Given a global cap, the boundaries of allocation can be established fairly easily. One extreme is to allocate permits on a *status quo* basis; that is, either in proportion to current emissions or to emissions in, say, 1990. This alternative can be dismissed as thoroughly unjust. It offends against every moral principle discussed in section III. DCs could not be expected to accept such a blatantly unfair scheme. The other extreme is to allocate *all* permits to DCs. This would imply that ACs would have to buy permits for all their emissions from DCs, which, in turn, would necessitate a large transfer from ACs to DCs, well in excess of what the latter would need to compensate them for the costs imposed on them by a high carbon price. Though this could certainly be justified on the basis of the theories outlined above, it is unrealistic in a world in which even the 0.7 per cent of GDP target for foreign aid remains massively under-fulfilled. The allocation of permits between the above two limits will be determined by bargaining and negotiation in which both moral considerations and naked self-interest would play their parts.

[17] Values cannot be logically derived from facts, but a change in the facts may constitute a strong reason for adopting or abandoning certain values. For example, the value judgement that 'people should be allowed to wear any clothes they like' may be abandoned if striped shirts begin to cause cancer in the eye of the beholder.

[18] Note that this is a minimal interpretation of the obligations of the ACs. The theories outlined above can support a strong moral case for large transfers to DCs, well beyond covering their mitigation costs. *A fortiori*, there is a strong moral case for the position we have taken in the context of climate change.

[19] An important objection to the case made above should be noted here. In practice, the redistribution of income implied in our conclusion would be from rich to poor states, not directly from rich to poor people. How can we be sure that poor people in poor states would actually benefit? Some faith in the benevolence of states is undoubtedly required.

[20] For a discussion of this issue, which has a different slant from ours, see Posner and Sunstein (2008).

Some intermediate allocative schemes deserve consideration. The first is an allocation that is based on equal *per capita* emissions.[21] This allocation would have the appealing moral feature that it would give every person on earth the same emissions rights over the atmospheric global commons. (Of course, the rights would in practice have to be given to states, not persons, but that concession to reality is unavoidable.) This allocative principle would in practice also have the advantage, broadly speaking, of favouring poor people worldwide since a large majority of them inhabit populous countries. But this is not invariably true; for example, the USA is a relatively populous country.[22] This last point suggests adoption of a criterion which is more explicitly in tune with egalitarian moral theories. Permits could be distributed in inverse proportion to *per capita* income.[23] This would be highly redistributive towards poor countries.[24]

Both the equal *per capita* emissions and inverse *per capita* income criteria would doubtless be criticized in the obvious quarters for 'overcompensating' DCs in the sense of rewarding them more than strictly required to pay for the costs inflicted by a globally appropriate carbon price. This suggests another criterion for permit allocation, viz. to allocate just enough permits to each DC to prevent the estimated welfare loss it would suffer from climate mitigation.[25] We are strongly attracted to this criterion as a reasonable compromise between fairness to DCs and acceptability to ACs. The criterion looks complex but has been implemented in a quantitative model, as we see below.

In practice, the politics of negotiating permit allocation will involve many other considerations: (i) countries' bargaining positions will depend on the benefits to them of avoiding climate change. The less vulnerable they are, the stronger their bargaining position, since they would lose less by walking away from a deal; (ii) bargaining positions will also depend on the strength of public opinion in different countries in favour of mitigation; (iii) ACs can be expected to resist an allocation of targets and permits that departs very drastically and quickly from the *status quo*; this is not unreasonable, perhaps not even ethically. The reason is that ACs' high carbon-dependency could imply significant dislocation of their economies, though they could soften the blow by making the transfers required to buy permits. They would doubtless also wish to minimize transfers. A compromise is unavoidable. The permit-allocation formula could incorporate

[21] Thus, consider a world of two countries, USA and India. If India's population were four times that of the USA, India would be allocated four-fifths of the world cap of permits.

[22] It has been argued by some that this criterion would also militate against long-run efficiency because it would create a perverse incentive to pursue high-fertility policies. This is implausible. There are many good reasons for countries not to pursue policies to maximize the size of the population.

[23] Thus, in a two-country world in which the US *per capita* income at purchasing power parity is 12 times that in India, India would receive approximately 92.3 per cent of permits, the USA 7.7 per cent.

[24] Like the equal *per capita* emissions criterion, this one, too, could be criticized on *ex ante* efficiency grounds, since it would create an incentive to remain poor. Again, implausible!

[25] Needless to add, this is a *gross* loss. There need be no net loss: indeed, there would, for most countries, be net gain because mitigation will bring benefits in due course. In principle, equitable allocation of permits should also allow for the differential eventual gross benefits that countries would enjoy. But this is a counsel of perfection and would introduce a large additional layer of complexity to the allocation decisions.

weights on population and *per capita* income that rise over time gradually, not abruptly; other constraints could also be built in, such as a cap on the loss suffered by any AC both in present-value terms and in any given year.[26]

Where does India stand in the negotiation game? Its moral position is strong since India is a heavily populated country with a low *per capita* income. Moreover, its expected growth rate is high, which means that it stands to lose a lot in the short run by sacrificing carbon-intensive development (unless it is compensated). All these points count heavily according to any respectable moral theory. Nevertheless, the importance of the high moral ground should not be exaggerated. India cannot expect to succeed in securing an allocation formula based purely on population and *per capita* income, because India's high vulnerability to climate change weakens its bargaining position.

Any bargaining would evidently have to be based on rough estimates of gains and losses to countries, given different assumed permit-allocation patterns. Such calculations may seem incredibly complicated but, in fact, there are several models around which have carried them out. The modelling strategy is straightforward. Two basic components are: the time profile of the global cap, and the global cost curve for mitigation, built up from the cost curves of constituent countries. The intersection of the two determines the equilibrium price of carbon and the marginal cost of mitigation. The third basic component is the allocation of permits. Given the carbon price and the permit allocation, each country is a buyer or seller of permits depending upon whether its marginal costs are higher or lower than the carbon price. The solution of the model yields the extent of carbon trading and the implied financing flows. Naturally the solution is heavily dependent on the shape and position of the global cost curve, which in turn depends on the assumptions made about technical progress. To this basic structure can be added various constraints that the solution has to satisfy.

We draw attention to three interesting modelling attempts, viz. Frankel (2008), Jacoby *et al.* (2008), and the WEO (IEA, 2008*b*). The Jacoby *et al.* model shows the implications of seven alternative schemes of permit allocation. India is explicitly included as one of the model's regions. Of the seven alternatives, six are of particular interest:

(i) a *status quo* allocation as of 2000, which is reduced over time up to 2050. In 2050, ACs', DCs', and global emissions targets would be, respectively, 30, 70, and 50 per cent of the 2000 baseline;

(ii) an allocation based on *per capita* emissions in 2000;

(iii) an allocation based on (the inverse of) *per capita* GDP in 2000;

(iv) an allocation (endogenously determined by the model) which would provide full compensation to DCs for the welfare cost of achieving the global

[26] It would be desirable, however, to specify the targets not, as currently done, on the basis of production-associated emissions, but in terms of consumption-associated emissions. The former would be unwarrantedly favourable to the ACs since they have achieved some of their 'progress' in reducing emissions so far by outsourcing the production of emissions to DCs (see Helm, Ch. 2).

target of 50 per cent emissions reduction by 2050, with the additional constraint that ACs are given equal amounts of permits as a proportion of their 2000 emissions;

(v) the same as (iv) but with a different additional constraint, specifically, ACs bear equal percentage costs in terms of GDP;

(vi) an allocation (endogenously determined by the model) such that compensation is paid to ensure that no DC's cost exceeds 3 per cent of GDP, with ACs given equal permits as a percentage of their 2000 allocations.

Allowance allocations, welfare effects, net transfers, and CO_2 price in the Jacoby *et al.* model for the USA and India for alternatives (i)–(v) in 2020 and 2050 are shown in Table 9.1. (Alternative (vi) is not presented since the transfers implied by it are not given in the Jacoby *et al.* paper, although it is clear that they would be smaller than those in alternatives (iv) and (v).) The numbers confirm our earlier surmises. Alternatives (ii), (iii), and (iv) score heavily over (i) from India's (and more generally the DCs') perspective but they involve significantly higher transfers than current flows of foreign aid. In addition, two other findings are notable. First, the *status quo* allocation that tapers down to 30/70 is, despite appearances, *not* favourable to India, which would receive negligible transfers and suffer high welfare costs. This is the result of India's expected high growth and hence its rapidly growing emissions under BAU. (A 70 per cent target for India in 2050 relative to 2000 emissions implies a target of about 25 per cent relative to BAU in 2050.) It would be unwise of India to accept a 30/70 target, or similar targets currently being bandied about. Second, since alternatives (ii) and (iii) would be unacceptable to ACs, it is interesting to observe that alternatives (iv), (v), and (vi), which are geared to keeping the welfare cost in DCs down to zero, involve, in 2020, much smaller welfare costs and outward transfers for the USA, and the ACs more generally, than (ii) and (iii).

We now turn to the Frankel model. This is explicitly intended to incorporate politically realistic constraints on the allocation of permits. The allocation formula allows for both AC and DC concerns. On the one hand, it gives significant weight to current emissions in the immediate future, thus protecting the ACs against a sudden and draconian reduction in emissions (or a sudden and large increase in transfers). On the other hand, it also incorporates rising weights over time for population and *per capita* income. The DCs agree immediately to quantitative targets but in the first few decades they merely copy their BAU paths. The DCs are not expected to reduce emissions below BAU until they cross certain income thresholds. Other realistic restrictions in the model include the requirement that welfare losses for each country, intertemporal as well as in any single year, should not exceed specified limits. *Per capita* emissions of ACs and DCs do converge, but only towards the end of the twenty-first century.

The solution of the model shows that the above path is feasible. We focus on the numbers for the USA and South Asia (Table 9.2). (Unfortunately, the model does not include India as a separate region.)

Table 9.1. Effects of alternative allocation schemes in 2020 (and 2050)

	(i)		(ii)		(iii)		(iv)		(v)	
	30/70		Population-based		GDP-based		Full compensation (*a*)		Full compensation (*b*)	
	USA	India	USA	India	USA	India	USA	India	USA	India
Welfare effect (% of GDP)	−0.1	−4.9	−2.8	20.9	−3.9	39.0	−1.3	0.0	−1.9	0.0
	(−2.6)	(−11.4)	(−5.5)	(21.0)	(−7.2)	(48.9)	(−7.4)	(0.0)	(−9.4)	(0.0)
Net transfer (US$ billion)	−30.3	10.1	−368.7	232.7	−483.5	439.7	−196.7	51.8	−264.5	52.3
	(−179.6)	(14.7)	(−668.8)	(513.9)	(−1,024.0)	(1,056.3)	(−1,239.4)	(176.4)	(−1,239.4)	(189.5)
Allowance allocation	80	98	20.5	265.4	1.7	405.2	49.3	127.6	37.3	129.5
(2000 emissions = 100)	(30)	(70)	(11.4)	(147.1)	(0.9)	(224.6)	(−8.3)	(93.3)	(−22.5)	(93.5)
CO_2e price (approx.)	75	75	75	75	75	75	n.a.	n.a.	75	75
(US$/t$Co_2e$)	(250)	(250)	(260)	(260)	(270)	(270)	n.a.	n.a	(270)	(270)

Source: Jacoby *et al.* (2008).

Table 9.2. Emissions targets and economic costs

	2010		2050		2100	
	USA	S. Asia	USA	S. Asia	USA	S. Asia
Emissions target 1990 = 1	1.30	2.04	0.42	7.33	0.01	3.62
Emission target *per capita* (tons of C)	5.96	0.25	1.51	0.63	0.03	0.32
Approximate economic cost (% of GDP)	Negligible	Negligible	1.00	−1.00	Small positive	Small negative

Source: Frankel (2008).

For the USA, target emissions relative to 1990 as well as *per capita* emissions fall sharply from 2010 to 2050. However, for South Asia they rise, since they follow the BAU path. From 2050 to 2100, the reductions in the USA are extremely severe; there are cuts in South Asia, too, but not quite so fierce.[27] There are negligible welfare costs for both USA and South Asia at the start; thereafter, the USA shows moderate losses, but South Asia gains somewhat as a result of sale of permits. A significant downside is that Frankel's algorithm delivers concentration stabilization of 500 parts per million (ppm) of CO_2 only in the last quarter of the century (and not by 2050, as in most other frameworks), which some mitigation enthusiasts may consider as too late.

Finally, the WEO in its latest report (IEA, 2008*b*) examines—for a shorter horizon compared to other studies—the implications of a reduction in energy-related CO_2 emissions under different *ad hoc* rules of allowance allocation. For the goal of a 10 per cent reduction in global emissions by 2020 (relative to WEO's reference scenario), Table 9.3 provides region-wise (including for India) calculations for three alternative allocation mechanisms—specifically, equal *per capita*, current level of emissions, and current GDP. For allowances based on a *per capita* basis, national allocations for many non-OECD countries, not surprisingly, would be substantially higher than their current and projected BAU emissions. Since the surplus countries would be able to generate income by trading the excess allowances, there is scope for substantial financial flows to developing economies. Countries in Africa and Latin America gain. So does India, which stands to garner as much as US$134 billion (about 5 per cent of GDP) in 2020.[28] In contrast, if the

[27] The related time-path of the world real price of CO_2 is intuitively plausible. In 2020, the price is at the lower end of extant estimates in the literature at US$30/tonne, it is then flat for a few decades due to the assumption that DCs do not undertake major emissions cuts before 2040, and subsequently climbs rapidly as targets begin to bite for DCs; the price of CO_2 crosses US$100/tonne by 2050, and levels off toward the end of the century at about US$700/tonne.

[28] Note that the large inward transfer associated with an equitable allocation for India could create a 'Dutch disease' problem characterized by real exchange-rate appreciation and contraction of the tradable sector. This would be a challenge for macroeconomic policy, albeit not an insuperable one.

Table 9.3. Change in 2020 of energy-related CO_2 emissions and associated financial flows under different allocation rules to achieve a 10 per cent reduction in emissions relative to the reference scenario

Region/country	Based on current emissions			Based on equal *per capita* emissions			Relative to current GDP		
	Emissions (Gt)	Change *vis-à-vis* reference scenario (Gt)	Potential financial flows (US$ billion)	Emissions (Gt)	Change *vis-à-vis* reference scenario (Gt)	Potential financial flows (US$ billion)	Emissions (Gt)	Change *vis-à-vis* reference scenario (Gt)	Potential financial flows (US$ billion)
USA	6.64	+0.87	+34.8	1.44	−4.33	−173.2	6.87	+1.10	+44.0
EU	4.62	+0.67	+26.8	2.09	−1.86	−74.4	6.99	+3.04	+121.6
Japan	1.41	+0.26	+10.6	0.52	−0.63	−25.2	2.13	+0.98	+39.2
Other OECD	2.32	−0.12	−4.9	1.24	−1.19	−22.8	3.00	+0.56	+22.4
China	6.6	−3.40	−13.6	5.90	−4.10	−164.0	3.30	−6.7	−268.0
India	1.47	−0.72	−28.8	5.54	+3.35	+134.0	1.40	−0.79	−31.6
Africa	0.99	−0.09	−3.5	5.16	+4.08	+163.2	1.18	+0.10	+4.0
Russia	1.84	−0.08	−3.2	0.56	−1.36	−54.4	0.98	−0.94	−37.6
Middle East	1.53	−0.56	−22.6	1.02	−1.07	−42.8	1.05	−1.04	−41.6
Latin America	1.24	−0.14	−5.6	2.42	+3.80	+152.0	1.38	–	–
Total change from 2020 reference scenario (in Gt)		−3.31			−3.31			−3.69	
(Change in per cent)		(−10%)			(−10%)			(−10%)	

Source: Calculations based on Tables 16.2 and 17.2, and a price of US$40/tonne of CO_2 in 2020 (all from WEO (IEA, 2008*b*)).

allocation is relative to current emissions or current GDP, then India will face a shortfall and have to purchase allowances worth around US$30 billion in 2020.

The results of these models are only as good as their assumptions, and they have to be taken with several pinches of salt. They suffice to show, however, that the models can accommodate realistic restrictions and produce solutions that may potentially be acceptable to all sides. Although permit allocations instantly geared to equal *per capita* emissions or permanently geared to current emissions would doubtless be unacceptable to ACs and DCs respectively, there is a large grey area between these boundaries which would be amenable to bargaining and negotiation.

V. UNDER-PROVISION OF ENERGY IN INDIA

Asking India (or, for that matter, DCs more generally) to 'contribute' towards emissions reduction, essentially by making energy more expensive (in the absence of financial compensation) is hardly tenable from any conventional dimension. Consider the following.

- The Indian power sector has about 160,000 MW of installed capacity, but its *per capita* electricity consumption is still among the lowest globally—for example, about a third of China's (see Patel and Bhattacharya, 2008, for a recent analysis of India's power sector).
- 44 per cent of the population is without access to electricity (GoI, 2008*c*).
- Nationwide shortage of electricity has been steadily rising; during 2008/9 (April–January) the average shortfall between demand and supply was 11 per cent, and the peak shortage in January was 12.3 per cent.[29]
- Over 70 per cent of the energy requirement of households (mainly for cooking) is satisfied by firewood and dung cake, which result in eye infections and respiratory problems linked with indoor pollution (GoI, 2006); the large health externality (not to mention, the resultant output loss) may warrant a household subsidy for fuel stoves and for liquefied petroleum gas (LPG) and kerosene.[30]
- India consumes 16 million Btu of primary energy *per capita*/year compared to 56 million Btu in China, 335 million Btu in the USA, and a world average of 72 million Btu.
- CO_2 intensity in tonnes/million 2000 US$ GDP is 287 for India, 544 for the USA, 693 for China, and 383 for OECD Europe (EIA, 2008*b*). Over the past decade, India's energy intensity has been declining by 4–5 per cent/year.
- India imposes significant energy taxes.

[29] *Source*: http://www.cea.nic.in/(the Indian fiscal year is 1 April–31 March).

[30] Black carbon and organic carbon emissions from kerosene and LPG stoves have been estimated to be lower than from those from biofuel stoves by a factor of 3–50; combustion of biofuels is a potentially significant source of atmospheric black carbon and associated climatic effects in South Asia (Venkataraman *et al.*, 2005).

Not only is India's recent emissions performance creditable, but even the BAU scenario for the period up to 2030, summarized in Appendix Tables 9.A1(*a*), 9.A1(*b*), 9.A2(*a*), and 9.A2(*b*), makes it clear that India will continue to be a relatively frugal consumer of energy on both a *per capita* and an output basis.[31]

There is a perception that energy consumption in India is (highly) subsidized (IEA, 2008*b*). Concurrently, availability of power at a reasonable price is often cited as the most important constraint to India's (industrial) growth prospects by foreign and domestic investors. While subsidies constitute one part of the fiscal overlay on the energy sector, taxes are another. We aggregated all energy-related taxes (that we could figure out) and compared the magnitude with (actual and implicit) subsidies on petroleum products, natural gas, electricity, and coal. It turns out that taxes on energy account for over a quarter of national indirect tax revenue, and close to a fifth of total (direct and indirect) tax revenue. Overall, the hydrocarbon sector is taxed even after deducting subsidies, albeit with sub-segments treated differently (see Table 9.4). In net terms, the petroleum sector is taxed most heavily, electricity consumers enjoy the largest subsidy,[32] and coal consumption is not subsidized. Against this background, any questioning of India's effort towards curtailing emissions would need to recognize, *inter alia*, the contribution to 'net carbon taxes' of present (and past), often heavy, taxation of energy (see Nordhaus, 2005; and Frankel, 2007). A rough-and-ready 'proxy' calculation indicates that the net taxation on petroleum entails an 'emissions tax' of about US$49/tonne of CO_2 emitted from this source in 2007. On the other hand, emissions from coal are (implicitly) 'taxed' at around one dollar per tonne, and for the energy sector as whole, emissions (on average) are 'taxed' at about US$6/tonne.[33]

VI. INESCAPABILITY OF COAL-GENERATED ELECTRICITY

(i) Coal is the Key: Unrivalled Intersection of Abundance, Affordability, and Energy Security

Given the legacy of the extant energy profile, overall energy demand growth in emerging markets, and broad availability and evolution of prices, it is accepted that despite increasing use of renewables, fossil fuels will continue to comprise

[31] It is instructive that even the benchmark (reference) multi-decadal scenarios for energy-related national and global emissions put out by credible sources differ significantly. For instance, the global BAU estimate for 2030 is lower by 1.75 Gt in WEO (IEA, 2008*b*) compared to the Energy Information Administration (EIA)/International Energy Outlook (IEO) projection, also made in 2008 (EIA, 2008*b*). On the other hand, for India the estimate for 2030 in WEO is larger by 1 Gt. The EIA assumes, for India, an annual GDP growth rate of 5.8 per cent (2005–30), while WEO deploys 6.4 per cent (2006–30).

[32] The subsidy has been declining in recent years.

[33] These 'tax' calculations should, of course, be treated with caution for obvious reasons. Indian CO_2 emissions for 2007 are taken to be 4 per cent higher than the figure for 2006 reported in WEO (IEA, 2008*b*), and the net taxation figures are from Table 9.4.

Table 9.4. Estimates of energy-sector tax and subsidy aggregates (Rs crores)

	2006/7	2007/8
Taxes		
Petroleum related:		
Central excise duty	58,821	54,769
State sales tax	53,949	55,677
Customs duty	10,043	12,625
Other centre taxes	4,822	12,569
Other state taxes	6,006	6,789
Tax and duty on electricity	8,559	9,052
Natural gas related[a]	2,400	2,500
Coal related[b]	3,025	3,500
Total	147,625	157,481
Subsidies		
Petroleum	48,000	73,000
Electricity	34,800	34,400
Natural gas[a]	16,800	18,700
Coal[b]	0	0
Total	99,600	126,100

Notes: 1 Rs crore = 10 million rupees.
[a] Domestic production of natural gas accounts for about $^3/_4$ of total consumption. India consumed in 2006/7 and 2007/8, respectively, 31,368 million metric standard cubic metres (MMSCM) and 34,328 MMSCM of gas. The (weighted) average ex-terminal price of gas sold in India is estimated at US$3.3/million British thermal units (MMBtu) (2006/7) and US$3.3/MMBtu (2007/8); the average international price—using the Henry Hub Index—is US$6.6 (2006/7) and US$7.3 (2007/8). For estimating the indirect tax burden on natural gas consumption, we have used a composite/weighted average rate of 16.5 per cent (comprising of state sales tax, central sales tax, and duty on imports, but excluding service tax on transportation and regasification services).
[b] India produces about 450 million tonnes of coal. The average price of coal supplied to the National Thermal Power Corporation (NTPC) in 2007/8 is estimated at Rs. 1,800/tonne (about US$45/tonne), which we have assumed for all customers (NTPC consumes 27 per cent of domestic coal production, and about 70 per cent of domestic production is used for electricity generation). The average calorific value of Indian coal is 3,500–4,000 kcal/kg, which is comparable to low-quality Indonesian coal (4,200 kcal/kg at a price of US$30–38/tonne for 2007/8). The average price of coal supplied to NTPC in 2006/7 is estimated at Rs.1,750/tonne (about US$39/tonne); and the average price of low quality Indonesian coal in 2006/7 was about US$28–31.5/tonne. Coal-related tax revenue reported in the table is an (interpolated) estimate comprised only of royalty payments by national coal companies, and is therefore an underestimate since the figure does not include mining-related cesses and taxes (such as entry tax, among others) imposed by various state governments at diverse rates, as also customs duty by the central government on imported non-coking coal.
Sources: Union budget documents (at http://finmin.nic.in/) GoI (2008*a*, *b*), (http://ppac.org.in/) and Ministry of Coal website.

a significant part of the global energy mix until 2030 (even for developed blocs such as Europe and the USA).[34] The single largest fossil fuel in the energy mix is coal, at 40 per cent of global energy consumption. Coal has major attributes: (i) it is the lowest-cost fuel source for base-load electricity generation; and (ii) coal

[34] With predicted increase in electricity demand—almost double by 2030 to 35.4 TWh—fossil fuel-based generation is also expected to double by this date, and the concomitant share of coal in electricity generation will increase from 40 to 45 per cent. (A 500 MW coal-fired power plant emits about 3 million tonnes of CO_2 annually.)

endowments are widely distributed around the world, hence, it supports the national energy security objectives of a number of large economies, including India.[35] Coal accounts for three-quarters of India's hydrocarbon reserves, and is the most abundant domestically available primary energy resource other than thorium and solar insolation.[36, 37]

(ii) Carbon Capture and Sequestration (CCS) Abatement Potential

Coal's contribution to total global CO_2 emissions declined to about 37 per cent early this decade (compared to 39 per cent in 1990), but is projected to exceed 40 per cent by 2030. In all scenarios, a major potential contributor to global emissions reduction by 2050 is the curtailment in CO_2 emissions from coal to half or less of today's level and to one-sixth or less of BAU projections.[38] CCS is the only known technology for capturing emissions from CO_2—not only from fossil-fuel power plants (coal and natural gas), but also from other industrial processes such as steel, cement, and refining; for most of these latter activities, at current knowledge, CO_2 cannot be avoided as a by-product.[39]

While many of the component technologies of CCS are relatively mature, to date there are no fully integrated power-generation-related commercial-scale CCS projects in operation (to the best of our knowledge). However, current knowledge gaps appear not to cast doubt on the essential feasibility of CCS (Deutch and Moniz, 2007). According to IPCC's 2005 report on CCS, the economic potential of CCS would be 200–2,200 Gt of CO_2, or 15–55 per cent of the cumulative global mitigation effort to 2100, under likely GHG stabilization scenarios of between 450 and 750 ppm, in a least-cost portfolio of mitigation options.

(iii) CCS is Very Expensive

CCS in the context of coal necessitates integration of coal combustion and conversion technologies to CO_2 capture and storage. It also entails transportation

[35] Fossil sources provide 80 per cent of global energy. Of the electricity generated in the USA, 50 per cent is from coal; in 2007 coal-based power generators in the USA emitted 1.98 Gt of CO_2 while generating 2.02 gWhr (EIA, 2008*a*).

[36] High-quality coal imports by India are forecast to be 120–770m tonnes by 2031/2 (GoI, 2006).

[37] While the recent civil nuclear agreements with various countries can facilitate huge investments in nuclear energy, the Indian government envisages a modest addition of 3,400 MW during the 11th Plan period (2007/8–2011/12). The high initial cost on account of up-front capital imports, as also the obvious implementation problems of a large-scale rollout in a sensitive sector (owing to concerns over security and safety) are plausible drivers for the government's cautious approach.

[38] There is a view (recently espoused, most notably, in *The Economist*, 14–20 March 2009) that CCS is unlikely to become a viable option as an instrument for climate-change mitigation.

[39] The cost of CCS for non-power applications has not received the same attention as it has for the power sector. The IEA estimates that applying CCS technology to cement kilns would increase production costs by 40–90 per cent, with expected investment costs in 2050 of US$150–200/tonne of CO_2 abated.

Table 9.5. Indicative carbon capture and storage system component costs

	Cost range (*a*)	Cost range (*b*)	Remarks
Capture from a coal- or gas-fired power plant	US\$15–75/tCO_2 net captured.	€30/tCO_2 (US\$40/tCO_2)	Net costs of captured CO_2 compared with the same plant without capture
Transportation	US\$1–8/tCO_2.	€5/tCO_2 (US\$6.7/tCO_2)	Transported per 250 km pipeline or shipping for mass flow rates of 5 (high end) to 40 (low end) Mt CO_2 in first year
Geological storage	US\$0.5–8/tCO_2.	€10/tCO_2 (US\$13.30/tCO_2)	Net injected excluding potential revenues from enhanced oil recovery or enhanced coal bed methane recovery
Geological storage: monitoring and verification	US\$0.1–0.3/tCO_2 injected.	—	This covers pre-injection, injection, and post-injection monitoring, and depends on the regulatory requirements

Sources: (*a*) IPCC (2005); (*b*) early commercial projects in McKinsey (2008).

of CO_2 produced at the coal-fired plant to the injection point at the reservoir site (onshore or offshore). In comparison to a *status quo* thermal power plant, CCS adds four supplementary costs: (i) installation of capture equipment; (ii) powering the capture process, which results in additional fuel use;[40] (iii) building a transport system; and (iv) storage of CO_2.[41] The cost ranges in Table 9.5 in part reflect the likelihood that individual project costs will vary significantly.

The bulk of the cost is attributable to (*a*) capturing the CO_2, viz. the additional capture-specific equipment, which raises required capital investment by about 50 per cent; and (*b*) an efficiency penalty (estimated at around 10 per cent), since energy absorbed in the capture process requires an increase in fuel consumption, as also an over-sizing of the plant to ensure the same electricity output.[42] Estimates of electricity costs from thermal power generation with CCS exhibit a fair dispersion, albeit around elevated levels compared to the *status quo*, as indicated in Tables 9.6 and 9.7 below.

[40] The three principal capture processes are oxy-fuel, post-combustion, and pre-combustion.

[41] The largest potential reservoirs for storing carbon are the deep oceans and geological reservoirs in the earth's upper crust. Storage is possible in diverse types of underground geological formations, including depleted oil and gas fields, depleted coal seams, and natural underground formations containing salty water, known as deep saline aquifers.

[42] Although at this stage estimates are largely theoretical, there is little doubt that it is the capture part of the process that represents the bulk of the costs (70–90 per cent, according to one source), while transport and storage are relatively minor contributors to overall costs. Another source states that overall additional capital expenditure would contribute more than half (up to two-thirds) of the CO_2 capture cost at €14–19/tonne (US\$18.50–25/tonne), while fixed and variable operational expenditure and fuel cost would be €5–7/tonne (US\$6.50–9.50/tonne) and €2–6/tonne (US\$2.60–8), respectively.

Table 9.6. Relative cost of electricity without and with CO_2 Capture[a]

	MIT	GTC	AEP	GE
PC no-capture, reference case	1.0	1.0	1.0	1.0
PC capture	1.60	1.69	1.84	1.58
IGCC no-capture	1.05	1.11	1.08	1.06
IGCC capture	1.35	1.39	1.52	1.33

Notes: PC: pulverized coal (super critical); IGCC: integrated gasification combined-cycle.

[a] Results reported in the MIT Coal Study (Deutch and Moniz, 2007), including from the Gasification Technology Council (GTC), General Electric (GE), and American Electric Power (AEP).

Table 9.7. Indicative costs—IPCC study (US$/kWh)

Power plant system	Natural gas Combined-cycle	Pulverized coal	Integrated gasification combined-cycle
Without capture (reference plant)	0.03–0.05	0.04–0.05	0.04–0.06
With capture and geological storage	0.04–0.08	0.06–0.10	0.05–0.09

Source: IPCC (2005).

DCs will find it very difficult (if not impossible) to deploy CCS without substantial financial support; they would simply not be able to afford electricity that is 66–100 per cent more expensive to produce compared to plants without CCS. Indeed, in the present context, the transfer of technology *per se* is not the critical issue; the principal challenge is who will pay for (eventually) decarbonizing thermal power generation in a country like India? (If the finance were available, the technology could be purchased when it becomes commercially available.)

(iv) Back-of-the-Envelope Calculation for India

During the seven years, 2000/1–2006/7, India's total installed capacity increased at an average annual rate of 4.9 per cent (and electricity shortage intensified), with thermal capacity addition of 4 per cent/annum over the same period (GoI, 2008*a*).[43] If we (simplistically) extrapolate capacity addition at the same growth

[43] Coal is the dominant fuel in India for electricity generation (about 70 per cent), with a share of over 40 per cent in the overall energy mix. Over time, the share of non-commercial energy (fuel wood, agricultural waste, and dung, essentially used by households for cooking) in total primary energy requirement is expected to decline from 28 per cent at present as households transit to cooking gas and electricity (GoI, 2006).

Table 9.8. Emissions intensity for thermal power generation (EU and US averages)

Fuel	Tonnes of CO_2/MWhr
EU:	
Coal	0.92
Oil	0.87
Gas	0.40
Lignite (old)	1.21
Lignite (new)	0.95
USA:	
Coal	0.98
Gas	0.42

Source: Citigroup (2007) and EIA.

rate up to 2030, then during the 2020s (when CCS could be commercially available) total thermal capacity addition over the decade would be 77.4 GW. On the basis of the above scenario (and industry estimates of CCS equipment cost of US$1 million/MW in 2020), India would have to undertake (on average) an annual expenditure in capture-specific capital of US$7.7 billion (at 2020 prices) over and above that for a thermal power plant. Indeed, this is an underestimate of total additional costs as it does not include the recurring costs of higher operating expenditure, extra fuel use for CCS-enabled power plants, and transport and storage of CO_2. It could be argued that installing 77.4 GW in the first decade that the technology is (possibly) commercially available, may be optimistic; if we were to trim it down to 50 GW, then the average annual capital investment would be obviously lower at US$5 billion/year.

Let us turn to estimating the financial implications (including compensation from an enhanced CDM outlined in the next sub-section) for India of abating CO_2. Coal-fired plants of India's largest thermal power utility, the NTPC, on average, emit 820g of carbon/kWh,[44] which compares favourably with plants elsewhere (see Table 9.8).

If we assume a plant load factor (PLF) of 75 per cent, 80 per cent of the capacity is coal-based, 20 per cent is natural-gas-based (where emissions/kWh is half of that from burning coal), and 90 per cent of emissions are captured (CO_2 prevented from being released into the atmosphere), then by 2030, 0.338 Gt of CO_2—about 15 per cent of total energy-related BAU emissions in 2030—will be captured annually from CCS-enabled plants with an aggregate capacity of 77.4 GW.[45] At the mid-point of (real) expected CO_2 prices in 2030 of €30–48/tonne (US$40–63), 0.338 Gt of CO_2 abated, if compensated fully, could result in an inflow of US$17.4 billion in 2030; at the higher end of this range (which would cover most of the CCS-related costs described in Table 9.5) the magnitude will be of the order of

[44] NTPC analysis as reported in Bhaskar (2008).

[45] The BAU emissions estimate of 2.24 Gt for 2030 is from EIA/IEO projections.

US$21.3 billion.[46] At a different price of CO_2—say in the mid-point of the range, US$40–45—the inflow will be about US$14.4 billion.[47] If 50 GW of CCS-enabled thermal plants are installed, then the abatement in 2030 would be 0.218 Gt (a tenth of 2030 BAU emissions), with associated financial flows at various expected CO_2 prices of US$11.2 billion (mid-point of US$40–63); US$13.7 billion (US$63); and US$9.3 billion (mid-point of US$40–45).

In the absence of outright subsidies and grants, the economics of CCS rests on the (expected) price of CO_2, which can vary and, of course, there are no guarantees in a cap-and-trade system. However, it may be feasible to design hedging mechanisms/insurance—say, long-dated put options—to alleviate some (tail risk) aspects of price fluctuations in this regard. Among the many X-factors inherent in CCS, including safety (and 'live' data from yet-to-be-built industry-scale pilot projects), the potential in India for storing CO_2 underground (in natural rock formations, depleted oil and gas fields, and depleted coal seams) is yet to be comprehensively assessed, but this task need not take an inordinate amount of time. The National Geophysical Research Institute is probably best placed, in conjunction with the Directorate General of Hydrocarbons, to carry out Geocapacity surveys.

(v) Modalities of Financing CCS: Carbon Trading or Enhanced CDM

The continuing importance of coal in the global energy portfolio (especially for electricity generation) implies that development and dissemination of CCS technology is essential for emissions control of any significant magnitude.[48] India's involvement in this process is critical for both India and the world. The main constraint is financial. The cleanest way to break the constraint from India's standpoint would be for India to be a full member of the carbon-trading mechanism, but with a generous allocation of permits that would enable it to sell them and buy the relevant technology.[49] (The same argument would apply to any DC that was willing to take on carbon targets.) Note also that countries with a cap under Kyoto have the option of 'Joint Implementation', whereby member states can acquire

[46] CO_2 price estimates are from Deutsche Bank, UBS, Soc Gen, New Carbon Finance, and Point Carbon.

[47] This latter price—a trajectory that starts at US$25/tonne of CO_2 in 2015 and increases thereafter at a real rate of 4 per cent—is from Deutch and Moniz (2007).

[48] The foot-dragging over funding demonstration projects and the relative paucity of encouragement from policy-makers to its importance is baffling, given CCS's potentially central role in mitigation. Both difficult technical design and economic issues have to be solved, and a functioning regulatory framework for CCS needs to be established. The list of outstanding issues is long and includes access to land to test potential sites and monitor existing sites; establishing rules for third-party access to infrastructure (transport, injection, or storage); competing land uses (between extractor and sequesterer); long-term liability over leakage; and CO_2 ownership. Governments may, at the least, be required to indemnify early developers from CO_2 leakage to kick start meaningful industry-scale (pilot) projects. For a planned project in Florida even permitting requirements have not been forthcoming, although the utility is ready to deploy CCS experimentally.

[49] A scheme in this spirit has been proposed by Wagner *et al.* (2008).

carbon credits by investing in emissions-reducing projects in other member states' markets. If India joined a mitigation treaty, such a scheme may have the potential to attract CCS investments into the country.

But the best should not become the enemy of the good. If India cannot get the right terms to join a mitigation treaty, it will have to obtain financing for CCS via the existing Clean Development Mechanism (CDM). CDM is at present the only market instrument in the Kyoto Protocol where DCs participate (China and India are, by far, the largest beneficiaries of the CDM). The CDM has been a modest success in terms of financing mitigation in DCs whereby Certified Emission Reductions (CERs), issued to developing country sponsors who can show that their projects will emit less than the stipulated baseline, can be bought by EU emitters so that the latter can emit beyond their allocation. In the most optimistic scenario, if the current 400-project per year capacity of the CDM is fully successful in terms of both registration and issuance of expected CERs, the resultant annual financial flows to developing countries will be in the region of US$6 billion at current carbon prices. Issues regarding the veracity of additionality of reduction in emissions, and the high transaction cost of the CDM have been discussed elsewhere (Stern, 2008*b*; Wagner *et al.*, 2008).

If CCS is ready for large-scale deployment by 2020, a CCS-specific facility for using the technology extensively in DCs is an option. A relatively uncomplicated course would be to expand the scope of the CDM, call it C-CDM, to incorporate sequestration of CO_2 as an offset that can be traded into a carbon-trading system. (Of course, the storage of CO_2 will need to be demonstrated/guaranteed for a minimum period of time to ensure that credits are justified on a scientific basis.) There is no obvious reason that CO_2 sequestered from sources such as cement plants, steel plants, etc. cannot also be incorporated in the C-CDM in due course. Others have gone even further. Teng *et al.* (2008) argue that to further incentivize carbon-efficient electricity generation, there is a case for inclusion in an expanded CDM of emissions 'saved' by installing natural-gas combined-cycle (NGCC) power capacity *without* CCS, since CO_2 emissions from gas-based plants are around half of those from coal (which is the alternative fuel).

Broadening the CDM to recognize CCS would enhance financial flows to DCs, and since thermal power plants entail large (and more or less similar) investments, the overhead cost related to CDM may turn out to be less onerous for these projects (a relatively easy cookie-cutter approach may be possible). In other words, reduction of transaction costs per unit of emissions—through greater learning-by-doing and learning-by-looking—linked with effective compliance, monitoring, verification, and trading is feasible with a wholesale or programmatic approach.[50] Second, additionality of abatement through a C-CDM will be genuine, whereas there are doubts over whether some segments of the present

[50] Power generation with CCS is 'big ticket' (500 MW and beyond), hence transaction costs are bearable (normalized by size of project); it is an archetypical concentrated, rather than dispersed, emission source. Currently, from validation to registration, the CDM regulatory process on average takes about 300 days, and the associated transaction costs can easily reach half a million dollars.

portfolio of projects that are eligible for credits actually constitute additionality in emissions reduction. Third, a credibly instituted C-CDM, including demonstration by ACs to pay for it, will imbue confidence about the extensive future demand for CCS—a couple of externally funded pilot projects in India and China will confirm intent—and hence catalyse R&D, investment, and entrepreneurship into the sector. On this count, economies of scale could be significant; for example, it is estimated that the total CCS cost (for new power installations) of abatement could be lower by US$6.50/tonne of CO_2 if there was a global roll-out of 500–550 projects by 2030 compared to a relatively limited roll-out in Europe of 80–120 projects.

VII. CONCLUDING REMARKS: INDIA'S NEGOTIATING POSITION

DCs feel that their economic progress will be curtailed by the extant stock of GHGs, most of which have been emitted by the ACs, and therefore that the costs of climate-change mitigation should squarely be borne by the latter. Given India's development imperatives and low *per capita* carbon footprint, it is not surprising that India subscribes to this view. The argument is even more compelling when we appreciate some specific Indian problems, for example hugely inadequate access to electricity for basic lighting, and dependence on non-traditional fuels for cooking. It is obvious that coal will continue to be the dominant fuel for power generation in India (and elsewhere) for reasons already outlined. CCS technology for decarbonization of thermal power generation is critical for meaningful emissions reduction by 2050. But CCS is expensive and will almost double the cost of electricity from coal-fired stations, which consumers in poor countries will simply not be able to pay for. Compensation to India for deploying this technology would be possible, *either* through the allocation of adequate emission allowances that can then be sold to defray the cost of CCS (among other costly abatement measures) and concomitantly reduce the cost to consumers of decarbonized power, *or* by widening the scope of the present project-oriented CDM. The former alternative is preferred because we favour India becoming a full member of a mitigation treaty, if it can secure the right terms.

India has so far been opposed to joining an international climate mitigation treaty. In our view, this negative stance should be abandoned. If India can get the appropriate terms, including an appropriate quantity of 'hot air' or 'headroom' in the allocation of permits, its interests would be best served by participation. We offer the following reasons for our view.

First, climate-change mitigation requires both a high price of carbon across the world as well as investment in clean-energy R&D. The former is a necessary condition for success in the latter and requires a global agreement with a tight overall cap. It is in India's interest to help achieve a comprehensive agreement, since India is particularly vulnerable to climate-change damage.

Second, neither the USA nor China would join a treaty without the other, and India is also a key player. India's willingness to join may play a catalytic role in motivating participation by the USA and China.

Third, India should join a treaty only if the terms are right, and this is, of course, a matter of negotiation. If India joins ahead of other DCs, it could secure a first-mover advantage in terms of obtaining a permit allocation with adequate 'headroom' to compensate it for the costs of mitigation. (India would doubtless push for permit allocations based on *per capita* emissions or *per capita* income. While this may serve as an initial bargaining move, its chances of success are negligible. A reasonable fall-back position would be to insist on an allocation with enough 'headroom' to compensate India fully for the welfare cost of undertaking its share of global mitigation.[51])

Fourth, India may be able to use its offer to join a treaty to get other things it wants—climate-related (for instance, credible long-term adaptation finance), and/or climate-unrelated (a seat on the UN Security Council? increased voting power in the IMF?). Note that when Russia joined the Kyoto agreement, it extracted the price of Western assistance in joining the WTO.

Fifth, unless the CDM is modified (given the problems associated with proving 'additionality' of emissions reductions), opposition to it may increase and the conditions surrounding it could become more circumscribed. One worry about expanded participation in the CDM which is frequently aired is that credits for India's 'low hanging fruit' projects would then be sold cheaply to ACs; the conclusion is drawn that such projects should be held back in case India eventually joins a mitigation treaty. However, the right inference is that India should join such a treaty soon. Permits in the European carbon-trading scheme currently trade at higher prices than CERs for a variety of reasons. If India were to join, and depending on the baselines accepted, it may get high prices for its 'low hanging fruit' projects. Why then does India fear joining a treaty? It is felt that it could be disadvantageous to India to be bound by emissions targets. This would not be the case if India could secure a permit allocation with adequate 'headroom', including built-in flexibility for upward revision if GDP growth turns out to be faster than expected.[52] (A 'zero welfare cost' criterion for permit allocation would of course cover this point.)

Sixth, if a treaty succeeds and India joins late, it faces the risk of being stuck with too many low-value, high-carbon assets. If India joins early and the treaty unravels, not much is lost since, assuming that the terms are right, India will have been compensated in the interim by the sale of permits.

Seventh, a mitigation treaty cannot succeed without some enforcement mechanism. The obvious one is trade restrictions against non-participants. This is a danger that India would avoid by joining a treaty.

[51] This underscores the importance of research to establish the magnitude of the welfare cost.

[52] Of course, it may well make sense for India to press for and make use of an expanded CDM (see section VI) *either* as a stepping-stone on the way to joining a mitigation treaty *or* as a fall-back position if the right terms cannot be obtained for treaty participation.

Lastly, India has to be wary of the changing dynamics of international *realpolitik*. While important developing countries such as China have hitherto taken a position in the climate-stabilization arena that is practically identical to India's, it cannot be ruled out that this may alter in the future. China's economy is substantially larger than India's, and China increasingly sees itself as a super power in-waiting; it could choose to enhance its standing—as a responsible aspiring power—by joining a treaty (to earn kudos, and/or secure some tangible *quid pro quo*[53]). If something akin to this comes to pass, it is not inconceivable that India could be isolated, and eventually be forced to accept an inferior 'done' deal.[54]

In sum, India should regard the issue of climate-change mitigation as a diplomatic challenge of getting the right terms, not as a bugbear to be feared and shunned. It should declare itself willing to negotiate to join a mitigation treaty, say in 2020, *provided* (i) the ACs demonstrate their good intent by making significant actual reductions in emissions by 2020; and (ii) the ACs are ready to admit India on equitable terms. The second condition involves agreeing on an allocation formula for permits which would compensate India for its mitigation costs for several decades.

[53] The latter could, for example, be a promise to keep India away from the diplomatic 'top table'.

[54] There is some 'chatter' about the USA and China working together on 'climate'.

DATA APPENDIX

Table 9.A1(*a*). Energy-related CO_2 emissions (in gigatonnes) and allied data

Region/country	1990	2005	2010	2020	2030	Average annual % change in CO_2 (2005–30)	PPP GDP in 2030 (in billion 2000 US$)	Average annual % change in GDP (2005–30)	Metric tonnes/million 2000 US$ PPP GDP (2030)	Average annual % change in carbon intensity (2005–30)
World	21.2	28.1	31.1	37.0	42.3	1.7	150,182	4.0	282	−2.2
USA	4.99	5.98	6.01	6.38	6.85	0.5	20,219	2.5	339	−1.7
OECD Europe	4.10	4.38	4.51	4.76	4.83	0.4	20,076	2.3	241	−1.8
OECD Asia	1.54	2.17	2.21	2.32	2.40	0.4	7,694	1.8		
Japan	1.01	1.23	1.20	1.20	1.17	−0.2	4,467	1.1	262	−1.2
Total OECD	11.40	13.57	13.83	14.74	15.54	0.5	52,542	2.3	296	−1.8
Non-OECD	9.83	14.49	17.27	22.30	26.79	2.5	97,640	5.2	274	−2.6
China	2.24	5.32	6.90	9.48	12.01	3.3	35,973	6.4	334	−2.9
Russia	2.38	1.70	1.79	1.98	2.12	0.9	5,404	4.0	392	−3.0
India	0.57	1.16	1.35	1.82	2.24	2.6	16,524	5.8	135	−3.0
Brazil	0.22	0.36	0.45	0.54	0.63	2.3	3,896	3.6	162	−1.2
Middle East	0.70	1.40	1.62	1.99	2.25	1.9	4,174	4.0	539	−2.6

Note: PPP is purchasing power parity.

Source: EIA (2008*b*).

Table 9.A1(*b*). *Per capita* energy-related CO_2 emissions (in tonnes)

Region/country	1990	2005	2010	2020	2030	Average annual % change (1990–2005)	Average annual % change (2005–30)
World	4.0	4.3	4.5	4.8	5.1	0.5	0.7
USA	19.6	20.1	19.3	18.9	18.7	0.2	−0.3
OECD Europe	8.3	8.2	8.3	8.5	8.5	−0.1	0.2
Japan	8.2	9.6	9.4	9.6	9.9	1.1	0.1
Total OECD	10.9	11.6	11.5	11.7	12.0	0.4	0.1
Every one else	2.3	2.7	3.0	3.5	3.8	1.1	1.4
China	2.0	4.1	5.1	6.7	8.2	5.0	2.9
Russia	16.0	11.8	12.7	15.0	17.1	−2.0	1.5
India	0.7	1.0	1.1	1.3	1.5	3.0	1.5
Brazil	1.4	1.9	2.3	2.5	2.7	1.9	1.4
Middle East	5.1	7.3	7.6	7.8	7.7	2.4	0.2

Source: Same as Table 9.A1(*a*).

Table 9.A2(*a*). Energy-related CO_2 emissions in the reference scenario (in gigatonnes)

Region/country	1980	1990	2000	2006	2020	2030
OECD	10.65	11.04	12.43	12.79	13.31	13.17
North America	5.30	5.57	6.54	6.62	6.95	7.06
USA	4.66	4.85	5.66	5.67	5.77	5.80
Europe	4.12	3.89	3.90	4.06	4.16	3.99
Pacific	1.23	1.58	1.99	2.11	2.21	2.11
Japan	0.88	1.07	1.19	1.21	1.15	1.06
Non-OECD	6.85	9.29	10.17	14.12	21.89	26.02
E.Europe/Eurasia	3.41	4.03	2.45	2.65	3.18	3.34
Russia	*n.a.*	2.18	1.50	1.57	1.92	2.00
Asia	2.14	3.52	5.20	8.36	14.17	17.30
China	1.42	2.24	3.08	5.65	10.00	11.71
India	0.29	0.59	0.98	1.25	2.19	3.29
Middle East	0.34	0.59	0.97	1.29	2.09	2.61
Africa	0.41	0.55	0.69	0.85	1.08	1.17
Latin America	0.55	0.60	0.86	0.97	1.38	1.60
Brazil	0.18	0.19	0.30	0.33	0.50	0.58
World[a]	18.05	20.95	23.41	27.89	36.40	40.55
EU	*n.a.*	4.04	3.08	3.94	3.95	3.76

Notes: [a] Includes emissions from international marine bunkers and international aviation; n.a.: not available.
Source: *World Energy Outlook* (IEA, 2008*b*).

Table 9.A2(*b*). *Per capita* energy-related CO_2 emissions in the reference scenario (in tonnes)

Region/country	1980	1990	2000	2006	2020	2030
OECD	11.0	10.5	11.0	10.8	10.5	10.1
North America	16.5	15.3	15.7	15.0	13.9	13.2
USA	20.2	19.1	19.7	18.6	16.8	15.8
Europe	8.7	7.8	7.5	7.5	7.4	7.0
Pacific	7.1	8.4	10.1	10.5	10.9	10.7
Japan	7.5	8.7	9.4	9.5	9.3	9.0
Non-OECD	2.0	2.2	2.1	2.6	3.5	3.8
E.Europe/Eurasia	10.6	11.6	7.1	7.8	9.6	10.4
Russia	n.a	14.7	10.3	11.0	14.6	16.3
Asia	0.9	1.3	1.6	2.4	3.6	4.1
China	1.4	2.0	2.4	4.3	7.0	8.0
India	0.4	0.7	1.0	1.1	1.6	2.3
Middle East	3.7	4.5	5.9	6.8	8.5	9.3
Africa	0.9	0.9	0.9	0.9	0.9	0.8
Latin America	1.9	1.7	2.1	2.1	2.6	2.8
Brazil	1.5	1.3	1.7	1.8	2.3	2.5
World*	4.1	4.0	3.9	4.3	4.8	4.9
EU	n.a	8.6	7.9	8.0	7.9	7.5

Source: See Table 9.A2(*a*).

10

Addressing Climate Change with a Comprehensive US Cap-and-trade System

*Robert N. Stavins**

I. INTRODUCTION

The impetus for a meaningful US climate policy is growing. Scientific evidence has increased (IPCC, 2007*a*, *c*), public concern has been magnified, and many people perceive what they believe to be evidence of climate change in progress. Such concern is reinforced by the aggressive positions of key advocacy groups, which are no longer limited on this issue to the usual environmental interest groups; religious lobbies, for example, have also been vocal. This has been reflected in greatly heightened attention by the news media. The overall result is that a large and growing share of the US population now believes that government action is warranted (Bannon *et al.*, 2007).

In the absence of federal policy, regions, states, and even cities have moved forward with their own proposals for policies intended to reduce the emissions of carbon dioxide (CO_2) and other greenhouse gases. Partly in response to fears of a fractured set of regional policies, an increasing number of large corporations, sometimes acting individually, and at other times in coalitions—together with environmental advocacy groups—have announced their support for serious national action. Building upon this is the April 2007 US Supreme Court decision that the Administration has the legislative authority to regulate CO_2 emissions,[1] as well as ongoing pressure from European and other nations for the United States to re-establish its international credibility in this realm by enacting a meaningful domestic climate policy.

Thus, momentum is clearly building towards the enaction of a domestic climate-change policy. But there should be no mistake about it—meaningful action to address global climate change will be costly. This is a key 'inconvenient truth' that must be recognized when policy-makers construct and evaluate

* John F. Kennedy School of Government, Harvard University, National Bureau of Economic Research, and Resources for the Future.

[1] Massachusetts *et al.* v. Environmental Protection Agency *et al.*, No. 05-1120, argued 29 November 2006, decided 2 April 2007.

proposals, because a policy's specific design will greatly affect its ability to achieve its environmental goals, its costs, and the distribution of those costs.

There is general consensus among economists and policy analysts that a market-based policy instrument targeting CO_2 emissions—and potentially some non-CO_2 greenhouse-gas (GHG) emissions—should be a central element of any domestic climate policy. This is reflected in international assessments of national policy instruments, as well (IPCC, 2007*d*). While there are trade-offs between two alternative market-based instruments—a cap-and-trade system and a carbon tax—the best and most likely approach for the short to medium term in the United States is a cap-and-trade system.

It is critical to identify the most effective, lowest-cost, and most equitable policy design at the outset, because any policy design once in place can be difficult to change (Repetto, 2007). The environmental integrity of a domestic cap-and-trade system for climate change can be maximized and its costs and risks minimized by: targeting all fossil-fuel-related CO_2 emissions through an upstream, economy-wide cap; setting a trajectory of caps over time that begins modestly and gradually becomes more stringent, establishing a long-run price signal to encourage investment; adopting mechanisms to protect against cost uncertainty; and including linkages with the climate-policy actions of other countries. Importantly, by providing the option to mitigate economic impacts through the distribution of emission allowances, this approach can establish consensus for a policy that achieves meaningful emission reductions. It is for these reasons and others that cap-and-trade systems have been used increasingly in the United States to address an array of environmental problems, including the phase-out of leaded gasoline in the 1980s, the reduction of sulphur dioxide (SO_2) and nitrogen oxide (NO_x) emissions from power plants beginning in 1995, and the phase-out of chlorofluorocarbons (CFCs) (Stavins, 2003).

A well-designed cap-and-trade system will minimize the costs of achieving any given emissions target. While firms have flexibility regarding precisely how much they emit, because they have to surrender an allowance for each ton of their emissions they will undertake all emission reductions that are less costly than the market price of an allowance. Through trading, this allowance price adjusts until emissions are brought down to the level of the cap. Firms' ability to trade emission allowances creates a market in which allowances migrate towards their highest-valued use, covering those emissions that are the most costly to reduce. Conversely, as a result of trading, the emission reductions undertaken to meet the cap are those that are least costly to achieve.

The cost of achieving significant emission reductions in future years will depend critically on the availability and cost of low- or non-emitting technologies. A cap-and-trade system that establishes caps extending decades into the future provides important price signals and hence incentives for firms to invest in the development and deployment of such technologies, thereby lowering the future costs of achieving emission reductions.

Even a credible long-run cap-and-trade system may provide insufficient incentives for investment in technology development because it would not address certain well-known factors (market failures) that discourage such investment, such as those associated with the public-good nature of the knowledge that comes from research and development efforts (Jaffe *et al.*, 2005; Newell, 2007). Thus, a cap-and-trade system alone will not encourage the socially desirable level of investment in research, development, and deployment of new technologies that could reduce future emission-reduction costs. To achieve this desired level of investment, additional policies may be necessary to provide additional government funding or to increase incentives for private funding of such research activities.

(i) Previous Use of Cap-and-trade Systems

Over the past two decades tradable permit systems have been adopted for pollution control with increasing frequency in the United States (Tietenberg, 1997), as well as other parts of the world. The first important example of a trading programme in the United States was the leaded gasoline phase-down that occurred in the 1980s. Although not strictly a cap-and-trade system, the phase-down included features, such as trading and banking of environmental credits, that brought it closer than other credit programmes to the cap-and-trade model and resulted in significant cost savings. The lead programme was successful in meeting its environmental targets, and the system was cost-effective, with estimated cost savings of about US$250 million per year (Nichols, 1997). Also, the programme provided measurable incentives for cost-saving technology diffusion (Kerr and Newell, 2000).

A cap-and-trade system was also used in the United States to help comply with the Montreal Protocol, an international agreement aimed at slowing the rate of stratospheric ozone depletion. The Protocol called for reductions in the use of CFCs and halons, the primary chemical groups thought to lead to depletion. The timetable for the phase-out of CFCs was accelerated, and the system appears to have been relatively cost-effective.

The most important application made in the United States of a market-based instrument for environmental protection is arguably the cap-and-trade system that regulates SO_2 emissions, the primary precursor of acid rain, established under the US Clean Air Act Amendments of 1990 (Ellerman *et al.*, 2000). The programme is intended to reduce SO_2 and nitrogen-oxide (NO_2) emissions by ten million tons and two million tons, respectively, from 1980 levels (Burtraw *et al.*, 1998). A robust market of SO_2 allowance trading emerged from the programme, resulting in cost savings of the order of US$1 billion annually, compared with the costs under some command-and-control regulatory alternatives (Carlson *et al.*, 2000). The programme has also had a significant environmental impact: SO_2 emissions from the power sector decreased from 15.7 million tons in 1990 to 10.2 million tons in 2005 (US EPA, 2005).

In 1994, California's South Coast Air Quality Management District launched a cap-and-trade programme to reduce nitrogen-oxide and SO_2 emissions in the

Los Angeles area (Harrison, 2003). This Regional Clean Air Incentives Market (RECLAIM) programme set an aggregate cap on NO_x and SO_2 emissions for all significant sources, with an ambitious goal of reducing aggregate emissions by 70 per cent by 2003. Trading under the RECLAIM programme was restricted in several ways, with positive and negative consequences. But despite problems, RECLAIM has generated environmental benefits, with NO_x emissions in the regulated area falling by 60 per cent and sulphurous oxide (SO_x) emissions by 50 per cent. Furthermore, the programme has reduced compliance costs for regulated facilities, with the best available analysis suggesting 42 per cent cost savings, amounting to US$58 million annually (Anderson, 1997).

Finally, in 1999, under US Environmental Protection Agency (EPA) guidance, 12 north-eastern states and the District of Columbia implemented a regional NO_x cap-and-trade system to reduce compliance costs associated with the Ozone Transport Commission (OTC) regulations of the 1990 Amendments to the Clean Air Act. Emissions caps for two zones from 1999 to 2003 were 35 and 45 per cent of 1990 emissions, respectively. Compliance cost savings of 40–47 per cent have been estimated for the period 1999–2003, compared to a base case of continued command-and-control regulation without trading or banking (Farrell *et al.*, 1999).

(ii) CO_2 and Greenhouse-gas Cap-and-trade Systems

Although cap-and-trade has proven to be a cost-effective means to control conventional air pollutants, it has a very limited history as a method of reducing CO_2 emissions. Several ambitious programmes are in the planning stages or have been launched. First, the Kyoto Protocol, the international agreement that was signed in Japan in 1997, includes a provision for an international cap-and-trade system among countries, as well as two systems of project-level offsets. The Protocol's provisions have set the stage for the member states of the European Union to address their commitments using a regional cap-and-trade system.

By far the largest existing active cap-and-trade programme in the world is the European Union Emissions Trading Scheme (EU ETS) for CO_2 allowances, which has operated for the past two years with considerable success, despite some initial—and predictable—problems (Ellerman and Buchner, 2007). The 11,500 emitters regulated by the downstream programme include large sources such as oil refineries, combustion installations, coke ovens, cement factories, ferrous metal production, glass and ceramics production, and pulp and paper production, but the programme does not cover sources in the transportation, commercial, or residential sectors. Although the first phase, a pilot programme from 2005 to 2007, allows trading only in CO_2, the second phase, from 2008 to 2012, potentially broadens the programme to include other GHGs. In its first two years of operation, the EU ETS has produced a functioning CO_2 market, with weekly trading volumes ranging between five million and 15 million tons, with spikes in trading activity occurring along with major price changes. Apart from some problems with the programme's design and early implementation, it is much too soon to provide a definitive assessment of the system's performance.

A frequently discussed US CO_2 cap-and-trade system that has not yet been implemented is the Regional Greenhouse Gas Initiative (RGGI), a programme among 10 north-eastern states that will be implemented in 2009 and begin to cut emissions in 2015. RGGI is a downstream cap-and-trade programme intended to limit CO_2 emissions from power-sector sources. Beginning in 2015, the emissions cap will decrease by 2.5 per cent each year until it reaches an ultimate level 10 per cent below current emissions in 2019. This goal will require a reduction that is approximately 35 per cent below business-as-usual, or, equivalently, 13 per cent below 1990 emissions levels. RGGI only limits emissions from the power sector, and so incremental monitoring costs are low, because US power plants are already required to report their hourly CO_2 emissions to the federal government (under provisions for continuous emissions monitoring as part of the SO_2 allowance trading programme). The programme requires participating states to auction at least 25 per cent of their allowances; the remaining 75 per cent of allowances may be auctioned or distributed freely. Given that the system will not come into effect until 2009, at the earliest, it is obviously not possible to assess its performance.

Finally, California's Greenhouse Gas Solutions Act (Assembly Bill 32) was signed into law in 2006, is intended to begin in 2012 to reduce emissions to their 1990 levels by 2020, and may employ a cap-and-trade approach. Although the Global Warming Solutions Act does not require the use of market-based instruments, it does allow for their use, albeit with restrictions that they must not result in increased emissions of conventional, local air pollutants or toxics, that they must maximize environmental and economic benefits in California, and that they must account for localized economic and environmental justice concerns. This mixed set of objectives potentially interferes with the development of a sound policy mechanism. The Governor's Market Advisory Committee (2007) has recommended the implementation of a cap-and-trade programme, with a gradual phase-in of caps covering most sectors of the economy, and an allowance distribution system that uses both free distribution and auctions of allowances, with a shift towards more auctions in later years.

(iii) Organization of Subsequent Sections

Section II of the chapter describes a comprehensive US CO_2 cap-and-trade system, including a description of its key elements: a gradual trajectory of emissions reductions; tradable allowances; up-stream regulation with economy-wide effects; mechanisms to reduce cost uncertainty; allowance allocations that combine auctions with free distribution, with auctions becoming more important over time; availability of offsets for underground and biological carbon sequestration; supremacy over state and regional systems; and linkage with international emission-reduction credit and cap-and-trade systems and climate policies in other countries. Section III provides an economic assessment of the cap-and-trade system. Section IV compares the system with alternative approaches to the same policy goal. Finally, section V concludes.

II. THE SYSTEM

The United States can launch a scientifically sound, economically rational, and politically feasible approach to reducing its contributions to the increase in atmospheric concentrations of greenhouse gases by adopting an up-stream, economy-wide CO_2 cap-and-trade system which implements a gradual trajectory of emissions reductions over time, and includes mechanisms to reduce cost uncertainty, such as multi-year compliance periods, provisions for banking and borrowing, and possibly a cost-containment mechanism to protect against any extreme price volatility.

The permits in the system should be allocated through a combination of free distribution and open auction, in order to balance, on the one hand, legitimate concerns by some sectors and individuals who will be particularly burdened by this (or any) climate policy, with, on the other hand, the opportunity to achieve important public purposes with generated funds. The share of allowances freely allocated should decrease over time, as the private sector is able to adjust to the carbon constraints, with all allowances being auctioned after 25 years.[2]

In addition, it is important that offsets be made available both for underground and biological carbon sequestration, to provide for both short-term cost-effectiveness and long-term incentives for appropriate technological change. The federal cap-and-trade system can provide for supremacy over US regional, state, and local systems, to avoid duplication, double counting, and conflicting requirements. At the same time, it is also important to provide for harmonization over time with selective emission reduction credit and cap-and-trade systems in other nations, as well as related international systems.

(i) Major Though not Exclusive Focus on CO_2

Fossil-fuel-related CO_2 emissions accounted for nearly 85 per cent of the 7,147 million metric tons of US GHG emissions in 2005, where tons are measured in CO_2-equivalent. Carbon-dioxide emissions arise from a broad range of activities involving the use of different fuels in many different economic sectors. In addition, biological sequestration and reductions in non-CO_2 GHG emissions can contribute substantially to minimizing the cost of limiting GHG concentrations (Reilly *et al.*, 2003; Stavins and Richards, 2005). Some non-CO_2 GHG emissions might be addressed under the same framework as CO_2 in a multi-gas cap-and-trade system.

[2] For a timely discussion of relevant auction design issues in carbon markets, see Burtraw *et al.* (2007).

(ii) A Gradually Increasing Trajectory of Emissions Reductions Over Time

The long-term nature of the climate problem offers significant flexibility regarding when emission reductions actually occur. Policies taking advantage of this 'when flexibility' by setting annual emission targets that gradually increase in stringency can avoid many costs associated with taking stringent action too quickly, *without sacrificing environmental benefits* (Wigley *et al.*, 1996). Premature retirement of existing capital stock and production and siting bottlenecks that can arise in the context of rapid capital stock transitions can be avoided. In addition, gradually phased-in targets provide time to incorporate advanced technologies into long-lived investments (Jaffe *et al.*, 1999; Goulder, 2004). Thus, for any given cumulative emission target or associated atmospheric GHG concentration objective, a climate policy's cost can be reduced by gradually phasing in efforts to reduce emissions.

Because of the long-term nature of the climate problem and because of the need for technological change to bring about lower-cost emissions reductions, it is essential that the caps constitute a long-term trajectory. The development and eventual adoption of new low-carbon and other relevant technologies will depend on the predictability of future carbon prices, themselves brought about by the cap's constraints. Therefore, the cap-and-trade policy should incorporate medium-term to long-term targets, not just short-term targets.

For illustrative purposes in the cost assessment, I adopt and assess a pair of trajectories for the period 2012–50 to establish a reasonable range of possibilities. The less ambitious trajectory involves *stabilizing* CO_2 emissions at their 2008 level over the period 2012–50. This trajectory, in terms of its cumulative cap, lies within the range defined by the 2004 and 2007 recommendations of the National Commission on Energy Policy (2004, 2007). The more ambitious trajectory—again defined over the years 2012–50—involves reducing CO_2 emissions from their 2008 level to *50 per cent below their 1990 level by 2050*. This trajectory—defined by its cumulative cap—is consistent with the lower end of the range proposed by the US Climate Action Partnership (2007). This range of trajectories is consistent with the frequently cited global goal of stabilizing atmospheric concentrations of CO_2 at between 450 parts per million (ppm) and 550 ppm *if* all nations were to take commensurate action.[3]

(iii) Upstream Point of Regulation and Economy-wide Scope of Coverage

In order to create *economy-wide coverage*, an *upstream point of regulation* should be employed, whereby allowances are surrendered based on the carbon content of fuels at the point of fossil-fuel extraction, import, processing, or distribution.

[3] 'Commensurate action' is defined as other countries taking action that is globally cost-effective, for example by employing cap-and-trade systems with the same allowance price or equivalent carbon taxes.

This can be thought of as a system where regulation is at the mine-mouth, well-head, and point of import. First sellers of fossil fuels could be required to hold allowances: for coal, at the mine shipping terminus; for petroleum, at the refinery gate; for natural gas, at the first distribution point; and for imports, at the point of importation. Such a cap will effectively cover all sources of CO_2 emissions throughout the economy.

The upstream programme should include a credit mechanism to address the small portion of fossil fuels that are not combusted and to address the use of post-combustion emission-reduction technologies, such as carbon capture and sequestration (CCS). In addition, upstream regulation should include a credit-based programme for fossil-fuel exports so that they are not at a competitive disadvantage relative to supply from other countries that do not face any allowance requirements.

An economy-wide cap provides the greatest certainty that national emission targets will be achieved. Limiting the scope of coverage to a subset of emission sources leads to emissions uncertainty through two channels. First, changes in emissions from unregulated sources can cause national emissions to deviate from expected levels. Second, a limited scope of coverage can cause 'leakage', in which market adjustments resulting from a regulation lead to increased emissions from unregulated sources outside the cap that partially offset reductions under the cap.

An emission cap with broad coverage of emission sources reduces the cost of achieving a particular national emissions target. Three factors contribute to lower costs. First, a broader cap expands the pool of low-cost emission-reduction opportunities that can contribute to meeting a national target. Second, an economy-wide cap provides important flexibility to achieve emission targets given uncertainties in emission-reduction costs across sectors. Third, an economy-wide cap creates incentives for innovation in all sectors of the economy.

The point of regulation decision is a primary determinant of a cap-and-trade system's administrative costs through its effect on the number of sources that must be regulated. As the number of regulated sources increases, the administrative costs to regulators and firms rise. The upstream point of regulation makes an economy-wide cap-and-trade system administratively feasible, making it possible to cap nearly all US CO_2 emissions through regulation of just 2,000 upstream entities (Bluestein, 2005). A key advantage of an upstream programme is that it eliminates the regulatory need for facility-level GHG emissions inventories, which would be essential for monitoring and enforcing a cap-and-trade system that is implemented downstream at the point of emissions.

(iv) Elements that Reduce Cost Uncertainty

Concern about cost uncertainty in the context of cap-and-trade systems derives from the possibility of unexpected, significant cost increases. The experience with the southern California RECLAIM cap-and-trade system for NO_x emissions is the frequently cited example. RECLAIM had *no* automatic mechanism to relax emission caps in the face of unexpectedly high costs and, in 2000, allowance prices spiked to more than 20 times their historical levels (Pizer, 2005). Cost uncertainty may increase the long-run cost of emission caps, because uncertainty about future allowance prices may deter firms from undertaking socially desirable, capital-intensive emission-reduction investments, forcing greater reliance on less capital-intensive, but more costly measures.

Allowance banking and borrowing can mitigate some of the undesirable consequences of cost uncertainty by giving firms the flexibility to shift the timing of emission reductions in the face of unexpectedly high or low costs. If the cost of achieving targets is unexpectedly and temporarily high, firms can use banked or borrowed allowances instead of undertaking costly reductions. Thus, banking and borrowing mitigate undesirable year-to-year variation in costs. Banking of allowances—undertaking extra emission reductions earlier, so that more allowances are available for use later—has added greatly to the cost effectiveness of previous cap-and-trade systems (Stavins, 2003), but banking provides little protection when costs remain high over extended periods, which could eventually lead to exhaustion of banked allowances. This problem may be particularly acute in a cap's early years, when relatively few allowances have been banked. Therefore, borrowing of allowances from future years' allocations can be a particularly useful form of cost protection in these early years. Of course, credible mechanisms need to be established to ensure that the use of borrowed allowances is offset through future emission reductions.

Banking and borrowing can be exceptionally important in reducing long-term cost uncertainty, but the possibility of dramatic short-term allowance-price volatility may call for the inclusion of a sensible cost-containment mechanism. Such a mechanism could allow capped sources to purchase additional allowances at a predetermined price, set sufficiently *high* to make it unlikely to have any effect unless allowance prices exhibited truly drastic spikes, *and* the revenues from the fee dedicated *exclusively* to financing emissions reductions by uncapped sources, such as of non-CO_2 greenhouse gases, or to buying back allowances in future years. This is very different from standard proposals for a 'safety valve,' both because environmental integrity (the cap) is maintained by using the fees exclusively to finance additional emissions reductions or buy back allowances in future years, and because the pre-determined price is set at a high level so that it has no effect unless there are drastic price spikes.

The pre-determined fee places a ceiling on allowance prices and hence on abatement costs, because no firms would undertake emission reductions more costly than the trigger price (Jacoby and Ellerman, 2002). To be used as an insurance mechanism, the fee should be set at the maximum incremental emission-reduction cost that society is willing to bear. At this level, the mechanism would be triggered only when costs are unexpectedly and unacceptably high.

(v) Allocation of Allowances

While all allocation decisions have significant distributional consequences, whether allowances are auctioned or freely distributed can affect the programme's overall cost. Generally speaking, the choice between auctioning and freely allocating allowances does not influence firms' production and emission-reduction decisions. Firms face the same emissions cost regardless of the allocation method. Even when using an allowance that was received for free, a firm loses the opportunity to sell that allowance, and thereby recognizes this 'opportunity cost' in deciding whether to use an allowance. Consequently, in many respects, this allocation choice will not influence a cap's overall costs. But there are two ways that the choice to distribute allowances freely can affect a cap's cost.

First, auction revenue may be used in ways that reduce the costs of the existing tax system or fund other socially beneficial policies. Free allocations forgo such opportunities. Second, free allocations may affect electricity prices in regulated cost-of-service electricity markets, and thereby affect the extent to which reduced electricity demand contributes to limiting emissions cost-effectively.

In discussions about whether to auction or freely distribute allowances, much attention has been given to the opportunity to use auction revenue to reduce existing distortionary taxes on labour and capital. Use of auction revenue to reduce these taxes can stimulate economic activity, offsetting some of a cap's costs. Studies indicate that 'recycling' auction revenue by reducing personal income tax rates could offset 40–50 per cent of the economy-wide social costs that a cap would impose if allowances were freely distributed (Bovenberg and Goulder, 2003).

Achieving such gains may be difficult in practice, because climate policy would need to be tied to particular types of tax reform. The estimated cost-reductions are for policies in which auction revenue is used to reduce marginal tax rates that diminish incentives to work and invest. If, instead, auction revenue funded deductions or fixed tax credits, such tax reform would have a lesser effect (and perhaps no effect) on incentives to work and invest.

In general, auctioning generates revenue that can be put towards innumerable uses. Use of auction revenue to reduce tax rates is just one example. Other socially valuable uses of revenue could include reduction of the federal debt (including offsetting a cap's potentially adverse fiscal impacts), or funding desirable spending programmes (for example, research and development). On the other hand, some government uses of auction revenue may generate less economic value than could be realized by private-sector use of those funds. Thus, the opportunity to reduce the aggregate cost of a climate policy through auctioning, rather than freely distributing allowances, depends fundamentally on the use to which auction revenues are ultimately put.

While auctioning has the potential to reduce a climate policy's economy-wide costs, depending on how auction revenues are used, free distribution of allowances provides an opportunity to address the distribution of a climate policy's economic impacts. Free distribution of allowances can be used to redistribute a cap's economic burdens in ways that mitigate impacts on the most affected entities, and a sensible principle for allocation would be to try to compensate the most burdened sectors and individuals. Such redistribution of impacts may help establish consensus on a climate policy that achieves meaningful emission reductions.

Because free allocations may increase a cap's overall cost, it is important to consider what share of allowances need to be freely distributed to meet specific compensation objectives. A permanent allocation of all allowances to affected firms would, in aggregate, significantly overcompensate them for their financial losses (Goulder, 2000; Smith *et al.*, 2002; Bovenberg and Goulder, 2003). This is the case because much of the cost that a cap-and-trade system initially imposes on firms will be passed on to consumers in the form of higher prices. In effect, before any free allocation, firms are already partially compensated by changes in prices that result from the cap. Thus, freely allocating *all* allowances in perpetuity to affected firms would both overcompensate them in aggregate, and use up resources that could otherwise be put towards other uses.

Faced with important differences in the implications of free allocation and an auction, the best alternative is to *begin* with a hybrid approach, wherein half of the allowances are *initially* auctioned and half are freely distributed to entities that are burdened by the policy, including suppliers of primary fuels, electric power producers, energy-intensive manufacturers, and particularly trade-sensitive sectors. The share of allowances that are freely distributed should decline over time, until there is no free allocation 25 years into the programme. This is because over time the private sector will have an opportunity to adjust to the carbon constraints, including industries with long-lived capital assets. Thus, the justification for free distribution diminishes over time.[4] In the short term, however, free distribution provides flexibility to address distributional concerns that might otherwise impede initial agreement on a policy. The half that are initially auctioned will generate revenue that can be used for public purposes, including compensation for programme impacts on low-income consumers, public spending for related research and development, reduction of the federal deficit, and reduction of distortionary taxes.

Why this particular pattern of beginning with a 50–50 auction-free allocation, moving to 100 per cent auction over 25 years? This time-path of the numerical division between the share of allowances that is freely allocated and the share that is auctioned is consistent with analyses which have been carried out of the share of allowances that would need to be distributed freely to compensate firms for equity losses. In a series of analyses that considered the share of allowances that would be required *in perpetuity* for full compensation, Bovenberg and Goulder (2003) found that 13 per cent would be sufficient for compensation of the fossil-fuel-extraction sectors, and in a scenario consistent with the Bovenberg and Goulder study, Smith *et al.* (2002) found that 21 per cent would be needed to compensate primary energy producers and electricity generators.

The time-path recommended here for an economy-wide programme—50 per cent of allowances initially distributed freely, with this share declining steadily (linearly) to zero after 25 years—is equivalent in terms of present discounted value to perpetual allocations (as those previously analysed) of 15, 19, and 22 per cent, at real interest rates of 3, 4, and 5 per cent, respectively. Hence, the recommended

[4] For discussion of the temporal dimension of climate policy, see Helm *et al.* (2005).

allocation is consistent with the principle of targeting free allocations to burdened sectors in proportion to their relative burdens. It is also pragmatic to be more generous with the allocation in the early years of the programme.

(vi) Credits (Offsets) for Specified Activities

The upstream programme should include selective use of the credit mechanism. First, credits should be issued for major non-combustion uses of fossil fuels, such as in some petrochemical feedstocks, as well as fuel exports. Second, credits should be issued for carbon capture and storage (CCS). Emission reductions from CCS technologies can be readily measured, and because there is no incentive to install CCS equipment absent a climate policy, emission reductions achieved by CCS are clearly additional. As CCS technologies may play a significant role in achieving long-run emission reduction goals (Deutch and Moniz, 2007; US Energy Information Administration, 2007), this credit mechanism is an essential component of the upstream cap.

Third, a programme of credits for selected cases of biological sequestration through land-use changes should be included. A cost-effective portfolio of climate technologies in the United States would include a substantial amount of biological carbon sequestration through afforestation and retarded deforestation (Stavins, 1999; Stavins and Richards, 2005; Lubowski *et al.*, 2006). Translating this into practical policy will be a considerable challenge, however, because of concerns about monitoring and enforcement, additionality, and permanence (Plantinga, 2007).

Fourth, provision should be made to provide coverage over time of non-CO_2 greenhouse gases. Although CO_2 is by far the most important anthropogenic greenhouse gas (84 per cent of radiative forcing linked with emissions in 2005), it is by no means the only greenhouse gas of concern. Carbon dioxide, methane (CH_4), nitrous oxide (N_2O), and three groups of fluorinated gases—sulphur hexafluoride (SF_6), hydrofluorocarbons (HFCs), and perfluorinated compounds PFCs—are the major greenhouse gases and the focus of the Kyoto Protocol. The non-CO_2 GHGs are significant in terms of their cumulative impact on climate change, representing about 16 per cent of radiative forcing in 2005. And because some emission reductions could be achieved at relatively low cost, their inclusion in a programme would be attractive in principle (Paltsev *et al.*, 2007*a*).

The sources of some of these gases are large in number and highly dispersed, making their inclusion in a cap-and-trade programme problematic. The answer may be to phase in regulation selectively over time with credit (offset) mechanisms, being careful to grant credits in CO_2-equivalent terms only for well-documented reductions. Over time, such approaches could be developed for industrial emissions of methane and NO_2 and for the manufacture of key industrial gases in the case of refrigerants (HFCs), circuits (PFCs), and transformers (SF_6). Thus, cap-and-trade of non-CO_2 GHGs would likely combine upstream and downstream points of regulation.

(vii) Linkage with other Cap-and-trade Systems and other Nations' Policies

Three distinct linkage issues are important. These are: the relationship of the national cap-and-trade system with existing state and regional systems in the United States; the linkage of the cap-and-trade system with other such systems in other parts of the world; and—more broadly—the relationship between the cap-and-trade system and other nations' climate policies.

First, there is the reality of various state and regional cap-and-trade systems for greenhouse gases in the United States. In the absence of a national climate policy, ten north-eastern states have developed a downstream cap-and-trade programme among electricity generators in their RGGI, and California is considering implementing a cap-and-trade programme at the state level. The economy-wide, national, upstream cap-and-trade system could take the place of any regional, state, and local systems to avoid duplication, double counting, and conflicting requirements (Stavins, 2007). It is likely that a decision will be reached on a national cap-and-trade system before any of the regional or state programmes have actually been implemented.

In the long run, linking of the US cap-and-trade system with such systems in other countries or regions, such as the EU ETS, will clearly be desirable to reduce the overall cost of reducing GHG emissions and achieving any global GHG concentration targets (Jaffe and Stavins, 2007). But there is a question of what level and type of linkage is desirable in the early years of the development of a US cap-and-trade system. In the short term, it may be best for the United States to focus on linkage with emission reduction credit (ERC) programmes, such as the Kyoto Protocol's Clean Development Mechanism (CDM), particularly if the CDM can be improved along the lines discussed at the 13th Conference of the Parties of the Framework Convention on Climate Change, in Bali, Indonesia, in December, 2007, namely to give greater emphasis to programme- and policy-based opportunities, as opposed to project-based opportunities, as a means to decrease the prevalence of additionality concerns.

First, by tapping low-cost emission-reduction opportunities in developing countries, linkage of the US system with CDM has a greater potential to achieve significant cost savings for the United States than does linkage with cap-and-trade systems in other industrialized countries (where abatement costs are more similar to those in the United States). Second, linkage with an ERC system such as CDM can only have the effect of decreasing domestic allowance prices, since transactions are uni-directional, i.e. US purchases of (low-cost) CDM credits. Third, the USA may have to choose between adopting a cost-containment mechanism and linking with cap-and-trade systems in other countries. It appears unlikely that the European Union would agree to linking its Emissions Trading Scheme with a US system that employed a safety valve or other such cost-containment measure. On the other hand, the USA could link with ERC systems, such as the CDM, even with a cost-containment measure in place.

Fourth, given that other cap-and-trade systems, such as that of the European Union, will likely be linked with CDM, linking the US system with CDM will have the effect of indirectly linking the US system with those other cap-and-trade systems, but in ways that avoid the short-term problems identified above. Fifth, such indirect linkage should reduce concerns about additionality normally associated with linking with CDM. If another country or region (for example, the European Union) has already linked with CDM, many of the credits that the US system would ultimately purchase would be used by other linked cap-and-trade systems if the United States did not link with CDM. Hence, for these credits, there is no incremental additionality concern regarding the US decision to link with CDM. Any US use of these credits would result in emission reductions in the other linked cap-and-trade systems that would otherwise have used the credits. Sixth, the indirect linkage created by a US link with CDM can achieve some and perhaps many of the cost savings that would arise from direct linkage with other cap-and-trade systems. This is because CDM credits can be sold on the secondary market, and so will ultimately go to the linked cap-and-trade system with the highest allowance price, pushing the allowance prices of the various cap-and-trade systems towards the convergence that would be achieved by direct linkage among cap-and-trade systems.

The fact that climate change is a global-commons phenomenon means that it can be sensible to condition the goals and operations of the US cap-and-trade programme on the GHG emissions reductions efforts that other countries are employing. One approach is to include a provision for the overall US emissions cap to be tightened when and if the President or the Congress determine that other major CO_2-emitting nations have taken specific climate-policy actions. Such 'issue linkage'—making the cap contingent upon the actions of other key countries—can make sense, particularly absent US participation in a binding international agreement. This links the *goals* of the US system with other countries' actions.

In addition, the *operation* of the cap-and-trade system should be linked with the actions of other key nations. As part of the cap-and-trade programme, imports of specific highly carbon-intensive goods (in terms of their emissions generated during manufacture) from countries which have not taken climate-policy actions comparable to those in the United States should be required to hold appropriate quantities of allowances (mirroring the allowance requirements on US sources). These allowances can be purchased from any participants in the domestic cap-and-trade system. This mechanism, if properly designed and implemented, can help establish a level playing-field in the market for domestically produced and imported products, and thereby can serve to reduce emissions leakage and induce key developing countries to join an international agreement (Morris and Hill, 2007).

There are some understandable concerns with such a mechanism. First, there is the economist's natural resistance to tampering with free international trade in order to achieve other ends. Second, there is the difficulty of making the needed calculations of appropriate quantities of allowances on imports of manufactured goods. Third, there is the inescapable irony that the United States might adopt a mechanism for use with other countries, which had recently been proposed by Europeans for use against the United States (although with a border tax) because of US non-ratification of the Kyoto Protocol. More broadly, there is the risk that this mechanism would be abused and inappropriately applied as a protectionist measure.

These concerns can be addressed by properly constraining the mechanism to apply only to primary highly energy-intensive commodities—such as iron and steel, aluminium, cement, bulk glass, paper, and, for that matter, fossil fuels. The requirement would not apply to countries that are taking comparable actions to reduce their GHG emissions, and exemptions could be provided for countries with very low levels of GHG emissions and the lowest levels of economic development.

In order to be compatible with World Trade Organization rules, it is key that the burden imposed on imported and domestic goods be roughly comparable, and that there not be discrimination among nations with similar conditions (Frankel, 2005; Pauwelyn, 2007). Also, this requirement should become binding only after 5–10 years, to allow time for an international climate agreement to be negotiated that includes all key countries in meaningful ways and thereby obviates the need for the mechanism (Aldy and Stavins, 2007).

(viii) Associated Climate Policies

The price signals generated by a well-functioning upstream cap-and-trade system will be insufficient for their purpose if there are remaining market failures that render those price signals ineffective. For example, there may be market failures other than the environmental externality of global climate change associated with energy-efficiency investments. If the magnitude of these non-environmental market failures is large enough and the cost of correcting them small enough to warrant policy intervention, then an argument can be made to attack these other market failures directly (Jaffe *et al.*, 1999).

Examples of such relevant market failures include information problems that lead consumers to under-value expected energy-cost savings when purchasing energy-consuming durable goods. Likewise, there is the principal-agent problem of landlords who may under-invest in energy-efficient appliances, because electricity costs are paid by tenants. Perhaps most important is the public-good nature of research and development, which leads to under-investment in R&D because knowledge generated may not be exclusive and so economic returns cannot be fully captured. To achieve the desired levels of investment, additional public policies—of various kinds, beyond the price signals generated by the cap-and-trade system—may be necessary (National Commission on Energy Policy, 2004, 2007).

III. ECONOMIC ASSESSMENT

A considerable number of analytical models have been employed over the past several years to estimate the aggregate costs (and in some cases, the distributional impacts) of a cost-effective set of emissions-reduction actions to achieve various national CO_2 and GHG targets. Two models have had a distinctly US focus, and have been used to give particular attention to the costs associated with domestic cap-and-trade systems: the National Energy Modeling System (NEMS) of the US Department of Energy (US Energy Information Administration, 2007), and the Emissions Prediction and Policy Analysis (EPPA) model of the Massachusetts Institute of Technology's Joint Program on the Science and Policy of Global Change (Paltsev *et al.*, 2007*a*, *b*).

To provide illustrative empirical cost estimates, I draw upon recent results from MIT's EPPA model, both because of the recent vintage of the analysis and because the model was applied by its authors (Paltsev *et al.*, 2007*a*, *b*) to examining an upstream cap-and-trade system that is—in its stylized form—close to what is described here.

The first illustrative trajectory involves stabilizing CO_2 emissions at their 2008 level over the period from 2012 to 2050. This trajectory, in terms of its cumulative cap, lies within the range defined by the 2004 and 2007 recommendations of the National Commission on Energy Policy (2004, 2007). The second illustrative trajectory—also defined over the years 2012–50—involves reducing CO_2 emissions from their 2008 level to 50 per cent below their 1990 level by 2050. This trajectory—defined by its cumulative cap—is consistent with the lower end of the range proposed by the US Climate Action Partnership (2007).

The tradable CO_2 allowances have value because of their scarcity, and it is their market-determined price that provides incentives for cost-effective emissions reductions and investments that bring down abatement costs over time. As the required emissions reductions (relative to 'business as usual' (BAU)) increase over time under both cap trajectories (Table 10.1), the market prices of the allowances also increase, rising from US$18/ton of CO_2 in 2015 to US$70/ton of CO_2 in 2050 for the less aggressive policy, and rising from US$41/ton of CO_2 in 2015 to US$161/ton of CO_2 in 2050 for the more aggressive policy (Table 10.2).

Fossil-fuel prices are also predicted to change as a result of the cap-and-trade system, because of effects on the supply and demand for those fuels in various markets. As Table 10.2 indicates, the net effect of both caps on coal and petroleum prices is to depress those prices *relative* to what they would be in the absence of climate policy, because of reduced fuel demand. It is important to note, however, that although these prices include the effects of allowance prices on fossil-fuel supply and demand, they do not include the cost of allowances *per se*.

As indicated above, the cap-and-trade system has the effect of reducing demand for fossil fuels relative to BAU conditions and hence reducing fossil-fuel prices *relative* to what those prices would be in the absence of policy. There is an important distinction, however, between the price of fuels themselves (Table 10.2) and the

Table 10.1. Anticipated CO_2 emissions reductions under two illustrative caps (million metric tons)

Scenario[a]		2005	2010	2015	2020	2025	2030	2035	2040	2045	2050
BAU	Emissions	5,984	6,517	6,995	7,357	7,915	8,518	9,283	10,013	10,871	11,656
Stabilize	Emissions	5,984	6,517	6,328	6,287	6,132	6,290	7,265	7,605	7,126	7,175
	Reduction[b]	0	0	−667	−1,070	−1,783	−2,228	−2,018	−2,408	3,745	−4,481
	% reduction[c]	0	0	−10	−15	−23	−26	−22	−24	−34	−38
50% b/1990	Emissions	5,984	6,517	5,740	5,443	4,914	4,085	5,169	4,650	3,588	2,945
	Reduction	0	0	−1,255	−1,914	−3,001	−4,433	−4,114	−5,363	−7,283	−8,711
	% reduction	0	0	−18	−26	−38	−52	−44	−54	−67	−75

Notes: [a] 'BAU' (business as usual) is the reference case from Paltsev *et al.* (2007*a*, *b*); 'Stabilize' is based on the 287 cumulative carbon-dioxide-equivalent billion metric ton (CO_2-e bmt) case from Paltsev *et al.* (2007*a*, *b*); and '50% b/1990' refers to 2050 emissions capped at 50 per cent below the 1990 level, and is based on the 203 cumulative CO_2-e bmt case from Paltsev *et al.* (2007*a*, *b*).
[b] Compared with BAU emissions in the same year.
[c] Compared with BAU emissions in the same year.
Source: Paltsev *et al.* (2007*b*, pp. 1, 2, 3).

cost of using those fuels, which is illustrated in Table 10.3. For sample allowance prices of US$25, US$50, and US$100/ton of CO_2, the added cost is estimated for major fuels, including crude oil, gasoline, heating oil, wellhead natural gas, residential natural gas, and utility coal. These added costs of allowances to fuel users (which do not include the adjustment for the effects of the cap-and-trade

Table 10.2. Predicted CO_2 and fossil fuel prices[a] under two illustrative caps

	Scenario[b]	2005	2010	2015	2020	2025	2030	2035	2040	2045	2050
CO_2 price[c]	BAU	0	0	0	0	0	0	0	0	0	0
	Stabilize	0	0	18	22	26	32	39	47	57	70
	50% b/1990	0	0	41	50	61	74	90	109	133	161
Petroleum product	BAU	1.0	1.2	1.3	1.5	1.7	1.9	2.0	2.1	2.2	2.3
	Stabilize	1.0	1.2	1.3	1.5	1.6	1.7	1.4	1.4	1.5	1.5
	50% b/1990	1.0	1.2	1.3	1.5	1.5	1.6	1.3	1.4	1.3	1.2
Natural gas	BAU	1.0	1.1	1.3	1.5	1.7	2.0	2.3	2.7	3.1	3.6
	Stabilize	1.0	1.1	1.2	1.5	1.9	2.4	2.5	2.8	2.8	2.8
	50% b/1990	1.0	1.1	1.2	1.4	1.8	2.1	2.1	2.2	2.2	2.0
Coal	BAU	1.0	1.0	1.1	1.1	1.1	1.2	1.2	1.2	1.3	1.3
	Stabilize	1.0	1.0	1.0	1.0	1.0	1.0	1.0	1.1	1.1	1.2
	50% b/1990	1.0	1.0	1.0	1.0	1.0	1.0	1.0	1.1	1.1	1.2

Notes: [a] All fossil fuel prices are price indices, with 2005 set equal to 1. Note that the price indices do not include the cost of allowances, but do include the effects of changes in fossil-fuel supply and demand (induced by impacts of allowance prices on downstream users of respective fossil fuels).
[b] 'BAU' (business as usual) is the reference case from Paltsev *et al.* (2007*a*, *b*), Stabilize' is based on the 287 cumulative CO_2-e bmt case from Paltsev *et al.* (2007*a*, *b*); and '50% b/1990 refers to 2050 emissions capped at 50 per cent below the 1990 level, and is based on the 203 cumulative CO_2-e bmt case from Paltsev *et al.* (2007*a*, *b*).
[c] Year 2005 dollars per ton of CO_2-equivalent.
Source: Paltsev *et al.* (2007*b*, pp. 1, 2, 3).

Table 10.3. Relationship between CO_2 allowance prices and recent fuel prices

Fuel	Average base price[a] 2002–6	Added fuel cost for various allowance prices[b]		
		US$25	US$50	US$100
Crude oil (US$/bbl)	$40.00	$11.30	$22.60	$45.20
		28%	57%	113%
Gasoline (US$/gallon)	$1.82	$0.24	$0.48	$0.96
		13%	26%	53%
Heating oil (US$/gallon)	$1.35	$0.27	$0.54	$1.08
		20%	40%	80%
Wellhead natural gas (US$/mcf)	$5.40	$1.38	$2.76	$5.52
		26%	51%	102%
Residential natural gas (US$/mcf)	$11.05	$1.39	$2.78	$5.56
		13%	25%	50%
Utility coal (US$/short ton)	$26.70	$51.20	$102.40	$204.80
		192%	384%	767%

Notes: [a] 2005 dollars.
[b] Added cost does not include adjustment for the effects of respective cap-and-trade policies on producer prices.
Source: For base prices, Paltsev *et al.* (2007*a*); added fuel costs are from author's calculations, drawing upon Table 5, p. 53, in the same source.

policies on producer prices from Table 10.2) are compared with the average price of the respective fuels over a recent period of time.

The cap-and-trade system, like any regulatory initiative, affects the behaviour of individuals and firms, causing reallocation of resources, and thereby causing economic output to grow more slowly than it would in the absence of the policy. Impacts on gross domestic product (GDP) are measured relative to no policy (BAU), and so reductions in GDP do not indicate that output would be lower than current levels, but rather that output would be lower than it would otherwise be expected to be (Table 10.4).

Consistent with findings from other studies, the analysis indicates significant but affordable impacts on GDP, generally reductions below BAU of less than

Table 10.4. Predicted aggregate costs: GDP impacts under two illustrative caps

	Scenario[a]	2005	2010	2015	2020	2025	2030	2035	2040	2045	2050
BAU[b]	GDP	11,981	14,339	16,921	19,773	22,846	26,459	30,534	34,929	39,530	44,210
% change GDP from BAU	Stabilize	0	0	−0.22	−0.38	−0.55	−0.68	−0.33	−0.29	−0.36	−0.28
	50% b/1990	0	0	−0.51	−0.79	−0.67	−0.56	−1.18	−1.00	−0.61	−0.48

Notes: [a] 'BAU' (business as usual) is the reference case from Paltsev *et al.* (2007*a*, *b*); 'Stabilize' is based on the 287 cumulative CO_2-e bmt case from Paltsev *et al.* (2007*a*, *b*); and '50% b/1990' refers to 2050 emissions capped at 50 per cent below the 1990 level, and is based on the 203 cumulative CO_2-e bmt case from Paltsev *et al.* (2007*a*, *b*).
[b] Billions of year 2005 dollars.
Source: Paltsev *et al.* (2007*b*, pp. 1, 2, 3).

one-half of 1 per cent in each year of the programme for the less aggressive cap trajectory and ranging up to 1 per cent below BAU each year for the more aggressive policy (Table 10.4). These impacts on GDP by 2050 are equivalent to average annual GDP growth in the BAU case of 2.901 per cent, and average annual GDP growth of 2.895 and 2.891 per cent, respectively, under the two cap trajectories.

Despite the fact that aggregate impacts on economic output (GDP) are relatively small, there can be very substantial impacts on particular sectors or groups of people. Regardless of how allowances are distributed, most of the cost of the programme will be borne by consumers, facing higher prices of products, including electricity and gasoline—impacts that will continue as long as the programme is in place. Also, workers and investors in the energy sectors and energy-intensive industries will experience losses in the form of lower wages, job losses, or reduced stock values. Such impacts are temporary, and workers or investors who enter an industry after the policy takes effect typically do not experience such losses (Dinan, 2007). The fact that the policy is phased in gradually provides more time for firms and people to adapt.

The cost impacts can be regressive, because lower-income households spend a larger share of their income than wealthier households, and energy products account for a larger share of spending by low-income households than wealthier households. But the distributional impacts will depend greatly on the specifics of policy design, including how allowances are allocated and how auction revenues are used.

Certain sectors and firms will be particularly affected, including fossil-fuel producers, the electricity sector, and energy-intensive industries. Coal production will be the most affected because coal is the most carbon-intensive fuel and opportunities exist for electricity generators and some industrial consumers to switch to less carbon-intensive fuels. Petroleum sector output will be less affected, partly because demand for gasoline and other petroleum products is fairly insensitive to increased prices, at least in the short term. And it is uncertain whether a cap would benefit or adversely affect output and profitability of natural gas producers (US Energy Information Administration, 2003, 2006).

Among firms that consume fossil fuels and electricity, impacts will likely be most pronounced in energy- and emissions-intensive industries (Jorgenson *et al.*, 2000; Smith *et al.*, 2002; Bovenberg and Goulder, 2003; US Energy Information Administration, 2003). For example, some of the most affected industries will be petroleum refiners and manufacturers of chemicals, primary metals, and paper. Refiners experience both increased production costs for their production-related emissions and reduced demand as consumers seek to limit emissions from the use of petroleum products. Among industries experiencing similar increases in their costs, impacts will be greatest in globally competitive industries that are least able to pass through higher costs without experiencing reduced demand for their output.

Industry-level impacts may obscure significant variation in firm-level impacts within an industry. The electricity sector offers an important example of this point. Regional variation in electricity-sector impacts will be greater than in many other sectors because of regional differences in the composition of power plants (including fuel type), physical limits on interregional electricity trading, and state regulation of electricity markets. Increases in the cost of electricity generation depend on the carbon-intensity of a region's generation, which varies widely across the country.

While attention often focuses on a cap's impacts on particular industries, the ultimate burden will be borne by households, primarily in the form of increased expenditures on energy and other goods and services, but also through changes in labour income (including job losses) and investment income (i.e. stock and mutual fund returns) that arise from impacts on firms. Higher fuel prices will likely have a regressive effect on households, although the degree of regressivity may not be very great (Dinan, 2007). Further, this regressivity may be counterbalanced by the fact that adverse impacts on investment returns resulting from a cap's effect on the profitability of firms will fall most heavily on high-income households.

There are also distributional implications of the allowance allocation, and the aggregate value of allowances will be much greater than the total cost burden to the economy. The value of allowances will be two to four times greater than the total cost of the programme in most years under either of the cap trajectories. Therefore, even a partial free distribution of allowances provides an opportunity to address the distributional cost burdens of the policy by using allowances to compensate the most burdened sectors and individuals.

IV. COMPARISON WITH ALTERNATIVE APPROACHES

The alternatives to the cap-and-trade approach most frequently considered by policy-makers for the purpose of reducing CO_2 and other GHG emissions are standards-based policies. In addition, among economists and some policy analysts, there has been discussion about the possible use of carbon taxes.

(i) Standards-based Policies

Technology or performance standards are a commonly proposed means of achieving emission reductions. Examples include efficiency standards for appliances, vehicle fuel-economy standards, best-available control technology standards, and renewable portfolio standards for electricity generators.

Because of practical limitations, most standards to address CO_2 emissions would target energy use or emission rates from new capital equipment, such as appliances, cars, or electricity generators. The fact that standards would affect new, but not existing equipment limits the opportunity for near-term emission reductions. It also makes the level and timing of those reductions dependent on the rate of capital stock turnover, and thereby difficult to predict. Moreover, by increasing the cost of new capital stock without affecting the cost of using the existing capital stock, standards on new sources have the perverse effect of creating incentives to delay replacement of existing capital stock, which can significantly delay the achievement of emission reductions (Stavins, 2006).

When considered as an alternative to a well-designed cap-and-trade system, standards-based approaches are less cost-effective. Administrative limitations constrain the scope of sources that can be covered by a standards-based approach, compared with an upstream, broad-based cap-and-trade system, and standards may not target all determinants of emissions from covered sources. Consequently, they may not bring about many types of potentially cost-effective emission reductions. Also, standards often impose uniform requirements, even though the cost of emission reductions achieved by such standards may vary widely across regulated entities (Newell and Stavins, 2003).

Standards have also been proposed as complements to market-based policies. On the one hand, standards may needlessly restrict the flexibility that allows market-based policies to minimize the cost of achieving emission targets. If standards are applied within the umbrella of an economy-wide CO_2 cap-and-trade system, the standards will offer no additional CO_2 benefits, as long as the cap-and-trade system is binding, but depending upon the nature of the standard and its associated costs, its placement can drive up aggregate costs. On the other hand, as emphasized above, some market failures affecting the development and adoption of less emissions-intensive technologies may not be addressed by a cap-and-trade (or carbon tax) policy. Simply increasing the cost of emitting GHGs will not address the core sources of such market failures.

(ii) Carbon Taxes

Both a carbon tax and a cap-and-trade system create a carbon price signal, but there is a fundamental difference in the way in which the level of that carbon price signal is determined. A carbon tax fixes the price of CO_2 emissions, and allows the quantity of emissions to adjust, whereas a cap-and-trade system fixes the quantity of aggregate emissions, and allows the price of CO_2 emissions to adjust.

A carbon tax (if implemented upstream and economy-wide) would appear to have some advantages over an equivalent upstream cap-and-trade system. First, is the simplicity of the carbon tax system, in which firms would not need to manage and trade allowances, and the government would not need to track allowance transactions and ownership. Experience with previous cap-and-trade systems, however, indicates that the costs of trading institutions are not significant. Whether a policy as significant as a meaningful national carbon tax would turn out to be simple in its implementation is an open question. Second, the tax approach avoids the political difficulties related to making allowance allocations among economic sectors, but would—on the other hand—create pressures for tax exemptions.

Third, a carbon tax would raise revenues that can be used for beneficial public purposes. Of course, an auction mechanism under a cap-and-trade system can do the same. Fourth, a tax approach eliminates the potential for price volatility that can exist under a cap-and-trade system. Some emissions-trading markets have exhibited significant volatility in their early years, including: the US NO_x Budget program (where prices increased in the presence of uncertainty about whether Maryland, a net supplier, would enter the programme on time); the RECLAIM programme in southern California (where price spikes were linked with flawed design and problems with electricity deregulation); and the EU ETS (where a dramatic price crash occurred when data revealed that the overall allocation had been *above* the BAU level). From an economic perspective, it makes sense to allow emissions to vary from year to year with economic conditions that affect aggregate abatement costs; and this happens automatically with a carbon tax. With a cap-and-trade system, this temporal flexibility needs to be built in through provisions for banking and borrowing, as described above.

There is also a set of apparent disadvantages of carbon taxes, relative to a cap-and-trade regime, that merits consideration. First among these is the over-riding resistance to new taxes in the current political climate. Second, in their simplest respective forms (a carbon tax *without* revenue recycling, and a cap-and-trade system *without* auctions), a carbon tax is more costly than a cap-and-trade system to the regulated sector, because with the former firms incur both abatement costs and the cost of tax payments to the government. In the case of the simplest cap-and-trade system, the regulated sector experiences only abatement costs, since the transfers associated with allowance purchase and sale remain within the private sector.

Third, cap-and-trade approaches leave distributional issues up to politicians, and provide a straightforward means to compensate burdened sectors. Of course, the compensation associated with free distribution of allowances based on historical activities can be mimicked under a tax regime, but it is legislatively more complex. The cap-and-trade approach avoids likely battles over tax exemptions among vulnerable industries and sectors that would drive up the costs of the programme, as more and more sources (emission-reduction opportunities) are exempted from the programme, thereby simultaneously compromising environmental integrity. Instead, a cap-and-trade system leads to battles over the allowance allocation, but these do not raise the overall cost of the programme nor affect its climate impacts. Some observers seem to worry about the political process's propensity under a cap-and-trade system to compensate sectors that effectively claim burdens (through free allowance allocations). A carbon tax is sensitive to the same pressures, and may be expected to succumb to them in ways that are ultimately much more harmful. This is the crucial political-economy distinction between the two approaches.

Fourth, a carbon tax provides much less certainty over emissions levels (in exchange for greater certainty over costs). Most climate policy proposals are for progressively greater cuts in emissions over time. Cap-and-trade is fundamentally well suited to this because it is a quantity-based approach. Progress under a carbon tax will be uncertain, mainly owing to variations in economic conditions.

Fifth and finally, a cap-and-trade system is much easier to harmonize with other countries' carbon mitigation programmes, which are more likely to employ cap-and-trade than tax approaches. Cap-and-trade systems generate a natural unit of exchange for harmonization: allowances denominated in units of carbon content of fossil fuels (or CO_2 emissions). In addition, cap-and-trade provides a convenient means—allowances traded between firms—to transfer resources for emissions reductions in developing countries. A carbon tax raises funds for the government that could likewise be used for this purpose, but such transfers would need to be between governments, and such transfers would be larger in magnitude than individual trades between sources under a cap-and-trade system, thereby reducing greatly the political feasibility of such arrangements.

Despite the differences between carbon taxes and cap-and-trade systems in specific implementations, the two approaches have much in common. Differences between the two approaches can begin to fade when various specific implementations of either programme are carried out. Hybrid schemes that include features of taxes and cap-and-trade systems blur the distinctions between the two (Parry and Pizer, 2007). In terms of the allocation mechanism, the government can auction allowances in a cap-and-trade system, thereby reproducing many of the properties of a tax approach. Mechanisms that deal with uncertainty in a cap-and-trade system also bring it close to a tax approach, including a cost-containment mechanism that places a cap on allowance prices, banking that creates a floor under prices, and borrowing that provides flexibility similar to a tax. To some degree, the dichotomous choice between taxes and permits can turn out to be a choice of design elements along a policy continuum.

In the meantime, debate continues among economists regarding cap-and-trade and carbon taxes. In a recent comparison of these two approaches, the Hamilton Project staff at the Brookings Institution concluded that a well-designed carbon tax and a well-designed cap-and-trade system would have similar economic effects (Furman *et al.*, 2007). Hence, they concluded, the two primary questions that should be used to decide between these two policy approaches are: (i) which is more politically feasible; and (ii) which is more likely to be well designed? In the context of the United States (and many other countries, for that matter), the answer to the first question is obvious. For the political-economy reasons I described above, the answer to the second question also favours cap-and-trade. In other words, it is important to identify and design policies that will be 'optimal in Washington', not just from the perspective of Cambridge, New Haven, or Berkeley.

V. SUMMARY AND CONCLUSIONS

The need for a domestic US policy that seriously addresses climate change is increasingly apparent. A cap-and-trade system is the best and most likely approach for the United States in the short to medium term. Besides providing greater certainty about emissions levels, cap-and-trade offers an easy means (partial free distribution of allowances) of compensating for the inevitably unequal burdens imposed by climate policy; it is straightforward to harmonize with other countries' climate policies; it avoids the current political aversion in the United States to taxes; and it has a history of successful adoption.

The system outlined in this chapter has several key features. It imposes an upstream cap on CO_2 emissions (carbon content measured at the point of fuel extraction, refining, distribution, or importation), with gradual inclusion of other greenhouse gases, to ensure economy-wide coverage while limiting the number of entities to be monitored. It sets a gradual downward trajectory of emissions ceilings over time, to minimize disruption and allow firms and households time to adapt. It also includes mechanisms to reduce cost uncertainty; these include provisions for banking and borrowing of allowances, and possibly a cost-containment mechanism (such as the sale of additional allowances during severe price spikes, with the revenues dedicated to bringing about additional emissions reductions) to protect against price volatility.

Initially, half of the programme's allowances would be allocated through auctioning and half through free distribution, primarily to those entities most burdened by the policy. This arrangement should help limit potential inequities while bolstering political support. The share distributed for free would phase out gradually over 25 years. The auctioned allowances would generate revenue that could be used for a variety of worthwhile public purposes. To increase the programme's short-term cost-effectiveness and create long-term incentives for technological development, entities that successfully implement carbon sequestration (biological or underground) would be eligible for offsets.

The system would operate at the federal level, eventually asserting supremacy over all regional, state, and local systems, while building on any institutions already developed at those levels. The system would also provide for linkage with international emissions-reduction credit arrangements, harmonization over time with effective cap-and-trade systems in other countries, and appropriate linkage with other actions taken abroad to maintain a level playing field between imports and import-competing domestic products. To address potential market failures that might render the system's price signals ineffective, certain complementary policies should be implemented, for example in the areas of consumer information and research and development.

Like other market-based emissions-reduction schemes, the one described here reduces compliance costs by offering regulated entities: rather than mandate specific measures on all sources, it allows emissions to be reduced however, wherever, and, to a great extent, whenever they are least costly. To illustrate the potential cost savings, this chapter has reported empirical cost estimates for two hypothetical time trajectories for emissions caps. The first stabilizes CO_2 emissions at their 2008 level by 2050, whereas the second reduces emissions from their 2008 level to 50 per cent below the 1990 level by 2050. Both are consistent with the often-cited global goal of stabilizing CO_2 atmospheric concentrations at between 450 and

550 ppm, provided all countries take commensurate action. The analysis found significant but affordable impacts on GDP under both trajectories: generally below 0.5 per cent a year for the less aggressive trajectory, and ranging up to 1 per cent a year for the more aggressive one.

We also explored the distributional implications of the programme. Illustrative estimates—which do not account for the offsetting effects of possible free allocation of allowances or redistribution of auction revenues—indicate a relatively small burden on fossil-fuel producers (about 4 per cent of the total), because most of the costs would be passed on to customers. Fossil-fuel-fired electricity generators also would bear a relatively small share, about 7 per cent, for analogous reasons. Business and industry would bear nearly 30 per cent of the total cost burden through their primary energy use, and about 25 per cent through their electricity use, for a total of about 55 per cent. The remaining roughly 35 per cent of costs would be borne by households.

The impact of any US policy will ultimately depend on the actions of other nations around the world. Without an effective global climate agreement, each country's optimal strategy is to free-ride on the actions of others. But if all countries do this, nothing will be accomplished, and the result will be the infamous tragedy of the commons. A cooperative solution—one that is scientifically sound, economically rational, and politically pragmatic—must remain the ultimate goal. Given these realities, a major strategic consideration in initiating a US climate policy should be to establish international credibility. The cap-and-trade system described and assessed in this chapter offers a way for the United States to demonstrate its commitment to an international solution while making its own real contribution to addressing climate change.

11

EU Climate-change Policy—A Critique

*Dieter Helm**

I. INTRODUCTION

Environmental issues in general, and climate change in particular, lend themselves to EU rather than national policy: many of the effects (such as acid rain and water pollution) are regional, and climate change is global. To date, the EU has had some notable successes, of which addressing the problem of acid rain is perhaps the most significant in both scale and impact. But when it comes to climate change, there has been much action but little effect. Even though the EU comprises over 20 per cent of world GDP, and despite its historical responsibility for a considerable amount of the carbon dioxide (CO_2) in the atmosphere, its efforts in the last two decades have probably not made as much as one part per million difference. Indeed, it is arguable that, even in comparison with the USA, the EU has not made much progress. The rhetoric, the plethora of initiatives, directives, and interventions have not been matched by outcomes.

It might be argued that to date this is not surprising: much of the policy has been largely a 'trial'—a process of learning by intervention, potentially leading to a significant future advance both within the EU and at the international level. The January 2008 Climate Change Package (CEC, 2008*a*) and the negotiated agreement at the December 2008 Summit (CEC, 2008*b*) argue that the new 2020-20-20 targets will deliver the desired effects.[1]

This critique focuses on the 2008 package of measures. The starting point is the measures taken so far, notably in respect of Kyoto, and its production-based measurement of emissions (section II). This sets up the context for the 20-20-20 package (section III) and the subsequent analysis of each of the main components: the EU Emissions Trading Scheme (EU ETS) (section IV), the renewables targets (section V), and the energy efficiency measures (section VI). Critiquing a particular package necessitates an analysis of the alternatives—what the EU has not done, but could have done. The notable components are nuclear, significant carbon capture and storage (CCS), and a serious R&D programme, as well as a carbon tax with a carbon import component (section VII). The critique and the

* New College, Oxford.

[1] The EU is committed to reducing its overall emissions to at least 20 per cent below 1990 levels and increasing the share of renewables in energy use to 20 per cent by 2020.

alternatives come together in an overall assessment of the EU's climate-change policy and provide the conclusions (section VIII).

II. THE STARTING POINT

The EU has from its foundation been primarily focused on trade and economic integration. Beginning with the Coal and Steel Community, it moved to a customs union. The political 'deal' at the heart of its foundation was the integration of Germany into the European economy after the Second World War, and the 'price' Germany paid was to support French agriculture. Unsurprisingly, therefore, the Common Agricultural Policy absorbed much of the EU's budget for decades. After the Gaullist stalling of further integration in the 1960s, the EU in the 1970s began to move towards a currency reform, eventually resulting in a currency union for the main economies. Liberalization played a part in completing the internal market—first through the 1992 programme and then with the Lisbon agenda. New members were added, as the southern dictatorships of Greece, Portugal, and Spain embraced democracy, and the Soviet Union imploded.

Along this path and with its preoccupations, the environment played at best a peripheral part. The EU was never until recently an environmental project. That does not mean that there were no attempts at EU-wide environmental policy. Rather they were focused on specific issues. Acid rain was one such example, and it was an EU matter because it was regional rather than national. The Large Combustion Plants Directive (LCPD) (CEC, 2001) proved to be a core measure, with the effects still playing out.

Similarly, energy has been primarily a national undertaking, with national champions playing a key role—notwithstanding the early Treaty Establishing the European Coal and Steel Community in 1951. As the 1992 programme to complete the internal market got under way and as privatization and liberalization were tried in the UK, the competition elements of energy policy became more important, though, as the Commission reported in January 2007 (CEC, 2007), attempts to create a competitive European-wide energy market have been largely a failure. Integration through network development has also been largely unsuccessful.

Climate change came very late to the EU, and its importance has transformed environmental issues from the periphery to the core. In 2008, the EU effectively made it its central policy focus. This centrality was partly a matter of expediency—the failure quickly to ratify the Lisbon Treaty left the EU short of initiatives in 2008, and, more importantly, climate change provided a way in which it could demonstrate relevance to the wider public, faced with widespread scepticism about the EU's performance. The impotence of the Commission in the face of the global economic downturn reinforced this.

Climate change provided not only an opportunity to demonstrate the Commission's relevance, but also a foreign policy role for the Commission. Indeed, the climate-change policy issues started off with the global negotiations following the Rio Summit in 1992, and then the Kyoto follow-up. In a crowded international space—with, notably, first Thatcher and then Blair championing the cause of abating emissions—the EU had to compete with the G8 and other international forums. Yet the decisive advantage the EU had was that it actually wanted to commit to Kyoto targets in a context in which others—notably China, India, and the USA—did not.

Why did the EU lead on Kyoto? A combination of factors contributed to the strategy. The wider political attractions were compounded by the fact that Kyoto targets were seen as achievable with little or no pain. The collapse of the Eastern European and Russian economies at the end of the 1980s played helpfully against the 1990 baseline. The targets were defined in terms of carbon production, rather than consumption, and that neatly avoided the need to make substantial north–south financial transfers. Finally, more narrowly, European governments entered the 1990s in the context of declining support for the major parties and hence coalitions were increasingly required to form governments, putting green votes in a powerful position, able to exercise political leverage beyond their voting base. In this they were supported by lobby groups backing particular technologies. In response, major parties scrambled to incorporate this green vote.

In playing this leadership role, the EU was isolated. The USA stood aside, as did most of the other major powers. Only by persuading Russia to join Kyoto could it be implemented, to meet the hurdle for participation. The EU therefore turned to Russia, and there followed a series of diplomatic initiatives which eventually brought Russian on board. These included support for World Trade Organization (WTO) membership. For Russia, the calculation was simple: the scale of its economic collapse in the early 1990s meant that it would be unlikely to bear significant costs, and there was also the calculation that Kyoto might be better than more effective action to tackle global warming, which, for a predominantly carbon economy, may have represented a significant threat.

The EU went much further than supporting Kyoto; it pursued two parallel policies which would eventually figure as central to the 2008 package: the EU ETS and the promotion of renewables. The EU ETS came about as a combination of the growing enthusiasm for market mechanisms, the recognition that there needed to be a carbon price, and the strong lobbying by polluters for a permits scheme rather than a tax. EU attempts to go down the carbon tax route in the early 1990s had failed to get off the ground, and the UK-only ETS experiment provided an example to draw upon. There was also the evidence from permit trading in the USA for sulphur, and a recognition not only of its success but also that it might be better than the regulation-driven LCPD in Europe.

The EU ETS started in 2005 for an initial trial period running until 2008. Permits were grandfathered (as industry had hoped), incumbents gained a strategic advantage, and there was an intense debate about whether the result was windfall profits. The carbon price proved volatile over the period, with a noticeable collapse, and this period coincided with rising oil and gas prices, too. There can be little doubt that lessons were learned—indeed, these have formed an important component of the proposals for the post-2012 period.

The other main component of early EU climate-change policy focused on renewables. Here, the EU was largely confined to exhortation, encouraging the spate of national initiatives, targets, and instruments. The result was a mishmash of support mechanisms, from feed-in tariffs to traded permits for renewables, and widely varying levels of penetration. Targets, such as the EU's 1997 target of generating 12 per cent gross domestic energy consumption from renewable sources by 2010 (CEC, 1997), made little initial progress, and the January 2007 'Renewable Energy Road Map' (CEC, 2006) listed the long history of initiatives on renewables. Until the 2008 package proposals, renewable remained in practice a national affair.

Perhaps of more importance in this early period was not what was done, but rather what was not done. Outside France, and some countries bordering on Russia (such as Finland), nuclear power was regarded with, at best, indifference and in many countries with outright hostility. Germany had a phase-out plan (as Sweden had had), the Netherlands showed no enthusiasm, and the UK effectively closed off the option in 2003. The memories of the Chernobyl nuclear accident in 1986 remained fresh, the oil price stayed low until 2000, and the green groups had a long anti-nuclear pedigree carried over from the Cold War. Renewable energy lobbyists also feared that a revival of nuclear would crowd their preferred technology out, and put the spotlight on its costs relative to nuclear.

The EU was also very slow off the mark on CCS technologies, and whereas the USA had, through the FutureGen initiative,[2] put the emphasis on R&D, in Europe the steps were tentative, and the European Institute of Technology concept—to rival the Massachusetts Institute of Technology (MIT)—came later, facing much national opposition. Finally agreed in November 2007, the Institute is only now getting set up (European Parliament and Council of the European Union, 2008). Thus key aspects of climate-change policy—base-load technologies and R&D—were not prioritized, and it remained for gas to fill the vacuum created. This comparative neglect carries over into the current context, as we see in section VII below.

The EU's attention to security of supply was negligible throughout much of the period from 1990 to 2006, while the contribution of the LCPD (which squeezed coal) and the impact of the renewables programme (which needed back-up for its intermittence) led to a further dash-for-gas. The fact that this gas increasingly came from less reliable sources did not seem to register on the EU's radar and, as we shall see, by 2008 the consequences were beginning to be felt, with inevitable implications for the generation mix, the future of coal, and, therefore, for future CO_2 emissions.

Finally, while security of supply was neglected, the liberalization agenda was being pursued with enthusiasm. The Commission took it for granted that

[2] FutureGen, launched in 2003, was one of the outcomes of the US National Energy Plan 2001. Another was the Nuclear Power 2010 programme. See the US Department of Energy website for details.

increasing competition and unbundling the networks would enhance both security of supply and carbon abatement—yet neither was necessarily true. Driving down the price of electricity and gas in the absence of an appropriate price of carbon may well have exacerbated distortions and increased emissions, while the unbundling process did not obviously improve Europe's bargaining power with Russia. At no point did those in charge of the liberalization of energy agenda appear seriously to consider the security and environmental consequences as they pursued the 'British model' of liberalization and competition. It was *asserted* that liberalization would increase security, but quite *how* remained unclear.

In 2006, the EU was still focused primarily on the liberalization agenda. The Commission carried out a study of competition and liberalization in the electricity and gas sectors, and concluded with a damning report in January 2007 (CEC, 2007), recommending the ownership unbundling of networks. Resistance from Germany and France was fierce, and by the end of the year it was evident that there would have to be significant compromises if directives were to be agreed.

A better way to reconnect with voters was through the climate-change agenda. Whereas the big three EU members could not agree on unbundling, they could on climate change. France had nuclear, Germany had its powerful Green Party and coalition formation issues, and the UK had its claim to international leadership. With the post-Kyoto negotiations gathering momentum through the various conferences and meetings of the parties to the Framework Convention, the EU turned its attention to its self-proclaimed leadership role in international negotiations at Bali. So was born the 20-20-20 programme, as the climate-change package in January 2008 was termed.

III. THE 20-20-20 PROGRAMME

Any package with a title of matching '20' numbers has got to be primarily political. The probability that the correct answer to the question of what to do about climate change is even approximately 20 per cent overall reductions, with 20 per cent from renewables—and then 20 per cent from energy efficiency—is close to zero. Its political resonance is matched by its economic inefficiency. Below, the renewables target and the role of the EU ETS are considered in greater detail. Here we concentrate on two aspects of the package: the 20 per cent overarching target and the extent to which the various elements fit together.

The overarching target of 20 per cent is a deceptively simple number. In practice, it is not at all clear what achieving it requires and, indeed, whether, if it were achieved, it would make much difference to global warming. The 20 per cent relates to the production of greenhouse-gas emissions within the EU as a minimum target. But why would this be a good number? Why not 10 or 30 or 50 per cent? What is the link to the stabilization objective of 550 parts per million (ppm) CO_2e by 2050?

The Commission itself does not think the 20 per cent target is adequate. It states that in order to limit global average temperatures to not more than 2°C above pre-industrial levels, developed countries as a group should reduce their emissions to 30 per cent below 1990 levels in 2020 (CEC, 2009, p. 2). Climate change is a global phenomenon, and it is far from obvious that the EU is the best location to make these reductions on this timescale. There may be much cheaper ways, for example by preserving tropical rainforests or decarbonizing China and India's rapid coal-based economic growth. But here the Commission sets the baseline for the contribution of the developing countries to 15–20 per cent below business-as-usual (BAU)—in China's case, presumably BAU represents the pre-recession 10 per cent + GDP growth per annum. The EU target does permit reductions from outside the EU to be counted towards the target—through the Clean Development Mechanism (CDM)—but, as we see below, it is far from clear that CDM reductions are equivalent to internal EU reductions.

This international dimension raises perhaps the most important aspect of the 20 per cent overall target: it is based on production of carbon within the EU, and not on consumption. Thus the EU can achieve its targets if it switches carbon production that would have taken place within the EU to overseas, and then imports back the goods and services which would have caused the emissions internally. And, to the extent that energy-intensive industrial production is shifting globally from developed to developing countries (which it is), the 20 per cent target can be achieved without reducing carbon concentrations globally by the implied amount. Indeed, if the production techniques in developing countries are less carbon-efficient than in developing countries, and if we add the emissions from shipping, aviation, and other transport, it could even increase emissions. There appears to be no clear analysis by the Commission along these lines, so it cannot assess what contribution a cut in carbon production of 20 per cent in the EU would make to mitigating global warming.

Worse still, by presenting the EU as taking a leadership role with its 20 per cent target, it sidesteps the substantial question at the heart of climate-change policy. This was set out in the Brundtland report (WCED, 1987) on sustainable development and the North–South divide. The key challenge for climate-change policy is how the developing world can raise its standards of living towards those of the developed countries and at the same time global carbon emissions and other environmental damage can be reduced. Brundtland understood that at the heart of this sustainable development problem is the transfer of resources from the North to the South—in money and technology. China can argue that its *per capita* emissions are much lower than those in Europe and the USA, and hence the developed countries should take the brunt of emissions reductions. Furthermore, since the developed countries are responsible for most of the stock of carbon in the atmosphere as a result of their industrialization, it is the developed countries which should pay China not to follow the same path. China can also argue that much of its emissions are caused by demand in developed countries—in effect, emissions have been outsourced.

The 20 per cent target is not just internally focused, it is designed with the explicit aim of facilitating an international post-Kyoto policy framework. The EU proposes that if the USA and others come on board, then the target will be increased to 30 per cent. Even more so than for the 20 per cent target, the Commission provides no serious analysis as to how it imagines that in just 10 years this might be achieved—since the USA and others will not agree before at least the Copenhagen Conference at the end of 2009, and possibly not until the 2012 deadline for Kyoto expires. To propose a further 10 per cent reduction in carbon emissions in less than a decade is not credible and, that being so, the EU is unlikely to achieve its objective of incentivizing other countries to take aggressive targets, too. Only a major long-term global recession for much of the period would make this sort of target plausible—and in such dire economic circumstances, it is far from obvious that the politics of global warming will be benign, given the costs of the interventions.

The 2020 date itself is a further serious flaw in the EU package: 2020 is so close that it is unlikely that there will be much technical change by then. In other words, the target is to be met by existing technologies. As a result, there are only two major candidates to meet the target on the energy side (in addition to outsourcing energy-intensive industries): renewables and demand reductions. In the renewables category, wind is likely to be the main technology. Energy efficiency might help to reduce demand, but not necessarily. If income rises sharply over the period, overall demand might also rise, even if energy efficiency goes down. And energy efficiency itself creates an income effect.[3] There is not much room for nuclear before 2020, or for CCS. Tidal power is not likely to make a significant contribution until post-2020, and the target itself provides no incentive towards the sorts of R&D required. For transport, the focus is on biofuels, since hydrogen and electric-based cars are unlikely to be significant pre-2020 technologies. The contribution of biofuels to reducing global warming is at best controversial and could even be adverse. Thus choosing a short-term target date induces a very powerful technology bias—with both short- and long-term consequences.

The package approach (take it or leave it), which the 20-20-20 programme measures represent, follows on from experience with monetary union and with the earlier completion of the internal market in the 1992 package. At the European Summit in December 2008, the components were brought together in this form. But packages tend to be created with political rather than economic requirements in mind, and the results in terms of the interaction between the component parts depend critically on the conceptual coherence. In both the internal market and monetary union cases, the overarching rationale was clear. Here, it is much less obvious how the various aspects cohere. At one level, there is a target and a price instrument—the EU ETS. The idea is that the high-level target is disaggregated into a stream of permits, so that the price of carbon emerges as a result of achieving the target. In theory, there is one target, and one instrument, with the market

[3] See Sorrell (Ch. 17 in this volume).

determining the most efficient ways on the supply and demand sides to meet the overall objective.

However, the package has multiple instruments. Not only is there the EU ETS, but also the renewables target and a host of ancillary policies. If the EU picks winning technologies, and legally enforces their deployment, the remaining target to be achieved by the EU ETS will be the residual of the combination of energy (and transport) demand and the emissions after renewables have been taken into account. The permits should add up to this residual, but they do not, and no attempt has been made to add up the parts. On the demand side, this is partly macroeconomic, and partly driven by policy.

Just to confuse the picture further, there is ambiguity both about the CDM contribution to the target, and about changes which might result from the international negotiations after 2012. Then there is the possibility that the renewables target might not be met. Finally, as no consideration has been given to the serious security-of-supply problems facing Europe in the next decade, it remains possible that the constraints on coal (notably the LCPD) might have to be relaxed to keep the lights on.

Thus the 2008 package targets an arbitrary number (20 per cent), and then for primarily political reasons applies this arbitrary number to renewables and energy efficiency as well. It is based on carbon production, not consumption, thereby sidestepping Europe's responsibilities towards the developing world. It has multiple instruments, the overlaps between which have not been adequately considered. It is short term (and shorter than the R&D horizon), and little account has been taken of security of supply. As a result, the package is very unlikely to have the intended effects, and it will be high cost. And, of greatest concern, it is not at all clear what impact, if any, it will have on the concentration of carbon in the atmosphere. Though politicians may legislate for the future, if the package lacks credibility it will almost certainly be revised *ex post*. To these criticisms of the overarching target and the coherence of the package we then need to add the problems with the main components—the EU ETS, renewables, and energy efficiency.

IV. THE EU ETS PHASE THREE

As with the overarching target, we need to ask: what is the question or questions to which the EU ETS is supposed to be an answer? The conventional response is that the global public bad—carbon emissions—should be priced to reflect its social marginal costs, and hence facilitate their internalization in decision-making.

It is immediately apparent that there are several alternative ways of achieving the internalization of the social marginal cost: in particular, that the carbon price could be fixed directly via a carbon tax rather than through a permits scheme, and that command-and-control regulation provides a third option. The choice of instruments is a topic which has been exhaustively researched in the literature, and two broad conclusions have been reached: that market-based mechanisms (tradable permits and carbon taxes) are generally better than command-and-control regulation; and between tradable permits and carbon taxes, the ranking depends upon the shapes of the costs and damages functions.[4] Put simply, under uncertainty, it depends whether the policy-maker is more worried about getting the damage or the costs wrong. In the climate-change case, a marginal increase in emissions is unlikely to make much difference to global warming, but a marginal increase in costs in the short run, above the expected level, might have big economic effects on competitiveness and economic output. Thus there is a strong case for arguing that taxes are better than permits for carbon emissions—a point which Nordhaus has made forcibly (Nordhaus, 2008).

Why, then, has the EU gone down the EU ETS rather than the carbon-tax route? The answer is almost entirely political. Following the tentative suggestion in the early 1990s that the tax route be followed, the policy process focused on the income effect—who gets the money. Under taxes, it goes to the governments; under permits, *if they are grandfathered*, the companies keep it. It is hardly surprising that for as long as the polluters expected grandfathering, they lobbied hard for this approach.

The politics has some twists, however, which affect the various interest groups. *Ex ante* auctions of permits give governments the capitalized value of what a carbon tax would have approximated. So if it is feasible to move from grandfathering to auctions, suddenly the income effect from the polluters' perspective is even worse under tradable permits than under taxes. However, if the revenues are ring-fenced—for example, for spending on particular technologies, such as CCS, renewables, and energy efficiency—a new set of vested interests has an incentive to argue for tradable permits since they now have a 'carbon pork barrel' to compete for.[5]

Rent-seeking is not confined to the technologies. A tradable permits regime creates new markets, which in turn create rents for participants. There is now a rapidly growing set of vested financial interests with every incentive to lobby for the retention and development of the EU ETS.

A further political argument relates to the role of the EU ETS in international negotiations. It is claimed that a tradable-permits scheme helps to achieve two additional objectives: to provide a way of integrating different countries' efforts to mitigate climate change; and to provide a mechanism for income transfer to developing countries. On the former, the argument is that other countries will be subject to the same political incentives, and hence will in any event construct their own tradable-permits schemes. The USA is the most significant case in point. Then fungibility between the EU and US schemes will lead to significant further efficiency gains. On the latter, the CDM has the considerable advantage that, in theory, it allows for cheaper ways of meeting carbon targets by bringing on board low-cost developing-country projects, and in the process facilitates some North–South transfers. The fact that these have very low visibility has the political

[4] See Hepburn (Ch. 18 in this volume). [5] See Helm (Ch. 2 in this volume).

advantage that voters will not see the consequences of the EU and particularly the USA transferring sums to the authoritarian regimes, such as China, and thereby increasing their competitiveness as decarbonization takes place.

As the EU prepared for the next phase of EU ETS, it argued strongly for a relatively simple 2012–20 phase-three regime with two principal innovations: many of the permits would be auctioned; and the domain of the permit scheme would be widened. Inevitably, this kicked off a political scramble for rents. The polluters lobbied again for grandfathering—especially in countries that are heavily coal dependent (in a context where the alternative up to 2020 is largely gas), and for sectors facing international competition from countries such as China with no such permit requirements. Then, in addition to grandfathering, a number of EU members argued that the EU ETS should have a cap and a floor. The argument had much to recommend it,[6] in that were the carbon price to rise sharply there would inevitably be considerable *ex post* difficulties which might trigger intervention. Furthermore, a very high price of carbon would lead to significant carbon leakage—to countries with lower pollution standards, such as China. And if the price of carbon were to fall sharply—for example, in a severe recession—then investors in low-carbon technologies would be out of the market.

Although there are practical difficulties with implementation, the caps-and-floors approach would have mitigated many of the economic and political problems with the EU ETS. The ceiling would be clear and transparent, whereas in practice what may now happen is that, if the price rises, the Commission will be under strong political pressures to add in more permits under the CDM, change the timing of permit release into the market, and at the limit suspend the EU ETS.[7] Indeed, in the negotiations for a post-Kyoto framework, the Commission may well offer such an enhanced CDM to induce developing countries to take on more demanding targets, and if countries join the trading regime after 2012, they will probably come with the inducement of a significant quantity of free permits or 'hot air'.

In respect of the floor, many EU countries face the problem of supporting low-carbon technologies post-2020, and to do this they will need a long-term price of carbon. A floor in the EU ETS as a carbon tax in addition to and separate from the EU ETS permit price would achieve this, if there were also agreement that it would never fall from its initial (low) level. In practice, many EU members are likely to introduce such a tax anyway, in part for reasons of raising general revenues to address their budget deficits. The difference between an EU ETS floor price and a series of national carbon taxes is that the former is uniform across the EU, while the latter is not—with the inefficiencies that will be created as a result. In addition, in the absence of the floor, governments will increasingly be under pressure to

[6] See Helm (2008); Philbert and IEA (2008).

[7] The final compromise on the package permitted external offsetting of around 8 per cent of a country's overall emissions reduction target. See Kérébel (2009) for a summary of the negotiation process.

subsidize low-carbon technologies which would otherwise have been supported by the floor price.

Having got the EU ETS up and running, there are now very powerful vested interests in not only perpetuating it, but also weighing in on its evolution. At the December 2008 EU Summit, these pressures were revealed, and the result has been at best very messy. The auctioning has been significantly reduced, the scope for *ex post* manipulation increased, and the resulting price expectation damaged. When combined with a sharp economic downturn and the associated demand destruction on the one hand, and with major security-of-supply problems in respect of Russian gas on the other, the EU ETS now looks a very shaky foundation on which to base the policy of decarbonization of the EU economy. The carbon price may even collapse, and very considerable volatility is already apparent. All of this will be accompanied by high transaction and administrative costs.

As time goes on towards 2012, the relative attractions of a carbon tax are likely to grow. A carbon tax provides a predictable and stable price of carbon, and it is not limited to 2020. It will enable some of the costs of the renewables programme to be absorbed through the tax base, and underpin the economics of new nuclear investments. It also has the merit of being able to take account of the price of oil: at US$147 a barrel, the case for a carbon tax on top was weak; at US$30 a barrel it is rather different. It might even be possible to make the tax broadly inverse to the oil price—thereby not only improving the efficiency of the tax itself, but also addressing some of the political constraints.[8]

The EU has therefore landed itself with a complex and relatively inefficient tradable permits system which maximizes the scope for vested interests to pursue the resulting economic rents. It provides no long-term price of carbon, and the short-term price that emerges is likely to remain highly volatile. It creates considerable problems for competitiveness which can only be met either by effectively reducing the impact on the exporting sectors, or by introducing a border carbon tariff or tax. Over time, it is possible that the EU ETS will move from centre stage towards the margins, though the vested interests will likely keep it going. A carbon tax as a floor price, extending to imports, is a plausible way in which the carbon price may be supported. This is especially likely if China and India, at Copenhagen and beyond, do not take on binding carbon constraints themselves.

V. RENEWABLES 20 PER CENT

For many, this rather gloomy assessment of the EU ETS is not of central importance. The main action, many argue, is with renewables (and, for some, nuclear). Neither technology is currently driven predominantly by the carbon price—both are very much the result of direct government intervention in the market. Indeed,

[8] Coal would have to be considered, too, however, as a high price of oil might encourage a switch to coal.

in the renewables case, the 20 per cent target sits rather oddly with the EU ETS—the former prescribes the share of a particular technology, while the latter leaves it to the market to sort out the relative shares of renewables, nuclear, energy efficiency, and switching from dirty to cleaner coal, and from coal to gas. The case for a market mechanism is precisely that policy-makers do not know the relative costs; the case for a renewables target is that they do, and, in particular, are able to calculate that it should be precisely 20 per cent. The consequence of having both appeals to those who argue that every mechanism available should be used, but it has significant efficiency costs.

As with the EU ETS, the starting point is to work out what is the question to which renewables are supposed to be the answer. It is far from obvious, and even less obvious why the answer is 20 per cent. Curiously, the very notion of a renewable is ambiguous: there is no clear definition—indeed, the concept itself is at best a relative one. It is not just a matter of semantics: the precise definition determines what is inside the protected domain and what is outside. And, of course, by varying (expanding) the definition over time, not only can the target be more easily met, but the returns to those projects well inside the domain are lowered as the supply of an increasing number of technologies goes up.

There are two approaches to this definitional question. The first is to try to find something intrinsic—that, in some way, the source of energy 'renews' itself. Wind and tides might fit into this category—the extraction of energy from them is argued not to reduce their future availability. The trouble with this sort of definition is that, on the one hand, it excludes a whole host of energy sources which policy-makers clearly want to include, such as biomass and biogas, and, on the other, fast-breeder nuclear reactors might almost qualify. The second approach is to define renewables as low carbon, but here again there are serious problems. For example, is the switch from coal to gas—which clearly *lowers* carbon emissions—'low carbon'? Or, more obviously, does nuclear qualify?

This ambiguity creates flexibility, which is politically very convenient, but also creates uncertainty for investors. If, however, the overarching question is about reducing carbon emissions—the justification for the high-level target—the only practical definition is the low-carbon one, and therefore one that includes at least nuclear. This result is one that most in the renewables camp wish to avoid, either because nuclear might turn out to be more economic than wind and tidal power, or for more ideological reasons and concerns about waste.

The next question is why renewables need a special reserved quota. If the EU ETS provides the price of carbon, as the Commission argues, then why is this not sufficient? Here a host of arguments are advanced. First and foremost is the 'infant industry' argument. The claim is that renewables are *new* technologies, subject to R&D, and as deployment expands the costs will fall. As a defence of the renewables targets across Europe by 2020, it is nonsense. Between now and the target date—less than 11 years—there is little scope for R&D resulting in deployed and operational assets. It is *after* 2020 that this argument would have traction. And in the next 11 years, much of the renewables will come from wind plus some biogas and biomass. In the wind case, the technology is well developed. There can be few who think that the renewables targets are necessary to incentivize a technical revolution in wind turbines in the next 11 years.

A second argument is that renewables need special protection because there are other (non-carbon) problems with their deployment, and they bring other advantages not reflected in the carbon price. These include the absence of transmission and distribution networks designed with decentralized generation in mind, and the claimed benefits to security of supply from local and national sources. On the former, these issues are best addressed through the regulated networks, which are charged additionally to customers. And, indeed, the Commission has made the additional requirement (on top of the 20 per cent target) that wind should be given priority access to networks. On the latter, there is much evidence to suggest that a dash-for-wind will, in the next 11 years, induce an associated dash-for-gas (reducing security). Or, if gas is deemed too insecure a fuel source, the result could be a dash-for-coal (increasing emissions).

These considerations indicate that the renewables target is less about addressing climate change in the most efficient and cost-effective way, and much more to do with politics, lobbying, and vested interests. In comparison, the case for a broader low-carbon obligation is a strong one, but this might lead to more nuclear, less wind, and a greater focus on alternatives such as coal-based methane and incinerated landfill.

Developing wind power is a coordination problem between networks, wind turbines, and customers. It is inherently intermittent, and especially vulnerable to high-pressure weather systems which tend to be associated with static, cold, continental air in winter. Not only does it require networks that take power from decentralized sources to customers, but it requires significant back-up generation capacity, and customers willing to absorb fluctuations in supply. In due course, battery storage and smart meters may help to solve these issues, but neither will have a noticeable effect before 2020.

Building the wind turbines before these technologies are widely available (and in the case of battery storage, even invented) is not only costly, but almost certainly more expensive than alternative ways of reducing emissions now. At the extreme, if all the extra subsidy that will go to wind in the next 11 years were instead to be invested in energy efficiency, the carbon reductions would be almost certainly significantly cheaper and greater. At the margin, although resources are being devoted to energy efficiency, there remains a trade-off. Furthermore, while the R&D on batteries and smart metering will take time to reach a deployable stage, the technologies for energy efficiency are largely mature.

The costs of the wind programme have been variously estimated. Looking back over the forecasts made by wind lobbyists is a revealing exercise. For those with an economic interest in capturing as much of the climate-change pork barrel as possible, there are two ways of presenting the costs in a favourable light: first, define the cost base as narrowly as possible; and, second, assume that the costs will fall over time with R&D and large-scale deployment. And, for good measure, when considering the alternatives, go for a wider cost base (for example, focusing on the full fuel-cycle costs of nuclear and coal-mining for coal generation) and assume that these technologies are mature, and even that costs might rise (for example, invoking the highly questionable 'peak oil hypothesis').

The correct way to do the analysis is to take the full-cost approach, and in the renewables case to include the full network costs and the back-up generation requirements. On this basis, most studies show wind power to be expensive relative to other fuels and, indeed, in many cases to achieve the dubious position of making nuclear power look cheap. On the back-up requirements, these can come through additional non-renewable generation (except where there is abundant hydro) and transmission interconnections over significant distances. In a national-only market, at the limit, if wind were 100 per cent of capacity when the wind was blowing, there would need to be another complete non-wind system in still periods. To put this in a more realistic context, whereas the UK's expected energy demand is met with a current installed capacity of around 70 GW, by 2020 with the wind power required to meet the 20 per cent energy from renewables target, and with a lower demand (assuming the energy efficiency measures actually reduce demand, rather than reduce only costs), National Grid predicts that at least 100 GW capacity will be needed (National Grid, 2008).

On the costs side, advocates of renewables have an incentive to claim that costs will fall over time for their preferred technologies, but not for others. This has turned out not to be the case so far: there is no evidence that wind costs have been falling—indeed, arguably they have risen significantly in recent years. The evidence to support the peak-oil hypothesis is highly questionable and, indeed, the predictions of oil at US$200 a barrel (in current prices) not only did not materialize when made confidently at the end of the 1970s, but also today remain suspect. There is much conventional oil to be discovered, much discovered but not brought to market, very significant gas reserves, lots of non-conventional sources, and, of course, several hundred years of coal reserves. It is less the concern about running out of fossil fuels that should trouble policy-makers, and more the possibility that these reserves might actually be burned.

These considerations do not apply equally across all EU member states. Where there is abundant and developed hydro (little new hydro could be built by 2020), there is scope for balancing the system without fossil fuels. In some countries, too, the nature of transmission and distribution systems lends itself more easily to decentralized and intermittent wind, and as climate (and wind patterns) vary, so, too, do the costs of intermittency. There is then a case for considerable variance across member countries, and the Commission has tried to capture these in the varying national targets. Yet, in calculating these, inevitably politics plays a role, too. Because there are only 11 years to meet the target, the starting point matters. So, for example, the UK has a target of only 15 per cent because its own national targets for 2010 are being missed.

In such circumstances, it might be expected that the Commission would want to replicate the EU ETS by a system of EU-wide tradable renewables certificates, to allow the market to find the cheapest European locations for a very rapid deployment. This, however, has not been pursued and, as a result, the allocation of national targets has been a political process which will almost certainly raise the costs of reaching the EU-wide 20 per cent.

The final issue to consider is whether the targets are *credible*. The EU has a history of setting targets well into the future for future politicians to address. Investors, however, have to evaluate the risks that the policy might be weakened, abandoned, or delayed, since this affects the economics of renewables projects. Why should any investor believe that these targets will be met?

In the design of this sort of regime, the key issues are: milestones, leakage, and penalties. It suits politicians to back-end load the renewables programmes and, indeed, that is inevitable given that there are only 11 years to go. Countries are required to lodge national energy action plans with the Commission by June 2010. This at least provides a basis for judging performance. Yet it is also reasonable to expect the EU to set precise milestones along the way to assess progress. These are, in practice, at best vague.

Second, credibility depends upon leakage, by broadening the definition of renewable through the inclusion of extra technologies, and including renewables investments from outside the EU. If, as the 2020 date approaches, the targets look like being missed, there will be a strong political temptation to broaden the definition, since it is possible to expand the definition of renewables to include just enough technologies to meet the target. Allowing greater scope for counting renewables from outside the EU will also be a way of meeting the target. Declaring success by changing the measuring stick is one way of dealing with the possibility that the wind investments are not made to time.

Third, there is the issue of penalties: what happens if members fail to hit the targets? The uncertainty here is considerable: what if only one country misses? What if those missing have plans to catch up? What happens if lots of countries miss the targets? The Commission will be hard pushed to punish credibly those who fail, unless most succeed. Since success is already in considerable doubt, so, too, is the credibility of enforcement.

To these standard questions of the design of the renewables regime, there is a further one: will the scheme as a whole be changed or even abandoned? By the middle years of the next decade, there may be major security-of-supply problems. As old capacity is retired, and as the EU LCPD and the EU ETS bear down on the existing old coal power stations, the EU may confront an ugly situation of a major (and increasing) reliance on gas in the context of a politically uncertain relationship with Russia. Wind makes this worse: it requires a high total capacity to address its intermittency. The possibility of an energy crunch by the mid-2010s has been widely suggested. Faced with quantity restrictions or very high and volatile prices, there will be political pressure to moderate the targets.

Then there is the economic recession. Suppose it lasts for years—as in Japan. Are European consumers willing to pay the much higher costs of wind generation as it becomes a significant part of total capacity (and bills), rather than making its present marginal contribution? The politics of energy prices will continue to play its part.

Finally, there is the issue of other technologies. By, say, 2015, it will probably be clear whether Europe is to see a major nuclear expansion in the years after 2020. The potential contribution of CCS will also be clearer. Suppose by then a combination of nuclear plus coal with CCS looks a viable long-term way forward. In such circumstances, would the Europeans carry on regardless with the back-end-loaded wind programme?

For these reasons, the national renewables targets themselves remain uncertain, and this will affect investor sentiments. The renewables target is not only an expensive way of reducing emissions in the short term, but it lacks credibility, too. Renewables have an important part to play, but a crash programme in wind is not obviously the best way to address global warming.

VI. ENERGY EFFICIENCY

Alongside the 20 per cent renewables target, the EU has a similar one for energy efficiency. The rationale for an energy-efficiency policy is well known: there are significant market failures which inhibit the take-up of energy-efficiency investments. As a result, it is argued that a host of projects with positive net present values are forgone. One of these market failures is carbon emissions, but, as we have seen, the EU ETS is designed to solve this particular failure by virtue of creating a price of carbon to be internalized. Thus, intervention might be justified to deal with other market failures, but in the climate-change arena it is only justified if the EU ETS price of carbon does not accurately represent the social marginal cost.

This overlap of policy instruments is typically ignored by the advocates of energy-efficiency measures. Indeed, many argue that energy efficiency is the main mechanism for reducing carbon emissions. No serious attempt has been made by the Commission to estimate how far the EU ETS fails to internalize these marginal costs, and hence how large a contribution the additional measures are required to make.

In the context of these other market failures, there is an extensive literature on the scale and magnitude of the net present values forgone. Much of this literature has been written from the perspective of advancing the case for further intervention. Little research has explored the possibilities that these positive net present values might be the consequence of ignoring costs—in other words, of policy appraisal optimism. If the net present values are so high, why do apparently rational consumers and firms ignore them, and why have not new economic agents appeared as intermediaries? Unless the rationality assumption is relaxed, the working hypothesis should be that some costs have been omitted.

To the extent that there are barriers to efficient take-up, it is far from clear why the appropriate domain of policy is the EU. Indeed, there are strong arguments to the contrary. The temperature varies greatly from Greece to Sweden, as does the rainfall between Spain and Ireland. Building designs are not optimally set on an EU-wide basis, and the information base for setting policy instruments is typically national or even local. Planning regimes differ widely. The degree of public housing varies not only in respect of the private sector, but also between national and local authorities. Even the housing finance markets vary considerably. For these reasons, the Commission is in a poor position to set optimal policy, and to adjudicate across countries. Given, too, that countries start with very different housing and building stocks, a common target has little economic rationale.

Reducing energy demand will, *ceteris paribus*, reduce emissions. The economic recession which began in 2008 is, indeed, having a notable impact—it is probably the single most important method of abatement in 2009. However, the Commission jumps from this observation to the much more contentious claim that increasing energy efficiency necessarily reduces emissions because it reduces demand. This is open to both theoretical and empirical objections.

If energy efficiency increases, then the amount of energy required to produce a given output goes down. However, as a result, the level of income goes up, since it now costs less to achieve the same output. It may also increase competitiveness if others improve energy efficiency less quickly. So, there is an income effect as well as a substitution effect. What then matters is what that income is spent on. It has been argued that, as energy efficiency goes up, consumers may spend some of the gains in income on energy-consuming activities.[9]

To these direct income effects, it is important to add in the effects of economic growth. Since the oil-price shocks of the 1970s (and particularly after the Iranian Revolution), the energy ratio has declined for many industrialized countries. Less energy is needed for incremental increases in GDP as economic growth continues. It is tempting to extrapolate this forward and, indeed, to use this extrapolation to set overarching targets. But this depends upon the composition of demand for final goods: for example, air-conditioning could pass a threshold cost against rising incomes and lead to an increase in energy intensity. As the price of energy falls relative to income, the demand may go up.

The above considerations suggest that energy efficiency may be important, but that demand reduction may be more so, as a policy to address climate change *in the short run* while the energy supply is dominated by fossil fuels. Demand reduction requires a higher price of carbon than energy efficiency because not only is the substitution from energy-intensive to less energy-intensive methods required, but there is also a requirement to offset the rebound effect and the broader impact of economic growth on energy demand. Energy-efficiency measures may be necessary, but they are not sufficient to address climate change.

[9] For example, the average temperature of houses in the UK has gone up from about 13°C in 1970 to around 18°C now (Committee of Climate Change, 2009). See also Sorrell (Ch. 17).

VII. WHAT IS LEFT OUT?

To sum up so far, the EU climate-change package is best regarded as a politically neat but economically inefficient set of targets. The '20' in all the targets is unlikely to be justified by the underlying costs and benefits: 2020 is short term, as is the supporting EU ETS and the renewables target. The critical component of a long-term price of carbon is therefore absent. The overlap between the price instrument and the renewables target has not been fully considered. On energy efficiency, it is not clear why the EU (as opposed to individual member states) has a target at all and, in particular, why in the short term it is targeting energy efficiency rather than energy demand.

These criticisms are serious: the package is flawed. But yet more serious is what is left out of the package—the policy measures which would otherwise form a core part of a credible EU climate-change package. These include: a long-term price of carbon; base-load technologies, notably nuclear and CCS; R&D; and a mechanism for addressing carbon consumption. There is little or no recognition that climate-change policy is not the only objective with respect to the energy sector—there is also little account taken of the implications for security of supply of the main climate-change targets. Market failures are multiple and, important though it is, climate change is not the only issue confronting governments and policy-makers in the energy sector.

Almost everyone agrees that a long-term price of carbon is an essential part of the architecture of a climate-change policy regime: it is necessary, but not sufficient (Stern, 2007, 2009). A price is needed to incentivize the demand and supply sides of the market, given that imperfect information pervades the economy, and the political economy of rent-seeking influencing public interventions. It needs to be long term for three reasons: climate change itself is a long-term problem; the capital stock in the energy sector is lumpy and long-lived; and R&D is an essential part of the solution.

Why then does the EU ETS make little provision for the longer term? In its defence, the Commission claims that the EU ETS is itself a long-term project: it does not end in 2020. So the 20-20-20 programme provides not only for the third-phase national allocation plans, but also the basis for an open-ended carbon regime. It argues that the commitment to the EU ETS should give confidence to investors whose time horizon is beyond 2020 that there will be a price.

This defence, however, places significant regulatory and political risk on private investors who are not well placed to bear it, and thereby raises the cost of capital. This risk is real: having witnessed the political debate in the run-up to the December 2008 Summit, it would be rational to conclude that the EU political commitment to the EU ETS is far from robust, and that the putting in place of mechanisms which enable *ex post* interventions signals that the EU support is tempered by the focus on the political acceptability of the resulting price of permits. Furthermore, there is not even a short-term stable price in the current EU ETS: it is volatile and in early 2009 much lower than the architects envisaged.

But the real political reason why there is no long-term price is that the Commission has repeatedly failed to advance the case for a carbon tax, and this, in turn, is tied up in the arguments about sovereignty over taxation. As a result, a major opportunity was missed in the design of the 20-20-20 package. As indicated above, a floor price could have been introduced—as a tax, rather than an internal mechanism to the EU ETS. It would be an external floor because, if internal to the EU ETS, it would have involved buying back permits at the floor price, which would have required public funds—in turn probably politically unacceptable. The long-term aspect could have been entrenched by an agreement to introduce the mechanism at a low initial level (given that the capital stock is fixed in the short run) and never to lower it in the future. Such a floor would have had the additional advantage that, should the EU ETS fail to develop as the central mechanism that the Commission envisages, it could be increased to take the strain of establishing a long-term carbon price.

As an alternative, had the Commission wished to entrench the EU ETS and give a longer-term price signal, it could have facilitated the auctioning of long-term carbon contracts, as advocated by Helm and Hepburn (2007). By holding partial future auctions of permits beyond 2020, there would be an intermediary between the sellers (the Commission or member states) and buyers for the period before the national allocation plans post-2020 were set. As a result, governments and the Commission would have a strong incentive to make sure that the EU ETS rolled forward after 2020 in order to transfer their (temporary) liabilities as counterparties to the auctioned contracts into the market.

To date, the Commission has vigorously opposed both floors (and ceilings) and long-term carbon auctions, in order to preserve the 'purity' of the existing scheme. The consequence for climate-change policy is very significant: there is no long-term price of carbon.

This absence of a long-term price of carbon bears down considerably on two base-load technologies which have the potential to play a major role in reducing emissions: nuclear and CCS. Nuclear power is a known, deployable, low-carbon technology, capable of producing large quantities of base-load electricity. It is therefore not surprising that several European countries, notably France and the UK, are embarking on large-scale expansions, with most other major European economies at least actively considering the option.

Nuclear power stations have several economic characteristics that present particular climate-change policy challenges. The stations are typically large-scale, capital-intensive projects which take around five years to complete and last for decades thereafter. They also have very long-term waste issues. These characteristics require, first, a long-term carbon price, and, second, some form of long-term contract which binds customers to honouring the sunk costs of the investments. The former condition, as we have seen, is absent. The latter is largely absent, too, since the competitive liberalized market that the Commission has mandated into EU law tends to favour short-term spot markets and short-term contracting. There is, in the European version of liberalized competitive markets, no mechanism to commit customers over the relevant time horizon.

These problems are acute in nuclear, but not unique. Renewables similarly raise issues of long-term contracts, and the member countries and the Commission have encouraged renewables obligations which provide such contracts. Interestingly, while such mechanisms are deemed essential for wind, and competition issues are therefore put aside, the same path is not followed for nuclear. An appropriate way of addressing this issue is through expanding the renewables obligation into a low-carbon obligation.[10]

Why has the Commission not pursued a level playing field for nuclear? As with the problem of a carbon tax, the answer is political. Several member states have political commitments to either phase out nuclear, or at least have a moratorium on future development. Germany is the key player here, and this position is a legacy of the Red–Green coalition under Chancellor Gerhard Schröder. The price of Green Party membership of the coalition was, in practice, the closure of at least one nuclear plant and an agreement to eventually get rid of the rest. It was a policy carried over to the Grand Coalition between the Christian Democratic Union/Christian Social Union and the Social Democratic Party.

The result of the anti-nuclear policies has been to create more room for renewables (as was intended by the supporters of renewables), and to encourage a further dash-for-gas across Europe—just as external gas dependency on Russia has become an increasingly serious problem for the EU. It is gas rather than coal, because the latter technology is under pressure for obvious environmental reasons, and the LCPD is forcing the closure of the coal industry across Europe. So just as the base-load capacity gap opens up across Europe, EU policies have been limiting the nuclear option (by failing to provide for either a long-term carbon price or long-term contracts) and accelerating the closure of coal.

As noted above, this will create major problems for both security of supply and climate change: by the middle of the next decade, the security-of-supply problem may turn out to be a binding constraint in Europe. Faced with the prospect of the lights going out, it is likely that the LCPD regime may have to be relaxed, both to provide that base-load and to provide back-up for the intermittency of a much greater share of wind.

The coal problem will not go away, however. Coal is the growing fuel globally, and hence it is the major problem for any effective global climate-change policy. Put simply, unless coal can be burnt in a less harmful way from a climate-change perspective, there will be little or no progress in abating global emissions. Any credible climate-change policy therefore has to have the coal problem at its core. The EU, by contrast, has it at the periphery.

The Commission has not entirely neglected coal. It is providing for a programme of demonstration plants for CCS technology, though the funding remains far from clear. But it is a question of scale and priority: the 20-20-20 programme places its overwhelming emphasis on renewables, and especially wind. The amount of resources to be devoted to wind across Europe up to 2020 dwarfs

[10] See Chapter 12 in this volume. Note that creating a level playing field does not of itself make nuclear power necessarily economic for the private sector.

any contribution on the coal front. There is virtually nothing in the programme which provides for CCS gas transmission, the establishment of large-scale storage, and the deployment of CCS technologies—other than up to 12 demonstration plants, probably not running before the middle of the next decade. There is little thought being given to how the lessons of the demonstration plants might be shared, or how the demonstration plants fit into wider international efforts. The contrast with the USA could not be greater. FutureGen has focused on R&D for large-scale technologies—notably nuclear, CCS, and hydrogen.[11]

R&D more generally is an area where the Commission would clearly like to have a larger role, but is hamstrung by the national approaches of member states (notably the UK) and lack of resources. The European MIT-type initiative is a case in point: jealous of national research funding, and of the loss of national expertise to a European institution, the original vision has been watered down considerably.

The comparative neglect of nuclear, CCS, and R&D provides a missed opportunity in tackling global warming. By concentrating on the EU ETS and renewables, the EU's contribution to addressing global warming between now and 2020 is likely to be marginal. Though there will be some emissions reductions as a result of these policies, they are likely to be partially offset by the need to rely on coal and other fossil fuels to back up the intermittency of wind. The EU ETS carbon price itself between now and 2020 will also have some effect, though at the low levels witnessed in 2009 it is likely to be swamped in its impact by volatility in the oil price.

While the EU focuses on the short-term carbon price and renewables, global emissions are likely to go on rising, driven by coal and by developing countries such as China and India. Both of these countries will increase their populations by one billion by 2050 and are heavily dependent on coal. Therefore, were the EU serious about climate change, the emphasis would be overwhelmingly on coal and China and India. But, as noted above, the production base for the 2020 20 per cent target (and for Kyoto) means that the measurement of 'success' is not the impact on global concentrations of CO_2 in the atmosphere, but the production of CO_2 in the EU. As also noted above, it is perfectly possible for the latter to go down, and the former to go up, and, indeed, possible that the consequence of reducing the latter might actually further exacerbate the former.

So why has the EU not taken seriously the China/India/coal problem? The answer is that there appears not to be the political will to do what would be implied: not only to make much larger cuts in EU carbon production, but also to make the large financial and technology transfers to the developed countries. On the contrary, the EU has been lulled into the false assumption that tackling global warming is cheap. Across the EU, the most widely quoted number from the Stern Review is that it will only cost 1 per cent GDP (Stern, 2007). Politicians drop the caveats about 'good policy' and have been very keen to assure voters

[11] The package includes a 'Directive on the Geological Storage of Carbon Dioxide', but this is primarily about the legal framework, not the delivery of a CCS industry.

that climate-change policy will not have a significant impact on their standard of living. They can have their cake and eat it: claiming that economic growth can go on at 2–3 per cent per annum for the rest of the century *and* the world (and not just Europe) can decarbonize.

The Stern Review cost estimates are seriously flawed. Even Stern himself acknowledges that once policy costs are taken into account 2 per cent may be more realistic (Stern, 2009). Probably the numbers are significantly higher. But it is the political interpretation of the number which has most damaged climate-change policy. For if the costs are much higher, voters have to be told that they will have to make greater sacrifices—that their current carbon consumption is unsustainably high, and that they will have to pay for the carbon embodied in the energy-intensive imports from countries such as China and India, and, in addition, pay for the industrialization of China and India in a less carbon-intensive way. Instead of the complacent line of 'no need to change living standards', the implication is a much more unpalatable one about having been living beyond our (carbon-constrained) means, and hence requiring an adjustment down in living standards in the West to accommodate the industrializing East.

This is a hard political 'sell', but probably necessary if climate change is to be addressed. It is the central challenge to the 'leadership' the EU has claimed, shaping global climate-change policy. It can be done by carrots and sticks. The carrots are direct transfers. These are, in part, included within the EU ETS through the CDM. But here the sums involved are trivial compared with the scale of the problem, and there are significant questions marks over the credibility of the projects financed in this way. More importantly, the CDM tries to go below the parapet of direct government-to-government agreements, and thus is unlikely to play a significant role.

The sticks are the use of border taxes and standards. A carbon consumption base could be constructed through a border carbon tax. This would internalize the consumption externality, and, indeed, it could be harmonized with a floor carbon price for the EU ETS, as discussed above. In effect, there would be a minimum carbon tax across the EU and at its borders. The objections are twofold: that it would be practically difficult to define and apply; and that it would encourage protectionism. There are obvious practical difficulties, but the perfect should not be allowed to over-rule the pragmatic: an upstream carbon intensity measure could be applied initially on crude bands of goods and then gradually refined. On protectionism, the objection is weak: the carbon problem is separate from the trade problem, and the border carbon tax improves the efficiency of trade since it prevents the artificial subsidy being applied implicitly in countries such as China by not pricing the carbon externality.

Taken together, a long-term carbon price via a floor price, a level playing field for all low-carbon technologies including nuclear, a major emphasis of CCS and R&D, and a border carbon tax would comprise an appropriate climate-change package for the EU. In comparison, a short-term emphasis on the EU ETS without a floor price and on renewables will have at best a marginal effect on global warming.

VIII. CONCLUSIONS

The EU has made climate change one of its principal concerns. It has recognized that an EU-wide approach is likely to be more efficient than a piecemeal national one, and that the EU as a whole has greater power in the process of forming global agreements. It is a major achievement to have gained acceptance of its role in climate-change policy among even its more Eurosceptic members.

The design of its 2008 climate-change package is inevitably flawed—all such packages are political, and they require negotiations and concessions. The initiatives began well with the recognition that the price of carbon has a central role to play in the process of decarbonization.

Yet the early promise of a market-based approach has been gradually emaciated by the politics. There is a history here. The Common Agricultural Policy was the EU's main project in the 1960s. Its aim was to stabilize agricultural markets, but over time it metamorphosed into a grossly distorting and expensive policy. The agricultural lobbyists captured the rents. The danger is that the climate-change policy will go the same way—as interested parties battle for the very considerable economic rents attached to the various components.

The 2008 climate-change package is the result of a political process. The 20-20-20 catchy title cannot be economically efficient. The rationale for the 20 per cent overarching production-based target is hard to fathom, and it is a short-term approach to a long-term problem. The EU ETS is flawed, though not irredeemably so. The renewables target is costly and unlikely to be met. The energy efficiency target is centralized rather than localized. And, most importantly, the package leaves out arguably the more important bits—the long-term price of carbon, base-load technologies, and R&D.

Policy, however, is rarely designed on a blank piece of paper. We are where we are, and the task now is to take what has been placed in legislation and try to improve its efficiency. Fortunately there are a number of steps which can be taken. A floor price of carbon can be placed on the EU ETS through a carbon tax, which can also serve as a border tax. The renewables target can be modified before its costs and almost inevitable failure to be delivered have serious consequences. Policy can be directed towards CCS, R&D, and even nuclear. Given the over-riding urgency of climate change, the EU has the scope to move on towards a more credible and better-designed policy framework.

Part III

Low-carbon Technologies

12

Nuclear Power, Climate Change, and Energy Policy

*Dieter Helm**

I. INTRODUCTION

Throughout the last quarter of a century, nuclear power has been largely on the back foot. In part this was a political reaction to events. The accidents at Three Mile Island and Chernobyl reinforced the idea that nuclear is a dangerous technology and that human error was both inevitable and potentially catastrophic, however good the technology. But in large part it was a reaction to the economics.

After the initial foray into civil nuclear power following the Second World War, the OPEC oil-price shocks (and the embargo) in the 1970s provided a platform of much higher fossil-fuel prices against which to compare nuclear economics. The early ideas that nuclear would be 'too cheap to measure' had been replaced by the new conventional wisdom that oil would be 'too expensive to buy'. In the 1970s, there was the additional impetus that the world was widely believed to be rapidly running out of raw materials—including fossil fuels—and that the price would continue to go up forever. Nuclear power had, in consequence, another renaissance.

The energy markets of the 1980s and 1990s put paid to this in almost every country except France. The conventional wisdom of the 1970s was turned on its head—now fossil fuels were regarded as abundant and cheap, and by the end of 1999 there was much speculation about a world with oil at perhaps $5 a barrel (*The Economist*, 1999). To add to nuclear's problems, natural gas went from being a premium fuel reserved for industrial purposes to the fuel of choice for electricity generation in Europe (and, to a lesser extent, globally where gas was available).

It seemed then that nuclear was a technology of the past, and a costly mistake for some countries, such as Britain, which had so badly mismanaged their investments. In 2003, the British government's White Paper, 'Our Energy Future', confined the dismal prospects for nuclear to just one paragraph (DTI, 2003), while Germany's red–green coalition started a phase-out.

Now conventional wisdom has again been turned on its head, and there is yet another renaissance in nuclear power well under way in both political and

* New College, Oxford.

corporate circles. Britain and the USA are prominent in this reversal, with France playing a catalyst's role in providing both technology and corporate leadership through AREVA and EDF, respectively, with Westinghouse providing the main competition from the USA.

This renaissance, like that of the 1970s, has been driven by rising fossil-fuel prices and a widespread prediction of an imminent oil price of $200 a barrel, and with it a concern about security of supply (in both price and quantity terms). But it has also been motivated by a wholly new factor—climate change. It is now argued that nuclear power is not only economic, but also environmentally benign.

This chapter provides an assessment of this nuclear renaissance, and in particular of how the lessons of the past and the economic fundamentals play out for the design of nuclear energy policy. Section II considers these lessons from the past, drawing in particular on the British experience to indicate how not to design policy in the future. Section III considers the market failures which policy seeks to address, and subsequent sections address each of the main market failures and the appropriate policy responses: sunk costs and long-term contracts; carbon and long-term carbon prices; and waste and liability management. Finally, the chapter concludes with a summary of the characteristics of a new energy-policy framework for nuclear, and the consequences of failing to get it right.

II. LESSONS FROM THE PAST

Civil nuclear power has been around for over half a century. It was a by-product of military technology, developed during the Second World War by the USA, quickly followed by the British and the Russians. In the early years, civil nuclear power was as much a means for the production of plutonium as it was a means of generating electricity. This was particularly true in the British case, where the Magnox reactor, with its graphite technology, produced enormous quantities of waste (Helm, 2004, ch. 5).

The military legacy had many important consequences. It conditioned not only the choice of technology, but also the central role of the state in nuclear development. It is no accident that it was the military nuclear powers which developed civil nuclear programmes, and a significant element of state planning went into the early programmes. This state role was fed through nationalized industries, where the concept of planning and the dominance of scientists and engineers provided an environment where project appraisal optimism prevailed.

The British case illustrates these determining factors most markedly, in part because Britain led the development of civil nuclear power and in part because of the particular characteristics of its energy sector. The first and second Magnox programmes were not subject to serious cost–benefit assessments, but rather driven by the assumption of low costs and the desire to take forward the 'white heat of technology'. In the 1970s, its approach to industrial interventions led the governments (Conservative and Labour) to support British construction consortia and, at the end of the 1970s, to make the fateful decision to push on with the British advanced gas-cooled reactor (AGR) technology rather than that of the US pressurized-water reactor (PWR). Despite considerable pressure from within the French government, the electricity industry in France resisted the arguments for home-made technology, and it bought into the PWR. The history of the two countries' nuclear programmes was thereby partly determined: Britain was thereafter locked into one of its worst investment decisions since the Second World War, with the AGRs being plagued by long delays and very poor performance, while France built PWRs largely on time, to budget, and with high subsequent load factors. The importance of making the wrong technological choice lives on into the twenty-first century: the financial collapse of British Energy in 2003 and its state rescue were the result of output failures in its AGRs (particularly the latest, Torness) and its eventual takeover by EDF reflected its AGR-related weakness, and hence its inability on its own to drive a new nuclear programme.

The AGR decision doomed the British nuclear sector, while the PWR decision in France provided a platform of performance. For France it was a necessary but not sufficient condition. France demonstrated a number of the other critical aspects of successful nuclear programmes. These included: the coordination of investment; state finance; and monopoly. All were backed up by a remarkable political consensus.

France took planning in the nuclear industry to a much higher degree than the British. The decision to go nuclear fed through into a roll-out plan over decades. To support this investment programme, it planned its manufacturing capability to sustain an ordered delivery of PWRs. As with wind power later in Denmark and Germany, manufacturers could rely on a steady flow of orders. Given the discrete and lumpy nature of each power station investment, and the need to invest in the manufacturing capability, France made sure these were broadly in line. It did this through state ownership of the entire technology chain, and for good measure provided the education and training for a long-term workforce. Finance by the state had obvious advantages: taxpayers ultimately absorbed the equity risk of what was explicitly a national project, and, because the risk was internalized within government, the cost of capital was lower. For practical purposes the balance sheets of the nuclear industry and those of the French government were the same. Taxpayers' exposure was further reduced by the back-to-back monopolies: there were no competitors and it was easy to pass costs through to final customers. When fossil-fuel prices collapsed in the 1980s, the nuclear industry remained substantially insulated from the impacts. And, finally, the programme risks were also insulated from political uncertainty: none of the major political parties in France wavered in its broad support for the programme, and their continued support was reinforced by the civil service and by the trade unions. As a result, having made the massive bet on nuclear power in the 1970s, and having chosen the right technology, France had the combination of an integrated and planned industry, financed through the state with cost pass-through and the broad support of politicians, civil servants, and unions.

The execution of this programme was not without its problems, but the contrast with Britain was obvious. This is perhaps surprising given that, at the outset, the Central Electricity Generating Board (CEGB) and Atomic Energy Authority (AEA) were also nationalized, and the concept of planning was similarly dominant in the supporting ministries in the 1960s and 1970s. Yet there were also important differences, especially from 1979 onwards. Unlike France, Britain had a powerful anti-nuclear lobby, with the Campaign for Nuclear Disarmament (CND) having deep roots in the Labour Party. Although primarily against military nuclear weapons, it spilled over into a distrust of civil nuclear power, too. It was a scepticism shared by many senior Labour politicians and most of the Liberals (carried over to the Liberal Democrats). In addition to this political opposition there were also economic doubts, born out of the early Magnox reactors and their costs.

Without political consensus, it was inevitable that Britain would want to judge each investment on its merits, on a case-by-case basis, in contrast to the programme decision taken in France. In the 1980s, the lack of commitment in nuclear came to the fore. Despite the Parliamentary announcement by the incoming Conservative government in 1981 of a programme of up to 10 PWRs, there followed a long drawn-out debate, with the result that only one was ever built: Sizewell B. From the 1981 decision to its commissioning, it took over a decade of inquiries (notably the Layfield Inquiry (Department of Energy, 1987)) to bring it on stream. In the meantime, the economic and political scaffolding had been knocked away. Liberalization and privatization removed the security of the monopoly for cost pass-through; privatization substantially increased the cost of capital; and as the political doubts about nuclear's future surfaced, there was no opportunity to plan for serial production.

Given this much less auspicious context, once fossil-fuel prices collapsed in the early 1980s Britain's nuclear industry faced the full force of the market when France's did not. France maintained its *de jure* monopoly as long as possible and kept a substantial state ownership presence even when part of EDF was sold. It lobbied hard against the European Commission for its particular vision of the energy markets and, by the time it eventually lost the *de jure* argument, its *de facto* market power remained powerfully entrenched. So when oil prices failed to continue ever upwards from the peak in 1979 (at US$39 a barrel), the nuclear programme remained insulated. In Britain, the fall in oil prices was disastrous for nuclear. Its (private) economics could not withstand the consequences, even as its coal costs remained high. For, in Britain, gas CCGTs filled the gap—although, given the scale of de-industrialization following the sharp recession in the early 1980s, very little additional capacity was in any event needed.

The lessons from the past point to the uneasy relationship between privatized and competitive markets on the one hand, and the peculiar economic characteristics of nuclear power on the other. But what this relationship requires is not that state ownership and monopoly are either necessary or jointly sufficient, but rather that the peculiar economics of nuclear power needs to be taken into account when designing the framework of energy policy within which markets operate.

The large scale and discrete nature of each nuclear investment, the high fixed costs, the inflexibility, the legacy waste, and the exposure to political controversy together create an extreme sensitivity to the cost of capital. In turn, this needs the careful allocation of equity risks between taxpayers, current and future customers, and shareholders. Energy policy and energy regulation are largely about how this allocation takes place. The first step in designing an appropriate energy policy for nuclear is therefore to understand this underlying economics and the risk-allocation issues.

III. THE ECONOMIC FUNDAMENTALS OF NUCLEAR POWER—MARKET FAILURES AND RISK

(i) Sunk Costs and the Cost of Capital

A nuclear power station is a capital-intensive and long-term investment. Its costs are sunk: there is little prospect of exit. Nuclear power stations take around five years to build, and then have an operating life of at least 30, and perhaps as many as 50, years. The average costs are high, the marginal costs are low, and hence the economics turns on how quickly the station can be built and the speed with which the gap between the nuclear marginal costs and the market price of electricity can pay back the capital costs. It is a trade-off between the cost of capital, the marginal costs, and the price of electricity. The electricity price is typically approximated by the costs of fossil fuels, and since gas and coal prices are loosely related to the oil price, the projected future oil price effectively determines the revenue line.

To these power station costs and revenues, three further items need to be added: the cost of nuclear fuel, the costs of dealing with spent fuel, and the costs of decommissioning the power station at the end of its life. The first comprises the uranium price and the costs of fuel fabrication. Uranium is in plentiful supply and, unlike oil and gas, widely dispersed across a range of countries, several of which are stable democracies. Fuel preparation tends to be in the country with the nuclear power stations. Spent fuel disposal is typically carried out by state-owned or heavily regulated domestic companies, and may be complicated by reprocessing. Disposal of nuclear waste is everywhere a state activity, with (as we see below) considerable uncertainty. Decommissioning is similarly under state control. It is far into the future and, at any positive discount rate, is not very significant in the project appraisal.

These economic characteristics dictate particular commercial consequences. Where the marginal and average costs diverge—and over such long periods—investors take the risk that future customers will pay. In a competitive market, they may opportunistically switch to non-nuclear suppliers if the oil price falls. Thus, it is natural for investors to seek long-term contracts from customers: in return for sinking their capital in such a long-term venture, customers are asked to pre-commit to buy the resulting output, thereby underwriting the sunk costs. Under monopoly, this is simply imposed on customers—the sunk costs are automatically passed through.

Monopoly is thus an extreme form of a long-term contract: it passes through all costs. It is, in effect, a rate-of-return-regulated regime—indeed, this is how the US nuclear programme was financed. But sunk costs are not all costs, and monopoly is more comprehensive than necessary. What is required is a long-term contract to cover only the sunk costs. France's state-owned and -directed nuclear industry with monopoly could internalize these costs. From the 1980s, Britain experimented with some elements of long-term contracts through the Non-Fossil Fuel Obligation (in effect, a nuclear obligation), but it was crude and poorly related to the sunk costs. It neither provided an appropriate and efficient mechanism to link the sunk costs to customers, nor was it robust against the politics.

The sunk costs therefore require some form of customer commitment and this, in turn, requires a long-term contract. Energy policy needs to correct for this peculiar economic feature.

(ii) Waste and Decommissioning

Nuclear waste comes in a variety of forms and toxicities. Much of it is suitable for conventional disposal, but there is a core which is very dangerous and takes thousands of years to decay. This cannot be left to markets: there is no mechanism by which private firms can fully internalize the interests of future generations, and the limited liability of companies would make bankruptcy the obvious strategy in the event of a serious problem. Put simply, private investors can ignore the small probability of serious consequences long into the future, since discounting reduces these risks effectively to zero, and they can simply walk away.

For these reasons, nuclear waste management is a public task, and the risk has to be socialized. Governments may claim that by requiring a fund to be created, companies are covering the risk. But since that risk is open-ended, there can be little credibility that any specific amount discharges this kind of risk. From the public perspective, the discount rate should be lower and, indeed, may be argued to be close to zero.[1]

Decommissioning might be argued to be more tractable, since it will begin to take place within a half century of the plant being built. Yet, even here, the risk is a public one. Decommissioning costs in respect of dismantling a nuclear power station may be estimated, but the residual wastes still have to be handled. Furthermore, the actual costs depend upon how fast the station is dismantled: if, for example, the core is simply covered in concrete and left for several hundred years, the costs will be lower than if it is completely decommissioned as soon as it reaches the end of life. Furthermore, technical change over half a century is

[1] See Hepburn and Stern (Ch. 3 in this volume) and Weitzman (2007*a*).

inevitable. Again, it is appropriate to transfer the equity risk to the public at the end of life, and any fund created from the revenues of the operation of the plant is likely to be somewhat arbitrary.

In both cases, it has been argued that risk aversion should dictate the scale of funds set aside. Again this is far from obvious: technical change may point to cost optimism and the spreading of the risk over entire populations and through time that a government achieves is very different from private risk spreading.

Risk transfer to government does, however, create problems of moral hazard: if the nuclear power plant developer faces a fixed-price contract for the waste and decommissioning, then it has little incentive to design and operate the plant with a view to minimizing these costs and risks. Thus risk transfer through fixed-price contracts requires careful regulation of the plant—including its choice of technology, design and operation. This is an important additional reason why nuclear requires intensive and intrusive regulation.

(iii) Security of Supply

Waste and decommissioning costs are examples of negative externalities which require internalizing. But nuclear has positive externalities and public goods, too. These include the benefits to security of supply. It is argued that by providing base-load domestic supplies of electricity, using diverse sources of fuel supply, nuclear reduces reliance on imported fossil fuels, notably gas. Recent developments in respect of the supply of Russian gas to Europe, and Europe's growing gas dependency add to the value of the security-of-supply benefit from nuclear power. Over time, as electricity provides a greater share of the transport sector, it will also reduce reliance on oil imports, too.

The security-of-supply argument has been a major reason why governments have pursued this technology in the past. It was uppermost in the mind of the French government in the 1970s, and in Mrs Thatcher's (failed) attempt to revive it in Britain in the 1980s as a diversification from reliance on the coal-mining unions. It is an explicit argument again now. Yet security of supply is a deceptively complex concept. Security is about quantity and price. Having 80 per cent of its electricity generated from nuclear power provided considerable security to the French in the face of the Russian–Ukrainian dispute in 2009. Indeed, several eastern European states argued that, as a result, they should be able to re-open old nuclear plants. But its 80 per cent reliance on nuclear left France exposed to its nuclear costs during the 1980s and 1990s when oil prices fell to US$10 a barrel. As nuclear is added, it provides a hedge against movements in fossil-fuel prices. But as the share rises, the diversification value falls, and it eventually renders the system highly exposed to a one-way bet on oil prices.

Security of supply is also about capacity margins and the ability to absorb demand and supply shocks. Nuclear has no unique role in this respect. Indeed, since it is inflexible in operation, it can reduce this kind of security. In Britain, this has been compounded by the generic failures in the AGRs. Ironically, although each AGR was developed with considerable first-of-a-kind features, the technology itself has experienced a sequence of generic faults. As a result, the possibility of the failure of one or more of the AGRs has been a major cause for security anxiety in recent years. In France, were the PWR to develop a generic fault, security would be seriously jeopardized—indeed, this is what happened in the heat wave in 2003 when the temperature of the water for cooling rose above the design assumptions.

(iv) Low Carbon

These considerations—of sunk costs, waste, and security—are all well rehearsed in the nuclear debate. But what has altered the landscape for nuclear is climate change. In the next two decades, nuclear is one of the very few large-scale deployable technologies producing low-carbon energy. This new dimension has led many who are otherwise sceptical or even hostile to nuclear to reconsider. Some go as far as to extend this argument to the large-scale production of hydrogen by nuclear, too.

Nuclear is not, of course, carbon-free: the mining of uranium, the construction of power stations, and the management of waste all create carbon emissions. Further out, reprocessing and fast-breeder reactors may reduce these carbon emissions, but such effects are uncertain and likely to have an impact on future rather than current power stations.

The price of carbon is an integral part of nuclear power economics. But unlike waste, it is not unique to nuclear technology. It applies to renewables and a host of intermediary technologies and it is, therefore, a generic market failure, not a technology-specific one. Hence, it points to a generic price of carbon. This, however, needs to reflect the time horizon of the technology, and therefore there needs to be a long-term price of carbon to integrate into the investment analysis. This, as we shall see, is singularly absent.

IV. A LOW-CARBON OBLIGATION AND THE SUNK COSTS

There are several ways in which the sunk-cost problem can be addressed—including the nationalized industries approach in the French and pre-1980 British programme, through rate-of-return regulation in the USA and a number of European countries, through market power and monopoly, and through an explicit obligation. All of these mechanisms transfer equity risk from shareholders—in most cases to customers (although nationalization in the presence of monopoly can include taxpayers).

The risk transfer is not necessarily confined to the sunk costs. In pure rate-of-return regulation, all cost risk is passed through. This may be modified by tests of efficiency applied to the cost pass-through—for example, through the US used-and-useful test. But in general, cost pass-through fails to separate out the different types of equity risk and to assign them to those best able to manage them. Thus, taxpayers are probably the only location for the risk of long-term waste costs, since it is government which determines such intergenerational issues. Governments also retain flexibility over how and over what timeframe decommissioning takes place. Transferring such obvious political and regulatory risks to shareholders is inefficient since their agents—the managers—are in no position to control them. On the other hand, building and operating a nuclear power station are the sorts of tasks and associated risks that managers can handle, and it is efficient for these risks to be borne by shareholders.

The sunk-cost risks are best transferred to customers—the future customers who will benefit from the electricity generated. Since the costs are sunk once the plant has been built, there is nothing that managers can do to mitigate them. They are then irreversible data. The equity risk here arises because, once sunk, the marginal cost is way below the average costs, and therefore the temptation of *ex post* opportunist behaviour will lead to the expropriation of the assets by customers. It is a time-inconsistency problem: customers may promise *ex ante* that if shareholders sink the capital they will pay, but without a contract to that effect they can *ex post* renege.

In a competitive market, the problem is solved by long-term, take-or-pay contracts. In the case of nuclear, this turns out to be practically impossible. The main reason is the time horizon. There is no obvious customer base with whom to write a contract for electricity delivered a minimum of five years in the future and for 30 or 40 years thereafter. In the absence of a customer base for contracts, it might be thought that other intermediaries could fit this role. The fossil-fuel price risk might in theory be hedged, but oil futures markets even a year ahead are thin, and after five years not a serious option. Large energy-intensive industries might form a contract base, especially where there is an element of market power in their own final products. The Finnish example is relevant here: in effect, the new nuclear plant is vertically integrated through contracts to a small number of large energy users. But a programme of ten or more reactors, such as that planned for Britain, is well beyond this sort of contracting base.

The problem is exacerbated by the rules of the liberalized market which has developed in Britain and is being extended across Europe. The essence of this market is the opportunity for customers to engage in short-term switching, using an increasing number of intermediates (often through websites) to search for the 'best deals'. Locking in customers has been severely restricted or even banned by regulators, creating problems not just for sunk costs in new power stations, but, for example, in providing energy-efficiency measures with payback periods of a few years.

This leaves one other option which has been deployed in the case of renewables—an obligation to purchase a fixed quantity of electricity from a particular technology source. The British Renewables Obligation (RO) is an example. Suppliers—as agents for customers—have fixed quotas, and they must produce sufficient Renewables Obligation Certificates (ROCs) to demonstrate compliance.

The British RO has a number of peculiar features. There is a buyout price and the price of the ROCs depends not on the costs of renewables generation, but on the scarcity of the renewables relative to the aggregation of the suppliers' targets and the wholesale price. The British RO in effect guarantees this scarcity price since the target is kept ahead of actual generation. The result is one of the most expensive renewables programme in the developed world—perhaps with only Italy as more expensive.

Note that the RO recovers a revenue flow through the ROCs, and makes no distinction between the sunk costs and the operating costs. Since the ROCs are so expensive, all costs are, in effect, recovered. To ensure that the sunk costs are remunerated—and hence avoid expropriation of these *ex post*—it would be possible to provide for them through a more limited obligation. The sunk costs could be established at the point of commissioning, and these could be passed into a supplier obligation and credited against the revenue stream from the sale of the electricity at the going market price. The shareholders would be permitted to recover these from an obligation account in the event that the revenue from the sale of the electricity fell short of this cost-recovery level. Such a mechanism would then significantly reduce the costs of renewables and nuclear to customers if the fossil-fuel price provided a stand-alone economic return, capping only the downside risk.

This sunk-cost only guarantee is analogous to the treatment of costs in the case of regulated utilities, which also display a wide gap between average and marginal costs and are large, lumpy, capital-intensive, and long-term. In the utilities case, the sunk costs are represented by the regulated asset base (RAB), and protected by the duty on regulators to ensure that the functions can be financed.

Consider the advantages of this limited obligation in respect of the sunk costs. Once the nuclear power station (or the wind farm, or tidal barrage) is completed, the sunk-cost risk transfers to customers. There is no equity risk in the sunk costs left with shareholders. Therefore, at this point, it can be entirely financed through debt. The overall cost of capital is lowered even though the equity risk is with customers because they have contracted through the obligation to underwrite the sunk costs. The risk that shareholders would have faced of the possibility of customers reneging has been dealt with—customers have committed not to do so. Compare this with the sunk-cost risk staying with shareholder. The gap between marginal and average costs is very great—hence the equity risk is great and the cost of capital high. For a capital-intensive project over a long lifetime, the effect of this (much higher) cost of capital overwhelmingly dominates the economics of the project. On a stand-alone basis, it is probably fatal to renewables, and possibly to nuclear, too.

Thus, a limited sunk-cost obligation is economically efficient. Its efficiency is enhanced if it is extended to all technologies with significant time-inconsistency characteristics. These include nuclear, renewables, and carbon capture and storage (CCS) projects, but not combined-cycle gas turbines (CCGTs). There may be borderline cases, too, such as non-CCS coal. The three main cases all turn out to be low-carbon, and hence a general low-carbon obligation (LCO) captures all main cases and avoids the discrimination between the technologies within this broad category.

The objection to broadening the RO to a LCO is that it would expose renewables to competition from nuclear (which arguably, in many cases, renewables would lose), and it would undermine the *ex ante* commitment already made to renewables that they can benefit from the extraordinarily generous ROCs system. The former is not a good argument. If there is something special about renewables beyond their low-carbon and sunk-costs characteristics (such as infant-industry arguments) then these should be addressed through other instruments, including subsidies where appropriate. The latter is important because to renege on the existing mechanism undermines the reliability of government commitments generally. Thus to preserve credibility, there is a case for grandfathering existing renewables which have already qualified for ROCs or buying out the implied property rights.

V. A LONG-TERM PRICE OF CARBON

The LCO outlined above is less about low carbon and more about sunk-cost obligations. It just so happens that the sunk-cost and low-carbon characteristics are held in common by the three technologies: nuclear, renewables, and CCS. The carbon dimension is a specific market failure, for which there are targets, and it is appropriate to have a dedicated instrument to address it. The obvious way to do this is through a carbon price.

Such a price exists—in the short run. It is the price of carbon permits under the EU Emissions Trading Scheme (EU ETS). The problem is that it has limited relevance to nuclear and other longer-term technologies. The EU ETS is a short-term mechanism which has significant imperfections. It gives only a weak signal in the medium to longer term.

The EU ETS was set up in 2005 for an initial three-year period. The second period is from 2008 to 2012, and a third period from 2012 to 2020 has just been negotiated through the 2008 EU Climate Change Package and agreed at the EU ministerial summit in December 2008. (CEC, 2008*a*, *b*). To date the price has fluctuated very considerably, most of the permits have been grandfathered, and for the post-2012 period a series of concessions have been made for sectors in internationally competitive markets. There can be little certainty that the rules of the game will not be changed between 2012 and 2020 and, indeed, in the very short term, the price of permits in 2009 fell below €10.[2]

The short-term nature and the volatility are inevitable components of the EU ETS. It is designed in such a way as to be administratively complex, and the carbon price varies with oil prices and the economic cycle. During 2008 and 2009, the

[2] See Helm (Ch. 11 in this volume).

oil price rose to US$147 and fell to around US$35 a barrel in the space of six months. The European economy contracted very sharply, well in excess of market expectations. The EU ETS is very sensitive to these movements—it is inherently volatile. An investor in nuclear power stations can draw few conclusions for the price of carbon in 2020 and beyond.

Fixing the quantity of carbon and letting the price be revealed via the EU ETS is an alternative to fixing the price and letting the quantity emerge. The latter is more direct and likely to be less volatile, and there are good theoretical reasons for preferring it as an instrument for addressing climate change. It has the further advantage that it is easier to use the price—a carbon tax—to address the longer term, since there can be an agreement at the outset to start with a low level which will never fall. It is thereby a floor price.[3]

Given that the EU ETS exists and is unlikely to go away, particularly as there are now so many powerful lobbies with a vested interest in its continuity, the floor price approach can co-exist alongside the EU ETS. The price of carbon would then be the floor price plus the EU ETS price. In the process, it would not only help to ameliorate the long-term pricing signal for investment in nuclear, but could also be extended to play the role of a border tax, thereby addressing the problems of international competitiveness in a context in which China and India do not adopt fixed carbon targets.[4]

The advantages of the floor price are relevant not just to nuclear, but to a whole range of post-2020 technologies. It would be particularly appropriate to CCS and next-generation renewable, and provides an incentive for R&D. It has the merit of being an instrument tied to a target which is technology neutral. There is then less scope for picking carbon winners, which in turn reduces the role of lobbyists who seek to capture the economic rents from the process of government intervention. It does not avoid such capture entirely, as there is an inevitable role for subsidies and specific supports for R&D, but it does at least strip out the sorts of capture activities which have characterized both nuclear and wind lobbying in recent years.

VI. FIXED-PRICE CONTRACTS AND WASTE MANAGEMENT

Waste management issues are, as argued above, inevitably long-term and open-ended. The costs of dealing with highly radioactive wastes cannot be determined *ex ante*. We do not know what future technologies will be available, and we do not even know whether at some future date these highly radioactive residues may even be deemed to be useful resources. Furthermore, the behaviour of governments is inevitably uncertain: future governments will inevitably change the

[3] On the general arguments for a carbon tax, see Nordhaus (2008). On the choice between price and quantity issues, see Hepburn (Ch. 18 in this volume).

[4] On the floor price, see Helm (2008*a*).

rules, and they may even use the materials to threaten others. Over centuries, we cannot assume that stable democracies will endure. In the twentieth century, the sheer scale of the disregard for human life displayed by Stalin, Mao, Hitler, Pol Pot, and a host of other dictators should induce considerable caution.

It is therefore somewhat alarming that, in a period of unprecedented peace, countries such as Britain and the USA cannot agree how to dispose of waste. Successive British governments have ducked the decision about a high-level waste depository, and it is clear that the location of such a depository has been driven as much by politics as geology.

A renaissance of nuclear power has to be considered against this disappointing and uncertain political background. It is apparent that such decisions cannot be left to limited liability companies, and decisions about the handling of waste must be placed in the hands of governments. Thus, a fixed-price contract between private nuclear companies and governments is inevitable as a mechanism for the transfer of equity risk. Such contracts need to reflect best *ex ante* guesses of the future costs, and they can only be guesses over an horizon in which technical change is likely. A degree of risk aversion is appropriate on the principle of sustainability—that future generations must be at least as well-off as ourselves, and in bequeathing them our waste, we should also transfer sufficient resources to them to deal with the consequences. Fortunately, if economic growth continues at say 2–3 per cent per annum for 50 years, a small sum now will be a big sum later. Hence, the contract price for transferring the risk should be small relative to the overall project costs. Of course, economic growth may not continue at this rate—indeed, climate change may be one of the factors limiting it—but that is a risk for society as a whole, not individual companies.

The design of the public bodies managing the waste is extremely important. Inside nationalized industries, the record is one of secrecy and, indeed, failure. The public sector AEA tried (with political connivance) to cover up the Windscale fire in the 1950s; the Russians tried to cover up the Chernobyl accident initially, resulting in many more deaths and radiation exposures in the critical first few days after the accident; and there have been numerous failures on a smaller scale, such as the dispute over the claimed fabrication of data in respect of Japanese spent-fuel reprocessing in the 1990s at Sellafield.

This poor history dictates an institutional entrenchment of transparency and openness. This is arguably best achieved where the roles of policy decision, regulation, and production are separated. It requires an independent regulatory body and private-sector contractors, where the contract provides a locus for reporting and assessment. Such separation of functions itself needs careful design. For example, if the government seeks to minimize costs through the promotion of competition in a situation in which the outputs are not easy to specify precisely, there may be a tendency towards shorter-term 'fixes' at the expense of longer term waste management. At the limit, costs may be cut at the expense of safety.

VII. FIXING SECURITY OF SUPPLY

Security of supply is a multi-dimensional public good. As discussed above, it encompasses price and quantity. As supply becomes scarce, price rises, and as the capacity margins tighten, prices become more volatile. Physical quantity interruptions are rare, but the impacts can be dramatic. Too little supply creates asymmetrically large costs when compared with too much supply.

Nuclear power brings a number of security benefits and some downsides. None is unique, and none requires a special nuclear policy intervention. The risk of inadequate capacity requires a capacity incentive, and a capacity market can meet this requirement. It can take a number of forms, and the further into the future the government wishes to be certain of adequate supply, the further out auctions of capacity slots can be organized. Nuclear has the opportunity to compete in such a market. Such quantity security is therefore best addressed through generic mechanisms, not technology-specific intervention.[5]

The price stability provided by nuclear can also be provided by other technologies, especially if they contract long for their fuel supplies. The required incentive mechanism here is much harder to design in the context of liberalized and competitive markets with short-term switching. One approach is to encourage the creation of capacity portfolios and to develop intermediaries which package the price stability into fixed-price contracts to consumers for limited periods. But as long as short-term switches have a significant role in the market, the scope for such fixed-price contracts in the retail sector is likely to remain small. The LCO, proposed above, includes nuclear and renewables and, as a result, the larger the LCO, the less the exposure to oil prices. However, it also includes CCS, and there is a linkage between coal and oil prices. Thus the LCO helps, but does not solve its problem. Hence there is a trade-off between the benefits of competition and price stability.

VIII. CONCLUSIONS

The design of nuclear policy starts with the allocation of equity risk. Investors are best placed to manage the construction and operation of a nuclear power station. They are less well placed to manage the risks of *ex post* opportunism, given the gap between marginal and average costs, and they cannot manage the risks associated with nuclear waste well into the future. For these reasons, efficient nuclear policy is a partnership between the private sector and government. Put another way, nuclear is always political and cannot be regarded as a purely private-sector activity. It requires both an explicit decision by government and a careful balance of risks and responsibilities between government and the private sector if it is to be efficiently delivered.

[5] For a discussion of the role of capacity markets in securing supplies, see Helm (2008*b*).

It is apparent that this allocation of equity risk has not been managed well in the past. The British example is one of the worst in the developed economies. By building and managing the nuclear power stations in the public sector, it internalized all the equity risk with government. The results have been power stations which have taken years to build (in the case of Dungeness B, 22 years to produce its first output), and with high operating costs. The French example has been better, in part because other aspects of the nuclear programme were better managed.

The basic equity-risk allocation sets up the economics of a power station contract. It is for commercial private-sector companies to contract for fuel supplies, to build, and to operate the plant. A fixed-price contract for spent fuel and waste transfers the equity risk in these areas to the public sector. The government guarantees the sunk costs through regulation, by requiring customers to commit to the sunk costs.

Translating this risk allocation into policy interventions, in addition to the public sector organizing waste management, the sunk costs are recovered by an obligation on customers, and in the British case this is best organized through an LCO, incorporating the three technologies where the sunk-cost problem is most acute: nuclear, renewables, and CCS. This obligation is only for sunk costs; it is not necessary to include other costs (particularly operating costs) and the carbon dimensions should be recovered elsewhere through a generic carbon price.

The carbon price should be long term, or at least far enough into the future to match the time dimensions of the technologies. This requires that it extends well beyond 2020. The EU ETS does not provide this carbon price, and therefore either longer-term carbon auctions are required, or a floor price of carbon should be created. The latter is, in effect, a carbon tax, and it could be extended into the future through commitment never to lower it. Additional sophistications could be added, such as inversely indexing it to the oil price above a floor level.

The security-of-supply issue is generic, too, and there are a number of generic mechanisms by which quantity and price security could be built into energy markets. A particular mechanism is the introduction of capacity markets over a medium-term horizon.

The combination of the allocation of equity risk, and functions, between the public and private sectors, and the pricing into the market of carbon and security of supply together provide an efficient basis for considering new nuclear investments. It is efficient because it allocates equity risk to those best able to manage its various dimensions, and hence lowers the cost of capital, which is, in such a capital-intensive technology, a dominating cost. In addition, where the policy interventions are generic, it avoids the government picking winners and in turn being captured by vested interests. In much of the post-Second World War period up until the 1980s, nuclear interests captured governments, notably in Britain and France. After 1980, they continued to do so in France, while in Britain they were (with coal) the losers in the privatization process. From the late 1990s, the wind lobby was successful to the exclusion of other low-carbon technologies, reaching the peak of its dominance over nuclear in the 2003 White Paper (DTI, 2003) and in support for the 2008 climate change package (CEC, 2008*a*, *b*).

With this structure in place—and, in particular, with an LCO (limited to the sunk costs), a long-term price of carbon, a capacity price, and a waste-management framework—nuclear will have a level playing field adjusted for the market failures. It may, or may not, as a result be economic. It is for the market to decide whether, in this appropriately designed context, it wishes to invest. But it is for government to decide whether it should be allowed to proceed, since the waste characteristics of nuclear power involve risks and costs to future generations, which can be resolved only through the political process.

Contrary to some assertions by nuclear interests, it is not necessary to have nuclear in the energy mix to meet climate-change objectives. There are a variety of ways of getting to a particular emissions target. But it may be economic to do so. If the political decision is favourable to nuclear, then it matters greatly that it is done properly. History provides some clear examples of how not to do this. A nuclear programme is not a discrete marginal undertaking. The policy framework required needs to be calibrated to the various components, as detailed above. But if the efficient components are neglected—as they are, for example, in the current British arrangements—then it may be better not to proceed. A well-designed programme—like that in France for the last three decades—is capable of containing the cost of capital, delivering power stations that work, and, as a result, making a major contribution to reducing emissions. A very badly designed programme—like that in Britain over the same period—has produced one of the worst investment outcomes since the Second World War—high cost, low performance, and a declining contribution to reducing emissions.

13

Carbon Dioxide Capture and Storage

*Howard Herzog**

I. INTRODUCTION

Carbon dioxide capture and storage (CCS) is the capture and secure storage of carbon dioxide (CO_2) that would otherwise be emitted to the atmosphere. Currently, the major CCS efforts focus on the removal of carbon dioxide directly from industrial or utility plants and subsequently storing it in secure geologic reservoirs. The rationale for CCS is to enable the use of fossil fuels while reducing the emissions of CO_2 into the atmosphere, and thereby mitigating global climate change.

At present, fossil fuels are the dominant source of the global primary energy supply, and will likely remain so for the rest of the century. Fossil fuels supply over 85 per cent of all primary energy; the rest is made up of nuclear, hydro-electricity, and renewable energy (commercial biomass, geothermal, wind, and solar energy).

While great efforts and investments are made by many nations to increase the share of renewable energy in the primary energy supply and to foster conservation and efficiency improvements of fossil-fuel usage, addressing climate-change concerns during the coming decades will likely require significant contributions from CCS. In his keynote address at the 9th International Conference on Greenhouse Gas Control Technologies (GHGT-9, November 2008), Jae Edmonds[1] reported that 'preparations for the IPCC 5th Assessment Report have indicated that meeting low carbon stabilization limits is only possible with CCS'.

The goals of this paper are to describe the fundamentals of CCS technology, to discuss the current status and costs of the technology, and to explore the policy context required for CCS to become a significant climate-change mitigation option. The paper is divided into sections as follows. Section II describes the major components of a CCS system and their commercial use today, while section III describes the CO_2 sources that are compatible with CCS. Sections IV (capture) and V (geologic storage) review the technological basis for CCS. Section VI looks at CCS costs. Section VII comments on China and CCS, while section VIII

* Massachusetts Institute of Technology, Energy Initiative.

I would like to thank three of my current research assistants who have helped in preparation of this chapter—Eleanor Ereira, Michael Hamilton, and Ashleigh Hildebrand.

[1] Chief Scientist, Joint Global Change Research Institute.

discusses the future of CCS in the context of climate policy. Some concluding comments and presented in section IX.

II. COMPONENTS OF A CCS SYSTEM

While there is no unique way to break down a CCS system into its component parts, typical components include the following.

- *Capture*. The separation of CO_2 from an effluent stream and its compression to a liquid or supercritical[2] state. In most cases today, the resulting CO_2 concentration is >99 per cent, though lower concentrations may be acceptable. Capture is generally required to be able to transport and store the CO_2 economically.
- *Transport*. The movement of the CO_2 from its source to the storage reservoir. While transport by truck, train, and ship are all possible, transporting large quantities is most economically achieved with a pipeline.
- *Injection*. Depositing CO_2 into the storage reservoir. Since the main storage reservoirs under consideration today are geological formations, these are the focus in this paper. Other potential reservoirs include the deep ocean, ocean sediments, or mineralization (conversion of CO_2 to minerals). While some commercial use of CO_2 may be possible, the amount that can be used compared to the amount of CO_2 that is emitted from power plants will be very small.
- *Monitoring*. Once the CO_2 is in the ground, it must be monitored. Since CO_2 is neither toxic nor flammable, it poses only a minimal environmental and health and safety risk. The main purpose of monitoring is to make sure that the sequestration operation is effective, meaning that almost all the CO_2 stays out of the atmosphere for centuries or longer.

It should be noted that all components of a CCS system are commercial today. The challenge for CCS to be considered commercial is to integrate and scale up these components. Below is a brief summary of the commercial use of each of the above components. Later sections discuss the technical aspects of both capture and storage.

(i) Capture

The idea of separating and capturing CO_2 from the flue gas of power plants did not originate out of concern about climate change. Rather, it gained attention as

[2] This means compression of CO_2 to above its critical pressure of 73.9 bar. At these pressures, CO_2 properties (e.g. density) are more like those of a liquid than of a gas.

a possible economic source of CO_2, especially for use in enhanced oil recovery (EOR) operations, where CO_2 is injected into oil reservoirs to increase the mobility of the oil and, thereby, the productivity of the reservoir. Several commercial CO_2-capture plants were constructed in the late 1970s and early 1980s in the USA. When the price of oil dropped in the mid-1980s, the recovered CO_2 was too expensive for EOR operations, forcing the closure of these capture facilities. However, the North American Chemical Plant in Trona, California, which uses this process to produce CO_2 for carbonation of brine, started operations in 1978 and is still operating today. Several more CO_2-capture plants have subsequently been built to produce CO_2 for commercial applications and markets.

All the above plants used post-combustion capture technology (discussed below). The amount of CO_2 captured ranged from a few hundred tons of CO_2 a day to just over a thousand tons a day. Deployment of post-combustion capture technologies for climate-change purposes will entail very substantial increases in scale, since a 500 MW coal-fired plant produces about 10,000 tons/day of CO_2.

(ii) Transport

There exist over 3,400 miles of CO_2 pipelines in the United States[3] (see Figure 13.1). Their main function is to transport CO_2 from naturally occurring reservoirs to the oil fields of West Texas and the Gulf Coast for enhanced oil recovery. The Wyoming/Colorado pipelines are fed by the LaBarge natural gas processing plant, where large quantities of CO_2 need to be separated from natural gas in order for the natural gas to meet commercial specifications, such as heating value. The North Dakota pipeline is fed by the Great Plains Synfuels Plant, which produces synthetic natural gas from coal, with large amounts of CO_2 as a by-product.

(iii) Injection

Though a relatively new idea in the context of climate-change mitigation, injecting CO_2 into geological formations has been practised for many years.

Acid-gas Injection

The major purpose of these injections is to dispose of 'acid gases', a mixture consisting primarily of H_2S (hydrogen sulphide) and CO_2 that is a by-product of oil and gas production. Acid-gas injection projects remove CO_2 and H_2S from the produced oil or gas stream, and compress and transport the gases via pipeline to an injection well, where they are injected into geological formations. In 2001, nearly 200 million cubic metres of acid gas were injected into formations across Alberta and British Columbia at more than 30 different locations. In most of these

[3] From the *Chemical Economics Handbook* (SRI Consulting).

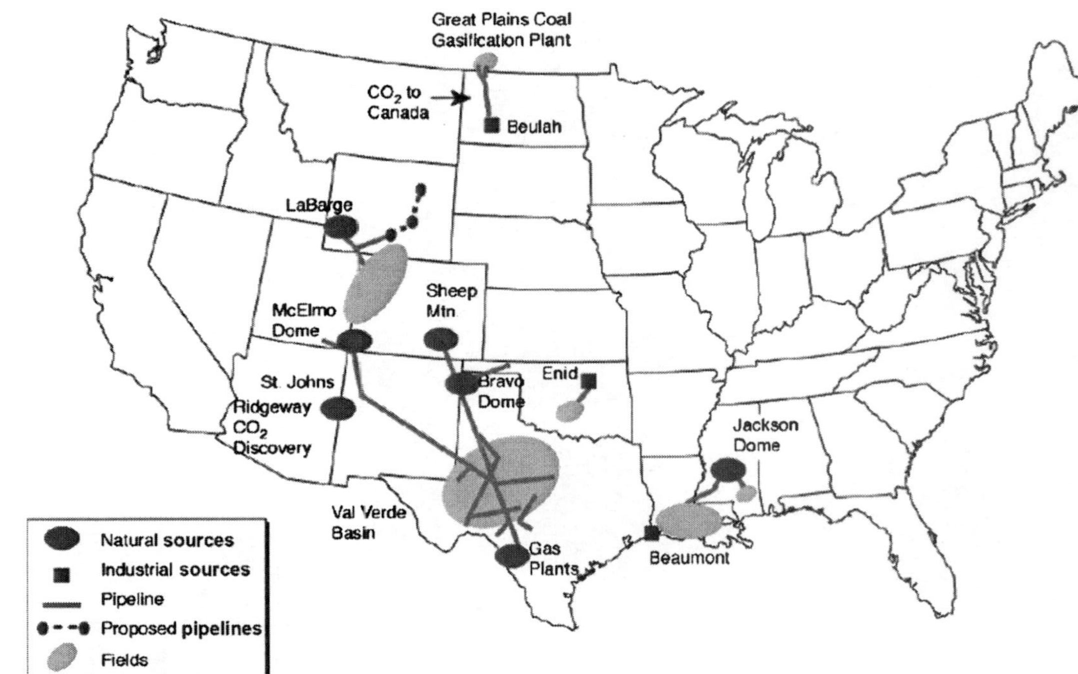

Figure 13.1. Existing CO_2 pipelines in the USA

Source: SRI Consulting, *Chemical Economics Handbook*, Carbon Dioxide Market Research Report, January 2007.

projects, CO_2 represents the largest component of the acid gas, consisting of up to 90 per cent of the total volume injected for some projects.

EOR

CO_2 injection into geological formations for enhanced oil recovery is a mature technology, having begun in 1972. In 2000, 84 commercial or research-level CO_2-EOR projects were operational worldwide. The United States, the technology leader, accounts for 72 of the 84 projects, most of which are located in the Permian Basin. Combined, these projects inject over 30 million tons of CO_2 per year. Outside the United States and Canada, CO_2-EOR projects have been implemented in Hungary, Turkey, and Trinidad.

In addition to acid-gas injection and EOR, natural-gas storage is also a commercial activity. Natural gas, like CO_2, is a buoyant fluid when injected into a geological formation, so their behaviour is similar. Natural gas was first injected and stored in a partially depleted gas reservoir in 1915. Since then, underground natural-gas storage has become a relatively safe and increasingly practised process to help meet seasonal as well as short-term peaks in demand. Because depleted oil and gas reservoirs were not readily available in the Midwest, saline aquifers were tested and developed for storage in the 1950s. Between 1955 and 1985 underground storage capacity grew from about 2.1 trillion cubic feet (Tcf) to 8 Tcf. Since CO_2 stored underground will be much denser than natural gas, 8 Tcf of natural gas capacity is roughly equivalent to the storage space needed to hold the CO_2 emitted annually from all the power plants in the United States.

(iv) Monitoring

Many tools and techniques used in oil and gas exploration and production are directly applicable to CO_2 storage.[4] Chief among these are several seismic techniques, including time-lapse 3D seismic monitoring, passive seismic monitoring, and crosswell seismic imaging. There are also many other methods, such as using tracers, sampling the reservoir brines, and soil gas sampling, illustrating the large variety of monitoring tools in use today that can be applied to CO_2 storage.

III. CARBON SOURCES

By far the largest potential sources today are fossil-fuelled power plants. Power plants are responsible for more than one-third of the CO_2 emissions worldwide. Power plants are usually built in large centralized units, typically delivering

[4] See section 5.6 of the IPCC Special Report, *Carbon Dioxide Capture and Storage* (IPCC, 2005), for a more detailed discussion on monitoring.

500–1,000 MW of electrical power. A 1,000 MW pulverized-coal-fired power plant emits 6–8 megatonnes (Mt)/year of CO_2, while a 1,000 MW natural-gas combined-cycle power plant will emit about half that amount. Coal-fired power plants represent by far the largest set of CO_2 sources that are compatible with CCS.

Several industrial processes produce highly concentrated streams of CO_2 as a byproduct. Although limited in quantity, they make a good capture target, because the CO_2 capture is integral to the total production process, resulting in relatively low incremental capture costs. For example, natural gas produced from the wells often contains a significant fraction of CO_2 that could be captured and stored. Other industrial processes that lend themselves to carbon capture are ammonia manufacturing, fermentation, and hydrogen production (e.g. in oil refining).

Fuel-conversion processes also offer opportunities for CO_2 capture. For example, producing oil from the oil sands in Canada is currently very carbon intensive. Adding CCS to parts of the production process can reduce the carbon intensity. Another example arises if we move towards a hydrogen economy. Opportunities for CO_2 capture will arise from producing hydrogen fuels from carbon-rich feedstocks, such as natural gas, coal, and biomass. The CO_2 by-product would be highly concentrated (in many cases, $>$99 per cent CO_2) and the incremental costs of carbon capture would be relatively low compared to capture from a power plant (usually just requiring compression).

Finally, coupling CCS with biomass feedstocks offers the potential for *negative net emissions*. Biomass contains carbon taken from the atmosphere and, in theory, we can capture and store the carbon in the biomass, resulting in a lowering of carbon concentrations in the atmosphere (i.e. negative emissions). Of course, one must account for the life-cycle emissions due to growing, harvesting, and processing the biomass. But if these emissions are kept low, net negative emissions can result.

IV. CAPTURE PROCESSES

CO_2 capture processes from power production fall into three general categories: (i) post-combustion capture; (ii) oxy-combustion capture; and (iii) pre-combustion capture. The first two categories are compatible with the existing pulverized coal (PC) power plant infrastructure that relies on combustion of fossil fuels. The last category is generally reserved for incorporation into an integrated gasification combined-cycle (IGCC) power plant.

(i) Post-combustion Capture

Post-combustion capture can be considered a form of flue-gas clean-up. The process is added to the back end of the power plant, after the other pollutant control

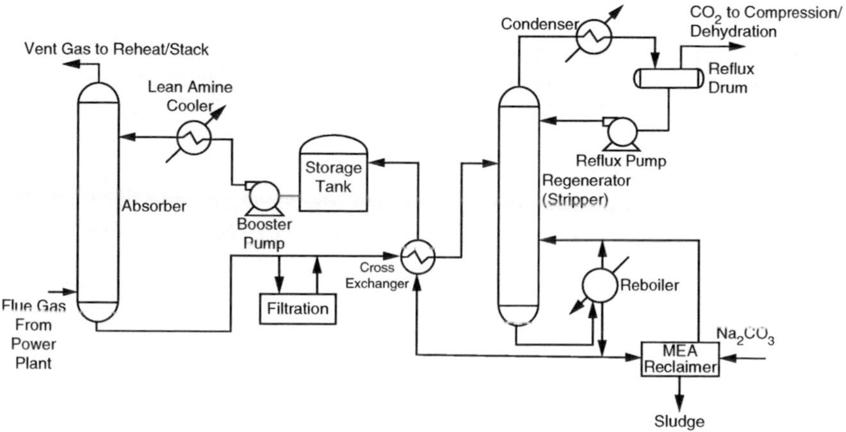

Figure 13.2. Process flow diagram for a typical amine separation process

systems (to control for particulates, sulphur dioxide (SO_2), and nitrous oxides (NO_x)). To be cost-effective, heat integration with the power plant is required.

To date, all commercial post-combustion CO_2-capture plants use chemical absorption processes with monoethanolamine (MEA)-based solvents. MEA was developed over 70 years ago as a general, non-selective solvent to remove acid gases, such as CO_2 and H_2S, from natural-gas streams. The process was modified to incorporate inhibitors that reduce solvent degradation and equipment corrosion when applied to CO_2 capture from flue gas. Considerations for degradation and corrosion also kept the solvent strength relatively low, resulting in relatively large equipment sizes and solvent regeneration costs.

As shown in Figure 13.2, which depicts a typical process flowsheet, flue gas contacts the MEA solution in an absorber. The MEA selectively absorbs the CO_2 and is then sent to a stripper. In the stripper, the CO_2-rich MEA solution is heated to release almost pure CO_2. The CO_2-lean MEA solution is then recycled to the absorber.

A later section discusses representative costs of a supercritical pulverized coal (SCPC) power plant, with and without capture, based on a modern amine system. A big part of the cost of post-combustion capture is the parasitic energy load. For capture of 90 per cent of the CO_2, the parasitic load for capture and compression will reduce the power plant output by about 25 per cent.

Research into new post-combustion capture technology is under way. The primary goal of these new processes is to reduce costs. This can be achieved by reducing the parasitic load, as well as reducing equipment sizes. Some approaches under way are:

- *Developing new solvents.* For example, two new processes based on ammonia as a solvent are currently being tested in pilot plants.

- *Using alternative separation processes.* These include adsorption and membrane-based processes. While theoretically possible, it is a difficult task due to the low CO_2 concentrations and pressures in the flue gas.
- *Developing new separation materials.* This is a new line of research that is still in the early stages of development. However, materials such as ionic liquids or metal organic frameworks (MOFs) are being applied to the CO_2-capture problem. They offer the possibility of significant cost reductions but not enough research has been carried out yet to judge whether they can be applied at the required scale and in the harsh flue-gas environment.

(ii) Oxy-combustion Capture

Because nitrogen is the major component of flue gas in power plants that burn coal in air (which nearly all existing plants do), post-combustion capture is essentially a nitrogen–carbon dioxide separation. If there were no nitrogen, CO_2 capture from flue gas would be greatly simplified. This is the thinking behind oxy-combustion capture: instead of air, the power plant is fed oxygen that is produced on site in an air separation plant. The resulting flue gas will be mostly CO_2 and H_2O, which are easily separable (the water condenses out in the compression process).

A few items about this process should be noted.

- The primary separation process has now shifted from the flue gas to the intake air, where oxygen is separated from nitrogen. This is done in a standard air separation unit (ASU), but it will have a large parasitic load of about 15 per cent of a power plant's electric output.
- A standard power boiler can be used for this process (making retrofits of this technology to standard PC plants possible), but a portion of the flue gas needs to be recycled into the combustion chamber in order to control the flame temperature.
- Once the water is separated out, the flue gas will be over 90 per cent CO_2. However, there will be minor impurities in the effluent, including SO_2, NO_x, and non-condensables such as oxygen and nitrogen. In general, these impurities will need to be cleaned up before the CO_2 is ready for transport and injection.

Studies show that oxy-combustion capture can be competitive with post-combustion capture. However, experience with oxy-combustion is limited. In September 2008, Vattenfall began operation of a 30 megawatt thermal (MW_{th}) oxy-combustion pilot plant at its Schwarze Pumpe site in Germany. The cost of this facility was about US$100 million and it is expected to provide critical operating data for the oxy-combustion process. Vattenfall projects that for full-scale operations, the cost of oxy-combustion capture will be 40 €/tonne CO_2 or less.

Future improvements in oxy-combustion can come from:

- specially designed boilers that increase efficiency and eliminate the need for the external recycle of flue gas;
- use of ionic transport membranes for oxygen production.

Other oxy-combustion technologies are:

- Chemical looping combustion, where solids flow between two fluidized bed reactors. In one reactor, the solid reacts with air (picking up oxygen). In the second reactor, it reacts with fuel (losing its oxygen). If successful, this process can essentially eliminate the cost of oxygen production.
- Clean Energy Systems has a process based on an 'oxygen turbine' (as opposed to oxygen boilers in the systems above). A pilot plant is currently under construction in California as part of the US Regional Partnership Program.

(iii) Pre-combustion Capture

Pre-combustion capture is usually applied in IGCC power plants. This process includes gasifying the coal to produce a synthesis gas composed of carbon monoxide (CO) and hydrogen (H_2); reacting the CO with water (in a water-gas shift reaction) to produce CO_2 and H_2; capturing the CO_2; and sending the H_2 to a turbine to produce electricity. Since the primary fuel sent to the gas turbine is now hydrogen, some can be bled off as a fuel for separate use, such as in hydrogen fuel cells to be used in transportation vehicles.

Capturing CO_2 before combustion offers some advantages. First, CO_2 is not yet diluted by the combustion air. Second, the CO_2-containing stream is usually at elevated pressure. Therefore, more efficient separation methods can be applied, for example using pressure-swing-absorption in physical solvents, such as methanol or polyethylene glycol (commercial brands are Rectisol and Selexol). One of the biggest barriers to this pathway is that currently electricity generation is cheaper in PC power plants than in IGCC plants. The pre-combustion process could also be used when natural gas is the primary fuel. Here, a synthesis gas is formed by reacting natural gas with steam to produce CO_2 and H_2. However, for the natural gas case, it is unproven whether pre-combustion capture is preferable to the standard post-combustion capture.

Worldwide, gasification facilities exist today that do not produce electricity, but synthesis gas and various other byproducts of coal gasification. In these facilities, CO_2 is separated after the gasification stage from the other gases, such as methane, hydrogen, or a mix of CO and hydrogen. The synthesis gas or hydrogen is used as a fuel or as a chemical raw material, e.g. for liquid fuel manufacturing or ammonia synthesis. The CO_2 can also be used as a chemical raw material, for dry-ice manufacturing, carbonated beverages, and EOR. For example, the Great Plains Synfuel Plant, near Beulah, North Dakota, gasifies 16,326 tonnes per day of lignite coal into 3.5 million standard cubic metres per day of combustible syngas, and close to 7 million standard cubic metres of CO_2. A part of the CO_2 is captured by a physical solvent based on methanol. The captured CO_2 is compressed and 2.7 million standard cubic metres per day are piped over a 325 km distance to the Weyburn, Saskatchewan, oil field, where the CO_2 is used for enhanced oil recovery.

V. GEOLOGICAL STORAGE

(i) Types of Formations

Geological sinks for CO_2 include oil and gas reservoirs, deep saline formations, and unminable coal seams. Together, these can hold hundreds to thousands of gigatons of carbon (GtC), and the technology to inject CO_2 into the ground is well established. CO_2 is stored in geologic formations by a number of different trapping mechanisms that depend on the formation type.

Oil and Gas Reservoirs

Depleted oil and gas reservoirs have proven that they can hold hydrocarbons for millions of years. This gives confidence that they can store CO_2 for a long time. Also, these reservoirs are relatively well characterized. However, some questions arise about whether the wells drilled into the reservoirs and the removal of the hydrocarbons have compromised their integrity. Active oil reservoirs have become a high priority target, since CO_2 storage can be combined with EOR.

Unmineable Coal Seams

Abandoned or uneconomic coal seams are another potential storage site. CO_2 diffuses through the pore structure of coal and is physically adsorbed to it. This process is similar to the way in which activated carbon removes impurities from air or water. The exposed coal surface has a preferential affinity for adsorption of CO_2 than for methane with a ratio of 2:1.

Deep Saline Formations

Deep saline formations, both subterranean and sub-seabed, may have the greatest CO_2 storage potential. These reservoirs are the most widespread and have the largest volumes. The density of CO_2 depends on the depth of injection, which determines the ambient temperature and pressure. The CO_2 must be injected below 800 m so that it is in a dense phase (either liquid or supercritical). When injected at these depths, the specific gravity of CO_2 ranges from 0.5 to 0.9, which is lower than that of the ambient aquifer brine. Therefore, CO_2 is buoyant and will naturally try to rise to the top of the reservoir.

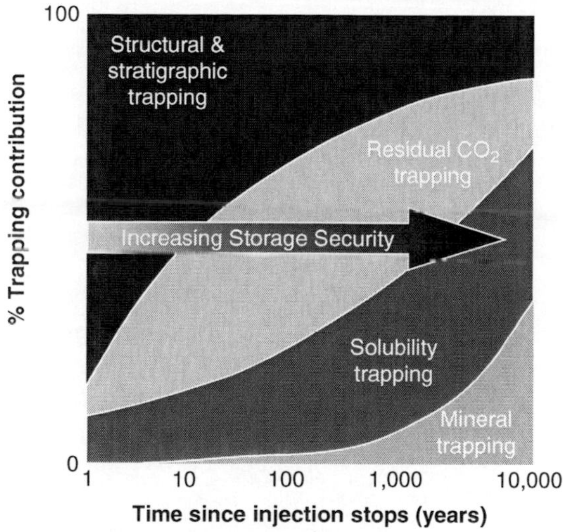

Figure 13.3. Schematic of the influence of different trapping mechanisms over time
Source: IPCC Special Report (2005), *Carbon Dioxide Capture and Storage*, figure 5.9, p. 208.

(ii) Trapping Mechanisms for Saline Formations

Unlike oil and gas reservoirs, deep saline formations have a limited history of use for storage, primarily from acid-gas injections or natural-gas storage. However, research has shown that there are a number of mechanisms that work to trap the CO_2. These mechanisms work on different time scales, but they work in such a way that the longer CO_2 stays in the ground, the smaller the chance of any leakage. This is shown schematically in Figure 13.3.

The four trapping mechanisms are described further below.

- *Structural and stratigraphic trapping*. The CO_2 is injected into a permeable reservoir, initially displacing the brine that is in the pores. The injection will generally cause a rise in pressure. This needs to be monitored to make sure it stays below the pressure at which the rock starts to fracture. The CO_2 will be buoyant in this environment, causing it to rise to the top of the reservoir. It is here that an impermeable caprock of the formation will trap the CO_2.
- *Residual CO_2 trapping*. As the CO_2 flows through the reservoir, some of it gets incorporated into the soil matrix. This is called residual CO_2 trapping. The CO_2 trapped in such a manner becomes immobile, and its storage can be considered permanent.
- *Solubility trapping*. Over timescales of decades to centuries, some of the CO_2 will dissolve in the brine. This is called solubility trapping. The timing and amount of CO_2 trapped in such a manner is very reservoir-dependent. This trapping removes the buoyancy from the CO_2, thus reducing the likelihood

of leakage. If the brine ever leaves the reservoir, the CO_2 will be released. However, this usually occurs on very long timescales.

- *Mineral trapping.* Over centuries to millennia, the injected CO_2 may react with the minerals in the reservoir. Essentially, CO_2 can get incorporated into the solid rocks and minerals in the reservoir. This is called mineral trapping and can be considered permanent storage.

(iii) Capacity

The IPCC Special Report, *Carbon Dioxide Capture and Storage*, concluded that 'available evidence suggests that, it is likely that there is a technical potential of at least about 2,000 GtCO_2 of storage capacity in geological formations'. This is a large number (about two orders of magnitude greater than total annual worldwide CO_2 emissions), indicating the potential of CCS to be a significant CO_2 mitigation strategy. It should be pointed out that some countries have an abundance of storage capacity (e.g. USA, Australia), while others have limited options (e.g. Japan).

The reservoirs with the largest potential capacity are the deep saline formations. At present, capacity estimates for CO_2 storage in deep saline formations are highly uncertain. This is because the data required to do rigorous capacity calculations are very sparse. Data are typically obtained through drilling wells. Unlike oil and gas reservoirs, deep saline formations have no commercial value, so the number of wells drilled into these formations is limited.

On the other hand, much more data exist for storage estimates in oil and gas reservoirs. However, owing to a current lack of field data needed to confirm the methodology used to calculate storage capacities, there is still uncertainty in these numbers.

Calculating storage capacities in coal seams is very difficult, in part because the feasibility of large-scale storage in coal seams has not been demonstrated. Any capacity estimates for these formations must be taken as very highly uncertain.

The US Department of Energy (DOE) has just completed a *Carbon Sequestration Atlas of the United States and Canada*.[5] It gives capacity estimates for oil and gas reservoirs as 82 GtCO_2. For saline formations, it gives a range of 920–3,400 GtCO_2. The high end of this range is greater than the worldwide capacity reported by the IPCC. It should be noted that the IPCC was being conservative in its estimates (saying 'at least'), but this does highlight the uncertainty in making these estimates.

In summary:

- At present, capacity estimates are highly uncertain;
- however, there is a broad consensus that the capacity will be large enough for CCS to be a significant CO_2 mitigation strategy;

[5] Available at http://www.netl.doe.gov/technologies/carbon_seq/refshelf/atlas/

Table 13.1. Existing large-scale storage operations

Project	Leader	Location	CO_2 source	CO_2 sink
Sleipner (1996)	Statoil	North Sea, Norway	Gas processing	Saline formation
Weyburn (2000)	Pan Canadian	Saskatchewan, Canada	Coal gasification	EOR
In Salah (2004)	BP	Algeria	Gas processing	Depleted gas reservoir
Snovit (2008)	Statoil	Barents Sea, Norway	Gas processing	Saline formation

- while potential storage reservoirs exist around the world, some countries will have better CCS opportunities than others.

(iv) Large-scale Projects

At present, four large-scale CO_2 storage projects are in operation (see Table 13.1). All of these projects are injecting in the order of 1m tonnes per year CO_2. Also, the source of CO_2 for all of these projects is an industrial by-product, so the cost of capture is relatively small. The number in parentheses next to the project is the year it started CO_2 injections.

The first commercial-scale project dedicated to geologic CO_2 storage is in operation at the Sleipner West gas field, operated by Statoil, located in the North Sea about 250 km off the coast of Norway. The natural gas produced at the field has a CO_2 content of about 9 per cent. In order to meet commercial specifications, the CO_2 content must be reduced to 2.5 per cent. At Sleipner, the separated CO_2 is compressed and injected via a single well into the Utsira Formation, a 250 m thick aquifer located at a depth of 800 m below the seabed. About 1 Mt of CO_2 have been stored annually at Sleipner since October 1996, equivalent to about 3 per cent of Norway's total annual CO_2 emissions. A total of 20 Mt of CO_2 is expected to be stored over the lifetime of the project. Over the years, the injected CO_2 has been monitored via time-lapse 3D seismic techniques. This has allowed researchers to get a better understanding of the behaviour of CO_2 in the reservoir. The seismic monitoring strongly suggests that the CO_2 is safely stored and not escaping the reservoir. However, the resolution of the seismic data is not great enough to definitively say that 100 per cent of the CO_2 has remained in the reservoir. Experiences at the other three sites are similar to that at Sleipner, in that they provide learning opportunities and demonstrate that CO_2 can be safely stored in geological formations.

(v) Regulatory and Legal Issues

While there is no comprehensive legal and regulatory framework for CO_2 storage *per se*, the US Environmental Protection Agency (EPA) has a regulatory framework governing most types of underground injection, the Underground Injection Control (UIC) Program. The UIC Program was created under the Safe Drinking Water Act of 1974 (SDWA) and establishes requirements to assure that underground injection activities will not endanger drinking-water sources. The UIC Program regulates underground injection under five different classes of injection wells, depending on the type of fluid being injected, the purpose of injection, and the subsurface location where the fluid is to remain. States are allowed to assume primary responsibility for implementing the UIC requirements in their borders as long as the state programme is consistent with EPA regulations and has received EPA approval. Injection operators are required to provide financial assurance in case they cease operations, with the level of assurance a function of the estimated cost of plugging and abandoning the injection well.

Recently, the EPA released a proposed rule for federal requirements under the UIC Program for CO_2 geologic sequestration (GS) wells.[6] Below is an excerpt from the EPA's fact sheet[7] on the new rules.

> EPA's proposed rule would establish a new class of injection well—Class VI—and technical criteria for geologic site characterization; area of review and corrective action; well construction and operation; mechanical integrity testing and monitoring; well plugging; post-injection site care; and site closure for the purposes of protecting underground sources of drinking water.
>
> The elements of today's proposal build upon the existing UIC regulatory framework, with modifications based on the unique nature of CO_2 injection for GS, including:
>
> - Geologic site characterization to ensure that GS wells are appropriately sited;
> - Requirements to construct wells with injectate-compatible materials and in a manner that prevents fluid movement into unintended zones;
> - Periodic re-evaluation of the area of review around the injection well to incorporate monitoring and operational data and verify that the CO_2 is moving as predicted within the subsurface;
> - Testing of the mechanical integrity of the injection well, ground water monitoring, and tracking of the location of the injected CO_2 to ensure protection of underground sources of drinking water;
> - Extended post-injection monitoring and site care to track the location of the injected CO_2 and monitor subsurface pressures; and
> - Financial responsibility requirements to assure that funds will be available for well plugging, site care, closure, and emergency and remedial response.

Beyond incorporation into existing regulations, CCS contains some items that go beyond the scope of the UIC Program. One item is legal access to the geologic formation. In most of the world, the pore space is owned by the state, so this is not a major problem. However, in the United States, this is not the case. While there may be some differences between the states, people that own mineral rights and/or

[6] See http://www.epa.gov/safewater/uic/wells_sequestration.html

[7] See http://www.epa.gov/safewater/uic/pdfs/fs_uic_co2_proposedrule.pdf

surface rights will have claim to ownership of the pore space. Under current law, the right to use the sub-surface would need to be acquired from every owner where the CO_2 plume migrates. This could become impractical in many situations, so new legislation may be needed to ease this process.

How to deal with the long-term stewardship and liability of the CO_2 is still an open issue. By long term, we mean centuries or longer. Questions on how to monitor the reservoir once it is closed and for how long need to be resolved. Liability would arise if CO_2 leaked out and caused environmental or health problems, but it is a highly unlikely that leaking CO_2 is a significant health or environmental risk. Of more concern, a leaking CO_2 reservoir becomes a CO_2 emissions source. We assume that there will be a charge for CO_2 emissions (through either a tax or cap-and-trade system), and someone would be liable for that charge. It has been suggested that a number of years after closure (in the order of 10 years) and assuming no significant leakage or operational problems, the long-term stewardship and liability would be taken over by the government. To help pay for this, companies injecting CO_2 into the ground would pay into a liability fund.

VI. COSTS[8]

In MIT's *The Future of Coal* report (MIT, 2007), detailed cost estimates were developed for all three of the CO_2-capture categories discussed in section IV. However, in the report, costs were based on analyses done in the 2000–4 timeframe, with costs given in 2005 US dollars. Since then, commodity and fuel costs have risen significantly, resulting in significant increases in costs. For example, CERA (Cambridge Energy Research Associates) reports that capital costs for coal-fired power plants have risen about 80 per cent over this timeframe.

Recently, we updated the cost estimates from *The Future of Coal* study. We only published the costs for supercritical pulverized coal (SCPC), since the recent literature and discussion with industry experts support these new estimates. We decided not to publish new cost estimates for IGCC and oxy-fuel combustion technology for two reasons. The first reason is the tremendous uncertainty regarding the true costs and performance characteristics of such new technologies. The second reason is that our discussion with industry experts indicates that any current IGCC cost estimate is highly uncertain since costs for IGCC may have doubled or tripled since 2004. To present a new estimate under such high uncertainty would be detrimental to the discussion about new-generation technology. This situation underscores the importance for new comprehensive design and cost studies reflecting the new technical knowledge about IGCC in this transient cost environment.

[8] This section is based on Hamilton *et al.* (2008) (see http://sequestration.mit.edu/pdf/GHGT9_Hamilton_Herzog_Parsons.pdf for more details).

Table 13.2. Updated costs for Nth plant SCPC generation

Reference plant	Units	SCPC
Total plant cost	\$/kWe	1,910
CO_2 emitted	kg/kWh	0.830
Heat rate (HHV)	Btu/kWh	8,868
Thermal efficiency (HHV)		38.5%
LCOE		
Capital	\$/MWh	38.8
Fuel	\$/MWh	15.9
O&M	\$/MWh	8.0
Total	\$/MWh	62.6
CO_2 capture plant		
Total plant cost	\$/kWe	3,080
CO_2 emitted @ 90% capture	kg/kWh	0.109
Heat rate (HHV)	Btu/kWh	11,652
Thermal efficiency (HHV)		29.3%
LCOE		
Capital	\$/MWh	62.4
Fuel	\$/MWh	20.9
O&M	\$/MWh	17.0
Total	\$/MWh	100.3
Mitigation cost		
\$/tonne CO_2 avoided	\$/tonne	52.2

Estimates of costs for SCPC have been updated to a 2007 US dollar basis according to estimates of recent escalation in capital, operating, and fuel costs (see Table 13.2). These costs are for an Nth plant (N may be in the range of 5–10). The first several CCS plants built will probably be more expensive, as typically happens with the introduction of new technologies. It should also be recognized that we are currently in a highly volatile market and costs are constantly changing.

In summarizing CCS costs for the SCPC case, the following should be noted.

- The mitigation cost for capture and compression is about US\$52/tonne CO_2. This does not include transport and storage costs, which are very site specific. However, we can estimate a typical range of US\$5–15/tonne CO_2. This implies a carbon price of about US\$60–65/tonne CO_2 is needed to make these plants economical in the marketplace.
- Adding capture to a power plant raises the cost of electricity by about 4¢/kWh. This represents an increase in the delivered price of electricity in the 25–50 per cent range.

It should be noted, that the cost of CCS from other sources (as discussed in section III) may be significantly less expensive than from coal-fired power plants and they may be good initial targets. However, their CO_2 emissions are much smaller than those from coal-fired power.

VII. CHINA

China has abundant coal reserves. Inexpensive coal has been crucial in powering China's rapid growth; on average, a new coal plant starts up every week in China. Since this trend is likely to continue (at perhaps a reduced rate), the question of whether CCS can be deployed in China is important.

Some specific points can be made about China and CCS.

- The CCS technology used in China will be essentially the same as is used in the USA and Europe.
- No authoritative studies have been conducted on potential geologic storage reservoirs in China. However, initial assessments suggest that, while not as abundant as in, say, the United States, there are significant resources available.
- China has shown a willingness to host CCS demonstration projects. China seems to have an easier time in developing infrastructure than the USA or Europe.

CCS, like most mitigation technologies, is very dependent on what China decides to do about climate policy in general. The MIT coal study (MIT, 2007) looked at China and concluded that it will probably lag the West in adoption of climate policies. How to integrate China and the rest of the developing world into an international climate regime is a difficult and critical issue, but beyond the scope of this paper.

The cost of CCS may also significantly slow its adoption by China, even after China implements a climate policy. Therefore, reducing costs for CCS becomes even more important in the China context.

VIII. THE POLICY CONTEXT AND THE FUTURE OF CCS

There are many roads CCS can take as we move forward. What path it takes depends not only on how the technology evolves, but also on how climate-change technology evolves. In this concluding section, CCS is discussed in this policy context.

First, it may be instructive to look at example scenarios for the growth of CCS. MIT (2007) presented simulations performed with its emissions predictions policy analysis (EPPA) model, a computable general equilibrium (CGE) model of the world economy. One set of simulations in the report contrast a business-as-usual (BAU) scenario, with two policy cases, one with a high global carbon price and one with a low price, implemented either through cap-and-trade or a carbon tax. The low carbon price is modelled as beginning in 2010 at US\$7/ton CO_2, increasing at a real rate of 5 per cent annually, and the high carbon price begins at US\$25/ton CO_2 in 2015, increasing at an annual rate of 4 per cent thereafter. Table 13.3 from the report shows the resulting coal CO_2 emissions, the coal consumption, and

Table 13.3. Implications for global coal consumption under alternative CO_2 price assumptions (from MIT, 2007)

	2000	BAU 2050	Low CO_2 price 2050	High CO_2 price 2050
Coal CO_2 emissions ($GtCO_2$/year)	9	32	15	5
Coal consumption (Exajoules (EJ)/year)	100	448	200	161
% Coal with CCS	0	0	4	60

the proportion of coal technologies that use CCS under the three scenarios. The simulations assume limited expansion of nuclear technologies and a reference gas price with no breakthroughs in liquefied natural gas (LNG) transport.

The model predicts that, under the BAU scenario, global CO_2 emissions from coal will reach 32$GtCO_2$/year by 2050. Under both CO_2 price scenarios, coal use grows from current levels, but not as much as under the BAU case. However, thanks to CCS, under a high CO_2 price, coal consumption still grows by over 60 per cent, but its emissions are almost cut in half.

The above simulation assumes that CCS has achieved both technological readiness and that policies are in place to create a market for CCS. Today, neither of these assumptions is valid. Below is an outline of the actions and policies necessary for CCS to move forward.

In the MIT study (MIT, 2007), conducting large-scale CCS demonstrations was identified as the key to achieving technological readiness:

> The central message of our study is that demonstration of technical, economic, and institutional features of carbon capture and sequestration at commercial scale coal combustion and conversion plants, will (1) give policymakers and the public confidence that a practical carbon mitigation control option exists, (2) shorten the deployment time and reduce the cost for carbon capture and sequestration should a carbon emission control policy be adopted, and (3) maintain opportunities for the lowest cost and most widely available energy form to be used to meet the world's pressing energy needs in an environmentally acceptable manner.

MIT called for 3–5 demonstration projects in the US in the next eight to ten years. More recently, at their 2008 meeting in Japan, the G-8 called for 20 demonstrations worldwide by 2020. The demonstration projects, coupled with a strong R&D programme, would help address the two biggest challenges for CCS:

- reducing or eliminating first-mover costs;
- reducing uncertainties primarily associated with storage at scale:
  - capacity
  - long-term integrity
  - regulatory framework
  - liability
  - public acceptance.

Assuming a successful demonstration programme, by 2020 CCS could be ready for large-scale deployment. However, an additional three key ingredients are necessary for CCS to be considered truly commercial.

(i) *Creating a market through climate policy*
As stated in section VI, a carbon price of about US$60–65/tonne CO_2 is needed to make CCS from power production economical in the marketplace. While a cap-and-trade system (or carbon tax) can create a carbon price, it is highly unlikely that climate policy will result in a carbon price greater than US$60/tonne CO_2 by 2020. Therefore, there will be a gap between the cost of CCS and the carbon price. Over time, the carbon price will rise and the cost of CCS may fall, giving hope that the gap will eventually disappear. However, for a decade or two, additional policy measures will be needed to promote CCS. These can take many forms—direct subsidies, production credits, bonus allowances, portfolio standards, etc.

(ii) *Providing a regulatory environment*
Companies will not enter a business with a high degree of regulatory uncertainty. As discussed in section V, there are three primary concerns that must be addressed:

- ownership of the pore space;
- regulations for site selection, injection operations, and site closure;
- resolution of the long-term liability issue.

(iii) *Development of a business structure*
While the two items above are primarily government tasks, this item is up to the private sector. It is the private sector that will build and operate CCS systems. It is the private sector that will make choices about technology and will spur future improvements. It is highly unlikely that one company will offer services for all parts of the CCS value chain. Today, quite a few companies are actively working to provide capture technology. Also, CO_2 transport companies exist. However, no companies exist to provide storage services or long-term stewardship. In addition, rules for how these companies interact still need to be developed.

IX. CONCLUSIONS

To summarize some of the key messages from this paper:

- there is a growing consensus that it will be impossible to achieve significant cuts in greenhouse-gas emissions (50–80 per cent below today's levels) without CCS. So while CCS may not be a silver bullet, it can be considered a 'keystone' technology;

- all components of a CCS system are commercially available and in operation today;
- the key technical challenge for CCS is the integration and scaling-up of the system components. This is a significant task that relies on major investments in the technology, but no technological breakthroughs are required.

The steps moving CCS to commercialization rely on making the necessary investments in the technology and involve both the private and public sectors. The four essential elements include:

- private–public partnerships are needed to build and operate approximately ten demonstration plants worldwide over the next decade;
- governments (with advice from the private sector) must create a market for CCS through climate policy. The policy should be technologically-neutral (i.e. avoid picking winners and losers);
- governments (with advice from the private sector) must provide a suitable regulatory environment for CCS. These regulations must be stringent enough to protect the public interests, but not overly stringent so as to stifle CCS development;
- the private sector must develop a business organization to address all components of the CCS value chain. The implementation of CCS, including decisions on the appropriate technologies, needs to be left up to the private sector.

BACKGROUND READING

Most of the material in this paper has been based on publications produced by the MIT Carbon Capture and Sequestration Program. These publications can be found at http://sequestration.mit.edu/
Several publications in particular were heavily relied upon:

de Figueiredo, M.A., Herzog, H. J., Joskow, P. L., Oye, K. A., and Reiner, D. M. (2007), 'Regulating Carbon Dioxide Capture and Storage', CEEPR WP-2007-003, April.

Hamilton, M., Herzog, H. J., and Parsons, J. (2008), 'Cost and US Public Policy for New Coal Power Plants with Carbon Capture and Sequestration', Presented at the 9th International Conference on Greenhouse Gas Control Technologies, Washington, DC, November.

Herzog, H. J., and Golomb, D. (2004), 'Carbon Capture and Storage from Fossil Fuel Use', in C. J. Cleveland (ed.), *Encyclopedia of Energy*, New York, Elsevier Science, 277–87.

MIT (2007), *The Future of Coal: Options for a Carbon Constrained World*, Massachusetts Institute of Technology (available at http://mit.edu/coal/).

In addition, two sources of additional reading are recommended for those who want to explore more deeply some of the topics discussed in this chapter:

IPCC (2005), *Carbon Dioxide Capture and Storage*, Intergovernmental Panel on Climate Change, Special Report, New York, Cambridge University Press (available at http://www.ipcc.ch/ipccreports/srccs.htm).

Proceedings of the 9th International Conference on Greenhouse Gas Control Technologies, Washington, DC, November 2008 available through Science Direct.

14

Climate-change Mitigation from Renewable Energy: Its Contribution and Cost

*Richard Green**

I. THE CONTEXT

The world has three main sources of energy. The most important at present is fossil fuels, providing more than 80 per cent of the world's energy in 2006 (IEA, 2008*b*). Fossil-fuel reserves are finite, but also abundant—we have more than 40 years of proven oil reserves at current rates of production, 60 years of gas, and 130 years of coal. The estimated reserves that are believed to exist but have not yet been proven (or even discovered) and unconventional oil sources, such as tar sands, should add substantially to these estimates (Ahlbrandt, 2006). These estimated reserve lives should be reduced to take account of likely future increases in demand, and marginal supplies of energy will become expensive long before the oil 'runs out'—a point made with respect to other natural resources by Dieter Helm in Chapter 2. Nevertheless, the world has adequate supplies of fossil fuels for many years to come.

The problem is that if we simply burn these supplies, the resulting carbon emissions will lead to unacceptable climate change. Low-carbon alternatives are needed. These include the other two main sources of energy at present: nuclear power (6 per cent of world energy in 2006) and renewable energy (13 per cent). Carbon capture and sequestration applied to fossil fuels will also be an option in future, as discussed by Howard Herzog (Ch. 13).

Nuclear power is discussed by Helm in Chapter 12. Nuclear fission is an established technology, and the world's reserves of uranium will allow for many centuries of its use if fast breeder reactors are adopted. Nonetheless, nuclear fission is highly controversial, given its problems of waste disposal and possible weapons

* University of Birmingham.

Support from the Engineering and Physical Sciences Research Council and our industrial partners through the Supergen Flexnet Consortium, grant EP/E04011X/1, is gratefully acknowledged. My thinking on this topic has developed while I was advising the House of Lords Economic Affairs Committee on their report 'The Economics of Renewable Energy', HL195 of 2007–8, and I would like to thank the Committee for giving me that opportunity. I would like to thank the editors and participants in seminars at the Department of Economics, University of Birmingham, and at the Birmingham Metallurgical Association for helpful comments. The views expressed are mine alone.

proliferation. Nuclear fusion offers potentially unlimited energy, but will not be available for decades, if ever.

Renewable energy can provide a sustainable source of low-carbon energy without the disadvantages of nuclear power. Developing renewable sources provides an extra technological option, alongside carbon capture and sequestration in the short term and nuclear fusion in the long term. The main disadvantage of most forms of renewable energy is that their costs are currently greater than those of fossil fuels, and some kind of government support is required to make them commercially viable.

The European Union (EU) has announced plans for a substantial increase in Europe's use of renewable energy, with a target that 20 per cent of the Union's energy should come from renewable sources in 2020 (European Commission (EC), 2008*b*). Other targets for that year, also attractively alliterative, are for a 20 per cent reduction in emissions of greenhouse gases and a 20 per cent increase in energy efficiency. In 2005, 8.5 per cent of the EU's final energy consumption came from renewable sources, but with great variation between member states: while Sweden took 39.8 per cent of its energy from renewable sources, the UK took just 1.3 per cent. The national targets started with the principle that each member state should increase its share of renewable energy by an equal amount, but these were then adjusted to require more expansion by the richer countries and less by those which had recently expanded their output of renewable energy significantly. The targets range from 10 per cent for Malta to 49 per cent for Sweden; the UK's target is 15 per cent.

The aim of this chapter is to examine the impacts of these targets on the energy system and on the cost of energy. It also discusses the design of policies to support renewable generation. First, however, it asks what renewable energy resources are available to the EU.

II. THE RESOURCE

Energy is used in three main ways—to provide heat, transport, and electricity (which can itself provide heat and transport). In the UK, heat and transport each take about two-fifths of final energy demand, and electricity one-fifth. The kinds of renewable energy available to substitute for each type of conventional energy differ.

For transport, the main alternative is bio-fuel, a range of liquid fuels usually derived from plants. At present, the so-called first-generation biofuels are derived from crops which would otherwise be used as food, and the additional demand has had the unfortunate side-effect of raising food prices, at least in the short term. In the longer term, palm oil plantations (for bio-diesel) may replace tropical rain forests, while corn grown for bio-ethanol in temperate climates requires fertilizer inputs involving significant emissions of greenhouse gases. The Gallagher Review for the UK government concluded that bio-fuel production risked becoming unsustainable (and even increasing emissions of greenhouse gases) if it was based on land diverted from food crops (Renewable Fuels Agency, 2008). The Review recommended that the UK's targets for bio-fuels should rise more slowly than previously planned, in order to reduce the pressure for land-use change. Second-generation biofuels are being developed, however, which would be derived from the woody parts of plants that are often wasted at present. If existing waste streams can be turned into energy, or new crops (such as jatropha) grown on currently marginal land, this will be more sustainable.

Biomass can also be burned to provide renewable heat. Burning waste (or the landfill gas produced by decomposing waste) would be sustainable, if the products had been produced in a sustainable manner. Energy crops can also be grown specifically to provide biomass for burning. The power of the sun can be used to heat water or another fluid to be used in a heat exchanger (solar thermal energy). Heat exchangers are also at the heart of heat pump technology, which cools a fluid, allows the energy in the air or ground to warm it up, and then extracts this energy to heat (or cool) a building. A good heat pump uses one unit of electrical energy to provide four units of heat.[1] Even though the efficiency with which primary energy is converted to electricity is only 45 per cent in the UK,[2] the heat pump still provides nearly two units of heat for each unit of primary energy. One drawback, however, is that the electrical distribution system would need a lot of reinforcement before it could cope with the induction loads created by the motors in a large number of heat pumps running simultaneously (Sterling, 2008).

Electricity is the sector with the highest penetration of renewable energy, in the UK and many other EU countries. The most significant source of renewable electricity within the EU is hydro-electricity, providing 66 per cent of renewable generation in 2006. Although hydro-electric plants are very flexible, there is little scope to expand large-scale hydro generation as most suitable sites have been developed: there is more potential for small-scale schemes. Any assessment of the potential for renewable energy has to take costs into account—as the amount required rises, so does the marginal cost. The higher the price we are willing to pay, the more renewable energy we can obtain. The estimates in this chapter are drawn from the EU Renewable Energy Road Map (EC, 2007), which is based on estimates of the potential supply (at various cost levels) in each member state. The potential outputs shown in Table 14.1 are based on a 'least-cost scenario' for achieving a 20 per cent share of renewable energy in 2020. In this scenario, the share of hydro generation will fall to 30 per cent of renewable electricity in 2020.

Biomass is the second greatest source of renewable generation (17 per cent of the total in 2006). Most of that comes from burning solid biomass (typically wood or wood waste), but a small proportion comes from the incineration of municipal waste, and a small part from collecting and burning the methane given

[1] Heat pumps with a coefficient of performance (ratio of energy output to input) of 4.9 are available in Japan (Mackay, 2008, p. 151).

[2] This is the ratio of primary energy input to final electricity consumption in 2007 (*Digest of UK Energy Statistics*, 2008, table 1.1).

Table 14.1. EU electricity generation from renewable sources

	Generation in 2006		Potential for 2020, Green-X model, least-cost scenario	
	TWh	%	TWh	%
Biomass	90	17	186	14
Geothermal	6	1	7	1
Hydro	344	66	398	30
Solar		0	62	5
Marine		0	124	9
Wind	82	16	545	41
	522	100	1,323	100

Source: EC (2007).

off at landfill sites. There is significant scope for expanding this last energy source (which also converts a more potent greenhouse gas into carbon dioxide (CO_2)), and while the share of biomass generation is predicted to decline, it only falls to 14 per cent of the total.[3]

In 2006, the share of wind generation was just behind that of biomass, at 16 per cent, but it has been rising rapidly and is predicted to reach 41 per cent in 2020. Wind turbines have been growing in size and efficiency, but have been the subject of complaints for their impact on the landscape. At present, a very small proportion of wind generation is located offshore, where the visual impacts attract less attention, but costs are significantly higher—not least because few turbines have been designed specifically for the taxing marine environment. By 2020, however, there could be almost as much offshore as onshore wind, according to the Renewable Energy Road Map.

Marine energy uses the tides and the waves. Tidal-range generation involves building a barrage across an estuary, and the scheme at La Rance in France has been operating since 1967. A similar barrage built across the Severn Estuary could provide nearly 5 per cent of the UK's electricity (DECC, 2009). Other marine technologies only exist as prototypes, however. These include tidal-stream generators (turbines that would be placed in areas of rapid tidal flows) and a variety of wave generators that can extract energy from the water's movement. Their costs are likely to be high, but the EU Renewable Energy Road Map predicts that marine energy could provide 9 per cent of the EU's renewable generation in 2020.

The amount of solar generation is currently very small, but could rise to 5 per cent of renewable generation by 2020. Solar photovoltaic power relies on light hitting a panel to create an electric current, while concentrating solar power uses

[3] The Road Map does not show any potential for an increase in electricity generation from biomass, but states that 'the allocation of the total biomass potential to the different sectors (electricity/heat/transport) is part of the optimization process in the applied modelling approach' (EC, 2007, p. 44).

Table 14.2. Scenarios for meeting the 20 per cent EU target

	Least-cost scenario		Balanced scenario	
	Mtoe	% penetration	Mtoe	% penetration
Electricity	125	43	99	34
Heat	95	16	121	21
Transport	38	11	43	12
	258	20	263	20

Note: Mtoe: million tonnes of oil equivalent.

Source: EC (2007).

mirrors to focus intense light on a boiler where a liquid can be converted to steam for use in a turbine. Given the UK's latitude, however, it will always be a relatively unattractive location for solar power.

The EU has analysed several scenarios for meeting the 20 per cent target. Two of them are described in Table 14.2. The transport sector is likely to have the smallest amount of renewable energy, both absolutely and as a proportion of its demand. The proportion of renewable energy will be highest in the electricity sector, but it is possible that the absolute amount of renewable energy will be greater in heat than in electricity.

III. SYSTEM IMPACTS

Some forms of renewable energy fit easily within the overall energy system. Power stations burning biomass can be dispatched in the same way as those burning fossil fuels. Heating a building using renewable, rather than conventional, energy has no implications for other nearby buildings. In the case of transport fuels, it will be important to match the proportion of biofuel mixed in with petrol or diesel to the capability of engines to burn such a mix. We may need to keep supplying some fuels with a low biofuel content, so that older vehicles with engines that are not adapted to burn a high proportion of biofuels can find a suitable fuel—assuming that we do not wish to force such vehicles off the road.

Some forms of renewable electricity, however, pose serious challenges for system integration. The output from a tidal generator will vary with the tides, although these are, at least, predictable. Wind-power stations depend (in a non-linear manner) on the strength of the wind, and this is very difficult to predict more than a short time ahead. Since electricity must, at present, be generated at the moment it is needed, a high proportion of wind generation would pose significant challenges for the electricity industry. Much of the additional generation needed if the EU is to meet its 2020 target is likely to come from wind power, and so this is a serious problem.

The intermittent nature of wind generation has two impacts on the electricity system. The first is the need for more balancing reserves, in case the output of other stations changes suddenly. System operators need to be able to react almost instantaneously if a significant amount of generation is lost, and then to bring other plants on line soon afterwards in order to restore their reserve margin. At present, the first need is met by running some stations at part load, able to increase output very fast (spinning reserve), while other stations are paid to act as replacement reserve and start soon after a problem occurs. The amount of spinning reserve required depends on the largest credible single loss of generation. In most EU countries, this would currently be given by the size of the largest generating unit, since it would be very unfortunate to lose two units in quick succession from independent causes. As the amount of wind generation rises, however, a single cause (a change in the wind) could lead to a larger loss of generation over a short period, and so more reserve plant is required.

The cost of this is equal to the amount of additional reserve plant (or demand response) needed, multiplied by its cost per megawatt-hour (MWh). For low levels of wind penetration, no extra reserve is needed, and so the cost is zero. As the amount of intermittent renewable output rises, however, it will start to determine the amount of reserve needed, and a cost will be imposed. Gross *et al.* (2006) surveyed a large number of studies of the cost of intermittency for the UK Energy Research Centre. They found that in studies relevant to the UK, the cost of the additional reserve needed for 20 per cent of renewable output was around £2–3 per MWh of renewable output. This cost is likely to increase with the level of renewable output, and National Grid, the electricity system operator for Great Britain, has estimated a cost of £3–7 per MWh of renewable output if the overall share is around 40 per cent (House of Lords, 2008, para. 102). Oswald *et al.* (2008) suggest that such figures exclude the cost to conventional generators of changing output more frequently to match the demand net of the fluctuating renewable output, and thus underestimate this aspect of the cost of intermittency.

The second impact of intermittency is that the amount of wind generation available at the time of the system peak may be well below the amount expected on average. The load factor of wind generators in the UK is around 27 per cent, and more than this in the peak winter months, but for around 10 per cent of the hours in January (when the peak is most likely to arise), a well-balanced portfolio of wind stations, dispersed around Great Britain, would produce less than 10 per cent of their capacity (Green and Vasilakos, 2008). This means that the wind generators cannot be counted on to contribute as much to meeting the peak level of demand as to providing energy over the year as a whole. Additional plant will be needed to reduce the risk of power cuts at the winter peak.

Demand at the winter peak may be higher than expected, and some conventional (fossil fuel and nuclear) power stations will turn out to be unavailable at that time, although failures at different plants ought to be uncorrelated.[4] Roughly

[4] An exception would be an interruption to fuel supplies, or a generic fault affecting a class of nuclear reactors.

speaking, a capacity of 20 per cent above the level of peak demand ought to be enough to keep the risk of power cuts at a very low level. In other words, to meet the UK's peak demand of around 60 GW, 72 GW of conventional power plants would be required. Wind generators can contribute towards this total, but only at around 10–20 per cent of their capacity. In other words, if the UK were to build 30 GW of wind power, this should be regarded as equivalent to between 3 and 6 GW of conventional plant from the point of view of meeting peak demand. As well as the wind capacity, 66–69 GW of conventional plant would be needed to give a total equivalent to the 72 GW required.

Building 10 GW of wind plant thus replaces only 1–2 GW of conventional plant, from the point of view of meeting the peak demand for capacity. If the only criterion was the total energy generated by the stations, the wind generators would be able to replace a larger amount of capacity. If the wind plant has a load factor of 28 per cent, for example, and a new conventional plant has a load factor of 80 per cent, then 3.5 GW of conventional plant would provide the same amount of energy as 10 GW of wind plant.[5] This means that between 1.5 and 2.5 GW of conventional plant is needed, not to provide energy, but because the intermittent plant does not provide much effective capacity. Gross *et al.* (2006) suggest that the best methodology for calculating this aspect of the cost of wind stations' intermittency is to take the cost of this additional capacity (the 1.5–2.5 GW in our example) and to spread it over the wind stations' output. They estimate this cost at between £3 and £5 per MWh of intermittent output, assuming a system similar to that of the UK which takes up to 20 per cent of its output from intermittent renewable sources.

Gross *et al.* (2006) base their estimate on the cost of new combined-cycle gas-turbine stations. In some circumstances, a country would meet its capacity needs, not by building new stations, but by keeping old stations open, which would be far cheaper. In the EU, however, large numbers of conventional stations will have to close before 2016, as it would not be economic for them to retrofit the pollution control equipment required by the Large Combustion Plant Directive. There will thus be no reserve of old stations to draw on. However, the cost of extra new capacity would be reduced if open-cycle gas turbines were built instead. While this might suggest that Gross *et al.*'s estimate is too high, the capacity credit of wind stations declines as the amount of intermittent generation rises. With a greater amount of intermittent generation than they assume, the amount of back-up capacity needed will be higher.

Future changes in technology could affect these costs. The most important development would be a cost-effective way of storing power (Dell and Rand, 2001). From the point of view of meeting the peak demand for electricity, a storage system is simply a substitute for a power station, and so the question is which would have the lower cost per MW of effective capacity. It would no longer be

[5] This is because 28% × 10 = 80% × 3.5. A load factor of 80 per cent is rather low, but allows us to use straightforward numbers in the example.

necessary to 'spill' wind output at times when demand was low.[6] The greatest advantage of energy storage, however, would come from its ability to smooth the load on conventional stations, and on the transmission system. At times when the output from intermittent renewable sources was unusually high, the excess would be put into storage, and taken out later when renewable output was lower. This would reduce the cost (in terms of fuel, and wear and tear) of changing the output from conventional stations. These benefits would, of course, have to be compared with the cost of building and operating the stores.

The cost of storing energy might be reduced to nearly zero, from the point of view of the electricity system, if the store is needed for some other reason. The most likely possibility would be an electrified transport system. If vehicles could charge their batteries at times when the system had surplus power, and the grid could draw on these batteries when it had a shortage, this would help to deal with intermittency (Kempton and Letendre, 1997). The question is how much energy could be stored and drawn down in this way. The cost and energy consumption of electric vehicles will be increased if their batteries are over-sized, and there must be a way of preventing a vehicle giving too much power to the system just before its driver wants to start a long journey.

Long-distance transmission could also reduce the cost of intermittency. The wider the geographic area covered by a group of wind farms, the lower the variation in their output. This makes transmission capacity another substitute for generation capacity and storage. Again, since transmission is expensive (and new lines often face public opposition), the question is whether it is a cost-effective substitute. The key issue would be the length of additional lines needed to bring power from an area sufficiently far away to reduce the correlation between wind speeds to a low level.

Significant changes to the electrical network may be needed in any case. Some of the best renewable resources are a long way from the centres of demand, and extra transmission capacity will be required. Many renewable generators will be small, and connected not to the transmission grid but to the distribution system. This is currently designed to take power from higher to lower voltages, and will need new operating techniques, and more protection equipment, to accept power flowing in the 'wrong' direction.

IV. THE COST OF RENEWABLE ENERGY

There are (at least) three measures of the cost of renewable energy, shown in Figure 14.1. The first is the cost of individual projects to the investor, in the

[6] It would be necessary to spill wind, not just when the wind output exceeded the total demand for power, but when it exceeded demand net of output from nuclear stations that cannot vary their output (something to be considered when designing new plants) and from conventional plants that must run part-loaded in order to provide spinning reserve, or when there was a constraint on the transmission system.

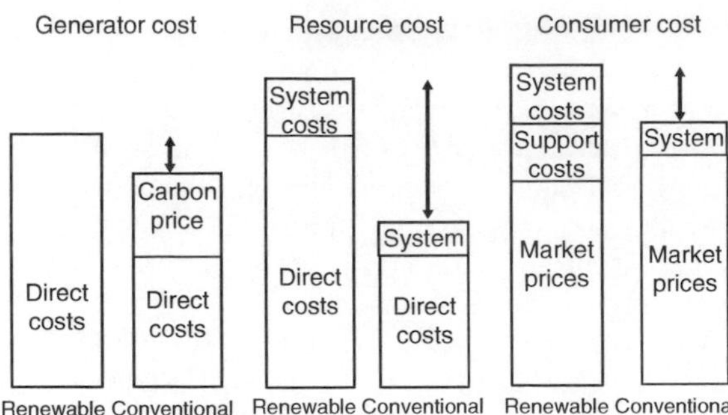

Figure 14.1. Cost comparisons

absence of support schemes. Since most forms of renewable energy are more expensive than conventional sources on this cost measure, some kind of support will be needed to make the projects viable. The second is the resource cost of using renewable energy rather than conventional sources. This could be assessed at the level of individual projects, but it is more useful to consider this cost at the level of the overall system, since this allows us to include the costs of accommodating renewable energy sources within the energy system. The third measure is the cost to energy consumers (or taxpayers). This will depend on the support schemes adopted, and the extent to which subsidies to renewable energy exceed their excess cost.

The cost of energy to the investor includes capital costs, fuel costs (if any), the cost of carbon emissions (if there are any, and if they are the subject of taxes or permits), and other operating costs, including labour and maintenance.[7] The split between these costs depends on the technology and on the load factor that the station is able to achieve. Many renewable technologies are capital intensive, but have no fuel costs. The cost per kW of installed capacity of onshore wind stations is similar to that of a coal-fired power station, for example, but their low output relative to this capacity (their output typically averages 30 per cent or less of their capacity over the year) means that they have much higher costs per kilowatt-hour (kWh) generated. Offshore wind stations have higher load factors than onshore stations, but their capital costs are also higher. As the proportionate increase in costs is greater than the proportionate increase in output, the cost per kWh of offshore wind stations is therefore higher than that of onshore stations. At the time of writing (early in 2009), turbine manufacturers are operating at full capacity, and are able to charge prices which may be above their long-term trend.

Most marine energy devices are only at the prototype stage, but also have high projected capital costs. Power stations to burn biomass have lower capital costs

[7] Figures given in UK studies typically also include the transmission charges paid by the generator. These are calculated on the basis of capacity, rather than output, and will thus raise the relative cost per kWh of renewable generators with low levels of output per kilowatt (kW) of installed capacity, such as wind.

Table 14.3. The cost of electricity to investors (at the power station)

	Coal	Gas	Nuclear	Biomass	Onshore wind	Offshore wind
Cost (pence per kWh)	5.6	4.6	4.5	9.0	7.3	8.1
Key assumptions:						
Construction cost (£ per kW of capacity)	£1,070	£523	£1,500	£1,837	£1,111	£1,574
Average output relative to capacity (load factor) (%)	81	81	77	80	27	37
Plant life (years)	25	20	30	20	20	20
Interest rate (%)	10	10	10	10	10	10
Fuel cost (pence per kWh of output)	0.74	1.38	0.44	4.6	0	0
Emissions of CO_2 (kg per kWh)	0.76	0.37		Nil at the station		
Cost of electricity (pence per kWh) given:						
Assumptions above	5.6	4.6	4.5	9.0	7.3	8.1
Capital cost up by 20%	6.0	4.8	5.1	9.7	8.4	9.3
Interest rate of 13%	6.1	4.9	5.6	9.9	8.4	9.5
Fuel price up by 50%	6.4	6.0	4.7	11.3	7.3	8.1
Carbon price of £50/tonne CO_2	7.9	5.7	4.5	9.0	7.3	8.1

Source: Adapted from House of Lords (2008, Table 2). All cases except the last include a carbon price of £20/tonne CO_2. This accounts for 1.5p/kWh of the cost of a coal-fired station, and 0.7p/kWh of the cost of a gas-fired station.

per kWh generated—because they can operate at high load factors—but typically have higher fuel costs than conventional stations.

The comparison between the costs of renewable and fossil-fuelled power is crucially dependent on the prices of fuel and carbon. If these prices are volatile (and in 2008, they certainly have been), the cost of generation from fossil fuels will be so, too. This is not necessarily a disadvantage to the investor, however, if the selling price of electricity moves with this cost. The profit margin of a fossil-fuelled generator is much less volatile than that of a nuclear (or renewable) generator with costs that are little affected by the price of fossil fuels (Roques *et al.*, 2006), a disadvantage for the latter that is magnified if carbon prices move with those of fossil fuels (Green, 2008).

Table 14.3 gives estimates of the cost of electricity from a range of generation types. These are based on figures used in recent studies for the UK government, with the exception of fuel prices, for which the actual prices paid in the 12 months to June 2008 were used. During this period, the price of oil averaged US$96 per barrel. The coal price was 0.74 pence per kWh (£54 per tonne) and the price of gas was 1.4 pence per kWh (40.6 pence per therm). The table gives the cost per kWh of electricity generated, based on a thermal efficiency of 45 per cent for a new coal-fired station, and 55 per cent for a new gas-fired station. For a biomass station, a fuel cost of 1.3 pence per kWh (£3.60 per gigajoule) and a thermal efficiency of 28 per cent were used. The price of carbon was set at £20 per tonne of CO_2. With these prices, nuclear power is just cheaper than gas (both cost around 4.5p/kWh), while coal-fired stations cost roughly 1p/kWh more. Onshore wind costs just over 7p/kWh, offshore wind just over 8p/kWh, and biomass in custom-built power stations costs about 9p/kWh. It should be noted that the capital-cost figures given in the table are well below those in press reports on the nuclear station being built at Oikuluoto in Finland (which may be suffering from 'first of a kind' costs) and on offshore wind projects (which may be suffering from a temporary bottleneck in supply chain capacity).

The table also shows the results of changing some key assumptions (one at a time). In almost every case, the renewable sources have higher costs than coal, gas, or nuclear stations. A very high carbon price would be needed to make even onshore wind power competitive with gas-fired electricity, and investors would need to believe that this carbon price would be maintained throughout the economic lifetime of the station. Very high fossil fuel prices would also make renewable energy competitive; a long period of low prices would give a greater cost disadvantage than in the figures presented here.

To estimate the resource cost of renewable energy, we need to consider the system as a whole. It is not possible for every power station to run at a load factor of 81 per cent, as the average demand for electricity in the UK is only two-thirds of its peak level.[8] Using a model that ranks power stations in order of increasing cost, it is possible to predict how much each one will actually generate. Stations with low variable costs will be used more intensively than those with high variable costs—as long as they are actually available. The stations with the lowest variable costs will be wind generators, but these are only available to the extent that the wind is blowing. Data on past wind speeds can be used to estimate the amount of wind generation that would be available, compared to the level of demand, and hence create an expected load-duration curve for the other power stations.

Such a load-duration curve can be used to predict the output patterns, and hence costs, of power stations. On top of these costs at the power station, we need to add the estimated cost of running additional reserve plant (to cope with changes in the wind speed) and holding additional capacity (to cope with low winds at the time of the peak demand)—the cost of intermittency. We should also add the cost of extra investment in the transmission and distribution networks. These costs were discussed in the previous section. Table 14.4 presents estimates for the UK with a renewable electricity share of 34 per cent in 2020.

According to these estimates, the resource cost of generating an extra 105 TWh a year of renewable electricity in 2020 will be an extra £6.8 billion a year, assuming the fuel prices of 2007–8. This is an extra cost of 6.4 pence per kWh of renewable electricity, over and above the level generated in 2007. With different fossil fuel prices, the additional cost of renewable energy changes—high fossil-fuel prices imply a lower additional resource cost, although the total cost of generation

[8] From 2003 to 2007, the average system load factor was 67 per cent (*Digest of UK Energy Statistics*, 2008, table 5.10).

Table 14.4. The resource cost of renewable generation

	Fuel prices 50% below 2007–8 levels (£ billion)	2007–8 fuel prices (£ billion)	Fuel prices 50% above 2007–8 levels (£ billion)
Predicted generation cost with 6% renewables (excluding CO_2 price)	12.7	16.2	19.6
Cost of balancing and the existing transmission system	1.5	1.5	1.5
Predicted total cost with 6% renewables	14.2	17.7	21.1
Extra costs of moving from 6 to 34% renewables			
Generation	6.3	4.3	3.0
Predicted additional costs of system integration			
Intermittency[a]	1.3	1.3	1.3
Transmission	1.2	1.2	1.2
Sub-total	8.8	6.8	5.5
Predicted overall cost of generation and transmission with 34% renewables (excluding CO_2 price)	23.0	24.5	26.6

Note: [a] The cost of intermittency is likely to vary with the cost of fuel, but no figures were available on its sensitivity to this.

Source: Adapted from House of Lords (2008, tables 3 and 4), plus author's calculations.

and transmission is still increasing in the price of fossil fuel. The resource cost estimates exclude any cost of carbon emissions, for they can then be used to estimate the cost of reducing emissions via renewable generation—in this case, emissions are reduced by 52 million tonnes of CO_2 a year. The implied cost is thus £130 per tonne of CO_2. This is well above the estimated damage caused by carbon emissions, which the Stern Review (Stern, 2007) put at US$85 per tonne of CO_2, for example.[9] The implication is that renewable energy is a high-cost way of reducing carbon emissions, although it brings other benefits and may deserve support on their account.

V. REASONS TO SUPPORT RENEWABLE ENERGY

Since most forms of renewable energy are clearly more expensive than the conventional alternatives, they will not be adopted on a wide scale without government support. There are four possible justifications for such support. First, since carbon emissions are a damaging externality, low-carbon generation could be subsidized

[9] This figure (based on 2000 prices) would equate to around £50 per tonne in 2007 prices at the exchange rate when the Stern Review was published (US$1.9 = £1), or to £64 per tonne at the current exchange rate of roughly US$1.5 = £1.

as a second-best policy for reducing them. The first-best policy, of course, would be to put a price on carbon emissions that reflected the full cost of the externality. In the presence of such a carbon price, the low-carbon status of renewable generators would not justify any additional support. If it is not politically feasible to raise the price of carbon emissions to the extent required to reduce them to sustainable levels, then giving extra support for renewable generators may prove a feasible way of making additional reductions.

The second justification recognizes that the cost of some renewable technologies is high because they are immature, and is likely to fall faster than the costs of alternatives, through research and development programmes or just via learning-by-doing (IEA, 2000). In many industries, companies are prepared to absorb development costs in the expectation of making greater profits when they have a mature product, and the price of a new product can reflect the cost of making it. Renewable energy competes directly with conventional energy sources, and would normally sell at the price of energy from those sources. Selling at such prices would involve heavy losses for the developers. If they are not sure that they can capture the gains from future cost reductions (if there are learning externalities) then extra support would be needed to cover these development costs. Neuhoff (2008) points out that subsidizing initial deployment can also bring benefits in allowing a greater expansion once the costs of renewable energy have fallen to a competitive level, if there is a limit to the rate at which the industry can grow.

The third justification for subsidizing renewable energy is that it adds diversity to a country's portfolio of energy sources. This can bring benefits from the point of view of security of supply. First, a country with a more diverse range of energy sources will be less exposed to increases in the price of one of them (Awerbuch, 2000). Second, if renewable energy implies less reliance on imports, a country's physical supplies of energy will be more secure. Offsetting this, however, is the risk that intermittent sources of renewable electricity generation, such as wind or marine (wave and tidal) energy will not be available in the short term when demand has to be met. If energy companies do not face the full consequences of an energy shortage, then they will under-invest in measures to prevent one, and some policy to correct this would normally be justified (Egenhofer *et al.*, 2004).

The fourth possible justification is related to the finite nature of fossil-fuel reserves—at some time in the future, we will need alternative energy sources. Although this may not be for many decades, starting to develop renewable energy now puts us in a better position for that eventual time, particularly if the alternative of nuclear fusion proves impractical.

There is something in each of these arguments, although the first—that renewables can act as a supplement to an inadequate carbon price in mitigating climate change—is explicitly a second-best policy, and government intervention in technology development (the second argument) has a long history of mixed success (see, for example, Henderson, 1977). The third and fourth arguments implicitly assume that there are externalities in energy shortages, not internalized by the companies that would otherwise make investment decisions.

VI. POLICIES TO SUPPORT RENEWABLE ENERGY

Assuming that specific government support is justified, what is the best way to provide it? The policies used by governments fall into three main groups: capital grants, feed-in tariffs, and obligation schemes. Capital grants address one of the main sources of cost disadvantage directly, reducing the amount that investors have to pay up front for renewable generators. With a feed-in tariff, the renewable generator receives a fixed price for each unit of output. With a certificate scheme, electricity companies have to obtain a set proportion of their power from renewable sources, or pay a penalty. Renewable generators obtain certificates that they can sell at a price linked to the penalty that the buyer can thus avoid paying. This gives the renewable generators an additional source of revenue.

Support policies can be assessed on two dimensions—how much renewable generation do they encourage (effectiveness), and what is the cost per MWh (efficiency)? The UK's Renewables Obligation, which effectively fixes the total amount of support for renewable generators, and then divides it among the actual output generated in a year, has been criticized for being both expensive in support per MWh generated and ineffective in bringing in new generation, although delays in the planning system have helped to keep the amount of new generation low. Germany's feed-in tariff for solar power has been effective in developing 3.8 GW of new capacity, but the efficiency of a scheme that paid €467/MWh might be questioned.[10] A competitive tender for new generation has the potential to be efficient, but if it only funds a small amount of new capacity, it may not be very effective.

A support policy is most likely to be effective and efficient if it is tailored to the cost characteristics of the renewable generator. Most renewable generators have relatively high capital costs, and as they are not much affected by changes in the price of fossil fuels, their total costs are not correlated with electricity prices. A support policy can reduce a generator's capital cost if it either reduces the up-front investment, as with a capital grant, or if it reduces the generator's cost of capital. A feed-in tariff can do this by separating the generator's income stream from the risky electricity price. Helm (2008*c*) has gone further, suggesting that renewable generation should be treated as a kind of utility, subject to a regulated return which customers would be required to finance. This would minimize post-construction risks, and hence the cost of capital. Given the importance of capital costs as a proportion of the total cost of renewable energy, keeping the cost of capital down will be vital if the EU is to meet its renewable targets in a cost-effective manner. In contrast, a tradable certificate scheme gives generators two income streams, from the certificate price and from electricity prices, which may both be volatile, raising their risks and cost of capital.[11] The EC (2008*c*) has found that well-designed

[10] Installations commissioned in 2008 will receive €467/MWh for 20 years through a feed-in tariff (IEA, 2008*a*). This level has been declining by 5 per cent a year since 2005.

[11] If the penalty for not having enough certificates was (formally) inversely correlated with electricity prices, this would make the combined income stream more like that from a feed-in tariff.

feed-in tariffs have generally been both more effective and more efficient than obligation schemes.

A further question is the degree to which support levels should be differentiated between generators. A support scheme that does not differentiate between technologies, or sites, will have to set the level of support to suit the most expensive generator required to achieve the desired amount of generation, and this will be well above the average level of support required. An overly differentiated scheme will cost more to administer, and is likely to be the subject of intense lobbying when the support levels are set. However, these costs are likely to be lower than the rents achieved by low-cost generators in an under-differentiated support scheme.

VII. THE COST OF RENEWABLE ENERGY TO CONSUMERS

We can now consider the third measure of the cost of renewable energy, which is the cost to energy consumers—how will the prices that they have to pay change? First, what will happen to the wholesale price of power? Second, how much will consumers have to pay to support the cost of renewable generation, over and above wholesale market prices? Third, how high will the additional system integration costs be?

If renewable capacity is added to an electricity market that already has adequate supplies of generation, we should expect prices to fall. Sensfuß *et al.* (2008) estimate that the reduction in German wholesale prices, owing to this effect, is approximately the same as the amount consumers pay to support renewable generators—in effect, the support for renewable power is paid by conventional generators. Sáenz de Miera *et al.* (2008) calculate a similar reduction in prices for the Spanish market, but point out that this is not a long-term equilibrium outcome. In the long term, generators need to expect to recover their costs from wholesale prices, and will tend to adjust capacity until this is possible. The time-weighted wholesale price would then equal the cost of the generators expected to run on base load, which should not be significantly affected by the amount of renewable generation. Increasing the amount of intermittent generation, however, will change the shape of the expected load-duration curve for the generators that are not expected to run throughout the year, and the optimal mix of plant types may change. In particular, there are likely to be more generators that are only expected to run for short periods during the year, and so technologies with relatively low fixed costs will gain market share over those with low running costs.[12]

[12] In electricity generation, there is typically a trade-off between fixed and running costs, so that plants with low fixed costs and high running costs are favoured to meet short-lived peaks in demand, and those with low running costs but high fixed costs are used to meet the base load throughout the year.

This will, in turn, affect the sector's overall revenue requirements, and hence the pattern of prices. Even if time-weighted prices are unchanged, consumers as a whole are exposed to the demand-weighted wholesale price, which may change.

The cost of support payments to renewable generators depends on the efficiency of the support scheme as well as on the amount by which market prices fall short of the generators' costs. At a minimum, the cost of support payments should equal the additional cost of renewable energy to investors, discussed in section IV, but an inefficient scheme will cost more than this.

The cost of system integration—balancing and reserve generation, and investment in the transmission system—was also discussed section IV. These costs will be incurred either by regulated transmission companies or in specialized markets for balancing and for capacity; in either case, it should be straightforward to pass them on to consumers without an excessive margin.

In the case of the UK, the cost of system integration has been estimated at £2.5 billion a year by 2020 (House of Lords, 2008, para. 127). The government is committed to retaining the Renewables Obligation, although it may be supplemented with a feed-in tariff for small-scale renewable generators. We have no information on how much support this tariff would provide, but it is safe to assume that it would be at least as generous as the Renewables Obligation is intended to be, given the higher costs of small-scale generation. A Renewables Obligation for 33 per cent of electricity generation would cost £4.4 billion a year. In future, however, the Obligation will be banded, providing more support to higher-cost technologies (and less to new plants using established technologies with lower costs), and if this increases the number of certificates relative to the level of renewable output, then the level of the Obligation will have to rise. An Obligation of 42 per cent would cost £5.6 billion a year.[13]

The EC (2008*a*, p. 35) has estimated that the EU renewables target would reduce the price of carbon in the EU Emissions Trading Scheme (ETS) by €10 per tonne of CO_2. This implies that the renewable energy is used as a substitute for other ways of reducing carbon emissions, rather than tightening the emissions target to take account of the contribution from renewable energy. The impact of this on electricity prices depends on whether coal- or gas-fired stations are setting the price—with a 50–50 mix, the wholesale price of power would fall by 0.52p/kWh or just under £2 billion, assuming the reduction in marginal cost is fully passed on to consumers. Overall, the UK's commitment to renewable electricity could cost its consumers £6.1 billion, or 4.8p/kWh of renewable power, in 2020.

[13] A possible mix of renewable technologies to deliver 34 per cent of renewable electricity by 2020 could produce certificates equal to 42 per cent of demand, given the banding levels for 2009–13. (There will be a high proportion of offshore wind, with 1.5 certificates per MWh.) For the next few years, the government is actually committed to setting the Obligation at least 8 per cent above the expected output of certificates, to prevent unusually high output levels creating a surplus and sending their price to zero. (The number of certificates per MWh of offshore wind was temporarily raised in the 2009 Budget, but the calculations here do not reflect this.)

VIII. CONCLUSIONS

The EU is committed to a dramatic increase in the level of renewable energy, with a very tight timetable. Achieving the target would make a significant contribution to the task of reducing carbon emissions, saving between 600 million and 900 million tonnes a year, according to studies carried out for the EC (2007, p. 20). Is the target at the right level? It is, obviously, a round number, and it would be surprising if a cost–benefit analysis were to come out with an answer that renewable energy should make up exactly 20 per cent of the EU's needs. In fact, the Commission's studies imply that, at the margin, renewable energy will require support of €45/MWh, on top of a carbon price of €39 per tonne of CO_2 (EC, 2008*a*, p.35). The cost per tonne of CO_2 saved from renewable energy depends on the carbon content of the conventional energy displaced. If this is electricity generated from a mix of (mostly) gas and coal, it might contain 0.5 tonnes of CO_2 per MWh. In this case, the resource cost of displacing the marginal tonne of CO_2 would be €129.[14] If the energy displaced has a lower carbon content, the cost per tonne of CO_2 saved will be higher (and vice versa).

This is similar to the estimated cost of carbon saved by renewable electricity generation in the UK. The study just cited implies that the EU can meet its target of a 20 per cent reduction in carbon emissions without expanding renewable energy (beyond a business-as-usual case), but that the carbon price required to do so would be higher without the contribution from renewable energy. However, if the ETS sectors have a marginal cost of carbon equal to €39 per tonne of CO_2, and the marginal cost of carbon saving from renewable energy is three times this amount, the allocation of carbon reductions between sectors would seem seriously sub-optimal. As discussed in section V, saving carbon emissions is not the only benefit of renewable energy. Nonetheless, the very high marginal cost per tonne of CO_2 saved suggests that the EU targets may be too ambitious. Furthermore, there is a danger that investing too much in the technologies available now might distract attention from other options that need more development, but could be more cost-effective in future.

This is not to say that there should be no expansion of renewable energy. If we expect fossil fuel prices to rise, renewable energy will become relatively cheaper.[15] The predicted average cost of the 20 per cent renewables target is much lower than its marginal cost, at around €50 per tonne of CO_2 saved. Given the high marginal cost, this implies that there must be substantial amounts of renewable energy available at a very low resource cost, well below the social cost of CO_2 emissions. These schemes should be pursued. Some renewable technologies that currently have high costs deserve support in the hope that their costs will soon

[14] The resource cost (assuming that the support is not excessive) is equal to the carbon price, plus the support for renewable energy per MWh, divided by the amount of CO_2 emitted per MWh of conventional energy displaced (€45/MWh ÷ 0.5 tonnes/MWh).

[15] The converse is also true—if low demand keeps fossil fuel prices low for the next few years, investment in renewable energy will look particularly unattractive at a time of tightened budgets.

fall to more economic levels, but if the costs remain high, the support for further investment should be withdrawn.

The support for renewable energy should be tailored to the pattern of its costs, and this means that a feed-in tariff will usually offer more effective support than a system of tradable green certificates. The feed-in tariff reduces the risk faced by the generator, cutting its cost of capital, and hence the cost to consumers. The feed-in tariff also ensures that the diversity benefit of renewable energy is passed on to customers, since it forms a fixed part of their bills, unaffected by fossil fuel prices. With tradable green certificates, generators face the risk of volatile certificate prices, and both generators and consumers are exposed to the market price for conventional energy. This double exposure to risk is the opposite to the metaphorical free lunch. One argument used in the UK to oppose a change in support policy is that the resulting uncertainty and delay to investments would make it impossible for the country to meet its share of the EU's target by 2020. If that target is, in fact, too ambitious, failing to meet it might be a good thing. Renewables clearly have a major role to play in our future energy system, but we need policies that support them in a cost-effective manner. Rushing to meet an artificial target, with a support mechanism that negates the diversity benefits of renewable energy, will not be a cost-effective policy.

15

The National Inventory Approach for International Forest-carbon Sequestration Management

Krister P. Andersson, Andrew J. Plantinga,** and Kenneth R. Richards****

I. INTRODUCTION

Forest-carbon management will be an important element of any international agreement on climate change (Plantinga and Richards, 2008). Forest-carbon flows comprise a significant part of overall global greenhouse-gas emissions. While global forests as a whole may be a net sink (Nabuurs and Masera, 2007), global emissions from deforestation contribute between 20 and 25 per cent of all greenhouse-gas emissions (Sedjo and Sohngen, 2007; Skutsch *et al.*, 2007). The size of the total global carbon pool in forest vegetation has been estimated at 359 gigatonnes of carbon (GtC), compared to annual global carbon emissions from industrial sources of approximately 6.3 GtC (IPCC, 2000*b*). The potential impact on the global carbon cycle of both natural and anthropogenic changes in forests is enormous.

An international forest-carbon management agreement can help sequester significant amounts of atmospheric carbon dioxide. To be effective, an agreement must induce countries to participate, provide landowners and governments with incentives to protect and expand stocks of carbon, and impose relatively low transaction costs while encouraging decision-makers to seek low-cost opportunities for sequestration.

The Kyoto Protocol (KP) has proven ineffective in this regard (Plantinga and Richards, 2008). Kyoto's Clean Development Mechanism (CDM) mechanism uses a project-by-project approach that excludes potentially beneficial projects, including those that could reduce deforestation (Santilli *et al.*, 2005). The total carbon effects of these *individual* forestry projects are difficult to measure, creating high transaction costs that have prevented widespread use of the CDM. In addition, the

* University of Colorado at Boulder.

** Agricultural and Resource Economics, Oregon State University.

*** School of Public and Environmental Affairs, Indiana University.

current approach under the KP may actually accelerate deforestation by shifting timber harvesting from Annex I to non-Annex I countries (Silva-Chavez, 2005).[1] This inter-country leakage cannot be addressed by a system that does not include global accounting of changes in forest use.

The impending expiration of the KP in 2012 invites a re-examination of how the global community can address forest-carbon management in the context of a climate-change agreement. There has also been a growing interest in identifying a mechanism for including avoided tropical deforestation under the KP or its successor (Gullison *et al.*, 2007; Myers 2007; Nepstad *et al.*, 2007; Skutsch *et al.*, 2007). At the ninth Conference of Parties meeting (COP9), a proposal for 'compensated reduction' (CR) in deforestation was advanced by a group of Brazilian non-governmental organizations (NGOs) (Santilli *et al.*, 2005) and endorsed by Papua New Guinea and Costa Rica (UN FCCC, 2005*c*).[2] Subsequently, participants at the COP11 meeting initiated a two-year study on reduced emissions from deforestation and degradation (REDD) to address the expansion of the KP to include this major source of emissions (UN FCCC, 2005*c*). While the CR and REDD proposals contain some attractive features, they also have a number of shortcomings that are redressed under the national inventory (NI) system first described by Andersson and Richards (2001).

The purpose of this chapter is to present the NI approach and provide a preliminary discussion of the major challenges that individual countries would face under an NI regime. While we recognize that the current political context is important for any forestry proposal, we do not want it to constrain the introduction and discussion of new ideas. Above all, we do not assume that the NI approach must be adopted within the existing framework of the KP.

In the next section we describe the NI approach and how it differs from prevailing approaches. Section III briefly reviews examples of national data on forests and forest carbon for ten different countries. In section IV we discuss the implications of country-specific circumstances and consider how those might affect both the direction of the negotiations that are at the base of the NI approach and the design of the programme itself. Given the importance of negotiations to the NI approach, we consider in detail how one important country—Brazil—might approach the negotiation process. We conclude that the national inventory approach provides a promising model for a future international agreement. It presents a substantial improvement over the current Kyoto regime and avoids many of the limitations of REDD. Its success hinges on (i) thoughtful use of the negotiated national base carbon stock as a mechanism for inducing participation; and (ii) improvements in the national forest-carbon inventory capabilities of many potential participants.

[1] Annex I countries under the 1992 Framework Convention on Climate Change are those industrialized countries that have agreed to reduce their greenhouse-gas emissions. Annex II countries are those Annex I countries that have also agreed to provide funds for non-Annex I developing countries to lower their greenhouse-gas emissions.

[2] Refinements and critiques of the CR approach are found in Schlamadinger *et al.* (2005), Myers (2007), Sedjo and Sohngen (2007) and Skutsch *et al.* (2007).

II. DESCRIPTION OF THE NATIONAL INVENTORY APPROACH

The NI approach is based on the concept of 'full carbon accounting' applied to measurable stocks. The distinguishing feature of this approach is that it calculates net changes in a nation's forest-carbon stocks and then awards emissions-reduction credits based on those changes. The approach requires periodic assessments of a nation's carbon stock to calculate net changes in carbon sequestration. The initial 'base carbon stock' or reference point may be negotiated to encourage nations to participate in the NI approach. Thereafter, the focus is on the change in a nation's *entire* forest-carbon stock rather than the change associated with particular carbon-sequestration projects or particular activities. In contrast to the approach used for Annex I countries under the KP, the NI approach does not differentiate between human-induced changes to carbon stocks and those that would have occurred naturally. The only issue that matters in calculating emission credits is the amount of carbon that has actually been transferred from the atmosphere to the country's forests.

We make several assumptions about how the NI approach might be linked with an international carbon-trading system. First, we assume that a country can opt into the forest sector programme even if it has not agreed to a cap on its energy- and industry-related emissions. The advantage of decoupling energy from forestry is that it reduces the entry barriers to the programme and, thus, increases the likelihood of having a large number of countries joining. Second, we assume that once a country has enrolled in the international forest-carbon programme, it is fully responsible for changes in its forest-carbon stocks relative to its negotiated base case. A net gain of a tonne in the inventory would be rewarded with a tonne of additional emissions allowances, but a net loss of a tonne from the inventory would have to be made up through an equivalent reduction in the country's emissions allowance allocation or by a purchase of allowances. Third, we assume that any allowances created in the base carbon stock negotiation process will be balanced with corresponding global emissions reductions targets.

Andersson and Richards (2001) identify the key characteristics that differentiate the NI approach from other methods of rewarding LULUCF (land use, land-use change, and forestry) activities. The key features of the NI approach are: (i) the identity of the participating parties and lands; (ii) the activities that are rewarded; (iii) the use of negotiated base carbon stocks; and (iv) the nature of measurement.

(i) Participating Parties and Lands

One of the chief distinguishing features of the NI approach compared to Kyoto, CR, and REDD is its potential to include more nations and more activities that promote terrestrial carbon sequestration within each nation. The NI approach is not limited to the developing world, so it can encourage net terrestrial carbon sequestration on a global scale. Moreover, by establishing the nation as the unit of analysis, the NI approach encourages a wide range of land management activities that can contribute to terrestrial carbon sequestration.

Under the NI approach, all land with sufficient contiguous area and a specified minimum forest cover would be included in the country's inventory. Because governments are the responsible parties, this approach can mobilize a wide range of policy instruments that create incentives for carbon sequestration. Governments would pursue a suite of domestic policies to augment carbon stocks as well as to satisfy other national objectives. While the financing of domestic activities would be the ultimate responsibility of a national government, funds could originate with the sale of offset credits from a previous evaluation period, or from the sale of carbon bonds at the start of an evaluation period (Santilli *et al.*, 2005).

(ii) Rewarded Activities

Under the NI approach, all increments in a country's measurable inventory would be counted, both positive and negative. At the international level, measured outcomes are rewarded—not the activities that produced the outcomes. At the national level, however, the NI approach can be used to encourage any activity that increases terrestrial forest-carbon stocks. The wide range of activities that could be covered under the NI approach include tree planting on non-forest lands (afforestation), reforesting harvested forestland, use of extended rotations, modifying harvest practices to reduce soil disturbance, preventing deforestation, and managing fire more effectively to avoid catastrophic loss. In some tropical countries, carbon sequestration might be increased by removing policies that promote deforestation (Santilli and Moutinho, 2005; Silva-Chavez, 2005). With current technology some carbon-sequestration activities are too costly to measure on a comprehensive basis, including changes in carbon stored in agricultural soil-carbon and wood products. Even with these present limitations, the NI approach can account for the most important terrestrial carbon sources and sinks.[3]

(iii) Setting the National Base Carbon Stock

For the NI approach, each nation is assigned an initial national base carbon stock inventory that the country is responsible for protecting and expanding. This is analogous to a project baseline. If at the end of the first measurement period a country's stock is higher (lower) than the national base stock it is awarded (debited) offset credits, each one of which is equal in value to an emissions allowance. Note that the assigned base carbon stock is a matter of negotiation. It may be either higher or lower than the actual stock at the beginning of the first period. Thus the

[3] According to IPCC (2000*b*), deforestation releases approximately 1.8 GtC per year, compared to a potential uptake of 0.4 GtC per year from the management of cropland and grazing land.

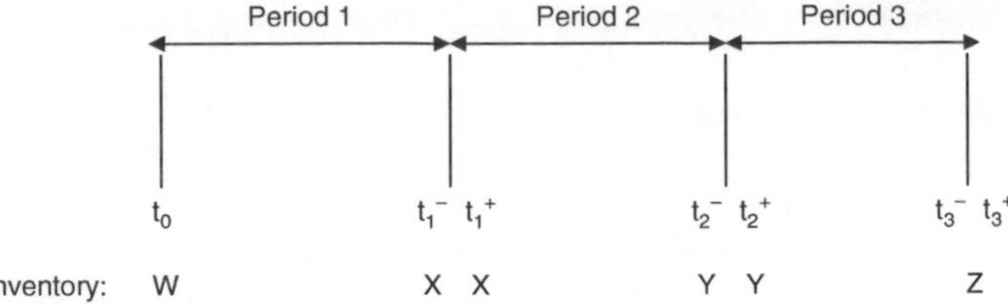

Figure 15.1. Measurement periods for NI approach

assignment of the base carbon stock can be used as an inducement to encourage non-Annex I countries to opt into the programme. Provided that the inducements for participation are matched with reductions elsewhere, such that the overall emissions-reduction goal is maintained, countries will still face the appropriate incentives on the margin to protect and expand national carbon sinks.

Consider the timeline in Figure 15.1. Suppose a country opts into the programme at the beginning of period 1, time t_0. As the result of negotiations, the country agrees to a national reference carbon stock of W. Future measurements of the country's actual stock will be evaluated relative to W to determine offset credits or debits. At time t_1^- the actual national carbon stock is estimated to be X. The country is awarded $(X - W)$ emissions offset credits. The country's reference carbon stock for period 2, at time t_1^+, is now X. At time t_2^- the country's measured forest-carbon stock is Y, so the country has earned an additional $(Y - X)$ offset credits in period 2 and $(Z - Y)$ in period 3.[4]

(iv) Measurement

One of the primary benefits of the NI approach is that it offers a conceptually simple measurement process. Previous approaches have struggled to determine whether a given forestry project was 'additional'—that is, whether the project would have occurred without the sequestration programme. In addition, previous approaches have hinged on whether forestry changes were anthropogenic or would have occurred naturally. National-level accounting addresses additionality and circumvents the problems raised by the requirement of differentiating human-induced and natural changes. These are not of central importance to the NI regime since this approach only considers the end result of net carbon change—regardless of its causes. While the NI approach is conceptually simpler, the measurement activities would still require significant effort and resources. The NI approach hinges on periodic and highly accurate measurement of changes in national carbon inventories. Highly accurate and comprehensive national carbon inventories can be developed only with significant expenditures on

[4] A country that has gained allowances for a rise in its stock during period 1 is responsible for at least maintaining the stock in period 2. Accepting the reward in period 1 hence carries a long-term obligation to maintain a stable forest-carbon stock.

field-based sampling. In contrast, low-cost inventories could be done through the processing of low-resolution satellite imagery using existing field data. However, this low-cost option is unlikely to have a level of accuracy that is suitable to the policy community (Andersson *et al.*, 2009).

A combination of remote sensing and 'ground-truthing' is likely to offer the degree of accuracy and cost-effectiveness needed for the NI approach to be effective. Ideally, countries should conduct an initial high-quality forest inventory. This inventory could then be correlated with data collected via remote sensing. Once these relationships are established, it becomes possible to infer land use and forest characteristics, and thus above-ground forest-carbon stocks, based on the remote-sensing data alone. Thereafter, remote-sensing techniques can be used to identify change in the spatial extent and characteristics of forests relative to the initial state.

Not all countries will have the financial resources or institutional capacity to conduct regular and credible national inventories. This is especially true for developing countries, with Brazil and India being important exceptions (Skutsch *et al.*, 2007). This suggests a role for an international organization, acting perhaps through the IPCC, in providing assistance to countries in developing their national inventories and documenting the results.[5]

For changes in national stocks of terrestrial carbon to be successfully linked to a permit-trading programme, frequent inventories will be needed for all participating countries. Accuracy is also important because of the linkage of carbon stocks to the permit-trading market. Given its sheer size, even small errors in the measurement of the global forest-carbon stock could exceed the total emissions reductions stipulated under a treaty.[6] Clearly, this uncertainty could undermine efforts to reduce net emissions if countries erroneously estimate that they have met their emissions-reduction targets based on changes in carbon stocks alone.

To help ensure that measured changes in stocks are due to actual changes, and not merely changes in methodologies, the same measurement protocol would be used within a country to estimate carbon stocks at the beginning and end of an evaluation period. However, over successive evaluation periods, new technologies could be employed to increase accuracy and reduce costs.

(v) Merits of NI Approach Relative to Alternatives

The primary advantage of the NI approach compared to others is that it has the potential to sequester more atmospheric carbon in the world's forests. The NI approach can achieve higher levels of sequestration by including more nations and

[5] Skutsch *et al.* (2007) suggest that the World Bank, among others, has indicated an interest in providing upfront financing for national inventories. These authors also suggest that Annex I parties, as the beneficiaries of deforestation offsets, might provide funding for forest inventories and domestic policies.

[6] When estimates based on existing carbon inventory techniques are subject to uncertainty analysis, it is not uncommon to see a 15 per cent or greater standard error in a country's forest-carbon pool estimates (Jonas *et al.*, 1999; Balzter and Shvidenko, 2000; Nilsson *et al.*, 2000).

forest management practices, by addressing leakage, and by offering a streamlined measurement and verification process.

Table 15.1 provides a summary of the important differences between the NI approach and other recent proposals.[7] The most noticeable difference is in the scope and the mechanism. Whereas all other proposals focus specifically on deforestation (and in some cases degradation), the NI approach recognizes that deforestation, afforestation, and other forest activities are all part of a mixture of practices that affect carbon stocks. As such, they should all be addressed under a single programme. To this end, the NI approach would replace all forestry provisions of the KP, including CDM, with a single approach based purely on outcomes.

There are also significant differences with respect to the reference levels. The NI approach concentrates on the national base carbon stock—a reference stock rather than a flow. It also recognizes both the equity implications and the fundamentally political nature of the choice of reference level. Hence issues such as identifying the 'growth cap' for low-emissions countries and inclusion or exclusion of credit for early action are rolled into the individually negotiated base carbon stock.

These negotiations can be used to address fairness and equity issues as well as to provide incentives for countries—in particular, countries with historically declining stocks—to participate in the agreement. Negotiations over reference carbon stocks can take into account existing wealth disparities that may be due, in part, to differences among countries in the historical exploitation of primary forests. As such, the negotiation process encourages participation by developing countries. It is better to have Brazil, Indonesia, and India in the capped group of countries, even if their base stocks are generously defined to allow for normal land-use changes, rather than having them left out entirely. The negotiated baseline of the NI approach offers an incentive for developing nations to participate that is missing from the REDD and CR proposals.

Moreover, once these nations have agreed to participate in the programme, the NI approach provides national governments with an incentive to improve forest management and a funding stream to implement forest policy. This gives developing nations an opportunity to meet internal environmental goals as well as carbon sequestration goals. Unlike the REDD and CR proposals, the NI approach rewards actual carbon uptake regardless of the causes of such outcomes. The straightforward outcome orientation provides strong incentives for countries to adopt comprehensive forest management policies. In addition, the NI approach places both responsibility and funding in the hands of national governments, who are best equipped to implement nationwide forest policies.

[7] The summary of the CR approach is based on Santilli *et al.* 2005. 'Papua New Guinea *et al.*' refers to the proposal submitted by a group of developing countries at the 11th Meeting of the Parties to the UN Convention on Climate Change (COP11) in 2005. The Joint Research Center proposal is described in Achard *et al.* (2006). 'Brazil' refers to the proposal submitted by Brazil at a workshop of interested parties in Rome in August 2006.

Table 15.1. Main features of the different proposals for voluntary approaches to reduced deforestation and degradation

	CDM	CR	Papua New Guinea *et al.*	Joint Research Center (JRC)	Brazil	NI
Scope	'Additional' reforestation and afforestation activities	Deforestation and implicitly degradation	Deforestation	Deforestation and degradation	Deforestation	All changes in forest-carbon stock
Mechanism under Kyoto or a separate protocol	KP	KP	Open	Not considered	Separate protocol	Separate protocol replacing KP
Reference level	Historical or reference case, as required by methodologies approved by CDM Executive Board	Historical, 'over some agreed period' (e.g. 1980s, 1990s, 1995–2005)	Historical	(Tropical) global conversion rate and historical national conversion rate	Historical	Negotiated in base carbon stock
'Growth cap' for historically low-emitting countries	No	Yes	Not considered	Yes	Not considered	Negotiated in base carbon stock
Liability	Temporary crediting, operational entities, national authorities	Banking and borrowing, insurance	Banking and borrowing	Temporary crediting	Banking and borrowing	Potential for banking
Financing	Credits sold to governments or private investors	Credits sold to governments or private investors	REDD as part of CDM is one option	Not considered	Voluntary fund by Annex II parties	Credits sold to governments or private investors
Price formation	Open	Nearly unrestricted access to allowance market	Open	Not considered	Contracted fixed price per tCO_2e[a]	Integration with allowance market
Early action	Not considered	Not considered	Yes	Not considered	Not considered	Negotiated in base carbon stock
Monitoring	As required by methodologies approved by CDM Executive Board	Remote sensing	Remote sensing	Remote sensing	Not considered	Remote sensing and on-ground measurement

Note: [a] tCO_2e is tonne of carbon-dioxide equivalent.

Sources: Modified from Andersson and Richards (2001) and Dutschke and Wolf (2007).

The NI system will also eliminate the risk that the carbon benefits of one project will be offset by deforestation elsewhere in the nation. Because a country's entire carbon stock is measured under NI, there is explicit accounting for this intra-country leakage. The problem of inter-country leakage to non-participating countries persists; however, this is not a problem particular to NI. Whenever there is less than full participation in an international treaty, there is the potential for unregulated actions by non-participating countries to counteract the treaty's objectives. Unlike other approaches, the NI approach can minimize this problem by encouraging greater participation and by measuring changes in forest use on a global scale.

Finally, the NI approach offers simplified implementation and verification, reducing costs per tonne of carbon sequestered when compared to the CDM. Implementation costs are minimized under NI by treating all forest-carbon sequestration activities under one seamless programme to the extent possible. The NI approach encourages terrestrial sequestration by use of familiar activities that are already integral to land-use management.

In addition, rather than potentially thousands of project-level measurements, fewer than 200 national inventories would need to be verified. This increases the prospects for the application of open and consistent methodologies. A smaller number of parties should also reduce transactions costs, though Skutsch *et al.* (2007) note that income generated nationally must still be distributed to domestic actors. Nepstad *et al.* (2007) suggest the use of three separate funds to channel offset payments to public and private entities in the Brazilian Amazon.

While the NI approach has many advantages over the project-by-project approach, it also has several disadvantages. Foremost among these is that the scope of carbon-sequestration activities that can be considered may be limited by the feasibility of measuring changes, particularly in the initial stages. Note, however, that adoption of the NI approach does not preclude the use of other mechanisms to treat the remaining carbon stocks.

In addition, placing responsibility with national governments is a relative disadvantage to the extent that a country lacks strong governmental institutions, government agencies are corrupt or poorly run, or the domestic policy-making process is captured by special interest groups. As well, CDM-type projects, whereby investors in one country fund carbon-sequestration projects in another, are unlikely to occur because credits are given on a national, rather than a project, basis.

Finally, while NI mitigates the problems with additionality and leakage with respect to carbon accounting for the international treaty mechanism, these problems resurface when countries pursue domestic policies. For example, if a national government provides subsidies for afforestation, it will be difficult to ensure that payments are given only for additional carbon sequestration. Likewise, there may be intra-country leakage associated with a domestic afforestation programme. Problems of this nature arise with many types of domestic policies. Although problems with additionality and leakage may raise the costs borne by national

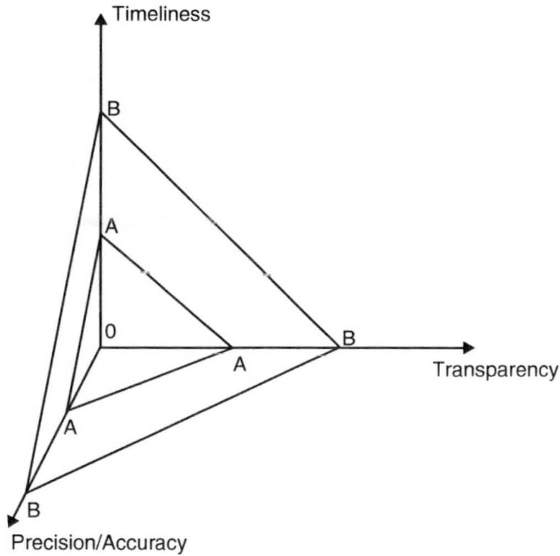

Figure 15.2. Isocost planes for timeliness, precision/accuracy, and transparency in national carbon inventory design

Source: Andersson *et al.* (2009).

governments, the NI approach helps to ensure that they do not undermine international efforts to combat climate change.

(vi) Information Requirements

To support implementation of the NI approach, the design of national forest-carbon stock estimation approaches will involve making explicit trade-offs between costs and three particular factors—timeliness, accuracy, and transparency. In the abstract, if we think of these three characteristics as being measured along three different dimensions, then it is possible to describe any national inventory programme as falling somewhere in 'inventory space' (this, of course, assumes we are holding constant other important factors, such as the number of participating actors in the programme). This inventory space is illustrated by Figure 15.2, which expresses the coordinates of this space as measures of timeliness, precision/accuracy, and transparency. Moreover, each point in this 'inventory space' will have a cost associated with it, which we might measure in dollars per year. Collecting all of the points in the space that have a given cost, say *A* dollars per year, will provide a hyperplane that economists call an 'isocost' curve. In Figure 15.2, the isocost hyperplane *A* is a collection of all combinations of programmes (each described in terms of timeliness, precision/accuracy, and transparency) that have a cost of *A* dollars per year. The hyperplane is depicted as flat, although the result could easily be a paraboloid.

This means that for any given cost, there is a host of inventory designs, each with a different level of timeliness, precision/accuracy, and transparency. Designing a programme for a given cost will involve making trade-offs among the three characteristics. For example, achieving increased precision and accuracy of inventory estimates might require managers to assign more resources to increase the sample size of field plots. Ensuring more transparency in the preparation and reporting of results also carries costs—more public scrutiny will require modifying working routines for data collection, analysis, processing, and communication of data, methods, and results (e.g. web-based database and library), as well as broader participation of non-governmental actors in all stages of the inventory. Finally, improving the timeliness of the reported results of the inventory will also require more resources to speed up the work during the data collection and processing stages.

Given these trade-offs, managers need to consider carefully which mix of these inventory attributes are the most important for achieving principal goals and will need to prioritize their resource allocation accordingly. If a fixed amount of resources is available for the inventories, the benefits associated with an investment to improve the accuracy and precision of estimates will come at the expense of transparency or timeliness of estimates, or both. It also means that to achieve simultaneous improvements on all three dimensions will require moving to a new, higher isocost curve, depicted in Figure 15.2 as isocost plane *B*.

III. EXAMPLES OF NATIONAL INVENTORIES

The Food and Agriculture Organization of the United Nations (FAO) undertakes a regular assessment of global forest resources, drawing on the best national inventory information available. The Forest Resources Assessment (FRA) report, most recently updated in 2006 (with 2005 data), is particularly useful for the present discussion. Although the report does not present the errors associated with the parameter estimates, it does provide insight into the general levels and variation of forest-carbon stocks for most of the world's countries, thus suggesting how negotiations regarding base carbon stocks might develop. The FRA report also illustrates the current limitations on assessing national forest-carbon inventories.

In this section we consider the data that are available from the FAO report. In the next section we consider how these data and other factors might influence the direction in international negotiations over national base carbon stocks.

(i) Sample Countries

To explore how the base carbon stock negotiations might unfold for individual countries, we consider several examples. These countries have been chosen to illustrate a cross-section of developing and industrialized countries of different

Table 15.2. Total, forested, and other wooded land areas, by country, 2005

	Land area 1,000 ha	Land area				
		Forest		Other wooded land 1,000 ha	Other land	
		1,000 ha	% of land area		Total 1,000 ha	With tree cover 1,000 ha
Australia	768,230	163,678	21.3	421,590	182,962	—
Bolivia	108,438	58,740	54.2	2,473	47,225	—
Brazil	845,942	477,698	57.2	—	357,858	—
Finland	30,459	22,500	73.9	802	7,145	177
India	297,319	67,701	22.8	4,110	225,508	815
Japan	36,450	24,868	68.2	—	11,582	—
Malaysia	32,855	20,890	63.6	—	11,965	—
Philippines	29,817	7,162	24.0	3,611	19,044	—
Uganda	19,710	3,627	18.4	1,150	14,933	—
United States	915,896	303,089	33.1	—	612,807	32,899

Source: FAO (2006).

sizes and population densities representing all five continents. Table 15.2 provides a summary of the amount of forested area in ten countries. Notice that while Australia, Brazil, and the United States have similar magnitudes of total land area, there is a substantial difference among them with respect to the amount of forest area in each—far more in both Brazil and the United States than in Australia. And while Finland, Japan, Malaysia, and the Philippines all have similar land areas, the first three have much more forest area than the last.

Notice also that while some countries, such as the United States and Malaysia, have no data available for the type referred to as 'other wooded land', the majority of Australian land and a significant amount of Philippines land is in that category. This suggests that any inventory methods developed under the NI approach will need to be able to account for all woodland types to induce participation of some countries.

Table 15.3 provides a summary of the changes in forest area and other wooded land from 1990 and 2005. Notice that Finland, India, and the United States all experienced growth in forested area over that period of time, although the rate of growth for all three has slowed. Japan has experienced virtually no change in its forest area. The other countries have all undergone reductions in forest area, with the Philippines and Uganda witnessing losses in the range of 2 per cent per year.

It is also interesting to note that while the area of other wooded land has remained constant in Australia and Bolivia, it has risen substantially in the Philippines, while dropping in Finland, India, and Uganda. If a programme treats the carbon stocks on forested land differently from those on other wooded land, or cannot even measure the carbon on the latter, it could work to the disadvantage of countries with similar characteristics as the last three countries.

Table 15.3. Change in forested area, by country, 1990–2005

	Forest							Other wooded land		
	Area			Annual change rate				Area		
	1990 1,000 ha	2000 1,000 ha	2005 1,000 ha	1990–2000 1,000 ha/year	1990–2000 %	2000–5 1,000 ha/year	2000–5 %	1990 1,000 ha	2000 1,000 ha	2005 1,000 ha
Australia	167,904	164,645	163,678	−326	−0.2	−193	−0.1	—	421,590	421,590
Bolivia	62,795	60,091	58,740	−270	−0.4	−270	−0.5	2,473	2,473	2,473
Brazil	520,027	493,213	477,698	−2,681	−0.5	−3,103	−0.6	—	—	—
Finland	22,194	22,475	22,500	28	0.1	5	n.s.	923	830	802
India	63,939	67,554	67,701	362	0.6	29	n.s.	5,894	4,732	4,110
Japan	24,950	24,876	24,868	−7	n.s.	−2	n.s.	—	—	—
Malaysia	22,376	21,591	20,890	−78	−0.4	−140	−0.7	—	—	—
Philippines	10,574	7,949	7,162	−262	−2.8	−157	−2.1	2,230	3,292	3,611
Uganda	4,924	4,059	3,627	−86	−1.9	−86	−2.2	1,404	1,235	1,150
United States	298,648	302,294	303,089	365	0.1	159	0.1	—	—	—

Note: n.s. is not significant.

Source: FAO (2006).

Table 15.4 provides carbon figures for forest and other wooded land, by carbon component. Carbon in both land types can be placed in one of five categories: above-ground biomass, below-ground biomass, deadwood, litter, and soils.

Perhaps the most striking element of Table 15.4 is the fact that Brazil's forest-carbon stock vastly exceeds that of all other countries. But there are other factors that may be more important for the design of an international forest-carbon programme. First, most of the countries do not have data for their soil-carbon stocks and carbon in litter. Second, for the three countries that do have soil-carbon data, the relative importance of that component varies significantly. In Brazil, soil carbon is approximately 48 per cent of the total forest biomass, whereas the figures for India and the United States are 72 and 37 per cent, respectively. Finally, only two of the countries have any figures for carbon stocks on the other wooded lands, and Australia, for which the category makes up over half of its total land area, has no data. In Uganda, the carbon on other wooded land is about 6 per cent of the total carbon stock on forested land.

Table 15.5, which summarizes the sources of data that the FAO has used to evaluate forest areas, stock, and biomass, provides insight into some of the challenges that might be presented by the data requirements of a national inventory approach. First, while the report was issued in 2006, the most recent remote-sensing data available were for 2004 for Brazil, and 2000–2 for the other countries. The field survey and mapping data dated from 1999 to 2003. Of the ten countries examined, for only three were both field-survey and remote-sensing data available. In fact, according to the report, only about 15 per cent of the world's developing countries actually carry out regular field-based forest inventories (FAO, 2006). In some cases the time series were based on data for only one point in time. Perhaps most importantly, there is no uniformity among the country estimates with respect to the methods or quality of data used to develop the national estimates of forest resources.

(ii) Data Challenges

The FAO report is not the only source of national forestry and carbon inventory data. For example, the United States and Finland have very sophisticated inventory programmes from which an international body might borrow both data and methods. But the FAO report does reflect the most comprehensive global effort to aggregate forest data. As such it provides insight into some of the challenges that might face a NI approach.

The brief look at the data above shows that there are significant differences among the countries with respect to their forest areas, carbon stocks, and the rates of change of each. There are also significant differences with respect to the availability and quality of data. While the FAO was able to develop estimates of the changes in forest area for all countries, the estimates for Bolivia and Uganda were based on a single point in time. Moreover, in several countries there was very little data to support estimates of the areas of non-forest wooded lands.

Table 15.4. National forest and other wooded land carbon stock, by component, 2005

	Forest					Other wooded land				
	Carbon in above-ground biomass M t	Carbon in below-ground biomass M t	Carbon in dead wood M t	Carbon in litter M t	Soil carbon M t	Carbon in above-ground biomass M t	Carbon in below-ground biomass M t	Carbon in dead wood M t	Carbon in litter M t	Soil carbon M t
Australia	5,824	2,515	2,209	—	—	—	—	—	—	—
Bolivia	3,926	1,370	581	—	—	—	—	—	—	—
Brazil	38,480	10,855	3,056	1,958	50,289	—	—	—	—	—
Finland	675	140	15	—	—	2	n.s.	n.s.	—	—
India	1,852	491	258	222	7,181	—	—	—	—	—
Japan	1,526	366	—	—	—	—	—	—	—	—
Malaysia	2,831	679	526	—	—	—	—	—	—	—
Philippines	783	188	107	15	—	—	—	—	—	—
Uganda	109	29	19	—	—	6	3	1	—	—
United States	15,826	3,138	2,675	4,657	15,732	—	—	—	—	—

Source: FAO (2006).

Table 15.5. Data sources and estimation methods, by country

	Most recent data on forest area			Forest area time series	Forest area projection	Growing stock time series	Biomass estimation
	Field survey/ mapping	Remote sensing	Expert estimate				
Australia	2002	2002	2005	MLT	MOD	NDA	NDA
Bolivia		2000		SIN	DEF	SIN	GPG
Brazil		2004		MLT	DEF	MLT	NAT
Finland	1999			MLT	MOD	MLT	NAT
India	2001	2001		MLT	REG	MLT	GNE
Japan	2002	2002		MLT	LEM	MLT	G&N
Malaysia	1997		2005	MLT	MOD	MLT	G&B
Philippines	2003			MLT	LEM	MLT	G&E
Uganda		2001		MLT	LEM	SIN	EXP
United States	2002			MLT	LEM	MLT	NAT

Notes:
Time series data:
SIN: Reported figures based on data for one point in time;
MLT: Reported figures based on data for two or more points in time.

Forest area estimation/forecasting:
DEF: Separate studies on deforestation or forest area changes used for estimation and forecasting; LEM: Linear interpolation or extrapolation; MOD: Model-based method of estimation between two or more points by making assumptions to modify linear trends; (use of plantation area, regeneration area, land-use matrix, or assuming no change, etc.).

Biomass and carbon estimation:
NAT: National factors developed by research; GPG: Factors from Good Practice Guidance (2003) of IPCC; EXP: Expert estimates; BWN: Expansion factors from FAO; G&B: Combination of GPG and BWN; G&E: Combination of GPG and EXP; G&N: Combination of GPG and NAT; GNE: Combination of GPG, NAT, and EXP; NDA: No data available.

Source: FAO (2006).

Calculating national carbon stocks will be more challenging still. The areas of forest and other woodlands are only one type of input to the calculation of the national carbon inventories. The FAO report did not supply time-series estimates for carbon stocks in forests, perhaps reflecting the difficulty in developing a historic record of carbon levels. And, while estimates for non-forest woodland areas are limited, the estimates for carbon are even more so. Finally, even within the forest-carbon estimates, the FAO was unable to provide estimates of soil carbon, a very sizable component of the inventory, for most countries.

There clearly are challenges for establishing historic records of national inventories of forest and woodland areas, forest carbon, and land-use change. But note that these challenges are not unique to the NI approach. Other REDD activities also depend upon a historic record, using models of past deforestation rates to imply losses in carbon.

The difference is that while the historic record is essential to the REDD process, with the NI approach the historic record is only used to imply potential future performance. Once a national inventory base is negotiated, the historic record is set aside. Thus, the NI approach places emphasis on improving the capacity to estimate current carbon inventories and changes in inventories rather than on the historic record.

IV. IMPLICATIONS FOR INTERNATIONAL NEGOTIATIONS

Assume that the inventories from the previous section are the best available—what does it suggest for possible negotiation issues? It is likely that the negotiations regarding each nation's carbon inventory base will involve not only the estimates of current inventories and recent changes in inventories, but a number of other factors as well, including expectations for future inventories, capacity and costs to influence future trends, institutional capability to undertake national inventories, and other related issues of national importance, such as poverty and environmental integrity.

(i) Assessment of Other Country Factors

While the FAO report does not provide time-series data for national carbon inventories, the inventories of forest and other wooded land suggest that only India, Finland, and the United States have increased their overall forest holdings since 1990. The losses in Brazil, however, dwarf all other changes among the countries combined.

Another factor that may affect the negotiations for setting national baselines is the capacity of countries to expand their forest holdings, particularly through the development of new plantations. In the past 15 years, the United States has increased its forest plantation area substantially, in both relative (70 per cent) and absolute (7,000,000 hectares) terms (Table 15.6). Australia, Brazil, India, and Uganda have also increased plantation areas significantly. In contrast, Malaysia and the Philippines have lost substantial areas. As with many of the factors, this observation raises the question of how to interpret the implications of recent plantation expansion. Does it indicate that a country has used up all opportunities, or that more opportunities exist?

The countries also differ with respect to the changes in the primary forests, defined as forests of native species with no clearly visible human activity and no significant ecological disturbance (Table 15.7). Brazil, for which primary forest is a large percentage of its total forest area, is experiencing a rapid decline in primary forest areas, while Japan's are expanding. The change in primary forest may indicate the extent to which a national government can control the actions of its citizens.

A country's ability to influence the direction of its national forest-carbon inventory may also be tied to the development of its forest-products industry. Large current removals may indicate a high demand for raw products, running counter

Table 15.6. Change in extent of forest plantations, 1990–2005

	Area of forest plantations			% of total forest area			Annual change rate	
	1990 1,000 ha	2000 1,000 ha	2005 1,000 ha	1990 %	2000 %	2005 %	1990–2000 ha/year	2000–5 ha/year
Australia	1,023	1,485	1,766	0.6	0.9	1.1	46,200	56,200
Bolivia	20	20	20	n.s.	n.s.	n.s.	0	0
Brazil	5,070	5,279	5,384	1.0	1.1	1.1	20,900	21,000
Finland	0	0	0	0	0	0	0	0
India	1,954	2,805	3,226	3.1	4.2	4.8	85,100	84,200
Japan	10,287	10,331	10,321	41.2	41.5	41.5	4,400	−2,000
Malaysia	1,956	1,659	1,573	8.7	7.7	7.5	−29,700	−17,200
Philippines	1,780	852	620	16.8	10.7	8.7	−92,800	−46,400
Uganda	33	35	36	0.7	0.9	1.0	200	200
United States	10,305	16,274	17,061	3.5	5.4	5.6	596,900	157,400

Source: FAO (2006).

to a policy to expand forest holdings. At the same time, countries that make long-term investments in growing stock will also experience a rise in carbon stock.

Finland, Japan, Malaysia, and the United States all have relatively high financial yields per hectare (Table 15.8), suggesting that investment in expansion of forest-lands could be justified on a combination of both forest-product and carbon-stock benefits. At the same time, with the exception of Australia and Uganda, employment in the forest sector is declining (Table 15.9).

Investment in expanding forest area may preserve some of the jobs lost in those countries with a declining forest sector.

Table 15.7. Change in extent of primary forests, 1990–2005

	Area of primary forest			% of total forest area			Annual change rate	
	1990 1,000 ha	2000 1,000 ha	2005 1,000 ha	1990 %	2000 %	2005 %	1990–2000 ha/year	2000–5 ha/year
Australia	—	5, 233	5, 233	—	3.2	3.2	—	0
Bolivia	31,388	30,036	29,360	50.0	50.0	50.0	−135,200	−135,200
Brazil	460,513	433,220	415,890	88.6	87.8	87.1	−2,729,300	−3,466,000
Finland	1,491	1,418	1,419	6.7	6.3	6.3	−7,300	200
India	—	—	—	—	—	—	—	—
Japan	3,764	4,054	4,591	15.1	16.3	18.5	29,000	107,400
Malaysia	3,820	3,820	3,820	17.1	17.7	18.3	0	0
Philippines	829	829	829	7.8	10.4	11.6	0	0
Uganda	—	—	—	—	—	—	—	—
United States	105,268	105,258	104,182	35.2	34.8	34.4	−1,000	−215,200

Source: FAO (2006).

Table 15.8. Value of wood and non-wood forest product (NWFP) removals, 2005

	Industrial roundwood US$1,000	Wood fuel US$1,000	NWFP US$ 1,000	Total	
				US$1,000	US$/ha
Australia	1,178,600	—	—	1,178,600	7
Bolivia	49,220	321	—	49,541	1
Brazil	2,897,019	942,020	193,131	4,032,170	8
Finland	2,614,351	151,450	154,656	2,920,457	130
India	208,644	8,023	179,132	395,799	6
Japan	2,864,500	—	34,506	2,899,006	117
Malaysia	2,081,000	69,000	—	2,150,000	103
Philippines	60,272	722	—	60,994	9
Uganda	—	70	—	70	n.s.
United States	18,682,708	309,226	34,200	19,026,134	63

Source: FAO (2006).

There will also be differences among countries with respect to the cost of labour and the availability of land. All things being equal, countries with lower labour costs and population density will likely find it easier to expand their forest area and carbon stock. For this reason India, Japan, the Philippines, Uganda, and, to a lesser extent, Malaysia may all find that population pressures limit their opportunities for expanding forest-carbon stock significantly (Table 15.10).

Similarly, Japan, the United States, Finland, and Australia may find the labour for establishing new forest plantations for carbon relatively expensive. Bolivia and Brazil, however, seem to be less constrained by population pressures and labour costs.

Table 15.9. Employment in forestry, 1990 and 2000 (in '000s of person-years)

	1990	2000			
	Total	Total	Production	Provision of services	Unspecified
Australia	15	17	13	4	—
Bolivia	—	23	14	—	9
Brazil	—	—	—	—	—
Finland	39	24	—	—	24
India	5,465	4,855	1,976	2,879	—
Japan	108	63	63	—	—
Malaysia	78	67	66	2	—
Philippines	—	—	—	—	—
Uganda	1	2	2	—	—
United States	311	281	221	50	10

Source: FAO (2006).

Table 15.10. Country demographics

	Land area (1,000 ha)	Population 2004				GDP 2004	
		Total (1,000)	Density (Pop./km^2)	Annual growth rate (%)	Rural (% of total)	*Per capita* (US$)	Annual growth rate (%)
Australia	768,230	20,120	2.6	1.2	7.7	22,074	3.0
Bolivia	108,438	8,986	8.3	1.9	36.1	1,036	3.6
Brazil	845,942	178,718	21.1	1.2	16.4	3,675	5.2
Finland	30,459	5,215	17.1	0.1	39.1	25,107	3.7
India	297,319	1,079,721	363.2	1.4	71.5	538	6.9
Japan	36,450	127,764	350.5	0.2	34.4	39,195	2.7
Malaysia	32,855	25,209	76.7	1.7	35.6	4,221	7.1
Philippines	29,817	82,987	278.3	1.8	38.2	1,079	6.2
Uganda	19,710	25,920	131.5	2.5	87.7	285	5.7
United States	915,896	293,507	32.1	0.9	19.6	36, 790	4.4

Source: FAO (2006).

Another factor that may prove important is the relative level of private versus public ownership of forest and other wooded land. Given that the national government will ultimately be responsible to the international forest-carbon sequestration programme, it may be easier for countries in which the government owns more of the forest land. If that is the case then, for example, India, Malaysia and the Philippines may find it easier to adopt policies that expand their national forest-carbon inventories (Table 15.11). But this is not a simple relation. For example, in the United States, government entities own more than 40 per cent of forests, but the vast majority of carbon sequestration opportunities are on private lands.

Table 15.11. Forest and other woodland ownership, by country, 2000

	Forest				Other wooded land			
	Total 1,000 ha	Public %	Private %	Other %	Total 1,000 ha	Public %	Private %	Other %
Australia	164,645	72.0	27.1	0.9	421,590	—	—	—
Bolivia	60,091	—	—	—	2,473	—	—	—
Brazil	493,213	—	—	—	—	—	—	—
Finland	22,475	32.1	67.8	0.1	830	68.9	31.0	0.1
India	67,554	98.4	1.6	0	4,732	98.4	1.6	0
Japan	24,876	41.9	58.1	0	—	—	—	—
Malaysia	21,591	93.4	6.6	0	—	—	—	—
Philippines	7,949	89.5	10.5	—	3,292	—	—	—
Uganda	4,059	29.8	70.2	—	1,235	20.8	79.2	—
United States	302,294	42.4	57.6	—	—	—	—	—

Source: FAO (2006).

Table 15.12. Forest function

	Forest						
	Total area 1,000 ha	**Production %**	**Protection %**	**Conservation %**	**Social services %**	**Multiple purpose %**	**None or unknown %**
Australia	163,678	8.0	—	13.1	—	77.6	1.3
Bolivia	58,740	0	0	20.0	0	80.0	0
Brazil	477,698	5.5	17.8	8.1	23.8	44.8	—
Finland	22,500	91.2	0	7.2	0.2	1.5	0
India	67,701	21.2	14.8	21.7	—	42.4	—
Japan	24,868	0	0	0	0	100.0	0
Malaysia	20,890	56.6	18.2	5.4	—	19.8	—
Philippines	7,162	75.0	11.0	12.0	—	—	2.0
Uganda	3,627	14.9	—	14.8	—	—	70.2
United States	303,089	12.0	—	19.8	—	68.1	—

Source: FAO (2006).

The difference is that the public lands are not particularly suitable for expanded carbon stocks.

Finally, it might be easier to expand carbon stock in those countries in which a significant portion of the forest land is already managed for multiple purposes. If that is the case, then Japan, Bolivia, Australia, and the United States may find expansion of carbon stocks relatively easier than for other countries in our list (Table 15.12).

(ii) Applying Country Factors to the Negotiations

To illustrate how the negotiated reference carbon stock might work, consider how Brazil might approach the negotiation process. Its 2005 forest-carbon stock appears to be around 105,000 million metric tonnes (MMT) of carbon. It has a total land area of 846 million hectares, of which 478m hectares are in forests. Of the forest area, 87 per cent is primary forest; only about 1 per cent is currently plantation. Since 1990, Brazil has lost about 8.2 per cent of its forest area: 0.5–0.6 per cent per year and accelerating in both absolute and percentage terms.

The forestry sector yields about 4 billion dollars per year in products and service. Forestland has a relatively low-value yield on a per-hectare basis (US$8/ha), but since *per capita* income is relatively low as well, the cost of establishing new forest plantations may be low. The country not only has a relatively low population density (21.1 persons/km^2), but a small percentage of the population is rural (16.4 per cent). Thus, if the Brazilian national government acted in earnest, it might be able to alter substantially the direction of its carbon stock. The situation is complicated, though, by the fact that there appears to be considerable ambiguity about the ownership of forest land in Brazil. Moreover, there appears to be considerable uncertainty regarding the amount of employment in the Brazilian forest sector.

Given this assessment, it appears that there is much that the Brazilian national government could potentially do to alter land-use patterns to decrease the losses of forest and eventually increase the stock of forest carbon. As a starting point in the negotiation, the country might suggest that the international community allow the country 10 years to reverse current trends. Thus, the country might argue, Brazil's original base carbon stock would be around 100,000 MMT.

Now consider how this scenario might unfold in subsequent commitment periods. Suppose at the end of the first five-year period, Brazil's forest-carbon stock is at 102,000 MMT. At that point Brazil would have earned a credit of 2,000 MMT of carbon—the difference between its reference carbon stock and its observed carbon stock. Its new base carbon stock for the coming five-year commitment period would shift to 102,000 MMT. If at the end of the second commitment period, its carbon stock is 101,000 MMT, the country would owe 1,000 MMT.

To put these figures in perspective, 2005 global net emissions were of the order of 7,800 MMT per year. Clearly, in this hypothetical scenario, the 2,000 MMT of carbon allowances awarded at the end of the first period and the 1,000 MMT debited at the end of the second would represent substantial resources. If carbon-dioxide allowances are trading at US\$10 per tonne, these two transfers would have a value of US\$72 $\times$ 10^9 and US\$36 $\times$ 10^9, respectively. This could be a powerful incentive for the government of Brazil to take the steps needed to stop the decline in its forest area and carbon stocks. It also presents the potential for abuse. Suppose that Brazil sold the allowances earned at the end of the first period, then refused to pay for the 1,000 MMT of allowances owed at the end of the second. Without explicit penalties for non-compliance, the international community would have little recourse. This suggests that it may be wise to pay out the award of allowances on a gradual basis, have countries post surety bonds against potential liabilities, require participants to maintain positive account balances, or institute other mechanisms to protect against programmatic defection.

V. CONCLUSIONS

The national inventory approach to an international forest-carbon sequestration agreement provides a promising, seamless approach that brings under one comprehensive programme a full range of sequestration efforts, without differentiation among countries. It helps overcome problems associated with causation and limited historic data. Moreover, it provides mechanisms to promote initial buy-in from countries that have declining stocks, even as it provides appropriate incentives to those countries to stem the losses and expand national forest-carbon stocks.

Key to the success of the programme will be the development of the capacity to carry out timely, accurate, and transparent inventories of national forest-carbon stocks. Current FAO periodic assessments suggest that the capacity is not available in all countries. However, recent work in the field suggests that it may be possible to develop the capacity for adequate national inventories with sufficient investment in large-scale field studies and national-level institutions.

16

On the Regulation of Geoengineering

*David G. Victor**

I. INTRODUCTION

Nearly all of the political debate around climate policy has focused on the mitigation of emissions. Until recently, this bias has been logical and appropriate because true solutions to the problem of climate change require a focused effort at the root cause. However, a mitigation-focused policy strategy is not enough. Actual mitigation efforts are already falling far short of what many analysts think is needed to avoid dangerous changes in climate (see IPCC, 2007*c*; Stern, 2007). These failings arise from a political logic that is difficult to rectify quickly. Deep cuts may be costly and thus politically difficult to organize and sustain; they imply radical changes in energy systems that will be difficult for many countries to administer effectively even if they could mobilize the needed political support. Moreover, it has proved extremely difficult to design competent international institutions for coordinating and enforcing worldwide efforts to mitigate emissions (Victor, 2001; Barrett, 2003, 2007*b*).

Such sobering facts have encouraged analysts to concentrate on adaptation as a complementary element of a climate-change strategy (IPCC, 2007*c*). They have also kindled nascent and uneasy interest in 'geoengineering'—that is, planetary-scale, active interventions in the climate system to offset the build-up of greenhouse gases.

Most geoengineering envisions increasing the reflectivity ('albedo') of the planet by injecting particles into the stratosphere. Modifying the albedo offers, in theory, large potential leverage on the heat balance; reducing incoming sunlight by just a few per cent could crudely offset the higher temperature caused by the build-up of greenhouse gases. Putting particles in the stratosphere (about 10–50 km

*University of California at San Diego.

I thank David Keith and Dan Schrag for the invitation to talk about the politics of geoengineering at their meeting on 8–9 November 2007, for which this chapter is an exploration of the ideas, and to my colleagues in vol. 24 no. 2 of the *Oxford Review of Economic Policy*, along with an anonymous reviewer, for discussions and comments. Thanks to Jay Apt, Michael Aziz, Martin Bunzl, Ken Calderia, Josh Cohen, Dieter Helm, Cameron Hepburn, Robert Keohane, Michael Levi, Gregg Marland, Granger Morgan, Burt Richter, Larry Summers, John Steinbruner, and Mark Thurber for comments on a draft; to Scott Barrett, Tom Schelling, and Marty Weitzman for sharing papers, and to Tom for talking strategically about this issue long before anyone else took it seriously.

above the Earth's surface) is attractive, in theory, because the stratosphere is stable and thus particles injected at that location will remain in place for one to three years before needing replenishment. Sulphate particles have attracted most attention because volcanoes already naturally inject large quantities of emissions that yield sulphate when they erupt, offering natural analogues for envisioning and studying possible man-made geoengineering systems. In addition to these ideas, other imagined schemes include putting diffraction gratings in outer space (which can deflect a bit of incoming sunlight away from the planet) or floating machines on the ocean that could blow water vapour into the atmosphere, which increases the cover of reflective bright clouds. It is also possible to change the albedo of large land areas from dark to light, such as by converting forests into more reflective grasslands. Many other schemes can also be imagined.[1]

The option of geoengineering is ridden with danger. All the most promising geoengineering methods have likely side effects that are worrisome. The unknown harms from large-scale tinkering with the planet could be even more grave than the predictable effects. Merely talking about geoengineering, say some, will take pressure off politicians to make serious efforts to mitigate emissions—its mere existence as an imagined option may thus assure its use. And yet geoengineering is inexorably rising in political salience. Formerly a freak show in otherwise serious discussions of climate science and policy, geoengineering today is a bedfellow, albeit one of which we are wary. The option may be needed as a hedge against unexpectedly harsh changes in climate (Weitzman, 2007*c*).

Geoengineering must be taken seriously because it turns the politics of climate protection upside down. The politics of actually stopping global climate change by mitigating emissions are nasty, brutish and endless. With today's technologies, achieving a deep cut in emissions will require costly investment for uncertain benefits that accrue mainly in the distant future—attributes that tend not to be rewarding for politicians.[2] The politics of mitigating emissions are additionally difficult because deep cuts in emissions are possible only with the collective action of many nations with diverging preferences.[3] The countries that are most keen to

[1] Keith (2000) provides a detailed survey of options and also explores the economics, politics, and ethics, and NAS (1992) provides a comprehensive (if now quite dated) look at the economics of climate-protection options including geoengineering. Bodansky (1996) points to many possible legal constraints; Barrett (2007*a*) examines the seemingly inexpensive economics of geoengineering and outlines a possible path for pursuing the option. Recent conference reports offer a useful catalogue of the complaints (Ames/Carnegie, 2006; Ricke *et al.*, 2008; Victor *et al.*, 2008), and Fleming's (2007) beautiful history of geoengineering is laden with warnings.

[2] Some studies have suggested that emissions control could be relatively inexpensive and amount to perhaps 1 per cent of GDP or less (IPCC, 2007*d*; Stern, 2007). That might be true for an optimally implemented policy that gives firms plenty of time to innovate and apply new technologies. But the cost of real policy could be a lot higher because political systems do not seem prone to make the needed complementary investments in research and development (e.g. EPRI, 2007). Least-cost strategies also usually envision the extensive use of 'offsets', which can encourage inexpensive emission controls in developing countries, that are proving difficult to administer (e.g. Paltsev *et al.*, 2007*a*, EPA, 2008). As real costs inflate so will the political challenges in adopting real policies.

[3] At first, perhaps just a dozen countries are needed and cooperation could emerge tacitly, which is less daunting than getting all nations on the planet to agree. However, even the core group of important

control their emissions, such as the west European nations and Japan, are a shrinking part of the problem because their economies expand at a relatively sluggish pace and their populations are in numerical decline. By contrast, the countries most wary about emission controls, such as China and India, are getting richer and expanding demographically much more rapidly (IEA, 2007*a*). Some nations that matter, such as frigid Russia as well as other fossil-fuel exporters, may conclude that they stand to lose massively if the rest of the planet actually makes deep cuts in emissions.

Geoengineering, by contrast, offers prompt benefits with seemingly small costs—attributes that greatly simplify the problem of collective action (Schelling, 1996). Most geoengineering methods involve deployment of technologies—for example, rocket launchers or large artillery units that could loft particles into the stratosphere or beyond—that prospective geoengineers, themselves, already control. Once particles are dispersed in the stratosphere it would be difficult for anti-geoengineers to remove them. Unlike collective efforts to control emissions, which are plagued by the constant threat of defection, the incentives to sustain cooperation are much stronger once geoengineering has begun, because failure to keep a geoengineering mask in place will lead to exceptionally rapid (and dangerous) climate change. Some estimates suggest that once a geoengineering scheme is in place, failure to sustain it could lead to climate warming at a pace 20 times greater than the warming evident today (Matthews and Caldeira, 2007). Once geoengineering has begun, even those who are hostile to the idea will reluctantly find they must support continued action.

Geoengineering may not require any collective international effort to have an impact on climate. One large nation might justify and fund an effort on its own. A lone Greenfinger, self-appointed protector of the planet and working with a small fraction of the Gates bank account, could force a lot of geoengineering on his own. Bond films of the future might struggle with the dilemma of unilateral planetary engineering.

With so many temptations, what can be done to impose useful discipline on geoengineers? Until recently, this question was not practically relevant because there had been so little effort to devise geoengineering systems; most analysts who examined the options closely had concluded that it would be reckless to mess with the planet. Today that is changing, and the question demands an answer.

Based on the experience with other international environmental challenges, the standard answer is that a legally binding regulatory treaty is needed, along with a careful global assessment that gives all nations the opportunity to participate formally in evaluating geoengineering science.[4] Applied to geoengineering, that

countries—such as China, the United States, the EU, and Russia—assign radically different preferences for economic growth and environmental protection (Victor, 2006). Eventually, explicit obligations that cover all nations are probably needed, because an open world economy makes it unlikely that important countries will tolerate high costs for long if their trading partners pay a lot less.

[4] That approach—binding treaties coupled to scientific assessments—has been successful in many other areas of international environmental cooperation, notably the depleting ozone layer (e.g.

answer would suggest the need for a comprehensive assessment by the Intergovernmental Panel on Climate Change (IPCC) as well as negotiations toward a binding treaty to constrain geoengineers of the future.

Here I suggest answers that point in very different directions. In brief, my conclusions are fourfold. First, most treaties on geoengineering will be useless or harmful because, at present, experts and governments do not know enough about the scope and hazards of possible geoengineering activities to frame a meaningful treaty negotiation. Diverging interests and the lack of knowledge about how to frame negotiations that focus on the most relevant topics will make it impossible to gain meaningful agreement.

Second, a taboo against geoengineering—as many of geoengineering's detractors imply is needed—would be the most dangerous policy. A taboo is likely to be most constraining on the countries (and their subjects) who are likely to do the most responsible testing, assessment, and (if needed) deployment of geoengineering systems. A taboo would leave less responsible governments and individuals—those most prone to ignore or avoid inconvenient international norms—to control the technology's fate. A much better approach would be an active geoengineering research programme, possibly including trial deployments, that is highly transparent and engages a wide range of countries that might have (or seek) geoengineering capabilities. That approach would be designed to explore the safest and most effective options while also socializing a community of responsible geoengineers. (Similar approaches have been followed in other international scientific collaborations that have had potentially hazardous side effects, such as the European Organization for Nuclear Research (CERN) and the Human Genome Project.)

Third, nearly all the geophysical analysis, to date, has focused on simple geoengineering options, such as tuning the planetary albedo, that are unlikely to be deployed in practice. If society ever deploys geoengineering it is likely to be in a more complex form—for example, albedo modification along with active efforts to offset ecological side effects, ocean acidification, and other harms that the simple primary geoengineering system cannot rectify. The economics, politics, and ethics surrounding these complex geoengineering systems are radically different from the simple geoengineering methods that occupy most technical analysis to date.

Fourth, at this stage the nature of the underlying science and geoengineering is particularly ill-suited to the consensus-oriented IPCC process. Instead, multiple competing assessments by small groups linked to active research programmes—reviewed and published openly—would be more effective.

Benedick, 1998). In time, it might prove helpful in addressing global warming. The standard response of treaty-making is so ingrained in the international environmental community that it is hard to identify a single definitive source that outlines this strategy, but for a thoughtful argument about the centrality of treaty-making as a response to environmental (and other) problems see Chayes and Chayes (1995). On the role of integrated assessments in addressing international environmental problems see Mitchell *et al.* (2006).

II. THE STATE OF GEOENGINEERING SCIENCE: THREE IMPLICATIONS

There is a small but growing literature on geoengineering methods. Careful reviews are published elsewhere (Keith, 2000; Ames and Carnegie, 2006; Ricke *et al.*, 2008). Three observations from that technical literature help to frame the options for the design of regulatory systems.

First, the option of geoengineering must be taken seriously because the cost of geoengineering systems that could crudely offset the human-caused build-up of greenhouse gases appears to be shockingly small. Early estimates suggest that the discounted present cost of a geoengineering programme extended into perpetuity is of the order of US$100 billion, which compares favourably with the US$1 trillion order-of-magnitude costs for mitigation. However, it is especially difficult to assess the cost of geoengineering schemes because humans have never tried to deploy such systems on a planetary scale.[5] Analogues with natural events, such as volcanoes, make it possible to calculate the scale of effort that would be needed to offset crudely some of the effects of some climate warming. Moreover, it is already possible to test some geoengineering methods at very low cost and without undue risk of irreversible effects on the planet. In short, it is possible to imagine actual development and deployment of geoengineering systems with today's technology, and likely innovation will probably lower those costs.

Second, the technical literature is highly stylized for many reasons. One is that nearly all studies evaluate the impacts of single interventions, such as pulsing the stratosphere with aerosols. However, it seems unlikely that such 'silver bullet' geoengineering will be deployed because the research demonstrates that all silver bullets have severe side effects. For example, attempting to offset rising emissions of greenhouse gases by modifying the albedo is likely to yield several harmful side effects, some of which have been analysed directly and others which can be inferred from analysis of analogous events such as volcanic eruptions:

- acidification of the oceans, which is due to the still-high concentration of carbon dioxide (CO_2) in the atmosphere (Ames/Carnegie, 2006);
- massive ozone depletion if the albedo scheme includes injection of particles into the stratosphere (Crutzen, 2006);
- possible changes in rainfall, with attendant risks for drought (Liepert *et al.*, 2004; Oman *et al.*, 2006; Trenberth and Dai, 2007);
- alteration of ecosystems due to effects such as the impact of dimming on light-sensitive plants, the availability of water, and fertilization of some plants in a CO_2-rich atmosphere (e.g. Stanhill and Cohen, 2001; Govindasamy *et al.*, 2002; Naik *et al.*, 2003; Mohan *et al.*, 2006; D'Arrigo *et al.*, 2007);

[5] This assessment is based on the first costing exercise in NAS (1992) and critical reviews of Keith (2000) and Ames and Carnegie (2006) which do not raise concerns that would alter the order of magnitude. With innovation and effort, total discounted present cost for a perpetual programme could be an order of magnitude smaller.

- uneven offsetting of climate change, since albedo adjustments do not perfectly mimic the spatial changes in climate that are induced by greenhouse gases (Govindasamy and Caldeira, 2000; Oman *et al.*, 2005).

In addition to this known list of side effects it is likely that other ills will appear once analysts start looking for them more aggressively.

Some of the geoengineering literature ignores such possible side effects, and by implication dismisses them as unimportant (e.g. Teller *et al.*, 1997). Other analysts of geoengineering pursue the opposite and equally extreme logic, concluding that the cure of geoengineering might be worse than the disease.[6] Most likely, however, is that the impacts of global climate change will have reached such a nasty state by the time societies deploy large-scale geoengineering that some side effects will be tolerated. These societies will be willing to spend handsomely on geoengineering, and the systems they deploy will not be a silver bullet but rather many interventions deployed in tandem—one to focus on the central disease and others to fix the ancillary harms. The strategy may be somewhat like the treatment of AIDS, with a constantly shifting 'cocktail' of drugs.

As the number of interventions rises so will the cost and complexity. More complex systems will be harder to assess because they will involve so many different interactions. To date, none of the technical or economic assessments of geoengineering have examined this kind of complex multi-faceted geoengineering—what I'll call 'cocktail geoengineering'. Moreover, the exact mix of interventions will pose difficult trade-offs. For example, simple modification of the albedo will not offset the ocean acidification caused by the build-up of CO_2 in the atmosphere. Liming the whole ocean to offset the acid appears to be impractical, but it might be feasible to buffer special highly valued zones; indeed, technologies have been imagined that could be deployed for exactly that purpose (e.g. House *et al.*, 2007). Perhaps a network of acid-offsetting pipes should be installed to rebalance special ecosystems such as the Great Barrier Reef and a few other gems. Fake reefs may need construction, as is already done for other reasons today. Similarly, the possibilities that albedo modification schemes might have an adverse impact on rainfall could animate countries to invest more heavily in water management systems. These are the real trade-offs for geoengineering. But how many patches should be added, and at what cost? The hardest trade-offs will involve ecosystems because they are difficult to value and thrive on complex and unpredictable interactions. It will be difficult to gain political agreement on the triage of nature. Moreover, ecosystem interventions will create special ethical challenges because, in the extreme, they turn the whole planet into a zoo of managed ecosystems.

[6] Most of the critical literature adopts this approach, though often with the caveat that the option should be explored in case climate changes are particularly severe. See, for example, Schneider (1996) who concludes uneasily that geoengineering merits some investigation but only if that does not become an excuse for sharply curtailing society's addiction to carbon fuels.

In short, the claim that geoengineering is remarkably cheap is based on simple assessments of silver-bullet geoengineering. In practice, however, the geoengineering cocktails that are likely to be deployed will not be cheap.[7]

Third, because it is hard to predict the effects of geoengineering—especially in its more plausible cocktail mode—today's discussions around investment in geoengineering systems have a ring of falsehood. Many studies seem to conclude that society should invest in enough knowledge about geoengineering to put the option 'on the shelf' in case it is needed if a climate emergency appears. The shelf analogy is misplaced for two reasons. One is a matter of incentives. Other than with nuclear weapons, societies have not spent massively to put an option on the proverbial 'shelf' and not use it.[8] Some partial exceptions to that rule include stockpiling of anthrax treatments and strategic oil stocks, though the difficulties in getting most countries to invest adequately in these options and to develop viable plans for deployment are a warning for those who think that societies will invest adequately to put geoengineering on the shelf. The brightest young minds and the most entrepreneurial organizations rarely mobilize themselves to put complex technologies on the shelf—especially when rival activities such as inventing the next YouTube offer greater rewards. The way societies usually get something on the shelf, politically and organizationally, is to use it.

The other weakness with the 'shelf' analogy is more important for our purposes. Long ago, Tom Schelling pointed out that most of the 'known' effects

[7] It might be useful to think of supply and demand for geoengineering in the context of a fuller climate strategy that includes mitigation and adaptation. If the y-axis is cost and the x-axis is climate protection, then the supply curve rises from the origin—the first flat segment is *simple geoengineering*, which costs little but has many side effects; as the curve rises to include additional patches it enters the much more costly realm of complex *geoengineering cocktails*. Similarly, it might be useful to think about the shape and location of the demand curve. Most discussion about geoengineering has imagined a dreamworld where geoengineering is interesting because it is cheap and because it is thought about largely in isolation from the economics of other policy options. In the real world, geoengineering is probably a price-taker that gets deployed at large scale when costly options to control emissions have failed. In that world, geoengineering is being weighed against still more costly options such as shutting down energy systems before the end of their useful lifetime or severe curtailment of demand. The former demand curve is nearly vertical and 'clears' only on the low-cost options; the latter demand curve is horizontal and clears deep in the territory of complex geoengineering.

[8] Nor is it clear that nuclear weapons have not been 'used'. Of course they were used against Japan in 1945, but even the investment in weapons since that date has been usable as a deterrent in some settings. Their mere existence altered outcomes—such as in Quemoy and Matsu (1950s), in Turkey and Cuba (1960s), probably in Israel (since the 1980s), and elsewhere. By contrast, geoengineering probably has no deterrent effect and may actually amplify the risks that give rise to its deployment. Gaia aside, the planet is geophysically unaware that it is being deterred from harmful climate outcomes when humans build geoengineering capabilities. But humans are aware of their own investments in geoengineering, and that awareness may make them less likely to invest mightily in controlling emissions and adapting to climate changes if they know geoengineering is available. The impact of such investments on human willingness to spend resources on controlling emissions is hard to assess; my impression, however, is that the option of geoengineering will not amplify the extent to which humans engage in reckless behaviour by not investing in emission controls. That's because careful assessments of geoengineering will show its many faults and side effects as well as unknown harms; indeed, identification of such harms has been the tenor of geoengineering research in recent years.

of atmospheric testing of nuclear weapons were not predicted. Electromagnetic pulse, for example, was discovered through atmospheric testing. The same insight probably applies to cocktail geoengineering. It is impossible to assess real geoengineering schemes—and thus put them on the shelf of practically available options—without actually testing them at scale. Readying the option for use in an emergency probably requires actually using it, at least for test deployments.

III. ASSESSMENT AND REGULATION

Finally we turn to the regulatory politics of geoengineering. Our starting point is the argument already made earlier and by other authors. Namely, geoengineering has the potential to transform the politics of the climate problem because countries, alone or in small groups, can pursue geoengineering with planetary effect. By contrast, mitigation of emissions requires many countries to participate. Thus the regulatory task in geoengineering requires the setting of norms that restrain all potential geoengineers as well as principles to govern the trade-offs that geoengineers will face as they decide, alone or in concert, which cocktails of geoengineering systems to deploy. (If geoengineering proves costly, then agreements might also be needed on how to share the expense.) Effective restraints and norms to govern trade-offs will require agreement on underlying scientific facts about geoengineering options and dangers. Here we explore these two issues—scientific assessment and regulation—and how effective systems for each could arise.

(i) Scientific Assessment

As geoengineering rises in prominence so will calls for a comprehensive international assessment. So far, however, essentially all comprehensive assessments of geoengineering—with the exception of the now dated NAS study (NAS, 1992), which was commissioned by the US government—have been the work of lone researchers pursuing interesting questions. Would a comprehensive international assessment be useful?

Comprehensive assessments have played an essential role in building consensus around important facts that, in turn, made future regulation more effective (e.g. Mitchell *et al.*, 2006; NAS, 2007). The IPCC is a testimony to the importance of these activities, as are the technical and economic assessments linked to the Montreal Protocol on the ozone layer and in many other areas, such as acid precipitation. But the fact that comprehensive assessments have played important roles in regulating some pollutants is not proof that such assessments work in all situations. Close attention is needed to the nature of underlying scientific knowledge to determine whether assessments actually produce usable knowledge.

Nearly all of the successful assessments reflect circumstances where the knowledge is relatively well structured and where 'normal' science can resolve controversies.[9] Thus the IPCC, for example, has done a very good job of reviewing the 'normal' and relatively well-understood effects of climate change on sea level through melting glaciers and thermal expansion of seawater. But it has fallen far short of providing useful knowledge about possible outlier effects that could yield much higher sea levels, such as the possibility that landed glaciers could melt and slide more rapidly than standard ice physics had traditionally estimated (Oppenheimer *et al.*, 2007). Similar arguments apply to the IPCC assessments of the effects of aerosols on climate forcing (for example, see Morgan *et al.*, 2006). For normal science, consensus-oriented assessments are useful; for scientific questions, where paradigms are weak or highly contested, such assessments produce either pabulum or silence (Cullenward and Victor, 2007). In general, consensus assessments have a harder time accurately portraying the long 'tails' that are pervasive in complex and poorly understood systems such as the climate. Yet the side effects of geoengineering that cause the greatest worries—for which assessment would be must useful—are in the tails.

Geoengineering is also particularly ill suited for standard assessments, such as through the IPCC, because some of the most important issues involve the evaluation of trade-offs, which is the realm of the social sciences. Outside of economics, the social sciences do not have strong enough and sufficiently well-accepted intellectual paradigms to yield usable knowledge through standard international assessments.[10]

The IPCC particularly struggles where paradigms are contested because it is, by design, an open and weak institution.[11] Without the aid of a strong paradigm, weak institutions have a hard time embracing novel ideas and conveying the true diversity of opinions in the 'tails' while, at the same time, keeping charlatans at bay.[12]

This suggests a different strategy for assessment of geoengineering. The IPCC (or any such consensus-based process) is unlikely to produce useful shared knowledge because a proper full evaluation of geoengineering options and their impacts is fundamentally ill suited for consensus. The penchant for IPCC to review

[9] By 'normal' I mean science pursued within a given intellectual paradigm or research programme with agreed boundaries (Kuhn, 1962; Lakatos and Musgrave, 1970). Where the boundaries of the paradigm are known and where the assessors can agree on core facts and theories (and on who qualifies as a 'scientist'), comprehensive assessment by the community of scientists is possible.

[10] The endless trials of IPCC's working group III supply many data points to support this hypothesis; some day, perhaps, the IPCC will wisely abandon its efforts in this area. The IPCC's nasty and inconclusive effort to evaluate trade-offs that involved assigning a value to lives lost in different economies is a warning of the hazards to researchers who attempt such work in a universal, comprehensive assessment.

[11] The term 'weak' is not intended pejoratively—rather, it is a factual statement of the ability of the institution itself to make decisions and steer outcomes. Most international institutions are 'weak'. Many governments are 'weak' by this same logic—including the US government, because, by design, it tends to gridlock and indecision. Most democracies, by design, have weak central institutions.

[12] Making the assessment institution stronger will not fix the problem because strong assessment institutions are prone to becoming captured by their masters. For its core tasks, the IPCC has the right design—a weak institution, charged with assessment of agreed science and open to scrutiny by anyone.

published literature—which is the standard method for determining the identity of accepted science—rather than formally to enlist new studies is an additional difficulty since the most interesting critiques and challenges to geoengineering will come from ideas that circulate in the unpublished grey literature.[13] Assessment, at this stage, is best combined with the ability to steer a research agenda. The actual published literature on geoengineering, in fact, is so short and can be read over a long weekend and there is little gain from a general synthesis and assessment; it is interesting more for its omissions than its robust findings.

A better approach would enlist multiple strong assessment institutions rather than a single, global, and weak institution. A few competent groups could prepare assessments in parallel—ideally groups that are connected to active scientific research in the area—and then compare the assessments. Their charge would include a special need to look at the many ways that geoengineering could go wrong. Academies of science are probably the best place to begin the process because they are usually well connected to the setting of research priorities and political decision-making. Russia is a good candidate because of that country's long history of dreaming about (and studying) climate modification and its role in heavy space lift (which is important for some geoengineering options). So is the USA, which must play a central role because most geoengineering science is, at the moment, American. To that small group China must be added, as that nation is building the capability to understand the issues and possibly deploy geoengineering systems. Maybe other countries should be added, with an eye to evaluating special options—for example, Brazil or other forested nations, if tinkering with the forests is envisioned. Throughout, the goal of these assessments would be a plurality of ideas and new evaluations, not consensus. Elsewhere, several colleagues and I have explored how such an academy-based assessment process could operate (Victor *et al.*, 2008).

(ii) Regulatory Treaties and Norms

As geoengineering is considered more seriously, the question of norms to govern deployment will arise. Norms might be needed not only to determine when such systems might be used but also the kinds of evaluations that geoengineers might be required to make before deployment, compensation for parties harmed, cost sharing, and commitments to maintain geoengineering systems once deployed. Bluntly, whose hands should be allowed on the thermostat?

[13] My goal is not to disparage the IPCC, for these problems are intrinsic to global omnibus assessments. Witness the magisterial *Global Biodiversity Assessment* (GBA), which remains, along with the Millennium Ecosystem Assessment, the most useful reference source on biodiversity. Yet the GBA, although originally conceived as policy-relevant, was largely orthogonal to the policy debate in the biodiversity treaty because the latter became focused on issues such as genetic engineering of crops and revenue-sharing for germplasm that were largely removed from the scientific debate. On the real hazards and trade-offs involved in such highly charged issues, the conservative consensus-oriented scientific process in the GBA had little to contribute. See Watson *et al.* (1995); Hassan *et al.* (2005).

The standard answer to the question of norm-creation, like most in the realm of international environmental regulation, looks to the treaty system to negotiate, codify, and enforce norms. Treaties undergo extensive review and ratification by governments before they become binding and thus represent the best-considered desires and capabilities of the governments that join them (Chayes and Chayes, 1998). These strengths of treaties, however, are also exactly their liability. They are the by-product of a negotiating process through which nations evaluate closely whether they can and will comply. Such processes are inherently conservative. Indeed, efforts to measure compliance with environmental treaties generally find that compliance is nearly perfect—because countries adjust their commitments to the point where they are sure that compliance is feasible and because they do not join when commitments are too demanding (Downs *et al.*, 1996; Victor *et al.*, 1998). The Kyoto process, which has yielded high formal legal compliance but little actual impact on global warming, is one manifestation of that general observation about treaty-making (Victor, 2001).

From today's vantage point, a treaty negotiation would yield inconclusive outcomes. Most nations would probably favour a ban on geoengineering because only a few countries actually have the capability to geoengineer on their own.[14] The rest have little to gain from being permissive and would be wary about letting the geoengineers tinker with the planet. Faced with pressure for a taboo, the few nations with unilateral geoengineering capabilities would seek favourable (i.e. vague) language; if unsuccessful, those countries could simply refuse to join. Exactly this outcome followed the hotly contested negotiations leading to the 1992 Convention on Biological Diversity (CBD), which contained European-inspired language that was hostile to genetically engineered crops and developing country-inspired language that demanded complicated revenue-sharing for some kinds of germplasm collections. The USA, world leader in these investments, simply refused to join the treaty. Investment in the genetic engineering and in new crops that faced complicated new revenue-sharing requirements was slowed, despite their large potential benefits.[15] A treaty on geoengineering, if attempted today, would follow a similar diplomatic pathway. Most countries would push for a ban, and most of the possible geoengineers would balk.

[14] Exactly how many nations could unilaterally geoengineer depends on the geoengineering system and on important practical considerations. Nations with space-lift capability, missiles, or other vehicles that could inject material into the stratosphere all have the capability, in principle, to geoengineer. That list could extend to a dozen today and perhaps two dozen with a decade or two of sustained investment. However, in practice, a large territory (or willingness to operate on the high seas in the face of acute disputes) and reliable lift systems would be needed for this to be done with global impact. That list of countries is much smaller and might include Australia, Brazil, China, India, the EU (if it could agree to act as one), Russia, and possibly Japan.

[15] For more on the CBD and its outcomes, see Raustiala and Victor (2004) and for its harm on crop innovation see Victor and Runge (2002). Other environmental treaties have similar histories. For example, the ban on some forms of ocean dumping under the 1972 London Dumping Convention effectively halted all significant research on sub-sea disposal of nuclear waste, which could have been an environmentally superior to the land-based disposal options that have dominated nearly all investment since that time.

In general, when it is not widely agreed how to frame the problem at hand, or if the framing creates strongly opposing interests, the outcome of treaty negotiations is stalemate. Sometimes that stalemate takes the form of vague language—a growing body of treaty language that might be called 'junk law', akin to the large amounts of 'junk DNA' that seems to serve no genomic purpose. In other instances, the outcome is a collapse of the treaty negotiations, as was the case for a planned treaty on forests in the early 1990s that could not yield agreement because important nations could not resolve how to frame and settle their disputes. Analysts and advocates are generally less mindful of these failures because they like to study success and there is no good theory of junk law. Thus bookshelves are filled with studies about the success in protecting the ozone layer, but few scholars study dormancy and death in the treaty-making process.

A treaty negotiation at this stage would also raise some questions that could become highly contested without purpose. For example, who owns the Lagrangian point L1—an orbit that affords uninterrupted position between Sun and Earth and thus could be an ideal site for space-based sunshades? At the moment, nobody knows how to assign property rights at L1, but surely some governments will imagine great riches and demand their share. That occurred, for example, when governments sought to allocate rights to deep-seabed minerals through the Law of the Sea (Sebenius, 1984). Imagined riches never appeared, despite a decade of wrangling over revenue-sharing agreements. Such negotiations can be distracting and are probably irrelevant if underlying circumstances make the deal that is reached inconvenient for important players. At this stage, attempting to allocate L1 would not be useful. It is not clear whether L1 is uniquely special because jostling hardware at that slot could be hazardous for the planet as a whole. Or perhaps L1 will become like geostationary orbits—once imagined to be scarce and thus highly valuable, but today much less scarce thanks to innovation in low-power satellites and higher gain antennas. Disputes over ownership of L1 could lead governments to question whether systems could ever be placed in that orbit, and that would lead them to forgo possibly useful investment in L1-based geoengineering options.

A more effective approach to building a relevant regulatory system would concentrate, today, on laying the groundwork for future negotiations over norms rather than attempting to codify immature norms now. Meaningful norms are not crafted from thin air. They can have effect if they make sense to pivotal players and then they become socialized through practice. To be sensible the norms must be based on evidence and reason; they must be relevant and responsive to core interests of pivotal players.

What can be done to craft sensible norms? Formal, singular scientific assessments, such as through the IPCC, seem unlikely to work for the reasons already discussed. Direct negotiation of norms, too, seems unlikely to bear fruit because not enough is known about geoengineering options and their effects to frame a useful formal negotiation. Here I explore a different approach, which is to build norms from the 'bottom–up'. The decentralized process of research and assessment, already outlined above, can generate the information needed to assess different geoengineering options. If done openly with extensive review as well as complementary funding to examine scenarios for actual geoengineering deployment, then such a process will likely create a base of accepted, shared information that could inform later formal efforts to create norms.

To be relevant, however, this decentralized process must contend with at least two inconvenient factors. First, the countries that are most wary about actually deploying geoengineering—more or less, the advanced industrialized countries—are the ones that are the best candidates to lead the effort because they are most likely to lade their programmes with prudent assessments. For these reasons, it is probably especially important not to create a taboo against geoengineering, for that would make it very difficult for these countries to mobilize the political support needed for funding geoengineering research and assessment. Second, assessments of geoengineering probably require some well-instrumented, trial deployments of geoengineering systems. Such deployments will be particularly controversial in those same countries whose engagement is most essential.

The process should be open enough so that scientists from prospective geoengineering nations see it as the main source of useful knowledge about geoengineering while, at the same time, become socialized with the prevailing norms and best practices. CERN and ITER come to mind as models, as do the joint efforts during the Cold War by Soviet and US scientists to conduct joint seismic research (which was relevant for monitoring of underground testing and helped governments craft workable test ban agreements). Such institutions do not guarantee that all governments will adhere to the emerging norms, but it is interesting to note that often it is the scientists who are in the midst of international scientific assessments and collaborations who become the strongest advocates for regulation and also best positioned within their governments to press for such outcomes. If successful, this effort would create the necessary base of information for lead countries to create their own capable domestic institutions to fund and regulate geoengineering. In time, those national efforts would link together in a transnational partnership of expert regulators, as has happened in many other areas where regulation rests on expert assessment and profits from international coordination (Slaughter, 2004).

Greenfingers might be invited to participate in this transnational assessment process, provided they subscribe to the emerging norms. The success of Craig Venter's for-profit Celera in applying a new method for sequencing the human genome (Venter's genome, to be precise) is a reminder that the world has entered a new era where big science is no longer solely the province of government. That experience is also a reminder that whatever regulatory system is created will be under constant pressure to be relevant—because if it fails or is overly restrictive then rival geoengineers could act on their own. Unlike other areas of R&D where there are promises of large commercial rewards, at present it seems unlikely that private-sector finance would play a major role in geoengineering.

There are no markets for geoengineering services, and if geoengineering systems were deployed at scale then governments would probably regulate the activity to prevent extranormal profits. However, if a few key capabilities for geoengineering could be identified, then prizes could be established for the parties that demonstrate them—akin to the X Prize that has encouraged private investment in space exploration, advanced automobiles, genomics, and other topics.

Along the way enough may be learned to create more formal treaties or other regulatory institutions. Exactly this 'bottom–up' process—ambitious norm-setting activities, backed by research and assessment—was followed in the North Sea regulatory process, leading eventually to a complex of precise regulatory treaties. Such systems often benefit from the use of flexible, non-binding agreements in the early stages of the effort when it is not clear which rules should be codified and how governments would implement them (Victor *et al.*, 1998; Victor, 2007).

IV. FINAL THOUGHTS

Growing attention to geoenginering will create pressure for regulation. I have suggested here that efforts to design strict regulations, at this stage, will probably fail to yield useful outcomes. And they may create a taboo against geoengineering that will have force in some countries. Taboos will make it hard for the countries that are most likely to sponsor informed and careful assessments of geoengineering to invest in the research and deployment of trial geoengineering systems that will be needed to generate useful and relevant knowledge.

Useful norms could arise through an intensive process of research and assessment that is probably best organized by the academies of sciences in the few countries with the potential to geoengineer.

I close by puzzling about what should be done if norm-setting from the bottom up is too plodding or does not work? A particular nation or Greenfinger might decide that harmful changes in climate compel unilateral action. Demarches and treaties will have little impact when highly concentrated benefits compel action. Trade sanctions, too, are unlikely to work—because they rarely work except when focused on small and vulnerable countries, which are the nations that are perhaps least likely to pursue unilateral geoengineering.

Such a scenario needs attention and careful assessment through techniques such as war games. For the countries not engaged in geoengineering, the best response to unilateral geoengineering might be a sharp increase in their own geoengineering effort. Such a breakout would make it easier to gain credible information on risks and also easier to re-establish norms. Unlike an arms race—in which breakout has the effect of making an adversary feel less secure, thus breeding further expenditure on weapons and rattling of sabres—a breakout in geoengineering could be stabilizing, because its transparent endpoint is to re-assert collective control over the technology. And once a unilateral geoengineer sees other countries engaged in similar efforts they will need to do less geoengineering on their own. But once the process of geoengineering begins—whether unilateral or collective—it is likely the world will be unable to stop. For whatever the ills of global climate change, it is probably even more dangerous to let the climate experience the even more rapid warming that would follow the dismantling of geoengineering systems.

17

Improving Energy Efficiency: Hidden Costs and Unintended Consequences

*Steve Sorrell**

I. INTRODUCTION

It is now widely accepted that global emissions of greenhouse gases must be more than halved by mid-century if the worst effects of climate change are to be avoided (IPCC, 2008; Stern, 2008*b*). Substantial further reductions will be required after 2050 and the most recent science suggests that faster and deeper cuts may be necessary (Anderson and Bows, 2008; Hansen, 2008). The scale and speed of the required transition poses an unprecedented challenge. Technically it should be achievable, but only through the rapid deployment of a wide range of low-carbon energy-supply technologies, in parallel with a reduction—or at least a significant curtailment in the growth—of global energy demand.

Both independent studies and official government policies assume that the primary mechanism for reducing energy demand will be the encouragement of energy efficiency throughout the economy—for example, through encouraging the adoption of thermal insulation and low-energy lighting in domestic buildings. The technical potential for such improvements is acknowledged to be extremely large and it is argued that the economics are very favourable, even without putting a price on carbon emissions (IPCC, 2007*d*). Moreover, unlike most energy-supply options, improvements in end-use efficiency are largely free of negative externalities. As a result, the encouragement of cost-effective energy-efficiency measures receives support from a wide range of stakeholders and forms a key element of climate policy at all levels.

The aggregate energy intensity of OECD economies has continually fallen over the last century, largely as a result of structural and technological change. But while this has contributed to a partial 'decoupling' of energy consumption from GDP, energy consumption has continued to increase, along with the associated carbon emissions. To reverse this trend, many argue for a substantial expansion of energy-efficiency policy—that is, to introduce more and better regulations, standards, information programmes, and subsidy schemes. However, owing in part to methodological difficulties, there is relatively little evidence on the energy

* Sussex Energy Group, SPRU (Science and Technology Policy Research), University of Sussex.

savings achieved by such policies, or their associated costs and benefits. As a result, some economists question the value of such approaches and argue that the economic potential for energy savings has been overestimated. Two leading explanations are that:

- the *hidden costs* associated with energy-efficiency improvements are neglected, so that they are more costly than they first appear; and/or
- the *rebound effects* of energy-efficiency improvements are neglected, so that the actual energy savings are less than those anticipated.

While both hidden costs and rebound effects may take a variety of forms, the relevant variables are difficult to measure and the causal relationships difficult to establish. As a result, debates over these issues tend to rely more upon theoretical arguments than empirical evidence. Also, these debates are highly polarized, with persistent disagreement over the appropriate concepts, definitions, and methodological tools. However, hidden costs differ from rebound effects in one crucial respect: while the former is well established in policy discourse, the latter is almost universally ignored. This is best illustrated by the Garnaut and Stern reviews, which devote whole chapters to hidden costs and related issues but manage to overlook rebound effects altogether (Stern, 2007; Garnaut, 2008*c*). Similarly, the IPCC (2007*d*) simply notes that the literature is divided on the magnitude of rebound effects. Given the potentially far-reaching implications of rebound effects, these are serious omissions.

This chapter summarizes the nature and consequences of both hidden costs and rebound effects and highlights their implications for climate policy. Given the partial and equivocal nature of the relevant empirical evidence, the focus is more upon clarifying the issues involved than on reaching a firm conclusion on their importance. It is suggested, however, that the economic potential for energy saving is more likely to be overestimated through the neglect of rebound effects than through the neglect of hidden costs. Complementary policy responses are available to address both of these problems and these can be effective in many circumstances. Nevertheless, the existence of non-trivial rebound effects raises some concerns about whether energy consumption can be significantly decoupled from economic growth.

II. HIDDEN COSTS

Energy-efficiency improvements frequently involve the adoption of established technologies whose performance is well proven and which appear to involve relatively little technical risk. It has long been claimed that the adoption of such technologies could be highly cost-effective for the individuals and organizations involved—with risk-adjusted rates of return greatly exceeding the cost of capital (Krause, 1996; Lovins and Lovins, 1997; Geller *et al.*, 2006).[1] While various

[1] For example, the IPCC (2007*d*) has suggested that 'no regrets' opportunities (i.e. those with net negative costs) have the potential to reduce emissions by around 6GtCO_2e/year by 2030.

factors may discourage the adoption of such technologies, proponents claim that these can be cost-effectively overcome through well-designed policy intervention. Support for such claims is derived from *ex post* policy evaluations (Eto *et al.*, 2000; Weil and McMahon, 2003; Anderson and Newell, 2004), observations of real-world energy decision-making (Romm, 1999), and 'bottom–up' energy-economic models that incorporate detailed information on the performance and cost of energy using equipment (Interlaboratory Working Group, 1997; Marsh *et al.*, 2003).

Many economists are sceptical of such claims, maintaining that if such opportunities are available, they should be readily adopted without the need for government intervention (Nichols, 1994; Stavins *et al.*, 2007). Many of the supposed 'barriers' to technology adoption may simply reflect real but *hidden* costs[2] which would be inappropriate to address through public policy. Only a subset of these costs may result from the market failures recognized by orthodox economic theory and only a subset of these may be cost-effectively reduced by public policy (Jaffe and Stavins, 1994*a*, *b*). Support for such claims is also derived from *ex post* policy evaluations (Kreitler, 1991; Loughran and Kulick, 2004), as well as from macroeconomic, or 'top–down' energy-economic models that typically represent technology abstractly through production or cost functions (EIA, 1998*b*; Weyant and Hill, 1999; Nordhaus, 2000).

Measurement problems make the 'hidden cost hypothesis' difficult to test and the available studies provide inconsistent results. While it is tautologous to assert that hidden costs *must* be present if particular technologies are not being adopted, there is disagreement over the nature and determinants of those costs, their magnitude in different circumstances, and their relevance for public policy (Sutherland, 1991, 1994, 1996; Joskow and Marron, 1992; Golove and Eto, 1996; Stavins *et al.*, 2007).

III. PERSPECTIVES ON HIDDEN COSTS

Underlying the debate on hidden costs are competing assumptions about the nature of human rationality, the appropriate role of markets, and the relative usefulness of different approaches to understanding economic behaviour. Scepticism about 'no regrets' opportunities derives largely from orthodox economics, which considers that policy intervention is only justified where the existence of market failures—such as negative externalities and asymmetric information—can clearly be demonstrated and where the benefits outweigh the costs. Market failures are pervasive in real-world decision-making, but of particular importance to energy efficiency is the cost of obtaining information, the asymmetric distribution of this information between different parties to a contract (e.g. buyers and sellers), and the tendency to use this information opportunistically (Milgrom, 1992).

[2] Hidden, that is, to the analyst but not to the individuals or organizations involved.

For example, in the absence of adequate oversight mechanisms, building contractors may substitute cheaper but less energy-efficient equipment to that required in the specification since the consequences are unlikely to be observed by the client (Lovins, 1992; Sorrell, 2003). Similarly, top management may require high rates of return from small, cost-saving projects in an attempt to prevent profits being dissipated through 'managerial slack' (Antle and Eppen, 1985; DeCanio, 1993, 1994). Problems such as these can prevent the take-up of energy-efficiency opportunities, but in the absence of asymmetric information and opportunism they would not arise.

Orthodox economics relies upon highly formalized mathematical models and unrealistic assumptions about cognitive ability. In contrast, *transaction cost economics* (TCE) assumes that individuals make satisfactory rather than optimal decisions and rely heavily on routines and rules of thumb (Simon, 1959; Williamson, 1985; Furubotn and Richter, 1997). Such rules may frequently be detrimental to energy efficiency, such as when engineers oversize heating, ventilation, and air-conditioning equipment, leading to inefficient operation on part load (Lovins, 1992; Sorrell, 2003). The combination of 'bounded rationality' and opportunism leads inevitably to transaction costs which are a necessary feature of all market, organizational, and contractual arrangements and which can impede energy-efficient and apparently cost-effective solutions. For example, in the absence of transaction costs, landlords and tenants could enter into contracts to share the costs and benefits of energy-efficiency investment. But if the potential gains are outweighed by the transaction costs of renegotiating the lease, the inefficiencies will remain (Sanstad, 1994). The landlord–tenant relationship is only the most prominent example of a principal–agent problem that pervades both market and organizational transactions and which separates the responsibility for specifying, installing, operating, and/or maintaining energy-using equipment from the accountability for energy costs (Sorrell *et al.*, 2004; IEA, 2007*d*).

Behavioural economics takes these arguments one stage further by arguing that decision-making is not just 'boundedly rational' but systematically biased and erroneous (Piattelli-Palmarini, 1994; Kahneman and Tversky, 2000). For example, individuals commonly exhibit 'loss aversion' and a '*status quo* bias' which can discourage them from undertaking cost-effective investments—such as the manager who declined to pursue a project with a 50–50 chance of either making US$300 thousand or losing US$60 thousand (Swalm, 1966; Samuelson and Zeckhauser, 1988; Thaler, 1991).[3] Experimental tests suggest that such biases are universal, predictable, and largely unaffected by either monetary incentives or learning (Kahneman and Tversky, 2000). Again, such behaviour can lead to departures from the

[3] Opportunity costs tend to be undervalued relative to out-of-pocket costs, and foregone gains are considered less painful than perceived losses. In the case of energy efficiency, individuals will consider themselves 'endowed' with their existing buildings, equipment, and energy bill (Hewett, 1998). The potential savings in energy costs from energy-efficiency improvements will be considered an opportunity cost, while the investment costs of energy-efficient equipment will be considered an out-of-pocket cost. Loss aversion will therefore tend to bias individuals against making such improvements.

Table 17.1. Market and organizational transaction costs

Type		Examples
Market (external)	Search and information costs	Searching for parties with whom to contract; communicating; gathering information about price and quality
	Bargaining and decision costs	Bargaining and negotiating costs; time and legal advice; costs of making any information gathered usable; compensation paid to advisers; cost of reaching decisions
	Supervision and enforcement costs	Monitoring contract terms; measuring product/service quality; measuring the attributes of what is being exchanged; protecting rights; enforcing contractual provisions
Organizational (internal)	Establishing organizations	Costs of setting up, maintaining, or changing and organizational design, including incentive design, information technology, public relations, lobbying, etc.
	Running organizations	Costs of decision-making, monitoring the execution of orders, measuring the performance of workers, agency costs, costs of information management, etc.

Source: Based on Furubotn and Richter (1997).

predictions of energy-economic models and prevent the adoption of apparently cost-effective energy-efficient technologies.

The different types of market and organizational transaction costs are summarized in Table 17.1. These costs form an important part of the hidden costs of energy-efficiency improvements and are difficult to incorporate within bottom–up energy-economic models. At the same time, there may be other types of hidden costs which may be more properly understood as part of the *production costs* of energy efficiency. The following sections examine these production and transaction costs in more detail, focusing in particular upon organizational decision-making on energy efficiency.

IV. PRODUCTION COSTS

The production costs of energy-efficiency improvements include all the associated capital, installation, staff, material, and energy costs. In principle, these should be included in bottom–up models, but in practice some elements could easily be underestimated or overlooked (Ostertag, 1999). Possible examples include design fees, civil engineering costs, the costs of re-routing pipework, the cost of new light fittings to accommodate compact fluorescents, and the cost of production interruptions during equipment installation. These costs are site- and project-specific and hence difficult to estimate, but individuals and organizations can be expected to take them into account when appraising investment opportunities.

A second group of costs relates to the inferior performance of some types of energy-efficient technology. For example, an energy-efficient production process may lead to increased noise; a variable speed drive may require extra maintenance; an energy-efficient motor may be less reliable; compact fluorescents may have poorer lighting quality and take longer to reach full intensity; and so on (Golove and Eto, 1996). While these considerations clearly apply to investments that are specifically designed to reduce energy consumption, they are likely to be more important when energy efficiency is only one of a number of attributes under consideration. Again, these costs could, in principle, be incorporated within bottom–up models, but in practice this may be difficult.

V. ORGANIZATIONAL TRANSACTION COSTS

Initiatives to improve energy efficiency will generally be associated with organizational transaction costs. For example, in relation to individual energy-saving projects, there may be costs associated with design and investment appraisal, approval of capital expenditures, specification and tendering, retraining of staff, and so on. There may also be 'overhead' costs of energy management, including the cost of employing specialist staff, maintaining and using energy information systems, and conducting energy audits. These costs are frequently cited as a major obstacle to cost-effective investment. For example, negotiated agreements between government and industry in the UK required the implementation of energy-efficiency projects with paybacks as short as three years. The primary reason given for the use of such strict investment criteria was the management time required to identify and implement such projects (ETSU, 2001). UK best-practice literature recommends that 5 per cent of an organization's annual energy expenditure be reserved for dedicated energy-efficiency investment (Energy Efficiency Office, 1993), but even for an organization with annual expenditure of £1 million, this is less than the salary costs of a full-time energy manager. Hence, stringent investment criteria for energy-efficiency improvements may partly be justified as a means to recover salary overheads.[4]

In case studies of 48 organizations in the brewing, mechanical engineering, and higher education sectors, Sorrell *et al.* (2004) found that the overhead costs of energy management provided the biggest obstacle to energy-efficiency improvements—especially for the smaller firms. This was most evident in the severe time constraints on the relevant staff, which were frequently considered

[4] However, in none of the 48 case studies undertaken by Sorrell *et al.* (2004) were overhead costs either explicitly quantified or used as a rationale for stringent investment criteria.

more important than capital constraints (as one interviewee observed: 'if we had more money, we wouldn't have time to spend it') (Sorrell *et al.*, 2004). Contracting out energy management to an energy service company (ESCO) only provides a partial solution, since there are transaction costs associated with searching for a supplier, negotiating and writing contracts, monitoring contract performance, enforcing compliance, negotiating changes when unforeseen circumstances arise, and resolving disputes. There are also costs associated with opportunistic behaviour by either party, such as when a contractor fails to maintain equipment to an adequate standard. For smaller organizations, these costs may outweigh the potential savings (Sorrell, 2007*a*).

VI. MARKET TRANSACTION COSTS

The identification, procurement, and installation of energy-efficient technologies will also be associated with market transaction costs. Improving energy efficiency often requires the procurement and installation of one or more complex, heterogeneous, and unfamiliar goods from markets with multiple suppliers and intermediaries. Since the lifetime of such products is long, the purchases are infrequent, and the rate of technical change is rapid relative to the purchase interval, the costs of information acquisition may be high.[5]

These costs may be reduced if the energy consumption of the product is clearly and credibly labelled and its performance is insensitive to installation, operation, and maintenance conditions. But information on energy consumption is frequently missing or ambiguous, making it difficult to compare the performance of different products. Even when rating schemes are available, the performance in use may depart significantly from the rated performance—for example, if technologies are operated on part load or are inadequately maintained. Furthermore, the performance of technologies such as control systems and variable speed drives may be difficult to evaluate even *after* purchase, since this requires low-level sub-metering, adjustment for variable factors such as occupancy, and careful analysis of consumption patterns over time. Absent these conditions, consumers will lack feedback on the consequences of different purchase decisions, with the result that energy costs will remain relatively invisible (Kempton and Layne, 1994; Hewett, 1998).

In practice, users frequently face a choice between an energy-efficient or -inefficient product when a decision is required anyway—for example, replacing a boiler which has come to the end of its life. What is relevant here is the

[5] In contrast, energy commodities such as gas and electricity represent a simple, unchanging, easy to understand, and homogeneous product which is purchased from a small number of large, well-established, and trusted firms. Purchases are made regularly, market information is widely available, and 'performance' is judged largely on price. Hence, the cost of information acquisition is much lower.

Box 17.1 Adverse selection in energy service markets

Asymmetric information in energy service markets may lead to the 'adverse selection' of energy inefficient goods (Akerlof, 1970). Take housing as an example (Jaffe and Stavins, 1994*a*). In a perfect market, the resale value of a house would reflect the discounted value of energy-efficiency investments. But buyers have difficulty in recognizing the potential energy savings and rarely account for this when making a price offer. Estate agents have greater resources than buyers, but similarly neglect energy efficiency when valuing a house. Since the operating cost of a house affects the ability of a borrower to repay the mortgage, this should be reflected in mortgage qualifications. Again, it is not. In all cases, one party (e.g. the builder or the seller) may have the relevant information, but transaction costs impede the transfer of that information to the potential purchaser. The result may be to discourage house builders from constructing energy-efficient houses, or to discourage homeowners from making energy-efficiency improvements, since they will not be able to capture the additional costs in the sale price.

The same processes are at work in a range of energy services markets. In some cases, producers may be unable to market desirable technologies since consumers are unable to observe their characteristics prior to sale (Howarth and Sanstad, 1995). In other cases, information asymmetries may create incentives for producers or suppliers to act opportunistically. For example, the energy efficiency of commercial buildings depends heavily on the detailed features of heating, ventilation, and control equipment. But in comparison to highly visible features, such as outward form and aesthetics, the performance of this equipment is extremely difficult for the customer to observe. Substitution of an inefficient or oversized piece of equipment in place of efficient equipment could be relatively easy, with the result that inefficient products drive efficient products off the market.

availability of information on the energy performance of the product as compared to the availability of information on other attributes of the product, such as capital costs. But energy efficiency may be expected to be a secondary attribute of many products and is likely to be determined by wide range of design and operational factors, the net effect of which may be difficult to assess. In the absence of clearly specified and comparable performance information, energy-efficiency considerations are likely to be outweighed by other more visible features. Hence, even if energy efficiency is valued by the consumer, the lack or cost of information may prevent this preference from being exercised. In some circumstances, efficient products may be driven off the market (Box 17.1).

VII. IMPLICATIONS OF HIDDEN COSTS

Hidden production and transaction costs are therefore a pervasive feature of market and organizational transactions on energy efficiency and in many cases could be significant. Since many of these costs depend upon contractual structures, procedures, incentives, and routines, they are difficult to incorporate within energy-economic models which represent costs purely in relation to individual technologies. In addition, since these costs are multidimensional and context-specific, they can be extremely difficult to measure. Such costs may better be explored by identifying their determinants and assessing the relative importance of these determinants in different contexts (Shelanski and Klein, 1995; Sorrell, 2007*a*), or by cross-sectional comparisons that seek to explain why some organizations, sectors, or countries are able to achieve higher levels of energy efficiency than others.

While competitive pressures should encourage an efficient choice of market, organizational, and contractual arrangements, this does not mean that all existing structures are optimal or that there is no room for improvement. Hence, the relevant policy question is not so much whether a market failure is present but whether it is possible to reduce transaction costs in a cost-effective manner. For example, minimum energy-efficiency standards can avoid the time and hassle of working out what 'bad' products to avoid. But whether this is desirable will depend on the welfare losses associated with removing cheap (but inefficient) products from the market and the costs of retooling for the relevant suppliers.

It is important to recognize that transaction costs will be incurred for both energy-efficient and -inefficient choices (e.g. purchasing both energy-efficient and -inefficient motors), so what matters is the difference between the two. Some types of transaction costs may only be relevant when decision-making routines are changed (e.g. when the shift is made from purchasing standard to high-frequency fluorescent lighting) and may also decrease over time as the relevant knowledge becomes embedded within organizations. Also, transaction costs need not increase in proportion to the volume of the transaction. So for example, the transaction costs associated with identifying and purchasing an energy-efficient motor will form a declining proportion of total life-cycle costs as the size of the motor increases (Ostertag, 2003). More generally, transaction costs are likely to be a significantly greater obstacle for smaller organizations and for households, which suggests that the benefits of policy intervention in these sectors may be correspondingly higher.

The debate on hidden costs would benefit greatly from more rigorous *ex post* evaluations of energy-efficiency policies. While the required methodologies are well established, applications to energy-efficiency policies are relatively rare (Train, 1994; Meyer, 1995; Frondel and Schmidt, 2001; Sorrell, 2005). Perhaps the most intensively studied area is utility demand-side management (DSM) programmes in the USA, where some of the better studies suggest that energy savings are significantly overestimated and costs underestimated (Joskow and Marron, 1992; Loughran and Kulick, 2004). However, other studies provide contradictory results and since the problems derive largely from 'free-riders', the conclusion cannot be extended to all types of energy-efficiency policy (Levine and Sonnenblick, 1994; Auffhammer *et al.*, 2008).

In a comprehensive review, Gillingham *et al.* (2006) concluded that DSM programmes appeared to be cost-effective, although concerns remained about hidden costs for consumers. Also, the free-rider effect was in part balanced by 'free-driver' effects and some of the better-designed programmes performed significantly

Box 17.2 The US Green Lights programme

In the US Green Lights programme, organizations in the public and private sector enter into voluntary agreements with the US Environmental Protection Authority (US EPA) which commit them to implementing energy-efficient lighting upgrades that satisfy conventional investment criteria while maintaining or improving lighting quality. In return, the US EPA provides information, software, and technical assistance, oversees compliance, and facilitates public recognition of the organization's efforts. Evaluations of this programme suggest that it has been a great success: for example, between 1991 and 1996, 2,300 participating organizations were estimated to have saved US$440m in energy costs at an average annual rate of return of 45 per cent (DeCanio, 1998; US EPA, 1998). In other words, the programme encouraged investments that the organizations should have been making anyway. While the costs to the EPA were not quantified, they appear to be relatively small since only a small number of staff were involved and the programme did not involve any subsidies.

Howarth *et al.* (2000) attribute the programme's success to its ability to overcome organizational failures, such as asymmetric information between senior managers and individual departments, and split incentives between production and facilities staff. As well as providing *credible* data on relevant investment opportunities to top management (who would otherwise pay little attention to such 'minor' cost-saving opportunities), it also provided wider benefits in terms of corporate image.

Box 17.3 Hidden benefits of energy-efficiency improvements

- Lovins and Lovins (1997) used case studies to argue that better visual, acoustic, and thermal comfort in well-designed, energy-efficient buildings can improve labour productivity by as much as 16 per cent. Since labour costs in commercial buildings are typically 25 times greater than energy costs, the resulting cost savings can potentially dwarf those from reduced energy consumption.
- Pye and McKane (1998) showed how the installation of energy-efficient motors reduced wear and tear, extended the lifetime of system components, and achieved savings in capital and labour costs that exceeded the reduction in energy costs.
- Sorrell *et al.* (2004) found a host of examples of the 'hidden benefits' of energy-efficiency improvements within 48 case studies of organizational energy management. For example, changes to defrosting regimes at a brewery led to energy savings, water savings, reduced maintenance, and reduced deterioration of building fabric.
- Worrell *et al.* (2003) analysed the cost savings from 52 energy-efficiency projects, including motor replacements, fans/duct/pipe insulation, improved controls, and heat recovery in a range of industrial sectors. The average payback period from energy savings alone was 4.2 years, but this fell to 1.9 years when the non-energy benefits were taken into account.

better than the average. Gillingham *et al.* also concluded that US appliance standards were cost-effective, and would remain so even if the omitted (i.e. hidden) costs were equal to those included in the evaluation. Box 17.2 illustrates how well-designed policy may reduce the transaction costs associated with energy efficiency, while Box 17.3 illustrates how these costs may sometimes be offset by *hidden benefits* that are equally difficult to incorporate into energy-economic models.

In summary, hidden costs are pervasive and, to the extent that many modelling studies continue to ignore them, they are likely to overstate the economic potential for energy saving. However, it does not necessarily follow that such costs cannot be reduced through carefully defined and targeted policies, such as subsidized energy audits and labelling schemes. Numerous studies suggest that such policies can be cost-effective, even when the environmental benefits are ignored (Anderson and Newell, 2004; Gillingham *et al.*, 2006). To date, however, researchers have paid too much attention to modelling what could be achieved and too little attention to evaluating what policy has (or has not) achieved—and why. Better evaluation practices should help to resolve the long-standing controversy about hidden costs as well as contributing to improved policy design.

VIII. UNINTENDED CONSEQUENCES

Insufficient evaluation of energy-efficiency policies is also relevant to the second reason for overestimating the economic potential for energy savings—the *rebound effects* from improved energy efficiency. Rebound effects encompass a variety of behavioural responses to lower-cost energy services. While generally neither anticipated or intended, their net effect is to reduce the energy savings achieved. An example of a rebound effect would be the driver who replaces a car with a fuel-efficient model, only to take advantage of its cheaper running costs to drive further and more often. As with hidden costs, such effects are generally overlooked by bottom–up energy-economic models.

Since energy-efficiency improvements reduce the marginal cost of energy services such as travel, the consumption of those services may be expected to increase, thereby offsetting some of the predicted reduction in energy consumption. This so-called *direct rebound effect* was first brought to the attention of energy economists by Khazzoom (1980) and has since been the focus of much research (Greening *et al.*, 2000; Sorrell and Dimitropoulos, 2007*b*). But even if there is no direct rebound effect for a particular energy service (e.g. even if consumers choose not to drive any further in their fuel-efficient car), there are a number of other reasons why the economy-wide reduction in energy consumption may be less than simple calculations suggest. For example, the money saved on motor-fuel consumption may be spent on other goods and services that also require energy to provide. These so-called *indirect rebound effects* can take a number of forms, as summarized in Box 17.4.

Box 17.4 Indirect rebound effects

- *Embodied energy effects*: The equipment used to improve energy efficiency (e.g. thermal insulation) will itself require energy to manufacture and install and this 'embodied' energy consumption will offset some of the lifetime energy savings achieved.
- *Re-spending effects*: Consumers may use the cost savings from energy-efficiency improvements to purchase other goods and services which themselves require energy to provide. For example, the cost savings from a more energy-efficient central heating system may be put towards an overseas holiday.
- *Output effects*: Producers may use the cost savings from energy-efficiency improvements to increase output, thereby increasing consumption of energy inputs as well as capital, labour, and material inputs which also require energy to provide. If the energy-efficiency improvements are sector wide, they may lead to lower product prices, increased consumption of the relevant products, and further increases in energy consumption. All such improvements will increase the overall productivity of the economy, thereby encouraging economic growth, increased consumption of goods and services, and increased energy consumption.
- *Composition effects*: Both the energy-efficiency improvements and the associated reductions in energy prices will reduce the cost of energy-intensive goods and services to a greater extent than non-energy-intensive goods and services, thereby encouraging consumer demand to shift towards the former.
- *Energy-market effects*: Large-scale reductions in energy demand may translate into lower energy prices which will encourage energy consumption to increase. The reduction in energy prices will also increase real income, thereby encouraging investment and generating an extra stimulus to aggregate output and energy use.

The *overall* or *economy-wide* rebound effect from an energy-efficiency improvement represents the sum of these direct and indirect effects. It is normally expressed as a percentage of the *expected* energy savings from an energy-efficiency improvement, where the latter is usually based upon simple engineering calculations. Hence, an economy-wide rebound effect of 20 per cent means that 20 per cent of the potential energy savings are 'taken back' through one or more of the above mechanisms. An economy-wide rebound effect of 100 per cent means that the expected energy savings are entirely offset, leading to zero net savings for the economy as a whole. *Backfire* means that the rebound effect exceeds 100 per cent, implying that energy-efficiency improvements lead to an overall *increase* in energy consumption. This possibility was first suggested by William Stanley Jevons and has since become known as Jevons Paradox:

> it is wholly a confusion of ideas to suppose that the economical use of fuel is equivalent to a diminished consumption. The very contrary is the truth.... Every improvement of the engine when effected will only accelerate anew the consumption of coal. (Jevons, 1865)

Box 17.5 Defining energy efficiency

Energy efficiency may be defined as the ratio of useful outputs to energy inputs for a system. The system in question may be an individual energy conversion device (e.g. a boiler), a building, an industrial process, a firm, a sector, or an entire economy. In all cases, the measure of energy efficiency will depend upon how 'useful' is defined and how inputs and outputs are measured (Patterson, 1996). The options include:

- *thermodynamic measures*: where the outputs are defined in terms of either heat content or the capacity to perform useful work;
- *physical measures*: where the outputs are defined in physical terms, such as vehicle kilometres or tonnes of steel; or
- *economic measures*: where the outputs (and sometimes also the inputs) are defined in economic terms, such as value-added or GDP.

When outputs are measured in thermodynamic or physical terms, the term energy efficiency tends to be used, but when outputs are measured in economic terms it is more common to use the term 'energy productivity'. The inverse of both measures is termed 'energy intensity'. Physical and economic measures of energy efficiency tend to be influenced by a greater range of variables than thermodynamic measures, as do measures appropriate to wider system boundaries.

Economists are primarily interested in energy-efficiency improvements that are consistent with the best use of all economic resources. These are conventionally divided into two categories: price-induced factor substitution and technical change. Only the latter is associated with improvements in overall, or 'total factor' productivity.

Rebound effects could make non-price energy-efficiency policies less effective in reducing energy consumption than is commonly assumed, while backfire could make them wholly counterproductive. Despite this, rebound effects tend to be almost universally ignored in official analyses of potential energy savings.

Rebound effects need to be defined in relation to particular *measures* of energy efficiency (Box 17.5) as well as to a particular *time frame* (e.g. short, medium, or long term) and *system boundary* for the relevant energy consumption (e.g. firm, sector, national economy). The economy-wide effect is normally defined in relation to a national economy, but if energy-efficiency improvements lead to changes in trade patterns and international energy prices, there may also be effects in other countries. Rebound effects may also be expected to increase over time as markets, technology, and behaviour adjust. For climate policy, what matters is the long-term effect of energy-efficiency improvements on global energy consumption.

IX. PERSPECTIVES ON REBOUND EFFECTS

A number of researchers have sought to quantify rebound effects. One approach uses either quasi-experimental or econometric methods to estimate the direct rebound effect for individual energy services, such as car travel. Such studies require high-quality data sets and face a number of methodological difficulties (Sorrell and Dimitropoulos, 2007*a*, *b*). The available evidence suggests that direct rebound effects from household energy services in the OECD are generally less than 30 per cent and may decline in the future as demand saturates and incomes increase (Sorrell *et al.*, 2009). However, these effects have only been studied over limited time periods and may be larger for low-income groups, for households in developing countries, and (most importantly) for producers.

Quantitative estimates of indirect and economy-wide rebound effects may be derived from top–down energy-economic models, but there are relatively few published studies and the dominant methodological approach has a number of weaknesses (Barker, 2005; Allan *et al.*, 2006; Sorrell, 2007*b*). The available studies relate solely to energy-efficiency improvements by producers and show clearly that the economy-wide rebound effect varies widely, depending upon the sector in which the energy-efficiency improvement takes place. All these studies estimate economy-wide effects in excess of 30 per cent and several predict backfire. Moreover, these estimates do not take into account the amplifying effect of any associated improvements in the productivity of capital, labour, or materials (Saunders, 2000).

Advocates of the Jevons Paradox tend to be sceptical of attempts to quantify rebound effects, relying instead on theoretical arguments, mathematical modelling, and 'suggestive' evidence from econometric analysis and economic history (Brookes, 2000, 2004; Saunders, 2000, 2008; Alcott, 2008). These different approaches are reviewed in detail by Sorrell and Dimitropoulos (2007*c*), who conclude that these arguments should be taken seriously, despite failing to provide a convincing case in favour of the universal applicability of the Jevons Paradox. Many of these arguments focus on the source of productivity improvements and the relationship between energy consumption and economic growth—a notoriously difficult topic.[6]

The conventional wisdom (as represented by both neoclassical and 'endogenous' growth theory) is that increases in energy inputs play a relatively minor role in economic growth, largely because energy accounts for a relatively small share of total costs (Denison, 1962; Gullickson and Harper, 1987; Barro and Sala-i-Martin, 1995; Jones, 2001). Economic growth is assumed to result instead from the combination of increased capital and labour inputs, changes in the quality of those inputs (e.g. better educated workers), and increases in total factor productivity that are commonly referred to as 'technical change'. From this perspective, improvements in energy productivity are unlikely to have a significant impact on economic output, so the corresponding output and compositional effects (Box 17.4) should be relatively small. Hence, the contribution to economy-wide rebound effects from this source should also be small.

[6] The extent to which growth in economic output can be considered a *cause* of increased energy consumption, or vice versa, is very difficult to establish. It seems likely that there is a synergistic relationship between the two, with each causing the other as part of a positive feedback mechanism (Ayres and Warr, 2002*b*).

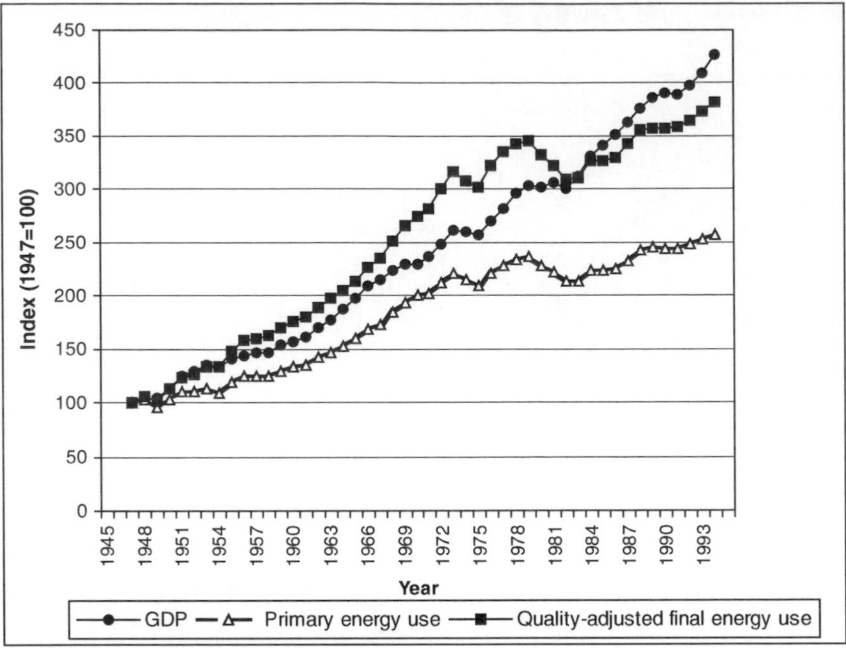

Figure 17.1. GDP and energy consumption in the United States

Note: Primary energy measured on the basis of thermal content. Final energy measured using a discrete Divisa index.
Source: Stern and Cleveland (2004).

A contrary view is provided by ecological economists, who argue that the increased availability of 'high quality' energy inputs has been the primary driver of economic growth over the last two centuries (Cleveland *et al.*, 1984; Kummel *et al.*, 1985, 2000; Hall *et al.*, 1986; Beaudreau, 1998, 2005). These authors emphasize that energy carriers differ both in their capacity to perform work (captured by the thermodynamic concept of 'exergy') and in their relative economic productivity—reflected by differences in price per kilowatt-hour (kWh) (Kaufmann, 1994; Cleveland *et al.*, 2000). So, for example, electricity represents a 'higher quality' form of energy than coal. In general, when the 'quality' of energy inputs are accounted for, aggregate measures of energy efficiency are found to be improving more slowly than is commonly supposed (Figure 17.1) (Hong, 1983; Zarnikau, 1999; Cleveland *et al.*, 2000). This conclusion is reinforced when the energy embodied in traded products is accounted for (Druckman *et al.*, 2008). An important implication of this perspective is that improvements in energy-productivity are likely to have a disproportionate impact on overall economic output. As a result, the contribution to economy-wide rebound effects from this source could be large.

Orthodox and ecological economists also make different assumptions about the scope for substituting capital or other inputs for energy (Stern, 1997). Ecological

Table 17.2. Conventional and ecological perspectives on energy, productivity, and economic growth

	Conventional view	Ecological view
Main source of productivity improvements	Exogenous or endogenous technical change	Increasing availability of high-quality energy, both directly and embodied in capital equipment and technology
Productivity of energy inputs	Proportional to share of energy in the value of output	Greater than the share of energy in the value of output
Input substitution in production	Scope for substitution indicated by substitution elasticities estimated at the sector level	Scope for substitution overestimated by substitution elasticities estimated at the sector level, since embodied energy neglected
Decoupling of energy consumption from GDP	Decoupling has already occurred in OECD economies and there is considerable scope for further decoupling	Conventional measures of energy inputs overstate the amount of decoupling. A strong link exists between *quality-adjusted* energy use and economic output and will continue to exist, both temporally and cross-sectionally
Economy-wide rebound effect	Likely to be small	Likely to be large

Sources: Cleveland *et al.* (1984); Ayres and Warr (2005).

economists emphasize how this is limited by the *indirect* energy consumption that is associated with those other inputs:

From an ecological perspective, substituting capital and/or labour for energy shifts energy use from the sector in which it is used to sectors of the economy that produce and support capital and/or labour. In other words, substituting capital and/or labour for energy increases energy use elsewhere in the economy. (Kaufmann and Azary-Lee, 1990)

These embodied energy effects are overlooked by models that estimate energy-saving potentials at the level of individual sectors and then aggregate the results to the level of the economy as a whole.

Table 17.2 compares the orthodox and ecological perspectives. The following sections provide some examples and evidence that appear to support the ecological perspective and highlight the potential implications.

X. HISTORICAL EXAMPLES OF BACKFIRE

Jevons based his arguments on the experience with steam turbines during the Industrial Revolution. He argued that the early Savory engine for pumping flood-water out of coal mines 'consumed no coal because its rate of consumption

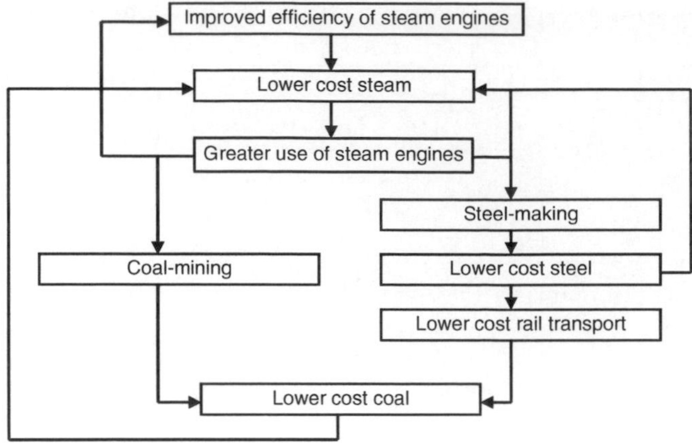

Figure 17.2. Energy efficiency, positive feedbacks, and economic growth

was too high' (Jevons, 1865). It was only with the subsequent improvements by Watt and others that steam engines became widespread in coal mines, facilitating greater production of lower-cost coal which in turn was used by comparable steam engines in a host of applications. One important application was to pump air into blast furnaces, thereby increasing the blast temperatures, reducing the quantity of coal needed to make iron, and reducing the cost of iron (Ayres, 2002). Lower-cost iron, in turn, reduced the cost of steam engines, creating a positive feedback cycle. It also contributed to the development of railways, which lowered the cost of transporting coal and iron, thereby increasing demand for both (Figure 17.2).

Rosenberg (1989) cites the comparable example of the Bessemer process for steel-making which:

> was one of the most fuel saving innovations in the history of metallurgy [but] made it possible to employ steel in a wide variety of uses that were not feasible before Bessemer, bringing with it large increases in demand. As a result, although the process sharply reduced fuel requirements per unit of output, its ultimate effect was to increase ... the demand for fuel. (Rosenberg, 1989)

The low-cost Bessemer steel initially found a large market in the production of steel rails, thereby facilitating the growth of the rail industry, and later in a much wider range of applications, including automobiles. However, the mild steel produced by the Bessemer process is a very different product to wrought iron (which has a high carbon content) and is suitable for a much wider range of applications. Hence, for both steel-making and steam engines, improvements in the energy efficiency of production processes were deeply entwined with broader developments in process and product technology.

Len Brookes (2000, 1990) cites the example of US productivity growth during the twentieth century. Energy prices were falling in real terms for much of this period, with the result that energy substituted for other factors of production, thereby *increasing* aggregate energy intensity. But these substitution effects were more than outweighed by the technological improvements facilitated by the availability of high-quality energy sources (notably electricity) which greatly improved the overall productive efficiency of the US economy. This meant that economic output increased much faster than energy consumption, owing to the greater productivity of capital and labour (Schurr *et al.*, 1960; Schurr, 1982, 1985). The net result was to produce *falling* energy intensity (as measured by the energy/GDP ratio) alongside *rising* energy consumption—as Jevons predicted.

The technological improvements that drove US productivity growth depended crucially upon the increased availability of more 'flexible' forms of energy (oil and electricity) at relatively low costs. These facilitated revolutionary changes in industrial processes, consumer products, and methods of industrial organization—for example, in transforming the sequence, layout, and efficiency of industrial production through the introduction of electric motors (Schurr, 1982). Brookes (2000) uses these observations argue that: (*i*) most improvements in energy productivity are associated with *proportionally greater* improvements in total factor productivity; (*ii*) these increase economic output, leading to a corresponding increase in demand for all inputs, including energy; and (*iii*) the resulting increase in demand for energy inputs more than offsets the reduced demand for energy per unit of output, with the result that aggregate energy productivity improves but energy consumption increases. Polimeni (2008) provides econometric evidence for this process for a number of countries and time periods.

These historical examples relate to energy-efficiency improvements in the early stages of development of energy-intensive process technologies (i.e. steam turbines, Bessemer process, electric motors) that are producing goods that have the potential for widespread use in multiple applications. The same consequences may not follow for energy-efficiency improvements in mature and/or non-energy-intensive process technologies that are producing goods that have a relatively narrow range of applications, or for energy-efficiency improvements in consumer technologies. Also, Brookes's example applies primarily to the causal effect of shifts to higher-quality energy carriers rather than other factors that affect aggregate energy productivity. Hence, it would be inappropriate to generalize from these examples to all types of energy-efficiency improvement. Nevertheless, these examples do suggest that the Jevons Paradox may hold in some important instances.

XI. EMPIRICAL EVIDENCE FOR BACKFIRE

Both Brookes and contemporary ecological economists claim that 'it is energy that drives modern economic systems rather than such systems creating a demand for energy' (Brookes, 1984). Some suggestive evidence in support of this claim may be derived from econometric studies and models of economic growth.

Kaufmann (1992, 2004) uses econometric analysis to argue that historical reductions in energy/GDP ratios owe more to shifts towards 'high-quality' fuels than to technological improvements in energy efficiency. He shows how these, together with changes in the proportion of household income spent on fuel, price-induced factor substitution, and a shift towards a service-based economy, explain most of the reduction in US energy intensity since 1929. Once this is controlled for, Kaufmann finds no statistically significant evidence for the 'energy saving technical change'[7] that is traditionally assumed in energy-economic models:

> Technical change has reduced the amount of energy (as measured in heat units) used to produce a unit of output. But characterizing that technical change as 'energy-saving' is misleading. Over the last 40 years, technical change has reduced the amount of energy used to produce a unit of output by developing new techniques for using oil, natural gas and primary electricity in place of coal. (Kaufmann, 1992)

Kaufmann's results also suggest that the *indirect* energy consumption associated with labour and capital inputs constituted a significant portion of the direct energy savings from energy-efficiency improvements over this period. Similarly, in a study of the US forest products industry, Kaufmann and Azary-Lee (1990) estimate that the indirect energy consumption offset between 18 and 83 per cent of the direct energy savings from input substitution.

Historical experience also provides little support for the claim that increases in income will lead to declining energy consumption (Stern, 2004; Stern and Cleveland, 2004; Richmond and Kaufmann, 2006). While the income elasticity of aggregate energy consumption may be both declining and less than one in OECD countries, there is no evidence that it is negative (or is soon to become negative). Again, neglect of changes in fuel mix and energy prices, together with the energy embodied in traded goods, may have led earlier studies to draw misleading conclusions regarding the extent to which energy consumption either has been or could be decoupled from GDP growth (Kaufmann, 2004). This includes, for example, Judson *et al.* (1999) whose results underpinned the estimates of abatement costs in the Stern Review (Anderson, 2006).

Ecological economists have also developed alternatives to conventional models of economic growth which depart from the traditional assumption that the productivity of each input is proportional to the share of that input in the value of output (Kummel, 1982, 1989; Kummel *et al.*, 1985, 2000, 2002; Beaudreau, 1995, 1998, 2005; Ayres, 1998; Ayres and Warr, 2002*a*, 2005, 2006; Ayres and van den Bergh, 2005). In contrast to orthodox theory, these models reproduce

[7] Improvements in total factor productivity should reduce the use of all inputs per unit of economic output. Hence, the amount of energy required to produce a unit of output should reduce over time. If technical change has an energy-saving bias, the degree of reduction should exceed that of other inputs. Energy-saving change is related to but not the same as the 'autonomous energy-efficiency index' (AEEI) which is a measure of the rate of growth of energy productivity, holding relative input prices constant (Sanstad *et al.*, 2006; Sorrell and Dimitropoulos, 2007*c*). The AEEI is a standard parameter in top–down energy-economic modelling, although technical change is increasingly being made endogenous (Gillingham *et al.*, 2008).

historical trends in economic growth extremely well, without attributing any role to technical change.[8] The alternative models find the marginal productivity of energy inputs to be around ten times larger than their cost share, implying that improvements in energy productivity could have a dramatic effect on output growth and therefore on economy-wide energy consumption.[9]

These studies challenge conventional theory and raise concerns about the potential for decoupling energy consumption from economic growth. However, the empirical evidence in support of this perspective remains patchy, inconsistent, and in some cases flawed (Sorrell and Dimitropoulos, 2007*c*). For example, the different variants of 'ecological growth models' rely upon an unusual and oddly behaved production function, provide results that are difficult to reconcile with each other, and appear vulnerable to bias from a number of sources (Sorrell and Dimitropoulos, 2007*c*). Similarly, life-cycle studies of building designs suggest that substantial reductions in energy consumption are achievable with only small increases in embodied energy (Feist, 1996; Winther and Hestnes, 1999). Hence, as with the historical example cited above, it would be inappropriate to draw general conclusions from this limited empirical basis—especially when evidence from other sources indicates that the size of the rebound effect varies with the nature and location of the energy-efficiency improvement.

A bridge between the orthodox and ecological perspectives could potentially be provided by Toman and Jemelkova's (2003) observation that increased energy inputs may frequently *enhance* the productivity of capital and labour:[10]

[8] Traditional neoclassical growth models estimate 'technical change' as the residual growth in output that is not explained by the growth of inputs. Early growth models attributed as much as 70 per cent of the growth in output to technical change, but later studies have shown how the proportion of growth that is attributed to technical change depends upon how the inputs are measured (Jorgenson and Griliches, 1967). In neoclassical growth models, technical change is typically represented by a simple time trend. Modern theories of economic growth seek to make the source and direction of technical change endogenous.

[9] Of particular interest is Ayres and Warr (2005), which combines historical data on the 'exergy' content of fuel inputs and second-law thermodynamic conversion efficiencies to develop a time series of the exergy output of conversion devices (useful work) in the US economy over the past century. They show that the useful work obtained from fuel resources has grown much faster than the consumption of fuels themselves, owing to substantial improvements in thermodynamic conversion efficiencies. By including useful work in their production function, rather than primary energy, Ayres and Warr (2005) obtain an extremely good fit to US GDP trends over the past century, thereby eliminating the need for a multiplier for technical change. The implication is that improvements in thermodynamic conversion efficiency provide a quantifiable surrogate for all forms of technical change that contribute to economic growth.

[10] Focusing in particular on households in developing countries, Toman and Jemolkova (2003) propose a number of ways in which this could occur. For example, cheaper and better lighting could allow greater flexibility in time allocation throughout the day and evening and enhance the productivity of education efforts. The increased availability of electricity could promote access to safe drinking water (e.g. in deeper wells), allow the refrigeration of food and medicine, and thereby improve both the health of workers and their economic productivity. Similarly, the increased availability of low-cost transport fuels could interact with investment in transport infrastructure to increase the geographic size, scale, and efficiency of markets.

when the supply of energy services is increased, there is not just more energy to be used by each skilled worker or machine; the productivity with which every unit of energy is used also rises. If all inputs to final production are increased in some proportion, final output would grow in greater proportion because of the effect on non-energy inputs. (Toman and Jemelkova, 2003)

It is commonly assumed that rebound effects must be small because the share of energy in total costs is small. But if energy efficiency improvements are associated with improvements in the productivity of other inputs, this need not necessarily be the case. Hence, the relevant empirical question is how frequently this occurs.

XII. IMPLICATIONS OF REBOUND EFFECTS

The possibility of large rebound effects has been dismissed by a number of leading energy analysts (Lovins, 1988, 1998; Howarth, 1997; Laitner, 2000; Schipper and Grubb, 2000) and many of the relevant mechanisms are poorly captured by standard models. But the evidence reviewed above suggests that there are grounds for taking this possibility seriously—at least for some types of energy efficiency improvement. Unfortunately, the persistent neglect of this topic has left us with insufficient understanding of the conditions under which rebound effects are more or less likely to be large.

The examples cited above suggest that backfire may be more likely to occur following improvements in the energy efficiency of 'general purpose technologies' (GPTs) such as steam turbines and computers, particularly when these are used by producers and when the improvements occur at an early stage of development and diffusion (Lipsey *et al.*, 2005).[11] In contrast, backfire may be less likely to occur following investment in 'dedicated energy-saving technologies', such as thermal insulation, particularly when these are used by consumers or when they play a subsidiary role in economic production. The implication is that non-price energy-efficiency policies should focus on encouraging the latter rather than the former. However, these categories are poorly defined, the boundaries between them are blurred, and GPTs seem likely to account for a significant portion of total energy consumption.

In principle, carbon taxes and emissions trading should mitigate rebound effects by ensuring that the cost of energy services remains relatively constant, while energy efficiency improves. To prevent carbon emissions from increasing, carbon prices will need to increase at a rate sufficient to accommodate

[11] According to Lipsey *et al.* (2005), GPTs have a wide scope for improvement and elaboration, are applicable across a broad range of uses, have potential for use in a wide variety of products and processes, and have strong complementarities with existing or potential new technologies. Steam engines provide a paradigmatic illustration of a GPT in the nineteenth century, while electric motors provide a comparable illustration for the early twentieth century. The former was used by Jevons to support the case for backfire, while the latter formed a key component of the US productivity improvements cited by Brookes.

both income growth and rebound effects, and will need to increase faster if emissions are to be reduced (Birol and Keppler, 2000). Cap-and-trade schemes are particularly attractive, since they focus directly on the relevant environmental goal (carbon emissions) rather than on one of the factors contributing to that goal (energy efficiency). With effective enforcement and mechanisms to prevent 'carbon leakage', such schemes should guarantee that the desired environmental outcome is achieved.

Orthodox analysis, as exemplified by the Stern Review (2007), assumes that rebound effects are small, mitigation is relatively cheap, and decoupling is achievable. In contrast, the perspective presented above suggests that rebound effects are large, mitigation is relatively expensive, and decoupling is difficult. While the available evidence is far from sufficient to demonstrate that this is the case, it does highlight some blind spots within orthodox theory. Since these are built into the assumptions and design of modelling tools, continued reliance on such tools may lead to falsely reassuring results.

XIII. SUMMARY

Hidden costs and rebound effects are of critical importance to future climate policy. If either or both are large, the economic potential for energy savings will be overestimated and the cost of meeting emissions targets will be underestimated. Since both are poorly captured by conventional modelling tools, this is a serious risk.

Fortunately, hidden costs can be partially addressed through the use of non-price policies such as labelling schemes, while rebound effects can be insured against through the use of carbon taxes or cap-and-trade schemes. This suggests a complementary policy mix that is consistent with current assumptions and which has some justification through *ex post* policy evaluations. Unfortunately, the majority of research continues to neglect these issues, preferring to estimate energy-saving potentials *ex ante* rather than evaluating them *ex post*. This contributes to continued uncertainty about the size of both hidden costs and rebound effects, which in turn fuels an unproductive and polarized debate.

While both issues are difficult to study empirically, our understanding of hidden costs is significantly better than our understanding of rebound effects. Also, it is not obvious that rebound effects are any more difficult to study than other relevant and well-researched issues, such as price-induced technical change. The continued neglect of rebound effects may result instead from the challenge they pose to conventional assumptions and/or their uncomfortable policy implications. Something is surely amiss when the most in-depth and influential studies (e.g. those by Stern, 2007; Garnaut, 2008*c*; and the IPCC, 2007*d*, 2008, overlook this important topic altogether. Too much is at stake for this to continue.

Part IV

National and International Instruments

18

Carbon Taxes, Emissions Trading, and Hybrid Schemes

*Cameron Hepburn**

I. INTRODUCTION

The scale and complexity of the climate challenge underlines the need for careful regulatory responses at the national and international level. In the United Kingdom, however, government has reacted with a proliferation of climate-change policies, targets, direct subsidies, market-based support, levies, pricing schemes, and various trading schemes. Some of these policies have reduced emissions, but others have delivered little and have potentially been counterproductive. Experience has been considerably less than perfect in many other countries as well.

One striking feature of current climate policy responses is that they are strongly guided by political factors, and only weakly guided by basic insights of economic theory which provide guidance on difficult questions of instrument choice—including theory on prices and quantities discussed in this chapter. Indeed, while great progress has been made over recent decades on the theory of environmental and climate-change economics, there is much more distance to travel on the practical application of economic theory to climate policy design. The time for this application is now ripe, because efficiency considerations will become more important as more ambitious climate targets are contemplated (Aidt and Dutta, 2004). Furthermore, climate policy is developing rapidly in various key regions, with new emissions trading schemes in action or in the process of passing through national legislatures. The core objective of climate policy must be to internalize the social cost of carbon in firms' decisions, such that firms profit when they adopt cleaner modes of production.

In this context, this chapter reviews the literature on the choice between carbon taxes (or 'price instruments') and cap-and-trade schemes (or 'quantity instruments'). It focuses narrowly on the use of instruments for reducing emissions from industry and energy, rather than on policies for, say, deforestation

* Smith School of Enterprise and the Environment, University of Oxford, and New College, Oxford.

This chapter builds upon research for the Stern Review on the Economics of Climate Change, published as Hepburn (2006).

(see Andersson *et al.*, ch. 15) or domestic energy efficiency (Sorrell, Ch. 17).[1] Section II provides a very brief and highly stylized outline of the regulatory process to provide context for the question of interest here, namely the choice of instrument to achieve a given climate target. Section III considers the broad choice between economic instruments and command-and-control regulation, and section IV reviews the basic concepts of price and quantity instruments, including their underlying duality. Section V provides a review of canonical economic theory on instrument choice, in addition to surveying some more recent results. The issues addressed are: efficiency under uncertainty (section V(i)), commitment, credibility, and flexibility (V(ii)), implementation (V(iii)), international issues (V(iv)), and political economy (V(v)). This is far from an exhaustive list—market structure is notable by its omission[2]—but represents some of the more important considerations. Section VI provides a direct and explicit application to climate policy. Section VII concludes.

II. THE REGULATORY PROCESS: OBJECTIVES, TARGETS, AND INSTRUMENTS

This chapter focuses upon the choice of policy *instrument* (e.g. a carbon tax) to achieve a particular *target* (e.g. limiting emissions of carbon dioxide to a fixed amount). The target has, with any luck, been carefully designed to meet an overarching policy *objective* (e.g. preventing dangerous climate change).[3] This chapter does not address the question of appropriate climate policy objectives[4] nor the justification for government intervention. Nor does it address the design of targets. These questions are clearly important—choosing the correct instrument is pointless if the target itself is ill-advised. For instance, suppose an accepted policy objective is to improve the performance of children at mathematics. A corresponding target might be expressed in terms of results achieved in mathematics exams. Given this target, instruments might then be proposed to provide schools with the incentives to achieve mathematics results targets—a 'price' might be put on good maths performance, or schools might be required to ensure that performance never falls below some specified quantity, with specified penalties for failure. Now, while the objective of improved mathematics competency is laudable (and would probably pass cost–benefit analysis at current levels of mathematical literacy),

[1] The focus is further narrowed to the economics of climate mitigation, rather than mechanisms to raise finance to support such mitigation (Hepburn, Ch. 20).

[2] The industrial economics literature deals with the choice between price and quantity instruments in the regulation of natural monopolies (e.g. Chen, 1990; De Fraja and Iossa, 1998). There, price-cap regulation has been preferred to rate-of-return regulation. While regulation of monopoly and market power is extremely important, it is not the focus of this chapter.

[3] The stylized sequence of policy-making implied here—define objectives, set targets, choose instruments—does not, of course, necessarily reflect practice. It may be easier to start with a focused discussion on the concrete measures to be adopted, before attempting to agree abstract objectives, even though the former conceptually follows the latter.

[4] See Hepburn and Stern (Ch. 3).

many people question the wisdom of setting exam performance targets. Without close auditing, exam targets may simply generate incentives to mark students leniently. Setting targets frequently leads to gaming and unintended outcomes,[5] and results are likely to be unsatisfactory when targets do not map closely with the desired objective. Furthermore, the imposition of explicit incentives can crowd out intrinsic incentives that are already present.[6] Many professionals in the health and education sectors, for instance, are already motivated by the knowledge that their work helps other people. Regulation creating explicit prices—such as the tax and trading schemes beloved by economists—may crowd out such motivation.[7] Softer policy interventions that account for and address cultural and institutional factors may be more appropriate.

As such, policy analysis requires assessing the merits of the stated objectives (which may differ from the actual objectives) as well as the merits of the targets, before the appropriate instrument can be properly determined. So, under the (non-trivial) assumption that the objectives and targets have been sensibly defined, we proceed to examine the choice between economic instruments[8] and traditional command-and-control regulation, before comparing price and quantity instruments in section IV.

III. ECONOMIC VERSUS COMMAND-AND-CONTROL INSTRUMENTS

Economic instruments provide an explicit price signal to regulated firms and individuals. They include price-based instruments (e.g. taxes and subsidies) where the price is set directly, and quantity-based instruments (e.g. cap-and-trade schemes) where the price emerges indirectly from trades in scarce permits or allowances. A key feature of economic instruments is that they exploit the capability of markets to aggregate information.

Economic instruments are especially useful when: (i) the appropriate response varies between different regulated firms; and (ii) there are information problems so the regulator does not have the necessary knowledge about firms' costs. In climate policy, for example, government has highly imperfect information about the costs of reducing greenhouse-gas emissions, and it is likely that some sectors can reduce emissions much more cheaply than others. Economic instruments are ideal under these circumstances.

[5] For instance, a UK target that patients should be able to see a medical general practitioner (GP) within 2 days appears to have resulted in GPs refusing to accept appointments more than 2 days in advance (Bevan and Hood, 2006). See also Bird *et al.* (2005).

[6] On general questions of school autonomy in the Finnish and British cases, see Webb *et al.* (1998).

[7] See Frey and Jegen (2001). The early theoretical debate came to prominence with Titmuss (1971) and Arrow (1972).

[8] These are also described as 'market-based instruments', because the government sets one variable (e.g. price) and leaves it to the market to reveal the other (e.g. quantity).

In contrast, command-and-control regulation requires firms or individuals to comply with specific standards, such as technology or performance standards. Command-and-control regulation should be preferred when the regulator has good quality information, when the risk of government failure is low, and when the desired objective is best achieved by imposing similar requirements upon different firms and individuals. For instance, if the optimal level of a certain pollutant is unequivocally zero, then the appropriate instrument is simply a ban—there is little point in constructing a sophisticated trading scheme or tax.

IV. PRICE VERSUS QUANTITY INSTRUMENTS

(i) Overview: The Duality of Prices and Quantities

Economists are familiar with the simple but essential symmetry between prices and quantities. Implementing a quantity constraint, whether by simple command-and-control regulation or by creation of a market, always imposes a corresponding (implicit) price.[9] If the regulated quantity is allocated and the allowances are traded, then under idealized conditions, the resulting allowance price will equal the optimum level of the price instrument (e.g. a tax). A more liberal allowance allocation is equivalent to setting a lower tax, and vice versa. As such, under idealized conditions, there is a one-to-one correspondence between price and quantity instruments.

(ii) Quantities

The most common form of regulation in many policy settings is command-and-control regulation by quantities. This includes quotas, targets, or specific commands, such as a regulation banning an activity (where the quantity cap is zero). Food standards specify maximum (or minimum) quantities of certain chemical compounds. The Civil Aviation Authority imposes minimum air-safety standards. Many environmental regulations specify upper limits (quantities) on pollution levels in effluent. Speed limits are another form of quantity regulation. More complicated quantity instruments may be a function of other measurable variables to be realized in the future.[10]

[9] This is true whether or not the price is directly revealed by a market that facilitates trading of the quantities. Even if the price is not directly revealed, there is a 'shadow' price. In the absence of a market these shadow prices may differ between regulated subjects according to their costs of compliance.

[10] Helfand (1991) provides an analysis of the economics of different types of quantity instruments in the context of different pollution standards. There is also a literature on *targets* that are expressed as a function of other variables to be realized in the future: see Aldy and Frankel (2004), McKitrick (2005), and Sue Wing *et al.* (2006) on the topic of emissions intensity targets. But Weitzman (1974) noted presciently that a 'contingency message', as he called it, is a 'complicated, specialized contract which is expensive to draw up and hard to understand'.

Some forms of quantity regulation occur by default. For instance, when public services are free at the point of use—as in the case of most roads and much health care—demand will often exceed supply, with the result that services are rationed. This rationing may be quite deliberate. According to Mattke (2000), limits on the number of hospital beds per specialty in the German regions are designed to create capacity constraints which force physicians to apply resources to patients with the greatest need.[11]

For some policy issues, the appropriate quantity may vary greatly between different individuals and/or firms—it is inefficient to impose the same quantity on all firms. However, the information required to determine the optimum distribution of quantities between firms is often unavailable. Under such conditions, as noted above, economic instruments are preferred, and it would make sense for the government to provide (or sell) *tradable* allowances that individuals or firms can exchange with one another, thus ensuring that the allowances end up with those who value them most highly. Indeed, if there are large differences in valuations between individuals, trade in the allowances is likely to occur, if not legally, then on a black market.[12] Creating a legal scheme involves at least three elements: (i) an aggregate quantity is fixed; (ii) allowances are allocated between individuals and firms, potentially through auctioning; and (iii) a mechanism is established for enforcing compliance with the scheme.[13]

(iii) Prices

Price schemes can also operate to ensure the efficient allocation of activity between firms, and some policy objectives are achieved through price instruments. For instance, rather than set a total quantity of cigarettes that can be consumed in Britain in a given year, the government employs the more indirect approach of taxing tobacco, increasing the price of cigarette consumption, and reducing the quantity consumed. Similarly, objectives in the labour market—such as the numbers of teachers, psychologists, nurses, etc.—are generally achieved by price instruments. These days, when more soldiers are needed, military wages are increased, rather than citizens being compulsorily conscripted.

When conditions are uncertain—as they always are—price instruments do not guarantee that a particular quantity target will be achieved. Equivalently the use of a quantity instrument will not guarantee that a particular price target will be achieved. However, as we shall see, simply because a target is expressed as a price

[11] There is some evidence that rationing may improve resource allocation. For instance, Selker *et al.* (1987) found that reducing the number of coronary care units in New England reduced admittances to the units, but did not increase mortality. However, according to Mattke (2000), Cuyler and Meads (1992) report in the United Kindom that implicit rationing also imposes costs by way of increased delay in treatment, and results in medical decisions based on the availability of resources rather than on clinical judgment.

[12] See Kay (2004) for some (unattributed) estimates of the price of British taxi licences.

[13] For a review of compliance issues, see Heyes (1998).

(quantity) does not mean that a price (quantity) instrument has to be employed to achieve it.

(iv) Hybrid Instruments

As Weitzman (1974) noted, there is 'no good *a priori* reason for limiting attention to just [prices and quantities]'. There is a wide range of more complicated instruments, including a schedule of prices, or a 'kinked' function by way of a two-tiered price system. The only reason for the focus on pure price and quantity instruments is their simplicity, and for some policy problems, the benefits of simplicity may be outweighed by the costs of inefficiency.

A hybrid instrument—a tailored combination of price and quantity instruments—is a small step up in complexity.[14] The most important form is a trading scheme with a price ceiling (also known as a 'safety valve') and/or price floor. Ceilings and floors can be implemented in several different ways. For instance, in the most direct form, the government could implement a price ceiling by committing to sell allowances at the ceiling price, and a price floor can be implemented by a commitment to buy allowances at the floor price. Alternatively, a price floor can also be established through a carbon tax (with or without a rebate for payments made for tradable allowances), which is politically more palatable for the public-sector finances, as it eliminates the need for funds to be available to buy back allowances should the price fall.

Furthermore, prices might be 'managed' without imposing absolute ceilings and floors. Hepburn *et al.* (2006*b*) show that setting a reserve price in allowance auctions can have the effect of establishing a soft price floor, provided a sufficiently large proportion of the allowances are auctioned at regular intervals.

Another form of hybrid scheme is the 'allowance reserve' proposal of Murray *et al.* (2009), in which a limited reserve of allowances, defined *ex ante*, would be released on to the market if prices exceeded a certain trigger point. This is effectively a limited ceiling price.

Some schemes contain an indirect form of ceiling price. In any tradable allowance scheme, there will be a penalty for non-compliance. Often the penalty is set proportional to the difference between actual performance and target. If payment of the penalty is an *alternative* to compliance, the penalty is effectively a price ceiling in a hybrid scheme (Jacoby and Ellerman, 2004). In contrast, if payment of the penalty does not amount to compliance—and the firm is still

[14] Hybrid instruments should be distinguished from the use of multiple instruments for the one problem (see section IV(v)). Hybrid instruments have recently generated a great deal of interest in the climate-change context, see, for example, Pizer (1997, 2002), Aldy *et al.* (2001), McKibbin and Wilcoxen (2002, 2004), and Jacoby and Ellerman (2004). The classic paper is Roberts and Spence (1976).

obliged to comply as soon as possible—then the scheme is not equivalent to a conventional hybrid scheme. For instance, although the European emissions trading scheme imposes penalties for non-compliance for Phases I and II of €40/tCO_2 and €100/tCO_2 respectively, excess emissions must also be offset in the following compliance period (European Commission, 2003). In contrast, the United Kingdom Renewables Obligation scheme is arguably a hybrid scheme, because firms can comply by simply paying the buy-out price.[15]

(v) Multiple Instruments

Regulations are often directed at internalizing externalities, and the simple theory of externalities indicates that only one instrument is needed to internalize one externality. Nevertheless, policies often involve multiple instruments, such as command-and-control regulation, subsidies, taxes, trading schemes, negotiated agreements, and information campaigns. In some instances, such as when there are multiple market failures, a 'package' of policy measures can make sense. However, in many instances, the use of multiple instruments to address a single problem reflects an *ad hoc* policy-accretion process, driven by the multiplicity of national institutions (Helm, 2005). Multiple instruments may also reflect the temptation of politicians to 'fix everything'—both price and quantity—even when policy is generally best served by fixing one and letting the market determine the other. This multiplicity of instruments is problematic when they are inconsistent with each other, and can result in perverse consequences if the interactions between different policies are not carefully considered. This should be contrasted with a carefully tailored hybrid scheme.

V. INSTRUMENT COMPARISON

(i) Efficiency Under Uncertainty

Under uncertainty, the duality of price and quantity instruments (see section III(i)) diverges.[16] In his classic paper, Weitzman (1974) demonstrated that when marginal costs of supplying a good are uncertain, using a price instrument is more (less) efficient than a quantity instrument when the marginal benefits of that good are relatively flat (steep) compared with the marginal costs.[17] As a rough heuristic,

[15] This scheme is unusual for another reason: revenues from the price ceiling (the buy-out price) are recycled to those in compliance, thus creating the possibility that the market price can rise above the price ceiling.

[16] Poole (1970) provides an early treatment of this divergence under uncertainty in the monetary policy context.

[17] Weitzman (1974) employs linear local approximations to the marginal cost and benefit functions. Most presentations follow Adar and Griffin (1976), who simply assume that the marginal cost and

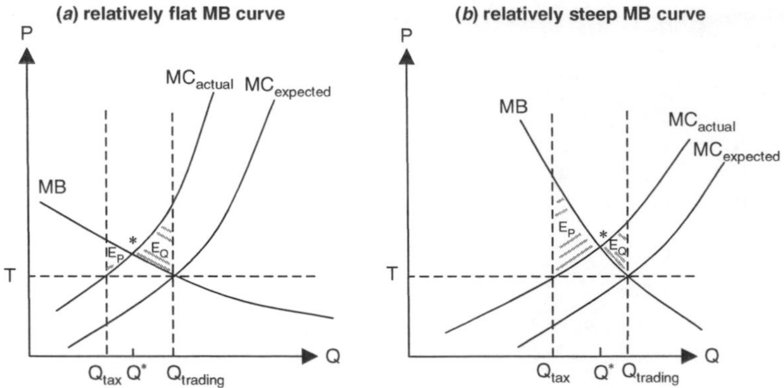

Figure 18.1. Simple illustration of the Weitzman (1974) result

this is because the instrument is intended to internalize the marginal benefit curve. A price instrument is horizontal (on the P–Q plane), so should be employed when the marginal benefit curve is relatively flat, while a quantity instrument is vertical and should be used when the marginal benefit curve is relatively steep. Figure 18.1 provides an illustration where the actual marginal costs of supplying the good are higher than originally expected. Here, the price instrument (tax, T), generates under-provision of the good ($Q_{\text{tax}} < Q^*$) leading to efficiency loss E_P, while the quantity instrument (trading scheme with cap Q_{trading}) leads to over-provision of the good ($Q_{\text{trading}} > Q^*$) with efficiency loss E_Q. As Figure 18.1 shows, the price instrument is preferable to the quantity instrument ($E_P < E_Q$) when the marginal benefit curve is relatively flat, and vice versa.

To illustrate, suppose the relevant good is the provision of prompt medical treatment. Suppose that reducing delay in medical treatment is costly, and that patients benefit from more rapid treatment. Suppose the marginal cost of reducing delay is uncertain, but is expected to increase quickly as delay is reduced (in the limit, the cost of treatment with zero delay is infinite). Suppose the marginal benefit of reducing delay is relatively constant—the medical condition is such that, without treatment, the patient's health will deteriorate gradually. In such circumstances, the Weitzman (1974) framework indicates that a price instrument is efficient—for this particular medical condition, the hospital should be paid a constant reward for each day of delay avoided (or have to pay a constant penalty for delay). In contrast, if the marginal benefit of reducing delay falls very quickly (perhaps because after a threshold delay, d, the patient will die), then the hospital should face a quantity instrument of the form 'no patient shall face a delay of more than d days', with a strict penalty attached for failure.

More pertinently, in the case of climate change, suppose the marginal cost of reducing emissions increases quickly as we move from eliminating the cheap, 'low

benefit functions are linear. See also Rose-Ackerman (1973), Fishelson (1976), and Roberts and Spence (1976).

hanging fruit' on to more difficult sources of emissions (e.g. aviation transport). Suppose also that, because damages from climate change are a function of the *stock* of greenhouse gases in the atmosphere, they are only a weak function of the *flow* of emissions over short periods (e.g. five years),[18] so that the marginal benefit from abatement is relatively flat.[19] In such circumstances, a price instrument—a carbon tax—is the appropriate instrument to use (Hoel and Karp, 2001, 2002; Pizer, 2002). In contrast, if instead we are on the brink of a tipping point, such that emissions now do substantially less damage than emissions in five years' time, then an immediate quantity restriction upon global emissions would be optimal.[20]

Note in both cases that it is not the *level* of the marginal cost curve that matters, but its relative *slope*.[21] It could be, for instance, that climate change is extremely dangerous in a manner that implies a high (but constant) marginal damage curve. A price instrument is still appropriate—the price should just be extremely high.[22]

Two further aspects of efficiency under uncertainty are relevant. First, Weitzman (1974) points out, and Stavins (1996) reminds us, that uncertainty in the marginal benefit function is also relevant if it is correlated with marginal costs. Where the correlation is positive (negative), quantities (prices) are relatively more efficient. Second, Baldursson and von der Fehr (2004) show that if regulation is being imposed upon risk-averse firms, prices may be more efficient than tradable allowances (*ceteris paribus*). This is because quantity regulation exposes firms to volatile allowance prices, which is avoided by direct price regulation.[23] Risk aversion encourages a net buyer of allowances to invest in technology that will reduce her need to buy allowances. Conversely, risk aversion leads a net seller to under-invest in such technology. The net effect is to reduce the trade in allowances, and thereby reduce the efficiency of the instrument relative to price regulation.

[18] The assumption that the marginal damage curve is flat is less valid over longer timeframes. Hoel and Karp (2002) find that the preference for quotas increases as the relevant time horizon of policy is increased.

[19] This is not to say that the damages from climate change are not high—they could be extremely high—only that they do not change rapidly as a function of additional emissions.

[20] Pizer (2002) finds that 'when damages rise from 1% to 9% as the mean global temperature rises from 3 to 4 degrees above historic levels, this is sufficient to encourage the use of quantity-based regulations over a 50-year policy horizon'.

[21] Weitzman (1974) examines the curvature of the cost and benefit functions, and employs local linear approximations to the marginal cost and benefit functions for simplicity. On the use of these approximations, see Malcomson (1978).

[22] The literature is not always clear here. For instance, McKibbin and Wilcoxen (2003) write that the 'trouble with a quantity-based approach like the Kyoto Protocol... is that it can be justified only under the most pessimistic assumptions about the dangers of climate change (a *steep* marginal benefit curve for abating emissions), or under the most optimistic assumptions about the cost of reducing emissions (a *flat* marginal cost curve)'. Pessimism about climate change certainly implies a high benefit of abatement curve—damages will be large—and possibly also a high marginal benefit curve—damages will rise quickly as we emit more greenhouse gases, but pessimism does not necessarily imply a *steep* marginal benefit curve.

[23] Of course, this depends upon the rule for tax adjustment—in practice taxes are adjusted in budgets which are an inherently political process, bringing its own uncertainties. Even if price regulation is credible, the flip side is that fixing prices creates quantity uncertainty.

In the case of climate change, price risk appears to reduce investment in long-term R&D into abatement technologies. Innovating firms already bear substantial technology development risk, and the addition of price risk reduces their incentive to innovate. This price risk might be broken down into three components: (i) political risk; (ii) risk of (optimal) policy adjustments as a result of new climate science; and (iii) market risks, such as competitors producing superior abatement technology. The government should probably bear political risk, and is possibly also in a better position to bear the climate science risk. Firms should probably bear the market risk. Nevertheless, given the public-goods nature of R&D, such innovations are probably already undersupplied. If the government shouldered all three risks by fixing carbon prices, this might be viewed as an implicit (second-best) subsidy to internalize the external benefits of innovation. Yet, in contrast, in the current EU emissions trading scheme, all three risks are arguably borne by firms, rather than governments.

(ii) Commitment, Credibility, and Flexibility

In many areas of public policy, uncertainties inevitably imply that policy will need to be adjusted over time in response to new technologies, new scientific information, and changed political realities. The discretion to adjust policy is therefore valuable. However, discretionary policy can also result in the following three problems:

(i) *The ratchet effect.* When firms have market power and respond strategically to regulation, discretion results in an incentive for firms to distort decisions to influence future regulation.[24] For instance, failure to meet a target arguably signals to the regulator that compliance is costly, thereby lending support for the negotiation of a more lenient target in the following period. In contrast, over-compliance signals that future targets should be tighter. These dynamic incentive problems are exacerbated if individual firms have the incentive to underperform now to gain a higher allowance allocation later.[25] In contrast, price instruments do not suffer from this problem.

(ii) *Credibility problems.* When the returns from irreversible investment depend upon future policy, and when the government faces different incentives *ex post* investment to those *ex ante*, the discretion to adjust policy creates a 'hold-up' problem.[26] For instance, energy regulators explicitly faces at least three competing objectives (energy prices, security of supply, and climate change), and once (irreversible) investment in low-carbon

[24] The basic ratchet effect is described by Freixas *et al.* (1985).

[25] This problem does not arise if allowances are auctioned, or grandfathered once and for all.

[26] See Kydland and Prescott (1977), Biglaiser *et al.* (1995), Kennedy and Laplante (1999), Karp and Zhang (2001), Moledina *et al.* (2003), Helm *et al.* (2004), Requate (2005), and Tarui and Polasky (2005*a*,*b*).

technology has occurred, the regulator has an incentive to reduce the pay-off for emission reductions so as to increase the pay-off for achieving the other objectives.

(iii) *Inappropriate risk allocation*. Discretion imposes the risk on the private sector that policy will be adjusted (whether optimally or not). It may not be appropriate for the private sector to bear policy risk, as discussed above. In either case, the required rate of return on investments reliant on a long-term revenue stream will be increased to reflect the additional policy risks.[27] The benefits of flexibility must therefore be balanced against the need to provide a fixed long-term policy regime (and price signal) to encourage investment. Risks must be allocated somewhere, so the question is where they are efficiently allocated. Efficiency probably requires the private sector to bear the risk of innovations by competitors. However, the government should probably bear policy risks arising from shifts in the political domain.

Obviously credibly committing to future policy solves all three problems—the distortion in investment decisions by the ratchet effect, the hold-up problem, and it also reduces the required rate of return—but it also eliminates the flexibility to adjust policy as new information emerges. Determining the optimal trade-off between commitment and discretion involves balancing the benefits of flexibility with the three costs outlined above.

The time horizon of committed policy should be short enough to be credible—a supposed 'commitment' which ignores the benefits of flexibility will not credible—and also to allow flexibility for policy-makers to respond to changes, and long enough to provide clear signals to the private sector and to address the other issues discussed above. In some policy areas, including climate policy, where the longest feasible commitment period may be too short to provide adequate incentives for long-term investment, the problem is finding a credible signal of future policy direction to firms. Credible signals are difficult to find, however, and by their very nature, they tend to be costly.

(iii) Implementation

Although there are differences in the implementation of price and quantity instruments, there is also a wide range of shared considerations. To start, an examination of the costs and benefits of the policies is required to determine the appropriate tax rate or number of allowances,[28] and a key insight is that 'generally speaking it is neither easier nor harder to name the right prices than the right quantities because in principle exactly the *same* information is needed to correctly specify either' (Weitzman, 1974). Both price and quantity instruments require detailed

[27] See Helm *et al.* (2003) and Helm and Hepburn (2005).

[28] Although as Helm (2005) notes, it is remarkable that the use of cost–benefit analysis still appears to be the exception rather than the rule. See also Pearce (1998).

regulation for their implementation. Both require careful attention to the incentives for compliance, including the specification of penalties for non-compliance and a monitoring and enforcement regime.[29] Just as a tradable allowance scheme requires the careful definition of the property right, so, too, the formal incidence of a tax must be clearly specified.

Some command-and-control regulation may be cheaper to implement and enforce than market-based instruments. For instance, although technology standards are (almost inevitably) less efficient than technology-neutral regulation, they have the countervailing advantage that enforcement is relatively straightforward. Rather than continuous measurement of firm performance, which can be costly, technology regulation can be enforced through simple spot checks that the appropriate equipment is installed.

Additional relevant issues which are important to implementation (and design), but do not necessarily guide in the choice between prices and quantities, include the requirements that: (i) agents have the information necessary to respond to the new incentives; (ii) agents have the capacity to respond to the incentives; and (iii) the behavioural response reflects the original assumptions underlying the intervention.[30] The first two considerations may imply that the implementation of the price or quantity instrument should be accompanied by an information/education programme.

Although various aspects of the implementation process are shared by price and quantity instruments, Helm (2005) notes that the institutional burden of constructing a tradable allowance scheme can exceed that of a tax. In addition to the elements described above, a tradable allowance scheme requires a mechanism for the initial allocation of property rights, and people (whether in government or the private sector) to create and ensure the continuation of the market. Additional regulation is required to ensure that the market is sufficiently competitive.

(iv) International Issues

Certain policy problems are fundamentally international in nature, such that all nation-states are better off if they can cooperate with each other. Climate change is the canonical example—mitigation is a global public good, but free-rider problems make full participation and compliance in any agreement extremely

[29] Nordhaus (2005) argues that taxes have a compliance advantage over permits because 'tax cheating is a zero-sum game for the two parties [the treasury and the taxpayer], while emissions evasion is a positive sum game for the two parties [the buyer and seller]'. However, permits must eventually be surrendered to the regulator, and if permit-holders are liable for non-compliance ('buyer liability') the incentives are similar to tax, and the market would reflect the risk of non-compliance with appropriate price signals (Victor, 1999).

[30] For instance, policies on energy efficiency previously assumed, reasonably enough, that the future energy savings were one of the main drivers behind the uptake of energy efficiency. A recent study by Oxera (2006), however, finds otherwise. Key positive factors include positive recommendations from friends and family and awareness of labelling; key negative factors were disruption and capital expenditure.

difficult (Barrett, 2003). Under such circumstances, efficiency considerations have to account for the need to encourage and sustain participation and compliance in an international agreement (Barrett and Stavins, 2003).

For a problem such as climate change, then, national policy must be designed to mesh with policies at the supranational level. This is particularly true in EU member states, where there are various EU directives and obligations under international treaties, but it is also true of the USA, China, India, and other nation-states. The choice of price or quantity instruments can be influenced rather strongly by arrangements at the supranational level. For instance, negotiations at the United Nations Framework Convention on Climate Change (UN FCCC) are, for better or worse, expressed in terms of quantities (emission reductions) rather than in carbon prices. if these quantity targets had significant penalties for non-compliance (which unfortunately they do not, and there is no global regulator to ensure compliance), then effectively the marginal benefit curve faced by any one nation state would be discontinuous at the target. In such circumstances, provided the penalty is large enough, the Weitzman framework would recommend using quantity instruments at the national level.

In the absence of a global regulator, the relevant question is whether price or quantity instruments yield differential incentives for participation and compliance. Barrett and Stavins (2003) identify three *positive* incentives for compliance and participation: explicit side payments, issue linkage, and the allocation of entitlements. Quantity schemes rely upon the allocation of entitlements to encourage participation, while price schemes, without such a mechanism, must employ explicit side payments.[31] There are clear advantages and disadvantages to both.[32] Harmonized taxes collected by national governments seem superficially fair—everyone is paying the same price—but the tricky questions of distributional effects are obscured, and must be dealt with indirectly with side payments. In contrast, negotiation over quantities places tricky distributional issues at the centre of the process, which again can be viewed as an advantage or a disadvantage. Negotiations, whether based around prices or quantities, are likely to be more successful if carefully linked in with other issues.

Barrett and Stavins (2003) also discuss three *negative* incentives supporting compliance and participation: reciprocal measures, financial penalties, and trade restrictions. The challenge here is that such incentives must be credible, and must be seen to be credible. This is problematic when punishment is itself a global public good, and therefore undersupplied. Again, it is not clear that there is a specific advantage to either price or quantity instruments in providing these negative incentives. Indeed, for climate change, Barrett (2003) and Barrett and Stavins (2003) argue that it is so difficult to construct a participation- and

[31] Endres and Finus (2002) show in a stylized two-country model that quotas are favoured over taxes when, along with other conditions, 'institutional restrictions' rule out side payments.

[32] The allocation of entitlements may amount to *implicit* side payments, raising negotiating difficulties that are magnified by the fact that the value of the entitlement is uncertain. See McKibbin and Wilcoxen (2002) on the advantages of resolving distributional issues by permit allocations, and Nordhaus (2005) on the disadvantages.

compliance-compatible regime that a voluntary R&D protocol is the best feasible outcome. Time will tell. At present, given the difficulties of achieving cooperation on climate change, there are persuasive arguments for building on existing achievements (Böhringer, 2003), rather than attempting to dismantle the institutional capabilities built over the last decade.

(v) Political Economy

The previous sections have largely focused on designing instruments to achieve efficient outcomes by correcting relative prices and inducing appropriate substitution effects. Such considerations are at the heart of the economic theory of instrument design. However, in practice, the instruments adopted depend more on political economy considerations than on economic theory, and the political economy of instrument design is driven by income transfers, rather than the substitution effect created by changes to relative prices.

Price, quantity, and hybrid instruments can all be designed to transfer wealth from the private sector to the public revenue, or vice versa. Subsidies and taxes (both price instruments) have opposite impacts on public finance. In theory, tax revenues can be returned to industry by hypothecation and recycling, but in practice this is difficult to achieve with any credibility. The public-finance impacts of quantity instruments are similar to taxes when tradable allowances are sold to the private sector (by auction or otherwise) and the market is (roughly) perfectly competitive. In contrast, if allowances are 'grandfathered' to incumbent operators for free (as in Phase 1 of the EU Emissions Trading Scheme (EU ETS)), quantity trading is similar to a tax where the revenues are fully recycled. In sum, theoretical considerations suggest that the public-finance implications of price and quantity instruments need not differ.

In practice, however, taxes tend to generate more public revenue than quantity instruments. Even when all the relevant allowances are auctioned, unless carefully designed, auctions may not raise the optimal amount of revenue (Klemperer, 2004). For instance, selling allowances in a series of industry-specific auctions may leave the process susceptible to manipulation. Moreover, grandfathered allowances have the additional benefit, as far as incumbent firms are concerned, of raising rivals' costs. Helm (2005) notes that providing for a 'new entrants' reserve' does not entirely solve the problem, because the trading scheme still creates risks which operate as additional barriers to entry. Incumbents, unlike new entrants, typically have physical hedges against such risks. Given these considerations, considerations of self-interest suggest that industry should be expected to lobby according to the following ranking: (i) subsidies; (ii) allowances grandfathered to incumbents; (iii) auctioned allowances; and then (iv) taxes.[33]

[33] A related point is the relative susceptibility of price and quantity instruments to regulatory capture, discussed by Helm (2006).

Nevertheless, the public interest would often be served by resisting this lobbying and raising revenue from instruments. This is particularly the case with instruments aimed at internalizing negative externalities, as has become clear from theoretical studies within environmental economics, which reveal at least five reasons to raise revenue from such instruments.[34]

First, raising revenue may generate a double dividend—the policy internalizes the negative externality, and the revenue raised can be recycled to offset other distortionary taxes.[35] This effect should not be overstated. Some policies—such as carbon pricing—can produce a 'tax interaction effect' by increasing product prices and reducing real wages and labour supply.[36] The tax interaction effect, while an indirect effect, can be relatively large.[37] Nevertheless, policies that internalize a carbon price without raising revenue also suffer from the tax interaction effect, without benefiting from the revenue-recycling effect.[38] As such, these considerations suggest that climate policies that raise revenue are preferable to policies which do not.

Second, raising revenue avoids distortions from perverse dynamic incentives. For instance, if allowances are allocated for free based on another variable (e.g. past emissions or output), firms have a dynamic incentive to increase that variable (e.g. increase emissions or output) now in order to be granted a larger allowance allocation in the future. In contrast, this effect does not arise with taxes or auctioned allowances.

Third, requiring payment from those who impose negative externalities on others probably reflects a fairer allocation of property rights. For instance, the polluter-pays principle starts from the premise that the right to a clean environment is owned by the public. If firms wish to pollute the environment, they must purchase the right to do so from the public.

Fourth, if allowances are grandfathered to firms (or taxes recycled), the rents ultimately accrue to shareholders, who tend to be wealthier than the general population.[39] As such, grandfathered allowances are a regressive instrument,

[34] Hepburn *et al.* (2006*b*) provide a review of the considerations for and against auctioning of European allowances in the EU ETS.

[35] A variety of different definitions of the double-dividend hypothesis are used in the literature, sometimes inconsistently. These definitions include 'weak', 'intermediate', and 'strong' forms. This terminology is avoided here because it is more confusing than it is helpful.

[36] See Bovenberg and de Mooij (1994), the critique by Fullerton (1997), and the reply by Bovenberg and de Mooij (1997). Also relevant are papers by Bovenberg and van der Ploeg (1994), Goulder (1995), Parry (1995), and Bovenberg and Goulder (1996).

[37] For climate-change policy, Parry (2003) notes that the tax interaction effect dominates the revenue recycling effect, which would be expected from the optimal tax theory result that broad taxes produce lower efficiency losses than narrow taxes (e.g. Diamond and Mirrlees, 1971). However, results appear to depend strongly upon assumptions about labour supply.

[38] Simple models, as in Parry *et al.* (1999) and Parry (2003), indicate that after accounting for the tax-interaction effect, grandfathered permits can generate striking welfare losses where auctioned permits produce gains. See also Goulder *et al.* (1997, 1999) and Fullerton and Metcalf (2001).

[39] Parry (2003) points out that in the USA the top income quintile owns 60 per cent of all shares with the bottom owning less than 2 per cent. He cites a finding that reducing US carbon emissions by 15 per cent using grandfathered permits would reduce the income of the bottom quintile by US$500 and increase that of the top quintile by US$1,500.

transferring wealth from poor to rich. Even if the government finds it politically necessary to preserve firm profits, theory and simulations suggest that no more than 50 per cent of allowances, and probably a much smaller percentage, should be allocated for free (Bovenberg *et al.*, 2005; Hepburn *et al.*, 2008).[40] An exception applies to firms competing against imports which are not subject to similar policies.[41]

Fifth, firms and individuals use heuristics and 'rules of thumb' to make decisions rather than by making calculations of optimality. Raising revenue directs management attention to climate-change policy, and is more likely to prompt an active response from firms. Furthermore, although firms should simply pass on a proportion of marginal costs to consumers, in practice prices may increase by a greater amount if firms also pay revenues to the government. Other things being equal, the demand response will be larger given a stronger price signal.

In sum, although economic theory provides several extremely good reasons—founded both on efficiency and equity—to raise revenue from the internalization of negative externalities, this frequently fails to occur for political economy reasons. Indeed, this point is more general. Economic theory has, justifiably, focused on providing guidance on instrument selection, under different conditions, to maximize social welfare. However, economists' theoretical prescriptions are rarely met in practice, for the simple reason that governments cannot design instruments without accounting for political realities (Pearce *et al.*, 2006). A more accurate explanation of why particular instruments are adopted requires the specification and analysis of a political welfare function, capturing the fact that politicians also want to retain the support of various lobby groups in order to stay in power, and implement their pet social or economic programmes.[42] With this framework, it is not at all surprising that instrument selection is better explained by political economy and the income effect than by considerations of economic efficiency (Helm, 2005).

VI. IMPLICATIONS FOR CLIMATE POLICY

It is an understatement to say that climate change is a difficult policy problem, and there is no room for pretence that it simply requires a blithe application of the theory of instrument choice. Nevertheless, basic economic theory has

[40] The essential reason for this is that, depending upon the market structure, firms will pass on a proportion of the marginal cost increase to consumers. As such, Vollebergh *et al.* (1997) recommend partial grandfathering and Bovenberg and Goulder (2000) examined the coal, oil, and gas industries in the United States and concluded that no more than 15 per cent of permits needed to be grandfathered for profit-neutrality. Oxera (2004) also finds that the EU ETS will produce windfall profits in sectors which are not subject to fierce international competition. Nevertheless, Hepburn *et al.* (2008) show that there are some market structures where individual firms could need an allocation representing *more than* 100 per cent of their emissions for profit neutrality.

[41] In the limit, fierce import competition would imply that firms are not able to pass through the marginal cost increase resulting from the emissions trading scheme.

[42] See, for example, Grossman and Helpman (1994), Aidt (1998), and Aidt and Dutta (2004).

some extremely important and useful insights. Assuming that the agreed target is to limit the *flow of emissions* within a given time period, as under the Kyoto Protocol,[43] the crucial question is which instrument (or combination) should be employed? Commentators and academics have responded to the incentive to have their names attached to the successful approach, and as such a plethora of different instruments have been suggested for consideration.[44] Nevertheless, a good starting point remains the choice between quantities (as under the Kyoto Protocol), prices (by way of an internationally harmonized carbon tax), or hybrid instruments.

In section V(i), the Weitzman (1974) framework was loosely applied to climate change with the conclusion that if the marginal cost of reducing emissions increases quickly, and damages from climate change are relatively insensitive to emissions over short periods (e.g. five years),[45] then a price instrument is the appropriate instrument to use.[46] Indeed, unless we are certain that we are on the brink of a tipping point, a carbon tax appears more efficient than tradable allowances. To be clear, this is not to say that climate change is not an urgent or an extremely concerning problem, nor is it to claim that climate damages are unlikely to be high. The central claim behind the recommendation of a price instrument—which might optimally be set extremely high—is simply that damages do not change rapidly as a function of additional emissions over the next few years. If the member states were prepared to agree to commitment periods of several decades (notwithstanding the discussion on flexibility and commitment in section V(ii)), then quantity instruments become more attractive (Hoel and Karp, 2002), precisely because it is more likely such a tipping point would be crossed over that period.

However, as discussed in section V(iv), for international problems such as climate change, this economic theory can only serve as a starting point. The absence of a global regulator implies that the feasible set of negotiated solutions is highly constrained. Achieving international collective action is crucial to organizing an effective response to climate change, and this requires the gradual development of institutions, trust, and credibility over time. This is important. Trust and credibility will not enhanced by large-scale, fundamental revisions to the direction of climate policy. As such, practical recommendations need to start from where we find ourselves, rather than where we might like to be. The institutions we

[43] This is far from being the only possible target. We might aim to prevent global mean *temperatures* from increasing by more than a certain amount, such as 2°C, or prevent concentrations of greenhouse gases in the atmosphere from rising beyond a specific point, such as 500ppmv, or even set a target to limit *cumulative anthropogenic emissions* (over all time periods) to less than 1,000 GtC. Frame *et al.* (2006) suggests that this last target might be better specified.

[44] See, for example, the reviews in Philibert (2005), Aldy *et al.* (2003), and Bodansky (2004)—the last providing summaries of over 40 different proposals.

[45] The assumption that the marginal damage curve is flat is less valid over longer timeframes. Hoel and Karp (2002) find that the preference for quotas increases as the relevant time horizon of policy is increased.

[46] For rigorous analyses that account for the stock pollutant nature of the problem, see Hoel and Karp (2001, 2002) and Pizer (2002).

have so far successfully developed are centred on emissions quantity targets and timetables. This approach has hard-won momentum, and a degree of institutional lock-in. Financial institutions within the emissions trading community, including some of the world's major banks and hedge funds, now have a vested interest in ensuring that emissions trading continues, with tighter caps to increase carbon prices and the value of their carbon assets. Policy-makers have gained useful insights by 'learning by doing', as international emissions trading schemes have been proposed, implemented, and iterated.

While such schemes are still far from perfect, the institutional switching costs of moving from a quantity-based to a price-based scheme, such as a harmonized tax, seem rather large. Substantial time and resources would need to be devoted to attempting to shift the current consensus away from targets and timetables. And there is no guarantee that a shift would be achieved, particularly given the environmental movement's resistance to leaving emissions uncapped, and industry resistance to additional taxes.[47] Even if an *agreement just to negotiate* a tax scheme were reached, the time and resource costs required to sort out the devilish details and to implement the scheme should not be underestimated.

Accepting a quantity-based regime as the platform for future climate policy, section V(v) implies several immediate recommendations. First, maximizing social welfare implies that a large proportion of the allowances should be auctioned. Second, it should be expected that industry will lobby ferociously against any auctioning. Results from the EU ETS indicate that industry won the first few rounds, and while the proportion of auctioning in the EU ETS has increased over time, the final compromise deal struck by the EU in December 2008 shows just how difficult it is to reduce the proportion of allowances available for free allocation.[48]

Furthermore, the theory on commitment and flexibility (section V(ii)) is especially relevant to climate policy setting. The costs imposed upon environmental innovators by retaining the flexibility to adjust climate policy are likely to be rather high. The benefits of the flexibility to respond to new climate science are difficult to estimate. As such, robust conclusions are unavailable. Nevertheless, while it is almost certain that the optimal commitment period is less than several decades (as this is the lifespan of most relevant plant), it is also unlikely that the optimal period is as short as five years. An analysis of longer commitment periods (e.g. ten years and beyond) is clearly called for.[49] The proposed Australian emissions trading scheme, called the Carbon Pollution Reduction Scheme, appears to strike a better balance (Australia, 2008). Scheme caps are set at least five years in advance, with the cap extended by one year, every year. Up to a further ten years of guidance is provided through 'gateways', or ranges, for future caps, which are extended for five years, every five years.

[47] Aldy and Frankel (2004) state that 'for all the criticism the Kyoto Protocol has received, the most feasible approach in future policy efforts may be to build on this foundation'.

[48] See http://www.consilium.europa.eu/ueDocs/cms_Data/docs/pressData/en/ec/104672.pdf

[49] McKibbin and Wilcoxen (2002) propose renegotiating their permit price once every decade.

Finally, accepting a quantity-based platform for future climate policy does not rule out the possibility of shifting to a hybrid instrument by adding a *price ceiling*, potentially through setting a reserve price in allowance auctions (Hepburn *et al.*, 2006*b*) and possibly also a *price floor*, potentially through carbon taxation. If economists are correct about the marginal benefits curve, this would lead to substantial efficiency gains, while avoiding the costs of a major switch from current arrangements. Additionally, a price ceiling may enhance policy credibility, because it caps the costs of compliance and thus reduces the risk of a policy reversal if abatement costs turn out to be injuriously high. The price floor guarantees a certain minimum return on investment in low-carbon technologies, reducing the risk faced by innovating firms.

Alternatively, as discussed in section IV(iv), prices might be 'managed' in other ways. For instance, Newell *et al.* (2005) note that in a multi-period system with banking and borrowing, prices could be managed by agreeing that the stringency of targets in the next period automatically depends upon the revealed price in the current period.

VII. CONCLUSION

Although economic considerations are not always paramount,[50] a large variety of policy problems, including climate policy, would benefit from a more systematic application of economic theories of regulation, including the theory of instrument choice presented here. Problems of decision-making under uncertainty, credible commitment and flexibility, implementation, and political economy arise in almost all settings, and increasingly international issues are also often relevant to national policy-makers. Economic theory has something to contribute in each of these areas.

There are at least six key lessons for climate policy from the theory of instrument choice. First, whenever government faces information problems, and the costs of response vary between regulated entities, economic instruments are likely to be preferable to command-and-control regulation. Second, under uncertainty, price instruments are more efficient than quantity instruments when the marginal benefit curve is flat relative to the marginal costs curve, but correlated uncertainty can reverse this preference. Third, perverse dynamic incentives (ratchet effects), hold-up problems, and the allocation of risk should be considered in making the (inevitable) trade-off between commitment and flexibility. Fourth, all instruments require enforcement, and some instruments (e.g. technology standards) may be simpler and cheaper to enforce than others. Fifth, instruments must be designed

[50] For instance, the decision to replace military conscription (effectively a quantity instrument) with an all-volunteer military force (effectively a price instrument) had little to do with the relative slopes of the marginal cost and benefits curves, and much more to do with philosophical reasons, as discussed by Galston (2003).

to mesh in with policies at the supranational level, and incentives for participation and compliance are crucial at the international level. Finally, and perhaps most importantly, political economic considerations appear to constrain the feasible set of instruments—industry has a strong preference for instruments that transfer income towards (or at least not away from) its shareholders and that enhance market power.

Political factors are more important than economic considerations in explaining why particular instruments are employed for particular problems. Helm (2006) provides a useful summary of regulatory capture in this context. To assume that politicians can maximize a representative social welfare function, rather than a 'political welfare function', is simply naïve, even if such an assumption was plausible in Platonic times.[51] However, as Pearce *et al.* (2006) put it, 'explaining the gap between actual and theoretical design is not to justify the gap'. For climate change, the gap between the sensible and the politically feasible may appear daunting, and no one would dispute that reducing global emissions by 50 per cent in 2050, with rich countries reducing their emissions by at least 75 per cent, is an enormous challenge. Nevertheless, the world is moving gradually towards global emissions trading, built by linking existing and new emissions-trading schemes, which could feasibly establish a shared global carbon price in due course. While lobbying for rents will persist, the establishment of a carbon price at the margin is an important step towards a more efficient and effective response to climate change.

[51] Russell (1946, Book 1, Part 2, ch. 14, final page) suggest that Plato's republic may have actually been intended to be founded. He notes that this 'was not so fantastic or impossible as it might naturally seem to us. Many of its provisions, including some that we should have thought quite impracticable, were actually realized at Sparta'.

19

Docking into a Global Carbon Market: Clean Investment Budgets to Finance Low-carbon Economic Development

*Gernot Wagner, Nathaniel Keohane, Annie Petsonk, James S. Wang**

I. INTRODUCTION

> Different actions by countries with different circumstances will need different docking stations of support. So what tools will you create within the climate change regime to deliver on adaptation and mitigation? How will you use those tools to develop a self-financing climate compact?
>
> (Yvo de Boer, Executive Secretary, United Nations Framework Convention on Climate Change)[1]

A central challenge of any new international climate agreement is financing the transition to low-carbon economic growth in developing countries. Avoiding dangerous climate change will require concerted global action to reduce greenhouse gas (GHG) emissions. Limiting the long-term increase in global mean temperature to two degrees Celsius (2°C) above pre-industrial levels—which many scientists identify as a key threshold to avoid catastrophic climate change—will not be possible without emissions reductions in all major emitting countries. Nor

* All at Environmental Defense Fund.

Our deepest appreciation goes to Sabeen Ali, Kevin Gorman, Stanislas de Margerie, Stephanie Mandell, and Clare Sierawski for their tireless research and assistance. Many thanks also to Richie Ahuja, Dan Dudek, Jason Funk, Peter Goldmark, Sasha Golub, Steve Hamburg, Jennifer Haverkamp, Kristen Hite, Ruben Lubowski, and Kyle Meng, as well as other current and former colleagues at Environmental Defense Fund for invaluable comments and suggestions. We are also indebted to Jos Cozijnsen, Leif K. Ervik, Jeff Frankel, Christian Hald-Mortensen, Cameron Hepburn, Michael Oppenheimer, Pedro Piris-Cabezas, José Eduardo Sanhueza, Christian Schumer, and others who have reviewed and commented on previous drafts of this proposal and provided feedback at discussions and presentations in Accra, Beijing, Cambridge, MA, London, New York, Poznan, and Washington, DC. Finally, we thank Stève Gervais and Pawel Olejarnik at the International Energy Agency (IEA) for providing emissions data. All remaining errors are our own.

[1] Statement at the high-level segment at the Conference of the Parties serving as the meeting of the Parties to the Kyoto Protocol, Poznan, Poland, 11 December 2008 (full remarks available at: http://unfccc.int/files/press/news_room/statements/application/pdf/cop_14_hls_statement_de_boer.pdf).

can that goal be achieved absent a framework that makes economic development an integral part of addressing climate change.

These twin challenges of emissions reductions and economic growth can both be addressed by channelling capital flows towards investments in emissions reductions in developing countries, resolving the usual tension between equity and efficiency. Developing countries offer a cornucopia of low-cost abatement opportunities, largely by decoupling economic development and carbon emissions. At the same time, the immediate and sizeable investments in low-carbon economic growth that are crucial to curbing emissions in the narrow time-window available for averting massive climate shifts can only happen with the engagement of capital markets in the world's advanced economies.

A framework that delivers substantial financing for low-carbon economic growth in emerging economies should satisfy four goals.

First, it should provide emerging economies sufficient access to capital to drive low-carbon economic growth. This capital cannot simply be delivered: it must be deployed in a way that decisively breaks the link between economic growth and carbon—driving economic growth up and GHG emissions down.

Second, the framework should prepare emerging economies for eventual participation as full partners in a global climate regime. A particular need is rapid development of the technical, institutional, and human capacity to limit effectively and ultimately reduce GHG emissions, starting with credible and comprehensive measurement, reporting, and verification (MRV) of current emissions.

Third, the framework must be commensurate with the capacity of nations and markets both to generate and to absorb this new set of resources. In particular, it needs to be consistent with maintaining the integrity of the core compliance market, which initially will largely consist of industrialized country markets.

Fourth, the framework must be consistent with environmental integrity defined by a goal of avoiding long-term warming in excess of 2°C above pre-industrial levels, which requires a reduction of global GHG emissions in the order of 50 per cent below current levels by 2050.[2] In taking this as our goal, we are explicitly adopting a science-based approach that treats climate change fundamentally as a problem of risk management rather than consumption smoothing.[3]

Many proposals have been put forward to meet these and similar goals. Some argue for massive increases in official development assistance (ODA). A second set of proposals revolves around shares of proceeds of auctions of the emissions allowances of industrialized nations and their firms. Third are levies on activities ranging from emissions trading transactions or financial transactions in general, to ones on aviation and shipping, among others. Fourth is compensation for

[2] See Appendix for more details on the science.

[3] See Yohe *et al.* (2004) and Weitzman (2009) on the point of risk management versus consumption smoothing. Keller *et al.* (2005) similarly employ economic analysis in the service of a science-based target.

reductions in emissions from deforestation and degradation (REDD) in developing countries. A fifth proposal focuses on maintaining the Kyoto Protocol's Clean Development Mechanism (CDM) but applying a discount to its certified emission reductions.[4]

All of these proposals are important. None on its own, or even in the aggregate, is likely to be sufficient either in terms of revenue generation or in terms of incentive delivery.[5] Moreover, it is not at all clear that taxpayers and politicians in industrialized nations will be willing to direct governmental instrumentalities to provide the necessary funds—a concern of particular relevance for the first three proposals. This paper outlines a new mechanism meant to build upon and complement the proposals above.

(i) A Proposal: Clean Investment Budgets

Under our proposal, emerging economies could voluntarily adopt domestically enforceable limits on the GHG emissions from a substantial fraction of their economies—with the limit set initially *above* current levels, consistent with a global 2°C goal. We call this approach adopting a 'clean investment budget' (CIB). In particular the growth increment, the portion of the CIB in excess of a nation's actual emissions, provides a pool of emissions allowances that could be leveraged in existing and future carbon markets in industrialized countries—financing investments in renewable and low-carbon energy generation, energy efficiency, and technology transfer. CIBs would thus reward early action by emerging economies, providing them with a source of capital to enable a rapid transition to a low-carbon economic development path.

Countries could use their CIB allowances in a variety of ways: for example, as collateral to secure private financing; to repay equity or debt finance in clean energy projects, with the payment tied to the emissions reductions achieved; or to provide grants for institutional capacity such as emissions registries and MRV capability. The flow of capital would increase as a country progressed through a series of performance benchmarks. Over time, as low-carbon investments matured, reductions in emissions would enable those nations to grow their clean investment capital accounts, making more surplus allowances available for leveraging even larger investments in new technologies and infrastructure.[6]

CIBs represent a particular application of a broader idea that has gained momentum in the international arena: 'docking stations', or flexible mechanisms to bring a wide range of countries into a global climate regime.[7] In the short time between Poznan and the 2009 Copenhagen Conference of the Parties, it is vital

[4] For CDM reform see Hepburn (Ch. 20 in this volume) and Petsonk (2007), among others, and our own more detailed discussion in section I(ii) below.

[5] See section III(i) on the need for funds and the inadequacy of the size of current financing proposals.

[6] See section III for more detail on financing and leveraging mechanisms.

[7] See Petsonk (2009) on the legal aspects of docking stations.

that nations elaborate the concept of docking stations further, and develop the notion into concrete tools that will enable a self-financing climate compact, as the United Nations Framework Convention on Climate Change (UN FCCC)'s Yvo de Boer proposes. To meet this challenge, docking stations could take on several forms. A new compact could enable tropical forest nations to dock into the carbon market if they practise REDD. Another version could use innovative tools to generate adaptation funding and enable small-island developing nations to dock into that funding. CIBs represent a third docking station, aimed at emerging economies.

(ii) Relationship to the Existing Literature

We are not the first to propose granting developing countries emissions targets that exceed current emissions. 'Premium budgets' were first proposed over a decade ago (EDF, 1997), and subsequently developed by Oppenheimer and Petsonk (2004), among others. Stewart and Wiener (2003) have also proposed allocating 'major developing countries allowances above their existing emissions. That would provide headroom—not hot air—for future growth and profitable allowance sales that attract investment while also reducing costs to industrialized countries'.[8] The contribution of this chapter is to present a detailed proposal for implementing the approach, show how it can be consistent with maintaining the core market integrity as well as a goal of limiting warming to 2°C, discuss the design of financing mechanisms that can provide 'carbon leverage', and explore practical issues of implementation.

By affording emerging economies clean investment budgets set initially above current emission levels, the CIB concept follows the principles of 'common but differentiated responsibility' and equity, as elaborated by Su Wei (2008), who noted the need to assure development space and carbon space for developing countries while promoting the transfer of environmentally friendly technologies from industrialized to developing countries. Zou Ji (2008) has developed one possible institutional design in the form of a body, parallel to the subsidiary bodies of the UN FCCC, that would develop public–private partnerships by linking public finance with carbon markets, capital markets, and technology markets, leveraging larger amounts of private finance by smaller initial amounts of public finance.

Hall *et al.* (2008) have laid out other ways for developing countries to engage in the international process, and group these efforts into three broad areas: domestic policy improvement; international financial mechanisms; and private and public diplomacy. CIBs fall chiefly into the second category but combine elements of all three.

[8] See Frankel (2008), who proposes 'growth budgets' with initial allowance allocations based on business-as-usual (BAU) paths for major emitting developing countries. Also see Olmstead and Stavins (2006) and Wiener (2008).

CIBs stand in clear opposition to other proposals that focus on more incremental measures to engage developing nations without generating large-scale capital flows for low-carbon development. Sectoral standards or technology requirements may have a place in domestic policy-making to achieve emissions reductions, especially in sectors (such as energy efficiency in commercial and residential buildings) where market imperfections appear to persist. But such command-and-control approaches are inadequate to meet the scale of the challenge: they fail to provide an economic incentive for cost-effective abatement, and tend to stifle rather than stimulate technological innovation. A second approach, intensity targets, may limit emissions per unit of economic output. But even if emissions intensity falls, emissions may continue to rise—especially in a context of robust economic growth. Moreover, a reduction in emissions intensity on its own does not yield a readily measured reduction in emissions, undermining trading and limiting the role for carbon markets, which would ultimately lead to more emissions.[9]

Approaches that rely on project-based offsets, such as the existing 'clean development mechanism' (CDM), suffer similar drawbacks. The CDM is insufficient to provide a supply of financing at scale, due to systemic bottlenecks in the approval process and the difficulty in proving 'additionality' (that is, whether credited activities provide real emissions reductions in addition to what would have occurred in the absence of a project).[10] At the same time, the CDM fails to provide any incentive or preparation for developing countries eventually to reduce their own emissions; indeed, it creates a perverse incentive for countries to refrain from accepting emissions targets in order to keep receiving funding from the CDM.

By contrast, CIBs have the potential to bring developing countries into a global carbon-market framework in a way that achieves early emissions reductions while respecting the principle of common but differentiated responsibilities. Limits on absolute emissions, initially set slightly above current levels and covering a substantial fraction of a nation's economy, can help ensure environmental integrity while simultaneously leveraging carbon markets in the industrialized world as a source of funds to drive low-carbon economic development.

(iii) Overview of the Chapter

The rest of the chapter proceeds as follows. Section II describes how CIBs might be determined and uses a simple numerical example for illustration. Section III discusses the design of mechanisms to deliver finance necessary to achieve maximum emissions reductions. Section IV lays out clear and measurable performance standards and discusses compliance and enforcement. Section V concludes.

9 See Hall *et al.* (2008) for a more detailed discussion of emissions standards and intensity targets.

10 Wara and Victor (2008) lay out some of the inadequacies of the existing CDM and offset tools in more detail. Axel Michaelowa (2005) and Cameron Hepburn (in this volume) provide perspectives for CDM reform that would address some of the current shortcomings.

II. DETERMINING CLEAN INVESTMENT BUDGETS

(i) Allocation of Emission Allowances above Current Levels

It is useful to think of a CIB as imposing a limit on emissions from a substantial fraction of a country's economy—with that limit initially set above current levels. In an international climate agreement that allows emission trading among countries (as the current Kyoto Protocol does, and as its successor likely will), however, no country truly accepts a *fixed* limit on its emissions: rather, each country commits itself to holding emission allowances at the end of each compliance period equal to the country's GHG emissions over that period.[11] A country accepting a CIB would take on the same fundamental commitment to cover its emissions with allowances in each compliance period. Note that this commitment is necessarily denominated in absolute terms—that is, in tons of emissions, rather than as an intensity standard or other rate-based measure.

The Kyoto Protocol itself provides a precedent for CIBs. Australia ratified the Protocol with an emissions budget set at 8 per cent above its 1990 baseline. Similarly, the European Union's Kyoto Protocol burden-sharing agreement set some countries' emissions above 1990 levels. As in the Kyoto Protocol, the initial CIB allocation would be expressed as a quantity of 'assigned amount units' (AAUs). Unlike the Protocol, however, a CIB country's obligation could either cover its emissions economy-wide, or cover emissions from its major emitting sectors only. Such a multi-sectoral approach would accommodate the difficulty of establishing a credible MRV system, and allow emerging economies to participate sooner. Of course, the sectors covered by a CIB would have to be chosen to represent a substantial fraction of the country's economy and to minimize the possibility of within-country leakage.

The actual CIB—the assigned allowance allocation—should be determined in advance for at least two successive commitment periods, to strengthen the incentive countries have to comply with their commitments in the first period.[12] The second period's budget could be set at or below the level of the first, to put CIB countries on a path toward a high-technology, low-carbon economy.

Figure 19.1 illustrates a hypothetical CIB over two five-year commitment periods starting in 2013. The rising dashed lines labelled 'Reference estimates' represents projected emissions under BAU. The lower solid line represents the

[11] We are indebted to Leif K. Ervik for succinctly expressing the nature of country obligations in an international climate regime. To state the matter precisely, article 3, para. 1 of the Kyoto Protocol commits each Party to emit no more than its allowable level. While Annex B of the Protocol sets out specific emissions targets relative to 1990 levels, these did not represent fixed limits: rather, those allowed amounts can be changed by a country's participation in one of the Kyoto flexibility mechanisms—e.g. CDM, joint implementation (JI), or emissions trading in AAUs.

[12] Helm *et al.* (2003) note the trade-off between commitment and flexibility: *ex ante* commitment to reduction targets spanning two commitment periods removes some options for readjusting policies within the two time periods.

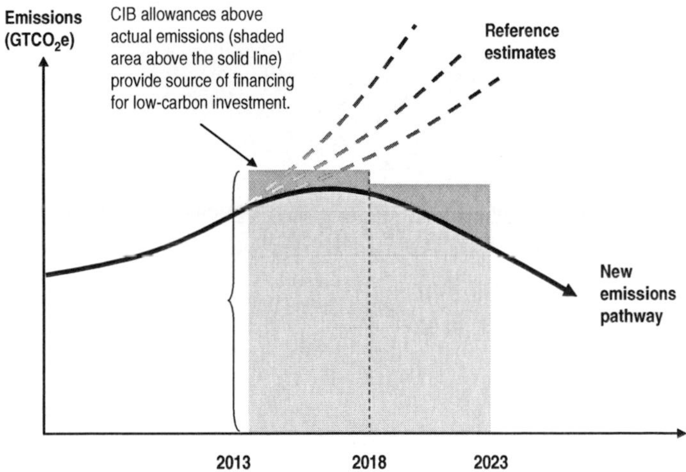

Figure 19.1. CIBs reward early action

emissions path after investments in low-carbon energy sources and energy efficiency, among others made possible by the CIB.

A CIB for an individual country would be set as a percentage above a historical base year, and would be above a reasonable expectation of BAU emissions during the early years of the programme.

Taken as a whole, meanwhile, the *sum* of CIBs must satisfy two constraints. The first is market integrity: compliance markets in industrialized countries must be able to absorb the number of surplus CIB allowances available for sale without significantly depressing the allowance price. The second constraint is environmental integrity: the sum of all nations' CIBs, in conjunction with commitments by industrialized nations, must be consistent with limiting global warming to 2°C above pre-industrial levels—what we refer to as a '2°C global emissions reductions pathway'. Before discussing those constraints in detail, however, we illustrate the concept with a simple quantitative example.

(ii) A Numerical Example

The concept of CIBs might be best illustrated via a numerical example. Suppose Mexico, for example, were to adopt a CIB beginning in 2013, and it negotiated a CIB set at 750 megatonnes (million metric tonnes) of carbon dioxide equivalent ($MtCO_2e$) per year, for ten years.[13] In this illustration, by joining the global carbon market on this 'early action' basis, Mexico would obtain immediate access to an

[13] 750 $MtCO_2e$ roughly corresponds to Mexico's BAU projections for 2016, allowing it a surplus component for the first three years of the programme. For simplicity, we are keeping the budget constant across two commitment periods.

amount of surplus allowances roughly equal to 80 $MtCO_2e$, the area above annual mid-range BAU projections and below the annual allocation of 750 $MtCO_2e$. At a price of US\$20/tCO_2e, the surplus would be immediately worth roughly US\$1.6 billion; at US\$30/tCO_2e, it would be worth roughly US\$2.4 billion. Leveraged at 50 per cent, Mexico could secure a loan of anywhere between US\$3 and US\$5 billion, depending on the allowance price.

This system could provide a significant amount of up-front capital to invest first in harvesting the low-end of the marginal abatement cost curve (MACC), where there are likely to be many no-regrets (i.e. low, no, and even negative cost) emission-reduction opportunities. If this source of financing could enable nations to access otherwise inaccessible rate-of-return abatement projects, whose success could in turn free up more surplus allowances to be added to the escrow amount to secure even more financing, it would begin to address the external financing needs identified by Mexico to pay for its recently proposed emissions reduction commitments.

(iii) Ensuring Market and Environmental Integrity

CIBs have demand and supply components. The demand for CIBs is given by the required upfront capital expenditures and a discounted stream of expected costs (net of potential gains) from emissions reductions. The supply side focuses on how many CIB allowances would be available in the first place. We focus on this second aspect of CIBs, and distinguish two constraints: the *economic* constraint represented by the ability of compliance carbon markets to absorb an influx of new allowances, and the *atmospheric* constraint implied by a global 2°C pathway. Because CIBs offer a 'premium' above actual emissions in the initial years of the programme, it is crucial that they be designed with these constraints in mind.

Several safeguards can help to ensure market integrity. First, the number of CIB allowances available for sale by developing countries could be tied to their progress in meeting performance benchmarks. In particular, nations that lack well-developed emissions measuring and monitoring systems could be required to hold significant portions of their CIBs in reserve to reduce the risk of over-selling; these reserve requirements could be loosened as the nations' abilities to measure and report actual emissions improve. This 'metering' of allowances would prevent a sudden influx of allowances into carbon markets, while at the same time providing continuing incentives for developing countries to improve their institutional capacities.

Second, as a practical matter, nations with CIBs might not wish to sell all of their surplus allowances at the outset. Three reasons account for this quasi self-regulation of the supply of allowances that flow into the market. For one, and most significantly, CIB allowances are most valuable when leveraged to generate a multiple of investment potential from the actual value of allowances.[14]

[14] See section III on leverage for a more detailed discussion of this concept.

Second, countries may wish to bank or save some allowances to cover potential emissions increases in the future, or to sell at a later date when they have reduced emissions even further and allowance prices have risen. The potential for banking to moderate and stabilize allowance markets has been explored in a variety of similar contexts, e.g. REDD markets and the EU Emissions Trading System (ETS).[15] Lastly, the market for credits from CDM projects has typically been a sellers' market; i.e. demand for credits exceeds supply (Wara and Victor, 2008). Such excess demand suggests that the market could absorb a further increase in supply without threatening market integrity or flooding compliance markets.

A full check of market integrity would require a complete model of the carbon market, ideally in a general-equilibrium framework. For present purposes we rely on a back-of-the-envelope calculation to derive an order-of-magnitude estimate of the total value of surplus CIB allowances consistent with market integrity. The global mandatory carbon market now largely consists of the EU ETS, which accounts for about 2 of 45 $GtCO_2e$ emitted globally in 2008. The United States would add another 6 $GtCO_2e$. A price of US\$20–30/tCO_2e would imply a value of US\$40–60 billion for EU ETS, compared to US\$160–240 billion for the EU plus US carbon markets.[16] If 10 per cent of a combined EU–US carbon market consisted of allowances from CIB countries, CIBs could deliver a total of US\$16–24 billion in a given year or, roughly speaking, emissions of 800 $MtCO_2e$ per year at a price of US\$20–30/tCO_2e.[17]

With an estimate in hand of how many allowances carbon markets could absorb, we can move on to an assessment of environmental integrity. Given the uncertainties associated with climate physics and the amount of past and future emissions, it is difficult to determine with precision the surplus allowances available for a given temperature goal. However, the number of tons derived through the back-of-the-envelope market calculation—8 GtCO2e over ten years—is small enough not to tip the physical balance one way or another. In the appendix, we demonstrate that CIBs of this magnitude could indeed be consistent with the 2°C target, using a standard climate model. Moreover, because CIBs are premised on a

[15] See, for example, Ellerman and Montero (2007) or Piris-Cabezas and Keohane (2008).

[16] Given the lack of a global carbon market and the lack of any compliance market beyond 2012, it is difficult to pinpoint an appropriate CIB carbon price. EU ETS allowances with a settlement date of December 2012 have traded at between €15 and €30/tCO_2e, or roughly US\$20–40/tCO_2e, between 2005 and 2008. January and February 2009 have seen prices decrease to €10 (or US\$13) due to the global economic slowdown, but prices are very likely to increase once longer-term economic projections become more optimistic. We take US\$20–30/tCO_2e, the lower range of the long-term price band, as a rough estimate of allowance prices beyond 2013.

[17] This is clearly a rough estimate. Several factors would influence the actual size, including if and when a domestic cap-and-trade system comes into force in the United States and how much room the system opens for international allowances. The back-of-the-envelope calculation also misses an important point a more comprehensive—possibly general equilibrium—analysis would consider: any country joining the carbon market through this programme necessarily expands the market itself. This is particularly true since not all allowances would be traded north–south but also within each region and country.

future of at least a decade or more of constraints on emissions—including mandatory, progressively more stringent caps on emissions in industrialized nations—the advent of CIBs would give rise to a powerful incentive to harvest emissions reductions in developing countries as soon as possible, and bank or save the resulting surplus allowances for the future, when the supply of emissions allowances will become more scarce. Bankability of CIB allowances, coupled with limits on the amount of CIBs allocated consistent with the 2°C constraint, can thus help ensure that CIBs satisfy and, in fact, advance the crucial criterion of environmental integrity.

III. DELIVERING FINANCING TO ACHIEVE MAXIMUM EMISSIONS REDUCTIONS

The primary goal of CIBs is to enable emerging economies to finance the transition to a low-carbon economy. Nations would be able to use CIB allowances to finance investments in a wide range of areas, such as energy-efficient buildings (or retrofits) and renewable electricity generation, among others.[18] CIB funds could also be used to fulfil the need for quick development of capacity for monitoring and independent verification of emissions. Initially, countries receiving CIBs may not be equipped to monitor, report, and verify emission reductions in line with best practice or even minimum standards to ensure the integrity of allowances and, thus, the core carbon market. A portion of CIB funds can and should be used to build these fundamental reporting tools and help the country move along the path towards full accession into the global carbon market.

Realizing the goals of the CIB proposal, however, requires more than simply granting these countries a generous allotment of allowances: a framework must be erected to ensure that CIB funding is well spent. This section discusses how CIB countries could access compliance markets, suggests how CIB allowances could be used to finance development, and discusses the range of financing mechanisms that could be employed.

A key goal in designing financing mechanisms is employing two types of leverage mechanisms: carbon and financial leverage. 'Carbon leverage'—essentially, price discrimination—allows getting more than one ton of emissions reductions (on average) for every CIB allowance sold into global carbon markets. Such leverage is made possible by the gap in abatement costs between industrialized countries and the developing world. Developing countries have abundant low-cost (or perhaps even negative-cost) opportunities for emissions reduction, but many of these opportunities require initial financing that simply is not available, particularly in credit-constrained economies. 'Financial leverage' refers to perhaps

[18] Some of these programmes could be modelled after existing mechanisms for 'green investment schemes' (GIS) of sales of AAUs mostly from Eastern Europe and Russia, possibly with additional safeguards.

a more traditional interpretation of leverage: using CIB allowances as collateral to gain access to more financing in the form of 'carbon loans' or other financing partnerships.

(i) Access to Compliance Markets as a Source of Carbon Finance

The cornerstone of the CIB approach is to provide emerging economies with a source of up-front capital, created by the value of their CIB allowances in excess of current emissions. Ultimately, once a credible and reliable system of emissions monitoring had been established, and a country had managed to bend its emissions trajectory downwards, a country accepting a CIB would be able to sell surplus allowances—those above their actual emissions but below their allowance allocation (recall the dark shaded area above the new emissions pathway in Figure 19.1).

In the initial years of the programme, however, a country's use of CIB allowances would be subject to additional oversight to help ensure that they financed reductions in long-run emissions. Rather than being issued directly to participating countries, CIB allowances could be held by an independent intermediary acting as trustee. This approach would balance the need to give developing countries access to capital with the imperative that the money be used to help countries transform their economies.[19]

One practical detail concerns the use of AAUs, since the AAU market (which involves country-to-country trades) has seen only a handful of trades to date. To boost liquidity, a nation might wish to hold its CIBs in escrow and borrow against them, or it might wish to devolve them to national firms and emitters, so that they could be freely traded. Liquidity could be increased further by allowing CIB allowances to be sold directly into compliance markets such as the EU-ETS and a future US emissions market. In any case, transfers of CIB allowances, and security interests in them arising from pledging them as security for loans, would need to be recorded in electronic registries, as is already done to a great extent under the registries of the Kyoto Protocol and other cap-and-trade systems.

Even with substantial safeguards in place, CIBs offer a potential solution to the current dramatic shortfall in carbon finance. Current sources of funding are roughly an order of magnitude smaller than what is required. UN FCCC (2007*c*) provides a comprehensive review of financing needs and derives a global figure in the order of US$200 billion per year by 2030, a third of which is needed in developing countries.[20] By comparison, existing multilateral funding is in the

[19] Developing countries may well argue that industrialized countries have 'borrowed' such tons all along, no strings attached. This is certainly true. However, this argument would miss the binding environmental imperative and the opportunities additional CIB funds can provide in the required global transition to a low-carbon economy.

[20] This US$200 billion figure assumes a mitigation scenario that achieves global GHG emissions reductions by 25 per cent below 2000 levels by 2030. Similarly, IEA (2008*c*) estimated the cumulative

Table 19.1. Current and proposed funding towards mitigation

	Per year, in billion US$
Existing	
Official Development Assistance (ODA)	<2
Global Environment Facility (GEF)	0.25
World Bank's Climate Investment Fund	6 (total pledged over 3 years)
CDM	6–13
Proposals	
CDM levy (EU, others)	0.2–1.7
JI, market levy (Colombia, LDCs)	<2.25
AAU auctions (Norway)	15–25
CO_2 tax (Switzerland)	18.4
Air travel levy (LDCs)	4–10
Bunker fuels levy (LDCs)	4–15

Sources: UN FCCC (2008*a*, table 3); Capoor and Ambrosi (2008).

order of a few billion dollars per year (Table 19.1). CDM stands out as the largest such source, with funds of US$6 billion in 2006 and US$13 billion in 2007 (Capoor and Ambrosi, 2008). UN FCCC (2008*a*) summarizes alternative policy proposals, which come closer to filling the gap, but are still not adequate by themselves (bottom half of Table 19.1).

CDM is the largest current source of funds for mitigation in developing countries. CDM reform is sorely needed, especially given current inefficiencies in the system. While the criticisms levelled at CDM often focus on operational considerations, such as high transactions costs and concerns about additionality, two other concerns are more fundamental (Hepburn, 2007). First, even in the best of circumstances CDM is a very expensive way to reduce emissions in the developing world: the price paid, which is currently driven by demand in the EU compliance market, is far above marginal cost. As a result, CDM cannot achieve the 'carbon leverage' crucial to reducing emissions at the required scale. Second, CDM currently not only fails to reduce net emissions but actively undermines the incentives for participating countries to commit to limiting their own emissions (Hepburn, 2007, and Ch. 20 in this volume).

A number of proposals have been advanced for addressing CDM's environmental shortcomings. The most important of these, CDM discounting, would be environmentally essential if, in the context of attempting to keep options open for limiting warming to 2°C, the Parties opted to reform the CDM primarily by broadening it to sectoral or programmatic CDM.[21] Expanding the CDM to

need of financing in non-OECD countries in the order of US$27 trillion by 2050 to decrease global emissions by at least 50 per cent below current levels by 2050.

[21] By CDM discounting, we refer to the proposition that industrialized nations would apply a discount to CERs from the CDM, so that emitters in industrialized nations would need to tender more than one CER for every ton of compliance crediting in their home countries. See Petsonk (2007) and Hepburn (Ch. 20 in this volume), among others.

programmatic and sectoral levels could increase the scope for financial transfers to developing countries. But the steep discount on certified emission reductions (CERs) that would have to accompany such expansion, in order to keep the 2°C option open, would necessarily diminish the extent to which an expanded CDM could help fill the funding gap. CIBs seek to capitalize on the broadening aspects of these CDM reform proposals, while narrowing the funding gap, all in the context of remaining fully consistent with a 2°C path. CIBs, therefore, have the potential to build on CDM reform proposals while enabling developing countries to tap the power of carbon markets further, faster, and more efficiently.

CIBs could help fill the funding gap while remaining consistent with a 2°C path. Recall our preliminary calculations above, estimating flows in the order of at least US$20 billion per year for ten years. This is larger than any CDM flows, at least one order of magnitude larger than other existing multilateral flows, and ranks among the highest proposed new funding mechanisms. Moreover, the US$20 billion estimate represents a lower bound, since the pool of CIB allowances could be leveraged to achieve a multiple of the initial figure.

(ii) 'Carbon Leverage'

'Carbon leverage' means achieving more than a ton of emissions reduction for each CIB allowance. To make this concept more concrete, consider Figure 19.2. The *minimum* abatement that a CIB could finance (setting aside uncertainty for the sake of exposition) would be that achieved on a ton-for-ton basis—i.e. if CIB allowances were simply sold and used to purchase emissions reductions in the CIB country at the world market price. Given the 'low-hanging fruit' available in emerging economies, however, the marginal cost of emissions reductions (depicted in the figure by the MACC) is likely to lie well below the world GHG price. As a result, a ton-for-ton approach would transfer a sizeable rent to the CIB country, while failing to maximize emissions reductions.[22]

With greater information about the MACC, of course, more emissions reductions could be purchased with the same amount of money. In the limit, perfect price discrimination would equate the area under the MACC with the value of the CIB at world prices. Such an outcome might be approximated in practice with a reverse auction, or through a form of third-degree price discrimination in which projects were differentiated by sector or other observable characteristics. Finally, even greater abatement could be achieved through financing mechanisms—such as using CIBs as collateral to secure traditional financing that would otherwise not be available (or would otherwise be too costly).

[22] See Hepburn (Ch. 20) for a discussion of 'carbon leverage', there referred to as 'price discrimination'.

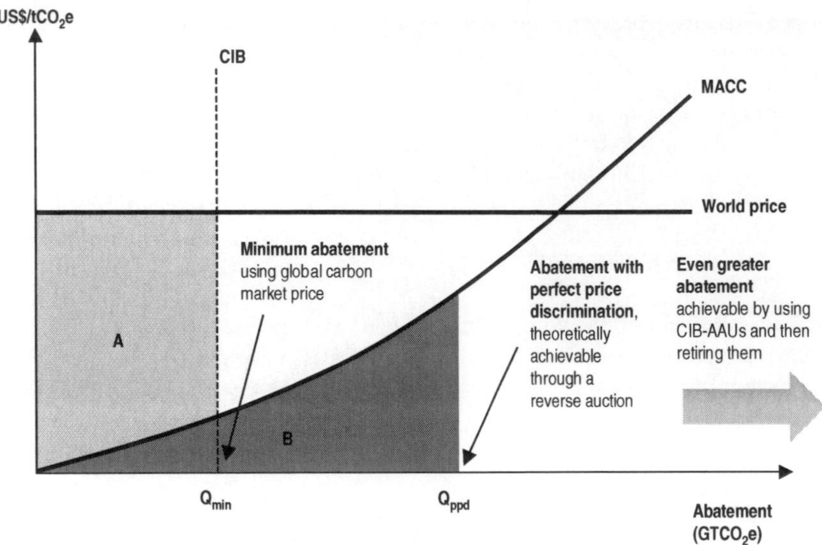

Figure 19.2. 'Carbon leverage' to increase abatement

(iii) Financing Mechanisms to Enable 'Financial Leverage'

The second kind of 'leverage' corresponds to the more traditional definition of 'financial leverage'. One could imagine three broad channels for disbursing CIB funds. First, CIB allowances could be used as collateral or as guaranteed debt service for commercial loans to secure traditional financing through private banks or perhaps export credit agencies. Used in this way, CIBs would facilitate financing by alleviating the need for alternative loan guarantees and expanding access to credit. Because the financiers would retain their incentive to assess the viability of projects and monitor performance, this approach would require relatively little oversight by the CIB trustee (the authority holding the CIB allowances) other than to perform due diligence on the banks providing the financing, and to ensure that the contract terms were not too generous. Since CIBs would be used only as collateral, a substantial fraction of them would be returned to the 'carbon capital account' after the completion of the underlying loan. Moreover, allowances could be (partially) retired after loan repayment to further strengthen the environmental integrity of the programme.

A second option—perhaps less leveraged but also more tightly overseen—could be a system of carbon loan payments or carbon dividends. In this case, the CIB allowances serve as a guaranteed stream of 'carbon cash flow'. Banks would provide incremental debt or equity financing for emissions reductions projects (in conjunction with other base financing).[23] The host country or project sponsor

[23] While incremental cost is an elusive concept in practice, given information asymmetries, it offers in principle a means of leveraging direct funding to supplement traditional sources of finance. For

would repay its debt (or pay out dividends) with CIB allowances. In the meantime, allowances would be held in escrow by the CIB trustee, who would disburse the funds and monitor compliance. The trustee (or another authority) would also be responsible for approving the projects and determining their expected yield of emissions reductions. Payments could still be structured to yield 'carbon leverage' of greater than ton-for-ton reductions. The International Finance Corporation (IFC), the private-sector lending arm of the World Bank, provides examples of systems following the first and second approach.

Finally, direct grants, funded by the proceeds from the sale of CIB allowances, would be the most tightly overseen and probably least-leveraged alternative. A grant mechanism could be modelled after the Multilateral Fund established by the Montreal Protocol to assist developing countries in reducing ozone-depleting substances, which is commonly seen as a success. As in that case, the responsibility of overseeing national action plans could be assigned to one central, international body, while other entities worked on a local level (the 'Implementing Agencies' in the Multilateral Fund) to approve funding and monitor projects. Grants could be directed at the incremental cost of emissions reductions.

While carbon leverage would be harder to achieve with grants than with alternative financing mechanisms, it could still be achieved by suitable selection of projects. An ideal mechanism would be a reverse auction. Given the desire of host countries to exercise significant control over investments, however, some sort of negotiated payment scheme might be more practical. For example, the size of a grant could be scaled to the expected emissions reductions, but with an initial payment per ton that was set well below the market allowance price. Or a portfolio of grants could be approved (perhaps at a programmatic or even sectoral level), with total payment tied to an estimate of the average cost per ton of avoided emissions. While there are obvious informational asymmetries, and hence a strong likelihood of significant information rents accruing to host countries, a greater than ton-for-ton reduction would probably be feasible.

None of these financing mechanisms is sufficient on its own; they are complements rather than substitutes. Using CIB allowances as collateral could appeal to countries with well-developed capital markets, and would be suited to projects where an incremental investment is easily identified and yields reliable and significant operating cost savings—for example, energy efficiency in commercial buildings. Carbon loan payments or dividends would be more appropriate to finance projects where (*i*) the incremental cost was fairly well-defined; (*ii*) the resulting emissions reductions could be accurately estimated and monitored; but (*iii*) those emissions reductions fail to translate into financial gains. Finally, grants could be used to finance policies or broader projects (e.g. transmission networks to support renewables) that contribute to long-term reductions in emissions but are less suited to conventional private-sector project finance.

example, traditional project finance might be available to fund a conventional coal-fired power plant; a CIB grant could provide the additional funding needed to improve drastically the plant's operating efficiency or to replace it with a renewable energy source.

IV. DESIGNING INSTITUTIONS TO PROMOTE PERFORMANCE

CIBs must be designed carefully to ensure that maximum financing flows toward low-carbon development projects and be able to achieve the twin goals of emissions reductions and economic growth. In particular, we need to define minimum criteria for participation, so that countries adopting CIBs are prepared to take full advantage of the financing provided; clear benchmarks for performance should be established, both to measure progress and to build confidence; and sharp incentives for compliance should be created.

(i) Minimum Criteria for Participation

To be allocated a CIB, a country would be required to meet a set of minimum criteria along the following lines.

(i) *Monitoring, reporting, and tracking requirements*
Ideally, nations taking CIBs will already have in place robust monitoring, tracking, and accounting systems for GHGs. However, the urgency of early action suggests that CIBs should be available to countries that are in the process of developing their GHG monitoring systems, even if those systems are not yet fully operational. The minimum criteria, therefore, might be (*a*) that a country have completed a current GHG inventory covering at least the sectors represented in the CIB;[24] and (*b*) that it be actively developing a GHG registry with associated emissions monitoring and reporting systems at the facility level.

(ii) *Institutional capacity*
At a minimum, countries taking CIBs should have demonstrated the ability to manage international donor funds or loans from international financial institutions such as the International Bank for Reconstruction and Development (IBRD) or the International Monetary Fund (IMF), and must express a willingness to accept international oversight of CIB financial flows.

(iii) *National action plans*
A prerequisite for participating countries to obtain financing under the CIB mechanism could be that they prepare national action plans defining a domestic strategy that will enable rapid shifts toward low-carbon pathways. These plans could include, among others: new or revised climate policies and regulations; plans to put in place operational GHG monitoring systems; projections of investments and financing needs; and timetables for emissions reductions. The plans would also set out performance benchmarks.

[24] Under the UN FCCC, non-Annex I countries submit GHG inventories as part of their 'national communications'. As of December 2008, however, only four countries have submitted more than one such communication—meaning that most countries lack updated, internationally vetted inventories. Hence the criterion suggested here would indeed be a binding one. Nonetheless, it could be met by gathering credible data on imports, production, and consumption of fossil fuels.

This approach could enable oversight bodies to assess a country's progress towards its commitments, while ensuring that all activities for which CIB financing will be requested remain consistent with a defined strategic framework.

(ii) Clear and Measurable Performance Benchmarks

The cornerstone of the CIB approach, and the key to maintaining its integrity, is to tie the availability of CIB allowances to measurable performance. A set of performance indicators or benchmarks should be established in advance on MRV and tracking of GHG emissions. Initially, a country's use of CIB allowances would be subject to a 'reserve requirement', with a substantial fraction of allowances withheld—similar to the 'commitment period reserve' allowances required under the Marrakech Accords (2001). In the CIB framework, these withheld allowances serve both as an incentive for the country to improve its MRV capabilities, and as a bond against the possibility of non-performance. As a country achieves each successive benchmark, the reserve requirement would be relaxed, giving the country access to a greater portion of its CIB allowances (and thus greater funding for low-carbon investment).

To build confidence in a country's ability to comply with its commitments, and to ensure an early start in reducing emissions, the criteria for progressing through the CIB mechanism could include requirements—or at least strong (financial) incentives—for complementary policies and measures to reduce emissions. CIB countries could, for example, be provided with funding and technical expertise to be able to demonstrate measurable progress in implementing building codes to promote energy efficiency, or minimum efficiency standards for certain consumer durables.

Over time, it is essential that comprehensive GHG inventories be available if compliance is to be assessed, and that the process does not go forward without accurate inventory data. Consequently, nations taking CIBs need to report their annual GHG emissions within a relatively short time period—for example, 3 years. The international community could usefully help these countries improve their emissions reporting and GHG inventories. Moreover, CIBs give participating nations incentives to improve the accuracy and transparency of their inventories, since it will enable them to attract more foreign investment.

(iii) Compliance and Enforcement

Compliance and enforcement are central issues in the design of *any* international regime; climate policy generally, and CIBs specifically, are no exception. In the context of CIBs, two distinct compliance problems can be identified. First, is the country using its CIB allotment to finance clean investment? Second, is the CIB country meeting its obligation to hold allowances sufficient to cover its emissions?

Each of these problems is individually familiar from international environmental policy. Multilateral development banks as well as private financiers face similar challenges in overseeing how grants and loans are spent in the context of economic development. As in that context, robust oversight of financial flows will be necessary to ensure that countries use their 'growth' budgets to fund long-term projects that will reduce GHG emissions in the long run. The stringency of such oversight would presumably vary depending on the financing mechanism used. In particular, when CIB allowances are effectively given to the recipient country as grants, the case for stringent oversight (on both normative and practical grounds) is strongest. When CIB allowances are used as collateral, with the prospect of eventually retiring them rather than releasing them into the market, the potential impact on the atmosphere is much reduced, and thus the need for oversight is as well. Moreover, in the case of private-sector involvement, some of the onus of compliance can be placed on the private-sector actor, who might be better equipped to monitor financial compliance.

With respect to compliance with emissions obligations, a CIB country could be treated much as Annex B parties are under the current system, once it had put in place an operational GHG monitoring system. (Recall that a country's incentive to put such a system in place is the prospect of accessing its CIB allowances.) In particular, a CIB country whose emissions exceeded allowable levels would be subject to the sanctions applicable to non-complying Annex B parties under the Marrakech Accords: i.e. the amount of its excess emissions would be subtracted from its emissions budget for the next commitment period, at a penalty rate of 1:1.3. When this provision was originally developed for inclusion in Kyoto context, it was intended to apply in the context of an agreement that comprised multiple commitment periods. The Kyoto Parties' failure to agree multiple commitment periods blunted the force of this 'seller liability' provision. This problem could be partially addressed by negotiating at least two consecutive compliance periods simultaneously, as we propose for CIBs.

While each compliance problem may be familiar from other settings, it is their combination that distinguishes CIBs from other compliance problems. Paradoxically this may be an advantage—in the same way that 'issue linkage' can enhance the potential for enforcement and compliance in other international regimes.[25]

For example, we have proposed that CIB allowances would be held in an 'escrow account' in order to allow for oversight. This, in turn, can serve as a key incentive for compliance, which ought to be especially effective in the early years of the programme: if a country has voluntarily taken on a CIB, presumably it will find it valuable in the first few years to comply with the requirements in order to continue to receive the withheld (escrowed) tons. This logic argues for giving large CIBs, but holding most allowances in reserve and releasing them only slowly over time. In this way the CIB can help solve not only the initial participation problem but also

[25] See Abrego *et al.* (2001) and Conconi and Perroni (2002); but see Barrett (Ch. 4 in this volume) for another view.

the ongoing dynamic participation (continuation) problem. It is also crucial that the escrow account be held as long as possible.

In theory, the escrow account can grow over time—to the extent that early investments 'bend the curve' downward, they will help free up more allowances under the CIB that can be invested in further projects. However, if the escrow account gets smaller as the date of 'full participation' (with a tighter cap) approaches, the incentive for compliance diminishes.

Ultimately, as in any agreement among sovereign nations, enforcement cannot be imposed entirely from without. The long-run solution to compliance, therefore, has to rest on changing the effective 'pay-off' for those who withdraw. CIBs need to finance investments that make it *more* attractive *ex post* to continue along the low-carbon path than to abandon the path and the commitments to it.

Again, the two compliance problems can work toward a mutual advantage. If financial oversight can be constructed in such a way as to assure proper investment incentives, then the investments made under CIBs will help increase the value from remaining in the international climate regime—akin to a 'low-carbon path dependency'.

Two analogies may be useful here. The first is the mobile phone network in the developing world. A stylized fact is that many developing countries have 'leapfrogged' development of a landline network with a mobile network. Once that happens there is little incentive to go back and develop the landline network. CIBs could help fund investments that leapfrog a high-carbon infrastructure in the same way. The case of distributed solar power versus a reliable, national electric-power grid comes to mind.

The politics and policy of international trade provide a second analogy. While the overall benefits of free trade to a country generally outweigh the costs, the political success or failure of a trade agreement depend on how it affects core domestic constituencies rather than aggregate net benefit. Initial participation in international trade agreements must overcome built-in domestic political resistance, because the losers from free trade (industries that have benefited from protectionist policies) will be more easily identified and better organized than the winners. However, once established, trade pacts can create an endogenous source of political support, by promoting the growth of export industries with new incentives and resources to engage in lobbying. The abstract aggregate benefits from freer trade are translated into concrete benefits for particular sectors and industries. Those domestic constituencies can then help to sustain the political will to comply with trade regimes going forward, even when such compliance comes at a cost to other interest groups. In effect, the act of participating in the regime helps to reshape incentives in favour of compliance.[26]

[26] See Gilligan (1997) and McGinnis and Movsesian (2000) for discussions of this effect in the context of US trade policy. Haggard (1988) presents a related institutional view (recounting how the passage of the Reciprocal Trade Act of 1934 favoured pro-free-trade domestic interests), while Frieden and Rogowski (1996) provide a succinct summary of how trade policy can affect the preferences of domestic interest groups by altering relative prices.

As the trade example makes particularly clear, the key to long-run compliance is to create the conditions within a country to sustain participation and involvement in a global carbon regime. That means creating domestic political constituencies that benefit from clean energy and from engagement with carbon markets in other countries.

V. CONCLUSION

Financing the transition to a low-carbon, high-efficiency economy is the key question of any international framework to address climate change and attempt to limit warming to 2°C above pre-industrial temperatures. Docking stations, in general, and CIBs, in particular, provide emerging economies with a voluntary mechanism to participate in global carbon markets on an early action basis.

CIBs achieve these twin challenges of emissions reductions and economic growth by giving countries allowances *above* current emissions in exchange for proper oversight and additional compliance mechanisms to enable the required rapid transition to cleaner development. The funds freed by CIBs could be quite significant—in the order of US$20 billion per year over ten years, without accounting for potential financial leveraging—and could provide an important element in the toolkit of available financing mechanisms for technological transfers and other mitigation options. CIBs reward early action, and do so in an environmentally sound and economically—and, thus, politically—viable fashion.

APPENDIX: DETAILS OF THE SCIENCE

The analysis laid out here shows that CIBs can be undertaken consistent with the goal of limiting global warming to 2°C above pre-industrial levels. Using peaking pathways, we generate sufficient atmospheric space under a global emissions-reduction pathway that meets the 2°C goal with a probability of 60 per cent and annual reductions after the peak of no more than 2.5 per cent.

Our analysis of global emissions reduction pathways builds on Meng *et al.* (2007) and Wang *et al.* (2007). We determined emission reduction pathways using the MAGICC model of greenhouse gases and climate (Wigley, 1993; Wigley and Raper, 2002; Wigley *et al.*, 2002), assuming the range of climate sensitivities recommended in the IPCC Fourth Assessment Report. The emissions in this paper include the six Kyoto gases (CO_2, methane, nitrous oxide, hydrofluorocarbons, perfluorocarbons, and sulphur hexafluoride). We aggregate them into units of CO_2 equivalent (CO_2e) using global warming potential values from the IPCC Second Assessment Report. We assume that emissions of other climatically important gases, including sulphur dioxide (SO_2) and tropospheric ozone precursors, follow the median of the IPCC Special Report on Emissions Scenarios (SRES). Through additional simulations, we found that concurrent abatement of these other gases under a global emission-reduction pathway would have only a small effect on temperature, as reductions in tropospheric ozone, a greenhouse gas, offset reductions in SO_2, a climate cooler.

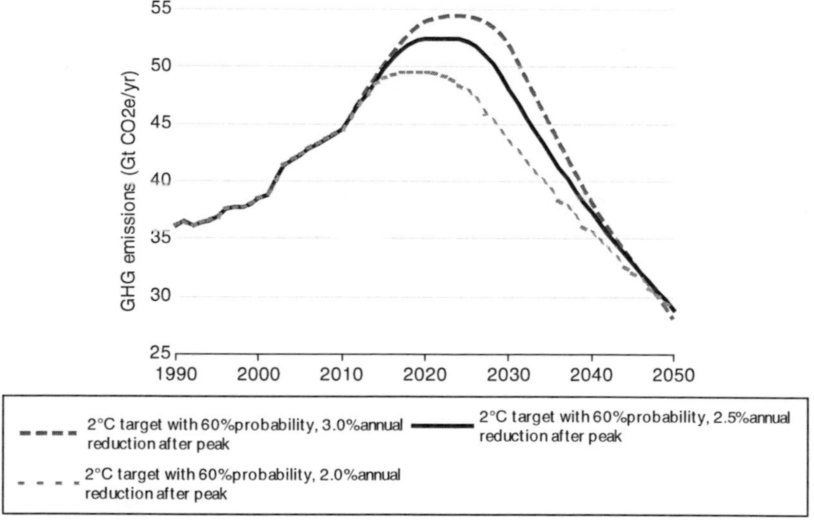

Figure 19.3. Global emissions reduction pathways with different annual reductions after the peak

Source: IEA and other emissions data; Environmental Defense Fund analysis.

The global emission reduction pathway considered in this paper avoids 2°C of warming with a probability of 60 per cent and a maximum annual emissions reduction rate of 2.5 per cent after the peak (Figure 19.3).[27] Various authors, including O'Neill and Oppenheimer (2002) and Oppenheimer and Petsonk (2005), have identified a warming of approximately 2°C above pre-industrial as a threshold beyond which the risk of dangerous climate change increases significantly. The pathway transitions from a peak to the maximum rate of reduction over a period of five years and corresponds to a total budget of 2,550 $GtCO_2e$ between 1990 and 2050, with approximately 1,770 $GtCO_2e$ remaining from 2009 onwards.

Note that we focus on concentration peaking pathways, rather than concentration stabilization pathways, in this analysis, similar to Meng *et al.* (2007) and Wang *et al.* (2007). Although stabilization pathways have been more commonly discussed in the scientific and policy arenas, there are other plausible pathways for avoiding dangerous levels of warming.[28] Peaking pathways have the additional benefit of allowing the possibility to bring concentrations, and eventually temperature, back down to or below today's level. However, a general guideline that should be followed is to choose as tight an overall emissions budget as possible to avoid a high *rate* of warming in the near term from a peaking pathway that may be acceptable in terms of the long-term *total* warming. Note that the main pathway

[27] We assumed that the probability of avoiding a particular temperature threshold is influenced mainly by the probability distribution function (PDF) for climate sensitivity, which we derived from the IPCC recommendation, with smaller effects from uncertainties in the carbon cycle, ocean-heat diffusivity, and the magnitude of sulphate aerosol radiative forcing (Meinshausen, 2006).

[28] See also Frame *et al.* (2006) for a critique of concentration stabilization pathways. Den Elzen and van Vuuren (2007) have also suggested peaking pathways as a more cost-effective alternative to stabilization pathways.

we consider in this paper, which gives a 60 per cent likelihood of avoiding 2°C of warming, entails a level of emissions reduction by 2050 equal to about 30 per cent below 1990 levels globally. This is comparable to a concentration stabilization pathway that gives a roughly 50 per cent likelihood of avoiding 2°C of warming (Meinshausen's 450 ppm CO_2e pathway that overshoots to 500 ppm[29]).

We also test sensitivity around the maximum annual reduction rates after the peak (changes in the slope), which corresponds to different levels of banking of emissions allowances (Figure 19.3).

We estimated historical emissions with data from various data sources: the IEA for CO_2 from fossil fuel combustion from 1990 to 2006 (OECD/IEA, 2008*a*); the EDGAR 4 database developed by the Netherlands Environmental Assessment Agency, the Joint Research Centre, and the Netherlands Organisation for Applied Scientific Research for other fossil CO_2 emissions from industrial processes, such as cement production, and from oil and natural gas wells from 1990 to 2005 (Olivier and Berdowski, 2001); Houghton (2008) for CO_2 emissions from land-use change and forestry (LUCF) from 1990 to 2005; and US Environmental Protection Agency (EPA) for non-CO_2 gases from 1990 to 2005 (US EPA, 2006). For projected BAU fuel combustion CO_2 emissions from 2007 to 2030, we used the IEA *World Energy Outlook* (OECD/IEA, 2008*b*), interpolating between the years for which data are provided. For other fossil CO_2 emissions, we simply assumed that they contribute the same fraction of total fossil CO_2 emissions going forward as they did during 1990–2005. For LUCF, we simply extrapolated the Houghton data using the average regional linear trends during 1990–2005. As the EPA estimates for non-CO_2 gases included projections through 2020, we used those projections, extrapolating to extend them beyond 2020.

Figure 19.4 displays the resulting historical and BAU greenhouse gas emissions for large emitting countries, regions, and LUCF.

Note that following BAU through 2030 would exceed a 2°C pathway with a greater than 80 per cent probability as well as a pathway that assures warming below 2°C with only 50 per cent probability.

We have also conducted sensitivity analysis using projected fossil CO_2 emissions from POLES (via the World Resources Institute's Climate Analysis Indicators Tool (CAIT)), which resulted in a larger amount of atmospheric space, owing to the lower projections given by POLES relative to IEA.

Table 19.2 lays out our assumptions for the future emissions from industrialized countries and deforestation under climate policy. Using these assumptions we find sufficient space under the 2°C pathway to support surplus CIB allowances with a total global volume of 12 $GtCO_2e$ in 2013, commensurate with the 8 $GtCO_2e$ budget needed over ten years to generate annual CIB flows of $20 billion.

The targets for the United States are based on the proposal by President Barack Obama stated at the Governors' Global Climate Summit on 18 November 2008. Those for OECD Europe are based on the EU's announced targets (with the weaker option for 2020). For Russia, we interpreted optimistically that their proposal to establish a post-Kyoto target along the lines of other Annex I countries, announced at the UN climate negotiations in Poznan in 2008, will amount to targets identical to those of the EU. For the rest of the industrialized countries, we assumed that they would adopt either the US or the EU targets. For tropical deforestation, the targets we assumed correspond roughly

[29] Various citations to Meinshausen *et al.*'s work are available at www.simcap.org

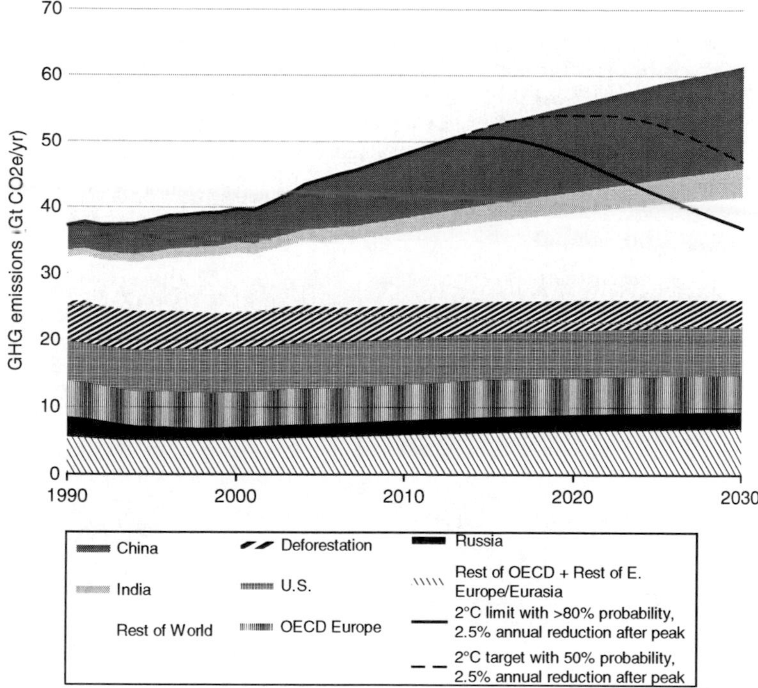

Figure 19.4. Global emissions at BAU to 2030

Source: IEA and other emissions data; Environmental Defense Fund analysis.

Table 19.2. Emissions targets assumed in analysis (% difference from 1990 base year)

Country/ Group	USA	OECD Europe	Russia	Canada, Japan, rest of OECD, Pacific	Rest of E. Europe / Eurasia	Tropical deforestation
2020	0	−20	−20	0	−20	−30
2050	−80	−60	−60	−80	−60	−80

to Brazil following through with its targets announced in Poznan and the rest of the tropical forest countries not acting until after 2020, when they, in turn, begin reducing deforestation. For all the aforementioned targets, we assumed that the new climate policies begin in 2013 and interpolated linearly between the emissions in 2012, 2020, and 2050.

Note that these targets necessarily assume that any emissions trading proceeds within the hypothesized caps set forth in the table. That is, this particular example assumes that neither the United States nor the EU authorizes the use of CERs, derived from reducing emissions in uncapped developing countries below BAU, to be used to offset increases in emissions in industrialized countries; and it necessarily assumes that no reductions in emissions from deforestation in Brazil are used to offset emissions increases above capped levels in industrialized countries. Of course, different scenarios entailing the use of CDM or REDD tons as offsets could be developed; however, they would entail more ambitious targets in other nations if the overall emissions constraints specified are to be met.

20

International Carbon Finance and the Clean Development Mechanism

*Cameron Hepburn**

I. INTRODUCTION

Many of the opportunities to reduce emissions at relatively low cost are located in developing countries. It appears that these opportunities must be seized to keep atmospheric carbon dioxide (CO_2) concentrations from exceeding the 450–550 parts per million (ppm) range suggested by Stern (2007). But poor countries are not immediately capable of taking all these opportunities;[1] they have other pressing priorities for their scarce resources. The simple conclusion is that rich countries must provide large-scale flows of 'carbon finance' to poor countries.

The international carbon-finance framework is thus at the heart of the global deal on climate change. The issues are complex. Carbon-finance transfers to poor countries are sometimes seen as compensation for harms caused by the emissions from rich nations. Others see international carbon finance as a 'cost containment' device, reflecting the relatively low-cost opportunities to prevent lock-in of fossil-fuel-based production and consumption. Yet others see carbon finance as an opportunity for low-carbon development. All these perspectives are involved in debates on the appropriate structure of the carbon-finance framework, adding complexity. Nevertheless, it is clear that for a 450–550ppm pathway to be attainable, the carbon-finance flows required to make the necessary emission reductions in developing countries are around US$100 billion or more, which is at least an order of magnitude greater than the flows occurring today.

A global deal on climate change must therefore create a framework to deliver funds efficiently, effectively, and fairly. Three key questions underpin the design of the international carbon-finance regime. First, roughly how many emission reductions should be paid for by rich nations—what is the scale of the financial flows? Second, what mechanisms should be employed to raise the necessarily funds? Third, how should the funds be allocated? The second and third questions are the main subject of this paper.

* Smith School of Enterprise and the Environment and New College, University of Oxford.

[1] This is not to suggest that developing countries are not taking any action to reduce emissions. There is lively discussion concerning 'nationally appropriate mitigation actions' (NAMAs).

The answers are not obvious. The first question, concerning the scale of financial flows, requires both empirical and normative analysis, along with an awareness of political reality. A rough order-of-magnitude estimate might be advanced as follows. In order to reach a 450ppm pathway, it is argued that reductions by developed countries of 25–40 per cent compared to 1990 levels are required by 2020, alongside a slower increase in emissions from developing countries, so that by 2020 emissions are around 15–30 per cent less than business-as-usual (BAU) (IPCC, 2007*d*; European Commission, 2009). Depending on the specific BAU scenario, this involves reductions of up to 10 Gt carbon-dioxide equivalent (CO_2e) per annum to occur in the developing world by 2020 (Höhne and Ellermann, 2008). As noted above, developing countries are only able and willing to pay for a portion of those reductions, and to bridge the gap the rich world would need to provide carbon finance for perhaps 5 $GtCO_2e$ annually.

The corresponding carbon financial flows are non-trivial. Even allowing for the fact that many of these reductions in developing countries might be secured at relatively low cost, the incremental financing flows required are at least in the order of many tens of billions of euros per annum. Indeed, the total carbon finance required is likely to be in the hundreds of billions of euros annually.[2]

By way of comparison, fossil-fuel subsidies are estimated to stand currently at over US$300 billion per annum, of which US$220 billion per annum is in 20 non-OECD countries (Barbier, 2009).[3] Eliminating these subsidies is difficult because they are often hidden, supported by powerful vested interests, and perceived (often inaccurately) to help the poor and to support energy security. Yet there are some phase-out success stories, and cancelling these subsidies alone would be expected to reduce emissions by 6 per cent (Barbier, 2009) and would raise public funds in the same order of magnitude as the carbon-finance flows required.

So the carbon-finance task is not necessarily impossible: governments intervene in and distort energy markets for alleged social purposes to a much greater extent every year. And nor are we starting from scratch on climate finance. Several mechanisms are already in place, including one market-based approach and a multilateral fund. By far the largest mechanism for delivering carbon finance from rich to poor countries to date has been the Clean Development Mechanism (CDM), which was incorporated into the Kyoto Protocol at the urging of US negotiators. The CDM operates as a 'no-lose' mechanism for poor countries; reductions in emissions from BAU may be eligible for credits, but poor countries

[2] Stern (2008) estimates that achieving climate stabilization would imply annual flows from developed to developing countries of up to US$100 billion by 2030. Project Catalyst (2009) estimates that €55–80 billion p.a. will be required in incremental financing flows, on top of €130 billion p.a. in incremental capital investment, averaged over the 2012–20 period, in order to achieve eventual stabilization at 450ppm.

[3] Russia alone has US$40 billion in energy subsidies annually, mostly for reducing the consumer price of natural gas, with Iran's energy subsidies at a similar level. China, Saudi Arabia, India, Indonesia, Ukraine, and Egypt each have subsidies in excess of US$10 billion per year.

are not obliged to make any specific reductions. The mechanism is expected to deliver around 300–400m Certified Emission Reductions (CERs) annually over the 2008–12 period, corresponding to international carbon financial flows of several billion euros annually.[4] This is not a bad start. But comparisons with the necessary reductions and financial flows discussed above indicate that international carbon finance need to be scaled up by at least an order of magnitude over the 2012–20 period.

In scaling up international carbon finance, several important problems need to be addressed. The CDM, while promising, is a long way from being a 'first-best' market mechanism, and reform is clearly needed. The problems are relatively clear: setting BAU baselines is dogged by uncertain and asymmetric information, there are potentially unhelpful dynamic incentives, and perverse interactions with national policies. Additionally, the allocation of funds through a market, at market prices, reduces the 'carbon leverage' of the system, or the tonnes of emission reductions delivered per euro of carbon finance.

Unfortunately, experience with multilateral carbon funds has been significantly less successful. The UN Global Environment Facility (GEF), for instance, is centralized, donor-dependent, faced with continuing political disputes,[5] and has simply been unable to raise and allocate carbon finance at anywhere near the level of the CDM.[6] Furthermore, poor countries have little reason to feel confident in proposals that rely upon directly raising public funds from rich-country treasuries—the poor record in delivering Overseas Development Assistance (ODA) for the Millennium Development Goals serves as one warning, but there are many other examples of solemn pledges that are blithely broken when the time comes to deliver.

This chapter addresses the design of an international carbon-finance framework for the 2012–20 period, with a focus on CDM reform and its complements and substitutes. It does not address financing for adaptation, or research and development of low-carbon technologies, or avoided deforestation (see Ch. 15 by Andersson, Plantinga, and Richards) or questions of governance (see Ch. 22 by Ghosh and Woods). Section II outlines how the CDM works, and reviews performance to date. Section III assesses the challenges faced by the international carbon-finance framework. It focuses on three key areas where the CDM has been less than perfect: environmental integrity; scale; and the provision of 'carbon leverage' to maximize the carbon 'bang for buck'. Section IV examines possible future directions of the carbon-finance framework. Incremental reform options are examined, such as improvements to staffing, governance, and the rules and

[4] The CDM and Joint Implementation (JI) combined are estimated to have generated annual investment of US$4.5–8.5 billion, and leveraged ten times as much in overall investment from the private sector, so that overall investment stimulated by CDM and JI is US$45–85 billion.

[5] See Fairman (1996) for some of the early issues, and Carbon Trust (2009).

[6] According to the UN Framework Convention on Climate Change (UN FCCC, 2008*b*), total funding since the establishment of the GEF in 1991 amounts to over US$2 billion, or about US$0.22 billion per year. However, it is estimated that the GEF leverages public- and private-sector financing at a level of US$1.15 billion per year.

functioning of programmatic CDM. More radical options are also considered, including CER discounting and sectoral approaches. Finally, altogether new institutional approaches are briefly discussed. Section V concludes.

II. REVIEW OF THE CLEAN DEVELOPMENT MECHANISM

(i) Overview

The CDM was established under Article 12 of the Kyoto Protocol to support projects that reduce emissions in poor countries (so-called 'non-Annex I' countries) and contribute to 'sustainable development'. The mechanism allows rich countries (so-called 'Annex I' countries) or their firms to purchase CERs from projects in non-Annex I countries, provided the project employs approaches and technologies approved by the CDM Executive Board (CDM EB), in Bonn, Germany. CERs are only created if the project is approved by the two host countries (one from Annex I and one from non-Annex I) and the CDM EB, whose approval is given after the project has satisfied a number of different procedural stages including 'validation', 'registration', and eventually 'issuance' of CERs (Hepburn, 2006). In particular, the emissions reductions must be judged by an independent verifier to be real, measurable, and 'additional' to any that would occur in the absence of the certified project activity.

Highly technical debates over this last concept of 'additionality' have generated a vast number of 'methodologies' to assess whether reductions would or would not have occurred without the CDM. As of 1 March 2009, almost 300 methodologies had been officially submitted to the CDM EB, and 120 different methodologies had been approved for use. The time and intellectual effort required to develop and agree these methodologies initially caused significant delays and frustration for market participants. Compounding this, the CDM EB was initially badly resourced, and inadequately staffed by part-time government secondees. In more recent times, however, the flow of fees from CER registration and issuance has enabled the CDM EB significantly to increase staff to more than 70 employees, allowing greater delegation of tasks and hopefully also improving consistency and speed of decision-making.

While it is tempting to see the cost of establishing these methodologies as a particular bureaucratic disadvantage of the CDM, the same conceptual issues arise under any 'no-lose' mechanism, where emissions reductions are determined relative to a BAU baseline.[7] Recognizing this, CDM methodologies now often serve as a point of reference for other schemes, including JI (another Kyoto flexible mechanism) and new schemes under development in the USA and elsewhere. In other words, the problematic aspect is the specification of baselines, which under

[7] For instance, a multilateral fund allocating finance between projects would also want to assess whether the projects would have happened anyway, without the funding, and hence the same issues of 'additionality' arise.

the CDM are defined by BAU. Designing and implementing a comprehensive cap-and-trade scheme would make this problem easier, but does not escape the need to set baselines, which are defined in negotiations over the cap and the allocation of allowances between regulated entities. As we have seen in the EU Emissions Trading Scheme (ETS), this political process of negotiating caps can be far from straightforward.[8]

(ii) Performance to Date

Despite the institutional bottlenecks and the time required to refine the inherently difficult notion of 'additionality', the CDM has actually been one of the success stories of the Kyoto regime. As at 1 March 2009, there were 4,660 CDM projects in the system, of which 1,424 had achieved registration with the CDM EB and 473 had issued CERs. Indeed, there has been a veritable explosion of project activity since the Kyoto protocol entered into force on 16 February 2005. Figure 20.1(*a*) shows projected CERs to 2012 from all projects by technology type. Notable is the market's initial focus on hydrofluorocarbon (HFC) and nitrous oxide (N_2O) gases, which have a high global-warming potential and provide an extremely cost-effective way to reduce tonnes of CO_2e. By December 2006, however, these opportunities had been all but exhausted, and Figure 20.1(*a*) shows that attention then moved to renewable energy projects, in particular wind and hydro. Other projects have focused on industrial reductions (e.g. cement, coal-mine methane), energy efficiency, and fuel switching, where the project-level carbon price signal provided by the CDM is well-suited to encouraging changes in firm behaviour. In contrast, the mechanism is poorly suited to more distributed activities in forestry, agriculture, transport, and building efficiency, where there has been hardly any progress under the CDM.

Figure 20.1(*b*) shows projected CERs by host country. After a slow start, China has now captured over 50 per cent of the CER market, driven by strong institutional support provided through the Chinese National Development and Reform Commission (NDRC), which requires Chinese asset owners to partner with a buyer from an Annex 1 country in the development of the project. Chinese firms have benefitted from this partnership with Western and international firms. By way of contrast, no such requirement is imposed in India, where project owners often attempt to bring projects though the UN FCCC system without outside assistance. Volumes are correspondingly lower. It is also notable that Africa only has around 2 per cent of the projects in the system, which might be seen to be disappointing, given that the mechanism was intended to promote sustainable development.

Actual deliveries of CERs are anticipated to be much lower than the simplistic estimates from Project Design Documents (PDD) shown in Figure 20.1. Downward revisions are appropriate to allow for: project delays in construction;

[8] Many economists argue that auctioning the allowances provides a superior solution along several dimensions: Hepburn *et al.* (2006*b*) provide a summary of the arguments.

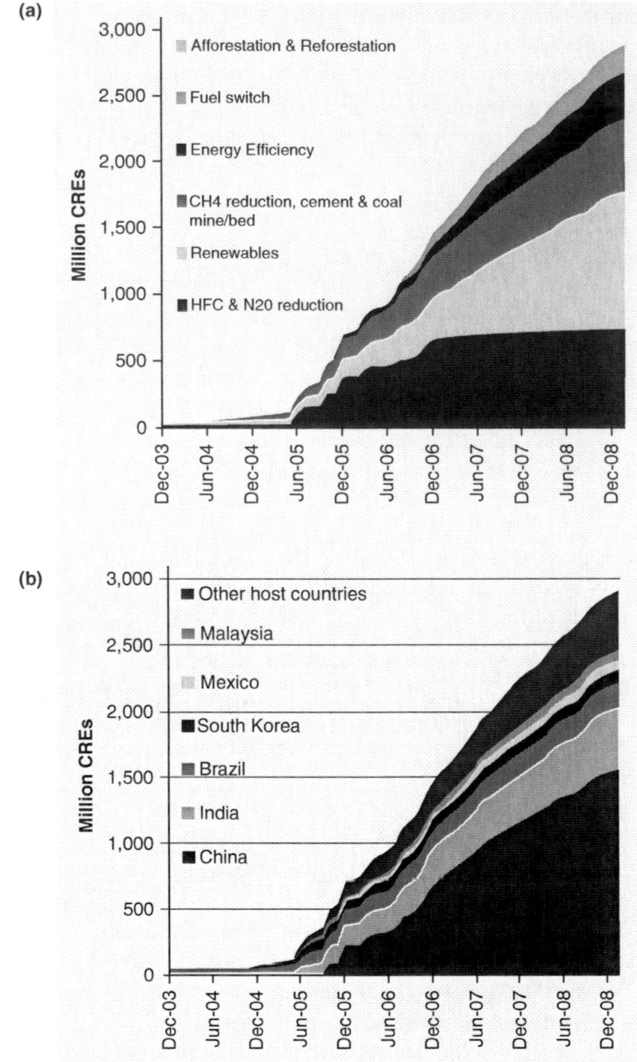

Figure 20.1. Accumulated CERs projected to deliver before 2012 by (*a*) project type; (*b*) host country

Note: Charts show the total CERs to be generated to 2012, based on estimates in the Project Design Document (PDD), and include volumes from all projects across all stages of the project cycle, from beginning validation through to issuance. Volumes are included from the date the project began its public-comment period in validation (marked on the horizontal axis).

Source: UNEP Risoe (2009).

optimism bias in performance once the project is up and running; procedural delays; and decisions by the CDM EB to reject more projects than originally anticipated. Indeed, compared with the 3,000 million CERs in Figure 20.1, industry forecasts for delivery between 2008 and 2012 tend to be somewhere in the range estimated by the World Bank of 1,400–2,200 million CERs, or roughly 300–400 million CERs annually (Capoor and Ambrosi, 2008). By comparison, at 1 March 2009, 250 million CERs had been issued.

Overall, the CDM has been surprisingly successful at delivering vast numbers of emission-reduction projects in key countries around the world. It has mobilized substantial amounts of private capital, and even with the various discounts discussed above, it will deliver substantial emission reductions. Furthermore, anecdotal evidence suggests the CDM has stimulated many emission-reduction projects that ultimately never went on to receive carbon finance because, after financial analysis, it turned out that the projects would be profitable without the CDM. However, the CDM has been significantly less successful at 'reputation management' and as the number of projects has grown, so, too, has the criticism in the public press and from parts of the academic community which are examined in section III.

III. CHALLENGES FOR CARBON FINANCE POST-2012

Criticisms of the CDM have been varied, but the important challenges tend to have been focused on three areas.[9] First, the environmental integrity of the emission reductions has been questioned, with the suspicion that some proportion of the credited activity would have happened even without the CDM. In other words, critics argue that a proportion of the CERs generated are not 'additional'. Second, while the private-sector response to the CDM has exceeded expectations, the mechanism is currently only capable of around 400 project registrations each year, and reductions of 300–400 $MtCO_2e$ annually are an order of magnitude lower than the 5 $GtCO_2e$ annual reductions required in a post-2012 carbon-finance framework. Third, debate continues over the desirability of the fact that early entrants have made substantial profits from cheap projects, such as those destroying HFC-23 gases. Constraints on the willingness and ability of the rich countries to transfer finance to poor countries, particularly in a financial crisis and a recession, imply that 'economic rents' or excess profits, should be minimized where possible, to maximize funds flowing directly to reducing emissions, and to increase the 'carbon leverage' of the finance provided. We consider these three criticisms in turn.

[9] This chapter does not address criticisms that non-Annex 1 host countries are not taking the requirement of 'sustainable development' seriously, which are outlined and addressed by Hepburn (2007), Boyd *et al.* (2007), Olsen (2007), and Schneider (2007). See also Wara (2007) and Wara and Victor (2008) for criticisms related to environmental integrity and rents.

(i) Environmental Integrity

Additionality

There is a fundamental asymmetry of information between CER project developers and the market regulator, the CDM EB. The CDM EB is reliant upon the project developer, and the independent verifiers, to provide an accurate assessment of the BAU scenario. The project developer must show that the project is not BAU, because of financial or other barriers to investment. The BAU is always uncertain, but the project developer is likely to have a better grasp of the most realistic BAU scenario than the CDM EB does from Bonn.

The consequences of uncertain and asymmetric information would be expected to be adverse selection (Akerlof, 1970). Non-additional projects are cheaper (since they were going to occur anyway), so the greater the information asymmetry, and the less reliable the verifiers, the higher the expected proportion of non-additional projects. While the independent verifiers conduct detailed (and relatively expensive) checks of the project data and the plausibility of its baselines, guaranteeing the 'additionality' of all of the 4,660 projects in the system is impossible, and few would disagree that CERs have been awarded to some projects that would have occurred anyway.

In many policy contexts, this is not necessarily considered to be a bad outcome. For instance, feed-in tariffs to incentivize renewable energy, commonly used in the USA, Germany, and other nations, pay generators irrespective of whether their renewable energy is 'additional' to what otherwise would have occurred. Payment is made simply for the provision of renewable energy to the grid. By increasing the returns of renewable generation, the policy encourages entry to the industry, and provides a stable price signal that encourages investment.

The CDM is arguably more economically efficient than a feed-in tariff, because in addition to providing payments to encourage provision of a desirable good (emission reductions), the payment is only made if the good would not have otherwise been delivered. However, the CDM is held to a higher standard than a feed-in tariff for the simple reason that it is an offset mechanism. The issuance of CERs allows for an increase of emissions by the (Annex I) country or firm that purchases the credits. As such, if CERs are issued when emissions have not actually been reduced, the net result is an increase in global emissions.

Perverse Policy Incentives

Projects mandated by law are arguably not 'additional' if the law requires them to occur irrespective of whether they receive carbon finance from the CDM. In theory, therefore, the CDM could create perverse incentives for national governments to delay the introduction of policies to reduce emissions, to ensure their firms remain eligible for CERs. Concerns about these potential policy disincentives have been expressed by many commentators (Samaniego and Figueres, 2002; Figueres, 2004; Bosi and Ellis, 2005; Cosbey *et al.*, 2005).

For these reasons, the CDM EB introduced two rules in 2004 to prevent countries from obtaining more CERs by passing bad environmental laws.[10] First, the 'E+ rule' states that the CDM baseline should ignore policies or regulations implemented since December 1997 that favour emissions-intensive activity. This reduces the perverse incentive for a host country to increase emissions, and then reduce the same emissions with support from the CDM. Second, the 'E− rule' states that the baseline should ignore policies or regulations implemented since November 2001 that favour less emissions-intensive activity. This reduces the perverse incentives for a host country not to reduce the baseline emissions. While the implementation of these two rules has not been perfect (Michaelowa *et al.*, 2008), they do reduce incentives for bad policy.

But there is a trade-off between a strict implementation of the E− rule and the notion of additionality. For instance, China's renewable energy programmes have helped support a significant increase in wind- and hydro-power projects. Under the E− rule, which protects China's incentive to roll out these policies, the renewable energy programmes are ignored for the purpose of determining CDM eligibility. Critics therefore argue that some renewable projects that have received CERs actually would have happened without the CDM, because of China's renewable-energy support policies.

(ii) Scale

As set out above, the post-2012 international carbon-finance framework needs to generate genuine emission reductions in the developing world, paid for by the developed world, of perhaps 5 $GtCO_2e$ annually. The current capacity of the CDM is around 300–400 $MtCO_2e$ annually. Similarly, the total financial value of activity stimulated by the CDM, including primary and secondary trade of CERs, was estimated in 2007 to be around US$13 billion (Capoor and Ambrosi, 2008), while the net financial flows required from developed to developing countries are in the tens of billions, if not greater. In other words, the international carbon-finance framework needs to be scaled up by at least an order of magnitude.

The consequences of the mismatch in scale of the problem and the solution are already beginning to be felt. For instance, the CDM has so far achieved relatively little to stop investment in high-carbon capital assets, which will be locked in for decades. China, in particular, despite its strong renewable programme, is well known to be increasing coal-fired power-generating capacity, most of which is likely still to be operating in several decades, and which may be costly to retrofit with carbon capture and sequestration (CCS) technology.

Scaling up the carbon-finance framework requires consideration of both the supply and the demand side of the equation. There is little point in constructing a mechanism able to supply up to 5 $GtCO_2e$ annually in carbon offsets from

[10] The Executive Board clarification of the E+/E− rules occurred at their 16th meeting (available at http://cdm.unfccc.int/EB/016/eb16repan3.pdf).

developing countries if developed countries do not create demand for the offsets and stand willing to pay for them. Demand for emission reductions (and the money to pay for them) might come through tighter developing-country targets with provision for greater use of offsets, auction revenues from EU allowances (EUAs) or 'assigned amount units' (AAUs), a levy on aviation and/or maritime emissions, or directly from public balance sheets. However, experience suggests that there will be many other political demands placed on publically accessible sources of funds, and that setting tighter targets and using the market may offer the most politically realistic alternative to create demand and funds to pay for emission reductions in developing countries.

(iii) Leverage and Rents

Given the limitations on developed countries' willingness to pay for emission reductions, it is vital that the funds available are spent effectively and are fully leveraged by private sector capital. Wagner *et al.* (Ch. 19) argue that there are two forms of leverage. First, 'carbon leverage' increases the number of emission reductions per unit of finance which amounts to price discrimination such that project developers are paid closer to their marginal abatement cost. Second, 'financial leverage', which is traditional leverage of carbon-related assets and expected revenue streams to raise debt and/or equity for emission-reduction projects. A particularly important financial leverage ratio is the ratio of private capital raised for every unit of public capital deployed.

The CDM in its current form does not provide a particularly high degree of carbon leverage. It rewards project developers on the basis of market prices, set through the interaction of supply of CERs, demand for CERs, and government interventions in the market, such as the unofficial Chinese floor price for CERs. As in any market, the market-clearing price can be substantially above marginal cost, creating economic rents as shown in Figure 20.2. These rents flow partly to project developers in poor countries, but also to financial intermediaries who add value, bear risk, but who also profit from information asymmetries.

There is nothing particularly surprising about a market generating profits for project developers who are able to reduce emissions. This is how markets work. However, using a market mechanism limits the potential for price discrimination, which is relevant when the funds available to pay for emission reductions are limited. For instance, Annex 1 governments could capture some of these rents, and reallocate them to purchase more emission reductions, as shown in Figure 20.2(*b*). To some extent, China already does this. For instance, it has introduced two measures designed to retain the profits from the CDM within the country:

- The 'unofficial' CER floor price of €8–9;
- A tax on CER projects at different rates to reflect the size of the rents available to international buyers, on the basis that CERs are 'national resources'. Tax rates are 65 per cent on HFC and perfluorocarbon (PFC) projects, 30 per cent on N_2O projects, and 2 per cent on renewable and other projects, with the revenues going to promote 'sustainable development'.

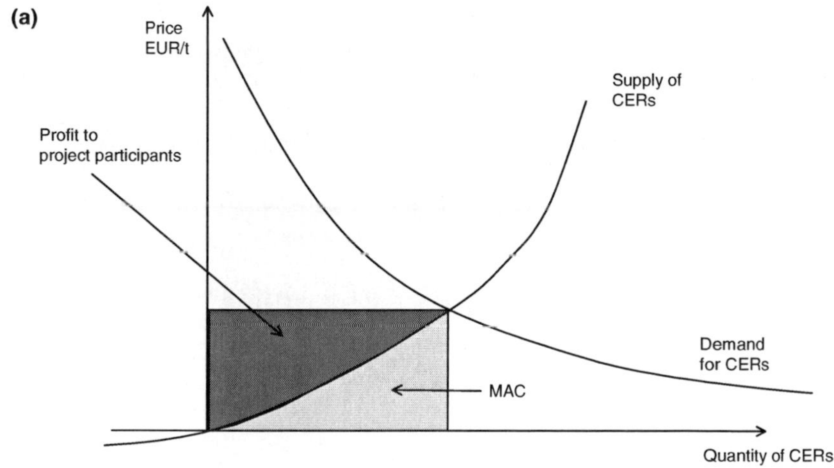

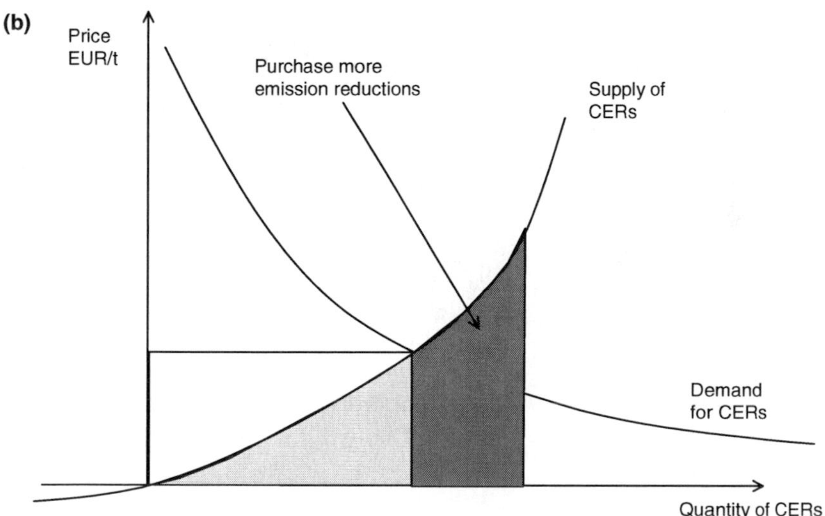

Figure 20.2. Price discrimination would reduce rents and increase 'carbon leverage'

As discussed above, however, governments do not have perfect information on marginal abatement costs, therefore paying just a small amount more than the marginal abatement cost for emission reductions is not possible unless a mechanism were introduced to induce developers to reveal their marginal abatement costs and a buyer's cartel was formed. This is easier said than done, given the potential for gaming and perverse incentives.

Even if perfect price discrimination were possible, it may not be desirable. Allowing rapidly-moving firms to initially make high profit margins does serve several useful functions: (*i*) it compensates new project developers for the risks involved in attempting to take projects through the (uncertain) CDM EB processes; (*ii*) it creates publicity and spreading awareness of the economic merits of reducing emissions; and (*iii*) it induces new entrants who compete away profit margins.

Those concerned by profits under a market-based approach are likely to favour a more centralized multilateral funding approach. An example is the World Bank's new Climate Investment Funds, which have had over US$6 billion pledged from rich donor countries.[11] The Climate Investment Funds are intended to provide a source of interim funding through which the Multilateral Development Banks will provide additional grants and concessional financing to developing countries to address urgent climate-change challenges. Time will tell whether the Climate Investment Funds succeed, but initial signals are relatively positive. In contrast, experience with the UN GEF is less encouraging. The Carbon Trust (2009) notes that the GEF has been constrained by politics, and that its centralized funding approach is not credible as the primary means for allocating carbon finance on the required scale. Further discussion is in section IV (iv), 'Multilateral carbon funds'.

IV. FUTURE DIRECTIONS

Critics of market-based approaches often struggle to articulate a credible and politically feasible alternative, lending support to the view that the underlying problem is intrinsically challenging. Indeed, much of the discussion has been focused on reforming, and adding to, the existing CDM, rather than replacing it entirely with some other framework.

Nevertheless, given the challenges experienced to date, it is clear that both CDM reform and additional carbon-finance frameworks will be needed. In particular, the CDM delivers a relatively low degree of 'carbon leverage', although the creation of a tradable asset (the CER) has enabled innovation in and high rates of 'financial leverage'. As noted above, the CDM in its current form is not particularly well suited to delivering emission reductions in forestry, agriculture, transport, and buildings. Other mechanisms and instruments need to be developed that are better adapted to these challenges.

(i) Criteria

Any new or reformed carbon-finance framework needs to improve upon the CDM's performance on the three issues discussed above: environmental integrity (section II(i)); scale (section II(ii)); and maximizing 'carbon leverage' (section III(iii)). In addition to these three, there are another two criteria to bear in mind.

[11] See http://www.worldbank.org/cif

Economic efficiency: The framework should remain as efficient as the CDM is now, in that the market seeks out the cheapest reductions.[12] Reformed or new schemes should aim to preserve efficiency to the extent possible. As a general rule, the greater the political involvement in decision-making over the allocation of funds, the less likely static economic efficiency will be achieved. Similarly, the framework should ensure that the incentives reach the specific people and firms making decisions. Multilateral or sectoral funding schemes are clearly inefficient if funds get lost within corrupt governments, diverted to other purposes, or generate diluted incentives for actual decision-makers.

Transitional/dynamic incentives: Because the current CDM does not generate emission reductions above and beyond developed-country targets, it can only ever serve a transitional function to some other arrangement. At this point, it appears possible that this other arrangement will involve internationally linked cap-and-trade schemes, with political negotiations on allowances substituting for the challenges of establishing BAU counterfactuals. As such, an important aspect of the post-2012 carbon-finance framework must be that it supports the transition from an offset mechanism to the mobilization of global emissions reductions through cap-and-trade schemes. The framework should support advanced developing countries to move towards developing their own schemes.

With these five criteria in mind—environmental integrity, scale, leverage, economic efficiency, and transitional incentives—we proceed to examine incremental and radical CDM reform options, and consider the potential role of new carbon-finance institutions.

(ii) Incremental CDM Reforms

There is a myriad of small reforms to the rules and the functioning of the CDM that would improve the system. We focus on two of the more important issues here. First, resolving governance problems is central to the future performance of the CDM on the critical criteria of scale and integrity. Second, an important point noted in section II(ii) is that the CDM has largely failed to deliver on emission reductions from sources that are widely dispersed. We therefore briefly consider progress on 'Programmatic CDM', which is intended to incentivize distributed emission reductions.

Governance of the CDM EB

The part-time members of the CDM EB simultaneously perform regulatory, executive, and quasi-judicial functions, and preside over a market worth €13 billion in 2007 (Capoor and Ambrosi, 2008). The International Emissions Trading Association (2008) notes that it is 'unlikely that any other regulatory agency charged with

[12] These six categories are not mutually exclusive—several of the other five categories impinge upon efficiency in one form or another.

such responsibility and working on a global scale employs such a small workforce, works on such an irregular schedule, and has a board involved in case-by-case decision-making'.

Indeed, the workload required of the CDM EB has been truly enormous, and has only increased in early 2009 since the board subjected more submitted projects to reviews, and suspended the accreditation of Det Norske Veritas, one of the CDM verifiers. Even without the need to scale up the system by an order of magnitude, it is widely agreed that a wholesale upgrade of the governance and resourcing of the CDM EB was required. Staff numbers have been increased and consistency in decision-making has begun to improve (Michaelowa *et al.*, 2008). Various proposals for separation of the different functions are now under consideration, as are proposals for the 'professionalization' of the board, and it is to be hoped that these issues are addressed irrespective of whether the more radical reform ideas come to fruition. Indeed, one of the most highly leveraged uses of public finance would be to resource the CDM EB better, as this would reduce project risk and encourage the deployment of more private capital.

Programmatic CDM

Programmatic CDM was intended to allow large numbers of small, distributed projects, which are monitored and verified jointly (rather than on a project-by-project basis) using appropriate sampling of results. This is intended to reduce transaction costs and allow the CDM to support many small, geographically and temporally dispersed activities where there are a large number of project owners (e.g. individual households). Examples of a Programme of Activities (PoA) include distribution of energy-efficient compact fluorescent light bulbs, or efficient or solar-powered cooking stoves to replace biomass cooking. While individually small, the large numbers of units in a programme can sum to significant reductions.

There are several constraints currently restricting the growth of programmatic CDM, and several parties, including the CDM EB and the Conference of the Parties (COP), are already working on removing these constraints to allow Programmatic CDM to make a more significant contribution. Key roadblocks include: the restriction on the use of one methodology per PoA; the low number of appropriate methodologies for programmatic CDM; the requirement of revalidation of the PoA if the baseline methodology is revised; and the problem that third-party validators are unwilling to accept substantial liabilities created by the current system (Michaelowa *et al.*, 2008). Efforts to improve Programmatic CDM are clearly welcome, and there is currently no compelling reason not to expand the possibilities of Programmatic CDM.

(iii) Substantial CDM Reforms

There are several more substantial reform ideas that build upon the experience to date with the CDM. We consider two of them. First, applying a discount to CERs from economically advanced and/or high emitting countries, or from technology types that are relatively low cost, might provide a form of carbon leverage and generate incentives for transition to wider cap and trade. Second, sectoral approaches, involving industry benchmarks, promise to radically simplify the CDM's 'additionality' requirements, and would simplify the transition to international cap and trade.

CER Discounting

The CDM currently functions on a 'commodity' basis, where every tonne of CO_2e reduced yields one CER. Discounting CERs, proposed for instance by Chung (2007), would reflect a move from a 'commodity' to a 'currency' basis, because one CER would potentially represent more than one tonne of CO_2e reduced, providing a clear and direct form of 'carbon leverage'. Discount factors for CERs might be set proportional to the level of *per capita* emissions and *per capita* GDP of a host country, or as a function of specific technology types.

For instance, Michaelowa *et al.* (2008) estimate that discounting CERs from countries with *per capita* emissions and GDP above world average levels could reduce CER supply by around 6 per cent over the 2013–20 period. Discounting CERs from countries above *half* the world average could reduce supply by around 28 per cent.

Some of the possible functions of CER discounting might be the following:

- reduce rents flowing to projects where marginal abatement costs are much lower than the market price, through a technology-specific discount rate (e.g. on HFC projects);
- increase carbon leverage for emission reductions from advanced emerging economies;
- provide a transitional incentive for more advanced developing countries to take on emissions caps (Chung, 2007; Michaelowa *et al.*, 2008). As the discount rate on CERs increases, countries would have a stronger incentive to join a cap-and-trade scheme to receive full credit for their reductions.[13]

At the aggregate level, discounting could potentially work to increase environmental integrity of the system. Suppose that only 50 per cent of claimed tonnes of CO_2e are additional. Suppose that CER discounting requires 2 tonnes of CO_2 in order to receive one CER. Then, in the aggregate, discounting would imply that the CDM was not increasing net emissions and would guarantee environmental integrity.

At the project level, however, discounting will probably have a negative, or at best neutral, effect on additionality. By definition, non-additional projects do not need the carbon finance (as they would have occurred anyway), and because their incremental costs of reducing emissions are zero, they would be willing to 'sell'

[13] Whether this incentive was greater than the general incentive to free-ride on others' actions would depend rather strongly on the level of the cap. For a general treatment of related issues, see Barrett (1994).

their CERs for trivially low prices. As prices fall, the proportion of non-additional projects would thus be expected to increase.[14] Discounting CERs weakens the effective price paid per tonne of CO_2e reduced, which would be expected to reduce the number of additional projects taking place. In contrast, a lower effective carbon price would not be expected to reduce the number of non-additional projects, because these projects were not relying on CER revenue in the first place.

In other words, discounting is likely to increase the proportion of non-additional projects. The greater the discount rate on CERs, the larger the endogenous reduction in the proportion of additional projects. In the limit, as the CER discount rate approaches 100 per cent, the proportion of non-additional projects also approaches 100 per cent. Empirically assessing the scale of this perverse effect is important. For instance, suppose it is believed that the percentage of non-additional projects is 20 per cent, prior to the introduction of CER discounting. From a policy perspective it matters enormously whether CER discounting at a given rate would increase the non-additional percentage to 25 or to 75 per cent, and more research is needed here.

CER discounting has the advantage that it may be used in combination with several of the other reform options discussed in the following sections. It has the disadvantage that it would require setting specific discount rates, which would presumably be subject to intensely political negotiations.

Sectoral Approaches

The international carbon finance might be scaled up by moving to a simpler, more 'wholesale' framework that is based on sectoral benchmarks (Delbeke and Zapfel, 2009). Under sectoral approaches, firms would receive credits for reducing their emissions intensity per unit output below a particular benchmark. Standardized emissions-intensity factors for specific sectors could speed up the approval and crediting process. In the short term, the framework would remain a 'no-lose', or one-sided, mechanism, so that developing countries receive benefits for reducing emissions but do not get penalized for BAU. As such, the benchmarks could be set ambitiously.

A sectoral approach might (Bodansky 2007):

- broaden participation;
- simplify negotiations;
- target critical areas (e.g. lock in); and
- address competitiveness concerns.

[14] A counter-argument is that, at present, some of the lowest-cost means of abatement (e.g. HFC 23 destruction) are also the most certain to be additional—the CER revenue is the only reason that these projects would be carried out. In contrast, some critics assert that renewable energy projects, which appear to be high-cost projects, are non-additional because they are already profitable after government incentives and revenue flows from power generation.

There are two main sectoral approaches. The first approach, often called 'sectoral CDM', envisages granting CERs to projects/installations which perform better than the 'additionality benchmark' defined for their sector. Project characteristics, such as technology choice and whether the plant is old or new build, might be included. Determining eligibility based on a benchmark represents a move away from the strict concept of additionality, and towards an instrument that looks closer to a feed-in tariff, as credits would automatically be given to all those private actors producing more efficiently than the benchmark, irrespective of whether the carbon finance was required. Determining the optimal stringency level of the 'additionality benchmark' is important. If the benchmark is too difficult to achieve, project developers will not bother to attempt to reduce emissions, while if the baseline is too loose, large volumes of non-additional CERs will be created. A stringent benchmark has the merit of reducing Type I errors (false positives) by rejecting non-additional projects, but it also increases Type II errors (false negatives) by rejecting additional projects.

Although sectoral benchmarks to determine *eligibility* represent a major change from the CDM as we know it, benchmarking *per se* is not unknown in the current CDM. It is already used in the power sector to determine the *quantity* of credits issued to eligible projects. This distinction between a 'crediting benchmark' (used to calculate the number of credits to be issued) and an 'additionality benchmark' (used to determine eligibility for credits) is important, and there may be advantages to conceptually separating the two. For instance, a tight 'additionality benchmark' might be married with a looser 'crediting benchmark', to minimize the proportion of non-additional projects, and to ensure that projects clearing the additionality hurdle are paid an adequate incentive.[15] The technicalities referring to baselines, monitoring, and verification, as well as the supervision and approval, would continue to be overseen by the CDM EB, but it would be likely that a relevant international industry association would conduct the analysis to support negotiations on appropriate benchmarks.

The second approach, called 'sectoral no-lose targets', envisages the CDM covering a whole sector of a country. CERs would be granted to *governments* for implementing policies and measures to reduce emissions in the sector, provided that emissions fall below the national sector baseline (for example, expressed as the emission intensity of the sector as a whole). Governments would agree sectoral benchmarks at COP level (rather than at the CDM EB level as in the sectoral CDM approach), and governments, not firms, would be granted credits for emission reductions relative to these sectoral benchmarks. This has the disadvantage that the incentives are not faced directly by firms, and it remains up to national governments to implement

[15] There are also various problems with this idea of 'double benchmarking', which is, in fact, just a special case of a more generalized two-part tariff, commonly used as a price-discrimination strategy. Many of the problems arise from the discontinuous incentives created at the point of the additionality benchmark.

appropriate policies domestically. If emissions in the sector exceeded the baseline, there would be no legal consequences; however, if emissions were below the baseline, then the state would receive emission-reduction credits that could be traded internationally.

A challenge with any sectoral approach is that confidential data are likely to be required in order to determine the appropriate level of the benchmark. Firms and countries may be reluctant to share these data, and if they do share data, firms with large market shares will have an incentive to inflate their emissions intensity figures to increase artificially the BAU emissions. Agreeing benchmarks is further complicated by the need to account for relevant local circumstances. For instance, production processes prevalent in each country and natural endowments of renewable energy will affect the feasibility of achieving particular benchmarks.

Benchmarks might work for industries that are the most emissions and energy intensive, such as refining, pulp and paper, metals, and cement. In sectors that are particularly subject to international competition, such as aluminium and steel, the benchmarks would probably mirror the efficiency levels expected from firms in industrialized countries (for example, those used in the allocation of allowances in an emissions-trading scheme). In some sectors this might take the form of global sector agreements. Standardized benchmarks would help to reduce the risk of carbon leakage,[16] alleviate competitiveness concerns, and thereby help to preserve free trade in these sectors.

(iv) New Carbon-finance Institutions

In addition to the more substantial reforms of the CDM discussed in the previous section, there are various proposals for new (and in some cases complementary) carbon institutions. We look at two. First, we consider the potential for new multilateral 'carbon funds' designed to achieve greater carbon leverage than the CDM. Second, we examine the appeal and feasibility of direct government-to-government deals on climate change.

Multilateral Carbon Funds

The two central challenges of carbon finance are (*i*) to raise the necessary funds for investment; and (*ii*) to spend those funds efficiently and effectively on reducing emissions. In the current political climate, with severe pressure on public balance sheets, raising the necessary funds will require leveraging private capital. Leveraging private capital is only possible if the private sector is offered an appropriate expected risk-adjusted return.

[16] Kallbekken (2007) estimates that the CDM in its current form has the potential to reduce the magnitude of carbon leakage by around 60 per cent.

The carbon markets have shown some promise in both leveraging private capital, and allocating the capital in an efficient manner. However, carbon markets may need to be supplemented by other mechanisms that achieve higher levels of carbon leverage, and which encourage investment at a much greater scale. Public-finance mechanisms that might leverage private-sector capital at scale potentially include guarantees, debt financing, credit lines, conditional grants, and so on. These mechanisms might be established and governed within the context of a multilateral carbon fund, with the intention of ensuring that the private sector is offered an appropriate long-term risk-adjusted return on low-carbon investment.

Importantly, the funds (and other forms of financial support) would be made available to the private sector on a competitive basis, so that the relevant private firms would bid for packages of support in a process resembling a reverse auction, which would yield helpful information about the desirability of different forms of financing mechanisms.[17] Some aspects of the arrangements might bear some resemblance to the Multilateral Fund of the Montreal Protocol, which was established to cover the agreed incremental costs of phasing out ozone-depleting substances.[18] A similar process might also achieve a rough form of price discrimination in situations where firms are bidding for public support for specific emission-reduction programmes or projects. Approximate information on abatement costs and financing needs across regions and technologies would be revealed by these competitive processes, extending the success of the existing carbon markets in revealing aggregate information about abatement costs.

Beyond the project level, public-finance mechanisms would be designed to support investment in carbon funds in a way that leverages the relatively patient capital held by large-scale pension funds. Understanding the types of competitive public-finance mechanisms that would leverage private capital, and the other public-institutional reforms (e.g. to the CDM) required to reduce risk for private investors, is likely to be an important area of research over the next year.

Government Deals

Victor and Wara (2008) propose a small number of government-to-government 'deals' as an element in a post-2012 regime, focusing on infrastructure development where money alone is inadequate. Jackson *et al.* (2006) provide two brief examples for nuclear technology in India and natural-gas-fired power

[17] Indeed, reverse auctions and/or tenders are already employed by some national governments as part of their CER procurement processes. EU member states including the Netherlands (see http://www.senternovem.nl/carboncredits/), Austria (see http://www.ji-cdm-austria.at/en/portal/index.php), and Norway (Norwegian Ministry of Finance, 2008), have high-profile CER-procurement programmes.

[18] See DeSombre and Kauffman (1996) (and updated information at http://www.multilateralfund.org/). Along similar lines, Wara and Victor (2008) briefly outline the idea of a climate fund for the USA and a cartel of developing countries.

plants in China. These proposed deals address climate change, energy development, and local pollution needs, and might be undertaken relatively cost-effectively.

However, the funds for these 'deals' are proposed to come directly from public-sector balance sheets in the developed world, which, as Hepburn and Stern (Ch. 3) note, are already stretched. Rich countries already appear likely to fail to meet the Millennium Development Goal targets of 0.7 per cent of GDP by 2015. The political challenges of raising public funds to finance the growth of future industrial competitors may be insurmountable. Nevertheless, if public funds can be found, a limited number of large-scale direct government-to-government deals may provide a valuable contribution to reducing emissions.

V. CONCLUSIONS

Developing countries must be at the centre of a global deal on climate change. They are neither responsible for creating the problem, nor are they capable of immediately addressing it, given their limited resources. But much of the mitigation potential at low cost lies within developing countries, and unless rich countries provide the necessary carbon finance, substantial low-carbon opportunities will be missed and high-carbon assets will be locked into place, implying that a 450–550ppm pathway will be almost impossible to achieve without a major unexpected technological breakthrough.

Carbon markets, in a reformed form, probably represent the most feasible model for supporting private financial flows for the developing world to reduce its emissions on the scale required. The CDM has made a promising start, and is already providing carbon finance of several billions of euros to the developing world, contributing to reducing the costs of compliance in Europe and other developed countries. Carbon trading provides a legitimate and coherent rationale for financial transfers on the scale necessary to shift China, India, and other developing economies on to cleaner growth pathways. Leveraging the carbon markets is likely to be more reliable than looking to strained public-sector balance sheets in a context where the politics of transferring resources abroad for aid are difficult, let alone transferring funds to stimulate the low-carbon growth of future competitors.

Nevertheless, the international carbon-finance framework needs reform and expansion before it can be deemed 'fit for purpose'. Five areas are critical—environmental integrity, scale, leverage, economic efficiency, and transitional incentives to international cap and trade. There is little doubt that the CDM, in its current form, performs well at achieving economic efficiency. However, the CDM is unable to achieve all five objectives across all sectors. A reformed programmatic CDM may contribute to providing incentives to reduce widely distributed emissions, it will nevertheless need to be complemented by other mechanisms and/or frameworks, at a minimum, to address forestry, agriculture, transport, and buildings.

Within the core areas of the current CDM, potential reform options range from the incremental to the radical. The four options reviewed here—governance reforms, programmatic CDM, CER discounting, and sectoral approaches—all have important attractions and, indeed, are not mutually exclusive. Governance reforms are required to enhance integrity and contribute to scale objectives. Programmatic CER increases the sectoral reach of the CDM. CER discounting would deliver on the requirements of carbon leverage and contribute to providing appropriate incentives to transition to international cap and trade. Multilateral carbon funds and innovative public-finance mechanisms are likely to be needed to leverage private capital on the necessary scale. If additional public funds are available, which seems unlikely, government-to-government deals on low-carbon infrastructure could sit alongside the post-2012 carbon finance architecture. Whatever directions are taken at the UN FCCC, it is critical that the resulting carbon financial framework operates at the service of developing countries.

Part V
Institutional Architecture

21

The Global Climate-change Regime: A Defence

Joanna Depledge and Farhana Yamin***

I. INTRODUCTION

It was more than 20 years ago that states first took collective action to address the threat of climate change. In December 1988, the UN General Assembly (UNGA) adopted a unanimous resolution (UNGA, 1988) acknowledging the potential severity of climate change, and endorsing the establishment of the Intergovernmental Panel on Climate Change (IPCC). Two decades on from that first UN resolution, the global climate-change regime now comprises a comprehensive set of rules, institutions, and procedures—founded on the 1992 Convention and 1997 Kyoto Protocol—guiding action on the problem over the long term. The Copenhagen negotiations are just the latest set of talks under the regime to strengthen commitments and improve the effectiveness of provisions.

Some scholars, however, now advocate abandoning the climate-change regime in favour of hypothetical alternatives (see, for example, Prins and Rayner, 2007; Victor, 2007). In support of their argument, such critics point to the large gap between the Protocol's existing targets and the deep emission cuts needed to stabilize greenhouse-gas concentrations at tolerable levels, along with weak implementation in many developed countries, flaws in the Protocol's compliance system, and loopholes in its market-based mechanisms (see Helm, Ch. 2, and Barrett, Ch. 4, in this volume). The effectiveness of regimes can certainly vary, and critical evaluations of the Kyoto Protocol and the broader regime are necessary and important to improving the international response to climate change. There is a danger, however, in judging the performance of the climate-change regime too narrowly. Regimes typically establish a long-term, institutional response to complex, persistent problems. As such, they have impacts and repercussions (positive and negative, intended and unintended) beyond the simple setting and attainment of short-term, first-round targets. In this respect, the often heard claim that the Kyoto Protocol has had little impact on climate change—before its first

* Lucy Cavendish College and Centre of International Studies, University of Cambridge.

** Institute of Development Studies, University of Sussex.

commitment period has even ended—risks misunderstanding the long-term purpose of regimes, and their multifaceted effects.

In response, this chapter assesses the climate-change regime through a wider lens and from a longer-term perspective than is usually employed by its critics. Unlike most analyses, this chapter focuses on the performance of the regime as a negotiating environment, rather than on the specifics of commitments (e.g. cap-and-trade versus alternatives). In doing so, the chapter defends the continuation of the climate-change regime in its basic current form, but puts forward several options for reform that could improve the regime's effectiveness.

The chapter begins by outlining the nature of regimes in general, before focusing on the climate-change regime itself. The chapter explores the historical antecedents of the regime, followed by a brief account of its current institutions and procedures. It then analyses the achievements and weaknesses of the regime as a negotiating environment, suggesting possible improvements. The chapter ends by underscoring the importance of the regime's global nature, before presenting conclusions.

II. REGIMES: PURPOSE AND FUNCTIONS

'Economists describe human induced climate change as an "externality" and the global climate as a "public good"' (Stern, 2007, p. v). Political scientists prescribe international collective action where the public good is transboundary in nature, and cannot be influenced through individual action alone—as is the case with the causes and consequences of climate change. International relations theory teaches us that, in such cases, more efficient outcomes can be achieved if states construct 'regimes'—sets of participation rules, institutions, and procedures—to coordinate their actions over the long term (Keohane, 1989; Zartman, 1993). The principal purpose of regimes is to facilitate collective action among states by providing a 'contractual environment' (Haas *et al.*, 1993) to advance negotiations. To this end, regimes supply a number of services to 'make agreement possible' (Keohane, 1989, p. 11). One such service, for example, is to minimize the high transaction costs involved in multilateral negotiations among many states—over 190 in global arenas—through the use of common procedural rules. By providing a forum for continuous negotiations, well-functioning regimes can also ensure continuity and generate momentum, enhancing flows of information and building trust among participants (Keohane, 1989; Underdal, 2002). Long-term relationships and iterative negotiations can, in turn, provide opportunities for complex reciprocity and learning over time. The point, therefore, is that regimes do not aim to solve the problem they are charged with through a single one-shot agreement. Typically, the problem in question, and the politics surrounding it, are far too complex for that. Instead, the purpose is to launch and facilitate a process that can gradually construct a comprehensive strategy and political bargain over time, whose specifics can be modified as conditions change. Like any institution, regimes can be designed more or less well, and even well-designed regimes can under-perform, or deteriorate in effectiveness over time (Barnett and Finnemore, 1999). It is important, therefore, constantly to keep in review the performance of a regime, in order to adjust its provisions as needed. Most regimes have built-in review mechanisms with this purpose in mind.

III. THE CLIMATE-CHANGE REGIME

(i) Historical and Institutional Context

The global climate-change regime is founded on the 1992 UN Framework Convention on Climate Change (FCCC), supplemented by its 1997 Kyoto Protocol. The regime, and the challenges it now faces, cannot be properly understood in isolation from its historical and institutional antecedents. Regimes, even those on entirely new issues, are rarely constructed on a blank slate. The climate-change regime was no exception. It has been shaped, and sometimes pulled in opposing directions, by two distinct framings and institutional reference points.

The first is the framing of climate change as an environmental/pollution-control issue, through a science-driven, targeted approach (see Yamin *et al.*, 2006). The environmental framing focuses on the damaging activities/substances, and tries to limit these to safe levels. Environmental approaches pay little attention to adaptation to the problem, as the priority is to halt the damage being done. Various policy responses are used to regulate the environmental pollution, notably target-setting or technology-based approaches, until a 'safe' level is reached. Institutionally, environmental regimes tend to be located in environmental ministries that are usually seen as 'opponents' of business-as-usual, over which they have little control. Typically, environmental approaches result in the setting up of expert groups to provide objective advice to policy-makers on what can be considered 'dangerous' and 'safe' pollution levels, and also on the technological and economic feasibility of response options. The best international example of a primarily environmental approach is the regime to combat stratospheric ozone depletion under the 1985 Vienna Convention and 1987 Montreal Protocol. The ozone precedent inevitably influenced the emerging political dynamics of climate change, and later the regime's design.

The second framing sees climate change as an issue integrally linked to the achievement of sustainable development, invoking a much broader set of conceptual and institutional linkages, domestically and internationally. Climate change emerged as an international issue in the late 1980s and early 1990s, when sustainable development was becoming the defining intellectual framing for how environmental protection and development could be achieved simultaneously, within the context of international cooperation. The term was used to revitalize not only the mandate of the UN but also global cooperation itself—North–South[1] as well as East–West—at a time when older ideological formations were crumbling.[2] A sustainable development framing highlights, in particular, issues of intra- and intergenerational equity, emphasizing that developing countries are small contributors to current global environmental problems, have lower capacities, and still have high levels of poverty that must remain their priority. All these features find clear expression in the climate-change regime.

From its very inception, the climate-change regime was firmly located in the UN system. Negotiations on a framework convention were launched in 1990 by the UNGA, prompted by the scientific findings of the IPCC, itself a joint body of the World Meteorological Organization (WMO) and the UN Environment Programme (UNEP). Despite pressure to assign climate change to UNEP (as was the case with ozone depletion and biodiversity loss), the wider linkages, development dimensions, and higher political stakes of the problem ensured that negotiations took place directly under the UNGA, thereby emphasizing its sustainable development, rather than environmental, framing (see Bodansky, 1993).

Individual scientific and political entrepreneurs acted through the UN system, encouraged and courted by a handful of small countries fearful of sea-level rise. These actors worked to ensure that climate change made it on to the international legislative calendar at a time when preparations were in full swing for the landmark 1992 UN Conference on Environment and Development (UNCED), itself prompted by the Brundtland Report of the World Commission on Environment and Development (1987). The simultaneous UNCED negotiations again ensured that climate change was considered in a broader sustainable developmental context, rather than a predominantly environmental one.

The formative years of the climate-change regime were thus heavily influenced by two different framings, with their distinctive mindsets and solution pathways. Negotiators would always look to the recently concluded negotiations on the Montreal Protocol, as this was one of the first treaties that addressed a global problem with significant equity dimensions, and on the basis of the precautionary principle. But there was always recognition that, with no quick technological fix in sight (as there was with ozone), climate change was a bigger, more complicated problem with implications for development itself—both in the developed and developing worlds.

(ii) Global Participation, Differentiated Commitments

One of the key tasks for regimes is to define participants and assign roles to them. The climate-change regime does this very clearly, but not without controversy. The

[1] The term 'North–South' is employed here as a stylistic shorthand, while recognizing that there are countries belonging to the political north located in the geographical south, and vice versa.

[2] For early analyses, see McCormick (1989) and Birnie (1993).

Convention allows any state to become a party (UN FCCC Article 22.1). This is the same for the Kyoto Protocol, with the proviso that countries must first be parties to the Convention (Kyoto Protocol Article 24.1; UN FCCC Article 17.4). Both the Convention and Protocol are thus *global* instruments, in the sense that they allow for, and seek, global participation in their governance processes. This model of global participation was derived from the UN setting and the powerful precedent of the ozone negotiations. As Hoffmann (2007) persuasively demonstrates, the ozone negotiations established a norm of universal participation so that, by the time climate change came on to the international agenda, this norm already 'pervaded the entire political context' (Hoffmann, 2007, p.130). It was not just a question of norm-internalization, but also hard politics. Developing countries had become newly involved in international environmental politics through the ozone negotiations, and wanted to sustain that involvement (Rowlands, 1995). Moreover, some were resentful at their lack of real engagement (that they were 'caught napping') in the early ozone talks, and felt that their interests had not been sufficiently addressed.[3] They were determined not to let that happen again in the climate-change context (Rowlands, 1995).

Within the model of global *participation*, the actual *commitments* of parties are heavily differentiated between developed and developing countries, resonating with the sustainable development framing, which gives weight to the aspirations of developing countries.[4] The Convention thus enshrines the principle of 'common but differentiated responsibilities and respective capabilities' (UN FCCC Article 3.1), establishing that, although climate change is of common concern, historical responsibility for causing the problem lies with the developed countries, and these also have greater resources to address the problem. The developed countries should, thus, 'take the lead in combating climate change and the adverse effects thereof'(UN FCCC Article 3.1).

This leadership paradigm is translated into the operational rules of the Convention, which includes a list of the countries concerned. These 41 'Annex I' countries include the members of the Organization for Economic Cooperation and Development (OECD) in 1990, along with countries of the former Soviet Union and Central and Eastern Europe[5] (the 'economies in transition', or EITs). Under the Convention, the Annex I parties had to 'aim' to return their emissions to 1990 levels by 2000 (UN FCCC Article 4.2(a)). The Kyoto Protocol is modelled on the same global/differentiated approach: participation is global, but commitments are (heavily) differentiated, with binding emission targets for the Annex I parties to be achieved by 2008–12. Neither the Convention nor the Protocol explicitly state that the 150-plus non-Annex I 'developing countries' will follow the lead—should it be demonstrated—of the Annex I parties. The inference, however, is there. The non-Annex I parties do have general commitments under both instruments, as well

[3] Rowlands (1995, pp. 170–1), citing a developing-country interviewee.

[4] For a more detailed examination of the rules, institutions, and procedures of the climate regime, see Yamin and Depledge (2004).

[5] Specifically, those that were members of the UN during the Convention negotiations.

as reporting requirements. A sub-set of the Annex I countries—'Annex II parties', composed only of the OECD members—are committed to providing financial and technological assistance to developing countries, while EITs are granted some flexibility in view of their more difficult economic circumstances. The regime also includes concessions for least developed countries (LDCs), and gives recognition to those considered highly vulnerable, notably small island developing states (SIDs).

(iii) Institutions and Procedures

The basic institutions and procedures of the climate-change regime are drawn from existing practice in the UN system. In terms of institutions, the Conference of the Parties (COP) serves as the supreme decision-making body for Convention affairs, and the COP, serving as the meeting of the Parties to the Kyoto Protocol (CMP), governs Protocol affairs. The COP and CMP are supported by two permanent subsidiary bodies—the Subsidiary Body for Scientific and Technological Advice (SBSTA) and the Subsidiary Body for Implementation (SBI), with additional bodies convened for particular negotiating rounds. All parties to the Convention are represented in these core institutions, but only Protocol parties may take part in decision-making on Protocol matters.

The regime also encompasses a raft of highly innovative limited-membership institutions, each with its own mandates and structures. Chief among these are the bodies that were established to govern the extensive carbon markets launched by the Kyoto Protocol, namely the Executive Board that oversees the day-to-day running of the clean development mechanism (CDM-EB) and the Supervisory Committee that performs a similar function for joint implementation (JI). The Kyoto Protocol also led to the creation of the Compliance Committee, which runs the compliance procedures, along with the more recently established Adaptation Board, that oversees the Adaptation Fund, itself financed by a ground-breaking levy on transactions under the CDM. There are also other expert groups under the Convention with advisory and analytical functions, for example, dealing with the special needs of LDCs, the promotion of technology transfer, and developing-country reporting issues.

The conduct of business is then governed by formal procedural rules, including those set out in the Convention, Protocol, and the 'draft rules of procedure' (UN FCCC, 1996). These determine procedures for intervening in debates, interpretation and translation, establishing informal groups, taking decisions, appointing chairpersons, and so on. They are supplemented by unwritten established practices that have developed over time both in the UN system in general and specifically in the climate-change regime. These procedural rules are distinctive in two main respects. The first is the regime's dubious distinction (which it shares with the Convention on Biological Diversity) in having failed formally to adopt its 'draft rules of procedure', owing to disagreement over the voting rule. The effect is that most decisions can only be taken by consensus. The second is the seat on the COP Bureau[6] reserved for SIDs, in recognition of their urgent stake in the regime's work. This measure has subsequently been incorporated into virtually all the limited-membership bodies established by the Convention and the Protocol. As discussed further below, the limited-membership bodies have their own procedural rules, including novel features quite distinct from the more traditional procedures of the broader regime.

IV. ACHIEVEMENTS

How has the climate-change regime performed over time? At one level, it has notched up considerable success, notably in generating momentum, enabling reciprocal deals, facilitating learning, and promoting reporting and verification.

(i) Momentum

The climate-change regime has unquestionably generated momentum, engaging parties, even the more reluctant ones, in a continuous move to advance the issue at hand. Reviews and deadlines scheduled in the Convention and Protocol have ensured that the strengthening of the regime regularly appears on the negotiating agenda. The negotiations that led to the Kyoto Protocol, for example, were launched in 1995 by a formal review mandated in the Convention. Negotiations on second-period targets were likewise launched at CMP 1 in Montreal in 2005, thanks to a deadline set in the Protocol itself.

Momentum, however, is more than diplomatic deadlines inscribed in legal text. The negotiating environment of a regime enmeshes delegations in a dense web of meetings, practices, processes, and rules, generating an inherent motivation among negotiators to advance the issue. The personal connection is significant, too. Long-standing climate-change delegates, of which there are many, have evolved into a distinct 'process community' (Sjostedt, 2003, p. 102), crisscrossed by personal relationships, sharing a common history, and, to some extent, working for a common purpose. This creates a form of peer pressure to reach agreements—or at least not to block a consensus. Another form of pressure is the visibility generated by regimes towards the outside world. Media coverage during negotiations can play an important contributory role—although rarely a decisive one—in inducing countries to strike a deal.

The momentum of the climate-change regime has been remarkably powerful throughout its history. It was momentum in July 2001 that propelled the climate-change parties to recover from the double-blow of a negotiating failure at COP6 in The Hague (November 2000), and the US repudiation of the Kyoto Protocol a few months later, to strike a political deal on the details of the Protocol. The

[6] An 11-person committee that advises the COP.

adoption of that deal reflected a clear sense of common determination among the remaining climate-change parties to save and advance the regime. It was also momentum that helped seal the final deal on the Bali Action Plan in December 2007. To recall, the USA initially rejected the proposed draft, and then appeared to change its mind and join the consensus, following strong and emotional appeals from other parties (ENB, 2007). It is important not to exaggerate the influence of regime-induced momentum, including an internal sense of community and outside media visibility, in this regard. To be clear, the USA did not change its mind in Bali because of internal pressure within the regime. What the internal momentum did do, however, is to exert strong pressure on the USA, and others, to intensify their efforts to find a solution. Indeed, the pressure felt by the USA has been unremitting since 2001. The continuity of the regime, and its forward movement, has meant that the USA has been utterly unable to ignore the issue of climate change. The effect is that the USA has continued to be engaged in the regime, not just under the Convention to which it remains a party, but also as an observer to the Kyoto Protocol. With over 120 members, the US delegation in Bali was larger even than in Kyoto. Several analysts have also pointed to the blossoming of actions to tackle climate change at many levels within the USA, despite the federal government's rejection of the Kyoto Protocol.[7] Would these many actions have emerged, in the absence of the climate-change regime? Would the incoming Obama administration even be contemplating stronger action on climate change if it were not for the regime?

The internal momentum of the regime has acted almost as a centrifugal force, keeping other reluctant states involved. Saudi Arabia, other oil-exporting allies, the Russian Federation, Canada (under recent administrations), even China and India: none of these states are inherently enthusiastic about tackling climate change, yet all have remained within the regime and engaged in each successive negotiating round. The case of Australia is particularly instructive. As soon as Kevin Rudd assumed office in late 2007, Australia rejoined the Kyoto Protocol, reflecting the 'pull' exerted by the regime.

(ii) Reciprocal Deals

The climate-change regime has also enabled complex reciprocal deals over time. The clearest example is the Bali Action Plan, which established that developing countries would now take on obligations beyond those in the Convention. This was an unmistakeable exercise in deferred reciprocity: in 1992, developed countries agreed to lead; in 2007, developing countries agreed to follow. How did this happen? The strengthening of rules within the regime, including entry into force of the Kyoto Protocol and the flourishing of the CDM, no doubt contributed to the sense among developing countries that leadership, of a sort, was being exercised by the Annex I parties. Of even greater importance was the 2005 launch of

[7] See, for example, Koehn (2008); also Pew Center (2006, 2008).

negotiations on second-period targets for developed countries under the Kyoto Protocol, without, at that stage, any undertaking on the part of developing countries. This represented a tremendous leap of faith on the part of developed countries (led by the EU), which was, in the end, vindicated in Bali. It is difficult to imagine such a politically sensitive deal being struck in the absence of the continuity and long-term relationships enabled by the regime. Learning over time, facilitated in part by the IPCC and exchange of information within the regime, also helped persuade developing countries of the need to move on from their Convention obligations.

(iii) Learning

Learning has been an important positive dynamic for the climate-change regime, feeding through to the Copenhagen negotiating round and beyond. The sheer amount of information and analysis passing through the regime in support of the negotiations is massive. There are several levels of such information. The IPCC provides the fundamental scientific basis for the continuation of the regime and (to a lesser extent) the setting of targets. The IPCC is independent, but maintains close links to the regime's policy organs, including through provision of common methodologies and data sets for states to work on. In this respect, the climate-change regime has proved to be well designed, safeguarding the IPCC's independence, yet ensuring its relevance. The importance and influence of the IPCC can be seen in debates on second-period targets under the Kyoto Protocol, where the Panel's figures have been cited as reference points for their determination. At another level, the regime has received a wealth of proposals from parties, seeking to share ideas on creative outcomes for the Copenhagen negotiations. Informal workshops have been held to discuss these proposals further, in a non-confrontational environment. Channels for input from civil society, notably side events on the fringes of the official negotiations, have enabled ideas developed in academia or among non-governmental organizations (NGOs) to move on to the political agenda.

Perhaps the most concrete proof of learning in the recent history of the regime lies in the market mechanisms of the CDM, JI, and emissions trading. Ten years ago, in Kyoto, the controversy generated by proposals on these mechanisms nearly brought the negotiations to collapse. JI was so politically sensitive it could not even be mentioned by name.[8] Today, the CDM is a massive multi-million dollar industry (notwithstanding its shortcomings), emissions trading is at the heart of the EU response to climate change (with the EU having been one of its sharpest critics in the 1990s), and 'joint implementation' has officially re-entered the vocabulary of the climate-change regime (UN FCCC, 2006, decision 10/CMP.1). Most remarkably, opposition to the market mechanisms on ideological grounds

[8] 'Activities implemented jointly' (under the Convention) and 'Article 6 projects' (under the Kyoto Protocol) were the terms used instead.

is now confined to the fringes of the climate-change debate. One of the very few early areas of agreement in the negotiations on second-period targets under the Kyoto Protocol was that the market mechanisms should 'continue to be available' to parties beyond 2012, with the focus on introducing improvements based on experience (UN FCCC, 2008*c*, para.18).

A further example of learning concerns reducing emissions from deforestation and forest degradation, or REDD. The rise of this issue up the climate-change agenda, since its proposal by Papua New Guinea and Costa Rica in 2005 (UN FCCC, 2005*b*), represents a considerable step forwards in addressing deforestation in developing countries. It was facilitated by methodological developments within the IPCC, research within the academic community and NGO advocacy linked to the regime, eventually reaching the formal negotiations themselves through concerned governments and informal NGO input. The REDD debate in the climate-change regime has moved further and faster in two years, than in 15 years of related discussions in other forest-specific regimes. Interestingly, it is also a case where the substantive incentives provided by the climate-change regime, notably market-based credits, have added a new, positive motivation to tackling this issue.

Other new ideas have moved from academic/think-tank debate into the political arena of the Copenhagen negotiations, notably SD-PAMs (sustainable development policies and measures), sectoral targets, sectoral-CDM, and levies on air transport to fund adaptation or mitigation activities in developing countries. All of these originated within the research community just a few years ago, but are now on the formal negotiating agenda, proving that the regime is able rapidly to absorb fresh thinking and approaches. On these and other proposals, the regime has demonstrably provided an open and effective forum for the development and spread of ideas.

Learning is also manifest in the new limited-membership bodies set up under the Kyoto Protocol. Acknowledging the inefficiencies of the regime's existing institutions, with their open participation and consensus decision-making, parties decided that the day-to-day governance of the CDM, JI, compliance system, and adaptation fund should be entrusted to much smaller, more nimble institutions (with a maximum of 20 participants). Unlike the COP and subsidiary bodies, the limited-membership bodies may resort to majority voting, and have pioneered innovative procedures, such as electronic decision-making. This is an example where the parties explicitly recognized the need to move away from existing practice, and try out new institutional models.

(iv) Reporting and Review

A major achievement of the climate-change regime, and one that is often overlooked, has been to establish perhaps the most rigorous and respected reporting and review system for developed countries of all multilateral environmental agreements (MEAs).[9] Since 1996, Annex I parties have been required to submit emissions data on an annual basis according to common rules and guidelines. These data are subject to individual and collective review, before being published on the Convention website and in official documentation. The reporting record, while not perfect, has improved considerably since the early days of the regime, especially among the EITs, where capacity for estimating emissions was limited at first. The reporting and review system has strengthened over time, and has now expanded to cater for verification of the Protocol's legally binding emission targets, along with the recording of credit exchanges under the market mechanisms. The CDM has similarly pioneered verification techniques, with the introduction of *ex ante* and *ex post* verification of emission credits generated by projects through independent, accredited organizations. The regime's use of private-sector entities to perform essential verification functions is a highly novel and significant feature. It demonstrates that, notwithstanding its location within the UN system, the regime is able to make use of new actors and the private sector where appropriate.

The collection and review of data in these myriad ways is critical to building confidence in the regime, providing the basis for assessing compliance with legally binding targets and for ensuring the validity of transactions under the market-based mechanisms. The availability of sound emissions data and a well-functioning reporting and review system is now taken for granted in the regime. Without it, however, effective action to tackle climate change would simply be impossible. If it were not for the climate-change regime, it is difficult to imagine that reporting and validation of emissions data would have progressed so far among such a wide range of countries. Emissions trading would also be impossible. The flipside, however, is that these achievements have yet to be matched by developing countries, as discussed further below.

V. WEAKNESSES

Despite its many achievements, the climate-change regime is not without significant weaknesses that hamper its effectiveness. These are discussed below.

(i) Dysfunctional North–South Politics

The regime's greatest weakness is the persistence of dysfunctional North–South politics. This is by no means the only axis upon which rancorous politics revolve. Indeed, conflict is rife within the developed countries, and also the developing countries, although this is usually kept behind closed doors. However, the split

[9] For a more detailed review and response to recent critiques, see Swart *et al.* (2007).

between the G-77 group[10] of developing countries on the one hand, and the richer, developed countries on the other, is the most potent of political divides. This two-way split is utterly at odds with the reality of country circumstances relative to climate change, instead reflecting longstanding ideological differences and historical political allegiances. This would not necessarily be a problem, if there were sufficient trust to enable developed and developing countries to communicate positively and constructively. Unfortunately, however, negotiations between the groups tend to be dominated by knee-jerk suspicion, defensiveness, and misunderstanding, which hinder the rational discussion of proposals (Depledge, 2006).

By its very nature, the climate-change issue was particularly prone to capture by North–South politics. However, the design of the climate-change regime has arguably made things worse. Rather than smoothing it over, the regime's rules may have contributed to entrenching, and even accentuating, the pre-existing North–South divide. Why is this? For a start, the Convention does not set a timeframe for the consideration of stronger developing-country obligations, or an objective yardstick by which to assess Annex I party leadership. Instead, this is left open-ended, with the obvious result that developed countries seek to bring forward the date when developing countries will assume commitments, and the developing countries seek to push it back. This is in contrast with the Montreal Protocol, which established a ten-year grace period, after which point developing countries would assume comparable commitments to those of developed countries. The fact that the climate-change regime did not emulate the ozone precedent in this regard was deliberate, and reflects the stronger leaning towards a sustainable development framework, as discussed above. It also reflects the greater wariness of the developing countries following their experience of the ozone negotiations.

Another problem is that all 150-plus countries that are not included in Annex I are treated *en masse* by the Convention's legal divisions (except for the 49 or so LDCs), despite their huge variations in circumstances. In terms of emissions alone, 19 non-Annex I parties have reported emissions under 1m tonnes of carbon-dioxide equivalent (tCO_2e), compared with 22 parties reporting emissions over 100m tCO_2e (see UN FCCC, 2005*a*). Politically, the non-Annex I group includes two OECD members (Mexico and South Korea), two EU members (Cyprus and Malta), and several Central Asian Republics, who consider themselves to be EITs, rather than developing countries. All of these, however, are subject to the same legal rules.

A related concern is the lack of dynamism built into the annex structure. Non-Annex I parties may voluntarily join Annex I, or otherwise assume the commitments of Annex I parties. A small handful of parties have done so, most of which are politically close to the EU.[11] However, there is no automatic

[10] The main developing-country grouping in the UN system, currently comprising over 130 members (see www.g77.org).

[11] Croatia, Liechtenstein, Monaco, and Slovenia joined Annex I in Kyoto in 1997. Kazakhstan declared it would take on the commitments of Annex I parties in 2000.

'graduation' process, nor objective criteria by which to judge whether countries might be ready to join Annex I. The Montreal Protocol, by contrast, set an automatic threshold of 0.3 kg of ozone-depleting substance (ODS) consumption *per capita*, above which developing countries had to forgo exemption under the grace period. The problem is particularly severe with respect to joining the Kyoto Protocol's Annex B, which lists Annex I parties and their emission targets. Here, the Protocol's rules were specifically designed to *prevent* easy amendment of the list. Because of onerous entry-into-force requirements,[12] it is, in practice, virtually impossible for any country to join Annex B under the current rules. The only country that has tried to do so, Belarus, is now stuck in a procedural no-man's land: as an Annex I party without an emissions target in Annex B, it cannot meaningfully participate in the Kyoto Protocol.[13] The upshot is that the regime's rules actively discourage non-Annex I parties from joining Annex I and Annex B. There are a handful of non-Annex I parties (especially those mentioned above that are not G-77 members) who might be tempted into joining Annex I and assuming an emissions target under Annex B. Kazakhstan, for example, has expressed an interest in taking on emission targets under the Kyoto Protocol. The difficulties in doing so, however, would deter any party from going down that road.

The stark division of countries between the two annexes thus reinforces and perpetuates the North–South political and ideological divide. Future differentiation of obligations among developing countries is virtually a prerequisite to any sensible engagement of so many vastly differing parties. This, however, is rendered infinitely more difficult, as it is entirely outside the existing framing of the climate-change regime.

The North–South divide also dampens initiatives by individual G-77 members, and hampers the emergence of more creative alliances between developed and developing countries that might share similar interests. During the Kyoto Protocol negotiations, for example, small island states, along with some Latin American countries, supported proposals that would have allowed individual developing countries to take on voluntary targets if and when they chose to do so. This was criticized by other major developing countries, and therefore quickly abandoned. More recently, South Africa faced criticism for deciding to limit its greenhouse gas emissions, on the grounds that this was a betrayal of its African and G-77 allegiances.[14]

Reporting of emissions data by developing countries has also suffered from the Annex I/non-Annex I division. Unlike the Annex I parties, who are engaged in rigorous and regular reporting, the vast majority of developing countries have only reported emissions data once since 1992. The result is the absence of comparable

[12] KP Articles 20 and 21. Three-quarters of the Protocol's parties must individually ratify any amendment to Annex B before it can enter into force. At present, this amounts to around 130 parties.

[13] For more on this topic, see Depledge (2009).

[14] 'S Africa criticised for unilateral commitment to set climate targets', 27 August 2008 (available at http://unfccc.int/files/meetings/intersessional/accra/press/application/pdf/pana_s_africa_criticised_for_unilateral_commitment_to_set_climate_targets.pdf).

time-series emissions data for some 150 parties to the climate-change regime. The more limited resources and capacities of developing countries, along with the leadership narrative, meant that the Convention rules for their reporting were inevitably more lenient. However, there has been almost no progress since then, for two main reasons. First, the issue of developing country reporting has become bound up with the politics surrounding developing country commitments: developing countries resisted scaling up their reporting, because this was seen as a new commitment. Second, inadequate funding has been forthcoming to enable most developing countries to set up permanent emissions-data collection systems in their own countries. The regime has held various workshops and capacity-building initiatives, but these have been insufficient. This deplorable failure to build up the capacity of most developing countries to estimate and record their emissions can be laid largely at the door of North–South politics, exacerbated by the regime's divisive narrative.

(ii) Complexity

A basic function of regimes is to help lower the huge transaction costs involved in global negotiations. Problems can arise, however, when the sheer number of participants and issues becomes overwhelming, and complexity begins to have an impact on the negotiations (Zartman, 1994). This is becoming an ever-greater risk in the climate-change context.

Each negotiating round in the climate-change regime has become more complex than the last. The Kyoto Protocol negotiations were seen, at the time, as immensely complicated. However, they appeared remarkably simple compared with the post-Kyoto negotiations, where detailed rules on the three market-based mechanisms, compliance, land-use change, and forestry, and reporting all had to be devised. At the time of writing, the ongoing Copenhagen negotiations were charged not only with deciding new emission targets for Annex I parties, alongside possible revisions to the Protocol's rules, but also a whole new architecture for developing-country involvement, and possibly that of the USA. To be acceptable to all interest groups, negotiations encompassed financial provisions, technology-transfer incentives, help for adaptation, new rules on REDD, new reporting guidelines for developing countries, provisions on carbon capture and storage, concessions to oil producers for the potential impacts of mitigation policies, possible sectoral elements, and a new 'shared vision'—to name just the central elements on the formal agenda.

As developing-country issues and obligations move centre stage, the climate-change negotiations must also increasingly address broader development linkages. In one sense, this strengthens the regime. Stronger linkages with development concerns bring new actors and potentially more resources and political momentum to the climate table. However, they also risk bogging the regime down in problems that are simply too big, and too deeply entrenched across the entire system of global governance, for climate institutions alone to resolve. In this respect, there is an urgent need for debate over the appropriate role of the climate regime in the broader fight for poverty reduction and development.

Complexity is an intrinsic problem with a global negotiation on such a multifarious and wide-ranging issue as climate change. It is made worse, however, by the absence of majority voting procedures (see also below), which might help filter out extreme, frivolous, repetitive, or filibustering proposals. The regime has also been unable to develop an effective process for prioritizing issues. Complexity arguably torpedoed (temporarily) the last round of comprehensive negotiations in The Hague in 2000, and may well do so again.

(iii) Unwieldy Decision-Making

The debating procedures of the climate-change regime do not encourage strong and brisk decision-making. Almost all decisions, including quite technical ones, are debated in bodies—either full plenaries, or informal groups—that are open to representatives from all parties. To recall, the SBSTA, the body responsible for scientific, technical, and technological issues, is fully open, and imposes no limits or criteria on membership or participation. In practice, it is rare that all the 190-plus parties and thousands of delegates are intimately involved in a negotiation on a particular topic, with active participants usually confined to 20–30 core individuals, often fewer. However, combined with the need to report back to coalitions (e.g. the EU, G-77), this is enough to make for a lengthy and complicated process. Small drafting groups and private informal consultations are used, but these do not have delegated decision-making power. The situation is not helped by the heavy politicization of the climate-change negotiations, which means that even the most minor, inconsequential, or highly technical decisions tend to be treated as political ones, requiring lengthy negotiation.

Furthermore, almost all decisions have to be taken by consensus. This leads to protracted debates, along with lowest-common-denominator outcomes, given that a handful of parties—usually the least enthusiastic—can always threaten to block a decision (Haas, 2002; Underdal, 2002). Although rarely used in practice, the existence of majority decision-making in other UN bodies and MEAs does force parties with more extreme positions to bargain, or risk being marginalized. In the climate context, however, such parties can, and do, hold up proceedings to breaking point, generally eroding the trust and give-and-take mentality that is needed if negotiations are to proceed.

(iv) Slow Learning

Learning within the climate-change regime is sometimes slowed down by the absence of an independent technical body, which could respond quickly to requests for analysis, or provide policy advice in a direct fashion. The IPCC is a highly important source of scientific assessment, but is itself an intergovernmental body, whose products must be mandated and approved by plenary meetings. The timeframe for the preparation of even the most targeted reports is at least a year. Moreover, the IPCC has no mandate to provide policy advice, and can only review the existing published literature (rather than having experts put forward their own considered opinions). The Convention secretariat can be a useful source of technical information on some issues, but the imperative for it to remain objective limits its impact. The main source of analysis thus comes from the parties themselves (or civil society) and is, unsurprisingly, often wildly contrasting, and cannot command widespread legitimacy. This institutional set-up contrasts, for example, with the leaner expert-based assessment panels of the ozone regime, which can prepare reports within a few months, and even make oral contributions on technical matters during negotiations. These panels are, at times, also mandated to provide specific policy advice. There are several current issues upon which independent technical advice and analysis would be useful, such as future emission projections in developed countries, current emission estimates and projections in developing countries, and the feasibility of options for the land-use change and forestry sector.

VI. OPTIONS FOR REFORM

There are many ways in which the climate-change regime could be reformed to improve its effectiveness. Indeed, this is in the very nature of regimes: to evolve continuously and adapt over time in response to changing circumstances.

The most important reform would be to remedy the rigid annex structure, making it easier for non-Annex-I Parties to join Annex I and assume an emissions target under Annex B. This might go some way to starting to dismantle—or at least to stop further entrenching—the toxic divide between developed and developing countries. The onerous entry-into-force requirements that are preventing movement into Annex B are currently being reviewed, and options have been put forward to inject greater flexibility. In one sense, therefore, the regime is displaying a capacity to identify problems, learn from experience, and develop new solutions. Political resistance to changing the rules, however, is strong, notably from powerful developing countries, who prefer not to make it too easy to take on new commitments, fearing they may be forced into policy choices that do not fit their specific circumstances. This illustrates well the interplay between regime design and politics. The annex system has ossified the divisions between developed and developing countries, and that division in turn makes it more difficult to reform the annex system.

Emissions data collection in developing countries could also be given greater priority. This would require a substantial (but not enormous) injection of financial, technological, and intellectual resources to ensure that *all* developing countries are able to set up permanent offices to monitor their emissions. It is worth noting that the emissions profiles of many developing countries are quite different to those of most developed countries, being more heavily skewed towards agricultural and land-use emissions. This will require extra, dedicated support.

An institutional change that might improve the negotiating environment would be to mandate the creation of smaller decision-making groups, with clearly circumscribed governance powers. These could address more technical or detailed issues, where multilateral diplomacy is inefficient and unhelpful. A limited-membership board/committee could be envisaged, for example, for technical rules on forestry issues (once a political deal has been struck) and also on reporting and review. This might help free up the negotiating environment of the COP, CMP, and subsidiary bodies for more efficient political decision-making. The climate-change regime has reached a stage when it is simply impossible for all issues to be dealt with effectively through multilateral negotiation in the open bodies. The problem is likely to worsen after Copenhagen, with new rules and processes on additional issues (e.g. new funds, REDD, and carbon capture and storage) almost certain to be launched. The institutional developments and majority-voting procedures implemented by the Kyoto Protocol's limited-membership bodies have been positive for the efficiency of the process, and should be replicated and extended to enable the regime to cope with the growing complexity of climate change.

In a similar vein, collective learning could be improved by establishing a new, independent technical body to provide analysis and advice in response to specific party requests. This body should be expert-based (rather than intergovernmental), with limited membership kept at a manageable level, and should have a mandate to provide policy advice, on request, on the technical feasibility of various options. It should be flexible enough to provide a response to requests in less than 12 months, as the normal annual cycle of the COP often requires rapid inputs. Obviously, parties will be under no obligation to accept its findings. However, there will have to be sufficient trust and acceptance of the new body for its findings at least to be respected as authoritative. One option could be for it to be an offshoot, or subsidiary, of the IPCC.

It is always tempting to advocate majority voting for a broader set of substantive issues as a means of unblocking political strangleholds and enabling faster and stronger decision-making. The problem is that voting generates its own difficulties. It is inherently alienating, with the defeated party left feeling aggrieved. It can, ironically, lead to deadlocks, when a decisive majority cannot be marshalled either in support, or opposition, to a proposal, and can lead to a party withdrawing altogether or simply choosing not to comply. In extreme cases, vote buying and bribery can even emerge. Interestingly, the International Whaling Commission, which has traditionally relied on voting for most decisions, has now amended its procedures to place greater onus on consensus. This does not mean, however, that there would be no benefit to introducing more majority voting in the climate-change regime. Indeed, voting has already been included in the rules of procedure for the CDM-EB and other boards/committees. If additional specialized governance bodies were established, as suggested above, majority voting should be extended to those bodies. In terms of the COP, CMP, and subsidiary bodies, the majority required for decisions would have to be carefully thought through, and probably weighted in some way, to ensure decisions commanded broad support across negotiating coalitions ('smart voting'). Voting could also be excluded, and consensus explicitly required, for certain particularly sensitive decisions. Unfortunately, discussion of such options has largely stalled in the climate-change regime, and carries considerable ideological baggage dating back to before the Convention's adoption. Reviving serious talks on voting issues should therefore only be contemplated if there if consensus over the merits of doing so, which is not currently the case.

The institutional options above suggest a significant expansion of the regime's institutional architecture. In the authors' view, this is unavoidable, and reflects the enormity and complexity of climate change, along with the sheer volume of work and existing institutional density. Eventually, the regime appears inexorably headed towards an expanded, permanent structure, with a number of standing expert and intergovernmental bodies that meet in almost continuous session, akin to the structure in the World Trade Organization. This might, eventually, encourage governments to establish permanent representations to the climate-change regime, resulting in a cadre of interdisciplinary climate experts that would hopefully facilitate more efficient decision-making. Such a vision might appear fanciful now, but the regime has nearly reached a stage of permanent session already: the regime's calendar shows meetings held nearly every week throughout much of 2008 and 2009. At present, such sessions are held all around the world and on an *ad hoc* basis. A standing 'international climate-change organization', in a single location, would surely be more efficient, less exhausting for delegates, and more climate-friendly, in terms of carbon air miles generated.

VII. IN DEFENCE OF THE GLOBAL

Fundamentally, many of the climate-change regime's weaknesses are due not to its specific design, but rather to the malignancy of climate change, combined with the inherent complexities of a *global* regime. This fact has led some to question whether a global approach was indeed the best response (Victor, 2006, 2007; Prins and Rayner, 2007; Haas, 2008). At the very start of the climate-change negotiations, Sebenius presciently wondered whether 'the complexities of a universal process' would 'threaten endless delay and impasse' (Sebenius, 1991, p. 144). These views were debated in the early 1990s, but quickly overtaken by the general enthusiasm for a global framework resulting from the precedence of the Montreal Protocol and the parallel UNCED negotiations (Stone, 1990; Hoffmann, 2007).

At first glance, arguments against a global regime appear to have some merit. Proponents of a more 'discriminating' regime[15] point out that about 20 countries account for some 80 per cent of fossil-fuel emissions. Agreement among these high emitters alone would go a long way to bringing down global emissions. A related suggestion is to confine initial negotiations to a core group of countries that already have strong relationships and are able to work well together (e.g. the OECD). The rationale behind both variants is that it would be easier to negotiate emission cuts and technological cooperation among 20 or so countries than among 190-plus (Victor, 2006; Prins and Rayner, 2007, p. 27). This is probably true, in terms of logistical complexity. In political terms, however, it is unlikely to work. First and foremost, this model excludes, or at least marginalizes, the main victims of climate change: the small island states, LDCs, and other poorer developing countries. If one aggregates causes and impacts, then climate change really is inescapably global. In any case, small emitters *are not the countries that are currently slowing down the negotiations*, and taking them out of the equation would not improve the political dynamics. Engaging only the main emitters would still generate the same political conflicts as in the global regime as, almost by definition, it is they who have the strongest positions. Even the economically and politically close OECD members tend to be split between Europeans and non-Europeans. The top 20 emitters also include Saudi Arabia, the main obstructionist in the negotiations (Depledge, 2008). Moreover, as noted above, the assumption that the climate-change negotiations always involve all 190-plus parties is erroneous; only 20–30 or so countries are ever deeply involved in the process anyway, to a large extent already replicating the limited-group idea.

Critics of the UN-based nature of the global regime tend to be hard-pressed to find a promising alternative setting (as they admit themselves— Victor (2007)). The OECD, G-8+,[16] and International Energy Agency (IEA), often cited,[17] may be good at research, analysis, promoting technological cooperation, and/or catalysing political commitment, but they have neither the mandate nor the experience in (successfully) negotiating legal obligations. Key players outside their membership—Russian Federation, China, India, Brazil, South Africa—may well balk at the idea of negotiating in these forums, inevitably with a different status to that of the core members. Regional bodies would not allow for cooperation among the range of countries required. Some commentators have suggested entirely new high-level political groupings.[18] The USA-led Major Economies process already constitutes such a group, but its value has been limited. A less controversial convening government may be more successful, but again

[15] For example, Prins and Rayner (2007); Victor (2007).

[16] The Group of 8 industrialized nations comprises Canada, France, Germany, Italy, Japan, the Russian Federation, the UK, and the USA. Recently, the G-8 has invited major industrializing nations to attend its meetings, notably Brazil, China, India, Mexico, and South Africa.

[17] See, for example, Haas (2008).

[18] See, for example, Victor (2007), citing former Canadian Prime Minister Paul Martin's proposal for an L20 'leaders' group, which Victor suggests could bring together the top 20 global emitters to work specifically on climate change.

more in terms of generating political commitment, than of striking concrete deals.

Fundamentally, a global regime may not be the most rational setting in theory, but in practice it is a *political* necessity. The main victims of climate change cannot be left out of the process simply because of their low emissions, limited leverage, and weak power. Their stake in the problem is immense. For a long time, attention to adaptation lagged behind that given to mitigation in the climate-change regime. Thanks to the perseverance of the small island states and LDCs, adaptation is now a major agenda item. This step forwards could not have happened in a limited-group regime involving only major emitters. Nor can those laggard countries that still fear a low-carbon economy simply be removed from the negotiations because they foment trouble (as suggested by Victor (2006, p. 96)). It is surely retrograde in the extreme to consider excluding those most affected by the outcome of negotiations.

The other critical dimension is the underlying desire of the G-77 to remain united or, at the very least, to determine its own dynamics. The fear that the developed countries will 'divide and rule' is precisely what has motivated their unity in the climate-change regime, and the UN more broadly. The desire for unity has to be respected, not least because any proposition that fails to do so will not work, and would exacerbate the North–South mistrust that has been so damaging. Involving large developing-country players in forums producing political declarations such as the G-8+ is one thing, but attempting to carve out substantive new deals with a select group of developing countries—without bringing any deals back to the climate-change regime—is unlikely to be accepted as legitimate. It is also unlikely to be workable in practice, because many business and private interests now involved in carbon markets need the legal certainty and global legitimacy that can only be provided by a *global* climate regime.

VIII. CONCLUSION

At the time of writing, in the run-up to the 2009 Copenhagen conference, debates were raging over the design of the next 'global deal' on climate change (see Chapter 3 by Hepburn and Stern in this volume). Whatever the outcome in Copenhagen, the climate-change problem is so complex and enduring that such debates are likely to continue way into the future. The main argument of this chapter is that, whatever substantive options are proffered, *they should be pursued within the framework of the existing global regime*, rather than seeking out new institutional structures. The 20-year-old regime has clocked up some important successes: keeping reluctant states engaged, sustaining the momentum of the process, enabling complex reciprocal deals, fostering collective learning, moving gradually ahead in strengthening commitments, and improving emissions data. These achievements are rarely acknowledged in the literature, but they are critical to building an effective long-term response to climate change. They must be sustained and supported, not abandoned. Alternatives to the change regime are attractive in principle, and might work in a perfectly rational world, where efficiency ruled, and messy politics and history did not intervene. In the *real* world, however, our best chance of avoiding dangerous climate change lies not in a fundamental rethink, but by reforming and continuously improving the existing global climate-change regime.

22

Governing Climate Change: Lessons from other Governance Regimes

Arunabha Ghosh and Ngaire Woods***

I. INTRODUCTION

At the heart of the existing climate-change regime is a divide between developed and developing countries. The UN Framework Convention on Climate Change (UN FCCC) enshrines 'common but differentiated responsibilities and respective capabilities' and in so doing recognizes that historical responsibility for climate change rests with developed countries and that they have greater capacity to address the problem. That said, the Convention specifies no timetable for the introduction of binding commitments on developing countries, nor any agreed procedures for 'graduating' countries from developing to developed status. As a result, progress in governing climate change rests heavily on finding a North–South agreement. That, in turn, rests on overcoming what Joanna Depledge and Farhana Yamin (Ch. 21 in this book) describe as 'the persistence of dysfunctional North–South politics . . . negotiations between the groups tend to be dominated by knee-jerk suspicion, defensiveness, and misunderstanding, which hinder the rational discussion of proposals'.

An 'integrated multi-track approach' has been proposed by Bodansky and Diringer (2008) as a possible way forward. All major emitters (developed and developing) would commit to reducing greenhouse gas (GHG) emissions, but they would have the flexibility to devise their own approaches (whether economy-wide targets, efficiency standards, efforts towards renewable energy, curbing deforestation, and so forth).[1] Many developing countries are concerned and sceptical about the prospect of new regulatory arrangements. They do not wish to become 'rule-takers' in yet another sphere of global politics which leaves them

* Woodrow Wilson School, Princeton University.

** University College, Oxford.

With thanks to Daniel Bodansky, not only for the inspiration of his superb work in this area but also for his generosity in giving comments.

[1] Bodansky and Diringer (2008). Unlike purely 'bottom–up' flexibilities, here the individual commitments of countries would be integrated in an over-arching framework to improve coordination among countries and facilitate trade-offs.

vulnerable to rules, monitoring, and enforcement which they see as having asymmetric impact to their disadvantage. We focus on the participation of developing countries in rule-making, and the monitoring, verification, and enforcement processes. As mentioned above, developing countries are concerned that a small group of powerful, industrialized countries will mostly 'do' the regulating, leaving them highly constrained, but marginalized, with little influence or control over the rules and their application. Below we draw out why developing countries might be concerned and what kinds of arrangements might reduce the risk that they will be marginalized from arrangements.

II. THE CHALLENGES OF PARTICIPATION IN RULE-MAKING

Until now, climate change negotiations have permitted participation from all countries. Within the UN FCCC, any state may become a party to the Convention. The underpinning existing treaties and arrangements are fully discussed in Chapter 21 by Depledge and Yamin. They underscore that in climate-change negotiations there is a 'norm of universal participation'. Progress towards the real objective of reducing GHG emissions has stalled because negotiators, including from major developing countries, are at a stand-off and unwilling to commit, let alone implement measures which in fact reduce GHG emissions. The prospects for resolving this stalemate through ongoing large-scale international negotiations look grim, especially when we consider the Doha Round of trade negotiations, which have been ongoing since 2001 and still have not reached a conclusion. The urgency of acting to mitigate climate change suggests that agreement among a small group of the largest emitters to reduce their GHG emissions is a crucial immediate step. However, the urgent deal among as few as four or five emitters needs buttressing with a wider deal to ensure that others do not immediately step into their shoes. Such a deal also needs buttressing with measures to alleviate the impacts of the failure to mitigate (to date) of the poorest countries in the world. These wider agreements will require institutional underpinnings to provide information, to monitor compliance, and to adjudicate disputes (Keohane, 1982). Indeed, some have called for a World Environment Organization to meet these needs (Esty and Ivanova, 2001; Newell, 2001). Whatever the institution, the challenge of engaging developing countries in the design and implementation of a global regime will be paramount. For these reasons we explore governance issues which will need to be addressed in the ongoing climate-change negotiations.

(i) Using Direct Incentives to Ensure Participation

Direct incentives offer one way to ensure greater engagement by developing countries who might otherwise avoid complying by simply avoiding participation in the regime (Barrett, 1999, p. 519). Several kinds of direct incentives are currently on the table, which include direct transfers (Barrett, 2001; Benedick, 2001, p. 71) or allocations of emission quotas (Bradford, 2001), or both (Hahn, 1998; Aldy *et al.*, 2001; Stewart and Wiener, 2001; Victor, 2003, p. 204). In the Montreal Protocol such side-payments were important. The London Amendment to the Protocol ensured increased participation, because rich countries offered to cover the incremental costs for developing countries to comply with the agreement. Much like the emission-reduction requirements, the Protocol obligated rich countries to transfer resources to a Multilateral Fund as payment to developing countries for the incremental costs of reducing the production of ozone-depleting substances (Barrett, 2005*a*, pp. 347, 349, 357).

New technology holds out another incentive for participation. Transfers from rich to poor countries would involve the adoption of new technology, whether related to cleaner coal with reduced emissions, or renewable sources of energy. The financing would come from developed countries (Benedick, 2001, p. 71) but the process could be strengthened with cooperative R&D and common international standards. But the transfer and use of technology has to be observable. The International Convention for the Prevention of Pollution from Ships (the MARPOL treaty) was effective because it was easier to monitor the adoption of a specific technology (segregated ballast tanks) than to observe actual pollution levels (Mitchell, 1994; Barrett, 2005*a*, pp. 393–6).

For developing countries the key concern over such promises to transfer resources or technology lies in a scepticism about whether these promises will be fulfilled. Theorists of cooperation have noted that when it comes to financial transfers, most countries prefer that others bear the cost (Barrett and Stavins, 2003, p. 358). More empirically, developing countries have learnt in other negotiations that where they can, developed countries avoid the costs. They look with hindsight at the Uruguay Round of trade negotiations and perceive that they accepted binding commitments in return for what proved to be discretionary future promises. In the final agreement, the priorities of industrialized countries, such as on intellectual property, were made into binding commitments. Meanwhile, progress on developing countries' priorities, such as the liberalization of trade in agriculture, cotton, and textiles, was promised at a future date. The disillusionment with this approach is one of the factors which has stymied further progress on the Doha Round of negotiations.

Another example of asymmetric commitments lies in the 2002 New Partnership for Africa's Development (NEPAD), which was agreed between countries of Sub-Saharan Africa and the G8 countries. On their side, the African leaders agreed to commit to a set of NEPAD political, economic, and corporate governance codes and standards contained in the *Declaration on Democracy, Political, Economic and Corporate Governance*, and created an African Peer Review Mechanism (APRM) to ensure adherence. In exchange for this pledge, the industrialized world committed to Africa's development with enhanced Overseas Development Assistance (ODA), debt relief, favourable trading terms, and direct foreign investments. However, the 'G8 Africa Plan of Action' was very slow in coming. What the G8 announced in 2002 boiled down to some uncoordinated and complex separate national initiatives on aid and trade access by the USA, Canada, and Britain, with no clear commitments on debt relief, market access, infrastructure development, and ODA reforms, nor was any discussion held of a mechanism to review whether the G8 was honouring its commitments. Three years later, at the G8 in Gleaneagles, larger promises were made, but many of these have not been honoured.

In the words of a former NEPAD Secretariat official, Khadija Bah, the slow and patchy progress in the delivery of the resources promised in the G8's pledges highlights that 'African leaders simply lack the leverage necessary to hold their industrialized partners accountable and make them deliver on their commitments'. While there is little African countries can do when the G8 fails to deliver, the G8 countries always have the option of suspending aid (Bah, 2009). For NEPAD to have been a genuine partnership, what was needed was 'symmetrical accountability', which would have required the conditions applying to Africa's industrialized partners to be clearly spelt out—for example, the size and composition of aid flows, the pace and sequencing of trade liberalization, and the flow of debt relief (Maxwell and Christiansen, 2002, p. 480).

The examples of the Uruguay Round and NEPAD explain developing-country demands in climate-change negotiations for verification and monitoring of any promised incentives. Some proposals have been made (Victor *et al.*, 1998). For example, in respect of technology transfers, developing countries are pushing for a multilateral financing and technology mechanism, to be supported by a Strategic Planning Committee, Technical Panels, Verification Group, and a Secretariat.[2] Experience suggests that systems to monitor financial contributions may be more difficult to put in place. Although monitoring financial and technology transfers might be technically easier,[3] to date reporting on financial contributions has been mixed at best, thanks to gaps in the data, multiple sources of funding, and inconsistencies in definitions (Breidenich and Bodansky, 2009, p. 16).

Similar monitoring problems have plagued other regimes. Reviews of 'aid-for-trade' found that measurements of actual funding flows were not only affected by multiple sources and double counting, but that there was little verification against commitments, and recipients had little say in the governance of funds. The OECD's Credit or Reporting System was also proposed for aid-for-trade, but poorer countries insisted on and secured a dedicated monitoring system. Similarly the OECD has developed a reporting standard for climate-related funding (the Rio Markers), but parties are not obliged to follow it.

Monitoring and verifying pledges to transfer resources and technology is not easy. However, efforts to secure a post-2012 climate deal will suffer unless developing countries have good reasons to trust that developed countries are both willing to make financing commitments and will, in fact, deliver on them. Centralized mechanisms which do not rely on appropriations from donor governments alleviate one concern about whether promised money is actually transferred.

[2] Proposal by the G77 and China for a Technology Mechanism under the UN FCCC (available at http://www.twnside.org.sg/title2/climate/info.service/20081111/G77-Tech%20Proposal%20Accra.pdf).

[3] Annex II parties are required to report in National Communications on their contributions to the Global Environment Facility or their bilateral climate-related aid.

To some degree the Adaptation Fund set up to complement the Clean Development Mechanism (CDM) is an example of such a centralized mechanism. One part of the fund is financed by a share of proceeds amounting to 2 per cent of certified emission reductions issued for a CDM project activity. That said, two additional issues arise in respect of a centralized funding mechanism. For developing countries, there is a concern about the automaticity of such funding or ensuring that this is not a conduit of World-Bank-style conditionality (the interim arrangements for the Adaptation Fund see it nested in the Global Environment Facility (GEF) with the World Bank as trustee). A second concern is the governance of such a centralized mechanism.

(ii) The Structure of Formal Decision-making

Participation will not be secured only by direct incentives. Equally vital is the structure of representation in decision-making that countries will face in governing climate change. As mentioned above, negotiations among 192 countries have proven difficult and frustrating. For some this highlights the need for an institution with a smaller decision-making body, such as the Executive Boards of the International Monetary Fund (IMF) and the World Bank. However, developing countries have long expressed dissatisfaction with the lack of votes and voice accorded to them in the Bretton Woods institutions which are dominated by the industrialized countries in large part because industrialized countries have a majority of votes on their Boards, and the United States a veto power. The fact that the institutions are located in Washington, DC, further underscores the sense of US dominance. The industrialized countries' grip on the IMF and World Bank has led developing countries to 'exit' when they can, in practical terms, from each institution by not borrowing and not taking advice from the institutions (whenever they can afford not to). In climate-change governance, 'exit' of this kind could render shared objectives unattainable. There is a further reason for ensuring that institutions governing climate change are not dominated by a small group of industrialized countries. Recall that the two tasks facing such institutions are: (*i*) a rule-based system on emissions; and (*ii*) effective financing for mitigation and adaptation. In respect of both tasks participation by developing countries and strong responsiveness to them will be crucial. There is evidence that international rules are more likely to be effectively implemented (as opposed to merely 'signed up to') by countries when they have been engaged in formulating the rules (and designing monitoring and enforcement mechanisms) themselves: the limited initial implementation of the IMF's codes and standards initiative in East Asia is one such example (Lombardi and Woods, 2008). Furthermore, to be effective in financing policies in developing countries, the institutions need to be maximally responsive. There is a strong temptation to design policies and finance packages for poorer countries, while sitting in Europe or North America. However, the experience of the past two decades highlights that in development financing 'ownership' is crucial to success. This does not mean 'persuading' governments to do things they would otherwise not do (which has a dismal record of failure). Rather, it means identifying in-country the projects and policies given priority by local communities and governments, and supporting those. To some degree these lessons have been taken on board.

The Adaptation Fund model has managed to avoid replicating the World Bank or GEF representation. The Adaptation Fund is governed by a Board composed of 16 members and 16 alternates representing the five United Nations regional groups (two from each), the small island developing states (one), the least developed countries (one), Annex I parties (two), and non-Annex-I parties (two). This gives formal representation to a range of countries and interests. That said, formal representation will not alone ensure that all parties' concerns and priorities are reflected in the policy and work of institutions governing climate change.

The regional development banks were created principally to ensure greater developing country 'ownership' and 'voice'. To this end they were structured in ways which ensured that developing countries from each region had a controlling share of votes, of capital, and staffing within their respective organization. Yet the early experience of these institutions was mixed, highlighting the importance of other conditions for exercising effective voice within an institution (Woods, 1999).

In the Inter-American Development Bank (IDB), regional members enjoyed formal control, holding a majority of the Bank's capital and votes and occupying the presidency, and the agency was perceived as being more 'in touch' with the region than the World Bank or the IMF. Yet it is also worth noting that in spite of the Latin American voting power within the Bank, the United States enjoyed enormous dominance through a veto on constitutional decisions, a provision that the Board's quorum required the presence of the US executive-director, the location of the bank in Washington, DC, the fact that one-quarter of its top management, its executive vice-president and usually also the financial manager and general counsel were from the USA, and the resources the US mission to the Bank used to present, argue, and lobby for particular positions or policies. The lesson to be drawn is that effective representation and participation requires not just representation in formal powers and structures. It also requires attention to other organization attributes, including staffing and location. At a subtler level, as evidenced by the experience of the Asian Development Bank, the counter-balancing of a dominant country's power by other powerful countries can create important space for a wider range of influences (Woods, 1999).

The experience of the African Development Bank is different but also instructive. From its inception in 1966 the Bank's capital, voting, and staff were structured to ensure African ownership and participation. Furthermore, the Bank was located in Abidjan, Côte d'Ivoire, with an African president and mostly African staff, and did not initially admit non-regional members. Yet for decades the Bank was found to be 'very distant from its African membership': to cite the report of the 1994 Task Force on Project Quality, the Bank had 'no systematic relations' with the African countries who are its majority share-holders. In the field, it was argued 'the Bank is absent when it should be present' (African Development Bank, 1994, p. 2). Furthermore, even within the boardroom, the African members of the Bank had a relatively low level of engagement in defining the Bank's overall direction, in questioning the institution's financial and operational strength, and in assuring the quality of its work and its contribution to African development. This was an institution whose formal structure attempted but failed to ensure the responsiveness and engagement of developing countries.

Developing countries' experience in international institutions highlights that formal 'seats at the table' or 'voting rights' are not enough to secure an effective voice and influence. Other organizational attributes are also important, including the role and selection of senior management, and the staffing and location of an organization. Equally important, however, is the capacity of developing countries to identify their own priorities, to 'politic' within institutions, to monitor and hold institutions to account for strategic goals and outputs, and to hold their own representatives to account, (Woods and Lombardi, 2006).

Holding representatives to account will become more important as negotiations on climate change proceed. Although negotiators ostensibly represent countries, in other institutions it is clear that over time representatives can too easily become more entrenched in their positions within their own governments, with their 'win-sets' becoming more defined and therefore more difficult to adjust. Ensuring that 'representatives' are held properly to account by those they represent is critical.

For many, the need to make big political decisions and trade-offs in climate change points to the need for engaging heads of government. For example, the G8 meeting of leaders at Gleneagles in 2005 launched a new level of political engagement in international negotiations by some of the major industrialized countries. Clearly, this was not a group endowed with formal representation or legitimacy but the leaders-level engagement made possible some linkage across issues. The G20 leaders meetings which were launched in Washington, DC, in 2008 to deal with the global financial crisis may well provide some impetus. Again the group does not represent more than a couple of dozen countries, meeting at the leaders' level, it may provide an important opportunity to shift the goalposts and agenda in climate-change negotiations, including on issues of concern to developing countries.

More formal decisions and agreements on rules and the like will require carefully framed decision-making rules and to date this has been every bit as contested (if not more) than participation itself. Members of the UN FCCC failed to adopt rules of procedure, principally because they could not agree on voting rules. The effect, as noted by Depledge and Yamin (Ch. 21 in this book), is that most decisions can only be taken by consensus. In the climate-change negotiations this has resulted in relatively small minorities (such as OPEC) regularly blocking agreement. The alternative would be to introduce some form of majority voting requirements, or to consider more closely the different ways that consensus operates in a number of different ways across different international organizations.

One version of 'consensus' is widely used in the UN Security Council. Formally the Council is made up of 15 members, five of whom are permanent (China, France, Russia, the UK, and the USA) and ten of whom are non-permanent representatives of various groupings of countries: the formal rule is that a minimum of nine votes is required for any decision, which must include the concurring vote of all five permanent members. Yet most of the Security Council's business is not carried out by formal voting, rather it is conducted in 'informal consultations of the whole', in which consensus decision-making replaces voting. By the late 1990s, it was said that this undoubtedly improved the capacity of the Council to despatch its business. It bred a much higher level of informal consultations, 'private straw votes', and meetings of small groups, according to members of the Council. Key decisions were taken outside of formal meetings. Even on procedural matters, when votes were taken they were 'so to speak, precooked in informal consultations': whereas there used to be frequent votes on the adoption of the agenda, by the late 1990s it was said that 'agendas are always agreed in advance... in informal consultations' (Wood, 1996). A serious problem with devolving decision to informal processes is that they are unrecorded and therefore in the absence of informal reporting (some of which emerged in the Security Council), they exclude many states.

Another form of 'consensus' operated from the early days in the World Trade Organization (WTO) where consensus came to mean decisions which reflect the mood of those *present at the meeting*. This prevents decision-making being held hostage by those not present. At the same time, however, it excludes those who cannot be present or who cannot afford to have a delegation at negotiations. A further variation on consensus decision-making within the WTO concerns decisions being made in lower Councils which had rules of procedure of their own. The practice emerged of ignoring these rules when consensus was not reached and instead decisions were 'bumped up' until consensus was reached at a higher level, if necessary going as far as the General Council.

In the climate-change negotiations, there are several forms of 'consensus' decision-making which could be used, or alternatively a form of majority decision-making. For example, double majority voting requires that the votes cast for a decision represent both a majority of countries as well as a majority of some other stake.[4] One possibility in climate-change negotiations would be to require that decisions command support from a majority of all countries, as well as a majority of the world's emitters (as measured, say in 1992 so as not to penalize those who have subsequently reduced emissions). The rationale for such voting rules is that they create incentives for countries and

[4] A range of measures is laid out in Dervis (2005).

groups of countries to consult with and to build up wider coalitions in favour of important issues, without permitting the emergence of relatively small blocking coalitions.

(iii) Supporting National Processes and National Priority-setting

Beyond the legal language and commitments embodied in international rules, the capacities that countries have to implement rules, or make use of exceptions varies hugely. Simply put, once agreements are struck, the same provisions do not impact in equal ways on developing countries.

For example, in the Agreement on Trade Related Aspects of Intellectual Property Rights (TRIPS), to which many developing countries signed up, there is provision for a variety of legal safeguards and options (the TRIPS 'flexibilities') which developing countries could use in the application of the agreement. Yet only a small number of developing countries have made use of legal safeguards and the 'flexibilities' inherent in the agreement. Curiously, some of the poorest and neediest countries who are signatories have opted for yet more onerous (TRIPs-plus) commitments. The reasons for this lie not in the legal language of the agreement but in the politics of implementation (Deere, 2008). An important part of the explanation lies in the way some smaller and poorer countries, such as those in West Africa, have not embedded their intellectual property laws and compliance into their broader national goals and institutions. As a result, the trade-offs between tight TRIPS-plus implementation and priorities such as national health, expenditure, and other development goals are not reflected in their law-making.

The experience of small states in trade negotiations highlights how crucial national capacities and processes are. Scholars have identified the extent to which small states are impaired by the absence of missions in Geneva, weak inter-governmental coordination, poor communication and information flows within government, and low levels of technical competence among officials (Blackhurst *et al.*, 2000; Ohiorhenuan, 2005). Administrative capacity is severely constrained in countries with small populations (Kotschwar, 1999, p. 14). Crucially, these problems have been magnified by the expanding scope of trade negotiations both within and beyond the WTO which demands ever greater institutional capacity (Tussie and Lengyel, 2002, p. 487).

The financing of climate-change mitigation and adaptation could play an important role in strengthening and supporting national and local processes. That said, there is a long history of efforts to 'incentivize' policy-makers in developing countries in the area of economic policy. Few have been successful. The main impact of 'structured incentives' or conditionality is to give 'assurance' to donor countries, offering a tempting mirage of policy change which lures them across the policy-equivalent of a desert. Far more likely to induce success is a careful examination (as already mentioned above) of how much local ownership there is of a project, and by whom. This can only be ascertained by investigating who initiated the project and what local resources are being dedicated to it. Similarly important is to ascertain the extent to which local expertise and institutions will be used to implement, report, and decide upon renewal (or not) of a project. Finally, countries promising finance should investigate themselves and, in particular, should ascertain whether the timing of disbursements, the certainty (or not) of finance, and its possible recurrence have been planned to suit the project and recipient of financing. Far too often projects fail because their financing has been arranged to suit a donor's budget cycle and reporting requirements. The lesson for developing countries in climate-change negotiations is one which underlines how important it is that their national positions be integrated across governments, so that the trade-offs for other national goals are properly considered, and so that implementation and enforcement cohere with other parts of government. For other countries in the climate-change regime, these elements of national ownership and coherence are vital for effective compliance.

III. THE CHALLENGES OF MONITORING

An effective information system is at the heart of regulation and the governance of mitigation. Effective monitoring which provides information and reduces uncertainties should facilitate international cooperation (Keohane, 1982, p. 325; Simmons, 2000, p. 819). The UN FCCC and the Kyoto Protocol have extensive provisions for monitoring, especially for the emissions of Annex I countries. But monitoring is still imperfect, both in terms of linking it to effective enforcement[5] and in broadening its scope to include issues of importance to developing countries. The Bali Action Plan explicitly recognizes the need for measurable, reportable, and verifiable (MRV) actions. It applies not only to 'mitigation commitments and actions' by developed countries but also to 'nationally appropriate mitigation actions' by developing countries '*supported and enabled by technology, financing and capacity-building, in a measurable, reportable and verifiable manner*'.[6] Yet, many of the new or alternative proposals for the climate regime either engage with monitoring only as a marginal question or not at all.

Monitoring and verification in the climate-change regime may be necessary but it will not be easy. In a world of sovereign states, monitoring is one of the most contested aspects of international regulation. No surprise, then, that it is a further area of concern for developing countries. On the one hand, developing countries do not want take on strong obligations for monitoring emissions, because they consider that to be a first step towards rule-bound commitments to

[5] Barrett and Stavins (2003, p. 366); Victor (2003, p. 204); Barrett (2005*a*, pp. 360, 396). Under Article 18 of the Protocol compliance cannot be enforced with 'binding consequences' without an amendment.

[6] Paras.1(b)(i) and 1(b)(ii) (emphasis added).

reduce emissions. Moreover, they recognize that building domestic systems for continuous emissions monitoring would entail significant costs. On the other hand, poor countries want improved monitoring of financial and technology transfers from rich countries. Thus, developing countries have an important stake in designing an MRV system for the climate regime. It is a precondition for improved compliance, which would not be limited only to measuring emission reductions but would apply transfers from rich to poor countries as well. Yet, their experiences in other monitoring regimes, discussed below, have put developing countries on guard.

(i) What Needs Monitoring?

Several aspects of the climate-change regime are likely to require monitoring. These include a global emission reduction and trading system, or linkages between national/regional trading schemes, or harmonized taxes, compliance, and enforcement. Each of these would be contingent on monitoring and reporting, verification, and procedures for peer pressure. Accurate, consistent, and internationally comparable data on emissions are essential for enabling member states to measure their performance against their commitments. This could include monitoring individual firms and sectors, evaluating performance against baselines, reporting and registering total emissions by states, and verifying the data via independent sources. Further, information on the best available technologies and the means to adapt to climate change is also needed to chart a path of sustainable development and to hold rich countries accountable for their promises to poorer ones.

Developing countries have concerns about their obligations for reporting and the legitimacy of procedures to promote compliance. The climate regime already has a complex set of obligations and voluntary requirements for monitoring and verification, which pertain to the supply of information. But the experience with designing effective monitoring mechanisms in international regimes suggests that it is equally important to understand the demand for information: who seeks information, of what kind, in what format, and how often. In an evolving climate regime, member states would have periodically to decide on the minimum standards for the information they seek from each other and from the UN FCCC Secretariat.

Economists tend to focus on the problem of asymmetric information, which makes parties unwilling to enter into an agreement (Akerlof, 1970, p. 488) or creates moral hazards when some actors free ride and increase the risk burden for others.[7] But the information problem in the climate regime has to be conceived not only in a relational sense (as asymmetries *between* parties) but also in an absolute sense (the absence of timely, relevant, and credible information for *all* parties). This is partly because of the uncertainties associated with the impact of

[7] Arrow, 1971. See also, Spence, 1973, p. 355; and Stiglitz, 1975, p. 283.

climate change on different countries, and partly due to the fact that the baselines, methods, and procedures for reporting and reviewing different aspects of the climate regime have not been fully resolved yet.

Provided a climate agreement is flexible (see previous section on rule-setting), uncertainties about the impact of climate change on specific regions might actually induce international cooperation (Koremenos *et al.*, 2001, pp. 778–9). Further, the reduction in uncertainty can also motivate parties to negotiate a deal by increasing awareness of the adverse consequences of inaction.[8]

Once countries have agreed on the need for mitigation actions, monitoring is needed in order to prevent free riding by individual states or other actors. Emission trading is central to several proposals for a global climate regime.[9] Some proposals recommend that countries undertake voluntary pledges regarding specific policies or actions (Schelling, 1998). A slightly different approach links tradable permit schemes across different jurisdictions to offer low-cost compliance options (Jaffe and Stavins, 2008).

Voluntary emissions cuts or not, the system would still require institutional monitoring to measure performance. At present, the provisions for annual national inventory reporting are limited to Annex I countries. If developing countries were to take on commitments for emission reductions, then emissions from all countries would have to be credibly verified (Barrett and Stavins, 2003, p. 359). In addition to measuring the quantity of emissions, the data also have to be comparable. Thus, emissions reporting cannot be the responsibility of governments alone. International institutions would need to ensure data quality for comparability because the trading of permits mixes the inventories from different countries (OECD, 2001, p. 37).

Another proposed design for the climate regime eschews emissions trading in favour of harmonized carbon taxes applied by all countries (Cooper, 2001, p. 11484; 2008, p. 1). Internationally determined taxes would be applied on domestic carbon use, while the rates could be set based on cost–benefit analyses (Nordhaus, 1998). A harmonized tax regime, in turn, would need monitoring of actual charges imposed by national regulatory agencies. One suggestion is for the IMF to include an assessment as part of its usual surveillance activities (Agarwala, 2008). The process would entail more inter-agency coordination between the IMF and UN FCCC. But a bigger threat to credibility would come from the asymmetric representation of members in the two institutions. Developing countries, with

[8] There are parallels between the Montreal Protocol and recent developments in climate change. For the former, a cost–benefit study from the US President's Council of Economic Advisers found the monetary benefits of reducing skin-cancer-related deaths outweighed the costs of reducing chlorofluorocarbons (CFCs) (Benedick, 1998, p. 63). Similarly, the Stern Review found that the cost of inaction far exceeded the costs of reducing GHG emissions (Stern, 2007).

[9] Variations include: formulas for gradual inclusion of developing countries (Frankel, 2008); hybrid systems with additional permits available at fixed prices (Aldy *et al.*, 2001); no fixed cap on emissions but regular purchasing and retiring of allowances by international agencies (Bradford, 2001); and separate domestic markets for trading in annual emissions and in endowments (McKibbin and Wilcoxen, 2000).

much less voting power in the IMF, would be unwilling to cede control to that organization to assess their compliance with carbon-tax obligations.[10]

The trade regime has also struggled with problems of comparability of data. Members submit data on tariff lines based on their own commodity classification standards. The WTO incorporates the data in a common database, but reviews are based on national data. More recently, however, databases on regional trade agreements (RTAs) and sanitary and phytosanitary standards (SPS) have sought to increase comparisons.

For the climate regime (cap-and-trade, linkage schemes, or taxes), the format and content of reporting from a disparate group of countries would need more attention. The UN FCCC's International Transaction Log, which tracks transactions for Assigned Amount Units, became fully operational only in 2008, so its performance has not been assessed yet (Breidenich and Bodansky, 2009, p. 14). Moreover, reporting of mitigation measures is subject to less critical review. Although Annex I parties are expected to submit detailed information on their policies and measures, there are no common standards to adhere to. The review teams do not verify the reported information.

(ii) Reporting and the Challenge of Building National Monitoring Systems

One of the functions of international regimes is to reduce hidden/inaccurate information about members' behaviour. For this purpose, regimes adopt various types of reporting mechanisms: self-reporting, other-reporting, institutional reporting, and non-state actor reporting.

When states are unwilling to cede sovereignty to the secretariat of an international regime, self-reporting systems emerge. Enforced properly, self-reporting is a valuable source of information and puts pressure on members to comply. The International Labour Organization (ILO) considers timely reporting by member states so important that it blacklists states that habitually fail in the task (Chayes and Chayes, 1995). The United Nations Convention on the Law of the Seas (UNCLOS) is the only major environmental agreement that has no formal reporting procedure, but here, too, the Secretariat requests information from states on straddling fish stocks.

In the General Agreement on Tariffs and Trade (GATT) and WTO, notifications have long been considered a principal way to improve transparency and promote compliance (GATT, 1990, para. 2). But the system of notifications, which the WTO inherited, has become increasingly problematic. Even rich countries, with fewer capacity constraints, fail to submit notifications on time. A recent review of agricultural subsidies resulted in an unprecedented number of questions on delayed notifications by developed countries. Developing countries fear that gaps

[10] Their experience of existing IMF surveillance is that it is highly asymmetric in its impact (Lombardi and Woods, 2008).

in notifications are no longer an issue of administrative capacity, but deliberate strategies to withhold information.

Under the UN FCCC, Annex I parties are expected to submit annual inventories of GHG emissions along with reports on methodologies and data sources. Non-Annex I (NAI) parties submit inventories as part of their national communications (which are less frequent) and are not bound by the same standards of data quality. The submissions do not include time-series data and cover only three GHGs, namely carbon dioxide, methane, and nitrous oxides.

Preliminary evidence, however, suggests difficulties in fulfilling these functions. The self-reporting structure is under strain, with both developed and developing countries having problems in maintaining accuracy and quality in their submissions (Kawamoto, 2005, p. 2). In the initial years, reports suffered from incomplete data or have under-reported emissions (Subak, 1998). National communications from developing countries have been delayed, in some cases, by more than 8 years.[11]

In other words, resource constraints within developing countries need more than marginal attention. At present there are no emissions-trading schemes in the developing world. For developing countries to participate in cap-and-trade schemes in future, they would have to maintain national registries and inventories, which have non-trivial cost implications.

In the trade regime, poor countries were shocked to discover the actual costs of improving their domestic regulatory capacities. Costs linked to implementing agreements on intellectual property, customs valuation, and SPS measures exceeded the annual development budget of a typical least-developed country (Finger and Schuler, 2000, p. 525). That experience has made them wary of agreeing to new obligations within the WTO.

Building capacity for domestic surveillance and external monitoring is not easy. Nearly 20 years after the WTO's Trade Policy Review Mechanism (TPRM) started operating, most developing countries still suffer from capacity constraints. A survey of 70 countries (just under half the WTO's membership) found that only a fifth of them had independent agencies for policies reviews. Even fewer had the ability to publish reports on other countries' trade barriers. Some of the larger developing countries have sought to build analytical capacity at home, but they, too, are forced to make trade-offs about which issues they can analyse (Ghosh, 2008).

It can be expected that high regulatory costs would affect countries' willingness to participate in the climate regime as well. Developing countries expect technical support from a Consultative Group of Experts (CGE) under the UN FCCC. But the resources allocated under the CGE were capped at US$100,000 per country. The assistance was provided only at the time of preparing national communications, not for collecting emissions data on a continuous basis. Moreover, its mandate, which expired in 2007, was not renewed until mid-2009.

[11] To date, 134 NAI parties have submitted their first communications, nine have submitted their second, and only one has submitted a third.

Thanks to the challenges with self-reporting, institutional reporting is often required. Institutional surveillance can be directed at individual countries, conducted regionally, or undertaken simultaneously for all member states. For example, the IMF conducts country-specific consultations periodically, along with comprehensive reports such as the *World Economic Outlook*. Among environmental regimes, the Convention on the International Trade in Endangered Species of Wild Fauna and Flora (CITES) is the only one that allows its secretariat to report on national performance.

Another response is reporting by non-state actors (non-governmental organizations (NGOs), firms, experts, and scientific institutions). But the division of responsibility for collecting and disseminating information is a deeply political issue.

In the climate regime, primary data is collected and disseminated by international organizations (UN Statistics Division, the Food and Agriculture Organization, the United Nations Environment Program, the World Bank), by national or regional agencies (Carbon Dioxide Information Analysis Centre, International Energy Agency, Eurostat, United States Environmental Protection Agency), by sectoral institutions (International Iron and Steel Institute), and by NGOs (World Resources Institute). Each of these options raises institutional design questions of sovereignty, availability of resources and capacity, and type and quality of data collected.

In the past, NGOs have also published emissions projections that differ by more than 5 per cent from official projections (Subak, 1998, p. 5). The role of NGOs serving as 'fire alarms' was enshrined in the North American Agreement on Environmental Cooperation (a North American Free Trade Agreement side-agreement), which introduced a Citizens Submissions Process (Raustiala, 2003–4, p. 389). NGOs can also monitor transfers of technology and financial resources to developing countries, thereby pressuring rich countries to comply with commitments.[12] Recent discussions on aid-for-trade monitoring found that poor countries had limited capacity to monitor flows. They demanded that NGOs be included in forums to discuss aid flows.

But there are questions about the political power of NGOs versus the capacity of developing countries. During the Kyoto Protocol negotiations NGOs used activist and advisory strategies to ensure that they would have a significant role in Enforcement Branch deliberations (Andresen and Gulbrandsen, 2003, p. 10). Developing countries have opposed NGO participation in multilateral institutions (such as the WTO) when their interests have clashed with those of developed-country-based organizations. Even for aid-for-trade, where interests converge, the WTO's role in monitoring was considered paramount. Similar apprehensions should be expected to prevail even in the climate regime.

A related challenge is the relationship between weak regulatory capacity and the role of non-state actors. Scholars have proposed buyer-liability systems to

[12] For instance, the World Bank includes NGOs in implementing technology-transfer projects through the Global Environment Facility.

put the burden of verification on the developed-country buyers of permits (Victor, 2001; Keohane and Raustiala, 2008). But the system would put a huge burden on permit-long (developing) countries to create the regulatory mechanisms that would ensure the validity of permits being sold from their territory. Further, the role of independent, non-governmental rating agencies would have to be specified when assessments of performance are carried out in intergovernmental settings. In the CDM, for instance, Brazil has been in favour of a National CDM Secretariat governed by state authorities. The United States, by contrast, prefers decentralized market mechanisms. As the current financial crisis demonstrates, however, decentralized systems are also susceptible to regulatory capture. Building institutions and processes to audit the auditors would put an additional burden on developing countries (Repetto, 2001, p. 303).

(iii) Assessment and Verification at the International Level

An effective climate regime needs to distinguish verification and review processes. The former is a technocratic certification of the validity of data; the latter is inherently a political process. Even without reference to legal judgments on compliance, peer reviews can potentially apply sufficient pressure on members to change their policies.

But restricted mandates can hamper even technocratic verifications. Trade policy reviews in the WTO, or IMF Article IV consultations suffer from the same weakness—namely that the assessments do not verify the quality and accuracy of the data. A new monitoring mechanism for RTAs also deliberately forsook examination procedures and the WTO Secretariat only got the mandate to prepare 'factual presentations'.

Among major multilateral environmental agreements, the Montreal Protocol is the only one that has dedicated non-compliance procedures. But it, too, does not permit the verification of the accuracy of nationally supplied data. Instead, the non-compliance procedures are *ad hoc* and rely on complaints brought by other parties. The CITES also has some features of a non-compliance procedure. In practice, compliance review in these regimes is treated as facilitative of compliance rather than merely as deterrence against non-compliance.

The climate regime also has various mechanisms: a compliance committee under the Kyoto Protocol, a supervisory committee for Joint Implementation activities, a CDM Executive Board, and the annual Conference of the Parties (COP) meetings.[13] Reviews by experts ascertain whether the methods used conform to the IPCC's Guidelines for National Greenhouse Gas Inventories (IPCC, 1996) and Good Practice Guidance and Uncertainty Management in national inventories (IPCC, 2001*b*). The reported data are also compared to data from other sources. But there is no provision in the UN FCCC for a final verification and

[13] Of course, at the project level, monitoring, evaluation, reporting, and verification present additional financial, management, and technological capacity hurdles, amounting to 5–10 per cent of a project's budget (see Vine and Sathaye, 1999, p. 43).

assessment of compliance under the Convention (OECD, 2001, p. 38). And there is no formal review process for GHG inventories from developing countries. If similarly high standards of data verification were applied to NAI parties in future, developing countries would be concerned that such detailed information could be used to impose new commitments for emission reductions.

Further, in order to evaluate the GHG-mitigation policies of Annex I parties, the issue of causality is critical. It is easier to measure changes in policy rather than establish the causal impact of the said policy. This is what makes the promotion of compliance via MRV mechanisms harder. The review process for national communications has no clear guidelines and is only facilitative: expert teams liaise with national officials but do not have the capacity credibly to verify the reported information (Breidenich and Bodansky, 2009, p. 15).

Part of the problem relates to the high cost of sending large teams for in-country missions, as the WTO has discovered. In the late 1990s at least four to five IMF staff members would go on country missions, although frequent rotation of staff members meant that there was lack of continuity. In 2005 the IMF used 9 per cent of its staff resources on multilateral surveillance and 29 per cent on bilateral monitoring (IMF, 1999, pp. 25, 31; Independent Evaluation Office of the IMF, 2006, p. 12). By contrast, the Trade Policy Review Division only accounts for 6 per cent of the WTO's staff. Given the small size of the teams and the range of countries to review, individual economists do not have the requisite expertise to engage with each country in depth. If expert teams in the UN FCCC had to verify reported emissions by Annex I *and* NAI parties and also review and assess their mitigation activities, there would have to be a proportionate increase in technical and financial resources in addition to an expanded political mandate to conduct in-depth reviews. Resource constraints would also affect any attempts to establish international reviews of non-target mitigation activities.

(iv) Compliance Promotion via Peer-to-peer Surveillance

What processes and forums do countries find legitimate to review each other's actions? Surveillance is interdependent with enforcement: information could be used to apply peer pressure during negotiations or it could be used as evidence in formal litigation/arbitration proceedings. Recent work has suggested three possible routes through which surveillance can influence a regime's members: by the direct provision of information, which reduces uncertainties for the states under review and for other actors; by peer reviews among regime members that produce social pressures to improve compliance; and by asymmetric power relations, which give the international institution more leverage over some members than others (Simmons *et al.*, 2006, p. 781; Lombardi and Woods, 2008).

An important question is who applies pressure for improved compliance. As enforcement mechanisms become more robust, countries would become more sensitive about the credibility of monitoring. In fact, too much legalization could undermine international agreements owing to concerns over the distribution of gains and losses (Goldstein and Martin, 2000, p. 606).

The IMF's influence under bilateral surveillance is at its most influential in respect of countries borrowing (or hoping to borrow) from the IMF, or relying on its stamp of approval to access other finance. For the rest of the membership, bilateral surveillance at best can provide some signal to the market rather than specific informational inputs that market participants use. There is some evidence that competition among peers has resulted in growing adoption of the IMF's voluntary standards and codes, but equally there is evidence that 'sign-up' to these standards provides little guarantee that members actually comply with them. Although the IMF emphasizes the value of 'learning' and dialogue within the context of IMF reviews, there are, in fact, few opportunities for peer-to-peer exchanges between government officials and IMF staff, in either bilateral or multilateral surveillance processes (Lombardi and Woods, 2008). This is, in part, a reflection of the way the IMF management has structured the surveillance process. Equally, however, it reflects how little authority the IMF's membership has delegated to the organization so that it might conduct surveillance effectively for its entire membership.[14]

Similarly, in highly legalized regimes (such as international trade), members have been reluctant to give much authority to the Secretariat and have undermined follow-up procedures. The WTO's TPRM aimed to institutionalize peer pressure and improve adherence to trade rules (Curzon Price, 1992, p. 87). At the same time, its mandate restricts the use of information from trade policy reviews in dispute settlement proceedings. But a perverse outcome has been that, thanks to the greater domestic capacity of rich countries to monitor others, the pressure on poor countries to comply is greater. An analysis of review meetings shows that much of the 'peer pressure' is directed from developed towards developing countries: developing countries get asked more questions both before and during meetings. Moreover, the majority of discussants for TPRs have also come from developed countries. In turn, developing countries are unable to apply similar pressure because they do not have the requisite information and the review meetings lack teeth. These dynamics have served to reduce the confidence of poor countries in trade policy surveillance (Ghosh, 2008).

Article 8 of the Kyoto Protocol creates the possibility for extensive peer review. It has provisions for expert review teams to verify inventories and national communications.[15] But it is also a step beyond technical assessments, because it demands that review teams should flag potential problems and implementation questions to the COP/MOP (Meeting of the Parties to the Kyoto Protocol). The idea is that both the Secretariat and the Parties would raise questions regarding a Party's non-implementation or non-compliance. This is a move away from the 'shared

[14] Elsewhere, however, the OECD's or the ILO's reports make non-binding recommendations, but they carry weight that states cannot ignore.

[15] In 1999 a Common Reporting Format was adopted for inventories, and inventories are subject to a three-stage review: initial checks, synthesis and assessment, and expert review (Tenner, 2000, p. 160).

learning' in non-confrontational settings that dominates other procedures under the UN FCCC.[16]

The Compliance Committee of the Kyoto Protocol (with its constituent Facilitative and Enforcement Branches) has balanced geographical representation. Representatives of NAI parties are also in a position to review the implementation of commitments by Annex I parties. But if NAI parties take on commitments in a post-2012 regime, then drawing on the experience of the IMF and the WTO, developing countries would be concerned about which countries participate regularly in reviews, which ones ask questions, and which countries become the targets of peer pressure. They would also want to establish strong review procedures for evaluating rich countries' performance with commitments to transfer financial and technological resources. The asymmetry of peer pressure and pressure from non-state actors in the WTO is a key reason why many members have stopped actively engaging with its monitoring mechanism, or why they have opposed opening up review processes to non-state actors.

In addition to assessing compliance by individual parties, regime members might want impact analyses and evaluations of the operation of the regime as a whole. General reviews are useful to monitor trends and systemic risks that tend to affect all members of a regime. In international finance, there has been a history of system-wide surveillance, whether as part of meetings of the G-7 finance ministers or more recently through the Financial Stability Forum. The IMF also undertakes general surveillance of international financial markets, reported in the *Global Financial Stability Report*, and of development-oriented issues via the *Global Monitoring Report* (Lombardi and Woods, 2008).

Similarly, information systems interpret rules, but in doing so they apply different yardsticks to individual countries and thereby suggest new rules. The evaluation of the regime and its impact on different categories of states is an iterative process of learning. The IMF's Article XVIII in the original Articles of Agreement explicitly provided for interpretation (questions were to be submitted to the Executive Directors). The ILO Governing Body has also been requested from time to time to interpret conventions. Although non-binding, such opinions are rarely challenged, giving them significant influence over compliance with labour conventions at the national level (Chayes and Chayes, 1995, p. 215). Similarly, GATT (and now WTO) dispute-settlement panel reports set precedents for how international trade law would be interpreted in future.

An interesting precedent in national environmental legislation relates to Sections 202 and 211 of the US Clean Air Act. The Environmental Protection Agency (EPA) has the authority to prescribe emissions standards for any air pollutant that it believes could 'endanger public health and welfare'. Such assessments are expected to draw on the latest scientific evidence from multiple sources, including IPCC reports, National Research Council reports, and peer-reviewed regional

[16] Note that although Article 8 provisions feed directly into Kyoto Protocol enforcement procedures, the Protocol itself does not provide strong incentives for participation or compliance (Barrett, 2008, p. 4).

assessments (Grundler, 2007). There have been recent controversies over delays in reporting after a Supreme Court judgment in 2007 asked the EPA to determine whether GHG emissions from new motor vehicles endangered public health or not. But the process underscores the importance of regime evaluation to reduce uncertainties and to develop improved regulatory standards.

In sum, the climate regime already has extensive provisions for monitoring, verification, and review, mostly targeted at Annex I parties. Extending those provisions to developing countries would mean confronting concerns about new commitments, enforcement procedures, and effective monitoring of financial and technological transfers. Developing countries' experience in other regimes, particularly with regard to the problems of reporting capacity, unbalanced reviews, and the lack of accountability for developed countries' commitments, has some bearing on the climate regime as well. The challenge of monitoring in the climate regime would be to determine the extent of differentiation in MRV obligations and processes: based on a country's domestic capacity; based on its systemic importance as regards the flows and stock of GHGs; and based on levels of responsibility for tackling all aspects of the climate-change problem.[17]

IV. THE CHALLENGES OF ENFORCEMENT

A final area of concern to developing countries in the structure of a new mitigation regime will be the nature and locus of enforcement. Without centralized review and adjudication at the international level, enforcement can take various forms.

The first option is to combine centralized adjudication with decentralized enforcement. In this model, the regime leaves it up to individual members (or actors within them) to pursue redress actions against an erring party. The multilateral trade regime is the foremost example. The reports of dispute settlement panels and the Appellate Body determine the extent of non-compliance and legitimate compensation. But whether the complainant actually imposes the sanctions or not depends on several factors, which render enforcement particularly difficult for small, developing countries (Nottage, 2009).

The most important constraint for developing countries is market-size. The market-restricting sanctions of many small economies are not sufficient to impose the pressures needed to change the behaviour of larger powers. Second, small economies, heavily dependent on trade, suffer potentially severe welfare losses if they try to impose sanctions on their larger trading partners. For many of these countries, the WTO's retaliation rules are 'virtually meaningless' (Footer, 2001, p. 94). However, one study finds that, even without retaliation, compliance with panel and Appellate Body reports is high (Davey, 2005, pp. 46–8). Thus, enforcement also depends, in part, on the domestic political economy within

[17] Thanks to Dan Bodansky for raising this important set of questions.

countries, as well as the desire for members to maintain their reputations in a rule-based global regime (Hudec, 2002, pp. 82–3).

The second option is centralized adjudication combined with centralized enforcement. The European Union's Stability and Growth Pact, which governs fiscal discipline within the euro-zone, adopts this approach. Under the Pact, the European Commission and the Council monitor the fiscal policies of member countries. States failing to limit their budget deficits to 3 per cent and national debt to 60 per cent of GDP, could be subject to sanctions, after several warnings. However, in this centralized system, the application of sanctions has not proven easy when powerful states are involved. The EU Council of Ministers has repeatedly failed to impose sanctions against France and Germany for violating the pact.

Other examples of centralized adjudication and enforcement include the Board of Governors of the International Atomic Energy Agency (IAEA) and the United Nations Security Council. However, in these cases enforcement relies on getting all necessary states to agree to resolutions which indicate non-compliance, or in the case of the Security Council can mandate enforcement measures. This has proven extremely difficult.

The third enforcement option is through linkage. Trade linkages have been proposed regularly to promote labour and environmental standards. Such linkage was originally conceived as negative sanctions: countries failing to adhere to commonly agreed standards could lose access to export markets. A frequently cited example of such linkage design was the NAFTA side-agreements. However, developing countries fear that linkage will too easily become a backdoor through which protectionist measures are introduced against them. More recent proposals have pushed for positive linkage, whereby countries committing to and delivering on higher standards would be rewarded with greater market access as well as direct financial transfers (Barry and Reddy, 2008). The main attraction of such proposals is that they create a potential win–win opportunity: a 'race to the bottom' of standards is avoided, which is a public good, and countries putting in the effort to raise standards receive additional rewards.

An effective and equitable climate regime would need to overcome the gaps highlighted in the above examples. If decentralized, the system would need to overcome the economic and political constraints on applying sanctions on bigger powers. The WTO Dispute Settlement Mechanism's activity is concentrated in a handful of regular users, all too few of which are developing countries.

With these concerns in mind, developing countries might prefer centralized enforcement in the climate regime. Centralized enforcement would, in turn, continue to face the difficulty of sanctioning powerful states. Further, the regime's members would have to determine whether sanctions should be applied against individual entities within a country's jurisdiction, or against countries as a whole. The difficulty in establishing the validity of permits traded by each single entity has given rise to proposals based on 'jurisdiction equality' (Keohane and Raustiala, 2008).

Finally, enforcement through trade linkages would come up against opposition from developing countries. Unlike international trade, where linkages are used to deter mercantilist behaviour, developing countries do not accept responsibility for mitigating climate change. Thus, linking their non-target mitigation actions to potential trade sanctions would be considered unethical and unfair.

V. CONCLUSIONS

An urgent reduction in GHG emissions is unlikely to be achieved in ongoing negotiations among nearly 200 countries. A small group of the world's largest emitters will need to take immediate action, individually and/or collectively. Longer term, however, actions by the largest emitters will need to be buttressed by global agreements which prevent other countries from becoming large emitters, and which offer assistance to poorer countries forced to adapt to the consequences of a failure to mitigate to date. The challenge for governing climate change at the global level is thus twofold: (*i*) to create, monitor, and enforce a rule-based regime to ensure emissions continue to reduce; and (*ii*) to channel financing to poorer countries for them to use to adapt or mitigate. To be effective, the global regime will need to be both participatory and responsive, especially towards developing countries.

In this chapter we have drawn out lessons which could inform progress towards this goal. The first lesson is that direct incentives to developing countries to induce their participation in the climate regime cannot be viewed as 'side payments'. The climate regime aims to provide a public good (the prevention of global warming). But action is necessary to solve a problem which developing countries had little part in creating. If their participation in a solution to the problem is now necessary, then negotiations on incentives have to be centre-stage and not treated as an afterthought. It bears remembering that, in these negotiations, poor countries have real veto power. They can stall the negotiations if the incentives to induce their participation lack guarantees, effective monitoring, and adequate accountability. In this instance, climate-change negotiations are not like the mercantilist trade negotiations of old, where developing countries were successfully pressured to agree to new standards and regulations in return for trade access.

A second lesson is that formal inclusion in a regime's governance structures is vital but offers no guarantee of voice, influence, or effective representation. Other organizational features are vital. Consensus decision-making in climate-change negotiations has permitted relatively small blocking-coalitions to prevent progress. In other organizations, consensus has been interpreted differently to permit more forward motion. More broadly, the lessons from other institutions demonstrate how quickly representatives or negotiators can get stuck, clinging to a narrow mission and within a structure which does not hold them adequately to account. Better transparency and formal accountability is one part of a solution. The other part may lie in manifestly less representative structures which are capable of opening up a broader agenda, such as the G20 meeting at leaders level. Finally, the experience of trade rules and their implementation highlights the importance of capacity—specifically the capacity of developing countries to formulate national and regional goals and strategies, and to have the trained personnel to pursue these in international negotiations is crucial to their influence.

Third, more attention has to be devoted to implementation concerns. Much of the discussion centres on trying to secure a deal. Just as the Kyoto Protocol suffered because negotiators postponed decisions on implementation and enforcement, the post-2012 regime might also stumble when countries have to implement their commitments. Here, the concerns of developing countries are two-fold: that they maintain the maximum flexibility to develop national policies while being in compliance with international rules; and that they build real capacity at home to integrate climate concerns into development plans and to regulate activities within their jurisdictions.

The concerns over reconciling domestic and international regulation are nowhere more politically problematic than for measuring, reporting, verifying, and reviewing performance. The fourth lesson is that the climate regime's information system has to respond directly to the information needs of developing countries. Rather than building elaborate reporting structures that increase the supply of information in the regime, a more honest appraisal is needed of the demand for different kinds of information. Thus, credible, timely, and relevant information is needed not only for GHG emissions, but also for trading schemes, tax structures, policies and measures, financial and technology transfers, and efforts towards adaptation. Developing countries are not interested in only providing data on their emissions (even though capacity-building efforts must be scaled up for that purpose). They are equally interested in getting information on policies, activities, and contributions of other countries. Were developing countries to become a part of a global emission-trading system, there would be additional questions about verifying the accuracy of reported data and compliance-promoting review mechanisms. Reviews and assessments of all countries' activities would gain credibility only when there is balanced representation and active participation in multilateral review meetings.

Finally, developing countries are right to worry about enforcement. While adjudication can (and probably should) be centralized, there is no easy lesson about how best to enforce rules, especially when it comes to enforcing them in respect of powerful countries. Decentralized enforcement, as in the WTO, has had some successes. It has been used by some developing countries, and provisions made for legal assistance and support are useful to those wishing to take cases. That said, even if small or poorer countries win their case and are granted rights to use retaliatory measures, it is unclear that these could be effective, or even conceivable to apply—nowhere is this more obvious than in considering the case of aid-dependent countries. More centralized enforcement options, such as that embedded in the European Union's Stability and Growth Pact, do not always sanction powerful states who fail to meet commitments. That said, a solution probably does lie with a centralized form of enforcement which may even be linked to economic incentive schemes.

Bibliography

Abrego, L., Perroni, C., Whalley, J., and Wigle, R. M. (2001), 'Trade and Environment: Bargaining Outcomes from Linked Negotiations', *Review of International Economics*, **9**(3), 414–28.

Achard, F., Belward, A., *et al.* (2006), 'Accounting for Avoided Conversion of Intact and Non-intact Forests: Technical Options and a Proposal for a Policy Tool', Report for Joint Research Centre of the European Commission.

Adar, Z., and Griffin, J. M. (1976), 'Uncertainty and the Choice of Pollution Control Instruments', *Journal of Environmental Economics and Management*, **3**, 178–88.

African Development Bank (1994), *The Question for Quality: Report of the Task Force on Project Quality for the African Development Bank.*

Agarwala, R. (2008), 'Towards a Global Compact for Managing Climate Change', Harvard Project on International Climate Agreements Discussion Paper.

Agerup, M. (2004), 'Climate Change Predictions: Bad Economics, Bad Science' (available at http://www.policynetwork.net/uploaded/pdf/martin-agerup-scenarios-april2004.pdf).

Ahlbrandt, T. S. (2006), 'Global Petroleum Reserves, Resources and Forecasts', in R. Mabro (ed.), *Oil in the 21st Century: Issues, Opportunities and Challenges*, Oxford, Oxford University Press, 128–77.

Ahmad, N., and Wyckoff, A. (2003), 'Carbon Dioxide Emissions Embodied in International Trade of Goods', OECD STI Working Papers, 2003/15.

Aidt, T. (1998), 'Political Internalisation of Economic Externalities and Environmental Policy', *Journal of Public Economics*, **69**, 1–16.

—— and Dutta, J. (2004), 'Transitional Politics: Emerging Incentive-based Instruments in Environmental Regulation', *Journal of Environmental Economics and Management*, **47**, 458–79.

Akerlof, G. A. (1970), 'The Market for Lemons: Quality Uncertainty and the Market Mechanism', *Quarterly Journal of Economics*, **84**, 488–500.

Alcott, B. (2008), 'Historical Overview of the Jevons Paradox in the Literature', in J. M. Polimeni, K. Mayumi, M. Giampoetro, and B. Alcott (eds), *The Jevons Paradox and the Myth of Resource Efficiency Improvements*, London, Earthscan.

Aldy, J. E., and Frankel, J. A. (2004), 'Designing a Regime of Emission Commitments for Developing Countries that is Cost-effective and Equitable', Note for G20 Leaders and Climate Change Conference at the Council of Foreign Relations, September.

—— and Stavins, R. N. (eds) (2007), *Architectures for Agreement: Addressing Global Climate Change in the Post-Kyoto World*, Cambridge, Cambridge University Press.

—— Barrett, S., and Stavins, R. N. (2003), 'Thirteen plus One: A Comparison of Global Climate Policy Architectures', *Climate Policy*, **3**, 373–97.

—— Orszag, P. R., and Stiglitz, J. E. (2001), 'Climate Change: An Agenda for Global Collective Action', Conference on 'The Timing of Climate Change Policies', Pew Center on Global Climate Change, October.

Allan, G., Hanley, N., McGregor, P. G., Swales, J. K., and Turner, K. (2006), 'UKERC Review of Evidence for the Rebound Effect—Technical Report 4: Computable General Equilibrium Modelling Studies', UK Energy Research Centre, London.

Allen, M. R., and Frame, D. J. (2007), 'Call Off the Quest', *Science*, **318**, 582–3.

Alpizar, F., Carlsson, F., and Johansson-Stenman, O. (2008), 'Anonymity, Reciprocity and Conformity: Evidence from Voluntary Contributions to a Natural Park in Costa Rica', *Journal of Public Economics*, **92**, 1047–60.

Ames/Carnegie (2006), 'The Ames/Carnegie Solar Radiation Management Workshop: Goals and Background', Conference report undated, from November 2006 workshop, mimeo.

Anderson, D. (2006), 'Cost and Finance of Abating Carbon Emissions in the Energy Sector', Supporting document for the *Stern Review on the Economics of Climate Change*, Imperial College, London (available from www.sternreview.org.uk).

Anderson, K., and Bows, A. (2008), 'Reframing the Climate Change Challenge in Light of Post-2000 Emission Trends', *Philosophical Transactions of the Royal Society—A: Mathematical, Physical and Engineering Sciences*, **366**, 3863–82.

Anderson, R. (1997), *The US Experience with Economic Incentives in Environmental Pollution Control Policy*, Washington, DC, Environmental Law Institute.

Anderson, S. T., and Newell, R. G. (2004), 'Information Programs for Technology Adoption: The Case of Energy-efficiency Audits', *Resource and Energy Economics*, **26**(1), 27–50.

Andersson, K., and Richards, K. (2001), 'Implementing an International Carbon Sequestration Program: Can the Leaky Sink Be Fixed?', *Climate Policy*, **1**, 73–88.

—— Evans, T. P., and Richards, K. R. (2009), 'National Forest Carbon Inventories: Policy Needs and Assessment Capacity', *Climatic Change*, **93**(1–2), 69–101.

Andresen, S., and Gulbrandsen, L. H. (2003), 'The Role of Green NGOs in Promoting Climate Compliance', Fridtjof Nansen Institute Report.

Anthoff, D., Hepburn, C., and Tol, R. (2009), 'Equity Weighting and the Marginal Damage Costs of Climate Change', *Ecological Economics*, **68**(3), 836–49.

Antle, R., and Eppen, G. D. (1985), 'Capital Rationing and Organizational Slack in Capital Budgeting', *Management Science*, **31**(2), 163–74.

Aronsson, T., and Johansson-Stenman, O. (2008), 'When the Joneses' Consumption Hurts: Optimal Public Good Provision and Nonlinear Income Taxation', *Journal of Public Economics*, **92**, 986–97.

Arrow, K. J. (1971), *Essays in the Theory of Risk Bearing*, Chicago, IL, Markham.

—— (1972), 'Gifts and Exchanges', *Philosophy and Public Affairs*, **1**(4), 343–62.

Asheim, G. B., Froyn, C., Bretteville, H. J., and Menz, F. C. (2006), 'Regional versus Global Cooperation for Climate Control', *Journal of Environmental Economics and Management*, **51**, 93–109.

Ashraf, N., Camerer, C. F., and Loewenstein, G. (2005), 'Adam Smith, Behavioral Economist', *Journal of Economic Perspectives*, **19**, 131–45.

Ashton, J., and Wang, X. (2003), 'Equity and Climate: In Principle and Practice', Pew Centre on Global Climate Change.

Auffhammer, M., and Carson, R. T. (2008), 'Forecasting the Path of China's CO_2 Emissions Using Province-level Information', *Journal of Environmental Economics and Management*, doi:10.1016/j.jeem.2007.10.002.

—— Blumstein, C., and Fowlie, M. (2008), 'Demand-side Management and Energy Efficiency Revisited', *Energy Journal*, **29**(3), 91–104.

Australia (2008), *Carbon Pollution Reduction Scheme: Australia's Low Pollution Future*, White Paper, 15 December, available at http://www.climatechange.gov.au/whitepaper/report/index.html

Awerbuch, S. (2000), 'Getting It Right: The Real Cost Impacts of a Renewables Portfolio Standard', *Public Utilities Fortnightly*, 15 February, 44–52.

Ayres, R. U. (1998), 'Towards a Disequilibrium Theory of Endogenous Economic Growth', *Environmental and Resource Economics*, **11**(3–4), 289–300.

—— (2002), 'Resources, Scarcity, Technology and Growth', Centre for the Management of Environmental Resources, INSEAD, Fontainebleau.

—— and van den Bergh, J. C. J. M. (2005), 'A Theory of Economic Growth with Material/Energy Resources and Dematerialization: Interaction of Three Growth Mechanisms', *Ecological Economics*, **55**(1), 96–118.

—— and Warr, B. (2002*a*), 'Useful Work and Information as Drivers of Growth', INSEAD, Fontainebleau.

—— —— (2002*b*), 'Two Paradigms of Production and Growth', INSEAD, Fontainebleau.

—— —— (2005), 'Accounting for Growth: The Role of Physical Work', *Structural Change and Economic Dynamics*, **16**(2), 181–209.

—— —— (2006), 'REXS: A Forecasting Model for Assessing the Impact of Natural Resource Consumption and Technological Change from Economic Growth', *Structural Change and Economic Dynamics*, **17**(3), 329–78.

Azar, C., and Sterner, T. (1996), 'Discounting and Distributional Considerations in the Context of Global Warming', *Ecological Economics*, **19**, 169–84.

Babcock, L., and Loewenstein, G. (1997), 'Explaining Bargaining Impasse: The Role of Self-serving Biases', *Journal of Economic Perspectives*, **11**, 109–26.

Bah, K. (2009), 'Africa's G-4: Altering the African Political Landscape and Africa's International Affairs', in L. Martinez-Diaz and N. Woods (eds), *Networks of Influence*, Oxford, Oxford University Press.

Baker, R., Barker, A., Johnson, A., and Kohlhaas, M. (2008), 'The Stern Review: An Assessment of Its Methodology', Australian Government Productivity Commission, Staff Working Paper, 24 January.

Baldursson, F. M., and von der Fehr, N.-H. M. (2004), 'Price Volatility and Risk Exposure: On Market-based Environmental Policy Instruments', *Journal of Environmental Economics and Management*, **48**, 682–704.

Balzter, H., and Shvidenko, A. (2000), 'Map Accuracy Report—SIBERIA Forest Cover Map, SIBERIA Working Note 58', Laxenburg, Austria, IIASA.

Bannon, B., DeBell, M., Krosnick, J., Kopp, R., and Aldhous, P. (2007), 'Americans' Evaluations of Policies to Reduce Greenhouse Gas Emissions', Working Paper, June.

Barbier, E. B. (2009), 'A Global Green New Deal', Report prepared for the Economics and Trade Branch, Division of Technology, Industry and Economics, United Nations Environment Programme, February.

Barker, T. (2005), 'The Transition to Sustainability: A Comparison of General Equilibrium and Space–Time Economics Approaches', Tyndall Centre for Climate Change Research.

—— Qureshi, M. S., and Köhler, J. (2006), 'The Costs of Greenhouse Gas Mitigation with Induced Technological Change: A Meta-analysis of Estimates in the Literature', Tyndall Centre for Climate Change Research Working Paper 89.

Barnes, P., Costanza, R., Hawken, P., Orr, D., Ostrom, E., Umaña, A., and Young, O. (2008), 'Creating an Earth Atmospheric Trust', *Science*, **319**, 724.

Barnett, M. N., and Finnemore, M. (1999), 'The Politics, Power and Pathologies of International Organizations', *International Organization*, **53**(4), 699–732.

Barrett, S. (1994), 'Self-enforcing International Environmental Agreements', *Oxford Economic Papers*, **46**, 878–94.

—— (1999), 'A Theory of Full International Cooperation', *Journal of Theoretical Politics*, **11**, 519–41.

——(2003), *Environment and Statecraft: The Strategy of Environmental Treaty Making*, Oxford, Oxford University Press.
——(2005*a*), *Environment and Statecraft: The Strategy of Environmental Treaty-making*, Oxford, Oxford University Press (paperback edition).
——(2005*b*), 'The Theory of International Environmental Agreements', ch. 28 in K.-G. Mäler and J. R. Vincent (eds), *Handbook of Environmental Economics*, vol. 3, Amsterdam, Elsevier.
——(2006), 'Climate Treaties and 'Breakthrough' Technologies', *American Economic Review (Papers and Proceedings)*, **96**(2), 22–5.
——(2007*a*), 'The Incredible Economics of Geoengineering', Manuscript, 18 March.
——(2007*b*), *Why Cooperate? The Incentive to Supply Global Public Goods*, Oxford, Oxford University Press.
——(2008), 'A Portfolio System of Climate Treaties', Harvard Project on International Climate Agreements Discussion Paper.
——and Stavins, R. (2003), 'Increasing Participation and Compliance in International Climate Change Agreements', *International Environmental Agreements: Politics, Law and Economics*, **3**, 349–76.
Barro, R. J. (2006), 'Rare Disasters and Asset Markets in the Twentieth Century', *Quarterly Journal of Economics*, **121**(3), 823–66.
——and Sala-i-Martin, X. (1995), *Economic Growth*, New York, McGraw-Hill.
Barry, B. (1995), *Justice as Impartiality*, Oxford, Oxford University Press.
Barry, C., and Reddy, S. (2008), *International Trade and Labor Standards: A Proposal for Linkage*, New York, Columbia University Press.
Baumeister, R. (1998), 'The Self', in D. Gilbert, S. Fiske, and G. Lindzey (eds), *Handbook of Social Psychology*, Boston, MA, McGraw Hill.
Beaudreau, B. C. (1995), 'The Impact of Electric Power on Productivity: A Study of US Manufacturing 1950–1984', *Energy Economics*, **17**(3), 231–6.
——(1998), *Energy and Organisation: Group and Distribution Re-examined*, Westport, CT, Greenwood Press.
——(2005), 'Engineering and Economic Growth', *Structural Change and Economic Dynamics*, **16**(2), 211–20.
Beckerman, W., and Hepburn, C. (2007), 'Ethics of the Discount Rate in the Stern Review on the Economics of Climate Change', *World Economics*, **8**(1), 187–210.
Benartzi, S., and Thaler, R. (1995), 'Myopic Loss Aversion and the Equity Premium Puzzle', *Quarterly Journal of Economics*, **110**, 73–92.
Benedick, R. E. (1998), *Ozone Diplomacy: New Directions In Safeguarding the Planet*, 2nd edn, Cambridge, MA, Harvard University Press.
——(2001), 'Striking a New Deal on Climate Change', *Issues in Science and Technology*, **18**, 71–6.
BERR (2008), 'Renewable Energy Strategy Consultation', London, Department for Business Enterprise and Regulatory Reform, 26 June.
Bevan, G., and Hood, C. (2006), 'Have Targets Improved Performance in the English NHS?', *British Medical Journal*, **332**, 419–22.
Bhaskar, U. (2008), 'Carbon Dioxide Emissions: Government Counters Report of US-based Think Tank', *Mint*, 28 August.
Biglaiser, G., Horowitz, J. K., and Quiggin, J. (1995), 'Dynamic Pollution Regulation', *Journal of Regulatory Economics*, **8**, 33–44.

Bird, S. M., Cox, D., Farewell, V. T., Goldstein, H., Holt, T., and Smith, P. C. (2005), 'Performance Indicators: Good, Bad, and Ugly', *Journal of the Royal Statistical Society, Series A*, **168**(1), 1–27.

Birnie, P. (1993), 'The UN and the Environment', in A. Roberts and B. Kingsbury (eds), *United Nations, Divided World: The UN's Role in International Relations*, 2nd edn, Oxford, Clarendon Press, 327–83.

Birol, F., and Keppler, J. H. (2000), 'Prices, Technology Development and the Rebound Effect', *Energy Policy*, **28**(6–7), 457–69.

Blackhurst, R., Lyakurwa, B., and Oyejide, A. (2000), 'Options for Improving Africa's Participation in the WTO', *The World Economy*, **23**, 491–510.

Bluestein, J. (2005), 'Upstream Regulation of CO2', Presentation to the National Commission on Energy Policy Workshop, Washington, DC, 16 September.

Bodansky, D. (1993), 'The United Nations Framework Convention on Climate Change: A Commentary', *Yale Journal of International Law*, **18**(2).

—— (1996), 'May We Engineer the Climate?', *Climatic Change*, **33**, 309–21.

—— (2004), *International Climate Efforts beyond 2012: A Survey of Approaches*, Pew Center on Global Climate Change, December.

—— (2007), 'International Sectoral Agreements in a Post-2012 Climate Framework', Working Paper prepared for the Pew Center on Global Climate Change, May.

—— and Diringer, E. (2008), 'Towards an Integrated Multi-track Climate Framework', Pew Center on Global Climate Change.

Böhringer, C. (2003), 'The Kyoto Protocol: A Review and Perspectives', *Oxford Review of Economic Policy*, **19**(3), 451–66.

Boko, M. I. *et al.* (2007), 'Africa', in M. L. Parry *et al.* (eds), *Climate Change 2007: Impacts, Adaptation and Vulnerability*, Contribution of Working Group II to the Fourth Assessment Report of the Intergovernmental Panel on Climate Change, Cambridge, Cambridge University Press.

Bosi, M., and Ellis J. (2005), 'Exploring Options for Sectoral Crediting Mechanisms', COM/ENV/EPOC/IEA/SLT(2005)1, Paris, OECD Environmental Directorate and International Energy Agency

Bovenberg, A. L., and de Mooij, R. A. (1994), 'Environmental Levies and Distortionary Taxation', *American Economic Review*, **84**(4), 1085–9.

—— —— (1997), 'Environmental Taxation and Distortionary Taxation: A Reply', *American Economic Review*, **87**(1), 252–3.

—— and Goulder, L. H. (1996), 'Optimal Environmental Taxation in the Presence of Other Taxes: General-equilibrium Analyses', *American Economic Review*, **86**(4), 985–1000.

—— —— (2000), 'Neutralising the Adverse Industry Impacts of CO2 Abatement Policies: What Does it Cost?', RFF Discussion Paper 00–27.

—— —— (2003), 'Confronting Industry-distributional Concerns in US Climate Change Policy', Discussion Paper (Les Séminaires de l'IDDRI no. 6), Institute on the Economics on the Environment and Sustainability.

—— and van der Ploeg, F. (1994), 'Environmental Policy, Public Finance and the Labour Market in a Second-best World', *Journal of Public Economics*, **55**, 349–90.

—— Goulder, L. H., and Gurney, D. J. (2005), 'Efficiency Costs of Meeting Industry-distributional Constraints under Environmental Permits and Taxes', *Rand Journal of Economics*, **36**(4), 951–71.

Boyd, E., Hultman, N. E., Roberts, J. T., Corbera, E., Ebeling, J., *et al.* (2007), 'The Future of the Clean Development Mechanism: An Assessment of Current Practice and Approaches for Policy', Working Paper 114, Tyndall Centre for Climate Change Research.

Boykoff, M. (2007), 'From Convergence to Contention: United States Mass Media Representations of Anthropogenic Climate Change Science', *Transactions of the Institute of British Geographers*, **32**, 477–89.

Bradford, D. F. (2001), 'Succeeding Kyoto: A No-cap but Trade Approach to GHG Control. Version 02a', Princeton University and NYU School of Law.

Bradley, R., Baumert, K. A., Childs, B., Herzog, T., and Pershing, J. (2007), *Slicing the Pie: Sector-based Approaches to International Climate Agreements*, Washington, DC, World Resources Institute.

Breidenich, C., and Bodansky, D. M. (2009), 'Measurement, Reporting and Verification Under the Bali Action Plan: Issues and Options', Pew Center on Global Climate Change.

Brekke, K. A., and Howarth, R. (2002), *Status Growth and the Environment*, Cheltenham, Edward Elgar.

—— Kverndokk, S., and Nyborg, K. (2002), 'An Economic Model of Moral Motivation', *Journal of Public Economics*, **87**, 1967–83.

Brennan, G., and Hamlin, A. (1998), 'Expressive Voting and Electoral Equilibrium', *Public Choice*, **95**(1), 149–75.

—— —— (2000), *Democratic Devices and Desires*, Cambridge, Cambridge University Press.

Broberg, T., Ellingsen, T., and Johannesson, M. (2007), 'Is Generosity?', *Economics*, **94**, 32–7.

Brock, W. A., and Taylor, S. M. (2004), 'The Green Solow Model', Working Paper No. 2004–16, Madison, WI, University of Wisconsin.

Broecker, W. S. (2007), 'Climate Change: CO2 Arithmetic', *Science*, **315**(5817), 1371.

Brookes, L. G. (1984), 'Long-term Equilibrium Effects of Constraints in Energy Supply', in L. Brookes and H. Motamen (eds), *The Economics of Nuclear Energy*, London, Chapman & Hall.

—— (1990), 'The Greenhouse Effect: The Fallacies in the Energy Efficiency Solution', *Energy Policy*, **18**(2), 199–201.

—— (2000), 'Energy Efficiency Fallacies Revisited', *Energy Policy*, **28**(6–7), 355–66.

—— (2004), 'Energy Efficiency Fallacies—A Postscript', *Energy Policy*, **32**(8), 945–7.

Brooks, N. (1998), 'Climate and History in West Africa', in G. Connah (ed.), *Transformations in Africa: Essays on Africa's Later Past*, London and Washington, Leicester University Press, 139–59.

—— (2004), 'Drought in the African Sahel: Long Term Perspectives and Future Prospects', Tyndall Centre for Climate Change Research, Working Paper 61 (available at http://www.tyndall.ac.uk/publications/working_papers/wp61.pdf).

Broome, J. (1992), *Counting the Cost of Global Warming*, Cambridge, White Horse Press.

Burtraw, D., Goeree, J., Holt, C., Palmer, K., and Shobe, W. (2007), 'Auction Design for Selling CO2 Emission Allowances Under the Regional Greenhouse Gas Initiative', Final Report produced for RGGI, October.

—— Krupnick, A., Mansur, E., Austin, D., and Farrell, D. (1998), 'The Costs and Benefits of Reducing Air Pollution Related to Acid Rain', *Contemporary Economic Policy*, **16**, 379–400.

Camerer, C., Issacharoff, S., Loewenstein, G., O'Donoghue, T., and Rabin, M. (2003), 'Regulation for Conservatives: Behavioral Economics and the Case for "Asymmetric Paternalism"', *University of Pennsylvania Law Review*, **151**, 1211–54.

Canadell, J. G., Le Quere, C., Raupach, M. R., Field, C. B., Buitehuis, E. T., Ciais, P., Conway, T. J., Gillett, N. P., Houghton, R. A., and Marland, G. (2007), 'Contributions to Accelerating Atmospheric CO_2 Growth from Economic Activity, Carbon Intensity, and Efficiency of Natural Sinks', *Proceedings of the National Academy of Sciences*, 0702737104.

Capoor, K., and Ambrosi, P. (2008), *State and Trends of the Carbon Market 2008*, Washington, DC, World Bank, May.

Carbon Trust (2009), *Global Carbon Mechanisms: Emerging Lessons and Implications*, UK, Carbon Trust, March.

Carlson, C., Burtraw, D., Cropper, M., and Palmer, K. L. (2000), 'Sulfur Dioxide Control by Electric Utilities: What Are the Gains from Trade?', *Journal of Political Economy*, **108**(6), 1292–326.

Carraro, C. and Siniscalco, D. (1998), 'International Institutions and Environmental Policy—Strategic Policy Issues', *European Economic Review*, **42**, 561–72.

Cason, T., and Mui, V.-L. (1997), 'A Laboratory Study of Group Polarization in the Team Dictator Game', *Economic Journal*, **107**, 1465–83.

Castles, I., and Henderson, D. (2003), 'The IPCC Emission Scenarios: An Economic-statistical Critique', *Energy and Environment*, **14**(2–3), 159–85.

CDIAC (2007), *National CO_2 Emissions from Fossil-Fuel Burning, Cement Manufacture, and Gas Flaring: 1751–2004* (available at ftp://cdiac.ornl.gov/pub/ndp030/nation.1751_2004.ems).

CEC (1997), 'Energy for the Future: Renewable Sources of Energy', White Paper for a Community Strategy and Action Plan, COM(97)599 final, 26 November, Commission of the European Communities.

—— (2001), 'Directive 2001/80/EC of the European Parliament and of the Council of 23 October 2001 on the Limitation of Emission of Certain Pollutants into the Air from Large Combustion Plants', *Official Journal*, L309/1, 27 November, Commission of the European Communities.

—— (2006), 'Renewable Energy Road Map. Renewable Energies in the 21st Century: Building a More Sustainable Future', COM(2006)848 final, Commission Communication of 10 January, Commission of the European Communities.

—— (2007), 'Report on Energy Sector Inquiry', 10 January SEC(2006)1724, DG Competition, Commission of the European Communities.

—— (2008*a*), 'Communication from the Commission to the European Parliament, the Council, the European Economic and Social Committee and the Committee of the Regions—20-20 by 2020—Europe's Climate Change Opportunity', COM(2008) 13 final, COM(2008) 16 final, COM(2008) 17 final, COM(2008) 18 final, COM(2008) 19 final, 23 January, Commission of the European Communities.

—— (2008*b*), 'Brussels European Council 11 and 12 December 2008: Presidency Conclusions', 17271/08, Commission of the European Communities.

—— (2009), 'Communication from the Commission to the European Parliament, the Council, the European Economic and Social Committee and the Committee of the Regions: Towards a Comprehensive Climate Change Agreement in Copenhagen', Brussels, 28 January, COM(2009) 39 final.

Challinor, A. J. *et al.* (2006), 'Assessing the Vulnerability of Crop Productivity to Climate Change Thresholds Using an Integrated Crop-climate Model', in J. Schellnhuber *et al.* (eds), *Avoiding Dangerous Climate Change*, Cambridge, Cambridge University Press, 187–94.

Chamon, M., Mauro, P., and Okawa, Y. (2008), 'Cars—Mass Car Ownership in the Emerging Market Giants', *Economic Policy*, **23**(54), 243–96.

Chayes, A., and Chayes, A. H. (1995), *The New Sovereignty: Compliance with International Regulatory Agreements*, Cambridge, MA, Harvard University Press.

Chen, P. (1990), 'Prices vs Quantities, and Delegating Pricing Authority to a Monopolist', *Review of Economic Studies*, **57**, 521–9.

Chung, H.-S. (2005), 'Balance of CO2 Emissions Embodied in International Trade: Can Korean Carbon Tax on its Imported Fossil Fuels Make Any Difference in BEET?', Paper presented at the economic model conference of 2005 (available at http://www.ecomod.net/conferences/ecomod2005/ecomod2005_papers/889.pdf).

Chung, R. K. (2007), 'A CER Discounting Scheme Could Save the Climate Change Regime after 2012', *Climate Policy*, **7**, 171–6.

Cialdini, R. (2001), *Influence. Science and Practice*, Boston, MA, Allyn & Bacon.

Citigroup (2007), 'Carbon Capture and Storage', Global Markets (Equity Research), December.

Clarke, L., Edmonds, J., Jacoby, H., Pitcher, H., Reilly, J., and Richels, R. (2007), 'Scenarios of Greenhouse Gas Emissions and Atmospheric Concentrations', Sub-report 2.1A of Synthesis and Assessment Product 2.1, US Climate Change Science Program and the Subcommittee on Global Change Research. Department of Energy, Office of Biological and Environmental Research, Washington, DC.

Cleveland, C. J., Kaufmann, R. K., and Stern, D. I. (2000), 'Aggregation and the Role of Energy in the Economy', *Ecological Economics*, **32**, 301–17.

—— Costanza, R., Hall, C. A. S., and Kaufmann, R. K. (1984), 'Energy and the US Economy: A Biophysical Perspective', *Science*, **225**, 890–7.

Cline, W. R. (2008), 'Global Warming and Agriculture', *Finance and Development*, **45**(1).

Coase, R. H. (1960), 'The Problem of Social Cost', *Journal of Law and Economics*, **3**, 1–44.

Cohen, L. R., and Noll, R. G. (1991), *The Technology Pork Barrel*, Washington, DC, The Brookings Institution.

Collier, P. (2006), 'Is Aid Oil?', *World Development*, **34**(9), 1482–97.

—— and Goderis, B. (2008*a*), 'Does Aid Mitigate External Shocks?', *Review of Development Economics*, forthcoming.

—— —— (2008*b*), 'Structural Policies for Shock-prone Commodity Exporters', Centre for the Study of African Economies, mimeo.

—— and Venables, A.J. (2007), 'Rethinking Trade Preferences: How Africa Can Diversify its Exports', *The World Economy*, **30**(8), 1326–45.

Committee of Climate Change (2009), 'Sectors, Emissions, Current Levels of Emissions' (available at http://www.theccc.org.uk/sectors/buildings/emissions-2).

Conconi, P., and Perroni, C. (2002), 'Issue Linkage and Issue Tie-in in Multilateral Negotiations', *Journal of International Economics*, **57**(2), 423–47.

Cooper, R. (2001), 'The Kyoto Protocol: A Flawed Concept', *Environmental Law Reporter*, **31**, 11484–92.

—— (2008), 'The Case for Charges on Greenhouse Gas Emissions', Harvard Project on International Climate Agreements Discussion Paper 08–10.

Copeland, B. R., and Taylor, M. S. (1994), 'North–South Trade and the Environment', *Quarterly Journal of Economics*, **109**(3), August.

—— —— (2003), 'Trade, Growth and the Environment' (available at http://www.ssc.wisc.edu/econ/archive/wp2003-10.pdf).

Cosbey, A., Bell, W., Murphy, D., Parry, J. E., Drexhage, J., Hammill, A., and Van Ham, J. (2005), *Which Way Forward? Issues in Developing an Effective Climate Regime after 2012*, Winnipeg, International Institute for Sustainable Development.

Council of Economic Advisors (1998), 'The Kyoto Protocol and the President's Policies to Address Climate Change: Administration Economic Analysis', Washington, DC.

Crutzen, P. J. (2006), 'Albedo Enhancement by Stratospheric Sulfur Injections: A Contribution to Resolve a Policy Dilemma?', *Climatic Change*, **77**, 211–20.

Cullenward, D., and Victor, D. G. (2007), 'Politicizing Climate Policy: The Limits of Consensus', *Climatic Change* (in press).

Curzon Price, V. (1992), 'New Institutional Developments in GATT', *Minnesota Journal of Global Trade*, **1**, 87–110.

Cuyler, A. J., and Meads, A. (1992), 'The United Kingdom: Effective, Efficient, Equitable?', *Journal of Health Politics, Policy and Law*, **17**, 667–88.

Dana, J., Cain, D. M., and Dawes, R. (2006), 'What You Don't Know Won't Hurt Me: Costly (but Quiet) Exit in a Dictator Game', *Organizational Behavior and Human Decision Processes*, **100**(2), 193–201.

—— Weber, R., and Kuang, J. X. (2007), 'Exploiting Moral Wriggle Room: Behavior Inconsistent with a Preference for Fair Outcomes', *Economic Theory*, **33**, 67–80.

Dannenberg, A., Sturm, B., and Vogt, C. (2007), 'Do Equity Preferences Matter in Climate Negotiations? An Experimental Investigation', Discussion Paper No. 07–063, Mannheim, Zentrum für Europäische Wirtschaftsforschung.

D'Arrigo, R., Wilson, R., Liepert, B., and Cherubini, P. (2007), 'On the "Divergence Problem" in Northern Forests: A Review of the Tree-ring Evidence and Possible Causes', *Global and Planetary Change*.

Dasgupta, P. (2001), *Human Well-being and the Natural Environment*, Oxford, Oxford University Press.

—— (2008*a*), 'Nature in Economics', *Environmental Resource Economics*, **39**, 1–7.

—— (2008*b*), 'Discounting Climate Change', *Journal of Risk and Uncertainty*, **37**(2–3), 141–69.

—— and Mäler, K-G. (2000), 'Net National Product, Wealth, and Social Well-being', *Environment and Development Economics*, **5**, 69–93.

Davey, W. J. (2005), 'The WTO Dispute Settlement System: The First Ten Years', *Journal of International Economic Law*, **8**, 17–50.

Deal, T. E. (2008), 'WTO Rules and Procedures and their Implication for the Kyoto Protocol', United States Council for International Business Discussion Paper, January.

DeCanio, S. J. (1993), 'Barriers within Firms to Energy Efficient Investments', *Energy Policy*, September, 906–14.

—— (1994), 'Agency as Control Problems in US Corporations: The Case of Energy Efficient Investment Projects', *Journal of the Economics of Business*, **1**(1).

—— (1998), 'The Efficiency Gap: Bureaucratic and Organisational Barriers to Profitable Energy Saving Investments', *Energy Policy*, **26**(5), 441–54.

DECC (2009), *Severn Tidal Power: Phase One Consultation*, London, Department of Energy and Climate Change.

Deere, C. (2008), *The Implementation Game: The TRIPS Agreement and the Global Politics of Intellectual Property Reform in Developing Countries*, Oxford, Oxford University Press.

De Fraja, G., and Iossa, E. (1998), 'Price Caps and Output Floors: A Comparison of Simple Regulatory Rules', **108**, 1404–21.

Delbeke, J., and Zapfel, P. (2009), 'An Evolving Role for International Offsets', *Environmental Finance*, March.

Dell, R. M., and Rand, D. A. J. (2001), 'Energy Storage—A Key Technology for Global Energy Sustainability', *Journal of Power Sources*, **100**(1–2), 2–17.

Dell, M., Jones, B. F., and Olken, B. A. (2008), 'Climate Change and Economic Growth: Evidence from the Last Half Century', NBER Working Paper No. 14132, June.

den Elzen, M. G. J., and van Vuuren, D. P. (2007), 'Peaking Profiles for Achieving Long-term Temperature Targets with more Likelihood at Lower Costs', *Proceedings of the National Academy of Sciences*, **104**, 17931–6.

Denison, E. F. (1962), 'Sources of Economic Growth in the United States and the Alternatives Before Us', Committee for Economic Development, New York.

Department for Transport (2003), 'The Future of Air Transport', White Paper, December, London, The Stationery Office.

Department of Energy (1987), 'Sizewell B Public Inquiry: Report by Sir Frank Layfield', *Volume V: The Economic Case*, London, HMSO.

Depledge, J. (2006), 'The Opposite of Learning: Ossification in the Climate Change Regime', *Global Environmental Politics*, **6**(1), 1–22.

—— (2008), 'Striving for No: Saudi Arabia in the Climate Change Regime', *Global Environmental Politics*, **8**(4), 9–35.

—— (2009), 'The Road Less Travelled: Difficulties in Moving between Annexes in the Climate Change Regime', *Climate Policy*, **9**, 273–87.

Dercon, S. (2002), 'Income Risk, Coping Strategies and Safety Nets', *World Bank Research Observer*, **17**, 141–66.

Dervis, K. (2005), *A Better Globalization: Legitimacy, Governance, and Reform*, with C. Ozer, Centre for Global Development and Brookings Institution Press.

DeSombre, E. R., and Kauffman, J. (1996), 'The Montreal Protocol Multilateral Fund: Partial Success Story', in R. O. Keohane and M. A. Levy (eds), *Institutions for Environmental Aid: Pitfalls and Promise*, Cambridge, MA, MIT Press, 89–126.

Deutch, J., and Moniz, E. J. (co-chairs) (2007), *The Future of Coal: Options for a Carbon-constrained World*, Cambridge, MA, MIT.

Diamond, P. A., and Mirrlees, J. A. (1971), 'Optimal Taxation and Public Production I: Production Efficiency and II: Tax Rules', *American Economic Review*, **61**, 8–27 and 261–78.

Dietz, S., and Stern, N. (2008), 'Why Economic Analysis Supports Strong Action on Climate Change: A Response to the Stern Review's Critics', *Review of Environmental Economics and Policy*, **2**, 94–113.

—— Hepburn, C., and Stern, N. (2008), 'Economics, Ethics and Climate Change', mimeo, London School of Economics, January.

—— —— —— (2009), 'Economics, Ethics and Climate Change', in K. Basu and R. Kanbur (eds), *Arguments for a Better World: Essays in Honour of Amartya Sen, vol. 2: Society, Institutions and Development*, Oxford, Oxford University Press.

Digest of UK Energy Statistics (2008), *Digest of UK Energy Statistics*, London, The Stationery Office.

Dimson, E., Marsh, P., and Staunton, M. (2007), 'The Worldwide Equity Premium: A Smaller Puzzle', ch. 11 in R. Mehra (ed.), *Handbook of the Equity Risk Premium*, Amsterdam, Elsevier.

Dinan, T. (2007), *Trade-offs in Allocating Allowances for CO2 Emissions*, Economic and Budget Issue Brief, Washington, DC, US Congressional Budget Office, 25 April.

Downs, G., Rocke, D., and Barsoom, P. (1996), 'Is the Good News about Compliance Good News about Cooperation?', *International Organization*, **50**, 379–406.

Dreber, A., Rand, D. G., Fudenberg, D., and Nowak, M. (2008), 'Winners Don't Punish', *Nature*, **452**(7185), 348–51.

Drèze, J., and Stern, N. (1987), 'The Theory of Cost–Benefit Analysis', in A. J. Auerbach and M. S. Feldstein (eds), *Handbook of Public Economics, Vol. 2*, Amsterdam, Elsevier, 909–89.

Drèze, J., and Stern, N. (1990), 'Policy Reform, Shadow Prices, and Market Prices', *Journal of Public Economics*, **42**(1), 1–45.

Druckman, A., Bradley, P., Papathanasopoulou, E., and Jackson, T. (2008), 'Measuring Progress towards Carbon Reduction in the UK', *Ecological Economics*, **66**(4), 594–604.

DTI (2003*a*), 'Our Energy Future—Creating a Low Carbon Economy', White Paper, London, Department of Trade and Industry.

—— (2003*b*), 'Options for a Low Carbon Future', Economics Paper No. 4, London, Department of Trade and Industry.

Dufwenberg, M., and Kirchsteiger, G. (2004), 'A Theory of Sequential Reciprocity', *Games and Economic Behavior*, **47**, 268–98.

Dutschke, M., and Wolf, R. (2007), 'Reducing Emissions from Deforestation in Developing Countries', Report for Deutsche Gesellschaft für Technische Zusammenarbeit (GTZ), Germany.

EC (2007), 'Renewable Energy Road Map: Renewable Energies in the 21st Century: Building a More Sustainable Future: Impact Assessment', Accompanying document to the 'Communication from the Commission to the Council and the European Parliament', SEC(2006) 1719/3, Brussels, Commission of the European Communities.

—— (2008*a*), 'Annex to the Impact Assessment: Commission Staff Working Document Accompanying The Package Of Implementation Measures For The EU's Objectives on Climate Change and Renewable Energy for 2020', Sec(2008) 85, Vol. II, Brussels, Commission of the European Communities.

—— (2008*b*), 'Proposal for a Directive of the European Parliament and of the Council on the Promotion of the Use of Energy from Renewable Sources', COM(2008) 19 final, Brussels, Commission of the European Communities.

—— (2008*c*), 'The Support of Electricity from Renewable Energy Sources', Accompanying document to the 'Proposal for a Directive of the European Parliament and of the Council on the Promotion of the Use of Energy from Renewable Sources', Commission Staff Working Document, SEC(2008) 57, Brussels, Commission of the European Communities.

ECIEP (2006), 'Integrated Energy Policy: Report of the Expert Committee', Expert Committee on Integrated Energy Policy, Government of India Planning Commission, New Delhi, August.

EDF (1997), *Building a Durable Climate Change Protocol: Participation of Developing Nations*, New York, Environmental Defense Fund.

EEA (2007), 'Greenhouse Gas Emission Trends and Projections in Europe 2007', EEA Report No 5/2007, Copenhagen, European Environment Agency, November.

Egenhofer, C., Gialoglu, K., Luciani, G., Boots, M., Scheepers, M., Constantini, V., Gracceva, F., Markandya, A., and Vicini, G., (2004), *Market-based Options for Security of Energy Supply*, Rome, Fondazione Eni Enrico Mattei, Nota Di Lavoro 117.2004.

EIA (1998*a*), *Natural Gas Issues and Trends*, Washington, DC, US Energy Information Administration.

—— (1998*b*), 'Impacts of the Kyoto Protocol on US Energy Use and Economic Activity', SR/OIAF/EIA-98-03, Washington, DC, Energy Information Administration.

—— (2008*a*), *International Energy Outlook 2008*, Washington, DC, US Energy Information Administration.

—— (2008*b*), EIA/IEO emission profiles, June, Washington, DC, US Energy Information Administration (available at http://www.eia.doe.gov/).

—— (various years), *International Energy Outlook,* various editions, Washington, DC, US Energy Information Administration.

Ellerman, A. D., and Montero, J.-P. (2007), 'The Efficiency and Robustness of Allowance Banking in the US Acid Rain Program', Cambridge, MA, Massachusetts Institute of Technology Center for Energy and Environmental Policy Research.

Ellerman, D., and Buchner, B. (2007), 'The European Union Emissions Trading Scheme: Origins, Allocation, and Early Results', *Review of Environmental Economics and Policy*, **1**, 66–87.

—— Joskow, P., Schmalensee, R., Montero, J.-P., and Bailey, E. (2000), *Markets for Clean Air: The US Acid Rain Program*, New York, Cambridge University Press.

Elster, J. (1999), *Alchemies of the Mind: Rationality and the Emotions*, Cambridge, Cambridge University Press.

ENB (2007), 'Summary of the Thirteenth Conference of Parties to the UN Framework Convention on Climate Change and Third Meeting of Parties to the Kyoto Protocol: 3–15 December 2007', *Earth Negotiations Bulletin*, **12**(354).

Endres, A., and Finus, M. (2002), 'Quotas May Beat Taxes in a Global Emission Game', *International Tax and Public Finance*, **9**(6), 687–707.

Energy Efficiency Office (1993), 'Organisational Aspects of Energy Management', General Information Report 12, ETSU, AEA Technology, Harwell.

Enkvist, P.-A., Nauclér, T., and Rosander, J. (2007), 'A Cost Curve for Greenhouse Gas Reduction', *The McKinsey Quarterly*, **1**, 35–45.

EPA (2006), *Global Mitigation of Non-CO2 Greenhouse Gases*, United States Environmental Protection Agency, June.

—— (2008), 'EPA Analysis of Lieberman–Warner Climate Security Act of 2008, S.2191 in 110th Congress', Washington, DC, US Environmental Protection Agency.

EPRI (2007), 'The Power to Reduce CO2 Emissions: The Full Portfolio', Palo Alto, CA, Electric Power Research Institute.

Eriksen, K. W., and Kvaløy, O. (2008), 'Myopic Investment Management', Working Paper, University of Stavanger.

Esty, D. C., and Ivanova, M. H. (2001), 'Making International Environmental Efforts Work: The Case for a Global Environmental Organization', Yale Center for Environmental Law and Policy, October.

Eto, J., Kito, S., Shown, L., and Sonnenblick, R. (2000), 'Where Did the Money Go? The Cost and Performance of the Largest Commercial Sector DSM Programs', *Energy Journal*, **21**(2), 23–49.

ETSU (2001), 'Climate Change Agreements—Sectoral Energy Efficiency Targets', ETSU, AEA Technology, Harwell.

EU (2008), '20–20 by 2020—Europe's Climate Change Opportunity', Climate Action and Renewable Energy Package, Commission to the European Parliament, the Council, the European Economic and Social Committee and the Committee of the Regions, 23 January.

European Commission (2003), 'Proposal for a Directive of the European Parliament of the Council Amending the Directive Establishing a Scheme for Greenhouse Gas Emission Allowance Trading within the Community, in respect of the Kyoto Protocol's Project Mechanisms', COM(2003) 403 Final, Brussels 23.7.

—— (2009), 'Towards a Comprehensive Climate Change Agreement in Copenhagen', Communication from the Commission to the European Parliament, the Council, the Economic and Social Committee of the Regions, COM(2009) 39 final, Brussels, 28 January.

European Parliament and Council of the European Union (2008), 'Regulation (EC) No 294/2008 of the European Parliament and of the Council establishing the European Institute of Innovation and Technology', *Official Journal*, L97/1, 9 April.

Evensky, J. (2005), 'Adam Smith's *Theory of Moral Sentiments:* On Morals and Why They Matter to a Liberal Society of Free People and Free Markets', *Journal of Economic Perspectives*, **19**, 109–30.

Fairman, D. (1996), 'The Global Environment Facility: Haunted by the Shadow of the Future', in R. O. Keohane and M. A. Levy (eds), *Institutions for Environmental Aid: Pitfalls and Promise*, Cambridge, MA, MIT Press, 55–87.

Falk, A. (2007), 'Gift Exchange in the Field', *Econometrica*, **75**, 1501–11.

—— and Fischbacher, U. (2006), 'A Theory of Reciprocity', *Games and Economic Behavior*, **54**, 293–315.

—— Fehr, E., and Fischbacher, U. (2008), 'Testing Theories of Fairness—Intentions Matter', *Games and Economic Behavior*, **62**, 287–303.

FAO (2006), 'Global Forest Resources Assessment 2005', Forestry Paper No. 147, Rome, UNFAO (Food and Agriculture Organization of the United Nations).

Farrell, A., Carter, R., and Raufer, R. (1999), 'The NOx Budget: Market-based Control of Tropospheric Ozone in the Northeastern United States', *Resource and Energy Economics*, **21**,103–24.

—— Keith, D.W., and Corbett, J. J. (2003), 'A Strategy for Introducing Hydrogen into Transportation', *Energy Policy*, **31**, 1357–67.

Fehr, E., and Gächter, S. (2000*a*), 'Fairness and Retaliation: The Economics of Reciprocity', *Journal of Economic Perspectives*, **14**, 159–81.

—— —— (2000*b*), 'Cooperation and Punishment in Public Goods Experiments', *American Economic Review*, **90**, 980–94.

—— Schmidt, K. M. (1999), 'A Theory of Fairness, Competition and Co-operation', *Quarterly Journal of Economics*, **114**, 817–68.

Feist, W. (1996), 'Life-cycle Energy Balances Compared: Low Energy House, Passive House, Self-sufficient House', *Proceedings of the International Symposium of CIB W67*, Vienna.

Festinger, L. (1957), *A Theory of Cognitive Dissonance*, Stanford, CA, Stanford University Press.

Figueres, C. (2004), 'Institutional Capacity to Integrate Economic Development and Climate Change Considerations—An assessment of DNAs in Latin America and the Caribbean', Draft submitted to the Inter-American Development Bank by Ecoenergy International.

Finger, J. M., and Schuler, P. (2000), 'Implementation of Uruguay Round Commitments: The Development Challenge', *The World Economy*, **23**, 511–25.

Fischbacher, U., Gächter, S., and Fehr, E. (2001), 'Are People Conditionally Cooperative? Evidence from Public Goods Experiment', *Economics Letters*, **71**, 397–404.

Fishelson, G. (1976), 'Emission Control Policies under Uncertainty', *Journal of Environmental Economics and Management*, **3**, 189–98.

Fisher, B. S., Nakicenovic, N., Alfsen, K., Corfee Morlot, J., de la Chesnaye, F., Hourcade, J.-C., Jiang, K., Kainuma, M., La Rovere, E., Matysek, A., Rana, A., Riahi, K., Richels, R., Rose, S., van Vuuren, D., and Warren, R. (2007), 'Issues Related to Mitigation in the Long Term Context', in B. Metz, O. R. Davidson, P. R. Bosch, R. Dave, L. A. Meyer (eds), *Climate Change 2007: Mitigation. Contribution of Working Group III to the Fourth Assessment Report of the Inter-governmental Panel on Climate Change*, Cambridge, Cambridge University Press.

Fleming, J. (2007), 'The Climate Engineers: Playing God to Save the Planet', *Wilson Quarterly*, Spring, 46–60.

Footer, M. E. (2001), 'Developing Country Practice in the Matter of WTO Dispute Settlement', *Journal of World Trade*, **35**, 55–98.

Frame, D. J., Stone, D. A., Stott, P. A., and Allen, M. R. (2006), 'Alternatives to Climate Sensitivity', *Geophysical Research Letters*, **33**, L14707.

Frankel, J. (2005), 'Climate and Trade: Links Between the Kyoto Protocol and WTO', *Environment*, **47**(7), 8–19, September.

—— (2007), 'Formulas for Quantitative Emission Targets', ch. 2 in J. Aldy and R. N. Stavins (eds), *Architectures for Agreement: Addressing Global Climate Change in the Post Kyoto World*, Cambridge, Cambridge University Press.

—— (2008), 'An Elaborated Proposal for Global Climate Policy Architecture: Specific Formulas and Emission Targets for all Countries in all Decades', Harvard Project on International Climate Agreements Working Paper 08–08.

Frey, B. S., and Jegen, R. (2001), 'Motivation Crowding Theory', *Journal of Economic Surveys*, **15**(5), 589–611.

Frey, B., and Meier, S. (2004), 'Social Comparisons and Pro-social Behavior: Testing "Conditional Cooperation" in a Field Experiment', *American Economic Review*, **94**, 1717–22.

—— and Oberholzer-Gee, F. (1997), 'The Cost of Price Incentives: An Empirical Analysis of Motivation Crowdingout', *American Economic Review*, **87**(4), 746–55.

Frieden, J. A., and Rogowski, R. (1996), 'The Impact of the International Economy on National Policies: An Analytical Overview', in R. O. Keohane and H. V. Milner (eds), *Internationalization and Domestic Politics*, New York, Cambridge University Press, 25–47.

Frondel, M., and Schmidt, C. M. (2001), 'Evaluating Environmental Programs: The Perspective of Modern Evaluation Research', *Ecological Economics*, **55**(4), 515–26.

Fudenberg, D., and Levine, D. M. (2006), 'A Dual-self Model of Impulse Control', *American Economic Review*, **96**, 1449–76.

Fullerton, D. (1997), 'Environmental Levies and Distortionary Taxation: Comment', *American Economic Review*, **87**(1), 245–51.

—— and Metcalf, G. (2001), 'Environmental Controls, Scarcity Rents, and Pre-existing Distortions', *Journal of Public Economics*, **80**, 249–68.

Furman, J., Bordoff, J. E., Deshpande, M., and Noel, P. J. (2007), 'An Economic Strategy to Address Climate Change and Promote Energy Security', The Hamilton Project, Strategy Paper, Washington, DC, The Brookings Institution, October.

Furubotn, E. G., and Richter, R. (1997), *Institutions and Economic Theory: The Contribution of the New Institutional Economics*, Ann Arbor, MI, University of Michigan Press.

Gächter, S. (2007), 'Conditional Cooperation. Behavioral Regularities from the Lab and the Field and Their Policy Implications', in B. S. Frey and A. Stutzer (eds), *Economics and Psychology. A Promising New Cross-disciplinary Field*, CESifo Seminar Series, Cambridge, MA, MIT Press.

Gallup, J. L., and Sachs, J. D. (2001), 'The Economic Burden of Malaria', *American Journal of Tropical Medicine and Hygiene*, **64**(1, suppl.), 85–96.

Galston, W. A. (2003), 'A Sketch of Some Arguments for Conscription', *Philosophy and Public Policy Quarterly*, **23**(3), 2–7.

Garnaut, R. (2007), 'Will Climate Change Bring an End to the Platinum Age?', Paper presented at the inaugural S. T. Lee Lecture on Asia & The Pacific, Australian National University, Canberra, 29 November.

Garnaut, R. (2008*a*), 'Will Climate Change Bring an End to the Platinum Age?', Paper presented at the inaugural S. T. Lee Lecture on Asia & the Pacific, Australian National University, 29 November 2007, published in *Asia Pacific Economic Literature*, **22**(1).

—— (2008*b*), *Garnaut Climate Change Review: Draft Report*, Commonwealth of Australia, June.

—— (2008*c*), *The Garnaut Climate Change Review*, Melbourne, Cambridge University Press (also available at www.garnautreview.org.au).

—— and Huang, Y. (2005), 'Is Growth Built on High Investment Sustainable?', in R. Garnaut and L. Song (eds), *The China Boom and its Discontents*, Canberra, Asia Pacific Press at the Australian National University.

—— —— (2007), 'Mature Chinese Growth Leads the Global Platinum Age', in R. Garnaut and Y. Huang (eds), *China: Linking Markets for Growth*, Canberra, Asia Pacific Press at the Australian National University.

—— and Song, L. (2006), 'China's Resource Demand at the Turning Point', in R. Garnaut and L. Song (eds), *The Turning Point in China's Economic Development*, Canberra, Asia Pacific Press at the Australian National University.

GATT (1990), 'Improvement of Notification Procedures—Note by the Secretariat', Negotiating Group on Functioning of the GATT System, General Agreement on Tariffs and Trade, MTN.GNG/NG14/W/39.

Geller, H., Harrington, P., Rosenfeld, A. H., Tanishima, S., and Unander, F. (2006), 'Policies for Increasing Energy Efficiency: Thirty Years of Experience in OECD Countries', *Energy Policy*, **34**, 556–73.

Ghosh, A. (2008), 'See No Evil, Speak No Evil? The WTO, the Trade Policy Review Mechanism, and Developing Countries', D. Phil. thesis, Oxford, University of Oxford.

Gilligan, M. J. (1997), *Empowering Exporters: Reciprocity, Delegation, and Collective Action in American Trade Policy*, Ann Arbor, MI, University of Michigan Press.

Gillingham, K., Newell, R. G., and Palmer, K. (2006), 'Energy Efficiency Policies: A Retrospective Examination', *Annual Review of Environment and Resources*, **31**, 161–92.

—— —— and Pizer, W. A. (2008), 'Modeling Endogenous Technological Change for Climate Policy Analysis', *Energy Economics*, **30**(6), 2734–53.

Gneezy, U., and Potters, J. (1997), 'An Experiment on Risk Taking and Evaluation Periods', *Quarterly Journal of Economics*, **102**, 631–45.

—— and Rustichini, A. (2000), 'A Fine is a Price', *Journal of Legal Studies*, **29**, 1–17.

—— Kapteyn, A., and Potters, J. (2003), 'Evaluation Periods and Asset Prices in a Market Experiment', *Journal of Finance*, **58**, 821–37.

GoI (2006), 'Integrated Energy Policy', Report of the Expert Committee, Planning Commission, Government of India, New Delhi, August.

—— (2008*a*), *Economic Survey 2007/08*, Ministry of Finance, Government of India, New Delhi, February.

—— (2008*b*), *Indian Public Finance Statistics 2007/08*, Ministry of Finance, Government of India, New Delhi, June.

—— (2008*c*), 'National Action Plan on Climate Change', Prime Minister's Council on Climate Change, Government of India, New Delhi.

—— (2008*d*), 'Submissions to UNFCCC', Various, Government of India, New Delhi.

Goldstein, J., and Martin, L. L. (2000), 'Legalization, Trade Liberalization, and Domestic Politics: A Cautionary Note', *International Organization*, **54**, 603–32.

Golove, W. H., and Eto, J. H. (1996), 'Market Barriers to Energy Efficiency: A Critical Reappraisal of the Rationale for Public Policies to Promote Energy Efficiency', Berkeley, CA, Lawrence Berkeley Laboratory, University of California.

Gomes, F. J., and Michaelides, A. (2008), 'Asset Pricing with Limited Risk Sharing and Heterogeneous Agents', *Review of Financial Studies*, **21**, 415–48.

Goulder, L. H. (1995), 'Environmental Taxation and the Double Dividend: A Readers' Guide', *International Tax and Public Finance*, **2**, 157–83.

—— (2000), 'Confronting the Adverse Industry Impacts of CO_2 Abatement Policies: What Does it Cost?', Climate Issues Brief No. 23, Washington, DC, Resources for the Future.

—— (2004), 'Induced Technological Change and Climate Policy', Arlington, VA, Pew Center on Global Climate Change.

—— Parry, I. W. H., and Burtraw, D. (1997), 'Revenue-raising vs Other Approaches to Environmental Protection: The Critical Significance of Pre-existing Tax Distortions', *RAND Journal of Economics*, **28**, 708–31.

—— Williams, R. C., and Burtraw, D. (1999), 'The Cost-effectiveness of Alternative Instruments for Environmental Protection in a Second-best Setting', *Journal of Public Economics*, **72**, 329–60.

Government of Canada (2005), *Moving Forward on Climate Change: A Plan for Honouring Our Kyoto Commitment*, Ottawa, Government of Canada.

Govindasamy, B., and Caldeira, K. (2000), 'Geoengineering Earth's Radiation Balance to Mitigate CO_2-induced Climate Change', *Geophysical Research Letters*, **27**, 2141–4.

—— Thompson, S., Duffy, P. B., Caldeira, K., and Delire, C. (2002), 'Impact of Geoengineering Systems on the Terrestrial Biosphere', *Geophysical Research Letters*, **29**, 2061.

Green, R. J. (2008), 'Carbon Tax or Carbon Permits: The Impact on Generators' Risks,' *Energy Journal*, **29**(3), 67–89.

—— and Vasilakos, N. (2008), 'Market Behaviour with Large Amounts of Intermittent Generation', Working Paper, Birmingham, Department of Economics, University of Birmingham.

Greening, L. A., Greene, D. L., and Difiglio, C. (2000), 'Energy Efficiency and Consumption—The Rebound Effect: A Survey', *Energy Policy*, **28**(6–7), 389–401.

Grether, J.-M., Mathys, N. A., and de Melo, J. (2006), 'Unravelling the World-wide Pollution Haven Effect', August.

Grieg-Gran, M. (2006), 'The Cost of Avoiding Deforestation', Report prepared for the Stern Review, International Institute for Environment and Development.

Griffin, J. (1996), *Value Judgement: Improving our Ethical Beliefs*, Oxford, Clarendon Press.

Gross, R., Heptonstall, P., Anderson, D., Green, T. C., Leach, M., and Skea, J. (2006), 'The Costs and Impacts of Intermittency: An Assessment of the Evidence on the Costs and Impacts of Intermittent Generation on the British Electricity Network', London, Imperial College.

Grossman, G., and Helpman, E. (1994), 'Protection for Sale', *American Economic Review*, **84**, 833–50.

Gruber, J., and Köszegi, B. (2001), 'Is Addiction "Rational"? Theory and Evidence', *Quarterly Journal of Economics*, **116**, 1261–303.

Grundler, C. (2007), 'Reducing Greenhouse Gases Under the Clean Air Act', 11th Biennial Conference on Transportation and Energy Policy, Asilomar.

Gullickson, W., and Harper, M. J. (1987), 'Multi Factor Productivity in US Manufacturing 1949–1983', *Monthly Labour Review*, October, 18–28.

Gullison, R. *et al.* (2007), 'Tropical Forests and Climate Policy', *Science*, **316**, 985–6.

Gupta, S., Tirpak, D. A., Burger, N., Gupta, J., Höhne, N., Boncheva, A. I., Kanoan, G. M., Kolstad, C., Kruger, J. A., Michaelowa, A., Murase, S., Pershing, J., Saijo, T., and Sari, A. (2007), 'Policies, Instruments and Co-operative Arrangements', in B. Metz, O. R.

Davidson, P. R. Bosch, R. Dave, and L. A. Meyer (eds), *Climate Change 2007: Mitigation. Contribution of Working Group III to the Fourth Assessment Report of the Intergovernmental Panel on Climate Change*, Cambridge and New York, Cambridge University Press.

Gürerk, Ö., Irlenbusch, B., and Rockenbach, B. (2006), 'The Competitive Advantage of Sanctioning Institutions', *Science*, **312**(5770), 108–11.

Haas, P. M. (2002), 'UN Conferences and Constructivist Governance of the Environment', *Global Governance*, **8**, 73–91.

——(2008), 'Climate Change Governance after Bali', *Global Environmental Politics*, **8**(3), 1–7.

——Keohane, R., and Levy, M. (1993), *Institutions for the Earth: Sources of Effective International Environmental Protection*, Cambridge, MA, MIT Press.

Habermas, J. (1990), *Moral Consciousness and Communicative Action*, Cambridge, MA, MIT Press.

Haggard, S. (1988), 'The Institutional Foundations of Hegemony: Explaining the Reciprocal Trade Agreements Act of 1934', *International Organization*, **42**(1), 91–119.

Hahn, R. W. (1998), *The Economics and Politics of Climate Change*, Washington, DC, AEI Press.

Hall, C. A. S., Cleveland, C. J., and Kaufmann, R. K. (1986), *Energy and Resource Quality: The Ecology of the Economic Process*, New York, Wiley Interscience.

Hall, D. S., Levi, M., Pizer, W. A., Ueno, T. (2008), 'Policies for Developing Country Engagement', Harvard Project on International Climate Agreements Working Paper 08–15.

Hamilton, M., Herzog, H. J., and Parsons, J. (2008), 'Cost and US Public Policy for New Coal Power Plants with Carbon Capture and Sequestration', Presented at the 9th International Conference on Greenhouse Gas Control Technologies, Washington, DC, November.

Hansen, J. (2008), 'Target Atmospheric CO_2: Where Should Humanity Aim?', *Open Atmospheric Science Journal*, **2**, 217–31.

——Sato, M., Ruedy, R., Lacis, A., and Oinas, V. (2000), 'Global Warming in the Twenty-first Century: An Alternative Scenario', *Proceedings of the National Academy of Sciences*, **97**(18), 9875–80.

Hare, R. M. (1971), *Essays on Philosophical Method*, Berkeley, CA, University of California Press.

Harrison, D., Jr (2003), 'Ex Post Evaluation of the RECLAIM Emission Trading Program for the Los Angeles Air Basin', Presented at Workshop on Ex Post Evaluation of Tradeable Permits: Methodological and Policy Issues, Paris, OECD Environment Directorate.

Harsanyi, J. C. (1982), 'Morality and the Theory of Rational Behavior', in A. K. Sen and B. Williams (eds), *Utilitarianism and Beyond*, Cambridge, Cambridge University Press, 39–62.

Hassan, R., Scholes, R., and Ash, N. (eds) (2005), *Ecosystems and Human Well-being: Current State and Trends, vol. 1*, Washington, DC, Island Press.

Hayami, H., and Nakamura, M. (2002), 'CO_2 Emissions of an Alternative Technology and Bilateral Trade between Japan and Canada: Relocating Production and an Implication for Joint Implementation', Discussion Paper 75, Tokyo, Keio Economic Observatory.

Helfand, G. E. (1991), 'Standards versus Standards: The Effects of Different Pollution Restrictions', *American Economic Review*, **81**(3), 622–34.

Helm, D. R. (2004), *Energy, the State, and the Market: British Energy Policy since 1979*, revised edn, Oxford, Oxford University Press.

——(2005), 'Economic Instruments and Environmental Policy', *Economic and Social Review*, **36**(3), 205–28.

—— (2006), 'Regulatory Reform, Capture, and the Regulatory Burden', *Oxford Review of Economic Policy*, **22**(2).

—— (2008*a*), 'Caps and Floors for the EU ETS—A Practical Carbon Price', Polish Office of the Committee for European Integration, 4 September (available at www.dieterhelm.co.uk).

—— (2008*b*), 'Credible Energy Policy: Meeting the Challenges of Security of Supply and Climate Change', London, Policy Exchange.

—— (2008*c*), 'Renewables—Time for a Rethink?', Commentary, 16 June (available at www.dieterhelm.co.uk/publications/Commentary_jun08.pdf).

Helm, D., and Hepburn, C. (2005), 'Carbon Contracts and Energy Policy: An Outline Proposal', Oxford University, mimeo.

Helm, D. R., and Hepburn, C. (2007), 'Carbon Contracts and Energy Policy: An Outline Proposal', ch. 3 in D. R. Helm (ed.), *The New Energy Paradigm*, Oxford, Oxford University Press.

—— —— and Mash, R. (2003), 'Credible Carbon Policy', *Oxford Review of Economic Policy*, **19**(3), 438–50.

—— —— —— (2004), 'Time-inconsistent Environmental Policy and Optimal Delegation', Oxford University Department of Economics Discussion Paper 175.

—— —— —— (2005), 'Credible Carbon Policy', in D. R. Helm (ed.), *Climate-change Policy*, Oxford, Oxford University Press, 305–21.

—— Phillips, J., and Smale, R. (2008), 'Too Good to be True? The UK's Climate Change Record', available at www.dieterhelm.co.uk

Henderson, P. D. (1977), 'Two British Errors: Their Probable Size and Some Possible Lessons', *Oxford Economic Papers*, **29**, 159–205.

Hepburn, C. (2006), 'Regulating by Prices, Quantities or Both: An Update and an Overview', *Oxford Review of Economic Policy*, **22**(2), 226–47.

—— (2007), 'Carbon Trading: A Review of the Kyoto Mechanisms', *Annual Review of Environment and Resources*, **32**, 375–93.

—— Quah, J. K.-H., and Ritz, R. A. (2006*a*), 'On Emissions Trading and Firm Profits', Oxford University Department of Economics Discussion Paper 295.

—— Grubb, M., Neuhoff, K., Matthes, F., and Tse, M. (2006*b*), 'Auctioning of EU ETS Phase II Allowances: How and Why?', *Climate Policy*, **6**, 137–60.

—— Quah, J. K.-H., and Ritz, R. A. (2008), 'Emissions Trading with Profit-neutral Permit Allocations', Economics Working Papers, 2008-W12, Nuffield College, University of Oxford.

—— Grubb, M., and Neuhoff, K. (2008), 'Emissions Trading will Profit-neutral Permit Allocations', Nuffield College Oxford Discussion Paper.

Hewett, M. J. (1998), 'Achieving Energy Efficiency in a Restructured Electric Utility Industry', Minneapolis, Center for Energy and Environment.

Heyes, A. G. (1998), 'Making Things Stick: Enforcement and Compliance', *Oxford Review of Economic Policy*, **14**(4), 50–63.

Hoel, M. (1996), 'Should a Carbon Tax be Differentiated Across Sectors?', *Journal of Public Economics*, **59**, 17–32.

—— and Karp, L. (2001), 'Taxes and Quotas for a Stock Pollutant with Multiplicative Uncertainty', *Journal of Public Economics*, **82**, 91–114.

—— —— (2002), 'Taxes versus Quotas for a Stock Pollutant', *Resource and Energy Economics*, **24**, 367–84.

Hoffert, M. I., Caldeira, K., Benford, G., Criswell, D. R., Green, C. *et al.* (2002), 'Advanced Technology Paths to Global Climate Stability: Energy for a Greenhouse Planet,' *Science*, **298**, 981–7.

Hoffmann, M. J. (2007), *Ozone Depletion and Climate Change: Constructing a Global Response*, Albany, NY, State University of New York Press.

Hofman, B., Zhao, M., and Ishihara, Y. (2007), 'Asian Development Strategies: China and Indonesia Compared', *Bulletin of Indonesian Economic Studies*, **43**(2), 171–200.

Höhne, N., and Ellermann, C. (2008), 'The EU's Emission Reduction Target, Intended Use of CDM and its +2°C', DG Internal Policies: Policy Department Economic and Scientific Policy, IP/A/ENVI/NT/2008–14.

Hong, N. V. (1983), 'Two Measures of Aggregate Energy Production Elasticities', *Energy Journal*, **4**(2), 172–7.

Hooijer, A., Silvius, M., Wösten, H., and Page, S. (2006), 'PEAT-CO2, Assessment of CO2 Emissions from Drained Peatlands in SE Asia', Delft Hydraulics Report Q3943.

Houghton, R. A. (2003), 'Emissions (and Sinks) of Carbon from Land-use Change (Estimates of National Sources and Sinks of Carbon Resulting from Changes in Land Use, 1950 to 2000)', Report to the World Resources Institute from the Woods Hole Research Center.

—— (2005), 'Tropical Deforestation as a Source of Greenhouse Gas Emissions', in P. Moutinho and S. Schwartzman (eds), *Deforestation and Climate Change*, Amazon Institute for Environmental Research, 13–21.

—— (2008), 'Carbon Flux to the Atmosphere from Land-use Changes: 1850–2005', in *TRENDS: A Compendium of Data on Global Change*, Oak Ridge, TN, Carbon Dioxide Information Analysis Center, Oak Ridge National Laboratory, US Department of Energy.

House, K. Z., House, C. H., Schrag, D. P., and Aziz, M. J. (2007), 'Electrochemical Acceleration of Chemical Weathering as an Energetically Feasible Approach to Mitigating Anthropogenic Climate Change', *Environmental Science and Technology*, **41**(21), 7558–63.

House of Commons Environmental Audit Committee (2008), 'Personal Carbon Trading', Fifth Report of Session 2007–08, HC 565, 26 May.

House of Lords (2005), 'The Economics of Climate Change', vol. I: Report, 6 July.

—— (2008), *The Economics of Renewable Energy, Economic Affairs Select Committee Fourth Report of Session 2007–8*, HL195 of 2007–8, London, The Stationery Office.

Howarth, R. B. (1997), 'Energy Efficiency and Economic Growth', *Contemporary Economic Policy*, **15**(4), 1.

—— (2003), 'Discounting and Uncertainty in Climate Change Policy Analysis', *Land Economics*, **79**, 369–81.

—— (2009), 'Rethinking the Theory of Discounting and Revealed Time Preference', *Land Economics*, **85**, 24–40.

—— and Sanstad, A. H. (1995), 'Discount Rates and Energy Efficiency', *Contemporary Economic Policy*, **13**(3), 101–9.

—— Haddad, B. M., and Paton, B. (2000), 'The Economics of Energy Efficiency: Insights from Voluntary Participation Programmes', *Energy Policy*, **28**(6–7).

Hudec, R. (2002), 'The Adequacy of WTO Dispute Settlement Remedies: A Developing Country Perspective', in B. M. Hoekman, A. Mattoo, and P. English (eds), *Development, Trade, and the WTO: A Handbook*, Washington, DC, World Bank, 81–91.

Hulme, M. *et al.* (2001), 'African Climate Change: 1900–2100', *Climate Research*, **17**(2), 145–68.

ICP (2008), *2005 International Comparison Program Tables of Final Results*, World Bank, International Comparison Program, February (available at http://siteresources.worldbank.org/ICPINT/Resources/ICP_final-results.pdf).

IEA (1992), *Climate Change Policy Initiatives*, Paris, Organization for Economic Cooperation and Development/ International Energy Agency.

—— (2000), *Experience Curves for Energy Technology Policy*, Paris, International Energy Agency.

—— (2006), 'Energy Technology Perspectives: Scenarios and Strategies to 2050', Paris, Organization for Economic Cooperation and Development / International Energy Agency.

—— (2007*a*), *World Energy Outlook 2007, China and India Insights*, Paris, Organization for Economic Cooperation and Development/International Energy Agency.

—— (2007*b*), *CO_2 Emissions from Fuel Combustion*, Paris, International Energy Agency.

—— (2007*c*), *IEA 2007 Energy Balances of Non-OECD Countries*, Paris, International Energy Agency.

—— (2007*d*), 'Mind the Gap: Quantifying Principal Agent Problems in Energy Efficiency', Paris, Organization for Economic Cooperation and Development / International Energy Agency.

—— (2008*a*), *Annual Report 2007: Implementing Agreement on Photovoltaic Power Systems*, Paris, International Energy Agency.

—— (2008*b*), *World Energy Outlook 2008, China and India Insights*, Paris, Organization for Economic Cooperation and Development / International Energy Agency.

—— (2008*c*), *Energy Technology Perspectives 2008: Scenarios and Strategies to 2050*, Paris, International Energy Agency.

IMF (1999), *External Evaluation of IMF Surveillance—Report by a Group of Independent Experts*, Washington, DC, International Monetary Fund.

—— (various years to 2008), *World Economic Outlook*, Washington, DC, International Monetary Fund.

—— (2008), *World Economic Outlook: Housing and the Business Cycle*, Washington, DC, International Monetary Fund, April.

Independent Evaluation Office of the IMF (2006), *An Evaluation of the IMF's Multilateral Surveillance*, Washington, DC, International Monetary Fund.

Interlaboratory Working Group (2000), *Scenarios for Clean Energy Future*, Berkeley, CA, Lawrence Berkeley National Laboratory (LBNL-44029).

International Emissions Trading Association (2008), *State of the CDM 2008: Facilitating a Smooth Transition into a Mature Environmental Financing Mechanism*, Geneva, International Emissions Trading Association.

IPCC (1995), *Climate Change 1995: The Science of Climate Change*, Geneva and Cambridge, Intergovernmental Panel on Climate Change and Cambridge University Press.

—— (1996), 'Revised 1996 IPCC Guidelines for National Greenhouse Gas Inventories' (available at http://www.ipcc-ggip.iges.or.jp/public/gl/invs1.html accessed March 2009).

—— (2000*a*), 'Emissions Scenarios: A Special Report of Working Group III of the Intergovernmental Panel on Climate Change', Cambridge, Cambridge University Press.

—— (2000*b*), 'Land Use, Land-Use Change, and Forestry', Special Report, Geneva, International Panel on Climate Change.

—— (2001*a*), 'Climate Change 2001: Synthesis Report', retrieved from Intergovernmental Panel on Climate Change (available at http://www.ipcc.ch/pub/reports.htm).

—— (2001*b*), 'Good Practice Guidance and Uncertainty Management in National Greenhouse Gas Inventories' (available at http://www.ipcc-nggip.iges.or.jp/public/gp/english/index.html, accessed March 2009).

IPCC (2005), *Carbon Dioxide Capture and Storage*, Intergovernmental Panel on Climate Change, Special Report, New York, Cambridge University Press (available at http://www.ipcc.ch/ipccreports/srccs.htm).

—— (2007*a*), 'Climate Change 2007: The Physical Science Basis', Intergovernmental Panel on Climate Change, Cambridge, Cambridge University Press.

—— (2007*b*), 'Summary for Policymakers', Working Group III Contribution to the Fourth Assessment Report, Intergovernmental Panel on Climate Change (available at http://www.ipcc.ch/SPM040507.pdf).

—— (2007*c*), 'Climate Change 2007—Impacts, Adaptation and Vulnerability', Working Group II Contribution to the Fourth Assessment Report of the IPCC, Cambridge, Cambridge University Press.

—— (2007*d*), 'Climate Change 2007—Mitigation of Climate Change', Working Group III Contribution to the Fourth Assessment Report of the IPCC, Cambridge, Cambridge University Press.

—— (2008), 'Climate Change 2007: Synthesis Report', Intergovernmental Panel on Climate Change.

Jackson, M., Joy, S., Heller, T. C., and Victor, D. G. (2006), 'Greenhouse Gas Implications in Large Scale Infrastructure Investments in Developing Countries: Examples from China and India', PESD Working Paper No. 54, March.

Jacoby, H. D., and Ellerman, A. D. (2002), 'The Safety Valve and Climate Policy', MIT Joint Program on the Science and Policy of Global Change, Report No. 83, Cambridge, MA.

—— —— (2004), 'The Safety Valve and Climate Policy', *Energy Policy*, **32**, 481–91.

—— Babiker, M. H., Paltsev, S., and Reilly, J. M. (2008), 'Sharing the Burden of GHG Reductions', The Harvard Project on International Climate Agreements, October.

Jaffe, A. B., and Stavins, R. N. (1994*a*), 'The Energy-efficiency Gap: What Does it Mean', *Energy Policy*, **22**(10), 804–10.

—— —— (1994*b*), 'Energy-efficiency Investments and Public Policy', *Energy Journal*, **15**(2), 43–65.

—— Newell, R. G., and Stavins, R. N. (1999), 'Energy-efficient Technologies and Climate Change Policies: Issues and Evidence', Climate Issues Brief No. 19, Washington, DC, Resources for the Future.

—— —— —— (2005), 'A Tale of Two Market Failures: Technology and Environmental Policy', *Ecological Economics*, **54**, 164–74.

Jaffe, J., and Stavins, R. N. (2007), 'Linking Emissions Trading Systems', Paper prepared for the International Emissions Trading Association, November.

—— —— (2008), 'Linkage of Tradable Permit Systems in International Climate Policy Architecture', Harvard Project on International Climate Agreements Discussion Paper 08–07.

Jang, B.-G., Koo, H. K., Liu, H., and Loewenstein, M. (2007), 'Liquidity Premia and Transaction Costs', *Journal of Finance*, **62**(5), 2329–66.

Jevons, W. S. (1865), 'The Coal Question: Can Britain Survive?', in A.W. Flux (ed.), *The Coal Question: An Inquiry Concerning the Progress of the Nation, and the Probable Exhaustion of Our Coal-mines*, New York, Augustus M. Kelley.

Johansson-Stenman, O. (2005), 'Distributional Weights in Cost–Benefit Analysis—Should We Forget about Them?', *Land Economics*, **81**, 337–52.

Jonas, M., Nilsson, S., Obersteiner, M., Gluck, M., and Ermoliev, Y. (1999), 'Verification Times Underlying the Kyoto Protocol: Global Benchmark Calculations', Interim Report IR-99062, Laxenburg, International Institute for Applied Systems Analysis.

Jones, C. J. (2001), *Introduction to Economic Growth*, New York, London, W.W. Norton.

Jorgenson, D. W., and Griliches, Z. (1967), 'The Explanation of Productivity Change', *Review of Economic Studies*, **34**(3), 249–82.

—— Goettle, R. J., Wilcoxen, P. J., and Ho, M. S. (2000), *The Role of Substitution in Understanding the Costs of Climate Change Policy*, Arlington, VA, Pew Center on Global Climate Change.

Joskow, P., and Marron, D. (1992), 'What Does a Megawatt Really Cost? Evidence from the Electric Utility Conservation Programmes', *Energy Journal*, **13**(4).

Jotzo, F., and Pezzey, J. (2007), 'Optimal Intensity Targets for Greenhouse Emissions Trading under Uncertainty', *Environmental and Resource Economics*, **38**(2), 259–84.

Judson, R. A., Schmalensee, R., and Stoker, T. M. (1999), 'Economic Development and the Structure of the Demand for Commercial Energy', *Energy Journal*, **20**, 29–58.

Kahneman, D., and Thaler, R. (2006), 'Anomalies: Utility Maximisation and Experienced Utility', *Journal of Economic Perspectives*, **20**, 221–34.

—— and Tversky, A. (1979), 'Prospect Theory: An Analysis of Decision under Risk', *Econometrica*, **47**, 263–91.

—— —— (2000), *Choices, Values and Frames*, Cambridge, Cambridge University Press.

—— Wakker, P., and Sarin, R. (1997), 'Back to Bentham? Explorations of Experienced Utility', *Quarterly Journal of Economics*, **112**, 375–406.

Kallbekken, S. (2007), 'Why the CDM Will Reduce Carbon Leakage', *Climate Policy*, **6**(7), 197–211.

—— and Hovi, J. (2007), 'The Price of Non-compliance with the Kyoto Protocol: The Remarkable Case of Norway', *International Environmental Agreements*, **7**, 1–15.

Kaniaru, D., Shende, R., Stone, S., and Zaelke, D. (2007), 'Strengthening the Montreal Protocol: Insurance Against Abrupt Climate Change', *Sustainable Development Law and Policy*, **3**.

Karp, L. (2005), 'Global Warming and Hyperbolic Discounting', *Journal of Public Economics*, **89**, 261–82.

—— and Zhang, J. (2001), 'Controlling a Stock Pollutant with Endogenous Investment and Asymmetric Information', Working Paper, Department of Agricultural and Resource Economics, University of California, Berkeley, CA.

Kaufmann, R. K. (1992), 'A Biophysical Analysis of the Energy/Real GDP Ratio: Implications for Substitution and Technical Change', *Ecological Economics*, **6**(1), 35–56.

—— (1994), 'The Relation between Marginal Product and Price in US Energy Markets: Implications for Climate Change Policy', *Energy Economics*, **16**(2), 145–58.

—— (2004), 'The Mechanisms of Autonomous Energy Efficiency Increases: A Cointegration Analysis of the US Energy/GDP Ratio', *Energy Journal*, **25**(1), 63–86.

—— and Azary-Lee, I. G. (1990), 'A Biophysical Analysis of Substitution: Does Substitution Save Energy in the US Forest Products Industry?', Proceedings of a workshop, *Ecological Economics: Its Implications for Forest Management and Research*, Swedish University of Agricultural Sciences, held in St Paul, MN.

Kawamoto, M. (2005), 'The Foundations of International Treaty Regime and the Roles of International Organizations: Compliance Facilitation Under the Climate Change Treaty Regime with Particular Attention to Reporting Obligation', Prepared for the 2005 Berlin Conference on the Human Dimensions of Global Environmental Change.

Kay, J. (2004), 'Nobody Wins When There Are Too Few Taxis', *Financial Times*, 28 January.

Kaya, Y., and Yokobori, K. (eds) (1997), *Environment, Energy, and Economy: Strategies for Sustainability*, United Nations University Press.

Keith, D. W. (2000), 'Geoengineering the Climate: History and Prospect', *Annual Review of Energy and the Environment*, **25**, 245–84.

Keller, K., Hall, M, Kim, S.-R., Bradford, D. F., and Oppenheimer, M. (2005), 'Avoiding Dangerous Anthropogenic Interference with the Climate System', *Climatic Change*, **73**, 227–38.

Kempton, W., and Layne, L. (1994), 'The Consumer's Energy Analysis Environment', *Energy Policy*, **22**(10), 857–66.

—— and Letendre, S. E. (1997), 'Electric Vehicles as a New Power Source for Electric Utilities', *Transportation Research Part D: Transport and Environment*, **2**(3), 157–75.

Kennedy, P. W., and Laplante, B. (1999), 'Environmental Policy and Time Consistency: Emission Taxes and Emissions Trading', in E. Petrakis, E. S. Sartzetakis, and A. Xepapadeas (eds), *Environmental Regulation and Market Power*, Cheltenham, Edward Elgar, 116–44.

Keohane, N., Revesz, R., and Stavins, R. N. (1998), 'The Choice of Regulatory Instruments in Environmental Policy', *Harvard Environmental Law Review*, **22**.

Keohane, R. O. (1982), 'The Demand for International Regimes', *International Organization*, **36**, 325–55.

—— (1989), *International Institutions and State Power: Essays in International Relations Theory*, Boulder, CO, Westview Press.

—— and Rautiala, K. (2008), 'Toward a Post-Kyoto Climate Architecture: A Political Analysis', Harvard Project on International Climate Agreements Discussion Paper 08–01.

Kérébel, C. (2009), 'The Results of Negotiations on the "Climate Change and Energy Package"', 18 February (available at http://www.ifri.org/frontDispatcher/ifri/publications/actuelles_de_l_ifri_1197584475485).

Kerr, S., and Newell, R. (2000), 'Policy-induced Technology Adoption: Evidence from the US Lead Phasedown', Washington, DC, Resources for the Future, draft manuscript.

Khazzoom, J. D. (1980), 'Economic Implications of Mandated Efficiency in Standards for Household Appliances', *Energy Journal*, **1**(4), 21–40.

Klemperer, P. D. (2004), *Auctions: Theory and Practice*, Princeton, NJ, Princeton University Press.

Kocherlakota, N. R. (1996), 'The Equity Premium: It's Still a Puzzle', *Journal of Economic Literature*, **34**(1), 42–71.

Koehn, P. H. (2008), 'Underneath Kyoto: Emerging Subnational Government Initiatives and Incipient Issue-bundling Opportunities in China and the United States', *Global Environmental Politics*, **8**(1), 53–77.

Koremenos, B., Lipson, C., and Snidal, D. (2001), 'The Rational Design of International Institutions', *International Organization*, **55**, 761–99.

Kotschwar, B. (1999), 'Small Countries and the FTAA', in M. Rodriguez Mendoza, P. Lowe, and B. Kotschwar (eds), *Trade Rules in the Making*, Washington, DC, Brookings Institution Press, 134–58.

Krause, F. (1996), 'The Costs of Mitigating Carbon Emissions: A Review of Methods and Findings from European Studies', *Energy Policy*, **24**(10–11), 899–915.

Kreitler, V. (1991), 'On Customer Choice and Free Ridership in Utility Programs', 5th International Energy Programme Evaluation Conference, Chicago, IL.

Kroll, S., Cherry, T. L., and Shogren, J. F. (2007), 'Voting, Punishment, and Public Goods', *Economic Inquiry*, **45**, 557–70.

Kuhn, T. S. (1962), *The Structure of Scientific Revolutions*, Chicago, IL, University of Chicago Press.

Kummel, R. (1982), 'The Impact of Energy on Industrial Growth', *Energy*, **7**(2), 189–203.

——(1989), 'Energy as a Factor of Production and Entropy as a Pollution Indicator in Macroeconomic Modelling', *Ecological Economics*, **1**(2), 161–80.

——Strassl, W., Gossner, A., and Eichhorn, W. (1985), 'Technical Progress and Energy Dependent Production Functions', *Nationalökonomie—Journal of Economics*, **3**, 285–311.

——Henn, J., and Lindenberger, D. (2002), 'Capital, Labor, Energy and Creativity: Modeling Innovation Diffusion', *Structural Change and Economic Dynamics*, **13**(4), 415–33.

——Lindenberger, D., and Eichhorn, W. (2000), 'The Productive Power of Energy and Economic Evolution', *Indian Journal of Applied Economics*, **8**, 231–62.

Kverndokk, S. (1995), 'Tradeable CO_2 Emission Permits: Initial Distribution as a Justice Problem', *Environmental Values*, **4**(2), 129–48.

Kydland, R. E., and Prescott, E. C. (1977), 'Rules rather than Discretion: The Inconsistency of Optimal Plans', *Journal of Political Economy*, **85**, 473–91.

Labour Party (1997), 'New Labour Because Britain Deserves Better', London, Labour Party, April.

Laitner, J. A. (2000), 'Energy Efficiency: Rebounding to a Sound Analytical Perspective', *Energy Policy*, **28**(6–7), 471–5.

Lakatos, I., and Musgrave, A. (1970), *Criticism and the Growth of Knowledge*, Cambridge, Cambridge University Press.

Lange, A., and Vogt, C. (2003), 'Cooperation in International Environmental Negotiations Due to a Preference for Equity', *Journal of Public Economics*, **87**, 2049–67.

——Löschel, A., Vogt, C., and Ziegler, A. (2007), 'On the Self-serving Use of Equity Principles in International Climate Negotiations', ZEW Discussion Papers 07–025, Mannheim, Zentrum für Europäische Wirtschaftsforschung.

Lawson, N. (2008), *An Appeal to Reason: A Cool Look at Global Warming*, London, Duckworth.

Lenzen, M. (1998), 'Primary Energy and Greenhouse Gas Embodied in Australian Final Consumption: An Input–Output Analysis', *Energy Policy*, **26**(6), 495–506.

Levine, M., and Sonnenblick, R. (1994), 'On the Assessment of Utility Demand-side Management Programmes', *Energy Policy*, **22**(10), 848–56.

Levitt, S., and List, J. (2007), 'What do Laboratory Experiments Tell Us about the Real World?', *Journal of Economic Perspectives*, **21**(2), 153–74.

Li, H., Pei Dong, Z., Chunyu, H., and Gang, W. (2007), 'Evaluating the Effects of Embodied Energy in International Trade on Ecological Footprint in China', *Ecological Economics*, **62**(1), 136–48.

Liepert, B., Feichter, J., Lohmann, U., and Roeckner, E. (2004), 'Can Aerosols Spin Down the Water Cycle in a Warmer and Moister World?', *Geophysical Research Letters*, **31**, L06207.

Limmeechokchai, B., and Suksuntornsiri, P. (2007), 'Embedded Energy and Total Greenhouse Gas Emissions in Final Consumptions within Thailand', *Renewable and Sustainable Energy Reviews*, **11**(2), 259–81.

Lintner, J. (1965), 'The Valuation of Risk Assets and the Selection of Risky Investments in Stock Portfolios and Capital Budgets', *Review of Economics and Statistics*, **47**(1), 13–37.

Lipsey, R. G., Carlaw, K. I., and Bekar, C. T. (2005), *Economic Transformations: General Purpose Technologies and Long-term Economic Growth*, Oxford, Oxford University Press.

Lombardi, D., and Woods, N. (2008), 'The Politics of Influence: An Analysis of IMF Surveillance', *Review of International Political Economy*, **15**, 711–39.

Loughran, D. S., and Kulick, J. (2004), 'Demand-side Management and Energy Efficiency in the United States', *Energy Journal*, **25**(1), 19–43.

Lovins, A. B. (1988), 'Energy Savings from More Efficient Appliances: Another View', *Energy Journal*, **9**(2), 155–62.

——(1992), 'Energy Efficient Buildings: Institutional Barriers and Opportunities', Strategic Issues Paper No. 1, E Source Inc., Boulder, CO.

——(1998), 'Further Comments on Red Herrings', *Letter to the New Scientist.*

——and Lovins, L. H. (1997), 'Climate: Making Sense and Making Money', Old Snowmass, CO, Rocky Mountain Institute.

Lubowski, R. N., Plantinga, A. J., and Stavins, R. N. (2006), 'Land-use Change and Carbon Sinks: Econometric Estimation of the Carbon Sequestration Supply Function', *Journal of Environmental Economics and Management*, **51**, 135–52.

Luhan, W. J., Kocher, M., and Sutter, M. (2009), 'Group Polarization in the Team Dictator Game Reconsidered', *Experimental Economics*, **12**(1), 26–41.

McCormick, J. (1989), *The Global Environmental Movement*, London, Belhaven.

McGinnis, J. O., and Movsesian, M. L. (2000), 'The World Trade Constitution', *Harvard Law Review*, **114**(2), 511–605.

Machado, G., Schaeffer, R., and Worrell, E. (2001), 'Energy and Carbon Embodied in the International Trade of Brazil: An Input–Output Approach', *Ecological Economics*, **39**(3), 409–24.

Mackay, D. J. C. (2008), *Sustainable Energy—Without the Hot Air*, Cambridge, UIT.

McKibbin, W. J., and Wilcoxen, P. J. (2000), 'Moving Beyond Kyoto', Brookings Policy Brief 66.

————(2002), 'The Role of Economics in Climate Change Policy', *Journal of Economic Perspectives*, **16**(2), 107–29.

————(2003), 'Reply to Michaelowa: Global Warming Policy', *Journal of Economic Perspectives*, **17**(3), 205–6.

————(2004), 'Estimates of the Costs of Kyoto: Marrakesh versus the McKibbin–Wilcoxen Blueprint', *Energy Policy*, **32**, 467–79.

McKibbin, W., Pearce, D., Stegman, A. (2004), 'Long Run Projections for Climate Change Scenarios', Lowy Institute Working Paper 1.04, Sydney.

McKinsey (2008), 'Carbon Capture and Storage: Assessing the Economics', Climate Change Initiative, September.

McKitrick, R. (2005), 'Decentralizing a Regulatory Standard Expressed in Ratio or Intensity Form', *Energy Journal*, **26**(4), 43–51.

Mäenpää, I., and Siikavirta, H. (2007), 'Greenhouse Gases Embodied in the International Trade and Final Consumption of Finland: An Input–Output Analysis', *Energy Policy*, **35**(1), 128–43.

Malcomson, J. (1978), 'Prices vs Quantities: A Critical Note on the Use of Approximations', *Review of Economic Studies*, **45**, 203–8.

Market Advisory Committee to the California Air Resources Board (2007), 'Recommendations for Designing a Greenhouse Gas Cap-and-trade System for California', 30 June.

Marrakech Accords (2001), 'Implementing the Kyoto Protocol on Climate Change', available at unfccc.int/cop7/documents/accords_draft.pdf

Marsh, G., Taylor, P., Anderson, D., Leach, M., and Gross, R. (2003), 'Options for a Low Carbon Future: Phase 2', Report for the Department of Trade and Industry, Harwell, AEA Technology.

Marshall Task Force (1998), 'Economic Instruments and the Business Use of Energy: Conclusions', November, Marshall Task Force on the Industrial Use of Energy.

Matthews, H. D., and Caldeira, K. (2007), 'Transient Climate-carbon Simulations of Planetary Geoengineering', *Proceedings of the National Academy of Sciences*, **104**, 9949–54.

Mattke, S. (2000), 'Cardiology and Cost Control: The Ethical Challenge for the New Millennium', *Zeitschrift für Kardiologie*, **89**(8), 649–57.

Maxwell, S., and Christiansen, K. (2002), 'Negotiation as Simultaneous Equation: Building a New Partnership with Africa', *International Affairs*, **78**, 477–91.

Mehra, R., and Prescott, E. C. (1985), 'The Equity Premium. A Puzzle', *Journal of Monetary Economics*, **15**, 145–61.

—— —— (2003), 'The Equity Premium Puzzle in Retrospect', in G. M. Constantinides, M. Harris, and R. Stulz (eds), *Handbook of the Economics of Finance*, Amsterdam, North Holland, 889–938.

Meinshausen, M. (2006), 'What Does a 2°C Target Mean for Greenhouse Gas Concentrations? A Brief Analysis Based on Multi-gas Emission Pathways and Several Climate Sensitivity Uncertainty Estimates', in J. S. Schellnhuber,W. Cramer, N. Nakicenovic, T. M. L. Wigley, and G. Yohe (eds), *Avoiding Dangerous Climate Change*, Cambridge, Cambridge University Press, 265–79.

Mendelsohn, R., Dinar, A., and Williams, L. (2006), 'The Distributional Impact of Climate Change', *Environment and Development Economics*, **11**, 159–78.

Meng, K., Dudek, D. J., Golub, A., Lugovoy, O., Petsonk, A., Strukova, E., Wang, J. (2007), 'Constructing a Post-2012 Pathway: Being on Track to Avoid Dangerous Climate Change', Environmental Defense Fund, New York.

Metcalf, G. E. (2008), 'Designing a Carbon Tax to Reduce US Greenhouse Gas Emissions', NBER Working Paper No. 13554, October.

Meyer, B. (1995), 'Natural and Quasi Experiments in Economics', *Journal of Business and Economic Statistics*, **13**(2), 151–60.

Michaelowa, A. (2005), 'CDM: Current Status and Possibilities for Reform', Hamburg Institute of International Economics (HWWI) Research Programme on International Climate Policy, Paper No. 3.

—— Hayashi, D., Jung, M., Müller, N., Bode, S., Castro, P., Dransfeld, B., and Höhne, N. (2008), 'A Review of the Current State and Options for Reform of the CDM', Report for UK Department of Environment, Food and Rural Affairs, July.

Milgrom, P., and Roberts, J. (1992), *Economics, Organisation and Management*, New Jersey, Prentice Hall.

Miller, D. (1999), *Principles of Social Justice*, Cambridge, MA, Harvard University Press.

Ministry of Sustainable Development (2005), *The Swedish Report on Demonstrable Progress Under the Kyoto Protocol* (available at http://www.sweden.gov.se/content/1/c6/05/47/62/24057533.pdf).

MIT (2007), *The Future of Coal: Options for a Carbon Constrained World*, Massachusetts Institute of Technology (available at http://mit.edu/coal/).

Mitchell, R. B. (1994), 'Regime Design Matters: Intentional Oil Pollution and Treaty Compliance', *International Organization*, **48**, 425–58.

—— Clark, W. C., Cash, D. W., and Dickson, N. M. (2006), *Global Environmental Assessments: Information and Influence*, Cambridge, MA, MIT Press.

Mohan, J. E., Ziska, L. H., Thomas, R. B., Sicher, R. C., George, K., Clark, J. S., and Schlesinger,W. H. (2006), 'Biomass and Toxicity Responses of Poison Ivy (*Toxicodendron radicans*) to Elevated Atmospheric CO2', *Proceedings of the National Academy of Sciences*, **103**(24), 9086–9.

Moledina, A. A., Coggins, J. S., Polasky, S., and Costello, C. (2003), 'Dynamic Environmental Policy with Strategic Firms: Prices versus Quantities', *Journal of Environmental Economics and Management*, **45**, 356–76.

Mongelli, I., Tassielli, G., and Notarnicola, B. (2006), 'Global Warming Agreements, International Trade and Energy/Carbon Embodiments: An Input–Output Approach to the Italian Case', *Energy Policy*, **34**, 88–100.

Morgan, M. G., Adams, P., and Keith, D. W. (2006), 'Elicitation of Expert Judgments of Aerosol Forcing', *Climatic Change*, **75**, 195–214.

Morris, M. G., and Hill, E. D. (2007), 'Trade is the Key to Climate Change', *The Energy Daily*, **35**(33), 20 February.

Morrison, S. A. (1986), 'A Survey of Road Pricing', *Transportation Research*, **20A**(2), 87–97.

Mossin, J. (1966), 'Equilibrium in a Capital Asset Market', *Econometrica*, **34**, 768–83.

Mueller, D. (2003), *Public Choice III*, Cambridge, Cambridge University Press.

Mukhopadhyay, K. (2004), 'Impact of Trade on Energy Use and Environment in India: An Input–Output Analysis', Paper submitted to the International Conference 'Input–Output and General Equilibrium: Data, Modeling, and Policy Analysis', Brussels, Free University of Brussels, 2–4 September (available at http://www.ecomod.net/conferences/iioa2004/iioa2004_papers/mukhopadhyay.pdf).

Müller, B., Michaelowa, A., and Vrolijk, C. (2001), 'Rejecting Kyoto: A Study of Proposed Alternatives to the Kyoto Protocol', Climate Strategies Report, London.

Muradian, R., O'Connor, M., and Martinez-Alier, J. (2002), 'Embodied Pollution in Trade: Estimating the "Environmental Load Displacement" of Industrialized Countries', *Ecological Economics*, **41**, 51–67.

Murray, B., Newell, R. G., and Pizer, W. A. (2009), 'Balancing Cost and Emissions Certainty: An Allowance Reserve for Cap-and-trade', *Review of Environmental Economics and Politics*, **3**(1), 84–103.

Myers, E. (2007), 'Policies to Reduce Emissions from Deforestation and Degradation (REDD) in Tropical Forests', Resources for the Future, RFF DP 07–50, Washington, DC.

Nabuurs, G. J., and Masera, O. (2007). 'Forestry', ch. 9 in *IPCC Climate Change 2007: Mitigation*, Cambridge, Cambridge University Press.

—— —— Andrasko, K., Benitez-Ponce, P., Boer, R., Dutschke, M., Elsiddig, E., Ford-Robertson, J., Frumhoff, P., Karjalainen, T., Krankina, O., Kurz, W. A., Matsumoto, M., Oyhantcabal, W., Ravindranath, N. H., Sanz Sanchez, M. J., and Zhang, X. (2007), 'Forestry', in B. Metz, O. R. Davidson, P. R. Bosch, R. Dave, and L. A. Meyer (eds), *Climate Change 2007: Mitigation. Contribution of Working Group III to the Fourth Assessment Report of the Intergovernmental Panel on Climate Change*, Cambridge and New York, Cambridge University Press.

Naik, V., Wuebbles, D. J., Delucia, E. H., and Foley, J. A. (2003), 'Influence of Geoengineered Climate on the Terrestrial Biosphere', *Environmental Management*, **32**, 373–81.

Nakiçenovic. N, and Swart R. (eds) (2000), *Special Report on Emissions Scenarios*, Cambridge, Cambridge University Press.

NAO (2005), 'Department of Trade and Industry: Renewable Industry', National Audit Office, London, The Stationery Office.

—— (2008), 'UK Greenhouse Gas Emissions: Measurement and Reporting', National Audit Office, London, The Stationery Office.

Narjoko, D. A., and Jotzo, F. (2007), 'Survey of Recent Developments', *Bulletin of Indonesian Economic Studies*, **43**(2), 143–69.

NAS (1992), 'Geoengineering', *Policy Implications of Greenhouse Warming: Mitigation, Adaptation and the Science Base*, National Academy of Sciences, Washington, DC, National Academies Press.

—— (2007), *Conducting Effective Global Change Assessments*, National Academy of Sciences, Washington, DC, National Academies Press.

National Commission on Energy Policy (2004), *Ending the Energy Stalemate: A Bipartisan Strategy to Meet America's Energy Challenges*, Washington, DC, December.

—— (2007), *Energy Policy Recommendations to the President and the 110th Congress*, Washington, DC, April.

National Grid (2008), 'GB Seven Year Statement', Table 5.1 (available at www.nationalgrid.com/uk/electricity/sys).

NBS (2006), *Input–Output Tables of China in 2002*, National Bureau of Statistics, Beijing, China (Statistic Press.

—— (2007*a*), *2007 China Statistical Yearbook*, National Bureau of Statistics of China.

—— (2007*b*), 'Communiqué on National Energy Consumption for Unit GDP in the First Half of 2007', National Bureau of Statistics of China (available at http://www.stats.gov.cn/english/newsandcomingevents/t20070731_402422194.htm).

—— (2008), 'Statistical Communiqué of the People's Republic of China on 2007', National Bureau of Statistics of China (available at http://www.stats.gov.cn/english/newsandcomingevents/t20080228_402465066.htm).

—— (various years), *The China Yearbook of Statistics*, 2001–7 edns, National Bureau of Statistics, Beijing (available at www.stats.gov.cn).

Nepstad, D., Soares-Filho, B., Merry, F., Moutinho, P., Rodriques, H. O., Bowman, M., Schwartzman, S., Almeida, O., and Rivero, S. (2007), 'The Costs and Benefits of Reducing Carbon Emissions from Deforestation and Forest Degradation in the Brazilian Amazon', Falmouth, MA, The Woods Hole Research Center.

Netherlands Environmental Assessment Agency (2007), 'China Now No. 1 in CO2 Emissions; USA in Second Position' (available at http://www.mnp.nl/en/dossiers/Climatechange/moreinfo/Chinanowno1inCO2emissionsUSAinsecondposition.html).

—— (2008), 'Global CO2 Emissions: Increase Continued in 2007' (available at http://www.pbl.nl/en/publications/2008/GlobalCO2emissionsthrough2007.html).

Neuhoff, K. (2008), 'Learning by Doing with Constrained Growth Rates: An Application to Energy Technology Policy', *The Energy Journal*, **29**, Special Issue, 165–82.

Newell, P. (2001), 'New Environmental Architecture and the Search for Effectiveness', *Global Environmental Politics*, **1**(1).

Newell, R. G. (2007), 'Climate Technology Policy', Resources for the Future Climate Backgrounder, Washington, DC.

—— and Stavins, R. N. (2003), 'Cost Heterogeneity and the Potential Savings from Market-based Policies', *Journal of Regulatory Economics*, **23**, 43–59.

—— Pizer, W., and Zhang, J. (2005), 'Managing Permit Markets to Stabilise Prices', *Environmental and Resource Economics*, **31**, 133–57.

Nguyen, T. T. A., and Keiichi, I. N. (2006), 'Analysis of Changing Hidden Energy Flow in Vietnam', *Energy Policy*, **34**(14).

Nichols, A. L. (1994), 'Demand-side Management: Overcoming Market Barriers or Obscuring Real Costs?', *Energy Policy*, **22**(10), 840–7.

Nichols, A. L. (1997), 'Lead in Gasoline', in R. Morgenstern (ed.), *Economic Analyses at EPA: Assessing Regulatory Impact*, Washington, DC, Resources for the Future, 49–86.

Nilsson, S., Shvidenko, A., Stolbovoi, V., Gluck, M., Jonas, M., and Obersteiner, M. (2000), 'Full Carbon Account for Russia', Interim Report IR-00-021, Laxenburg, IIASA.

Nisbet, M., and Myers, T. (2007), 'The Polls—Trends: Twenty Years of Public Opinion about Global Warming', *Public Opinion Quarterly*, **71**(3), 1–27.

Nordhaus, W. D. (1998), 'Is the Kyoto Protocol a Dead Duck? Are there any Live Ducks Around? Comparison of Alternative Global Tradable Emissions Regimes', Department of Economics, Yale University, Working Paper.

—— (2000), *Warming the World: Economic Models of Global Warming*, Cambridge, MA, MIT Press.

—— (2005), 'Life after Kyoto: Alternative Approaches to Global Warming Policies', NBER Working Paper No. 11889, December.

—— (2007*a*), 'A Review of *The Stern Review on the Economics of Climate Change*', *Journal of Economic Literature*, **45**(3), 686–702.

—— (2007*b*), 'The Challenge of Global Warming: Economic Models and Environmental Policy', Yale University, New Haven, CT (available at http://nordhaus.econ.yale.edu/dice_mss_072407_all.pdf).

—— (2008), *A Question of Balance: Weighing the Options on Global Warming Policies*, New Haven, CT, Yale University Press.

—— and Boyer, J. (2000), 'Warming the World: Economic Models of Global Warming', Cambridge, MA, MIT Press.

Nottage, H. (2009), 'Developing Countries in the WTO Dispute Settlement System', Global Economic Governance Programme Working Paper 2009/47.

Norwegian Ministry of Finance (2008), *Carbon Neutral Norway*, Norwegian Ministry of Finance Carbon scheme, Norwegian Ministry of Finance, Oslo (available at http://www.carbonneutralnorway.no/).

Nyborg, K. (2007), 'I Don't Want to Hear About It: Rational Ignorance among Duty-oriented Consumers', Working Paper, University of Oslo.

Obersteiner, M. (2006), 'Economics of Avoiding Deforestation', International Institute for Applied Analysis, Austria.

OECD (2001), 'Kyoto Mechanisms, Monitoring and Compliance: From Kyoto to the Hague', Paris, Organization for Economic Cooperation and Development Environment Directorate and International Energy Agency.

—— (2005), *OECD in Figures*, 2005 edn, Statistics on the member countries (available at http://213.253.134.43/oecd/pdfs/browseit/0105061E.pdf).

—— and IEA (2008*a*), *CO2 Emissions from Fuel Combustion*, Paris, Organization for Economic Cooperation and Development and International Energy Agency.

—— —— (2008*b*), *World Energy Outlook 2008*, Paris, Organization for Economic Cooperation and Development and International Energy Agency.

Office of National Statistics (2008), *Regional Trends*, London, Palgrave Macmillan.

Ohiorhenuan, J. F. E. (2005), 'Capacity Building Implications of Enhanced African Participation in Global Rules-making and Arrangements', in A. Oyejide and W. Lyakurwa (eds), *Africa and the World Trading System*, Trenton, Africa World Press.

Oliveira-Martins, J., Burniaux, J.-M., and Martin, J. P. (1992), 'Trade and the Effectiveness of Unilateral CO2 Abatement Policies: Evidence from GREEN', *OECD Economic Studies*, No. 19, 123–40.

Olivier, J. G. J., and Berdowski, J. J. M. (2001), 'Global Emissions Sources and Sinks', in J. Berdowski, R. Guicherit, and B. J. Heij (eds), *The Climate System*, Lisse, A. A. Balkema / Swets & Zeitlinger, 33–78.

Olmstead, S. M., and Stavins, R. N. (2006), 'An International Policy Architecture for the Post-Kyoto Era', *American Economic Review Papers and Proceedings*, **96**(2), 35–8.

Olsen, K. H. (2007), 'The Clean Development Mechanism's Contribution to Sustainable Development: A Review of the Literature', *Climatic Change*, **84**, 59–73.

——— and Thordarson, T. (2006), 'High-latitude Eruptions Cast Shadow Over the African Monsoon and the Flow of the Nile', *Geophysical Research Letters*, **33**, L18711.

Oman, L., Robock, A., Stenchikov, G. L., Schmidt, G. A., and Ruedy, R. (2005), 'Climatic Response to High-latitude Volcanic Eruptions', *Journal of Geophysical Research*, **110**, D13103.

O'Neill, B. C., and Oppenheimer, M. (2002), 'Dangerous Climate Impacts and the Kyoto Protocol', *Science*, **296**, 1971–2.

Oppenheimer, M., and Petsonk, A. (2004), 'Reinvigorating the Kyoto System and Beyond: Maintaining the Fundamental Architecture, Meeting Long-term Goals', Paper prepared for Leaders' Summit on Post-Kyoto Architecture: Toward an L20?, Council on Foreign Relations, New York City, 20–21 September.

—— —— (2005), 'Article 2 of the UNFCCC: Historical Origins and Recent Interpretations', *Climatic Change*, **73**, 195–226.

—— O'Neill, B. C., Webster, M., Agrawala, S. (2007), 'The Limits of Consensus', *Science*, **317**, 1505–16.

Ostertag, K. (2003), *No-regrets Potentials in Energy Conservation: An Analysis of their Relevance, Size and Determinants*, Heidelberg and New York, Physica.

Ostrom, E. (1990), *Governing the Commons: The Evolution of Institutions for Collective Action*, Cambridge, Cambridge University Press.

Oswald, J., Raine, M., and Ashraf-Ball, H. (2008), 'Will British Weather Provide Reliable Electricity?', *Energy Policy*, **36**(8), 3212–25.

Oura, H. (2007), 'Wild or Tamed? India's Potential Growth', IMF Working Paper, WP/07/224.

Oxera (2004), 'CO_2 Emissions Trading: How will it Affect UK Industry?', Oxford, Oxera Consulting, July.

—— (2006), 'Policies for Energy Efficiency in the UK Household Sector', Report prepared for Defra, Oxera Consulting, January.

Pachauri, R. (2007), 'Conference of the Parties to the UNFCCC serving as the meeting of the Parties to the Kyoto Protocol (COP/MOP), Opening Ceremony 12 December 2007—WMO/UNEP Intergovernmental Panel on Climate Change, Mr Rajendra Pachauri, Chairman', Video presentation (available at http://www.un.org/webcast/unfccc/2007/index.asp?go=09071212).

Page, S. E., Siegert, F., Rieley, J. O., Boehm, H.-D. V., Jaya, A., and Limin, S. (2002), 'The Amount of Carbon Released from Peat and Forest Fires in Indonesia during 1997', *Nature*, **420**, 61–5.

Paltsev, S., Reilly, J. M., Jacoby, H. D., Gurgel, A. C., Metcalf, G. E., Sokolov, A. P., and Holak, J. F. (2007*a*), 'Assessment of US Cap-and-trade Proposals', Working Paper 13176, Cambridge, MA, National Bureau of Economic Research, June.

—— Gurgel, A. C., Metcalf, G. E., Sokolov, A. P., and Holak, J. F. (2007*b*), 'Appendix C—Assessment of US Cap-and-trade Proposals: Details of Simulation Results,' Cambridge, MA, National Bureau of Economic Research, June.

Pan, J. (2008), 'Carbon Budget for Basic Needs Satisfaction and its Implications for International Equity and Sustainability', *World Economics and Politics*, **1**, 35–42 (in Chinese).

Parikh, K. S. (2006), *Integrated Energy Policy: Report of the Expert Committee*, Planning Commission, Government of India, New Delhi.

Parry, I. W. H. (1995), 'Pollution Taxes and Revenue Recycling', *Journal of Environmental Economics and Management*, **29**, S64–S77.

—— (2003), 'Fiscal Interactions and the Case for Carbon Taxes over Grandfathered Carbon Permits', *Oxford Review of Economic Policy*, **19**(3), 385–99.

—— and Pizer, W. A. (2007), 'Emissions Trading Versus CO_2 Taxes', mimeo.

—— Williams, R. C., and Goulder, L. H. (1999), 'When Can Carbon Abatement Policies Increase Welfare? The Fundamental Role of Distorted Factor Markets', *Journal of Environmental Economics and Management*, **37**, 52–84.

Pascual, M. *et al.* (2006), 'Malaria Resurgences in the East Africa Highlands: Temperature Trends Revisited', *Proceedings of the National Academy of Sciences*, **103**, 5829–34.

Patel, U. R., and Bhattacharya, S. (2008), 'Infrastructure in India: The Economics of Transition from Public to Private Provision', April, prepared for China–India special issue of *Journal of Comparative Economics*.

Patterson, M. G. (1996), 'What is Energy Efficiency: Concepts, Indicators and Methodological Issues', *Energy Policy*, **24**(5), 377–90.

Pauwelyn, J. (2007), 'US Federal Climate Policy and Competitiveness Concerns: The Limits and Options of International Trade Law', Working Paper 07-02, Nicholas Institute, Duke University.

Pearce, D. (1998), 'Environmental Appraisal and Environmental Policy in the European Union', *Environmental and Resource Economics*, **11**(3–4), 489–501.

—— Atkinson, G., and Mourato, S. (2006), *Cost–Benefit Analysis and the Environment: Recent Developments*, Paris, Organization for Economic Cooperation and Development.

Perkins, and Rawski, T. (2008), 'Forecasting China's Economic Growth over the Next Two Decades', in L. Brandt and T. G. Rawski (eds), *China's Great Economic Transformation*, Cambridge, Cambridge University Press.

Peters, G. P., and Hertwich, E. G. (2008), 'Post-Kyoto Greenhouse Gas Inventories: Production versus Consumption', *Climatic Change*, **86**, 51–66.

Petsonk, A. (2007), 'Climate Change—International Issues, Engaging Developing Countries', Testimony before the Subcommittee on Energy and Air Quality, Committee on Energy and Commerce, US House of Representatives, 27 March.

—— (2009), ' "Docking Stations": Designing a More Welcoming Architecture for a Post-2012 Framework to Combat Climate Change', *Duke Journal of Comparative and International Law*, May, **19**(3), 433–66.

Pew Center (2006, 2008 (update)), 'Learning from State Action on Climate Change', *Climate Change 101: State Action* (available at www.pewclimate.org).

Philibert, C. (2005), 'Approaches for Future International Co-operation', OECD Environment Directorate / International Energy Agency, COM/ENV/EPOC/IEA/SLT(2005)6.

—— and IEA (2008), 'Price Caps and Price Floors in Climate Policy: A Quantitative Assessment', International Energy Agency Information Paper, December (available at http://www.iea.org/textbase/papers/2008/price_caps_floors_web.pdf).

Piattelli-Palmarini, M. (1994), *Inevitable Illusions: How Mistakes of Reason Rule our Minds*, New York, John Wiley & Sons.

Pielke, R., Wigley, T., and Green, C. (2008), 'Dangerous Assumptions', *Nature*, **452**, 531–2.

Pigou, A.C. (1932), *The Economics of Welfare*, 4th edn, London, Macmillan.

Pijoan-Mas, J. (2007), 'Pricing Risk in Economies with Heterogeneous Agents and Incomplete Markets', *Journal of the European Economic Association*, **5**(5), 987–1015.

Piris-Cabezas, P., and Keohane, N. (2008), 'Reducing Emissions from Deforestation and Forest Degradation in Developing Countries (REDD): Implications for the Carbon Market', Environmental Defense Fund, New York.

Pizer, W. A. (1997), 'Prices vs. Quantities Revisited: The Case of Climate Change', RFF Discussion Paper 98-02, Washington, DC, Resources for the Future.

—— (2002), 'Combining Price and Quantity Controls to Mitigate Global Climate Change', *Journal of Public Economics*, **85**, 409–34.

—— (2005), 'Climate Policy Design Under Uncertainty', Discussion Paper No. 05–44, Resources for the Future, Washington, DC.

Plantinga, A. J. (2007), 'Land-use Change and Biological Carbon Sequestration', Presentation at Workshop on Carbon Sequestration in Agriculture and Forestry, Thessaloniki, 27 June.

—— and Richards, K. R. (2008), 'International Forest Carbon Sequestration in a Post-Kyoto Agreement', Discussion Paper 2008–11, Cambridge, MA, Harvard Project on International Climate Agreements, October.

Polimeni, J. M. (2008), 'Empirical Evidence for the Jevons Paradox', in J. M. Polimeni, K. Mayumi, M. Giampietro, and B. Alcott (eds), *The Jevons Paradox and the Myth of Resource Efficiency Improvements*, London, Earthscan.

Poole, W. (1970), 'Optimal Choice of Monetary Policy Instruments in a Simple Stochastic Macro Model', *Quarterly Journal of Economics*, **84**(2), 197–216.

Posner, E., and Sunstein, C. (2008), 'Justice and Climate Change', Cambridge, MA, Harvard Project on International Climate Agreements, September.

Prins, G., and Rayner, S. (2007), 'The Wrong Trousers: Radically Rethinking Climate Policy', Joint discussion paper of the James Martin Institute for Science and Civilization, Oxford, University of Oxford, and the MacKinder Centre for the Study of Long-wave events, London, London School of Economies and Political Science.

Project Catalyst (2009), *Financing a Global Deal*, Climate Works Foundation, 28 February.

Pye, M., and McKane, A. (1998), 'Enhancing Shareholder Value: Making a More Compelling Energy Efficiency Case to Industry by Quantifying Non-energy Benefits', *Proceedings of 1999 Summer Study on Energy Efficiency in Industry*, Washington, DC, American Council for a Energy Efficient Economy, 325–36.

Rabin, M. (1993), 'Incorporating Fairness into Game Theory', *American Economic Review*, **83**, 1281–302.

—— (2000), 'Risk Aversion and Expected-utility Theory: A Calibration Theorem', *Econometrica*, **68**, 1281–92.

—— and Schrag, J. (1999), 'First Impressions Matter: A Model of Confirmatory Bias', *Quarterly Journal of Economics*, **114**(1), 37–82.

—— and Thaler, R. (2001), 'Anomalies: Risk Aversion', *Journal of Economic Perspectives*, **15**, 219–32.

Ramsey, F. (1928), 'A Mathematical Theory of Saving', *Economic Journal*, **38**(152), 543–59.

Raupach, M. R., Marland, G., Ciais, P., Le Quere, C., Canadell, J. G., Klepper, G., and Field, C. B. (2007), 'Global and Regional Drivers of Accelerating CO_2 Emissions', *Proceedings of the National Academy of Sciences*, 0700609104.

Raustiala, K. (2003–4), 'Police Patrols and Fire Alarms in the NAAEC', *Loyola of Los Angeles International and Comparative Law Review*, **26**, 389–413.

Raustiala, K. and Victor, D. G. (2004), 'The Regime Complex for Plant Genetic Resources', *International Organization*, **58**(2), 277–309.

Rawls, J. (1971), *A Theory of Justice*, Oxford, Oxford University Press.

Reilly, J., Jacoby, H., and Prinn, R. (2003), 'Multi-gas Contributors to Global Climate Change: Climate Impacts and Mitigation Costs of Non-CO2 Gases', Arlington, VA, Pew Center on Global Climate Change.

Renewable Fuels Agency (2008), *The Gallagher Review of the Indirect Effects of Bio-fuels Production*, St Leonards-on-Sea, Renewable Fuels Agency.

Repetto, R. (2001), 'The Clean Development Mechanism: Institutional Breakthrough Or Institutional Nightmare?', *Policy Sciences*, **34**, 303.

—— (2007), 'National Climate Policy: Choosing the Right Architecture', Boston, MA, Yale School of Forestry and Environmental Studies, June.

Requate, T. (2005), 'Dynamic Incentives by Environmental Policy—A Survey', *Ecological Economics*, **54**, 175–95.

Richiardi, M. G. (2005), 'On the Virtues of the Shame Lane', *Topics in Economic Analysis and Policy*, **5**(1), Article 8.

Richmond, A. K., and Kaufmann, R. K. (2006), 'Is There a Turning Point in the Relationship between Income and Energy Use and/or Carbon Emissions?', *Ecological Economics*, **56**(2), 176–89.

Ricke, K., Morgan, M. G., Apt, J., Victor, D. G., and Steinbruner, J. (2008), 'Unilateral Geoengineering', Briefing notes for a workshop at the Council on Foreign Relations, 5 May.

Roberts, M. J., and Spence, M. (1976), 'Effluent Charges and Licences under Uncertainty', *Journal of Public Economics*, **5**, 193–208.

Rodrik, D., and Subramaniam, A. (2004), 'From "Hindu Growth" to Productivity Surge: The Mystery of the Indian Growth Transition', IMF Working Paper 04/77.

Rogner, H.-H., Zhou, D., Bradley. R., Crabbé, P., Edenhofer, O., Hare, B. (Australia), Kuijpers, L., and Yamaguchi, M. (2007), 'Introduction', in B. Metz, O. R. Davidson, P. R. Bosch, R. Dave, and L. A. Meyer (eds), *Climate Change 2007: Mitigation. Contribution of Working Group III to the Fourth Assessment Report of the Intergovernmental Panel on Climate Change*, Cambridge and New York, Cambridge University Press.

Romm, J. J. (1999), *Cool Companies: How the Best Businesses Boost Profits and Productivity by Cutting Greenhouse Gas Emissions*, Washington, DC, Island Press.

Roques, F. A., Nuttall, W. J., Newbery, D. M., de Neufville, R., and Connors, S. (2006), 'Nuclear Power: A Hedge against Uncertain Gas and Carbon Prices?', *Energy Journal*, **27**(4), 1–23.

Rose-Ackerman, S. (1973), 'Effluent Charges: A Critique', *Canadian Journal of Economics*, **6**, 512–27.

Rosen, D. H. and Houser, T. (2007), 'China Energy: A Guide for the Perplexed', Washington, DC, Peterson Institute for International Economics, May (available at www.iie.com/publications/papers/rosen0507.pdf).

Rosenberg, N. (1989), 'Energy Efficient Technologies: Past, Present and Future Perspectives', Paper presented at the conference, 'How Far Can the World Get on Energy Efficiency Alone?', Oak Ridge National Laboratory.

Rouwendal J., Verhoef E., Rietveld P., and Zwart B. (2002), 'A Stochastic Model of Congestion Caused by Speed Differences', *Journal of Transport Economics and Policy*, **36**(3), 407–45.

Rowlands, I. H. (1995), *Politics of Global Atmospheric Change*, Manchester, Manchester University Press.

Russell, B. (1946), *History of Western Philosophy*, London, Routledge, reprinted 1994.

Sachs, J. (2001), 'Tropical Underdevelopment', NBER Working Paper No. 8119.

Saelen, H., Atkinson, G., Dietz, S., Helgeson, J., and Hepburn, C. (2008), 'Risk, Inequality and Time in the Welfare Economics of Climate Change: Is the Workhorse Model Underspecified?', Department of Economics Working Paper 400, Oxford, University of Oxford.

Sáenz de Miera, G., del Río González, P., and Vizcaíno, I. (2008), 'Analysing the Impact of Renewable Electricity Support Schemes on Power Prices: The Case of Wind Electricity in Spain', *Energy Policy*, **36**(9), 3345–59.

Samaniego, J., and Figueres, C., (2002), 'Evolving to a Sector-based Clean Development Mechanism', ch. 4 in K. A. Baumert *et al.* (eds), *Building on the Kyoto Protocol: Options for Protecting the Climate*, Washington, DC, World Resources Institute.

Samuelson, P. A. (1963), 'Risk and Uncertainty: The Fallacy of Large Numbers', *Scientia*, **48**, 108–13.

Samuelson, W., and Zeckhauser, R. (1988), 'Status Quo Bias in Decision-making', *Journal of Risk and Uncertainty*, **1**(1), 7–59.

Sánchez-Chóliz, J., and Duarte, R. (2004), 'CO_2 Emissions Embodied in International Trade: Evidence for Spain', *Energy Policy*, **32**(18), 1999–2005.

Sanstad, A. H. and Howarth, R. B. (1994), '"Normal" Markets, Market Imperfections and Energy Efficiency', *Energy Policy*, 22(10), 811–18.

—— Roy, J., and Sathaye, S. (2006), 'Estimating Energy-augmenting Technological Change in Developing Country Industries', *Energy Economics*, **28**, 720–9.

Santilli, M. and Moutinho, P. (2005), 'National Compacts to Reduce Deforestation', in P. Moutinho and S. Schwartzman (eds), *Tropical Deforestation and Climate Change*, Amazon Institute for Environmental Research and Environmental Defense.

—— —— Schwartzman, S., Nepstad, D., Curran, L., and Nobre, C. (2005), 'Tropical Deforestation and the Kyoto Protocol: An Editorial Essay', *Climatic Change*, **71**, 267–76.

Sathaye, J., Makundi, W., Dale, L., Chan, P., and Andrasko, K. (2006), 'GHG Mitigation Potential, Costs and Benefits in Global Forests: A Dynamic Partial Equilibrium Approach', *Energy Journal*, Multi-Greenhouse Gas Mitigation and Climate Policy Special Issue, 95–124.

Saunders, H. D. (2000), 'A View from the Macro Side: Rebound, Backfire, and Khazzoom–Brookes', *Energy Policy*, **28**(6–7), 439–49.

—— (2008), 'Fuel Conserving (and Using) Production Function', *Energy Economics*, **30**(5), 2184–235.

Schelling, T. C. (1996), 'The Economic Diplomacy of Geoengineering', *Climatic Change*, **33**, 303–7.

—— (1998), *Costs and Benefits of Greenhouse Gas Reduction*, Washington, DC, AEI Press.

Schipper, L., and Grubb, M. (2000), 'On the Rebound? Feedback between Energy Intensities and Energy Uses in IEA Countries', *Energy Policy*, **28**(6–7), 367–88.

Schlamadinger, B., Ciccarese, L., Dutschke, M., Fearnside, P. M., Brown, S., and Murdiyarso, D. (2005), 'Should We Include Avoidance of Deforestation in the International Response to Climate Change?', in P. Moutinho and S. Schwartzman (eds), *Tropical Deforestation and Climate Change*, Amazon Institute for Environmental Research and Environmental Defense.

Schneider, S. H. (1996), 'Geoengineering: Could—or Should—We Do It?', *Climatic Change*, **33**, 291–302.

Schneider, L. (2007), 'Is the CDM Fulfilling its Environmental and Sustainable Development Objective? An Evaluation of the CDM and Options for Improvement', Berlin, Öko-Institut.

Schurr, S. (1982), 'Energy Efficiency and Productive Efficiency: Some Thoughts Based on American Experience', *Energy Journal*, **3**(3), 3–14.

——(1985), 'Energy Conservation and Productivity Growth: Can We Have Both?', *Energy Policy*, **13**(2), 126–32.

——Netschert, B. C., Eliasberg, V. E., Lerner, J., and Landsberg, H. H. (1960), *Energy in the American Economy*, Resources for the Future, Baltimore, MD, John Hopkins University Press.

Sebenius, J. (1984), *Negotiating the Law of the Sea: Lessons in the Art and Science of Reaching Agreement*, Cambridge, MA, Harvard University Press.

——(1991), 'Designing Negotiations Towards a New Regime: The Case of Global Warming', *International Security*, **15**(4), 110–48.

Sedjo, R. A. and Sohngen, B. (2007), 'Carbon Credits for Avoided Deforestation', Discussion Paper DP 07–47, Washington, DC, Resources for the Future.

Selker, H. P., Griffith, J. L., Dorey, F. J., and D'Agostino, R. B. (1987), 'How do Physicians Adapt when the Coronary Care Unit is Full? A Prospective Multicenter Study', *Journal of the American Medical Association*, **257**(9), 1181–5.

Sen, A. K. (1999), *Development as Freedom*, New York, Knopf.

Sensfuß, F., Ragwitz, M., and Genoese, M. (2008), 'The Merit-order Effect: A Detailed Analysis of the Price Effect of Renewable Electricity Generation on Spot Market Prices in Germany', *Energy Policy*, **36**(8), 3076–84.

Shang, J., and Croson, R. (2006), 'Field Experiments in Charitable Contribution: The Impact of Social Influence on the Voluntary Provision of Public Goods', Unpublished manuscript.

Sharpe, W. F. (1964), 'Capital Asset Prices: A Theory of Market Equilibrium Under Conditions of Risk', *Journal of Finance*, **19**(3), 425–42.

Sheehan, P. (2008), 'The New Global Growth Path: Implications for Climate Change Analysis and Policy', *Climatic Change*, **19**(3–4), 211–31.

——Sun, F. (2007), 'Energy Use and CO_2 Emissions in China: Interpreting Changing Trends and Future Directions', CSES Climate Change Working Paper No. 13, Centre for Strategic Economic Studies, Melbourne, Victoria University.

——Jones, R., Jolley, A., Preston, B., Clarke, M., Durack, P., Islam, S. M. N., and Whetton, P. (2008), 'Climate Change and the New World Economy: Implications for the Nature and Timing of Policy Responses', *Global Environmental Change*, **18**(3), 380–96.

Shelanski, H. A., and Klein, P. G. (1995), 'Empirical Research in Transaction Cost Economics: A Review and Assessment', *Journal of Law, Economics and Organisation*, **11**(2), 335–61.

Shiv, B., and Fedorikhin, A. (1999), 'Heart and Mind in Conflict: Interplay of Affect and Cognition in Consumer Decision Making', *Journal of Consumer Research*, **26**, 278–82.

Shui, B., and Harriss, R. (2006), 'The Role of CO_2 Embodiment in US–China Trade', *Energy Policy*, **34**, 4063–8.

Silva-Chavez, G. A. (2005), 'Reducing Greenhouse Gas Emissions from Tropical Deforestation by Applying Compensated Reduction to Bolivia', in P. Moutinho and S. Schwartzman (eds), *Tropical Deforestation and Climate Change*, Amazon Institute for Environmental Research and Environmental Defense.

Simmons, B. A. (2000), 'International Law and State Behavior: Commitment and Compliance in International Monetary Affairs', *American Political Science Review*, **94**, 819–35.

——Dobbin, F., and Garrett, G. (2006), 'Introduction: The International Diffusion of Liberalism', *International Organization*, **60**, 781–810.

Simon, H. A. (1959), 'Theories of Decision-making in Economics and Behavioural Science', *American Economic Review*, **49**, 253–83.

Sjöstedt, G. (2003), 'Norms and Principles as Support to Post-negotiation and Rule Implementation', in B. I. Spector and I. W. Zartman (eds), *Getting it Done: Post-agreement Negotiation and International Regimes*, Washington, DC, US Institute of Peace, 89–114.

Skutsch, M., Bird, N., Trines, E., Dutschke, M., Frumhoff, P., de Jong, B. H. J., van Laake, P., Masera, O., and Murdiyarso, D. (2007), 'Clearing the Way for Reducing Emissions from Tropical Deforestation', *Environmental Science and Policy*, **10**, 322–34.

Slaughter, A. M. (2004), *A New World Order*, Princeton, NJ, Princeton University Press.

Smale, R., Hartley, M., Hepburn, C., Ward, J., and Grubb, M. (2006), 'The Impact of CO_2 Emissions Trading on Firm Profits and Market Prices', *Climate Policy*, **6**(1), 29–46.

Smith, A., Ross, M., and Montgomery, D. (2002), 'Implications of Trading Implementation Design for Equity–Efficiency Trade-offs in Carbon Permit Allocations', Working Paper, Washington, DC, Charles River Associates.

Sobel, R. S., and Wagner, G. A. (2004), 'Expressive Voting and Government Redistribution: Testing Tullock's "Charity of the Uncharitable" ', *Public Choice*, **119**, 143–59.

Sorrell, S. (2003), 'Making the Link: Climate Policy and the Reform of the UK Construction Industry', *Energy Policy*, **31**(9), 865–78.

—— (2005), 'The Role of Evidence in Energy Policy: What Can Be Learnt from Evidence Based Policy and Practice?', SPRU, Brighton, University of Sussex.

—— (2007*a*), 'The Economics of Energy Service Contracts', *Energy Policy*, **35**(1), 507–21.

—— (2007*b*), 'The Rebound Effect: An Assessment of the Evidence for Economy-wide Energy Savings from Improved Energy Efficiency', London, UK Energy Research Centre.

—— and Dimitropoulos, J. (2007*a*), 'The Rebound Effect: Definitions, Limitations and Extensions', *Ecological Economics*, **65**(3), 636–49.

—— —— (2007*b*), 'UKERC Review of Evidence for the Rebound Effect: Technical Report 3—Econometric Studies', London, UK Energy Research Centre.

—— —— (2007*c*), 'UKERC Review of Evidence for the Rebound Effect: Technical Report 5—Energy Productivity and Economic Growth Studies', London, UK Energy Research Centre.

—— O'Malley, E., Schleich, J., and Scott, S. (2004), *The Economics of Energy Efficiency: Barriers to Cost-effective Investment*, Cheltenham, Edward Elgar.

—— —— and Sommerville, M. (2009), 'Empirical Estimates of Direct Rebound Effects', *Energy Policy*, **37**(4), 1356–71.

Spence, A. M. (1973), 'Job Market Signaling', *Quarterly Journal of Economics*, **87**, 355–74.

Stainforth, D., Aina, T., Christensen, C., Collins, M., Faull, N., Frame, D. J., Kettleborough, J. A., Knight, S., Martin, A., Murphy, J. M., Piani, C., Sexton, D., Smith, L. A., Spicer, R. A., Thorpe, A. J., and Allen, M. R. (2005), 'Uncertainty in Predictions of the Climate Response to Rising Levels of Greenhouse Gases', *Nature*, **433**, January, 403–6.

Stanhill, G., and Cohen, S. (2001), 'Global Dimming: A Review of the Evidence for a Widespread and Significant Reduction in Global Radiation with Discussion of its Probable Causes and Possible Agricultural Consequences', *Agricultural and Forest Meteorology*, **107**, 255–78.

Starmer, C. (2000), 'Developments in Nonexpected-utility Theory: The Hunt for a Descriptive Theory of Choice Under Risk', *Journal of Economic Literature*, **38**, 332–82.

Stavins, R. N. (1996), 'Correlated Uncertainty and Policy Instrument Choice', *Journal of Environmental Economics and Management*, **30**, 218–32.

Stavins, R. N. (1999), 'The Costs of Carbon Sequestration: A Revealed-preference Approach', *American Economic Review*, **89**(4), 994–1009.

—— (2003), 'Experience with Market-based Environmental Policy Instruments', ch. 9 in K.-G. Mäler and J. Vincent (eds), *Handbook of Environmental Economics*, vol. I, Amsterdam, Elsevier Science, 355–435.

—— (2006), 'Vintage-differentiated Environmental Regulation', *Stanford Environmental Law Journal*, **25**(1), 29–63.

—— (2007), 'A US Cap-and-trade System to Address Global Climate Change', The Hamilton Project Discussion Paper 2007–13. Washington, DC, The Brookings Institution, October.

—— Richards, K. R. (2005), *The Cost of US Forest-based Carbon Sequestration*, Arlington, VA, Pew Center on Global Climate Change, January.

—— Jaffee, J., and Schatzki, T. (2007), 'Too Good to be True: An Examination of Three Economic Assessments of California Climate Change Policy', Washington, DC, Resources for the Future.

Stephan, M. (2002), 'Environmental Information Disclosure Programs: They Work, but Why?', *Social Science Quarterly*, **83**, 190–205.

Sterling, M. J. H. (2008), 'Effects of Heat Pump Motors on the Distribution System', Personal communication, 19 September.

Stern, D. I. (1997), 'Limits to Substitution in the Irreversibility in Production and Consumption: A Neoclassical Interpretation of Ecological Economics', *Ecological Economics*, **21**, 197–215.

—— (2004), 'The Rise and Fall of the Environmental Kuznets Curve', *World Development*, **32**(8), 1419–39.

—— and Cleveland, C. J. (2004), 'Energy and Economic Growth', Troy, NY, Rensselaer Polytechnic Institute.

Stern, N. (2007), *The Economics of Climate Change: The Stern Review*, Cambridge, Cambridge University Press.

—— (2008*a*), 'The Economics of Climate Change', *American Economic Review*, **98**(2), 1–37.

—— (2008*b*), 'Key Elements of a Global Deal on Climate Change', Grantham Research Institute on Climate Change and the Environment, London, London School of Economics and Political Science, May.

—— (2009), 'Time for a Green Industrial Revolution', *New Scientist*, 2692, 21 January.

Sterner, T., and Persson, U. M. (2007), 'An Even Sterner Review Introducing Relative Prices into the Discounting Debate', Resources for the Future Discussion Paper 07–37, July.

Stewart, R. B., and Wiener, J. B. (2001), 'Reconstructing Climate Policy: The Paths Ahead', *Policy Matters*.

—— —— (2003), 'Practical Climate Change Policy', *Issues in Science and Technology*, **20**, 71–8 (available at http://www.issues.org/20.2/stewart.html).

Stiglitz, J. E. (1975), 'The Theory of "Screening" Education, and the Distribution of Income', *American Economic Review*, **65**, 283–300.

—— (2006), 'A New Agenda for Global Warming', *The Economists' Voice*, **3**(7), Art. 3 (available at http://www.bepress.com/ev/vol3/iss7/art3).

Stoll-Kleemann, S., O'Riordan, T., and Jaeger, C. C. (2001), 'The Psychology of Denial Concerning Climate Mitigation Measures: Evidence from Swiss Focus Groups', *Global Environmental Change*, **11**, 107–17.

Stone, C. (1990), 'The Global Warming Crisis, If There is One, and the Law', *American Journal of International Law and Policy*, **5**(2).

Straumann, R. (2003), 'Exporting Pollution? Calculating the Embodied Emissions in Trade for Norway', *Statistics Norway*, Reports 2003 /17.

Subak, S. (1998), 'Evaluating Accuracy of National Inventories and Actions After Kyoto', Centre for Social and Economic Research on the Global Environment Working Paper.

Sue Wing, I., Ellerman, A. D., and Song, J. (2006), 'Absolute vs. Intensity Limits for CO_2 Emission Controls: Performance under Uncertainty', MIT Joint Program on the Science and Policy of Global Change, Report 130.

Sutherland, R. J. (1991), 'Market Barriers to Energy Efficiency Investments', *Energy Journal*, **12**(3), 15–34.

——(1994), 'Energy Efficiency or the Efficient Use of Energy Resources?', *Energy Sources*, **16**, 257–68.

——(1996), 'The Economics of Energy Conservation Policy', *Energy Policy*, **24**(4), 361–70.

Su Wei (2008), 'The UN–China Climate Change Partnership', Side event presentation at the UN Climate Change Conference, Poznan, 9 December.

Swalm, R. O. (1966), 'Utility Theory: Insights into Risk-taking', *Harvard Business Review*, **44**, 39–60.

Swart, R., Bergamaschi, P., Pulles, T., and Raes, F. (2007), 'Are National Greenhouse Gas Emissions Reports Scientifically Valid?', *Climate Policy*, **7**(6), 535–8.

Tarui, N., and Polasky, S. (2005*a*), 'Environmental Regulation with Strategic Investment, Technology Spillovers and Learning', Columbia Earth Institute and Department of Applied Economics, University of Minnesota, mimeo.

————(2005*b*), 'Environmental Regulation with Technology Adoption, Learning and Strategic Behavior', *Journal of Environmental Economics and Management*, **50**, 447–67.

Teller, E., Wood, L., and Hyde, R. (1997), 'Global Warming and Ice Ages: I. Prospects for Physics-based Modulation of Global Change', Lawrence Livermore National Laboratory preprint, 15 August.

Teng, F, Chen, W., and He, J. (2008), 'Possible Development of a Technology Clean Development Mechanism in a Post-2012 Regime', The Harvard Project on International Climate Agreements, December.

Tenner, C. (2000), 'Verification and Compliance Systems in the Climate Change Regime', *Verification Yearbook*, London, Verification Research, Training and Information Centre (VERTIC).

Thaler, R. H. (1991), *Quasi Rational Economics*, New York, Russell Sage Foundation.

——and Benartzi, S. (2004), 'Save More Tomorrow™: Using Behavioral Economics to Increase Employee Savings', *Journal of Political Economy*, **112**(1), S164–87.

——and Sherfin, H. (1981), 'An Economic Theory of Self-control', *Journal of Political Economy*, **89**, 392–406.

——and Sunstein, C. R. (2003), 'Libertarian Paternalism', *American Economic Review, Papers and Proceedings*, **93**(2), 175–79.

————(2008), *Nudge: Improving Decisions About Health, Wealth, and Happiness*, New Haven, CT, Yale University Press.

The Economist (1999), 'The Next Shock', 3 March.

Thomson, J. M. (1998), 'Reflections on the Economics of Traffic Congestion', *Journal of Transport Economics and Policy*, **32**(1), 93–112.

Tietenberg, T. (1997), 'Tradeable Permits and the Control of Air Pollution in the United States', paper prepared for the 10th Anniversary Jubilee edition of *Zeitschrift F¨urangewandte Umweltforschung*.

Titmuss, R. (1971), *The Gift Relationship: From Human Blood to Social Policy*, London, LSE Books.

Tol, R. S. J., and Yohe, G. W. (2006), 'A Review of the Stern Review', *World Economics*, **7**(4), 233–51.

Toman, M., and Jemelkova, B. (2003), 'Energy and Economic Development: An Assessment of the State of Knowledge', *Energy Journal*, **24**(4).

Tomaselli, I. (2006), 'Brief Study on Funding and Finance for Forestry and the Forest-based Sector', Final Report to the United Nations Forum on Forests Secretariat, New York, United Nations.

Train, K. E. (1994), 'Estimation of Net Savings from Energy-conservation Programs', *Energy*, **19**(4), 423–41.

Trenberth, K. E., and Dai, A. (2007), 'Effects of Mount Pinatubo Eruption on the Hydrologic Cycle as an Analog of Geoengineering', *Geophyscial Research Letters*, **34**, L15702.

Tussie, D., and Lengyel, M. F. (2002): 'Developing Countries: Turning Participation into Influence', in B. Hoekman, A. Mattoo, and P. English (eds), *Development, Trade, and the WTO: A Handbook*, Washington, DC, World Bank.

Tyran, J.-R. (2004), 'Voting when Money and Morals Conflict. An Experimental Test of Expressive Voting', *Journal of Public Economics*, **88**(7), 1645–64.

—— and Sausgruber, R. (2006), 'A Little Fairness may Induce a Lot of Redistribution in Democracy', *European Economic Review*, **50**, 469–85.

UN, UN Commodity Trade Statistics Database (available at http://comtrade.un.org/db).

Underdal, A. (2002), 'One Question, Two Answers', in E. Miles *et al.*, *Environmental Regime Effectiveness: Confronting Theory with Evidence*, Cambridge, MA, MIT Press.

UNDP (2007), *Human Development Report 2007/8002. Fighting Climate Change: Human Solidarity in a Divided World*, United Nations Development Programme, New York, Palgrave.

UNEP Risoe (2009), *CDM/JI Pipeline Analysis and Database*, 1 March (available at http://www.cdmpipeline.org/).

UN FCCC (1992), 'United Nations Framework Convention on Climate Change', New York, 9 May 1992, in force 21 March 1994, 31 ILM 849.

—— (1996), 'Draft Rules of Procedure', FCCC/CP/1996/2.

—— (1998), 'Kyoto Protocol to the United Nations Framework Convention on Climate Change', FCCC/CP/L.7/Add.1.

—— (2005*a*), 'Sixth Compilation and Synthesis of Initial National Communications from Parties not Included in Annex I to the Convention. Inventories of Anthropogenic Emissions by Sources and Removals by Sinks of Greenhouse Gases', FCCC/SBI/2005/18/Add.2.

—— (2005*b*), 'Reducing Emissions from Deforestation in Developing Countries. Approaches to Stimulate Action', FCCC/CP/2005/MISC.1.

—— (2005*c*), 'Reducing Emissions from Deforestation in Developing Countries: Approaches to Stimulate Action', UN FCCC, FCCC/CP/2005/MISC.1.

—— (2006), 'Report of the Conference of the Parties Serving as the Meeting of the Parties to the Kyoto Protocol on its First Session, Held at Montreal, from 28 November to 10 December 2005', FCCC/KP/CMP/2005/8/Add.2.

—— (2007*a*), 'Climate Change: Impacts, Vulnerabilities and Adaptation in Developing Countries' (available at http://unfccc.int/files/essential_background/background_publications_htmlpdf/application/txt/pub_07_impacts.pdf).

—— (2007*b*), 'Ad Hoc Working Group on Long-term Cooperative Action under the Convention: Proposal by the President', FCCC/CP/2007/L.7/Rev.1, Bali, UN Framework Convention on Climate Change.

—— (2007*c*), 'Investment and Financial Flows to Address Climate Change', Bonn, United Nations Framework Convention on Climate Change.

—— (2008*a*), 'Investment and Financial Flows to Address Climate Change: An Update', Technical Paper FCCC/TP/2008/7, Bonn, United Nations Framework Convention on Climate Change.

—— (2008*b*), 'Identifying, Analysing and Assessing Existing and Potential New Financing Resources and Relevant Vehicles to Support the Development, Deployment, Diffusion and Transfer of Environmentally Sound Technologies', FCCC/S B/2008/INF.7, 20 November.

—— (2008*c*), 'Report of the Ad Hoc Working Group on Further Commitments for Annex I Parties under the Kyoto Protocol on the First Part of its Fifth Session, Held in Bangkok from 31 March to 4 April 2008', FCCC/KP/AWG/2008/2.

UNGA (1988), 'Protection of the Global Climate for Present and Future Generations of Mankind', Resolution A/RES/43/53, 6 December.

US Climate Action Partnership (2007), *A Call for Action—Consensus Principles and Recommendations from the US Climate Action Partnership: A Business and NGO Partnership*, Washington, DC, 22 January.

US Energy Information Administration (2003), *Analysis of S.139, the Climate Stewardship Act of 2003*, Washington, DC, US Department of Energy.

—— (2006), *Energy Market Impacts of Alternative Greenhouse Gas Intensity Reduction Goals*, Washington, DC, US Department of Energy, March.

—— (2007), *Energy Market and Economic Impacts of a Proposal to Reduce Greenhouse Gas Intensity with a Cap and Trade System*, Washington, DC, US Department of Energy, January.

US EPA (1998), 'Building on Our Success: Green Lights and Energy Star Buildings: 1996 Year in Review', US EPA, Office of Air and Radiation, Washington, DC.

—— (2005), *Acid Rain Program: 2005 Progress Report*, Washington, DC, US EPA, Office of Air and Radiation, Clean Air Markets Division.

—— (2006), 'Global Anthropogenic Non-CO_2 Greenhouse Gas Emissions: 1990–2020', Office of Atmospheric Programs, Climate Change Division, United States Environmental Protection Agency.

Van der Eng, P. (2006), 'Accounting for Indonesia's Economic Growth: Recent Past and Near Future', Paper presented at the Seminar on World Economic Performance: Past, Present and Future—Long Term Performance and Prospects of Australia and Major Asian Economies, on the occasion of Angus Maddison's 80th birthday, University of Queensland, Brisbane, 5–6 December.

Van Vuuren, D., and O'Neill, B. (2006), 'The Consistency of IPCC's SRES Scenarios to 1900–2000: Trends and Recent Projections', *Climatic Change*, **75**, 9–46.

Velders, G. J. M., Anderson, S. O., Daniel, J. S., Fahey, D.W., and McFarland, M. (2007), 'The Importance of the Montreal Protocol in Protecting Climate', *Proceedings of the National Academy of Sciences*, **104**(12), 4814–19.

Venkataraman, C. *et al.* (2005), 'Residential Biofuels in South Asia: Carbonaceous Aerosol Emissions and Climate Impacts', *Science*, March.

Verhoef, E., and Rouwendal, J. (2003), 'A Structural Model of Traffic Congestion: Endogenising Speed Choice, Traffic Safety and Time Losses', Tinbergen Institute Discussion Paper TI2001-026/3.

Victor, D. G. (1999), 'Enforcing International Law: Implications for an Effective Global Warming Regime', *Duke Environmental Law & Policy Forum*, **10**(1), 147–84.

Victor, D. G. (2001), *Collapse of the Kyoto Protocol and the Struggle to Slow Global Warming*, Princeton, NJ, Princeton University Press.

—— (2003), 'International Agreements and the Struggle to Tame Carbon', in J. M. Griffin (ed.), *Global Climate Change: The Science, Economics and* Politics, Cheltenham, Edward Elgar, 204–29.

—— (2006), 'Toward Effective International Cooperation on Climate Change: Numbers, Interests and Institutions', *Global Environmental Politics*, **6** (**3**), 90–103.

—— (2007), 'Fragmented Carbon Markets and Reluctant Nations: Implications for the Design of Effective Architectures', ch. 4 in J. E. Aldy and R. N. Stavins (eds), *Architectures for Agreement: Addressing Global Climate Change in the Post-Kyoto World*, Cambridge, Cambridge University Press, 133–60.

—— Runge, C. F. (2002), *Sustaining a Revolution: A Policy Strategy for Crop Engineering*, a Council on Foreign Relations Study, New York, Council on Foreign Relations.

—— Raustiala, K., and Skolnikoff, E. B. (eds) (1998), *The Implementation and Effectiveness of International Environmental Commitments: Theory and Practice*, Cambridge, MA, and London, MIT Press.

—— Morgan, M. G., Apt, J., Steinbruner, J., and Ricke, K. (2008), 'Constraining the Climate Engineers', mimeo, 14 July.

Vine, E., and Sathaye, J. (1999), 'The Monitoring, Evaluation, Reporting and Verification of Climate Change Projects', *Mitigation and Adaptation Strategies for Global Change*, **4**, 43–60.

Vissing-Jørgensen, A. (2002), 'Limited Asset Market Participation and the Elasticity of Intertemporal Substitution', *Journal of Political Economy*, **4**, 825–53.

Vollebergh, H. R. J., de Vries, J. L., and Koutstaal, P. R. (1997), 'Hybrid Carbon Incentive Mechanisms and Political Acceptability', *Environmental and Resource Economics*, **9**, 43–63.

Wagner, G., Keohane, N., Petsonk, A., and Wang, J. (2008), 'Docking into a Global Carbon Market: Clean Investment Budgets to Encourage Emerging Economy Participation', Environmental Defense Fund, December.

Wan, Y. (2006), 'China's Energy Efficiency Policy in Industry', Paper presented at the 'Working Together to Respond to Climate Change', Annex I Expert Group Seminar in Conjunction with the OECD Global Forum on Sustainable Development, Paris, 27–28 March.

Wang, T., and Watson, J. (2007), 'Who Owns China's Carbon Emissions?', *Tyndall Centre Briefing Note*, No. 23, October.

Wang, J. S., O'Neill, B. C., and Chameides, W. L. (2007), 'Linking Mid-century Concentration Targets to Long-term Climate Change Outcomes', Interim Report IR-07-022, Laxenburg, IIASA.

Wara, M. (2007), 'Is the Global Carbon Market Working?', *Nature*, **445**, 595–6.

—— and Victor, D. G. (2008), 'A Realistic Policy on International Carbon Offsets', Program on Energy and Sustainable Development Working Paper No. 74, Stanford, CA, Stanford University.

Ward, M. (2005), 'Implications for Climate Change Policy of Trends in Exports and Imports of Energy Commodities and Manufactured Goods', *Global Climate Change Consultancy*, Wellington, New Zealand, November.

Ward, P. D. (2006), 'Impact from the Deep', *Scientific American*, **295**, 64–71.

Warde, P. (2007), 'Facing the Challenge of Climate Change: Energy Efficiency and Energy Consumption', *History and Policy*, Policy Paper 65, October (available at http://www.historyandpolicy.org/archive/policy_paper_65.html).

Warren, R. *et al.* (2006), 'Understanding the Regional Impacts of Climate Change', Research report prepared for the Stern Review on the Economics of Climate Change, Tyndall Centre for Climate Change Research, Working Paper 90.

Watson, R. T., Heywood, V. H., Baste, I., Dias, B., Gamez, R., Janetos, T., Reid, W., and Ruark, R. (eds) (1995), *Global Biodiversity Assessment*, Cambridge, Cambridge University Press.

WCED (1987), 'Our Common Future', Brundtland Report, World Commission on Environment and Development.

Webb, R., Vulliamy, G., Hakkinen, K., and Hamalainen, S. (1998), 'External Inspection or School Self-Evaluation? A Comparative Analysis of Policy and Practice in Primary Schools in England and Finland', *British Educational Research Journal*, **24**(5), 539–56.

Weil, P. (1989), 'The Equity Premium Puzzle and the Risk-free Rate Puzzle', *Journal of Monetary Economics*, **24**, 401–21.

Weil, S., and McMahon, J. (2003), 'Governments Should Implement Energy Efficiency Standards and Labels—Cautiously', *Energy Policy*, **31**(13), 1403–15.

Weitzman, M. (1974), 'Prices vs Quantities', *Review of Economic Studies*, 41(4), 477–91.

—— (2001), 'Gamma Discounting', *American Economic Review*, **91**, 261–71.

—— (2007*a*), 'A Review of the *Stern Review on the Economics of Climate Change*', *Journal of Economic Literature*, **45**(3), September.

—— (2007*b*), 'Subjective Expectations and Asset-return Puzzles', *American Economic Review*, **97**(4), 1102–30.

—— (2007*c*), 'On Modeling and Interpreting the Economics of Catastrophic Climate Change', mimeo, 4 November.

—— (2009), 'On Modeling and Interpreting the Economics of Catastrophic Climate Change', *Review of Economics and Statistics*, **91**(1), 1–19.

Weyant, J. P., and Hill, J. (1999), 'Introduction and Overview', in 'The Costs of the Kyoto Protocol: A Multi-model Evaluation', special issue of *The Energy Journal*, vii–xliv.

—— De la Chesnaye, F. C., and Blanford, G. (2006), 'Overview of EMF–21: Multi-gas Mitigation and Climate Change', *Energy Journal*, 22 November.

Wiedmann, T., Wood, R., Lenzen, M., Minx, J., Guan, D., and Barrett, J. (2008), *Development of an Embedded Carbon Emissions Indicator*, Report to the UK Department for Environment, Food and Rural Affairs by the Stockholm Environment Institute at the University of York and the Centre for Integrated Sustainability Analysis at the University of Sydney, June.

Wiener, J. B. (2008), 'Climate Change Policy and Policy Change In China', *UCLA Law Review*, **55**, 1805–26.

Wigley, T. M. L. (1993), 'Balancing the Carbon Budget. Implications for Projections of Future Carbon Dioxide Concentration Changes', *Tellus B*, **45**(5), 409–25.

—— (2007), 'CO_2 Emissions: A Piece of Pie', *Science*, **316**(5826), 829–30.

—— Raper, S. C. B. (2002), 'Reasons for Larger Warming Projections in the IPCC Third Assessment Report', *Journal of Climate*, **15**, 2945–52.

—— Richels, R., and Edmonds, J. (1996), 'Economic and Environmental Choices in the Stabilization of Atmospheric CO_2 Concentrations', *Nature*, **379**(18), 240–3.

—— Smith, S. J., and Prather, M. J. (2002), 'Radiative Forcing Due to Reactive Gas Emissions', *Journal of Climate*, **15**, 2690–6.

Williamson, O. E. (1985), *The Economic Institutions of Capitalism*, New York, Free Press.

Winther, B. N., and Hestnes, A. G. (1999), 'Solar versus Green: The Analysis of a Norwegian Row House', *Solar Energy*, **66**(6), 387–93.

Wood, M. (1996), 'Security Council: Procedural Developments', *International and Comparative Law Quarterly*, **45**, 150–61.

Woods, N. (1999), 'Good Governance in International Organizations', *Global Governance*, **5**, 39–61.

—— and Lombardi, D. (2006), 'Uneven Patterns of Governance: How Developing Countries are Represented in the IMF', *Review of International Political Economy*, **13**, 480–515.

World Bank (2004), 'Sustaining Forests: A Development Strategy', Washington, DC, World Bank.

World Commission on Environment and Development (1987), *Our Common Future*, Oxford, Oxford University Press.

Worrell, E., Laitner, J. A., Ruth, M., and Finman, H. E. (2003), 'Productivity Benefits of Industrial Energy Efficiency Measures', *Energy*, 1081–98.

Yamin, F., and Depledge, J. (2004), *The International Climate Change Regime, A Guide to Rules, Institutions and Procedures*, Cambridge, Cambridge University Press.

—— with Smith, J., and Burton, I. (2006), 'Perspectives on "Dangerous Anthropogenic Interference"; or How to Operationalize Article 2 of the UN Framework Convention on Climate Change', in H. J. Schellnhuber *et al.* (eds), *Avoiding Dangerous Climate Change*, Cambridge, Cambridge University Press.

Yohe, G., Andronova, N., and Schlesinger, M. (2004), 'To Hedge or Not Against an Uncertain Climate Future?', *Science*, **306**, 416–7.

Zarnikau, J. (1999), 'Will Tomorrow's Energy Efficiency Indices Prove Useful in Economic Studies?', *Energy Journal*, **20**(3), 139–45.

Zartman, I. W. (1993), 'Lessons for Analysis and Practice', in G. Sjöstedt (ed.), *International Environmental Negotiation*, London, Sage, 262–74.

—— (ed.) (1994), *International Multilateral Negotiation: Approaches to the Management of Complexity*, San Francisco, CA, Jossey-Bass.

—— (2003), 'Negotiating the Rapids: The Dynamics of Regime Formation', in B. I. Spector and I. W. Zartman, *Getting it Done: Post-agreement Negotiation and International Regimes*, Washington, DC, US Institute of Peace, 13–50.

Zou Ji (2008), 'The UN–China Climate Change Partnership', Side event presentation at the UN Climate Change Conference, Poznan, 9 December.

Index